Growing Up Abolitionist

GROWING UP *ABOLITIONIST*

The Story of the Garrison Children

Harriet Hyman Alonso

UNIVERSITY OF
MASSACHUSETTS PRESS

Amherst and Boston

Printed in the United States of America

LC 2002007122

ISBN 1-55849-233-X (cloth); 381-6 (paper)

Designed by Milenda Nan Ok Lee
Set in Adobe Garamond by Graphic Composition, Inc.
Printed and bound by Thomson-Shore, Inc.

Library of Congress Cataloging-in-Publication Data

Alonso, Harriet Hyman.
Growing up abolitionist : the story of the Garrison children / Harriet Hyman Alonso
p. cm.
Includes bibliographical references and index.
ISBN 1-55849-233-X (alk. paper) — 1-55849-381-6 (pbk. : alk. paper)
1. Garrison family. 2. Garrison, William Lloyd, 1805–1879—Family.
3. Abolitionists—United States—Biography. 4. Antislavery movements—United States—History—19th century. I. Title.
E449 .A46 2002
973.7'114'0922—dc21

2002007122

British Library Cataloguing in Publication data are available.

This book is published with the support and cooperation of the
City College of New York, City University of New York.

For Miguel and Pablo

CONTENTS

Garrison family tree appears on page 6; illustrations follow page 134.

Growing Up Abolitionist

PROLOGUE

> I have lived over again in my thoughts all the experience of that day when the first break was made in our family circle.—"Break" is not the right word, after all. . . . I am sure they are both here, Father & Mother, and that we can never have a *break* in the family, and that as children the bond between us must ever be as close & strong as when our precious parents were here in the flesh to cement it.
>
> Francis Jackson Garrison to Fanny Garrison Villard, 1880

On May 24, 1879, the great antislavery leader William Lloyd Garrison lay dying. His beloved wife and partner, Helen Eliza Benson Garrison, had passed from his life three years earlier, and he still felt her loss most profoundly. Garrison, however, was not alone during his final days. Surrounding him with care and love were his five adult children: George, William, Wendell, Fanny, and Frank. These offspring had grown up adoring their dissident parents and appreciating the gift of political awareness handed down to them. All had, in their separate ways, molded their parents' beliefs and behavior to fit their adult lives. Collectively and individually, they carried on their parents' values in the civil rights, peace, and woman suffrage movements.

In the final weeks of his life, Garrison had traveled from his home in Boston to Fanny's domicile in New York City. There Fanny lived with her husband, the financier, publisher, and railroad magnate Henry Villard, and their three children: Helen, Harold, and Oswald. The seventy-four-year-old Garrison had been feeling ill for some time, and Fanny wished him to see her physician, Leonard Weber, who diagnosed kidney disease. For most of May, the tired old activist's health fluctuated. By the third week of his stay, it became clear to Fanny that her father did not have long to live. She summoned her brothers, who came as quickly as possible. William's wife, Ellie, accompanied him. George's wife, Annie, had just given birth and was unable to travel. Wendell's wife, Lucy, had succumbed in 1877 after a long illness. Henry Villard was in California on business and unable to return home. Frank was still single.

As Wendell related in a letter to his brother-in-law, Henry, the "death struggle" took fifteen hours, largely because Garrison continued to invoke his "tremendous vitality." The children were unable to sleep, afraid to miss their father's final moment. As their dear parent lay propped up on pillows with his feet touching the floor, his limbs grew weaker and his heart and lungs began "their irregular rivalry." Ellie and Frank, hoping to soothe him, began singing some of Garrison's favorite hymns. He, in turn, at first beat the time feebly with his hands and then with his feet, which his children uncovered to make the small movements easier. Wendell felt that this was "the one joyous moment preluding a night of horror."[1] Their wait ended at eleven o'clock that evening.

William Lloyd Garrison's detailed obituaries appeared in newspapers throughout the United States and Europe. His children, always aware of their father's importance to the landscape of U.S. history, made sure that he received postmortem recognition. As Fanny soon wrote to the British abolitionist Elizabeth Pease Nichol, an intimate friend of her father, "In our grief we seem to have the sympathy of the country, for his loss is regarded as a national one." "Yet," she added, "how few can know the beauty of his private life, so gentle, so sweet, so true!" Fanny pledged that she and her brothers would preserve both their father's memory and his inestimable reputation: "The parting from our Father is indeed hard to bear, but we feel proud of the record of his glorious life, and grateful that we are permitted to be his children. We can only strive to keep his name bright and unsullied, and that we shall do."[2]

The Garrison children understood that their father and mother's abolitionism included many issues that today we would term "social justice," including the ending of racial and sexual oppression, the struggle against imperialism, and the embracing of nonviolence. Before their parents' deaths, however, each had assumed his or her own mantle of activism. Although rejecting nonviolence, the eldest son, George, had so taken to heart the abolitionist cause that he volunteered to serve in the 55th Regiment of Massachusetts Volunteer Infantry during the Civil War, the second black regiment to be organized in the state. Although his action upset his strictly nonresistant father and brothers, who opposed violence to such a degree that they would not cooperate with the institutions that fostered it, George answered to his own sense of justice, arguing that the war was necessary. During his almost two-year stint, he also upheld his parents' conviction in racial justice, struggling to see that the men of the 55th received the same wages as white soldiers and voicing his disdain for the racist commanding officers who passed over competent black soldiers for promotion.

George's brother William also embraced his parents' causes. Like his father, he preferred to carry on his political work from home, always living near his parents and dedicating much of his effort to being a responsible husband, father, and son. In the 1860s, however, he took to lecturing and writing, first against slavery and later in support of woman's rights, becoming a noted figure in the Massachusetts suffrage movement. Along with his brothers Wendell and Frank and his sister, Fanny, he lobbied for Reconstruction legislation that would guarantee citizenship rights and education to the newly freed population in the South. Finally, in 1888, William embraced Henry George's single-tax movement, which not only brought his political positions under a common umbrella but led him to the campaign against imperialism, a cause that his father had also embraced.

Wendell, the most politically conservative of the Garrison children, worked for forty years as an editor on the *Nation,* the newspaper founded in 1865 by abolitionists interested in fostering civil rights. Although educated in the prestigious Boston Latin School and Harvard College, Wendell schooled himself in journalism by writing columns for his father's paper, the *Liberator.* At first Wendell appeared to adopt his father's views completely, but his exposure to the *Nation*'s rather conservative editor, E. L. Godkin, turned him into somewhat of an intellectual snob, which created tension with his father. Wendell's habit of belittling suffragists and his acquiescence to Godkin's claim that the South's problem was simply corrupt government also irked his brothers and sister. In the end, however, Wendell chose to embrace his radical upbringing by seeing to it that the abolitionist movement's history did not fall into obscurity. Wendell ensured that many stories were preserved, including those of his mother's family (the Bensons), his in-laws (the McKims), and his own parents.

In this effort, he worked closely with the youngest of the Garrison children, Frank. In 1871 Frank had accepted a position with the publishing firm that later became Houghton Mifflin. Throughout his forty-four years with the company, he eased the way for the publication of several abolitionist memoirs and other documents under the Riverside Press imprint. Unlike Wendell, Frank was deeply involved with the post–Civil War work of Reconstruction, forming a close relationship with Booker T. Washington. When, in the children's opinion, Washington became too accommodating to wealthy white leaders and businessmen, Frank, along with William and Fanny, threw his support behind W. E. B. Du Bois. In 1909, together with other white and black activists, including Fanny's son Oswald, they formed the National Association for the Advancement of Colored People (NAACP). Frank worked continuously with the organization's Boston branch until his death.

Fanny, the only surviving daughter of William Lloyd and Helen Benson Garrison, was no less an activist than her brothers, although her truly productive period came after her husband's death in 1900. Like her mother, Fanny had embraced the Victorian-era ideal that a woman's main role was to be a wife and mother. Yet she could not turn her back on her activist roots. While her children were young, the wealthy Fanny Garrison Villard generally expressed her politics in letters to her brothers and through various forms of benevolent reform work. She became particularly active in achieving higher education for women, taking part in the efforts to open Barnard College in New York and Radcliffe College in Cambridge. But she also worked for racial justice by funding and supporting the building of schools for African Americans in the segregated South and in fostering the work of the NAACP. For over twenty-five years she served as president of the Diet Kitchen Association, an organization that provided fresh and healthy milk and food products for New York's ill and needy. Fanny's best-known and most respected work, however, was her fifteen years in the woman suffrage movement (her organizing efforts centered on New York City and nearby Westchester County) and her antiwar work in the Woman's Peace Party and the Women's Peace Society. In all of her peace and suffrage work, Fanny stood by her father's belief in nonresistance.

The Garrison family formed a close-knit unit. The bond, in fact, was so strong that it kept the spirits of two Garrison children who died young (Charley and Elizabeth) alive and present in the everyday lives of the survivors. The children's belief systems reflected their upbringing within the antebellum abolitionist community. As adults, the children adhered to their parents' political and Christian beliefs while not aligning with any specific church or denomination. Sometimes the strength of the attachment proved problematic, however, and pressure was exerted on one child or another to uphold the family's expectations. Yet the children felt it their filial obligation to dissent. George's insistence on going to war and Wendell's stubborn support of E. L. Godkin, no matter how disconcerting, could not rupture the bond holding parents, brothers, and sister together. Neither could Fanny's insistence on marrying an "outsider"—a cigar-smoking, beer- and wine-drinking German—lessen their hold on her. The many years that she lived in Germany were filled with gifts, letters, and visits from one side of the ocean to the other. When their parents died, the siblings remained emotionally and practically attached.

The Garrison children did indeed uphold their father's (and mother's) reputations, whether through their own political organizing or their efforts to trace and record their family's history. Neither Helen nor William Lloyd Garrison kept a journal or wrote an autobiography. The *Liberator,* which appeared weekly from January 1831 through December 1865, was as close to a journal as the man produced. The children saw to it that several entire runs of the newspaper were placed in libraries; that letters were collected, organized, and preserved; that family history was traced and published. When Fanny and William spoke or wrote about civil rights, peace, and suffrage, they invoked their father's image and utilized his ideas. George, the least political of the offspring, gave his mite in verbal support for his siblings' causes. Together, Wendell and Frank produced a four-volume biography of their father which, in the most reverent of terms, preserved the history of the abolitionist movement. Titled *William Lloyd Garrison, 1805–1879, The Story of His Life Told by His Children,* the work included excerpts from the many letters, journals, and articles found among their father's papers.[3] In addition, Wendell and Frank conducted a physical search for information that might throw light on their parents' backgrounds. In their effort to cover the complete scope of their mother and father's lives, they uncovered much about themselves—information that helped them to understand how they had matured into the adults that they were.

Growing Up Abolitionist is devoted to the Garrison children and the people and issues they cared about. It includes their search for their grandparents' histories and their recollections of their own experiences as abolitionist children. Theirs were lives shaped within the context of the great nineteenth-century campaigns against slavery, racism, violence, war, imperialism, and the repression of women. They, as children, became apprentices of these movements. They observed and learned from some of the greatest reformers of their day: Frederick Douglass, Susan B. Anthony, Henry C. Wright, Sojourner Truth, Lucretia and James Mott, Lucy Stone, Thomas Wentworth Higginson, George Thompson . . . and, of course, their own parents. They grew up in a loving family, but one that experimented with medical treatments, was enticed by spiritualism, followed the temperance line, disdained traditional religion while being staunchly Christian, and appreciated the joys of life. The lessons they learned from their parents and their friends—and the knowledge they gained about them—became the foundations for their lives.

THE GARRISON FAMILY

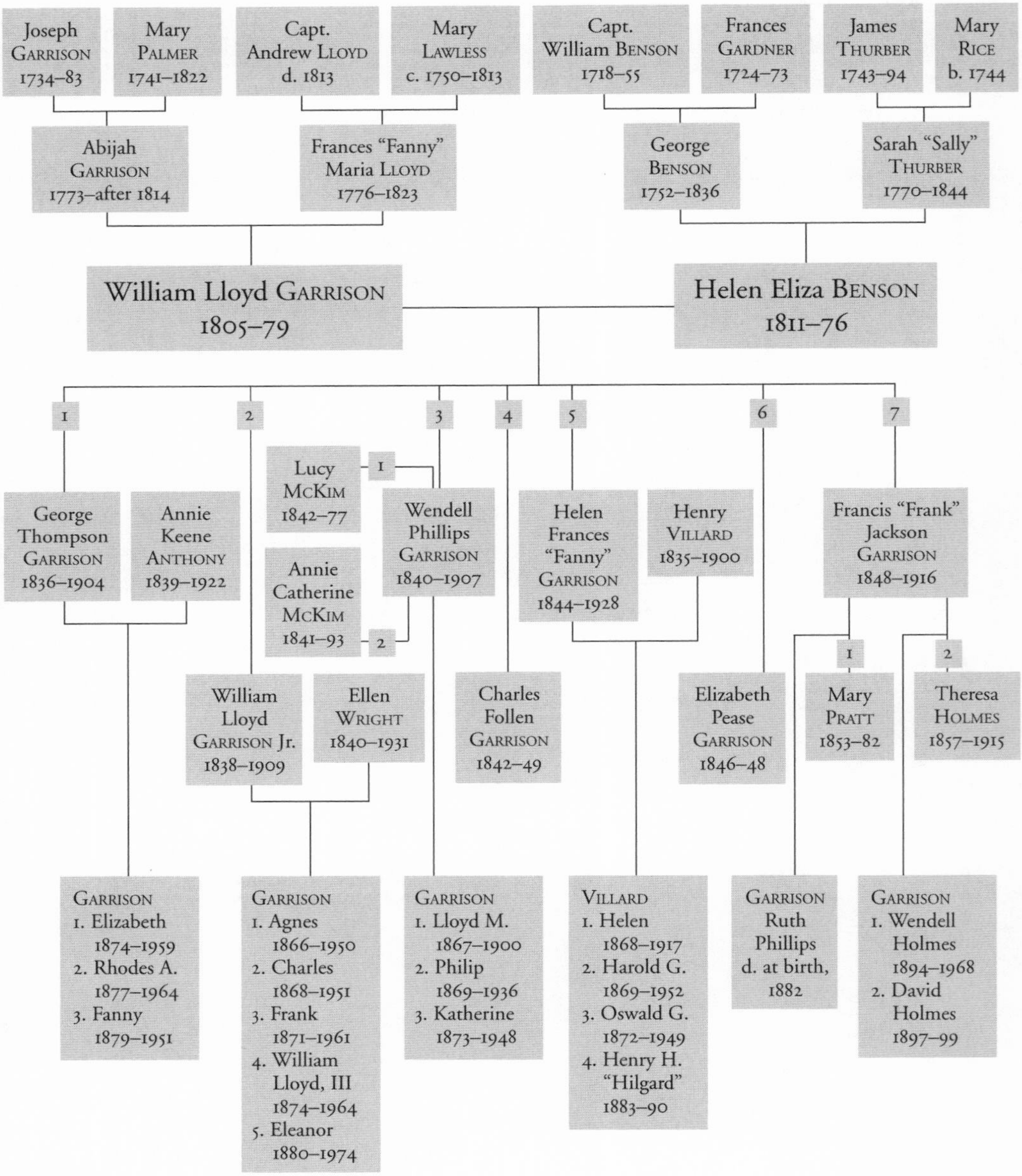

Garrison family tree. Courtesy of James W. Gould.

ROOTS

FANNY'S STORY

The first two I desire to meet "on the other side of Jordan" are your fond mother and my own.

William Lloyd Garrison to his son, Wendell, 1878

CHAPTER I

Throughout childhood the Garrison children were taught to honor "Grandmother Garrison," who had died long before they were born. Their father told them tales of Frances (Fanny) Lloyd Garrison's beauty, her religiosity, and her difficult life. Rarely did they hear about their grandfather Abijah, except in terms of the pitfalls and evils of alcoholism, which had driven a wedge between him and Fanny and caused his desertion of the family. In the mid-nineteenth century, when spiritualism became the rage, Grandmother Garrison often appeared to family members through the aid of a planchette board and mediums at seances. Indeed, so strong was William Lloyd Garrison's emotional connection with his mother that his sons Wendell and Frank made every effort to unearth her story and to fit her into their legacy of Christian ethics and political activism. Learning the truth, however, was no easy task, for much of Fanny's correspondence and nearly all of Abijah's had been lost.

Even with careful research and contact with long-lost relatives, the brothers unearthed little about Fanny Lloyd's early years in New Brunswick, Canada. They learned that her father earned a decent living as the pilot of a schooner, carrying salted fish, lumber, and furs among eastern Canadian ports, and that Fanny, like other pioneer children, learned domestic skills and simple farming tasks, such as tending her parents' goats. But they also discovered that the most defining feature of their grandmother's life was her religious conviction. Fanny's Irish-immigrant parents raised their daughter in a strict Episcopalian manner, teaching her to distrust all other believers, especially Baptists.[1] One day, for a lark, she and some church friends decided to attend a service conducted by a traveling Baptist preacher.[2] Although her peers scoffed, Fanny was deeply touched by the simplicity of the meetinghouse and the emotional involvement of each individual in the practice of the faith. Much to her parents' chagrin, she announced her intention to become a Baptist. According to family history as it was passed along to Wendell and Frank, Fanny was banished from her family home and was saved from destitution only by a sympathetic uncle.

Fanny was certainly not alone in her attraction to this new faith. In the last quarter of the eighteenth century, a Great Awakening spread from England to the colonies. People who felt constrained by the older, traditional religions embraced the more intensely individual and emotional cloak of Baptism with its emphasis on the conversion experience. Through prayer, belief, and study, they connected with God until, hopefully, in one especially ecstatic moment, they felt a spiritual union which bound them to the religious community. Women were very attracted to the Baptist faith, as it was one of the only institutions at the time where they could exercise authority in such roles as itinerant preachers, decision makers, and local organizers. Certainly Fanny's faith turned her into an independent and assertive woman. In Eastport, where she was one of the few literate members of the Baptist community, she often conducted religious meetings on the Sabbath when no minister was available to officiate.

Abijah Garrison, a young seaman of English, Irish, and French Huguenot extraction, found himself attracted to Fanny's intelligence, independence, and beauty.[3] As her son William Lloyd (or "Lloyd," as he preferred) fondly recalled, during his boyish years his mother appeared as "a tall, majestic figure, singularly graceful in deportment and carriage" with fine features and "hair so luxuriant and rich that, when she unbound it, like that of Godiva of old, it fell around her like a veil."[4] Fanny, for her part, was as taken by Abijah's appearance as he was by hers. Lloyd, who was a mere three years old when he last saw his father, could as an adult somehow call up the image of a balding, tall young man with light hair, fair skin, a reddish beard, and a "very noticeable scar on his face, a birth-mark," which ran "from ear to ear and under the chin, like a muffler" and was "sometimes as red as blood."[5] A rather formal but distant courtship followed, until Fanny and Abijah wed in Waterborough in December 1798 and began their life together in a town on the Jemseg River in New Brunswick. Wendell's and Frank's inquiries and research revealed that the couple had a daughter, Mary Ann, who died in infancy, but they found no written record of the birth or death. What is certain, however, is that in 1801 the couple settled in St. John, where, on July 10 of that year, Fanny gave birth to a son, James Holley. In 1803 a second daughter, Caroline Eliza, was born.

For several years, the marriage of Fanny and Abijah seemed happy. Together, they were able to face the difficult life of New Brunswick with its frigid winters and frontier conditions. Abijah, a ship's pilot who eventually reached the rank of sailing master, made innumerable long voyages along the East Coast to the West Indies, most likely as part of the codfish and lumber trade. As time passed, however, he grew worried about the effect the Napoleonic Wars were having on his ability to be a good provider. The disruptions in trade and the lack of prosperity had resulted in people migrating from Canada to the United States. Abijah, too, wanted to resettle in a place where he felt he would be "less expos'd to the Ravages of war and stagnation of business."[6] Hence, in 1805 the small Garrison family left Canada for the prosperous and booming seaport town of Newburyport, Massachusetts, which by the 1750s was touted as New England's greatest shipping center.[7] During the warm months, schooners carried men to catch and cure codfish; when the weather turned cold, they transported their cargo of fish and lumber to the West Indies, where they exchanged it for sugar, molasses, coffee, and cocoa.[8]

Abijah and Fanny felt renewed hope for their future in this new location, especially after they rented rooms from David and Martha Farnham. Because David's life as a sea captain also often kept him away from home, Fanny and Martha, who were only two years apart in age and both devoted Baptists, quickly became friends. The Farnhams' two-story, saltbox-style wooden house was just a few steps from the rear of the First Presbyterian Church on Federal Street. Just a few short blocks down the slope, the street ended at the wharves, where Fanny could look out at the serene water, protected from the open ocean by Plum Island, and forget for awhile the growing number of taverns and flophouses serving the sailors. If she preferred, she could cross Federal Street and walk a few blocks west to the bustling market area and business district. There was another route Fanny could easily take from her home, and that was uphill on Federal Street to High Street and its mansions belonging to the investors, industrialists, and merchants who had made huge profits over the years from 1756 to 1807. High Street, perhaps at first a fanciful avenue to walk along, later became a bleak reminder to Fanny of her own lost dreams.

For two years, life passed rather peacefully for the Garrisons. On December 10 or 12, 1805, Fanny gave birth at home to her second son, William Lloyd.[9] Because Abijah sent her most of his earnings while at sea, she did not have to scurry around trying to earn extra money as many seamen's wives did. Her life with her children could therefore revolve around the First Baptist Church, founded in Newburyport in the spring of 1805, and the weekly prayer meetings that she and Martha conducted in their home. In December 1807, however, the effects of war and foreign diplomacy, which had forced the family out of Canada, struck them again in Newburyport.[10] Prosperity came to a halt when Congress passed the Embargo Act, legislation that kept the nation from becoming entangled in the war between

France and England, but virtually banned U.S. vessels from leaving port. Two supplementary acts in January and March 1808 prohibited the export of both U.S. products and foreign imports by land or sea. These laws proved to be disastrous for the East Coast ports. Within a year, export trade dropped by 80 percent and import trade by more than 50 percent. For Newburyport alone, by the end of the year, all but fourteen of the town's ships lay idle. As the Newburyport *Herald* reported that July, "Our wharves have now the stillness of the grave. . . . Nothing flourishes on them but vegetation."[11]

The economic failure of Newburyport rang a death knell for the marriage of Fanny and Abijah Garrison, largely because Abijah could not ply his trade, nor could he find any other work. For escape, comfort, and the companionship of other idle seamen, he turned increasingly to drink. At first this choice was socially acceptable and seemingly logical; alcoholic beverages were part of everyday life, and the tavern was a common meeting place for many working men. In 1810, in fact, liquor was the third most important industrial product in the United States. By 1830 the average adult in the country consumed 5.2 gallons of absolute alcohol a year. Since Newburyport housed numerous distilleries, rum, domestic whiskey, and beer were popular and cheap. Baptists, unfortunately for Abijah and Fanny, constituted one of the few groups who considered liberal alcohol consumption a sin.[12] Abijah's earlier life had included a certain amount of drinking, which Fanny apparently tolerated. As one of his relatives later wrote to Frank and Wendell, "It was the fashion of the day to use alcoholic spirit in all places of honor and trust. We had it at all our ordinations, weddings, births, and funerals, and the decanter was brought on the table to greet our friends with when they came, and was not forgotten when they left; and if they could stand the test and not reel, they were called sober men."[13]

Abijah's drunkenness and idleness, however, were not the only challenges facing Fanny. When the embargo began, she was in the early months of her fifth pregnancy. Lloyd, her youngest child, was just two and a half; Caroline was four, and James, six. On June 18, 1808, tragedy struck when Caroline died after eating poisonous flowers in her neighbor's yard. A few weeks later, on July 3, Elizabeth Knowlton was born.[14] The combined factors—poverty, a husband becoming an alcoholic, a child's death, pregnancy, and a birth—turned Fanny's life upside down. Although she had her own outlet as Abijah had his, they were incompatible, for the more that Abijah drank, the more Fanny relied upon her church for comfort and support. As time passed, the tensions between the pair worsened. Violent arguments ensued, and not long after Elizabeth's birth Abijah walked out of Fanny's life. Neither she nor their children ever heard from him again.

Abijah's departure is clouded in mystery. According to family legend, some sailor friends came over to drink with him one evening. Fanny, with all the indignation of an angry Baptist temperance wife, threw the men out, shut the door in their faces, and smashed the bottles of liquor. A volatile scene followed, after which Abijah stormed out of the house. Wendell and Frank, in their retelling of this episode, were content to portray the couple as having only one major confrontation. They were quick to excuse Abijah, claiming no proof of his constant intemperance while extolling Fanny's Christian righteousness. Whatever the reality, the result was that Fanny, at the age of thirty-two, found herself alone with three young children to support, no employment, and no prospects. Although Abijah carried the stigma of the drunk, Fanny became the woman who had failed at marriage, also a considerable disgrace. Later, in the eyes of society if not to her son or grandchildren, she became the woman who failed at motherhood as well. Abijah, however much he may have regretted his choice, was free to create a new, unburdened, life for himself.

In the early nineteenth century, women did not have many serious options for earning a living. Although some elderly women, especially widows, took in younger children in "dame schools" (similar to today's home daycare providers), Fanny's living situation was not suitable for this work. Other Newburyport women who earned wages relied on seamstressing, laundering, keeping a boarding house or dry goods store, or nursing. Although Fanny possessed the rudimentary sewing and embroidery skills expected of young women, nursing, which consisted of providing nonmedical care for ill people, appealed to her the most, and over the next decade and a half she relied on it and housekeeping to provide her family with a livelihood. There is no indication that Fanny received any financial help from her family in Canada. As a man of twenty-nine, Lloyd vaguely remembered that in 1810 his mother took him for a visit to New Brunswick. Apparently finding little sympathy, she quickly returned to Massachusetts. In the absence of family support, Martha Farnham proved herself a good friend by assuring Fanny that neither she nor her children would ever be homeless. During those times when Fanny was forced to be away from home to take care of a patient, "Aunt Farnham" took care of the three youngsters. Martha's daughter, Harriet, treated Lloyd and Elizabeth like a brother and sister. When no nursing assignments were available, Fanny made molasses candy, sending James and Lloyd out to sell it on holidays or at festivals. In more desperate moments, Lloyd was sent to a mansion on State Street to pick up meal leftovers saved specifically for Fanny.

Because job opportunities were sporadic, Fanny eventually had to make use of the help offered to the "dependent poor." As early as 1793, Massachusetts had instituted a comprehensive poor law, requiring each town "to relieve and support all poor and indigent persons, lawfully settled thereof."[15] With the Embargo Act severely affecting the local community, the town took steps to meet this traditional obligation by establishing temporary soup kitchens. As the situation worsened, more prosperous residents agreed to donate supplies, which were then distributed by the town's overseers. Fanny's case was unique for the town leaders, as she was the only abandoned wife and female head of household who approached them.[16] Four years after Abijah left her, the overseers' minutes of April 1812 indicate, she asked for their help; she had decided that in order to earn a living she would leave the two youngest children in Newburyport and take James with her to Lynn. The overseers granted her $1.25 per week for both Lloyd and Elizabeth, the former taking up residence with a Baptist deacon, Ezekial Bartlett, and the latter remaining with Martha Farnham. This decision was a most difficult one for Fanny. Her children and her church were her only joys, and from this point on, no matter how hard she tried, she would never be close to either again. Instead, one bad choice led to another. Her lifestyle became more transient, her relationships less long-lasting or stable, and her health unsteady.

Fanny's choice of Lynn, Massachusetts, was logical. First, Lynn was only about thirty miles from Newburyport, although roads were rough and travel too expensive for frequent visits. Second, Fanny wanted James, now eleven, to be apprenticed to a shoemaker so that he would have room and board and, by the age of eighteen or nineteen, a livelihood. Third, at a time when the seaport towns were languishing, Lynn was flourishing as a shoe center.[17] The town had developed from a haven of small shops to a manufacturing center of larger shops which employed hundreds of workers. In 1813 one of the master craftsmen in Lynn, Christopher Robinson, agreed to apprentice James, probably as a result of his and Fanny's shared Baptist affiliation. James spent a year with this "teetotaler" before moving on to the shop of Samuel Mansfield, where his troubles began.[18] According to his memoirs, written near the end of his life when he was residing in Lloyd's home, he was only twelve or thirteen years old when his fellow apprentices and master introduced him to "black strap," a combination of New England rum and molasses. As he later recalled, "I took a drink, it was sweet, and from that fatal hour I became a drunkard."[19] Instead of minding his mother's advice as to the pitfalls of alcohol abuse, he took to going on drinking sprees, gambling, and running around with girls his own age and young women. Drinking usually led to fighting and then to the loss of his job—a pattern repeated throughout his life. James, it seemed, was destined to turn out worse than his father, becoming addicted to alcohol and running off for what turned out to be an arduous and heart-wrenching life at sea. His tragic circumstances later served as a cautionary tale for his brother's children.

James's behavior was the most likely cause for Fanny's dislike of Lynn. Another was her great sense of loneliness. James was no comfort to her, and she missed her other two children dreadfully. She wrote constantly to Martha Farnham and to Lloyd, expressing concern for the children's well-being, trying to have some voice in their care, and reiterating her desire to reunite with them. Fanny was always careful to acknowledge Martha's help and to assure her of "the Lord's Smile" on her "kind endeavours."[20] Another reason for Fanny's disliking Lynn was her failure to find secure work. She had a string of nursing and domestic assignments, none of which were very long or satisfying. She was often "tired from Slavish work" and insulted by the way she was treated. As her grandsons were told, however, Fanny had dignity. In 1814 she left one employer, a Mrs. Gardner, because she felt the woman treated her "as dirt hardly fit for her to walk on."[21] After three months of intermittent work, Fanny found another position, which paid only in room and board. Lastly, Fanny missed her church, her most important emotional support. In letters home, she constantly inquired about her community and expressed her great sense of loss in being "cast on the protecting hand of a Divine providence in a Strange place."[22] When the trials she suffered in Lynn depressed her, she reprimanded herself for doubting "the Lord goodness to me."[23] She wrote to a church "Brother" that her heart felt very heavy, all her "former happiness . . . gone never to be recalld." She was, in truth, homeless, "a wanderer . . . a Pilgrim," who might hopefully find a happier, more sanctified existence.[24] As time passed and her ties to Newburyport lessened, Fanny's references to religion became more abstract and inner-directed. This shift reflected her lost self-esteem and newly acquired sense of degradation. Expression of this began in Lynn when she referred to her "unworthiness" and her need to learn "Submission by adversity."[25] Such self-deprecation, a common enough sentiment within the Baptist faith, became more frequent and intense as her life became more difficult.

While Fanny and James were meeting their personal trials in Lynn, little Lloyd and Elizabeth were quite safe in Newburyport. Although separated from their mother and older brother, they were in familiar surroundings and well cared for. Elizabeth, in fact, came to see Martha Farnham as a mother figure. Lloyd, from age seven to ten, was equally fortunate, considering the circumstances. Ezekial and Salome Bartlett and their two daughters treated him kindly, and he lived only a few blocks away from Elizabeth and Martha. As devout Baptists, the Bartletts saw to it that Lloyd attended church and even, for some months, the grammar school on High Street. When he was with his mother, Lloyd had sporadically attended the primary school opposite the Farnhams' home, but, according to his sons, he had had trouble mastering the alphabet, although he did finally learn to spell, read, and write. His major problem was that he was left-handed, and his teacher forced him to use his right hand, making studying awkward and time consuming. As an adult, he charmed his children with his ambidextrous talents.

Lloyd's education was not cut short by any malicious intent on the part of the Bartletts. Rather, Ezekial needed his help in earning his keep and income for the entire household. Most children worked either in their own family settings or for neighbors, so this was not an unusual expectation. The deacon earned his living by sawing wood, sharpening saws, making lasts, and selling apples each autumn from his own small stand. Young Lloyd became his right-hand man, a job unsuitable at that time for either of Ezekial's daughters. Despite hard work, however, there were good times for the boy as well. Lloyd related to his children how when Fanny was poor, other boys taunted him for begging for food, but once in the Bartlett home, he gained respectability. He now had friends with whom he flew kites and played marbles and "bat-the-ball."[26] He enjoyed swimming and boating in the summer and ice skating and snowball fights in the winter. He liked singing, at first with Fanny and Aunt Farnham at home and then later with the choir of the Baptist Church. It was also the boy's pleasure at this time to have pet cats, a passion that lasted throughout his lifetime. The animals offered him affection, and he happily responded to them. He later told his sons how one pet woke him by bringing her latest litter of kittens into his bed. "My eyes moistened when I realized what she had done, and we all slept in one bed that night."[27] Lloyd loved his Newburyport life even though he had lost his immediate family.

Fanny, however, missed her children so much that in mid-1815, she devised a plan to bring Lloyd to Lynn to apprentice for Gamaliel W. Oliver, a Quaker who had a shoe workshop adjoining his house. Unlike James, nine-year-old Lloyd showed little aptness for this particular occupation. Small for his age and not strong enough to sustain the work, he succeeded in making several shoes, although his fingers and knees grew sore from pounding the soles on a heavy lapstone. Despite Oliver's kindness, Lloyd felt miserable. Although he had also worked hard in Newburyport, he made friends there and had time to play. In Lynn, Fanny, who did not live with Lloyd, was too preoccupied looking for work and dealing with James's bouts of drinking and fighting to comprehend her younger son's situation. To make matters worse, without a second thought she accepted the offer of a successful Lynn shoe manufacturer, Paul Newhall, to travel with him and his workers to his new factory in Baltimore. Wendell and Frank Garrison tried to find out exactly why their grandmother had been invited to participate in this project. In the 1870s they interviewed former Newhall workers who claimed they liked to listen to Fanny espouse moral and religious views and that they called her "Mother."[28] Apparently, Newhall recognized the value of bringing along a housekeeper who would also provide a compassionate ear for his crew. Fanny's new course, however, took her further away from Newburyport and her daughter.

On October 21, after thirteen days at sea, Fanny, James, and Lloyd found themselves in Baltimore, Maryland, where by 1815 approximately eight hundred new residents were arriving every month, the majority, like Fanny, emigrating from the North.[29] Here, in what Fanny saw as a "place of Confusion," construction was booming, businesses flourishing, and, as a result, rents and the cost of food had doubled within a few years.[30] Unfortunately for her, the arrangement Fanny relied upon with the Newhalls did not last more than a few months, throwing her once again upon the uncertainties of day labor. Her only sense of stability came from her faith. Utilizing a letter from Pastor John Peak of the Newburyport church, she quickly found a congregation, and by the next September had established a

Baptist female prayer meeting which met every Saturday afternoon. Once again, she took up itinerant preaching, walking thirteen miles every Sunday to sermonize; yet she still felt lonely and alone and spent much of her time worrying about James and Lloyd. James, as was his wont, found trouble immediately. At the age of fourteen, his alcoholism was growing worse, and after being fired from two jobs because of violent episodes, Fanny sent him back to Lynn. For over two years she had no word from or about him until he returned to Baltimore in September 1818 to request her aid in preparing for a life at sea. Fanny arranged with Joseph Mudge, a seaman of some experience, to take James along on his schooner. Just before his leave-taking, she took her son's hand, kissed him, and gave him her blessing. They never saw each other again.

Meanwhile, Lloyd was experiencing his own difficulties in adjusting to life in Baltimore. Even after Fanny moved on to another establishment, he continued to live with the Newhalls, paying for his keep by doing odd jobs. He certainly must have felt some sense of abandonment and, therefore, longed for his life with the Bartletts and for the one place he considered "home"—Newburyport. Fanny, although busy with James, worried about Lloyd. If she could not be as active as she wished in his upbringing, might he not end up like his brother? Hence, contrary to her own desires, Fanny contacted Ezekial Bartlett and made arrangements to send Lloyd home for the next year, after which she promised herself that she would reunite with him. The boy was ecstatic, dreaming about returning to school and regaining his friendships. For Fanny, his move meant more financial responsibility, as she needed to again send money to both the Bartletts and the Farnhams, money she rarely had as her own life continued on its downward spiral. She moved from job to job, seemed endlessly depressed, often wished for release from her earthly misery, and experienced a deterioration in her health, caused either by tuberculosis or possibly lung cancer.

Once Lloyd was back in Newburyport, Fanny requested that Ezekial Bartlett place him in an apprenticeship. He complied by arranging a situation with Moses Short, a cabinetmaker in Haverhill, Massachusetts. Although the Short family was quite kind to the now pubescent young man, he was so unhappy that after six weeks he climbed out of his bedroom window with his possessions tied in a large bandanna and struck out for Newburyport, a distance of about twelve miles. A compassionate and reasonable man, Short released Lloyd from his contract and returned him to the Bartletts. Fanny was not pleased with this turn of events, for she would once again have to provide for his support, but in his own defense Lloyd told his mother that he wanted to find a trade he enjoyed and could do well at so that he could take care of her. As it happened, Ephraim W. Allen, the editor and publisher of the Newburyport *Herald,* a semiweekly newspaper, announced that he was looking for a male apprentice to learn the printing trade. Most likely, it was Ezekial Bartlett who put Lloyd forward as a candidate, for on October 18,

1818, just six weeks shy of his thirteenth birthday, he began the usual seven-year term, moving into the Allens' home and a world of physical comfort, exciting conversation, and eclectic reading. Fanny felt great relief upon learning that he had finally found work he liked.

Fanny and Lloyd maintained a regular correspondence. Many of her letters passed on from Lloyd to his sons, but unfortunately only one of Lloyd's replies survived the years. In this instance, he apparently rejected his mother's pleas that he relocate to Baltimore in order to help her out during her declining years. Fanny's response in May 1819 indicated a deep sense of hurt: "All things considered, I think you have acted wisely in staying and learning your trade. Your dear Sister must have felt the loss of your company, and your prospect here was not the best, although you might have had a chance of doing well."[31] Five months later, she again complained to him, this time for neglecting to write to her on a regular basis: "How painful to a Mothers feelings—my love for you is still the same—and at this important moment I write as one perhaps that may not be privileged to address you again."[32] Although not even fourteen years old, Lloyd chose to distance himself from his mother in order to protect his own future prospects.

As 1819 drew to a close and Fanny accepted that Lloyd was not coming to Baltimore, she became obsessed with thoughts about Elizabeth, now eleven years old. Although she had not seen her since 1812, Fanny felt as close to her daughter as if she had been with her every day of her life. For Elizabeth, however, Fanny only existed through occasional gifts, letters, or stories from Lloyd. Not of an age to make decisions for herself and not as assertive as her two brothers, Elizabeth became vulnerable to Fanny's desires and needs. Ill and lonely, Fanny saw in her daughter her last hope in being able to recapture some semblance of family life. Now that her youngest child had reached an age where she could be useful rather than totally dependent, Fanny wanted her by her side. Hence, she began her mental preparation for their reunion by imagining that her daughter needed her, when it was actually she who needed Elizabeth. In November 1819 she wrote to Lloyd that she felt "uneasy" about his sister, as she had the "most wretched dreams about her and alas I am afraid all is not well."[33] But she was unable to act upon her fears because of her own poor physical condition. In January 1820, Fanny became so ill that no one around her thought she would survive. She experienced "dropsy in the Chest" and had bled "Copious," unable to leave her room for days on end.[34] In May, she coughed up enough blood to wet two large handkerchiefs.

Fanny's declining health and long, idle days gave her plenty of time to ruminate over Elizabeth, especially after Martha insisted that Fanny remove her daughter from her care—she was tired of doing the job out of pure Christian charity when she, herself, needed money. So Fanny requested that Lloyd and Martha send her daughter to her in July. Like her brother, however, Elizabeth was reluctant to leave Newburyport. Lloyd, her self-proclaimed protector, wrote his mother about his sister's feelings. Fanny, in turn, tried to reassure him that Elizabeth would be better off with her. To Elizabeth, she voiced her sorrow in hearing that her daughter did not want to join her and added that although she could understand Elizabeth's attachment to Martha and her children, "your dear Aunt F. cannot keep you and I wish to relieve her of that burden before I die."[35] Finally, after several disappointing months, Elizabeth unexpectedly appeared in Baltimore in early September. She had made the trip alone, arriving "in a raging fever, scarce sensible that she had a parent's protection." Fanny, however, was not much of a caretaker; rather, as she reported to Lloyd, "some ladies" had become interested in her own case and had taken her under their wing in order to prevent her being sent to the poorhouse.[36] Elizabeth, in turn, ended up going out daily to clean other women's homes.

In 1822 Fanny again asked Lloyd to visit her. It had been six years since they had been together. Would he come? Apparently, he avoided the issue, for she wrote again, telling her son that she was "emaciated" after having been confined to her bed for ten "long" months. At present, she could not even dress or undress herself without help and had become totally dependent on "the charity of friends." This deeply humiliated her. She had tried so hard over the years to remain self-sufficient, but now her pride was "mortified" and her spirits low.[37] Lloyd, however, begged off, claiming he could not leave Newburyport because of his apprenticeship. This was the one chance he had to learn a trade he really liked. He could not jeopardize his future. Ephraim Allen had made him the office foreman, and in his spare time he took to reading novels and poetry, studying the works of Byron, Pope, and Scott. He became enthralled with politics and, believing himself to be a budding Federalist, tried to learn everything he could about the Newburyport branch of the Party.

Lloyd also tried his hand at writing. Adopting the pseudonym "An Old Bachelor," he submitted letters to the Newburyport *Herald* on subjects ranging from marriage to foreign policy to the colonization of free blacks, letters that his sons later traced and eagerly read. When Lloyd told Fanny of his actions, she was supportive even though she could not understand why he kept his identity a secret. As she wrote him in July, "If Mr. Allen approves of it why you have nothing to fear; but I hope you consulted him on the publication of them. I am pleased myself with the idea, provided that nothing wrong should result from it." She then requested copies of his articles, so she could judge for herself whether Lloyd was "an old Bachelor, or whether you are AOB, as A may stand for an ass, and O for oaf and B for blockhead."[38] Considering their father's position as a respected writer and editor, however poor, Wendell and Frank must have found it amusing that, the next year, their grandmother gave her son another tongue-lashing about his choice of a probable low-paying profession. She had approved of his apprenticeship to learn printing, not writing. "Next your turning Author," she wrote, "you have no doubt read—and heard the fate of such Characters that they generally starve to death in some garret or place that no one inhabits—so you may see what fortune and luck belongs to you if you are of their Class of people—." As for his delving into political issues, Fanny felt his time would be better spent if he "studied the *Bible*."[39]

Lloyd's happiness was momentarily shattered in December 1822, when he learned that Elizabeth had died of yellow fever.[40] Fanny wished him to come to her, but it took him more than a year and a half to arrange it, partly because Ephraim Allen was reluctant to let him go and partly because Lloyd himself did not want to make the trip. Finally, on July 5, 1823, after seven long years, mother and son were reunited. Lloyd was astounded by the change in Fanny. As he wrote to Ephraim Allen, "I found her in tears—but, o God, so altered, so emaciated, that I should never have recognized her, had I not known that there were none else in the room. Instead of the tall, robust woman, blooming in health, whom I saw last, she is now bent up by 'fell disease,' pined away to almost a skeleton, and unable to walk. She is under the necessity of being bolstered up in bed, being incompetent to lie down, as it would immediately choke her."[41] Lloyd stayed with Fanny for two or three weeks. Soon after he left, she was operated on for a cancerous tumor near her chest. Never able to rally, she steadily drifted toward death, which took her on September 3, 1823. She was buried in the cemetery of the First Baptist Society in Baltimore. Lloyd marked his mother's passing with a brief notice in the Newburyport *Herald,* the Eastport *Sentinel,* and the St. John *Star.* It said simply, "DIED. In Baltimore, 3rd inst., after a long and distressing illness, which she bore with Christian fortitude and resignation, Mrs. Frances Maria Garrison, relict of the late Captain Abijah G., formerly of this town, aged 45."[42] Rather than identify his mother as an abandoned woman, he listed his father as deceased.

Fanny's story does not really end with her death, for three other people's stories are intertwined with her own: Abijah's, James's, and Lloyd's. As far as historians and the Garrison children have told it, the only one of the Garrison branch of the family to live to old age was Lloyd. However, there remains a question about Abijah's fate. As an adult researching his father's history, Wendell found out some interesting information. On a trip to St. John, New Brunswick, in 1873, a cousin, Joanne Palmer, shared a letter she had received from Abijah in 1814. It proved he was in Lundey, Canada, in the parish of Waterborough.[43] Later rumors included that he had returned to the sea, taken up teaching, and/or begun a new family. Even more compelling, however, and, understandably, absent from the sons' laudatory biography, is the fact that one William Augustus Garrison, a music teacher in St. John, claimed to be Lloyd's half-brother. As Wendell wrote to his sister, Fanny, "The story is a long one, and it is enough to say here that he was a son of Abijah by his second cousin Nancy Palmer, and that he was born in Dec. 1809, just five years after Father, to whom he bears a striking resemblance." Lloyd had met William A. in 1840 and 1845, but thought him to be "a sort of cousin, & never dreamed of the nearer relationship."[44] Several months after Wendell's visit, William A. wrote how the purpose of the visit, that of discovering family history, convinced him to reveal his parentage, a story not even his wife had known. He felt humiliated for not coming forward earlier with the tale of his "unfortunate mother."[45] After his confession, he attempted to restore contact with Lloyd, but his letters went unanswered. What became of Abijah is unknown.

James's fate, however, was easily traceable. For years he shifted around, his life always following the same pattern: a job at sea, drinking, fights or cruel treatment at the hand of some sadistic sea captain, jail, and then guilt. From time to time, he wrote to Lloyd or vice versa, but there seems to have been no regular contact until the fall of 1839, when Lloyd came to James's rescue. Learning that his brother had become disabled, because of what Lloyd described as "a fistulous abscess, of a cancerous nature, situated at the base of the back bone, and badly affecting the spine," he appealed to Commodore John Downes of the United States Navy to allow James a leave so that he could recover his health at Lloyd's Cambridgeport home.[46] After three months with no improvement, Lloyd began a process of appeals for James's discharge, in which he succeeded in April 1840. James remained in the care of Lloyd and his wife of six years, Helen, both of whom showed him great warmth and compassion. A very young George, William, and Wendell met their uncle, but only George could vaguely recollect him. As diehard temperance advocates and good Christians, Helen and Lloyd expected James not only to abstain from alcohol but also to repent for his so-called sins. Sounding very much like his mother, Lloyd told his brother that "without repentance there can be no reconciliation; and unless we are reconciled to God, how can we be happy?"[47] James tried to live the good life, even writing his memoirs, which were eventually published in 1954 as *Behold Me Once More: The Confessions of James Holley Garrison, Brother of William Lloyd Garrison.* The memoirs, which read like a temperance tract, present a good argument for nonviolence, for James's life was riddled with brutality. In the spring of 1842, like his mother, he developed an abscess on his chest. His fate followed hers, and on October 14, with his brother by his side, James died. He was only forty-one years old.

As for Lloyd, in the few years following Fanny's death, he graduated from his apprenticeship at the *Herald* and established his own Newburyport paper, the *Free Press,* in the process, discovering the young poet John Greenleaf Whittier. The venture was not profitable, however, and Lloyd moved on, first to Boston to edit the *National Philanthropist,* where he met the great abolitionist Benjamin Lundy, and then, in 1828, to Bennington, Vermont, to edit the *Journal of the Times.* Lloyd's future as a great abolitionist leader really began in 1829 at the age of just twenty-four, when Lundy convinced him to take on the coeditorship of his newspaper, the *Genius of Universal Emancipation,* an abolitionist publication in which

Lloyd, as William Lloyd Garrison, expressed his belief in the immediate emancipation of all slaves.[48] Ironically, the journal was published in Baltimore, the city he so fervently avoided in his youth, but where he stayed for about a year before returning to Boston and establishing the *Liberator* in 1831.

Lloyd grew into a man of tremendous insight, compassion, and political awareness. He embraced many reforms of his day, the most telling being abolitionism, feminism, temperance, and nonviolence—all, in his case, related to the traumas he experienced as a child. As his own children matured, they came to accept that their father's early traumas were actually a part of their own heritage. Lloyd's involvement in temperance was easy for them to understand. Alcohol had destroyed his childhood, had ripped his parents apart, and then stolen his brother. Nonviolence also seemed obvious. His home had been torn asunder by violence between his parents; he himself perhaps had experienced physical or psychological violence firsthand. In his adult life, Lloyd never allowed anyone to use violence toward his children, and he and Helen never raised their voices at each other. His ties to feminism were less obvious, but Lloyd must have, in a very real way, understood that Fanny's struggles might not have been as serious had there been equality for women. Throughout his adult years he respected strong, independent abolitionist women who, like his mother, spoke their minds. He wanted equality for these women, and he especially wanted it for his own daughter, Helen Frances (or Fanny), although he preferred she find happiness as a wife and mother. Furthermore, both the early temperance and woman's rights movements addressed the need for easier divorce laws for women married to alcoholics, a cause Lloyd could easily embrace.

Lloyd's devotion to abolitionism was more difficult for his children to trace back to his early years. Clearly, as a child, he w`itnessed slavery in Baltimore, but except for the mention of one slave woman who had treated her kindly, neither mother nor son mentioned slavery in their letters, making it impossible to know just what he had experienced. He most likely witnessed human cruelty, humiliation, and powerlessness. Certainly, while later working for Benjamin Lundy, he learned firsthand from free blacks and slaves the meaning of the "peculiar institution." Indeed, in the spring of 1830 Lloyd spent forty-nine days in a Baltimore jail for libeling Francis Todd, a Massachusetts shipowner who, Lloyd alleged, allowed his ships to carry slaves. Whatever his youthful thoughts about slavery, Fanny's own inability to improve her lot also taught Lloyd about exploitation and hopelessness. Fanny took menial jobs, was often treated badly, and had few other options. As he wrote about slaves to a friend, Harriet Minot, in 1833, "It is the lowness of their estate, in the estimation of the world, which exalts them in my eyes. It is the distance which separates them from the blessings and privileges of society, which brings them so closely to my affections."[49] This quotation could very well reflect upon Fanny's life as well as that of the slaves.

For the Garrison children, Lloyd's real and romanticized images of Fanny as a long-suffering poor and abused Christian wife and mother served as lessons against alcohol abuse, violence, and poverty. Fanny's story provided them with a concrete and personal example of suffering from which they could better understand the lives of slaves, the impoverished, and the oppressed. But her life also served as a reminder of their own father's struggles to avoid these evils and carve out his exemplary career. Their grandmother's image, constantly evoked in their family history, became one of their personal reference points for their future political work in benevolent, woman's rights, peace, and racial justice movements, not to mention their firm commitment to nonviolence.

LLOYD AND HELEN

> What, indeed, strikes the reader of the fourth volume of the *Liberator,* from the very beginning, is the frequency, fulness, and animation of the editorial articles. . . . But one is made aware of a special exaltation seeking a vent in verse—mainly in sonnets—of which the last two, "Helen, if thus we tenderly deplore," and "Thou mistress of my heart! my chosen one!" reveal the cause.
>
> Wendell Phillips Garrison and Francis Jackson Garrison,
> *William Lloyd Garrison*

CHAPTER II

It was essential for the Garrison children to know their maternal grandparents' history, for therein lay the roots of their mother's abolitionist beliefs and the key to understanding the deep connection that blossomed between their own parents in 1834. Since they knew their Benson grandparents only slightly, they had to learn about them secondhand, the way they had learned about Fanny Garrison. George Benson, their grandfather, died in 1836, when Helen and Lloyd's eldest son, George, was less than a year old; their grandmother, Sarah (Sally) Thurber Benson, died eight years later, making it possible for her grandsons George, William, Wendell, and Charley to know her in varying degrees. One would suppose that the Bensons' middle-class status would have made it easy for Wendell and Frank Garrison to reconstruct their story. Such was not the case, however, for the Bensons, although educated, prosperous, and influential, preserved little of their correspondence and none of their diaries or journals. Therefore, their story took as much investigation as had Fanny's.

As a result of his research, Wendell arranged to have his record of the family's genealogy privately published in 1872. In *The Benson Family of Newport, Rhode Island,* he traced his mother's family line in this country as far back as the 1690s.[1] Wendell was sure that John Benson, a shipowner or captain, came to the Newport area sometime after May 1692, the same year as the Salem witch trials in

Massachusetts. In 1714 John married Anna Collins. Considering the Benson family's later prominence in the antislavery movement, it is interesting to note that John and Anna's son, William, was involved in trade that included slave labor and slave-made products. Two of William's five sons, Martin and John, continued the family business, and the youngest son, George, although an antislavery advocate, also conducted business with slave owners.

At the age of twenty, George, born in Newport on August 20, 1752, moved to Providence, Rhode Island, a prosperous port city, to work as a clerk with the trading firm of Nicholas Brown & Company. He stayed with the business until sometime after the war of independence from England began, whereupon he joined the revolutionary forces. After the war and a brief time in Boston, George returned to Providence, where by the end of 1783 he had joined with his former boss, Nicholas Brown, in a business renamed Brown & Benson, which in 1792 became Brown, Benson & Ives. Although Brown, Benson & Ives prospered, some of the owners' endeavors contradicted George Benson's antislavery sentiment and his family's preference for alcohol abstinence. For instance, in the early 1790s Brown & Benson held a business interest in a rum distillery owned by John Brown of Providence and imported molasses from Surinam.[2] When Brown took to distilling his own gin in 1794, Benson's firm made even more money. Tobacco was another of the company's major business interests tying it to Southern slaveholders.

After Brown, Benson & Ives purchased its own ships, its reach expanded to Europe, South Asia, and China.[3] But natural disasters and wars added such great risk that George Benson chose to keep his hard-earned profits and resign from the company rather than continue to participate in shaky expansion plans.[4] During his years at Brown, Benson & Ives, George Benson had become a prominent citizen of Providence. In 1792, for example, he was elected a director of the Providence Bank. So once he retired from Brown, Benson & Ives at the age of forty-four, the business world was still open to him. He immediately became director and secretary of the newly established Washington Insurance Company of Providence, and for some years he served as a trustee of Brown University.

It was not until January 27, 1793, when he was forty, that George Benson wed Sarah (Sally) Thurber, then only twenty-three. Since the average age of marriage at the time was twenty-two for women and twenty-six for men, he would have been considered by many as a diehard bachelor. However, oblivious of the seventeen-year difference in their ages, they built a solid and close-knit family, eventually producing nine children, six girls and three boys. Helen, born in 1811, was next to the youngest.[5] Prosperous and influential, the Benson family lived in an elegant house at 64 Angell Street, which reaped a $6,500 profit when sold in 1826.[6] A beautiful two-story Georgian-style, with third-floor attic rooms and a widow's walk, it was a typical affluent home in Providence at that time but a stark contrast to William Lloyd Garrison's own early Newburyport home on School Street. For twenty-nine years the Benson family grew in this house until, in 1823, George, feeling that land was a "more secure property than trade," purchased a sixty-four-acre farm in Brooklyn, Connecticut. Twelve years later, he somewhat regretted his choice, for his farm gave him "little, very little profit."[7]

Although the Garrison children had little firsthand knowledge of Brooklyn, the town grew to mythical proportions in their minds, for it was here that their parents courted and wed and that their own abolitionist roots started. A rural village in the northeastern corner of Connecticut and the seat of Windham County, Brooklyn was perfectly located for the Bensons—approximately thirty miles from their beloved Providence, thirty-nine from Worcester, and seventy-seven from Boston. Their property, later characterized as low and swampy, included on it a two-story, four-bedroom house, a blacksmith's shop, two barns, and a carriage house, and was a mere quarter of a mile from the town common, upon which sat the Unitarian and Congregationalist churches.[8]

One reason why the Bensons may have left Providence was George's conscience-stricken feelings about his complicity in the institution of slavery. According to Wendell, his grandfather had expressed concern about the issue as early as 1775, when a letter appearing in the Providence *Gazette* on September 9 of that year, signed "A Friend of America," was attributed to him. In it, George proffered support for a petition to the General Assembly of Rhode Island to pass an act "for prohibiting the importation of negroes into this colony, and asserting the right of freedom of all those hereafter born or manumitted within the same."[9] During the Independence era and in the years following the end of the war in 1781, many Northern states abolished slavery. These actions were not necessarily based upon an antipathy toward slavery; rather they often reflected the spirit of newfound national liberation in an area not economically dependent on slave labor. In 1790, six years after Rhode Island outlawed slavery, George joined in the truly committed antislavery voice in the nation by signing a document establishing the Providence Society for Promoting the Abolition of Slavery for the Relief of Persons Unlawfully held in Bondage, and for Improving the Condition of the African Race. Two years later, he was made an honorary member of the similarly titled Pennsylvania society, an organization whose first president was none other than Benjamin Franklin. George's early sense of the injustice of slavery may have partially led to his withdrawal from Brown, Benson & Ives, but it did not impinge upon his family's comfortable lifestyle, made possible in part by slavery.

Unlike Providence, Brooklyn had evolved into an abolitionist town, a brave and important action since the final emancipation of slaves in the state of Connecticut, which had begun as a gradual policy in 1792, did not become law until 1848. In fact, at the time the Bensons moved to Brooklyn, abolitionists and free African Americans were generally disliked in Connecticut. Blacks were not permitted to vote although the 1818 state constitution granted them citizenship, and antislavery activists, black or white, were seen as troublemakers, especially as cotton mills grew in number. In Brooklyn the Benson family joined the Unitarian minister, Samuel J. May, and other like-minded people in the work of the Underground Railroad, the Brooklyn Anti-Slavery Society (formed in 1834), and the Brooklyn Female Anti-Slavery Society (formed in 1835). The Underground Railroad was an especially important endeavor, since Brooklyn was on the route which ran north from New London through Massachusetts, New Hampshire, and Vermont to Canada and freedom. The Bensons, Mays, and other local residents acted as "agents" and "conductors" who aided fugitive "passengers" in getting from one "station" to another and in raising money to see that those in flight had the means to travel and then to settle in their new homes.[10]

Besides being abolitionists, George Benson and Samuel J. May were also pacifists, which at that time signified a Christian commitment to nonviolent solutions in one's personal life as well as in the political world.[11] Together, in 1826, they founded the Windham County Peace Society. May's Unitarian church, where peace and justice were preached each Sunday, was a favorite place for the Benson family to hear sermons, and they and the Mays became close friends. Indeed, it was a friendship that extended itself into the future Garrison family. The Bensons were unusual in their religious habits, however, and not every member of the family attended any one church. George and Sally Benson had entered their marriage as Baptists, but after Sally quarreled with the minister of the Providence church the couple left the Baptist community. They both then began attending Quaker meetings and continued to do so, although they never officially joined a Friends' Meeting. The Benson children were raised as staunch Christians, but each was allowed to choose her or his denomination, a practice that Helen and Lloyd adopted with their own offspring. Mary and Anna Benson became Quakers; George W., a utopianist; Helen, first a Unitarian and then nonaffiliated. All, however, attended services that appealed to their abolitionist beliefs, no matter what the sect.

The first contact that anyone from Brooklyn had with the then twenty-four-year-old William Lloyd Garrison occurred on October 16, 1830, when Samuel J. May attended a lecture at Julien Hall in Boston.[12] There he met the very modest young man whose slight, five-foot ten-inch build, pale complexion, yellowish-hazel eyes, thinning dark-brown hair, and round spectacles presented a most benign and sincere figure. Taken by Lloyd's passion, May and his cousin, Samuel E. Sewall, encouraged him to give more speeches, which he did, but what primarily interested Lloyd was finding a place to launch his own newspaper.[13] Boston, in his home state of Massachusetts and only thirty-five miles from Newburyport, presented an attractive possibility. With the encouragement of May, Sewall, and another Boston acquaintance, the wealthy lawyer Ellis Gray Loring, Lloyd made plans to start business. He convinced a former printer friend from Newburyport, Isaac Knapp, to join him, and the two set out to find an office, buy supplies, and raise money. Their first business success was achieved when on January 1, 1831, the *Liberator* made its debut with Lloyd writing his now well-known opening editorial (his children could recite it by heart), which read in part: "I am aware, that many object to the severity of my language; but is there not cause for severity? I *will be* as harsh as truth, and as uncompromising as justice. On this subject I do not wish to think, or speak, or write, with moderation. . . . I am in earnest—I will not equivocate—I will not excuse—I will not retreat a single inch—AND I WILL BE HEARD."[14]

This strong statement clearly set Lloyd apart from the American Colonization Society, which supported the removal of free blacks from the United States to Liberia. The society, which had several slaveholding members, claimed to wish for the elimination of slavery through compensating owners for their loss of property, but Lloyd and other abolitionists believed the ultimate goal of the society was to eliminate only free African Americans from the United States while maintaining the institution of slavery indefinitely. Lloyd particulary distrusted the society's members, claiming that they had no desire to live in a biracial society, and, in fact, believed that such a plan was untenable.

The Garrison children loved to hear how Lloyd and Samuel J. May's friendship led their father to the Benson family, first to the youngest Benson, seventeen-year-old Henry, who became an agent for the *Liberator,* and then to Henry's older brother, George W., a wool merchant in Providence, with whom Lloyd felt an instant camaraderie. Lloyd came to depend on Henry for a myriad of activities, from selling newspapers to reporting on important news events, especially since he himself could not edit, print, sell newspapers, and do investigative reporting at the same time. Henry and George W. also helped Lloyd to organize the New England Anti-Slavery Society, founded on January 6, 1832, in Boston. Soon after, other "Garrisonian" societies emerged, and Lloyd became a popular figure among antislavery advocates. By the end of the year, he felt a great sense of accomplishment as his hard work had spawned an expanding network of antislavery societies throughout the Northeast, and the *Liberator* was ready to start its second year of publication.

For a young man from such poor roots, Lloyd was certainly making a success of his life. His mother, Fanny, might have still questioned his pecuniary straits, but she would have been unable to suppress her pride in her son's deep sense of Christian morality and the respect which a number of both rich and poor people showed him. Although his nondenominational approach to religion and the absence of a conversion experience might have worried her, she would have felt great joy in hearing him describe himself as one of God's workers ready for any sacrifice, even martyrdom. Actually, on a very personal level, Lloyd was delighted with his ability to attract people to his way of thinking and with his position of authority at the *Liberator* and in the abolitionist movement named after him. Years later, although they knew their father was deeply committed to the ideal of personal sacrifice for his cause, his children clearly recognized that he enjoyed the life he had created for himself. The world had opened itself to Lloyd, and he eagerly accepted its gifts of intellectual growth, personal friendships, and moral challenges.

Two new worlds opened for Lloyd in 1833. In that year he made his initial voyage to England to meet with British abolitionists, and, even more important, he met his future wife—Helen Eliza Benson. To gain funding for the trip, the young abolitionist went on a lecture tour throughout the Northeast. One of his stops was Providence, where George W. and Henry brought their sister, Helen, to hear him speak at the African Church. The next day, according to the version their parents told their entranced children, Lloyd and Helen met at George W.'s store.[15] At twenty-two, Helen seemed to Lloyd very sweet; to her, the twenty-seven year old Lloyd was nothing short of charismatic. Wendell and Frank related in their father's biography how their mother was "riveted to the spot, lingering long to hear him converse, and bidding him farewell, perhaps forever, with a dull weight upon the mind."[16] From Providence, however, George W. took Lloyd to Brooklyn, where he spent the weekend as a guest of the Bensons, becoming better acquainted with all the family, although his attention kept returning to Helen.

Lloyd's visit coincided with a great turmoil surrounding the harassment of Prudence Crandall for operating a school for African-American girls.[17] In the summer of 1831, Crandall had been appointed by a group of citizens in nearby Canterbury to open a private academy for local young ladies (assumed to be white). The interested parties purchased the Luther Paine house, originally constructed in 1805 on the Canterbury Green, and in January 1832 the academy opened its doors to students, who were then instructed in reading, writing, arithmetic, English grammar, geography, history, moral philosophy, chemistry, and astronomy. All went well at the school until the fall of its first year, when Crandall admitted Sarah Harris, the sister of the school's African-American domestic worker. Many of the community people, including parents of enrolled students, were appalled and outraged by this racial mixing. Their efforts to force Crandall to dismiss her student led this antislavery daughter to close her white academy in order to redesign it as a school for African-American young ladies, the first such school in New England.

While Lloyd was in Brooklyn, Crandall and her sister, Almeria, stopped by for a visit with him and their good friends, the Benson sisters, all of whom expressed undying support for the project. Soon after, Lloyd left to continue his lecture tour and travel to England while the Benson and May families spent a great deal of their time and effort in trying to help Prudence Crandall save her school. Crandall, in fact, found such great comfort at the Benson home that she nicknamed it "Friendship's Vale." The name stuck, first as "Friendship's Valley" and then as "Friendship Valley," which it is still called today. Meanwhile the Connecticut state government took quick action against Crandall's school for "young ladies and little misses of color" and any other similar future project. On May 24, 1833, the General Assembly passed the "Black Law," which made it illegal for anyone to establish a school or academy for "colored persons who are not inhabitants of this State."[18] Until 1838, when the law was repealed, any such person was fined one hundred dollars for the first offense, two hundred for the second, and a double penalty for each offense after that.

Although there are no extant records stating the exact number and names of out-of-state students Crandall taught between May 1833 and September 1834, historians at the Prudence Crandall Museum in Canterbury have tracked down at least twenty-five names of students from Connecticut as well as from Pennsylvania, Rhode Island, New York City, and places unknown. On June 27, 1833, Crandall was arrested for her supposed crime and locked up in the jail in Brooklyn, where Anna Benson insisted on staying with her for the night. It took three court trials before the case was dismissed on a technicality in July 1834. During that time, while Lloyd and the Connecticut abolitionists led a campaign to support Crandall, her opponents attempted to physically destroy the academy. They threw manure into the well to contaminate the water, set a corner of the building ablaze, and then broke ninety of the building's windowpanes. Crandall, fearing for her charges' lives, decided to give up. Soon afterward, she and her new husband, Calvin Philleo, left Canterbury.

Lloyd, meanwhile, had returned to Boston at the end of the summer of 1833. Throughout his European jaunt and once home, he could not stop thinking about Helen. Finally, in November, he wrote George W. of his desire to visit Brooklyn where he could find "the soft blue eyes and pleasant countenance of Miss Ellen."[19] Lloyd would later claim, "If it was not 'love at first sight,' on my part, it was something very like it—a magnetic influence being exerted which became irresistible on further acquaintance."[20] The Garrison children must have found it amusing that their lovesick father did not remember his true love's name correctly, but they overlooked the misunderstanding, knowing that Lloyd had met his ideal partner: a quiet, shy young woman who was physically appealing, politically compatible, and part of a family for which he already felt great affection.

In 1828, when Lloyd was writing under the pseudonym "An Old Bachelor," he described his fantasy of the perfect wife and mother. His description matched the typical Victorian-era perception of "true womanhood," a woman who was pious, pure, domestic, and voluntarily submissive to her husband, father, or other men who held power over her, a woman who bore little resemblance to his own poor mother.[21] As he wrote then:

> No one has more respect than myself for the character of woman, when she is employed in exerting her proper influence and doing her proper duty. In early life, she

is to be the peculiar solace of her parents. She is in truth to pass her *whole* life in softening the character, exciting the affections, and rewarding with a love beyond all price the toils of man. She is to educate her children. She is to develop those powers which as she has taught them to reach forward to good or bad objects, will be a curse or a blessing to the world. Above all, on the mother it depends (as far indeed as such a thing can depend on earthly power) whether her children shall be happy or miserable forever. This is her appropriate sphere of duty, but beside this, she is to be the hand-maiden of charity and of religion.[22]

Helen Eliza Benson's own mother, Sally, fit this description quite well. According to Lloyd, Sally "combined all the best qualities—sound discretion, admirable economic prudence, cheerful self-denial, retiring modesty, a 'meek and quiet spirit,' and a rare capacity for the faithful discharge of all household responsibilities."[23] She also shared her husband's belief in temperance, pacifism, and abolitionism and taught these values to her children.

According to sons Wendell and Frank, when their father and mother met, she was "a plump and rosy creature, with blue eyes and fair brown hair," whom her family sometimes called "Peace and Plenty" because she was both "placid" and endlessly cheerful. Helen dressed simply, believed in such experimental health treatments as using cold water baths and drinks, and was praised for her kindness and attentiveness to others. Although the sons learned little about their mother's childhood, they knew she had received some, though not an extensive, education with a sound grounding in Christian and abolitionist thought. They also observed that she loved to read and turned out to be one of the most informed people they knew in terms of the news of the day. Always, however, she was very "self-distrustful," some would say "self-deprecating," others "modest."[24] In any case, although Lloyd found himself inexplicably attracted to her, his own lack of knowledge of courting rituals prevented him from asserting himself into her life. While in Brooklyn in May 1833, for instance, he wanted to escort Helen on a carriage ride to Canterbury, but was too bashful to ask. Indeed, it was not until January 1834 that he goaded himself to begin courting, and then, most of their romance took place through the mails, although as the relationship intensified, Lloyd made several visits to Friendship Valley. The Garrison children loved to hear stories of their parents' romance and, years later, saw to it that the correspondence between Helen and Lloyd was carefully preserved.

Lloyd opened the way to wooing Helen on January 18, 1834, when he wrote her the first of many letters. In it, he drew a vivid picture of his happy mood precipitated by the January thaw, a brief period each winter when New England weather eases a bit and there are hints of spring in the air. "My spirit is perfectly bird-like—not merely hopping from twig to twig, and tree to tree," he wrote, "but soaring upward and onward with a stronger flight and with better pinions than an eagle's. Where has it not been? It has flown to Providence, and been refreshed with a smile from you, and with the gratulations of George, and Henry, and all the dear friends." He went on to wax poetic about the four seasons and about his own letter writing. Finally, however, he posed a political challenge to Helen, one that would give him some information about her public persona. He wanted to know if she had aspirations of becoming an activist. "I shall look to you," he stated, "for the formation of a Female Anti-Slavery Society in Providence. You know, or must know, that I rely upon female influence to break the shackles of the bleeding slave." The letter was signed, "Your friend and well-wisher, William Lloyd Garrison."[25] Helen did not respond until February 11, but her tone and message were just what Lloyd wanted to hear and what her children later expected of her behavior. Very modestly, she explained to him that she did not consider herself to be influential enough to begin such a society. She knew only the people within her family circle in Providence and very few others. Helen was apparently greatly flattered by Lloyd's advances, but she did not fancy herself a public person. Little did she know that Lloyd was looking for a partner who would take care of the home and become his companion (and a good abolitionist) rather than an independent political performer such as Lucretia Mott or, later, Abby Kelley, who often left home for conventions and lectures.

After this first interchange, every week or two, a letter left Lloyd's small home, "Freedom's Cottage," in Roxbury, just outside Boston, and Helen's home in Brooklyn. Each correspondent eagerly awaited the next missive, which would reveal some new piece of information about the other. Lloyd was full of compliments about Helen's letters. He immediately told her how he loved her "frankness," her "contemplative spirit," and her lack of "affectation."[26] At the end of February he made an official trip to Brooklyn to answer charges of libel for statements made during the Prudence Crandall episode. But once there, he found that the trial had been postponed. (The charges were eventually dropped.) Lloyd was not unhappy about making the unnecessary journey, however, for he and Helen had the opportunity to be together. From this brief visit, Lloyd decided that Helen was the woman he wanted for a wife; in fact, he wanted to claim the entire family as his own, confessing on March 8, "All of you have got possession of my heart."[27]

At first, Lloyd's aggressive pursuit of Helen unsettled her. She was flattered by the attentions of this rather famous and controversial man but unsure whether she wanted to move along with the relationship so quickly. Rebuffed, Lloyd momentarily retreated. He insisted that Helen not worry about answering all of his letters, as he had no "claim" upon her time. He then filled his pages with melancholy love poems by Byron, Thomas Moore, and his favorite poet, Felicia Dorothea Hemans, to which he added his own lament: "And therefore I wept in sadness and in solitude. Is it ever thus to be? Alas! all may be mated but me—I have no attractions to enkindle or secure love—there is none in the wide world whose heart

I am authorised to claim—none, into whose bosom I can pour the wealth of my affections."[28] Helen's reaction to this dramatic pronouncement was once again just what Lloyd had wished for. She apologized for causing him any grief, and then confessed, "Sincerely do I reciprocate the affectionate feelings of your heart, and am happy to know that I am the favored one, whom you have selected; and in whose heart, you may 'pour the wealth of your affection.'" Embarrassed by her emotional outburst, she asked Lloyd to burn the letter. Of course, she could have done this herself and rewritten it, but courtship always contains the element of risk that lovers so enjoy. "I have opened my heart to you!" Helen concluded, "perhaps have expressed too much, and have now erred on the other side."[29]

In reading their parents' courtship letters, the Garrison children could witness the intricacies of the dance of love, when two people start circling widely but with each twist and turn move ever closer. There was some faltering, some backtracking, but basically the children knew the exciting conclusion—that the dancers would eventually come together, their lives entwining. More than any other previous communication, Helen's declaration of affection moved the relationship forward. Lloyd's next missive burst with pleasure, from its opening, "Dearest Helen," to its closing, "Your affectionate lover." "Those tender, affectionate, ardent confessions of yours!—they are all that I could desire. . . . You may confide in my fidelity—in the singleness and devotedness of my heart—in the purity and holiness of my love," he responded. At their first meeting, he had been struck by Helen's "sweet countenance." He had thought about her continuously during his trip to England, and when they rode together to Canterbury, he wished to tell her of his feelings, but his "tongue was tied" and his heart "timorous."[30] He exposed his lack of confidence to her, a side of him few people experienced. This, indeed, was a deeply personal gift.

Now that Helen and Lloyd had reached an unspoken understanding that they were heading toward marriage, he was bursting to tell someone. He had no family of his own; James was nowhere in sight, so he turned to a man he wished to have as a brother—George W. Benson. "The case, then, is briefly this," he wrote. "From the first moment I ever saw your gentle sister Helen, and had the pleasure of enjoying her society, I was most favorably impressed, in relation to her personal, mental, and moral worth. . . . At each successive interview, I felt a growing attachment, but I disclosed my feelings and predilections to no one." He described their most recent exchange of letters and the joy he felt at Helen's avowal of love. He felt it his "duty" to tell George W., but begged him not to share the information with anyone else except his wife, Catharine, and his sisters. He assumed that George Sr., Sally, and Henry had already been informed. Lloyd hoped for the approval of the entire Benson clan: "Until this be granted to me, my happiness will not be complete."[31] His next job was to draft a letter to Helen's parents properly requesting their permission to marry their daughter and for their blessing.

Helen was equally ecstatic about their plans and also confessional. In the letter which sons Wendell and Frank later paraphrased, she recalled to Lloyd how much she had anticipated seeing him that first time at the African Church in Providence. She had heard so much about him and had very high expectations of this "noble" being. She had not been disappointed; indeed, Lloyd was "all and even more" than she imagined he would be. The next day, when she met him again at her brother's store, she revealed, "I was riveted to the spot and lingered long to see—and hear you converse, and when I took leave of you, and thought it might be the last time I should ever behold you again on earth, I knew not why, but my mind seemed shrouded in gloom, which I could not dispel."[32] From that moment on, she had noted his whereabouts, read his articles in the *Liberator*, and worried about his well-being.

From April 5, 1834, until their wedding on September 4, letters passed constantly between Roxbury and Brooklyn. Some were philosophical, dealing with such issues as religion, politics, and the meaning of marriage. Some were conversational, about the arrangements for the wedding and the establishment of their home in Roxbury. Some were revealing of friendships, embarrassing incidents, and differences of opinion. All contained romantic expressions of the couple's initial love and growing attachment, and each tested and measured his or her compatibility with the other. For their children, each letter provided tantalizing information about their parents' youthful beliefs and dreams. From this correspondence, for example, they discovered how deeply religious their parents had always been, even though they stood by no sect. Lloyd was very vocal about his Christian beliefs. Fanny, Martha Farnham, and the Bartletts had certainly set a strong example for him, and he had learned much from his exposure to the Baptists. Helen, although less forthcoming, had similar feelings. Even though she liked to attend services in Samuel J. May's Unitarian church and imitated her mother's and sisters' Quaker speech patterns, she also embraced no specific sect. Yet, through their courtship letters, the two were able to establish their mutual belief in God. In early April, Lloyd wrote, "What may be our joys, or what our sorrows, He only knows who sees the end from the beginning. Come what may, however, if we have given first the supreme homage of our hearts to HIM, and then their pure affections to each other, we cannot but be happy."[33]

The children knew from their own experiences that agreeing on abolitionism and race consciousness were of prime importance if their parents' marriage was to be successful. Lloyd's professional and personal life revolved around them. If Helen had *any* qualms about Lloyd's mission in life, the couple either needed to resolve them before marriage or give up any plans of spending their lives together. Fortunately, Helen's upbringing had prepared her for such a role. Certainly, her great support of Prudence Crandall proved her to be a well-raised abolitionist daughter; in addition, it provided her and Lloyd with a common experience. Lloyd filled his letters with abolitionist news, such as meetings concerning the antislavery societies and the *Liberator,* and with messages for Samuel J. May and the Benson activists, particularly George Sr., George W., and Henry. Helen relayed all messages and commented on various points, largely supporting Lloyd's positions and sympathizing with his beliefs. She confessed feeling awed by the responsibility she was assuming by becoming "Garrison's wife." In May, in an effort to show her beau that she understood the importance of the role she was assuming, she wrote of her belief that "the class" he had "so long labored to elevate and enlighten" would look to her as a role model, a task she felt confident she could perform well. However, Helen's obvious lack of connection with black abolitionists showed through in her elaboration of her point: "I have been considering how much the colored people think of dress, and how much of their profits are expended for useless ornaments, that foolishly tend to make a show or parade. . . . So . . . to set a good example, I must endeavor to be exceedingly plain in my deportment, and very simple in my dress."[34]

Through the letters, the Garrison children learned that even though their mother had experienced Prudence Crandall's traumas, she was still very naive about the African-American community, a quality that did not totally please their father. But Lloyd did not consider Helen's comments a breach of abolitionist conduct. Rather, he took them as a sign that she meant well but needed more education about the nature of racism. While he agreed with her that some members of the free black community had "a passion for gaudy finery," this, he felt, was a natural result of being degraded by other members of society.[35] Once slavery was abolished and prejudices eliminated, he stressed, the cause for such ostentation would disappear. Victorian-era Christian modesty would flourish. What neither Lloyd nor Helen nor their children after them perceived was that their patronizing attitude toward blacks was laced with classism as well as racism. Neither parent would have made such disrespectful comments about individual people, such as James Forten, Robert Purvis, Sarah Parker Remond, Sarah Douglass, Charlotte Forten, or any others, many of whom had far more money than they did and, in fact, by constituting the majority of subscribers, continued to assure that the *Liberator* remained in circulation.

Lloyd, however, did not differentiate among slavery, poverty, and racism in his thoughts to Helen. All he imparted to her were his feelings about the slaves' plight. Loving Helen, he wrote, made him fully realize "how dreadful a thing it is for lover to be torn away from lover, and husband from wife, and parents from children." If he was forced to be separated from her for life, he could not bear it. Did she not agree? "O, *we* can, and *we* will, sympathize with the poor slave, dear Helen, let others scoff as they please."[36] Through gentle reasoning and persuasion, behavior expected of respectable middle-class husbands, Lloyd helped Helen to grow into the mature abolitionist she later became. During their married years when her social world expanded to include African Americans, she learned more about the nature of racism in a free society and passed on her newfound understanding to her children.

Interestingly, Helen and Lloyd's greatest difference rested in their beliefs governing women's role in society. While it was true that Lloyd's personal preference was for a traditional Victorian-era helpmate who had no desire to be a public figure, his political stance was woman-rightist, or feminist, as it was later termed, and his children were raised to adopt this same sentiment. Lloyd expressed the belief that women should be equal within personal relationships and in the public sphere as well. Indeed, he thought of his upcoming marriage as one between equals, although he saw a clear gender division regarding responsibilities. Helen would be primarily responsible for the home, largely because Lloyd had a cause to lead. But Lloyd expected he would assume a share of the domestic responsibilities once the couple started having children. He did not see this as a chore but as a welcome part of being in a loving family. Helen, however, never expected to help in the pecuniary maintenance of the family.

Being raised to embrace the cause of woman's rights, the children must have been amused by the argument their parents had over the proper behavior for women in the world of courting. This difference of opinion regarding women's roles emerged after a rather assertive Quaker woman by the name of Leah Fell wrote Lloyd proposing that the two of them get married. Lloyd considered the matter a serious one, for it threw him into the position of having to hurt Fell's feelings. He told Helen that he had responded immediately, informing Leah Fell that he had long since given his heart to Helen, whom he loved "beyond any other human being." How sad it was, he ruminated, "to love, and get nothing in return but bitter disappointment."[37] Helen, however, was not so sympathetic. She was "astonished" by the news. "I cannot believe that one of my sex would venture thus far." Someone must have been playing an evil trick on Fell. "I am sure no young lady with the least delicacy of feeling, and in her right senses would have written such a letter." Helen claimed to feel no jealousy, just "pity" for such a "wretched" soul who was about to be thoroughly humiliated.[38] Indeed, on May 30, Lloyd reported that his admirer had responded apologetically for her letter. She had not realized that he was engaged. "She writes," Lloyd added in his report to Helen, "as if her mind was in a state of painful confusion, in consequence of the discovery she had made."[39]

A few days later, still disturbed by Helen's reaction, Lloyd broached the subject again. "Why," he asked her, "should not females as freely communicate their love as the other sex?" Did this question surprise her, he wondered? He pursued the issue further:

> Is it reasonable that overtures should always be made on the part of men? True, custom so decides it; but ought custom to rule in so exclusive and despotic a manner? Will it be said that delicacy ought to deter a woman from first avowing her love? Is not this tantamount to saying that there is something indelicate in a marriage proposal? Why, then, should the other sex be called upon to make it? Tenderly loving you, my dear H., —yet ignorant as to the state of your own heart,— I made bold to throw myself at your feet, and avow my passion. Happily, for my peace of mind, you did not reject me, but, on the contrary, confessed a kindred attachment. —Suppose that I had remained silent, and your love had gone on increasing until it had become insupportable—would you not, or rather, ought you not to have made me acquainted with the state of your heart, and endeavored to ascertain whether I could reciprocate your affection? Ah! how many lovely females have gone down to the grave broken-hearted, in consequence of having studiously refrained from acknowledging their attachment![40]

The exchange over female assertiveness versus traditional passiveness was one of the most heated between the two lovers and one that showed the children just how strong an influence their father had on their mother's ideas. Helen admitted her uncertainty in knowing if there was really anything "indelicate in a lady's offering herself to a gentleman," but for sure this was what she and all young men and women had been taught throughout their lives. Hence she found the idea "revolting." Helen would *never* have found herself in the same position as Leah Fell, for she would never have given her heart to anyone unless asked to do so. Had she been as much in love as Leah Fell, she would never have revealed the fact to a living soul, "but kept it locked as treasure in the deep recesses of the heart until the tomb received me broken hearted." Helen firmly believed that had she declared her "passionate attachment" without being asked, she would have deserved to be spurned "for transgressing the bounds of propriety." Helen had had her say, but as a nineteenth-century woman trained for a subordinate role in marriage, one in which she might express her own ideas but would bend to the wiser judgment of her husband, she added, "Perhaps I am wrong, if so set me right. I am always willing to be led by your greater experience of the world, and of course better judgment. When I have considered of it more I may change my opinion, but at present I cannot."[41] Within a week, she conceded more: "I see you are determined still to think a lady ought to choose a husband for herself. And I will allow that custom & the criticism of the world is all that seems to preclude her from so doing and were it only the fashion I suppose we should think nothing about it. So I have half a mind to think with you there is nothing so improper in it."[42]

As their children later concurred, Helen and Lloyd were a perfect match. He guided, she followed. He taught, she learned. He never bullied, neither did she. He was the leading abolitionist in the nation, she was abolitionist-raised. Neither drank nor smoked. Both were open to alternative medicines and diets. Both were avid readers, both knowledgeable about politics. As the wedding plans gained in momentum, their passion for each other grew in leaps and bounds. Each continued to learn about the other's thoughts and dreams. Helen, shy and a bit reserved, was quite struck by Lloyd's openness, his sentimentality, and his romantic outpourings. She basked in the fact that Lloyd continuously plied her with love poetry, some of which graced the pages of the *Liberator* as well as arriving in his letters.[43] Poems that appeared in the paper made the courtship a public event, even when Helen's name was purposefully omitted from the text. Such was the case in "A Letter, My Love," which spoke of their long-distance courtship and read, in part:

> A Letter, my Love! that shall breathe thy name,
> To prove thou art fondly and truly the same,
>   And say but 'I am well;'
> To bring sweets from thy lip, and the balm of thy sigh,
> The blush of thy cheek, and the flash of thine eye!
> I'll think thou art present, and sorrow shall fly,
>   While wrapped in fancy's spell.
> A Letter, my Love! Oh, send to me
> One blessed thought, or a word from thee,
>   And with joy my heart shall swell.[44]

The sentiment in the verses was quickly picked up by the abolitionist community. When Lloyd visited Philadelphia in May, Mary Sharpless, the wife of his friend, Joseph Sharpless, teasingly inquired of him, "What is her name, William? They say it is Helen Benson, a sister of George—I wish thee much joy!" Lloyd responded, "You are quizzical, Mary, and there is some meaning to such language, if one could only find it out." Such playful repartee was popular among Lloyd's friends and *Liberator* readers. "My Sonnets to you seem to have awakened suspicion universally, and caused much speculation among my male and female friends as to the chosen one," he wrote a most likely mortified Helen. Lloyd loved the public nature of his courtship as well as its private aspects. He enjoyed the speculation over whom his intended might be, but as his children knew, the lucky bride *must* be an abolitionist, just as their own future mates should be. Lloyd responded to one such quip, "And do you think for one moment, that I would choose any other than a good abolitionist?"[45]

The Garrison children saw that their father appreciated his and Helen's courtship on several levels. The previously lonely and somewhat abandoned child they had discovered their father to be had become the object of great adoration and love. Not only had he captured the heart of a most desirable woman, but he had also won her family's love and respect as well. Lloyd looked forward to all the commitments marriage called for. This courtship had also warmed the hearts of abolitionists who read Lloyd's sonnets in the *Liberator*. In effect, although he had become a much lauded and admired political activist, Lloyd and Helen's courtship conveyed his romantic and human side to a community that valued these traits. Since most abolitionists and reformers considered the nuclear family the center of life, Helen and Lloyd's courtship added an important credential to his resume; it offered credibility. Lloyd not only gained the Bensons as a family but also found acceptance as part of the abolitionist extended family structure.

Lloyd also basked in his ability to excel in the practice of courting. Not having been raised in a social circle that utilized letters, poems, and sentimental gifts to gain a mate, he had had to observe and learn how to play the game. As evidenced by their own courtships, the children benefited from his and Helen's exercise. They had no doubt that their father's and mother's feelings for each other were sincere, but they also learned that their parents' courtship pattern was styled to fit the times (as, later on, their own would be). In no letter was this more clearly laid out than on May 23, when Lloyd extolled the pleasures of the love letter, a means of expression he had thoroughly mastered. To Helen, he wrote:

> O, what magic there is in a genuine love-letter! How the bosom heaves, how the heart throbs, how the pulse leaps, how the hand trembles, on the receipt of it! First, the outward superscription fixes the eye—then the sacred seal, which hides the mysterious contents, is eagerly broken—and then every word, and syllable, and letter, that is revealed, operates for a moment like a spell. Then impatient love goes over the pages, like a young race-horse over the course, eager to arrive at the goal of victory. Or, peradventure, covetous of every sentence, and loath to arrive at the conclusion of that which is so precious, it reads slowly and deliberately to the end, in despite of its strong desires. Dear Helen, is not this a true picture?[46]

Helen's modest description of her own love letters reflected her acceptance of the role of the secondary partner, one who remains in the background and never makes a public spectacle of herself. "Be sure you never let any eye but your own, glance at *my imperfect letters,*" she wrote, "for it is bad enough to have *you see them.* . . . I always feel dissatisfied with them; if I read them over after they are written, I want to commit them to the flames, instead of sending them to you."[47]

The courtship letters inevitably led to planning the wedding, a process that enlightened the children about their parents' way of addressing practical matters and their growing trust in each other's judgment. Helen expressed her sadness about the prospect of leaving her parents' home. As she wrote to Lloyd, the thought of becoming his wife gave her "unspeakable delight"; yet, "the dread of parting from home, and the beloved objects" that "entwined" her heart, often filled her with such sorrow that it dampened the joys that seemed "in reserve" for her. Besides losing the constant companionship of her mother and sisters, Helen feared a certain loss of closeness with her brothers, especially after Henry said to her, "Do not tell a *married woman* any *thing*; for *she will tell her husband*."[48] Although Henry was most likely teasing his much-loved sister, Helen interpreted his sentiment to mean that she was no longer welcome to sit in on family conversations. Helen also expressed doubts in her ability to be a good wife. "Be assured that nothing arduous, or excessive, or difficult, will be required of you as the wife of W.L.G.," Lloyd responded, "I am a plain man—at least, I mean to be; my habits are, like yours, very simple and abstemious."[49] Lloyd claimed to like solitude and not receiving many visitors. He promised Helen a quiet, domestic homelife, a pledge he would be unable to keep when his popularity grew and hospitality was expected from him in exchange for all he received in kind.

In July, on a brief speaking tour meant to connect abolitionism with Independence Day celebrations, Lloyd took the opportunity to visit Helen in Brooklyn. While with her, he shared some disconcerting news he had heard of mob action against abolitionists in New York City. The trouble had begun on July 4, quieted down, then burst forth again from the seventh to the tenth. The Old Chapel on Chatham Street, where an antislavery meeting had been held, was vandalized, and several homes were damaged, including those of Lewis Tappan and the Reverend Dr. Samuel H. Cox. Lloyd was greatly dismayed by the news, although calm. He had no doubt that such actions would simply further the cause of antislavery as an increasing number of people grew indignant about the violence. Helen was happy that Lloyd had not been there. She wanted him to remain safe, but Lloyd's agitator life could not guarantee this. His notoriety had surfaced the same year that the *Liberator* had begun publication, especially after the Nat Turner rebellion of August 21, 1831. Turner, a literate Virginia slave, believed that he was spiritually chosen to lead other slaves to freedom. Among his neighbors, he was perceived as a charismatic force, and several slaves followed him with great fervor. On one fateful night, Turner's rebels killed thirteen men, eighteen women, and twenty-four children of the slaveholding class. It took three days to quell the revolt, at which point Turner went into hiding. He was soon found, tried, and sentenced to death. Lloyd, although a nonresister who believed that all violent solutions were wrong, had serious questions about the right of slaves to achieve their freedom by any accessible means. He expressed his opinions in the *Liberator* and published many detailed articles about Turner, blaming the country as a whole for the slaughter, since federal policy supported and protected slavery.

In retrospect, the Garrison children recognized that Nat Turner's rebellion had placed their own father's life in danger. The *Liberator*'s coverage of the affair brought Lloyd to the attention of Southern slaveholders. In their minds, he graduated from being a Northern pest to posing a real threat. His name appeared quite often in Southern newspapers, several of them either hinting at or outrightly accusing him of inciting the revolt. Threatening letters were sent to the *Liberator*, and its sale was prohibited in several places. The Georgia legislature went as far as passing a bill offering a reward of an unspecified sum (later set at $5,000) to any person who could arrest Lloyd and deliver him to the state for trial on the grounds of treason. The penalty for such a crime, of course, was death. Lloyd was not intimidated by what became basically a war of words. By the time he met Helen, he had become nonchalant about threats to his life, expressing the possibility of his own bodily harm in terms of Christian martyrdom. Certainly, during their courtship, the issue of impending violence had never been voiced. Although Helen was aware of the dangers of Lloyd's being an outspoken abolitionist leader, it was only after they were married that she realized that threats against her husband would be an everyday reality for her and any children they might produce.

In spite of his escalating notoriety and increasing activist responsibilities, Lloyd secured Freedom's Cottage as their home and then, with Helen's advice and approval, furnished it. Truly, this would be his first real home since the day his mother left Newburyport for Lynn in 1812. For over twenty years, he had boarded in other people's houses or, for a while, stayed in the *Liberator* office with Isaac Knapp. As a boy, Newburyport meant home to him, but now home would be a real house with furniture—a real family life with Helen and their eventual seven children. This was, perhaps, one of the happiest periods in his life. By August 11, Lloyd had contentedly settled into their new home. Then, at eight o'clock in the morning on September 4, Samuel J. May wedded him and Helen. As Lloyd later observed, "The dear minister's heart was deeply affected, and almost too full for clear, unembarrassed utterance. His expressions of friendship for us both were ardent and tender—his parental and social admonitions valuable and timely—his wishes for our happiness large and multifarious."[50] By nine o'clock, the travelers were in their cariole heading for Worcester and then Boston.

For the next seven months, Helen and Lloyd settled into married life in Freedom's Cottage with housemates Isaac Knapp and his sister, Abigail, and guests such as Helen's friend Eliza Chace, her sister Anna, and the visiting British abolitionist George Thompson and his wife. Helen was immediately swept up in Lloyd's world. The *Liberator*, although primarily constructed at the antislavery offices on Washington Street, became part of family life. Lloyd enjoyed being home, and he took to reading proofs and writing articles there, a practice he continued throughout his life. Indeed, for the couple's children, their father's abolitionist work was part of their everyday reality. So were the constant demands upon their mother to play hostess to any number of abolitionists passing through town. In fact, as Lloyd noted, there was "rarely a day when there was an unoccupied bed in the house."[51]

Helen appeared to enjoy life near Boston, although at times she worried about her husband's safety. Abolitionists were a minority in Massachusetts; yet Lloyd openly condemned anyone who supported slavery. Many businesses in the state depended upon slave labor in the South to turn a profit. Mill owners needed cotton; rum makers required sugarcane; shop owners depended on products like tobacco and rice to make money. In spite of tremendous opposition, Lloyd continued his campaign, soon rejecting the entire U.S. political structure as well as the Constitution for upholding the "peculiar institution," and so Helen worried, but she did not criticize. Rather, as she had promised, she wholeheartedly supported her husband's (and her own) cause. Also, as she had indicated to Lloyd in her letters, she did not desire any public role for herself, but she did attend meetings of the Boston Female Anti-Slavery Society and volunteered her assistance in organizing the annual December antislavery fairs, one of the largest fundraising efforts of the movement. Helen's main place of activism, however, was her home—making life as comfortable as possible for Lloyd, taking care of a growing family, most of the time with the help of only one domestic worker, and hosting the nonstop stream of guests seeking dinner, entertainment, a place to sleep, and at times, for those fleeing slavery, a place of refuge. Hence, in May 1835, when their lease expired, Helen, Lloyd, and the Knapps moved from Freedom's Cottage to a larger house at 23 Brighton Street in Boston's West End.

The Garrison children were always painfully aware that one of the biggest adjustments for their mother was the decline in her economic status. Upon marriage, she willingly accepted the life of near poverty of which Lloyd had forewarned her. He was not yet receiving a salary from the New England Anti-Slavery Society (renamed the Massachusetts Anti-Slavery Society in 1835) for publishing the *Liberator.* Rather, his earnings were supposed to come as a result of sales and subscriptions. In January 1835, just a few months into their marriage, he also faced the possibility of the newspaper's termination. Subscribers were late in payments, and although the number of individual copies sold was decent, the agents were not conscientious about sending in their revenue. This scenario became familiar in Helen's and the children's lives; money was always tight, but wealthier abolitionists constantly came to the newspaper's or Lloyd's aid. Wendell Phillips, Francis Jackson, Ellis Gray Loring, Robert Purvis, the Boston Female Anti-Slavery Society, and brother George W. Benson were just a few of the sources who helped keep the family housed, clothed, and fed. Helen learned immediately that she was no longer a privileged middle-class lady. In reality, she became a poor housewife whose family lived off the dedication of others to her husband and his work as a very capable antislavery leader.[52]

By the summer of 1835, Helen was pregnant with their first child, and the couple began to look forward to building their family. Political life, however, continued to add a note of apprehension for her. George Thompson's reception in the United States had not been friendly. From his arrival the previous September to his departure that November, his path was strewn with criticism, rocks, and brickbats. Thompson was a strong and committed reformer, however, who kept speaking even under threat of untold violence. As the man who had invited Thompson to U.S. shores and who sang his praises, Lloyd also became more of a target of attack. On the night of September 10, while the vacationing Helen and Lloyd slept soundly in the Benson home in Brooklyn, a group of men erected a gallows suited for two in front of their Brighton Street home, where Helen's brother Henry and Isaac Knapp were staying. Helen's fears mounted. As Lloyd wrote to Henry, "Helen is filled with anxiety and alarm on my account. She trembles when she thinks of returning to Boston."[53]

For months previous to this affront, Helen had been plagued with news of attacks on Thompson, Arthur and Lewis Tappan, and her own brother George W., who had spent a night in a Providence jail in order to remain safe from "enemies." A meeting in Haverhill, Massachusetts, led by Samuel J. May, was broken up by a "shower of brickbats"; George Thompson had "a narrow escape" from a mob in Concord, and John Greenleaf Whittier, the poet, had mud and stones thrown at him.[54] Word was that several slave states had supported the creation of "Vigilance Committees and Lynch Clubs" to harass and abduct abolitionists.[55] As Lloyd later attested, Helen lived in constant fear that some harm would come to him, and, indeed, in October 1835 she experienced true terror when an angry mob threatened to lynch her husband.

FAMILY LIFE

ESTABLISHING THE FAMILY

My inherited principles of Non-Resistance . . . seem as essential to me as the breath of life and paramount to all others.

Fanny Garrison Villard,
William Lloyd Garrison on Non-Resistance

CHAPTER III

George Thompson Garrison was not yet born when on October 21, 1835, an angry antiabolitionist mob threatened Lloyd's life. In the Garrison home on every anniversary of that event, the children gathered around their parents for a dramatic retelling of the "broadcloth mob" episode. Hearing it, they were reminded of their father's bravery and commitment to justice and of their mother's acceptance of the ultimate sacrifice their father might perform for his beliefs, one he claimed to be willing to make even though he loved life and his family beyond words. So ingrained was this date in the children's minds that the first volume of Wendell and Frank's biography of their father noted its completion on "the 50th anniversary of the Boston Mob, 1885."[1]

The fabled event unfolded on a bright, crisp, New England autumn day. For Helen it promised to be a day to spend sociably with other abolitionist women at a meeting of the interracial Boston Female Anti-Slavery Society.[2] Formed two years previously, the organization consisted of women who gave their wholehearted support to the male-dominated Massachusetts Anti-Slavery Society. Two of the women, Maria Weston Chapman and Lydia Maria Child, were close allies of Lloyd, Chapman often acting as coordinator of the Boston abolitionists' social world, while Child wrote numerous articles, essays, and stories on the evils of slavery. These women, although central to Lloyd's life, were not Helen's preferred friends. She tended to shy away from the assertive leaders to form close relationships with Ann Terry Greene Phillips, the young invalid wife of Lloyd's close friend and fellow coagitator Wendell Phillips; with Thankful Southwick, a forty-ish woman, and her then fourteen-year-old daughter Sarah; and with Eliza Follen, married to the abolitionist Charles Follen. Since she was not scheduled to meet the other women at 46 Washington Street until two o'clock, Helen had time to take care of her chores, relax, and think about the child she was carrying. Lloyd, who was to replace George Thompson as the scheduled speaker, had left home several hours earlier.

While George Thompson had followed Lloyd's advice to leave Boston for a while, agitation against him continued to escalate, for even though in 1780 Massachusetts had become the first state to outlaw slavery, many of its residents feared that the abolitionist agenda would result in a legislatively forced mixing of races, which they would not tolerate. In the hopes of stirring up antiabolitionist feeling, on the morning of the female antislavery meeting, two merchants, Isaac Stevens and Isaac Means, published five hundred copies of a handbill falsely announcing Thompson's appearance at the gathering. The flyer offered a one-hundred-dollar reward to anyone who could deliver Thompson up for an evening tar-and-feather party. By the time the women gathered, an angry and curious crowd had formed outside the building.

As the meeting room filled, Lloyd watched the contrasting forces taking shape. On one side he saw about fifteen to twenty "ladies . . . sitting with serene countenances"; on the other, "a crowd of noisy intruders (mostly young men) gazing upon them."[3] At first, he attempted to disperse the men, singling out one group which was crowding menacingly by the door. "This is a meeting of the Boston *female* Anti-Slavery Society," he stated calmly. "If, *gentlemen,* any of you are *ladies*—in disguise—why, only apprise me of the fact, give me your names, and I will introduce you to the rest of your sex, and you can take your seats among them accordingly."[4] Not amused, the men grew restless and agitated because they could not find the promised George Thompson, whose capture meant collecting the reward. The only abolitionist man they saw was Lloyd, and, at first, he had little appeal for them. Promptly at two o'clock, the president of the organization, Mary Parker, called the meeting to order, even though several members, including Helen, had not been able to reach the building.

Lloyd stared in admiration as the women proceeded with their business while the mob's chants for "Thompson" grew increasingly hysterical. Finally, the intruders moved into the hall, followed by Boston's mayor, Theodore Lyman, who pushed his way to the front of the room. Desperate to keep the peace, he informed the crowd that George Thompson was not there and ordered them to leave. They did not. He then turned on the women, ordering them to halt their meeting. On behalf of the society, Maria Weston Chapman refused. Often characterized as "Garrison's chief lieutenant," she replied, "If this is the last bulwark of freedom, we may as well die here as anywhere."[5] For several minutes, it appeared as if all sides were at a stalemate, until after great discussion with the mayor, the women agreed to leave. Black and white women, linked arm in arm, one white woman on either side of a black woman, walked calmly through the angry crowd to Chapman's house at 11 West Street, where they continued their meeting. What astonished them was that the crowd of ruffians that appeared so frightening included a fair number of businessmen whom they knew and had always considered supporters. Meanwhile, this "broadcloth mob," named for its businessmen participants, turned its attention to the next leading abolitionist on the premises—Lloyd—who, on Parker's insistence, had left the meeting room. Going into the adjoining antislavery office, he and his friend, Charles C. Burleigh, locked the door to prevent the crowd from entering and destroying their supply of abolitionist publications.

Once the women were safely out of sight, the mob turned its full attention to Lloyd. Perceiving the danger he was in, he tried to leave the building through Wilson's Lane. He and a friend, John Reid Campbell, dropped from a back window of the building onto a shed in an alleyway, Lloyd barely preventing himself from falling head-first to the ground. The mob, however, blocked the street. Upon seeing the two abolitionists enter a carpenter's shop, they let out a shriek and ran toward them. Only the quick action of a workman who closed the door to the shop kept them at bay. Lloyd later claimed that he was ready to martyr himself to the crowd, but the fact that his friend easily convinced him to return upstairs and hide contradicts his words. So did his next action, after two or three rioters discovered him, tied a rope around his waist, and forced him down a ladder. While descending, Lloyd managed to extricate himself, but before he could escape he was quickly seized by two or three other men and dragged along the street. Nearly all his clothes were ripped or torn from his body as he was pushed through Wilson's Lane into State Street to the rear of City Hall.

Just at this moment of deep humiliation, Mayor Lyman came to Lloyd's rescue and guided him into his office. A kindly post office worker in the same building lent him a pair of pantaloons; another gave him a coat; a third, a scarf; a fourth, a cap, and so on until he was suitably attired. The mayor then ordered that a carriage take him to the Leverett Street jail for a night of protective custody. Lloyd remained calm even while the crowd, in an attempt to reach him, assaulted the carriage. They clung to the wheels, pushed open the doors, seized hold of the horses, and tried to upset the vehicle, all the while being pushed back by the police. At last, Lloyd was placed in a locked cell, where he spent a quiet and enjoyable evening, except for an "occasional throb of anxiety" over Helen.[6] After a nice, sound sleep, he awakened refreshed to eat a full breakfast, after which he was released.

Helen, meanwhile, had to face this traumatic episode on her own. Caught in the crowd and turned away from the meeting by an agitated spectator, she naturally feared that something had gone amiss. However, after running into Caroline

Weston, Maria Weston Chapman's sister, on Court Street and being assured that Lloyd had left the meeting, she relaxed, imagining him safely chatting at a companion's house. Feeling no fear, she stopped to visit a friend and then hastened home, as she said, "with the fond anticipation of meeting him." When she arrived, her domestic worker informed her that an "exceedingly agitated" Samuel E. Sewall, whose wife, Louisa, was at the meeting, was looking for her.[7] Within minutes, he returned to describe Lloyd's rescue by the mayor and to assure Helen that he was fine, a fact she wanted to prove for herself. Putting on her coat, she dashed off for the jail, stopping only when some concerned friends convinced her that such a potentially violent and dangerous scene could harm her baby. With great hesitancy, Helen accompanied her friend Lydia Fuller to her home to await news.

Largely because of Helen's pregnancy, the broadcloth mob incident created great upheaval in the couple's existence. With the atmosphere of violence still strong, both the mayor and the abolitionist community insisted that the Garrisons leave town. Within a day, Helen and Lloyd had arrived in Brooklyn, their intention being to remain in Connecticut only until after their child's birth in February and Helen's recovery. Lack of money, however, kept them there for almost a year, even though Lloyd made monthly visits to Boston to oversee the *Liberator* and prepare for the family's return. Meanwhile, Francis Jackson, a well-to-do merchant who proved a dear friend and steady financial supporter of the Garrison family, offered his home to the Boston Female Anti-Slavery Society since no public space would open its doors to them. Even though the *Liberator*'s creditors, fearing its demise, called in for payment and the paper's records, equipment, and materials were, for a time, scattered around various storage areas, Lloyd, of course, was adamant that the periodical not only survive but also remain in Boston. He had devoted four years to its development; more important, it represented his beliefs and provided his family's basic means of support. Without it, how would he earn a living? Brooklyn was only a temporary solution to his problems. Hence, he returned to Boston on November 4 to orchestrate the storing of his and Helen's furniture and goods and the working out of arrangements to secure the newspaper's future until he could return to the city permanently. He found the atmosphere surprisingly quiet, not a person paying him any undue attention. George Thompson, also back in Boston, was visiting peacefully with Thankful Southwick and her husband, Joseph. Three days later Lloyd went to the Anti-Slavery Society offices. (His own printing equipment was in storage and the *Liberator* was being produced out of several other shops.) By then he had become used to being just another anonymous face in a big city. At headquarters, he spoke with Thompson about his imminent departure for England and to the Weston sisters, who agreed to adopt his cat, find space for his furniture in their own home until they could sell it, and hire the Garrisons' domestic helper, Christina. His business completed, Lloyd returned to Brooklyn.

Besides creating immediate havoc, the October 21, 1835, mob incident marked a major turning point in Lloyd's life. By the end of the year, he and Isaac Knapp had dissolved their partnership, making Lloyd the sole editor of the paper and Knapp the publisher, a responsibility he kept until the beginning of 1840, when debt and alcohol addiction forced him into an early retirement. Furthermore, when Lloyd returned to Boston in September 1836, he was a family man, a status he cherished so greatly that it affected every subsequent decision he made. In total, Helen and Lloyd had seven children, Helen's pregnancies following the common spacing of approximately two years apart. Like many white women raised in the middle-class at that time, she nursed each child for approximately a year and a half, after which she soon became pregnant.[8] Apparently, although the Garrisons faced constant economic hardship and favored the use of nontraditional medicines and diets, they appeared to forego family planning.[9] This was a conscious decision, not one based upon ignorance. Helen and Lloyd showed great interest in the ideas of such utopianists as Robert Dale Owen, who in 1831 published the first notable U.S. tract on birth control, *Moral Physiology; or, A Brief and Plain Treatise on the Population Question,* which encouraged coitus interruptus for effective family planning. They also could not possibly have missed the 1832 publication of the Massachusetts physician Charles Knowlton's *Fruits of Philosophy; or, The Private Companion of Young Married People,* a highly controversial book that sold over seven thousand copies within five years in spite of the state government's efforts to suppress it. Withdrawal, douching, vaginal sponges, and periodic abstinence were birth control measures available to Helen and Lloyd, but until their last child, Frank, was born in 1848 the couple apparently chose to use them rarely or not at all. This may have been a result of Lloyd's need for a close-knit family to make up for his lonely childhood and Helen's desire to help her husband gain the stability he craved. Both apparently agreed with most people of the time that the arrival of each child was a loving gift from God.

The couple's first successful effort in creating their family came on February 13, 1836, when after nearly fourteen hours of labor, Helen gave birth to a son they named George Thompson, after their British abolitionist friend. Lloyd was beside himself with joy, ecstatic over holding his son and taking care of him, often claiming that "if there was one thing he was fitted for, it was to tend babies."[10] After Lloyd's death, Oliver Johnson noted, probably with some exaggeration and no nod to Helen's mothering, "Did one of the children cry in the night, it was in his [Lloyd's] arms that it was caressed and comforted . . . he made his home a heaven into which it was a delight to enter."[11] Meanwhile, as in the case of his courtship and marriage, when Lloyd's personal life became entwined with his political role, he shared his happiness with his adoring abolitionist public. The February 20th edition of the *Liberator* bore five sonnets honoring his newborn son and rededicating his own life to antislavery work. "Sonnet I" expressed Lloyd's joy in having received, "Heaven's long-desired gift!" With the 1835 mob still fresh in his thoughts, he contemplated what it meant to have a child who would follow in his footsteps should he himself die before the slaves were freed:

> For if, amid this conflict, fierce and wild,
> With stout foes of God and man, I fall,
> Then shalt thou early fill my vacant post . . .[12]

Lloyd pledged young George's life to the cause, indicating in the second sonnet that George would be raised to hate oppression, love liberty, and embrace the teachings of Jesus Christ. In a more personal tone, the third sonnet expressed his deep emotional response to becoming a father, his realization that loving this child made him despise slavery even more:

> Bear witness, Heaven! do I hate Slavery less,—
> Do I not hate it more, intensely more,—
> Now this dear babe I to my bosom press?
> My soul is stirred within me—ne'er before
> Have horrors filled it with such dire excess,
> Nor pangs so deep pierced to its inmost core!

He continued in this vein in "Sonnet IV," contemplating the link between his cause and his newfound role as a parent:

> Yet is the Negro's babe as dear as mine—
> Formed in as pure and glorious a mould;
> But, ah! inhumanly 'tis seized and sold!

Indeed, he concluded, African-American babies were created in God's image the same as his own son and were entitled "to reign— / As high in dignity and worth to tower!" In the final sonnet, Lloyd put himself in the slave parents' shoes. He claimed to identify with their desperation in seeing their child in bondage, perhaps sold away from them:

> O, dearest child of all this populous earth!
> Yet no more precious than the meanest slave!
> To rescue thee from bondage, I would brave
> All dangers, and count life of little worth,
> And make of stakes and gibbets scornful mirth!

To identify fully with the slave and to bond his son to the cause, Lloyd ended his sonnets with a portrait of himself as a victim of public ridicule because of his political work. His wish for his son was that he also be dedicated to freedom, but not subjected to harassment:

Yet I am covered with reproach and scorn,
  And branded as a madman through the land!
But, loving thee, FREE ONE, my own first-born,
  I feel for all who wear an iron band—
So Heaven regard my son when I am gone,
  And aid and bless him with a liberal hand!

Lloyd and Helen welcomed six other Garrison children just as joyfully as they did George. The second to enter the family was William Lloyd Jr., born on January 21, 1838. Among the names considered for him was Abijah, but in the end the babe was named after his own father. Affectionately called "Willie," the child looked just like George, "as two twin-cherries upon one stem"—and so this pattern repeated itself with each son. Weighing a hefty nine pounds, Willie was a demanding nurser, "disposed to grumble" if he did not get as much of his mother's milk as he wanted. Helen and Lloyd were thrilled that brother George took to his new sibling with ease. As Lloyd wrote to his mother-in-law, "As for George Thompson, his brother throws him into ecstacies. He smoothes his bald head very tenderly, covers his fat cheeks with kisses, throws his arms around him, and performs a variety of other brotherly pranks."[13]

Wendell Phillips Garrison, nicknamed "Wendy," arrived on June 4, 1840. Helen—although attended by a woman physician, a nurse, her mother, her sister Anna, Oliver Johnson's wife Mary Ann, and Helen's domestic helper Caroline—felt emotionally very much alone, for at the time of Wendy's birth Lloyd was on a ship near the Grand Banks on his way to the World's Anti-Slavery Convention in London. He had no knowledge of the new arrival until July 3, when he received a letter from Oliver Johnson. Lloyd expressed to Helen his great relief that all had gone well and his pleasure of having received a lock of his new son's hair, which he "gazed upon . . . with rapturous delight."[14] Yet, having wished for a girl, both Lloyd and Helen felt a sense of disappointment. Moreover, for Helen this birth had been full of anxiety. Although on the decline, death during delivery was still a threat to women. Lloyd's absence, which began around May 11 when he headed off to New York City to attend the annual convention of the American Anti-Slavery Society, left her in deep dread. From there, Lloyd left for Europe, sending constant letters home describing his exciting meetings in the same breath as lamenting his separation from Helen and the children for the next three or four months. On May 15 he wrote from New York, "I assure you that nothing but a strong sense of duty will ever lead me to separate myself from you; for there is no place so dear to me in the world as my home, and I am never so happy as when by your side."[15]

The next day Lloyd wrote that he had almost made a quick turnaround trip to Boston just to see them all briefly before leaving for Europe, but he "feared if we should meet again to be again separated in the course of forty-eight hours, our hearts would be lacerated afresh."[16] A few days later he reiterated that any separation from Helen was like a "bereavement."[17] He could not sleep, and being far from the children made him feel as if they had been taken from him.

Although Helen clearly reciprocated Lloyd's feelings of love and attachment, during this particular time, she felt some anger and resentment at his willingness to leave her for such an extended period. Her family could not truly substitute for the husband who shared her everyday life in such a caring manner. All of Lloyd's expressions of loneliness seemed inconsistent with his lively descriptions of his travels, and Helen balked, indicating that if Lloyd was so unhappy without her, why did he not simply remain home? In response, he wrote,

> Dear Helen, I can truly affirm that I have never absented myself one hour from you as a matter of choice, but only as duty and friendship imperatively demanded the sacrifice. The strength of my love you will probably never fully know; for I am not accustomed to the use of fond terms, and feel a thousand fold more than I can express. Sometimes you have hinted that I was too ready to go away from home; and such a charge would have made me often very unhappy, if I could have persuaded myself that you meant it as a reproach. I have always excused it on the ground of your affection for me, which I know to be pure and intense; and happy am I that my presence at all times is a delight to your heart.[18]

In spite of his protests, Lloyd appeared to welcome the break. He rationalized this impulse by blaming Helen. As he wrote to Elizabeth Pease, a dear British abolitionist friend, "I tell Helen that the only fear I have is, that her attachment for me is carried to an undue extent. She always feels my absence so keenly, that I never leave home without great reluctance."[19] Helen's annoyance was clearly tied to her sense of abandonment at this particular time and to the heavy demands placed upon her at home. She had little, if any, relief from her routine and envied Lloyd his ability to change his venue. Had she experienced them, she might have decided that his journeys were not as physically or emotionally pleasant as she imagined them to be.

Lloyd arrived home on August 15, Helen having been alone with Wendy, William, and George for over two months. Profoundly happy to see him, she repressed her anger even though in addition to his absence, he procrastinated in naming the child, a task not completed until mid-September, a month after Lloyd returned home. Conflicts between the pair, however, were infrequent and did not interfere with the family's growth. On September 9, 1842, Helen again delivered a boy, Charles Follen, named after her friend Eliza's husband, the abolitionist clergyman and Harvard professor who had drowned nearly three years earlier when the steamer *Lexington* was shipwrecked in Long Island Sound. Much to his parents' delight, Charley was born just a few days after Helen's brother George W. and his wife, Catherine, also produced a new child. Weighing ten pounds at birth, Charley, although as welcome as his three brothers, was still somewhat of a disappointment to his father, who continued to long for a daughter. Helen, meantime, was happy and relieved that her labor had been so easy. She felt the first pains at eight o'clock in the morning, and by eleven the child had arrived. "This was quick work," Lloyd wrote his brother-in-law, "and seemed almost like a dream."[20]

On December 16, 1844, Helen and Lloyd finally welcomed the daughter they had so long desired. Lloyd wrote to his longtime supporter Louisa Gilman Loring, "We think she is a bud of promise—a tolerable pretty babe—and deserving of all the kisses we bestow on her—of course!" This wonderful gift from God was named Helen Frances, after her mother and maternal grandmother and immediately nicknamed "Fanny," a sign of Lloyd's desire to honor his mother's memory.[21] This Fanny, however, was born with the promise of love, care, and parental protection from all the ills that had befallen her namesake. "We shall demand for her," Lloyd continued, "the rights of a human being, though she be a female."[22] Almost two years to the day, on December 11, 1846, Helen and Lloyd welcomed another daughter, "the finest babe ever yet born in Boston!"[23] From July 16 to November 17, most of Helen's late stage of pregnancy, however, Lloyd had again been in England. There he cemented his great friendship with Elizabeth Pease, after whom he named the new child. Elizabeth Pease Garrison, or "Lizzy," was a beautiful child, with "a sweet face and mild blue eyes," but from the first, she was more delicate and fragile than her siblings. When she was almost four months old, Lloyd wrote to her namesake that all his other children doted upon Lizzy. To please them, he composed a "jingle" describing a bit about the baby's life but which also seemed to foreshadow her early death the next year. The poem, "Lizzy Pease," begins:

> There sits mother at her ease,
> With her baby, Lizzy Pease,
> Lying softly on her knees.—

Then followed allusions to his other five children's shenanigans, instructing them how to handle the baby:

> Kiss the darling, if you please—
> Her lips are "like wine on the lees"—
> But be careful not to tease,
> Though she'll bear a gentle squeeze.—

He concluded with a prophetic warning:

Keep her warm, else she may freeze,
Or take a sudden cold, and sneeze,
And day and night shall cough and wheeze,
Till her little spirit flees,
(By the tyrant Death's decrees,
Who is never cheated of his fees,)
To where St. Peter turns the keys![24]

Over the next year, it became apparent that Lizzy's lungs were not healthy. When in the spring of 1848 she came down with a severe case of the flu, Lloyd and Helen called in their physician, Christian F. Geist, a German-born homeopathic healer who had begun his Boston practice in 1842 and who remained the family's chief medical consultant for most of Lloyd and Helen's lives. Under Geist's care, Lizzy appeared to improve, but on April 19 she took a turn for the worse, and at one o'clock the next morning she died peacefully in the arms of Eliza Jackson Meriam, a friend who had come to help out with her care. Two days later Helen and Lloyd asked Theodore Parker, the Unitarian clergyman and family friend, to say a few words at her small funeral.

Lizzy's death at the age of sixteen months had a profound effect on her parents, who looked to themselves for blame. The previous year, Lloyd had traveled through Pennsylvania and Ohio on an antislavery speaking tour, largely in the company of the abolitionist and former slave Frederick Douglass, but from early August to early December he was quite ill from symptoms resembling typhoid fever. For five weeks he remained bedridden in the home of Robert F. Wallcut and his wife, losing twenty pounds and usually being too weak to write to Helen. As a result, Helen's own life was thrown into turmoil. The reports that she received made it sound quite possible that Lloyd would die, so her first instinct was to pack, find friends and family to remain with the children, and run to his side. Heavy home responsibilities and advice from other abolitionists convinced her not to make the journey, but because of the chaos, it is likely that her supply of breast milk was seriously affected. As a result, she could no longer nurse Lizzy. As Lloyd wrote to Elizabeth Pease, "from that time to the hour of her flight, [Lizzy] made very little progress in health, strength, or size."[25] Even teething became unusually painful for her. Could the premature weaning, the parents asked themselves, have resulted in her inability to fight off the flu?

Lloyd's personal grief was profound. To Pease, he continued, "The event which has happened to us is a very common one indeed, in this mutable world." However, "though millions of parents have anticipated us in a similar bereavement, it comes to us as though we were first in the painful experience." For six months

Lloyd had watched Helen hover over Lizzy as the baby wasted away. She had practically exhausted herself by tending to the infant's every need day and night. During the last two and a half months of Lizzy's life, Helen was again with child and experiencing all the fatigue and symptoms of early pregnancy. When Lizzy died, she was overcome with grief and exhaustion. As Lloyd observed, "To see the cradle vacant—to be unable to clasp her babe to her bosom—to wake up in the night, and find no little one nestling by her side—all this seems to leave her almost solitary, although there are still five others left, each of whom she loves just as tenderly."[26] In August, while she and Lloyd were in Northampton, Massachusetts, visiting her brother George W., who had settled there, Helen was still trying to deal with her grief. The presence of George W. and Catherine's own two month old did not help. As she wrote to her dear friend Ann Greene Phillips, "Dear little Lisea I miss more and more every hour. . . . I feel lost without her and look about me with regret to think our circle not complete."[27] Grief was alleviated a bit on October 29, when Helen and Lloyd's fifth son and last child was born. Helen had a difficult labor, so much so that her usual midwife, Mary Margaret Alexander, tried the use of ether, a new anesthetic introduced in 1846. Rather than dull Helen's pains, however, the drug exacerbated them, so it was abandoned. Francis Jackson, "Franky," named after one of his parents' most attentive benefactors, appeared at two o'clock in the morning, weighed ten and a half pounds, and had black hair and dark eyes. Lloyd felt great relief, as he always did, that the trial had ended successfully. Now, he and Helen just prayed for a healthy start to this new life.

Unfortunately, this period of establishing their family ended on another sad note when just a year after losing Lizzy, the family experienced a tragic blow with the death of seven-year-old Charley. The boy's demise plagued Helen and Lloyd for the rest of their lives, for while there was no evidence that Lizzy had died because of any negligence on her parents' part, Charley's death may in fact have been caused by unintentional parental carelessness and naiveté in believing that they could cure his illness themselves. Throughout their years together, Helen and especially Lloyd looked to unconventional methods of health care for themselves and for their children. They were not unusual in this regard, especially since the medical professionals were not highly respected, and hospitals were often places people went to only when they expected to die. Illnesses were better treated at home unless isolation was required.[28] For most of his adult life, Lloyd had experimented with treatments for his various ills. In fact, his children later joked about their father's adventures with the Thomsonian cure, hydropathy, and even homeopathy, a system they themselves often followed. The Thomsonian cure, created by Samuel Thomson, the self-educated son of a New Hampshire farmer, consisted of a patented system of botanical medicines. By 1839, Thomson claimed to have sold 100,000 permissions for establishments to use his method. His theory was basic: illness was caused by cold; therefore, it could be cured by heat. Purgatives and other substances were taken or applied to unblock the gastric system and stimulate perspiration. Common treatments included the use of the purgative calomel, cayenne pepper, and Indian tobacco (*Lobelia inflata,* a violent emetic). Steam and hot baths were also essential to create the needed perspiration.

In March 1838, Lloyd visited a Thomsonian infirmary in Boston to treat a long-lasting head cold which had badly affected his ears and created a swelling of his face. He took a fellow abolitionist, the Reverend Joshua Vaughan Himes, with him. The two began their day at ten o'clock with a hot cup of Thomsonian "coffee," followed by a session in a steam room, where the temperature ranged from 110 to 114 degrees. "Never did I know what it is to perspire until then," Lloyd wrote his brother-in-law George W. "What a shower of rain poured from my neck to my heels!" Yet the effect was quite pleasant. Lloyd remained in the bath about fifteen minutes and then went "dripping" to bed where he rested until three o'clock. Throughout the day, he was plied with hot liquids filled with lobelia and cayenne. This mixture was meant to keep him vomiting and sweating for some time. Finally, the two men joined other patients for a dinner of "good beafsteak" and then went home, Lloyd feeling greatly relieved of his ills.[29] He continued to take the cure, even though he knew all along that Samuel Thomson was publicly recognized as somewhat of a quack, frequently sued, once charged with murder but acquitted, and another time sent to prison for six weeks.

Lloyd's dependence on another form of alternative medicine was less unusual. The opposite of Thomsonianism, hydropathy, based on the cold water cure, came to Lloyd through the abolitionist community.[30] In 1842 George W. became involved in the establishment of the utopian community known as the Northampton Association of Education and Industry. One of the residents of the community was David Ruggles, an African-American abolitionist with extensive experience as an agent for the *Liberator* and a participant in the Underground Railroad in New York. Between 1835 and 1839, Ruggles helped some six hundred slaves (including Frederick Douglass) to freedom through his work for the New York Committee of Vigilance. By 1842, however, he was not in very good health and had lost much of his eyesight. Lloyd and George W. arranged for Ruggles to move to the Northampton community, where he was welcomed warmly and, through the use of alternative cures, nursed back to health. Learning about diet reform through Sylvester Graham, who visited the community, and the German-imported hydropathy movement through a course of self-study, Ruggles became a skilled hydropathic healer. He then established the Northampton Water Cure, where he limited his patients to those who applied to him in writing. Ruggles, however, had made it clear to Lloyd that he would be most honored to treat him any time he wished. After his own long illness and Lizzy's death, Lloyd considered the summer of 1848 the perfect time to take Ruggles up on his offer.

Lloyd arrived at Ruggles's establishment on July 17 and began the cold water treatment the next morning along with eighteen other patients already there. Although treatments varied depending on the complaint, the basic concept of hydropathy stated that by ingesting cold water or applying it through baths, wraps, or sprays, aches and pains would be relieved and the body rid of illness. Exposure to fresh air, following a predominantly vegetarian diet, abstaining from alcohol and caffeine, wearing loose-fitting lightweight clothing, exercising regularly, and avoiding too much emotional and sexual stimulation all led to good health. Each day of the treatment followed a similar rhythm, "a half bath at 5 o'clock. A.M.; rubbed down with a wet sheet thrown over the body at 11 o'clock; a sitz bath at 4, P.M.; a foot-bath at half past 8, P.M."[31] For several weeks, Lloyd spent most of his time in cold water, causing him to miss the first U.S. woman's rights convention held in Seneca Falls, New York, on July 19 and 20. Finally, he experienced his "crisis," which was followed by fever and the diarrhea that Ruggles claimed would "carry the humors off."[32]

Homeopathy was the third important medical belief for the Garrisons. Introduced to the United States in 1825 by Samuel Hahnemann, a German physician, homeopathy became very popular in the 1840s. Like hydropathy, homeopathy encouraged fresh air, healthy food, lots of water, and an avoidance of stimulants. Its basic concept was that disease was a matter of the spirit, nearly all illnesses being caused by a suppressed itch, or "psora." The object of the treatment was to displace a patient's natural disease by a weaker, artificial one that the body could more easily dispose of. Homeopathists, believing that "like cures like," worked to discover substances that would produce in a healthy person the same symptoms a disease would in a sick person. The substance would then be diluted many times to a strength where it would not produce any symptoms in a healthy person. When given to the patient, it was believed the medicine would cancel out the sickness. In many cases, however, because the medicines were so diluted, they alleviated the symptoms without curing the disease itself.

Considering Lloyd and Helen's medical beliefs, it is not surprising that when the usually healthy and robust Charley became ill with the flu in April 1849, they were both open to any suggestions of alternate medical treatments to cure him. Indeed, for four days, Lloyd and Helen nursed him themselves, trying to ease his muscle aches, fever, and frequent vomiting. They wrapped the sick boy in a wet sheet three or four times with no result and then consulted their homeopathic books to find some remedies based on his symptoms. Lloyd later admitted that this was not a wise path, since both he and Helen lacked adequate skill and knowledge to treat their child on their own, and, therefore, their treatments did no good. When a friend (unnamed in all the correspondence surrounding the issue) told him about a medicated vapor bath that his wife had administered several times with great success, Lloyd decided to try it, procuring the necessary chair and apparatus. The next evening, the woman arrived to help him. Up to this time, Charley had remained coherent and cooperative during his parents' many treatments, although his illness had worsened so that when his arms and legs were moved, he hollered in agony. Nevertheless, in good faith, Lloyd and his friend's wife placed him in the chair and began the hot water treatment. After about fifteen minutes, the boy started squirming, then screaming, begging his father to take him out of the seat. Helen, who was most likely not within earshot, was unaware of what was going on. As Lloyd later told Elizabeth Pease, "No other person was in the room, except the lady and myself." Never considering that the woman had turned the temperature up too high, Lloyd appealed to his son's "little manhood . . . urging him to bear it all with fortitude."[33] Finally, when the child's cries became unbearable, the two removed him from the tub. Much to their horror, they discovered that he had been severely burned on his buttocks, the skin on one side having been entirely destroyed. From the moment of his removal from the vapor bath, Charley became delirious. In four days, on April 8, he died, his mother and father by his side. Again, Theodore Parker was asked to join a small group of family and friends to lay a Garrison child to rest.

Helen and Lloyd were beside themselves with grief and guilt, Lloyd wanting nothing more than to repress his culpability, which he could not. How awful to consider that he had killed his own child! Perhaps he recalled his anger with his mother for supposedly causing the death of his sister, Elizabeth. Fanny's responsibility, however, had been in bringing her daughter to Baltimore; Lloyd's was much more horrendous. In an effort to rationalize the situation, he told Pease that for all anybody knew, Charley might have died anyway. "The fever struck upon the brain with great force from the beginning," he wrote, "and it therefore made his case a critical one, as he was a child full of warm blood and nervous excitability." The loss to the entire family was so great that even little four-and-a-half-year-old Fanny, who had adored her brother, constantly asked if she could join him and "dear Lizzie." The strength of Fanny's youthful desire to be with her deceased brother and sister frightened her parents, who almost feared it was a sign that she, too, would "early be called away."[34]

Lloyd was so distraught about his role in Charley's death that he could not even bear to have a daguerreotype made of his son before his burial, a fact he later regretted. Instead, he offered Pease his own final portrait of his child:

> He was a beautiful boy, but in no frail or delicate sense. He had a fine intellectual and moral development, with great bodily energy; he seemed born to take a century upon his shoulders, without stooping; his eyes were large, lustrous, and charged with electric light; his voice was clear as a bugle, melodious, and ever ringing in our ears, from the dawn of day to the ushering in of night—so that since it has been stilled, our dwelling has seemed to be almost without an occupant. But, above all, he was re-

> markable for the strength and fervor of his affection. He loved with all his soul, mind, and might. In this respect, I have never seen his equal. All the friends who have visited us for the last three or four years have had the strongest proofs of his attachment. He would almost smother them beneath a tornado of kisses; his embraces were given with intense vital energy, and "with a will." He had not a vicious quality.[35]

Helen was nearly out of her mind with grief. Three months after Charley's death, she wrote Ann Phillips of her lack of enthusiasm for the annual Fourth of July celebrations. All she could imagine was young Charley's "bright happy face" the previous year. She felt nothing but "an aching void" in her heart.[36] Unlike her husband, she did not absolve herself of blame; in fact, the guilt ate at her day after day. She could easily have placed all responsibility for the scalding on Lloyd's shoulders, but she did not. Rather, she turned it inward, never forgiving herself, perhaps faulting herself for going along with her husband's experimental solutions rather than calling for a doctor early on in the illness. In mid-July, Helen wrote a letter to their intimate friend Henry C. Wright, "Every hour, indeed every moment, he is before me; in all his beauty and freshness, and I long to clasp him to my heart." She had tried to resign herself to her son's death, she told Wright, and to be outwardly cheerful, but "it is all forced my heart is ready to break. . . . I desire no consolation from any source, for I feel certain the vapor-bath caused his death. I have read from several writers since Charlies death of the effect of the bath upon the brain, and how quick the disease is sent to the head by them." To this, she added a rare expression of anger toward her husband: "Then that scald, what treatment from those who were trying to restore him, could anything be worse." Too horror stricken to continue, she ended her thought, "I cannot dwell upon it. I sometimes think I will never mention his name, for I can seldom speak of him composedly and without weeping."[37]

Helen remained profoundly depressed into October. At times she wished she could die so the pain would cease. She must have expressed these feelings to her dear Philadelphia friend, Mary Grew, a relation of Wendell and Ann Phillips, for Grew returned a letter that was filled with deep concern. "You say that you can scarcely wait for the reunion with your child," she wrote. "I know how very painful must be your reflections; how frequently the thought *will* come. Had we done differently, it might not have been thus. Let me entreat you to *strive earnestly* to banish that agonizing thought." Grew tried to convince Helen that, in fact, no matter what she and Lloyd had tried, they might not have been able to save their son. They had simply done their best, "and, now, surely, your hearts should resist every feeling akin to self-reproach."[38]

Years later, when the remaining five Garrison children reflected upon their early homelife, they came to understand the important role their father's political world played in their development into adults. During the period from 1836 to 1849, much of Lloyd and Helen's time revolved around creating a warm family environment for their children. But the siblings learned early on that their father, the designated breadwinner for the clan, was a main political leader in the antislavery movement, and that his obligations often took him away from their immediate world. In addition to agitation around the issue of slavery, their father had committed himself to several other issues, which he introduced into his home: anti-sabbatarianism, peace, anti-imperialism, and woman's rights—all which had a great impact on his family. When the mob of 1835 ruled, Lloyd seemed unconcerned for his personal welfare, but after becoming a father, his sense of responsibility for his children's futures affected every move he made. The personal and political became even more inseparable, both for him and the entire family. But for the young children, their father's world, although exciting and varied, was too complex to understand.

Several portraits and political cartoons from the 1830s and 1840s depict the children's balding, thinnish abolitionist father. But perhaps the best image of Lloyd as a public person derives from a description of him written by the British author Harriet Martineau. Martineau wrote several articles and books about her journeys through the young United States, her best known being *Society in America.* Her book *Retrospect of Western Travel,* which describes New England village and city life in great detail, portrays the abolitionist community most sympathetically.[39] Although written before George's birth, Martineau's description of their father later greatly tickled the children. The author, for example, at first envisioned Lloyd as somewhat of a zealot, particularly after hearing about the 1835 Boston mob scene. Eager to meet this much adored but seemingly eccentric man, she appealed to an acquaintance, Ezra Stiles Gannett, to arrange a meeting. Lloyd arrived at Gannett's home at ten o'clock in the morning on December 30, 1835, during one of his visits to Boston from Brooklyn. Expecting a dour, grim fanatic, Martineau was "wholly taken by surprise" to see "a countenance glowing with health and wholly expressive of purity, animation, and gentleness" who reminded her of the many Quakers she had met on her travels. After several enjoyable conversations, Martineau decided that Lloyd was a man who expressed himself from the heart, one with a mission to expose fallacies and denounce hypocrisy. However, he was also puzzling, for while he often used the pages of the *Liberator* to harshly criticize those less radical than himself, when he spoke of them in person he was most gentle. This apparent contradiction struck her very much as an issue of masculinity. In person, Lloyd appeared to have "a want of manliness," she told one of his Boston supporters, who agreed that "a kind look and shake of the hand from a stranger unmanned" Lloyd for a moment before he regained his bearing.

Lloyd's children later realized that Martineau's observation, although not intended to be mean-spirited, reflected the opinions of those who despised the abolitionists. Opponents constantly accused the men in the movement of unmasculine (even feminine) behavior in the hopes these insults would either lead to physical confrontation or discourage other men from joining. This perception was often based on the placid, nonviolent posturing of the male leaders. (On the other hand, antiabolitionists also liked to characterize the women as pushy and masculine.) These attacks meant nothing to Lloyd. In his personal dealings with loved ones, fellow travelers, and acquaintances, he clearly chose to adopt a gentle, nonviolent persona, one that was directly opposite to his father's, perhaps even his mother's. In an adversarial situation, he used a similar manner of calm, quiet strength. He wished to instill this same attitude in his own sons, hence, his urging of poor young Charley to act like a man in the face of adversity, to be calm, quiet, and determined. For Lloyd, strength and manhood came through the soul, not the fists.

As he evolved into the role model of a political activist for his children, the calm, purposeful Lloyd that Harriet Martineau met developed other radical ideas which came to define him both publicly and privately. Fortunately, Helen agreed with these positions, as spousal harmony was probably the most important example the two wished to establish for their children. Lloyd wanted his children to understand how certain issues were both political and deeply personal, and each of these was continuously discussed at home. The first concerned religion, especially as it pertained to particular sects and then to the sabbath. While they tended to favor Quakerism or Unitarianism, Helen and Lloyd, and then the children, attended church on an irregular basis, frequenting any establishment, white or black, offering a good antislavery sermon, making them rather free-spirited in terms of institutionalized religion. As a result, the children grew up to be good nonsectarian Christians with a curiosity, but wariness, of organized religion. For example, in 1857, when Willie was nineteen years old, he attended a Methodist revival meeting. His reaction was somewhat cynical. He reported to his brother Wendell that he "witnessed the operation by which good saints are manufactured from bad sinners. Such a howling and excited audience I never saw before."[40] In addition, even though Lloyd knew the Bible intimately, neither he nor Helen foisted it upon their children, as most God-fearing Christian parents did. When in 1859 his father presented the adult William with a gift of the Holy Scriptures, his son remarked that he would like to become "thoroughly acquainted with it" as he had up to then found it "the most difficult of books to read . . . partly [due] to my lack of thought on religious matters."[41]

Sixteen years later, Lloyd again presented his son with a Bible, this time making it crystal clear that the book was to be considered a guide rather than law. His inscription read: "From his affectionate father, who presents it not as 'the Word of God,' as it is by many dogmatically assumed to be . . . but as a volume to be studied, criticized, and judged, without prejudice, credulity, superstition, or regard to any popular or prevailing interpretation thereof, and with the same freedom as any other book or compilation of ancient manuscripts; in which case, reason and conscience holding mastery over it, it will still be found deserving of the highest consideration for its incomparable truths, solemn warnings, and precious promises."[42]

After their marriage, Lloyd and Helen also chose to cease the practice of honoring the Sunday sabbath. From their perspective, every day was meant to honor God, making the one-day sabbath meaningless in their lives. Perhaps the first expression of Lloyd's own move toward antisabbatarianism came in November 1835, soon after the people of Connecticut gorged themselves on food during an official day of Thanksgiving. As Lloyd playfully wrote his brother-in-law George W., there was "an immense slaughter among the turkeys, geese and chickens, who were destroyed by the jaw-bones of the people without the slightest remorse." Besides the fowl, there were potato, mince, and apple pies and various puddings, all adding up to a gigantic "insurrection of the stomache." On a more serious note, however, Lloyd had his doubts about the sincerity of this and other "outward forms and ceremonies and observances, as a religious duty."[43]

Lloyd's distancing himself from the church may have resulted from both his upbringing and the difficulties he had convincing influential clergymen to support his political work. Both factors led him to develop his own private religious practice, which he and Helen then passed on to their children. Raised in a very strict Baptist tradition, Lloyd resented the unbending and sometimes contradictory practices that had affected his mother's life. Whether in Newburyport, Lynn, or Baltimore, Fanny had taken him with her to weekly services or women's meetings. After she arranged for him to remain in Newburyport with Deacon Ezekial Bartlett, Lloyd was expected to attend weekly services and encouraged to sing in the church choir. Bartlett and Martha Farnham were key to Lloyd's passage from boyhood to manhood, but each expressed anger and frustration with Fanny's inability to solve her personal problems and meet her financial obligations to them. From Lloyd's perspective, Martha, by forcing Fanny to take responsibility for her own daughter, may have been, in fact, indirectly responsible for Elizabeth's death. These God-fearing people who were both charitable and punishing at the same time created in Lloyd a skepticism of institutionalized church communities.

Once a father, Lloyd clarified his religious position. Faith was of great importance to him, and he and Helen planned on raising Christian children. But they would not allow their offspring to be exposed to petty hypocrisies. Lloyd's personal antagonism toward formal religion was exacerbated by the reception his political ideas received from church leaders. The Baptist churches generally avoided the antislavery issue to mollify congregations in the South. Other sects agreed with the idea of abolishing slavery but did not appreciate the militant voice of the Massachusetts Anti-Slavery Society. In 1835 Lloyd made a special effort to win over the Unitarian minister William Ellery Channing of the Federal Street Church, but Channing, although sympathetic to the cause, felt that the slave owners themselves had to end the practice. Lloyd publicly criticized Channing in the *Liberator* for his moderate beliefs. Lyman Beecher, another well-known preacher, also claimed Lloyd was too fervent and outspoken, and he too received Lloyd's anger through his newspaper. Lloyd and Helen's way of ensuring that their children were not exposed to sermons against their father was to take them only to Garrison-friendly institutions. In this way, they were guaranteed a pleasant experience as well as exposure to an antislavery Christian ethic.

Lloyd's religious beliefs determined another rather unfavorable political position he held, that of nonresistance, a belief that all violence was wrong, and that people should not participate in institutional state violence, such as war and slavery. Nonresisters often refused to pay taxes or cooperate when called for militia training, took public positions against violence, and, above all, did not take part in the electoral process, a position that caused great controversy among abolitionists themselves.[44] The political stance of nonresistance, when coupled with a personal commitment to nonviolence, determined how husband and wife interacted, how children were raised, how fellow workers were treated, even how animals were handled. These ideals permeated the Garrison household and, more than any other doctrine, became the underpinning of the children's adult personal and political lives.

Lloyd awakened to the political uses of nonresistance and its cohort, peace, as early as 1828 when he became acquainted with the newly founded American Peace Society.[45] A retired sea captain, William Ladd, had formed the organization in an effort to unite Christians who had a moral aversion to war and institutionalized violence. By 1829, Lloyd had surpassed the American Peace Society's relatively mild program of pacifism-through-persuasion by moving closer to a position of noncooperation. While writing for the *Genius of Universal Emancipation,* he identified the militia as a system that benefited the rich while penalizing the poor, an idea that Ladd had not conceptualized. Lloyd recalled how his own failure to show up for a "muster" in Boston had resulted in a fine, even though his near-sightedness and belief in nonresistance should have excused him. He vowed he would rather serve time in prison than cooperate with the militia or any other armed effort.[46] While Lloyd never expected to deviate from his belief, he did not necessarily expect others to live by it. When David Walker's 1829 *Appeal to the Coloured Citizens of the World* called for slave uprisings or when Nat Turner led his 1831 slave insurrection, Lloyd, although reticent to sanction their work, expressed some understanding, claiming that the white government and slaveholders' practices were to blame for this extreme counteraction. Also, when in 1837 the Reverend Elijah Lovejoy died at the hands of an Illinois mob while defending himself and his abolitionist press with arms, Lloyd expressed regret over his resorting to violence but did not deny him his choice. In effect, violent antislavery actions were taken in self-defense, and although not the preferred Christian way, they were understandable, perhaps even necessary. Lloyd would repeat this position on several occasions, the most controversial being his personal abhorrence yet public support of the Civil War.

Lloyd's Christian nonresister stance led logically to a belief in anti-imperialism, which his children strongly echoed in their adult lives. In 1837 this concern was distinctly tied to arguments surrounding the possible annexation of Texas, which in 1836 had declared its independence from Mexico, thanks largely to a war supported by slaveholders. When the new republic immediately applied for admission into the United States, there were an equal number of thirteen slave and free states, and Northern congressmen did not favor creating an imbalance. Obviously, Lloyd opposed the entry of Texas into the Union because it was a slavocracy, but he also feared a war with Mexico, which refused to recognize Texas's independence. These feelings, clearly based on his opposition to violence, were also anti-imperialistic. "As a nation," he wrote, "we have evinced the basest perfidy towards Mexico; we have openly violated the faith of treaties; we have encouraged our citizens to invade and revolutionize a part of her territory; we have rashly and impudently recognized the independence of that territory; and we have been fertile in devising plots and expedients to provoke her to declare war on us."[47] His concern over tensions with Mexico did not ease, so that in 1845, when President James K. Polk invited Texas to join the Union and war ensued, Lloyd again expressed great sympathy for the so-called enemy. He kept this stance throughout the war. In 1847, almost a year before the Treaty of Guadalupe Hidalgo was signed to end the conflict, he wrote, "I desire to see human life at all times held sacred; but in a struggle like this,—so horribly unjust and offensive on our part, so purely one of self-defence against lawless invaders on the part of the Mexicans,—I feel as a matter of justice, to desire the overwhelming defeat of the American troops, and the success of the injured Mexicans."[48]

In this vein, Lloyd attacked the British government for its treatment of the peoples of Ireland and India and Louis Napoleon for his tyrannical hold on the French. "You rightly judge my character," he wrote to John W. LeBarnes, "I am not only an abolitionist for the chattelized slave, but an emancipationist for the whole human race."[49] Lloyd also considered the relationship between the U.S. government and Native Americans as imperialistic. In 1837 he lamented the previous two hundred years of repression against the native peoples whose "blood warm and fresh" had stained the nation's history, a country "now engaged in completing the extinction of the red men of the forest, once the occupants and owners of her soil, once multitudinous and powerful!"[50] Eight years later, he again addressed the issue. "Have the Cherokees, have the Seminoles and the other Indian tribes, lost not 'a foot of land' by our plundering disposition?" he questioned U.S.

senator Levi Woodbury, who had defended the forceful removal of Native Americans from their lands. "Are not their cries continually going up to Heaven, that a righteous retribution may fall upon us for our horrid cruelties toward them—for driving them from their fertile lands, extinguishing their council fires, spilling their blood, and conspiring for their extermination?"[51] Through his defense of the exploited against the power of the United States, Lloyd not only set a political example for his children but also hoped to teach them compassion for the underdogs of the world.

As Lloyd's stands on nonresistance and anti-imperialism grew stronger, his respect for the American Peace Society weakened, resulting in his proposal that a general peace meeting be called to address his deeper concerns. Hence, in September 1838 a Peace Convention was held where Garrisonians and more traditionally minded American Peace Society members confronted one another over two issues—nonresistance and equal participation for women within the organization. Both issues later resonated strongly in Lloyd's children's personal and political lives. Although the feminist aspect of Lloyd's beliefs had surfaced several times during his courtship with Helen and in the pages of the *Liberator,* it had taken center stage in the early summer of 1837 when two sisters, Angelina and Sarah Grimké, arrived in New England to lecture for the Massachusetts Anti-Slavery Society. Born in a slaveholding home in South Carolina, the two sisters had emigrated to the North (Sarah in 1821, Angelina in 1829), forsaking their wealthy Southern Episcopal heritage for a more sedate and philanthropic life as Quakers.[52] In February 1835, Angelina joined the Philadelphia Female Anti-Slavery Society, a Garrisonian organization founded in 1833, and soon she and Sarah were heavily involved in abolitionist work. Of course, the very fact that they were exiles from the South who had firsthand knowledge of the slave experience made the sisters an invaluable resource for the movement. Lloyd had helped to introduce their ideas to the public when he published an antislavery letter Angelina had written to him in September 1835.

Once ensconced in the movement, Angelina, the more assertive of the sisters, began to use her Southern identity to foster her work. In early 1836 the American Anti-Slavery Society published her pamphlet *An Appeal to the Christian Women of the South.* In this long essay she explained to Southern women the unchristian nature of slavery, appealing to their motherly hearts to reexamine their feelings toward the "peculiar institution." She implored them to "1. Read then on the subject of slavery," in the Bible, books, and newspapers. "2. Pray over the subject. . . . 3. Speak on this subject"—to friends, relatives, acquaintances. But, largely, they should "4. Act on this subject."[53] If women owned slaves and believed slavery to be a sin, they needed to free them. Freed people who chose to stay on as wage earners must then be educated. The Southern response to Angelina's tract was quick and decisive. The state governments ordered postmasters to destroy the pamphlets, and Grimké was told never to return to her home in Charleston, the implication being that she would be physically harmed or arrested and tried for treason. The tract, however, also led to the thirty-one-year-old woman's acceptance of a position as lecturer (to women) for the American Anti-Slavery Society in New York City. Sarah, also a convincing writer and speaker who was unwilling to be separated from her sister, left her conservative Quaker Meeting in Philadelphia to join her. The two remained together for the rest of their lives, even after Angelina's marriage to the abolitionist educator Theodore Weld on May 14, 1838.

Meanwhile, Angelina's female meetings in New York proved so popular that both sisters were soon speaking before larger groups in churches. Men as well as women were attracted by their Southern experiences, and soon they found themselves addressing what was then called "promiscuous" audiences, a combination of women and men. For nineteenth-century women to take on this public role was most scandalous, placing the Grimké sisters right in the middle of one of the first woman's rights controversies in U.S. history. Soon after they arrived in Massachusetts in 1837, the Congregational clergymen wrote a "Pastoral Letter" to their congregations decrying the Grimkés' unconventional behavior. The document urged ministers to ban all traveling lecturers from their churches, especially women who spoke before promiscuous audiences. Three "Clerical Appeals" followed, which condemned Lloyd for publishing attacks of these ministers and rebuked the Grimkés for their outrageous behavior or both. Lloyd enjoyed the controversy, using the pages of the *Liberator* to air his views. He repeated all his previous complaints about the clergy's mediocre support of abolitionism, but, even more important to the development of his own public position on woman's rights, he aired the Grimkés' woman-rightist ideas as well.

When the Peace Convention met in 1838, the air was charged with tension. Greatly influenced by the assertiveness of the Grimké sisters, the Chapman sisters, Lucretia Mott, Sarah Douglass, Margaretta Forten, and Abby Kelley (who had recently joined the antislavery lecture circuit), Lloyd decided it was time for a man to take a stand on women's right to equal participation within the abolitionist and peace movements. He was astute enough to recognize that without the participation of women, his efforts would never succeed. As he wrote in 1833, "Whose influence is so potent as Woman's? . . . Whose benevolent heroism, or moral excellence, or tender sensibility, or deep devotion is comparable to hers? . . . The destiny of the slaves is in the hands of the American women, and complete emancipation can never take place without their co-operation."[54] In hindsight, Lloyd's move for decisive action at the Peace Convention might have come as a reaction to the destruction of Pennsylvania Hall that May.[55] Intended as a space for meetings, public forums, and free-produce stores (which refused to sell slave-made items) and for publishing the *Pennsylvania Freeman,* an abolitionist newspaper, the building had been constructed in response to the closing of many public spaces as a result of the gag rule, a decision made by the House of Representatives not to debate antislavery petitions. Dedicated on May 14, 1838, Pennsylvania Hall was immediately used for the Second Anti-Slavery Convention of American Women.

The Philadelphia antislavery community had always been racially integrated, perhaps more so than others. The easy camaraderie between black and white activists, however, did not please the majority of Philadelphians, who feared intermarriage as well as social and economic parity. Economic problems, exacerbated by the Panic of 1837, fueled the fires of racial hatred, especially among the working class. When the opening of Pennsylvania Hall was announced, many citizens of Philadelphia turned hostile. Spectators gathered, angry men muttering epithets at black and white women conventioneers hurrying in and out of the building. On the second day, the mayor of Philadelphia suggested that African-American women stop attending, an idea that was adamantly rejected. However, for purposes of self-protection, when the women left the hall, they did so in pairs, one white woman linked arm in arm with a black woman, a strategy similar to the one used by the Boston women in October 1835. That night, with the mob numbering about seventeen thousand, the mayor ordered the hall locked but left it unguarded. The mob broke through the doors, piled up the books and benches and set them ablaze. To ensure total destruction, they broke the gas pipes. Within hours, the building was nothing but smoking ash and rubble. Lloyd was a witness to the events, but, at the insistence of his friends Robert Purvis, Joseph Parrish Jr., and Israel H. Johnson, was whisked out of town at two o'clock in the morning. James Mott saw that Maria Chapman and Anne Weston also left safely. During the night, the restless crowd looked for someplace else to vent its anger. At first, they hoped to attack the Motts' home, but a family friend, pretending to be an antiabolitionist, led the mob in the opposite direction. Unable to find any abolitionists to throttle, they aimed their wrath at the black Mother Bethel Church and then upon the Shelter for Colored Orphans. The Philadelphia police were nowhere in sight.

If previous to this incident, Lloyd had perceived women as a morally blessed, gentle volunteer corps, he could not help but see that they were far more than that. All around him women activists were showing their courage, assertiveness, dedication, and intelligence. Had he not taken a stand before his fellow male reformers, he might have lost the admiration of these invaluable women—and so he acted, and as a result drew this dynamic female cadre closer to him. The step that Lloyd took at the Peace Convention in the September following the torching of Pennsylvania Hall was designed to guarantee women equal rights within the organization. As he related to Helen, "When the roll of members was about being made out, I rose and suggested, that, as mistakes often occur in procuring signatures, each individual should write his or *her* name on a slip of paper, &c.; thus mooting the vexed 'woman question' at the very outset."[56] Although there were many unhappy faces among the male members, the suggestion was adopted, thus acknowledging women as members with the right to speak out and vote. Soon after, a business committee was established which included Abby Kelley and Susanna Sisson. Many men were disgruntled by these actions, but they did not rebel until, during an afternoon meeting, Kelley had the audacity to call the Reverend George C. Beckwith to order. At this point, he and most of the other male American Peace Society members in attendance walked out of the convention. Left remaining were Garrisonians who then formed the New England Non-Resistance Society. Effingham L. Capron agreed to be president; Lloyd, corresponding secretary; Maria Chapman, recording secretary, and Thankful Southwick and Anne Weston, the female members of the executive committee.

The *Declaration of Sentiments,* which Lloyd wrote and which was unanimously accepted by the new organization, stated his philosophy about war. Except for his son George, who fought in the Civil War, all of the Garrison children embraced this code, making it part of their personal creed. The paragraph that became especially meaningful to them read:

> We register our testimony, not only against all wars, whether offensive or defensive, but all preparations for war; against every naval ship, every arsenal, every fortification; against the militia system and a standing army; against all military chieftains and soldiers; against all monuments commemorative of victory over a fallen foe, all trophies won in battle, all celebrations in honor of military or naval exploits; against all appropriations for the defence of a nation by force and arms, on the part of any legislative body; against every edict of government requiring of its subjects military service. Hence, we deem it unlawful to bear arms, or to hold a military office.[57]

The New-England Non-Resistance Society lasted until 1849. A newspaper, the *Non-Resistant,* was published until 1842, and Henry C. Wright, an important influence upon the children's lives, became the society's leading proponent, taking on the self-assigned role of peace agent. Adin Ballou, the founder of the Christian utopian society of Hopedale in 1842 (a later educational site for son George), also took on much of the society's work. Many abolitionists felt that nonresistance and woman's rights watered down their stance, but Lloyd continued to incorporate them into his life. Indeed, in 1840, when Lloyd left pregnant Helen alone to attend the American Anti-Slavery Society annual meeting in New York and then the World Anti-Slavery Convention in London, the issue of woman's rights was again forced into the spotlight. The New York meeting was rife with tension from the start, for one of the first actions Lloyd initiated that Tuesday morning, May 12, was the nomination of Abby Kelley to the organization's business committee, a ploy that had worked in his favor at the Peace Convention. The vote came out as 571 in her favor and 451 against her. Those who could not abide having women in prominent positions seceded to form the American and Foreign Anti-Slavery

Society. Once again, whether intentionally or not, Lloyd had orchestrated the move to include women while at the same time purging his ranks of dissenters. His luck did not hold up in London.

Owing to the fog and poor sailing conditions, Lloyd arrived in London after the conference had begun. Much to his chagrin, he found that the British abolitionists had refused to allow the U.S. women delegates, including Ann Greene Phillips, Lucretia Mott, Mary Grew, Sarah Pugh, and others, to take seats as active participants. Rather, they were relegated to a separate section from which women could observe, but not participate in, the proceedings. Lloyd had anticipated such an occurrence. As he wrote to Oliver Johnson from aboard ship on his way to England, he had no idea how the British would handle a mixed constituency. "The object of the Convention," he said, "is to promote the interests of Humanity. It is, then, a common object, in which all who wear the human form have a right to participate, without regard to color, sex or clime. With a young woman placed on the throne of Great Britain, will the philanthropists of that country presume to object to the female delegates from the United States, as members of the Convention, on the ground of their sex? In what assembly, however august or select, is that almost peerless woman, LUCRETIA MOTT, not qualified to take an equal part?"[58] As a result of the British behavior, Lloyd, Nathaniel Rogers, Charles Remond, and William Adams, who had arrived together, refused to participate in the discussions. Rather, they sat with the exiled women delegates in a display of solidarity.

Throughout the 1830s, Lloyd's activism had embraced a multipronged agenda of abolitionism, woman's rights, nonresistance, peace, anti-imperialism, and antisabbatarianism. All of these included philosophical and political positions he wished to pass on to his children . . . and did. Lloyd's willingness to attack many issues at a time reflected his vast interest in what was going on around him. However, his diversity did not please many abolitionists who simply felt that Garrisonianism was losing its focus and becoming too extreme. As a result, the movement retained its 1840 split into the Garrisonian American Anti-Slavery Society and the New York–based American and Foreign Anti-Slavery Society headed by Arthur and Lewis Tappan, James G. Birney, and Henry B. Stanton. Those who remained with Lloyd held on to their ideas of immediate emancipation for slaves, nonresistance, and equal participation for women. In January 1843 they also took on the mantle of disunion, claiming that since the U.S. Constitution sanctioned slavery, it was an immoral, unchristian document. There could be no union between North and South as long as slavery existed. The American Anti-Slavery Society took on the motto "No Union with Slaveholders," which also appeared on the masthead of the *Liberator*.

Some abolitionists, particularly in upstate New York, felt that the U.S. Constitution did not sanction slavery but rather, through its provision to end the foreign slave trade in 1808, pointed the way toward the eventual end of the evil institution. These men, including Gerrit Smith, Alvan Steward, and Myron Holley, supported the idea of an antislavery political party to work within the governmental system to achieve abolition. The organization, the Liberty Party, formed in 1840, attracted numbers of activists who could not accept Lloyd's radical perceptions. Furthermore, other abolitionist men, especially those who gathered around the Tappan brothers, found Lloyd's feelings against the church too unappealing. Theodore Weld, for one, leaned more toward this position than any other. Hence, in the early 1840s, Lloyd's circle grew smaller; yet it was as fervent as ever, and it was certainly the one that attracted the most diverse and socially adventurous people.

At the core of Lloyd's work was, of course, race. This was the most complex issue for him, not only on the political level, but also in his and Helen's personal lives. While the couple tried to foster a colorblind philosophy of life for their children to emulate, they were not always successful. During the early years of his abolitionist organizing, Lloyd often relied on the African-American community to feed and house him on his travels as well as to support the *Liberator*.[59] Indeed, by April 1834 three-fourths of the 2,300 subscribers were African-American, and so were several of the agents, including Richard Johnson of New Bedford, Massachusetts; Jehiel C. Beman of Middletown, Connecticut; Abraham D. Shadd of Wilmington; Philip A. Bell of New York City, and John B. Vashon of Pittsburgh. Black women's antislavery organizations also pledged material support for the periodical. The constitution of the Female Anti-Slavery Society of Salem, Massachusetts, for example, clearly stated:

> Resolved, That as we believe the Boston Liberator to have been the means of enlightening the minds of many, in regard to the ungenerous scheme of African colonization, and also removing the monster prejudice from the minds of many, in regard to the free people of color, by representing things in their true light, we are determined to support it and all antislavery publications.[60]

The organization resolved to seek donations to send to deserving publishers.

Close African-American male associates of Lloyd included Robert Purvis and James Forten of Philadelphia, John and Charles Lenox Remond of Salem, and Nathaniel Paul of Boston. Purvis, who was born in South Carolina, had inherited a large sum of money from his white father. By 1850 he held real estate worth $35,000. Forten, an antislavery activist since 1817, was even wealthier. As a well-known sailmaker, he had amassed savings worth $100,000 by the 1830s, a considerable sum in those days. Both families lived in fashionable homes that Lloyd could only dream of having. John Remond and his son, Charles, benefited from the sizable profits attained through the family's catering business in Salem. Nathaniel

Paul lived the less remunerative life of a clergyman. Lloyd also enjoyed the association, if not close friendship, of many black female compatriots including Sarah Douglass of Philadelphia and Eunice Davis, Julia Williams, Susan Paul, Martha and Lucy Ball of Boston, and Sarah Parker Remond of Salem. Susan Paul ran a school for African-American children and created the Garrison Juvenile Choir, which was quite popular within the movement. Youths such as Charlotte Forten adored Lloyd. As Forten wrote upon dining with him in 1854, "At the table, I watched earnestly the expression of that noble face, as he spoke beautifully in support of the non-resistant principles to which he has kept firm; his is indeed the very highest Christian spirit, to which I cannot hope to reach."[61]

Indeed, Helen's early fears that Lloyd might be physically attacked on his way home from work might have been allayed had she known that cudgel-bearing black abolitionists accompanied and protected him, remaining out of sight so that even Lloyd was unaware of them. He, in turn, tried to foster racial equality by hiring African-American male workers, the most prominent being William Cooper Nell, a man whom the Garrison children knew well. Born in Boston on December 20, 1816, Nell's parents raised him with a consciousness about racism. His father was a founding member and vice-president of the Massachusetts General Colored Association, an antislavery society formed in 1826. By the age of sixteen, Nell was secretary of the Juvenile Garrison Independent Society, a group of black youth dedicated to education, community service, and self-help. Nell's effective public speaking came to Lloyd's attention in 1831, and he asked the adolescent if he would like to work as an errand boy for the *Liberator*. Soon after, at a time when racially integrated shops were hardly ever heard of, Lloyd promoted Nell to the rank of apprentice, where he trained with Lloyd and his printer, James Yerrinton. But Nell was also an activist, giving talks and organizing against slavery. He was the key player in the 1855 Massachusetts decision to integrate public schools. That same year, he published *Colored Patriots of the American Revolution*, a book considered to be the first serious historical study of African Americans. Throughout Nell's tenure, the *Liberator* was an important means by which both black and white abolitionists shared information and sustained a united community. It was also the conduit for discussion and debate over political issues.

Intimacy across racial lines, however, was a different story. Although Lloyd socialized with members of the black community in his own home and often spent nights in the Forten, Purvis, and Remond residences, there was a certain line of closeness that was not crossed. Lloyd's formality could have simply been New England reserve or, in some cases, a discomfort caused by class. In a letter to a friend, his sense of an undefined difference separating him from his black supporters seemed evident. Upon a visit to Robert and Harriet Purvis's home in Philadelphia, he noted, "I wish you had been with me in Philadelphia to see what I saw, to hear what I heard, and to experience what I felt in associating with many colored families. There are colored men and women, young men and young ladies, in that city, who have few superiors in refinement, in moral worth, and in all that makes the human character worthy of admiration and praise."[62] In spite of his admiration for the Purvises and Fortens, William C. Nell, even after twenty years in a close working relationship, referred to Lloyd as "Mr. Garrison" and never appeared to be a frequent guest in his home. The Remonds, Purvises, and Fortens did not spend long periods as guests either. In later years, Sojourner Truth, the famed itinerant preacher who spoke out against slavery and for woman's rights, traveled through Boston and spent a few nights at the Garrisons' home, but she was more of a respected oddity than a close friend. Lloyd's intimate working and social circle, known as the "Boston Clique," included Wendell Phillips, Samuel J. May, Francis Jackson, Maria Weston Chapman and her sisters Anne, Deborah, and Caroline Weston, Oliver Johnson, Charles Follen, and other Massachusetts abolitionists but did not include any African Americans. For Lloyd, racial equality was a political issue to which he was deeply committed, but like woman's rights, it was also an issue that reached only so far into his personal life. His children later adopted the same philosophy and practice.

Lloyd's discomfort with racial intermixing was a part of his personality which he did not openly discuss. On the surface, he tried very hard to conquer his own sense of difference as evidenced by his constant reaching out to and dependence on the black abolitionist community. In 1843, for example, Lloyd supported that community's successful campaign to repeal a state law prohibiting interracial marriages. However, even though he was most radical for his times, like many white and black abolitionists, he personally felt that such unions were not wise. His own children were raised to date and marry whites only, a practice handed down through the generations. As his great-grandson David Lloyd Garrison explained, the family was not racist, but there were no interracial couples because they all believed that the children of such unions would "suffer" from social ostracism.[63] In spite of this belief in a limit to interracial relationships, Lloyd fought against racism and tried to set a good example for his children. If he achieved the mission of abolishing slavery, he wanted a new generation of activists to take on the next struggle for civil rights.

Lloyd had his own regrettable experiences, however, and one of them involved the very popular runaway slave by the assumed name of Frederick Douglass.[64] Born around 1817 to a slave mother and a father rumored to be white, Douglass escaped from his owners in 1838. For a time, he and his wife, Anna, a free woman who came from Baltimore to join him, settled in New Bedford, Massachusetts, where they assimilated into free Northern society. While there, an agent for the *Liberator* offered Douglass a free trial subscription. Reading the newspaper brought the newly freed man into the world of abolitionism. On April 16, 1839, Douglass heard Lloyd speak and decided that he, too, wanted to devote his life to the antislavery cause. For Douglass, of course, this was a major decision. If he began to publicly tell his own story and his face became well known, slave hunters might very well attempt to kidnap him and collect the reward for returning a fugitive slave to his owners. However, the die had been cast, and Douglass began talking to local groups about his life in the South. In the spring of 1841, William C. Coffin, a Nantucket Quaker, heard Douglass speak and invited him to return to the island with him for a meeting of the Massachusetts Anti-Slavery Society. This he readily did, giving his first nonlocal address before such famous leaders as Lloyd, Wendell Phillips, Parker Pillsbury, Edmund Quincy, and Samuel J. May. Lloyd was tremendously excited by Douglass, whose charismatic presence, good looks, and deep voice were evidence that he would be a great addition to the movement. Douglass, himself, was awestruck. The man he had grown to admire so much had now turned his attention to him. Douglass was immediately recruited for the abolitionist lecture circuit.

Frederick Douglass, as a former slave, faced a greater degree of condescension than free black abolitionists did. When he began lecturing, for example, Lloyd and other abolitionists presented him to the public as a former "chattel" who had become "a man" through freedom.[65] Douglass took such references to slaves not being real men in stride, sometimes even using the same language in his own speeches. Yet, he also continued developing as a lecturer on his own terms and in his own style. Even though he kept Northern racism in the forefront of his thoughts, Douglass came to trust Lloyd and other leaders who often stood by his side when he encountered discrimination. Wendell Phillips, for instance, spent a long night on the deck of a boat to New York accompanying Douglass, who had been denied a berth. For several years, Douglass tramped the lecture trail with various white speakers. Quite often, Abby Kelley joined him, receiving a great deal of public criticism herself for doing so. Although wearing conservative Quaker-like attire (a gray dress, white collar, and shawl), Kelley was blasphemed for traveling in the company of men and speaking before promiscuous audiences. Rumors constantly circulated about her alleged deviance. Traveling with Douglass made matters even worse for her as the public had a heyday with her seeming audacity in crossing the unspoken color line. Regardless of their unconventional pairing, however, both were popular speakers. Douglass's story was so well received, in fact, that in 1845, it was published as the *Narrative of the Life of Frederick Douglass,* with a preface by Lloyd and a letter of endorsement by Wendell Phillips. Following the publication of his book, Douglass spent two years in England and Ireland speaking against slavery and raising money for the U.S. movement. For part of that time, in 1846, Lloyd was with him. While there, British abolitionists raised the money to buy Douglass's freedom from his former owner, Thomas Auld.

In August 1847, Douglass and Lloyd traveled west together on a speaking tour. It was on this trip that Lloyd became so desperately ill that Douglass had to travel on without him. Unbeknownst to Lloyd, Douglass had begun making plans to leave Massachusetts to move to Rochester, New York, where he wanted to establish his own newspaper. Indeed, the plan was hatched while he was abroad, and along with his freedom his British supporters had given him five hundred English pounds for his new enterprise. In 1846, when he first mentioned his plan for a newspaper, Lloyd, Maria Chapman, Edmund Quincy, and Wendell Phillips tried to talk him out of it. Lloyd had specific fears about a rival paper produced by Douglass. First, the new paper might very well pull enough supporters away from the *Liberator* to put it out of business. While it was true that several other antislavery papers existed, at least four published by black abolitionists, no one with as great a public image as Douglass had ever entered the competition. In real bread-and-butter terms, a smaller subscription base could not feed the rather large Garrison family. Second, Frederick Douglass was an indispensable lecturer. He was one of the most dynamic speakers of the movement, whereas Lloyd, although popular, was more noted for his great writing than his eloquence, often reading from a written text rather than extemporizing.

Third, Lloyd felt hurt that Douglass had seemingly abandoned their friendship in the process of creating his paper. Loyalty was something Lloyd depended upon. As he wrote to Helen from Cleveland, "Is it not strange that Douglass has not written a single line to me, or to anyone, in this place, inquiring after my health, since he left me on a bed of illness? It will also greatly surprise our friends in Boston to hear, that, in regard to his project for establishing a paper here, to be called 'The North Star,' he never opened to me his lips on the subject, nor asked my advice in any particular whatever. Such conduct grieves me to the heart."[66] Lloyd dealt with his feelings by working hard to overcome them. The *North Star* began publication on December 3, 1847, and by the end of the next month, Lloyd had praised it in the *Liberator* and wished it every success. In 1849 William C. Nell joined the staff of the *North Star* as its printer, but felt compelled to defend Lloyd's reputation during his ten months there. He eventually returned to the *Liberator* in 1853 with a newfound dedication to Garrisonianism. Although Douglass and Lloyd remained respectful of each other, their relationship never completely repaired itself. This may have been partly due to Douglass's later interpretation of the U.S. Constitution as antislavery and his eventual defection from the disunion position to supporting the Liberty Party.

From 1836 through 1848, during the years that Lloyd and Helen established their family, Lloyd also developed his political agenda, the ideals upon which his and Helen's children were to be raised. This included a wide range of issues—antislavery, antiracism, nonviolence, peace, anti-imperialism, feminism, and antisabbatarianism. He also supported or showed interest in such movements as temperance, homeopathy, utopianism, spiritualism, and diet reform. His objectives were both political and personal—to build a socially just world for his children and to train them to carry on any unfinished reform work. Of course, Lloyd could not accomplish this task alone. Although he was deeply involved in his children's lives, he depended on his "helpmeet," Helen, to assume the major task of daily child care and education. Together, they built a solid family unit dedicated to addressing the world's ills.

RAISING LITTLE GARRISONS

I do not forget the trouble we caused her [Helen] as boys, nor her occasional weariness and loss of heart; but scolding did not come natural to her, and her discipline seems, as I look back on it, to have been only mild and gracious.

Wendell Phillips Garrison to his father, 1876

CHAPTER IV

In her remembrances of her father published in 1924, Fanny Garrison (then Villard) paid tribute to the parenting skills of both her mother and her father. Her parents, she said, taught their children compassion, joy, generosity, selflessness, and a morality that embraced worthy, though unpopular, causes of the time. Fanny wrote that "these exceptional qualities were ours to emulate in the daily round of our home life. A greater legacy, a richer moral inheritance, I cannot believe was ever bestowed upon children by both parents than that which was so abundantly ours."[1] At one time or another, each of the Garrison children praised their parents for raising them to love and care for each other and also to become progressive reformers of the next generation.

Helen and Lloyd's belief in the great value of a strong nuclear family and their philosophy of child rearing reflected those of other abolitionists.[2] For their movement, for the future health of the nation, and for their own joy, it was important that both mother and father be actively involved in the children's upbringing. It was also essential that the parents be of one accord on the issue of slavery and that the use of violence be abhorred on the personal and political levels. In some abolitionist marriages, both partners spoke on the lecture circuit and attended meetings. Such was the well-known case of Abby Kelley and Stephen Foster, whose daughter, Alla, was cared for by the parent remaining at home or by Foster's sister, Caroline, who frequently stepped in to lend a hand. In the case of Lucretia and James Mott, Lucretia was often the leading light in terms of traveling and speaking; her extended family helped with child care. Lucy Stone and Henry Blackwell both traveled until Lucy decided to remain home with her child. In 1848, after the women's movement gave new life to women lecturers, a rising number of wives and mothers journeyed from their homes for speaking engagements and conventions. Included in that initial group were Martha Wright, Paulina Wright Davis, and Elizabeth Cady Stanton (Stanton's large family curtailed her activities). In many cases, abolitionist women preferred to keep their activism close to home so that they could maintain the traditional familial roles while supporting the cause. Sarah Douglass, Margaretta Forten, and Elizabeth Buffum Chace all adopted this pattern.

Lloyd and Helen's preference was not unique; in many abolitionist families, husbands and wives assumed the age-old roles of provider and homemaker. James Miller and Sarah McKim and Oliver and Mary Ann Johnson followed this model. Once married and a parent, Angelina Grimké Weld opted to leave the lecture circuit to become a full-time homemaker, mother, and teacher to abolitionist children who boarded at her school. The difference between Helen and these other women is that she was less self-confident; the difference between Lloyd and the other men is that he played a more active role at home. Part of the reason for this was his deep emotional need to have a family and a stable home life. As he put it, "I like home infinitely better than any other place in the world."[3] Lloyd also loved children, especially his own. He and Helen were not bothered by the fact that the Garrison family with seven youngsters was larger than the average abolitionist family at the time, which counted about 3.7 children.[4]

While Lloyd was an unusually involved father for the nineteenth century, it was Helen who was the primary homemaker and nurturer, an arrangement that suited the couple well. Although she enjoyed being an abolitionist, Helen had never wanted to be in the public eye. Rather, her roles as a mother, which included teaching her children the political and moral values of the movement, and as a supporter of her husband matched her unassuming personality and modest desires. They also fit in well with the early-nineteenth-century belief that the new republic of the United States needed to educate its youth to ensure its continued independence and prosperity. It was particularly important for mothers of the time to foster "republican" values. Helen's continued self-education ensured her effectiveness in that role. She kept abreast of all the news of the day, devouring the contents of the many periodicals that Lloyd brought home, attending meetings whenever she could, and enjoying the company of the innumerable activists who stayed with the family when they visited Boston. While she sometimes tired of having a home that resembled a hotel, she greatly appreciated the interchange with the fascinating people she had little chance to see otherwise.

Life for the couple, however, was not always easy. The years 1832 through 1850, although generally happy, were sometimes emotionally trying, especially for Helen. During that period she courted, married, birthed her seven children, and lost two of them. She also saw her parents and five of her siblings die. Eighteen thirty-six, the year George was born, was the same year Helen's father, George, died, adding responsibility for her mother and unmarried sisters, Anna, Mary, and Sarah, to the Garrison family. The next year, 1837, saw the death of her twenty-three-year-old brother, Henry, from a long-lasting respiratory illness. Henry had been the first Benson to join Lloyd in his crusade against slavery, working as an agent for the *Liberator,* then as a reporter, and finally as one of Lloyd's closest confidants and assistants. During his illness, he stayed for extended periods of time with Helen and Lloyd, good-naturedly allowing his brother-in-law to subject him to innumerable alternative medical treatments.

Helen's grief over each loss was profound, but her household responsibilities kept her so busy that she was unable to attend all the funerals. In 1842 alone, while tending three children, she experienced the death of her sister Mary on January 29; the birth of son Charles on September 9, and the death of Lloyd's brother, James, on October 14. James spent his final days in Helen and Lloyd's care, Helen having barely recovered from childbearing at the time of his death. The next September, Helen's sister Anna died, followed in 1844 by her mother. By 1850, when Helen's sister Sarah passed away, the Benson family, once totaling nine children, had been reduced to three—Helen, George W., and Charlotte. Charlotte lived in Providence with her husband and children, too far for daily contact, while George W. moved from Brooklyn to Northampton, then to New York City, and finally to Kansas, distances that separated him from his sisters for long periods of time. After James's death, Lloyd still had his aunt Charlotte, who eventually came to live with the family for a brief time before her own death in 1857. The result of this shrinking of family ties was twofold: first, Helen and Lloyd grew to rely increasingly upon each other for their primary emotional support, and, second, the care of their growing family had to be assumed almost completely by themselves, the lack of resources limiting their ability to hire help. From time to time, Charlotte visited from Providence or a friend came to assist them, but basically the growing Garrison clan had only one another to rely on, one of the reasons why Lloyd did not spend too much time on the lecture circuit. Between the *Liberator* and his family, he had enough responsibility to keep him in the Boston area.

Besides bearing children and burying family, the Garrisons always seemed to be contending with ill health. Lloyd constantly suffered from one ailment or another. In the summer of 1836, a low-grade fever and lack of appetite resulted in a weight loss of twelve pounds, down from 158 pounds to 146 within a few months. That same summer, he suffered from a sore on his leg which took weeks to improve. In 1838 he was plagued with violent headaches, sore throats, and scrofula (accompanied by a high fever), which recurred several times and resulted in an extreme swelling of his right fingers and hands, making writing very laborious. Severe headaches again plagued him in 1839 and 1842, while in 1843 he experienced swelling on his left side causing him great pain and discomfort. Recurring laryngitis and backaches also disabled him. In 1856 his "spinal attacks" landed him in bed for ten days. This pattern continued throughout Lloyd's life. The abolitionist community shared some concern about the family's health and frequently commented among themselves about their situation. In 1843, for example, Edmund Quincy notified Richard D. Webb in Ireland that Lloyd was "as ill, I suppose, as a man could be and live." Indeed, the entire family had been "in much trouble" for a year, first with scarlet fever, then the children with "lung or brain fever" and Helen with "the rheumatic fever."[5] Two years later, Laura Boyle told Abby Kelley that Lloyd's health was so poor that she feared he would have to retire "before the poor bleeding slave is rescued." Boyle lamented that, in fact, the entire Garrison clan were "some of them sick almost constantly."[6] Even Wendell Phillips noted in 1846 that Lloyd's health needed, "every few years, that he should throw completely off the burdens of his paper."[7]

Lloyd's constant practice of seeking out alternative cures was well known by his fellow activists, since he himself often described his trials to them. In 1843 he related to Phoebe Jackson his various efforts to rid himself of a severe cold, cough, and swelling on his left side. Lloyd consulted four specialists. Robert Wesselhoeft, a German-trained physician who embraced Priessnitz's water cure, diagnosed a tumor under the ribs. Clark Greene, a Harvard-trained physician, demurred; he claimed the problem was an enlarged spleen. Henry Bowditch, associated with Massachusetts General Hospital, disagreed with the first two but could not say what it was, and John Warren, a surgeon at Harvard Medical School, opted for an enlargement of the colon. In frustration, Lloyd decided to consult with two clairvoyants, Fanny Wilkins and Elizabeth Gleason. Gleason felt nothing was wrong on the left side, only on Lloyd's right, and Wilkins identified a "collection of brownish matter near the heart" that could bring on sudden death. Unsatisfied, Lloyd told Jackson he planned on visiting a third clairvoyant.[8] It is no wonder that sometimes Lloyd's friends joked about his quest for a cure-all for his physical complaints. In 1853 Edmund Quincy related to Richard Webb, "He is quite ignorant of physiology and has no belief in hygiene, or in anything pertaining to the body except *quack medicines.* That he has survived all he has taken is proof of an excellent constitution." Lloyd would certainly have been shocked by Quincy's knowledge about one drug he had swallowed called "Dr. Clark's Anti-Scrofulous Panacea," for, as Quincy told Webb, Lloyd praised the medicine, saying that he felt it "permeating the whole system in the most delightful manner." "'Permeating the system!' said Hervey Weston, with the malice of a regular practitioner; 'why, it was the first time he had taken a glass of grog, and he didn't know how good it was!'"[9] Two years before, Lloyd had claimed that the same medicine resulted in his recovered health and weight gain. As he had written to Dr. Clark, "I used some half dozen bottles. . . . I have repeatedly recommended it in my paper, and among my friends and acquaintances."[10]

Helen, in the meantime, sometimes experienced bouts of influenza and colds, but largely suffered from chronic fatigue; the children the usual afflictions of teething, influenza, and the then life-threatening childhood diseases, such as whooping cough, scarlet fever, scarletina, bowel disorders, and measles. Helen's own personal trauma of the 1840s and 1850s, besides childbearing, was a dislocated bone in her arm caused by a carriage accident in 1843. Lloyd, who was managing the wagon carrying Helen, infant Wendy, Sally Benson, and himself when it overturned during a visit to Northampton, felt tortured by his sense of his own carelessness. He spared no expense in finding appropriate medical care for Helen, but he had to borrow money from friends. In September, several weeks after the accident, Lloyd discovered that the physician who initially treated Helen had mistaken a dislocation of the elbow for a fracture and actually caused her more pain than she would otherwise have experienced. He searched until he discovered a "natural bonesetter," Dr. Stephen Sweet, whose family's reputation, dating back to the seventeenth century, was legendary in New England. Sweet set the bone and prescribed lineament rubs, but it took many months before Helen could use her arm, and she never fully recovered. Wendell and Frank remembered that their father usually loaded their plates with food and cut their meat because of Helen's bad arm. In 1857, almost fourteen years after the accident, Lloyd, on one of his travels, warned his wife against writing too often, lest she "exert that dislocated arm." His sense of guilt still plagued him, as he noted, "Having been the unfortunate cause of that dislocation, I ought to be willing to release you from all obligation to write to me."[11] Because of the accident, throughout 1843, Helen primarily relied upon Lloyd and a few friends to assist her with the children. Thankful Southwick happily shared the care of young Wendell and Charley with Angelette, the Garrison family's domestic helper. Helen's disabled arm also meant that George and Willie spent extended vacations in Northampton with their uncle George W. and aunt Catherine.

In spite of their physical and emotional setbacks, Helen and Lloyd devoted much thought and energy to raising their active group of children to be healthy, happy, and well educated in all ways, whether it be book learning, manners, political causes, or religious beliefs. Although it was a common nineteenth-century practice for mothers to keep a journal of the daily activities and development of their children, Helen did not do so, perhaps because she did not like to "commit" her "thoughts on paper."[12] However, Lloyd's letters, the children's memories, and other information from the period makes it possible to reconstruct what life was like growing up in the Garrison household. Three facets of their lives have already been established. First, the children grew up in a poor household, which took on the veneer of middle-class respectability largely through the generous monetary support of wealthier abolitionists. Second, there was a good deal of illness and death during their years of growing up; yet their homelife was cheerful and secure. Third, their lives were filled with the drama of the antislavery struggle as well as other causes with which their father was aligned. Other factors contributed to making them into the adults they became, however. First, their parents followed a clear philosophy of child rearing, one supported by several manuals available at the time. Second, their homelife included exposure to many famous activists of the day as well as to fugitive slaves on their way through Boston to Canada. Third, their parents supplied them with the necessary education to ensure their movement into the middle class and their dedication to social justice causes.

On June 1, 1836, when George was three and a half months old, Lloyd told Helen about a recently published book, *The Young Mother, or Management of Children in Regard to Health,* an instant success and a "most instructive work, just what you and all mothers need."[13] He was most likely attracted to the work because its author, William Andrus Alcott, an 1825 graduate of the Yale Medical School, was a cousin of Bronson Alcott, a utopianist acquaintance of the Garrisons. Since the book dealt largely with infant and child health care, it answered the needs of a father who spent a great deal of his own time investigating cures and alternative philosophies of medicine. Alcott's book was, in fact, a very practical polemic. Its chapters dealt with such issues as ventilation and temperature in the nursery, children's clothing, cleanliness, food, medicine, and behavior. Although Helen and Lloyd were not wealthy, they could see to it that their children had cheerful, cool, and clean quarters, although not separate rooms for each child, as Alcott advised. They could also afford brightly colored curtains, blankets, and toys to encourage the children's curiosity. There was little problem in following Alcott's advice that children not be dressed in too many clothes and that clothing be loose and comfortable. Fanny recalled that her mother made all the children's clothes herself, since they could not afford to hire someone else to do it.[14] But while Helen may have easily adapted to the concept of loose clothing, she most likely resisted the idea that a child's head be kept bare because caps could cause disease. After all, New England winters were cold, and the summer sun was strong. Another idea that Helen and Lloyd might have dismissed was Alcott's belief that cold water baths be used sparingly, if at all. Lloyd's experience at David Ruggles's Northampton Water Cure proved his faith in cold water whose use he sanctioned for his own children, both for cleanliness and good health. Fanny recalled asking her father if she had been baptized, as she was questioned about this in her school and did not know the answer. Lloyd responded, "No, my darling, you have had a good bath every morning, and that is a great deal better." When Fanny related this answer to her teachers, they replied, "Oh, yes! You are the daughter of an infidel."[15]

Alcott's nutritional advice was also taken cautiously. Helen nursed each of her children, except Elizabeth, for approximately eighteen months. While Alcott recommended feeding a baby every three hours and not utilizing the breast for quieting a child, Helen and Lloyd's aversion to human suffering might indicate that she fed them on demand. As for regular foods, Alcott's ideas easily matched the Garrisons' own. Once children were weaned, preferably in the spring, it was best that they eat fresh fruit (especially apples) and vegetables, not too much bread, sweet cakes, or candies, and no drinks such as tea, coffee, chocolate, or beer—all of them stimulants. Water was by far the healthiest drink a growing child could consume. According to Alcott, nine out of ten childhood diseases were caused by eating and drinking the wrong foods. Besides watching their children's eating habits, parents had to control how a child was physically handled. A young infant who was tossed in the air or carried while the parents were running or jumping could easily be harmed; so could a child who was allowed to sit up at too early an age. The Garrison children were encouraged to be active, just as Alcott recommended. Crawling or walking, the physician claimed, was healthy exercise for a child's development. Learning how to read, write, and do arithmetic was also recommended, although lessons for younger children needed to be short. As children developed intellectually and emotionally, they required ways to express themselves. For Alcott, of great importance was a child's right to cry. Since Lloyd openly acknowledged his own tendency toward tears, he could easily support this idea. Even more enthusiastically could he accept Alcott's claim that laughter was the greatest ingredient to raising a healthy child. Rest was next. Once out of infancy, a child needed to sleep at night in a cool room and a comfortable bed, but not one with feathers. Rising early was healthy; sleeping late was seen as a means for lazy parents to keep children out of their way. In fact, Alcott characterized sleeping late as a form of child abuse. Garrison children rose early, had a good bath and breakfast, and played rambunctiously.

The Young Mother was the kind of practical guide to parenting that Lloyd appreciated. However, there were many other maternal advice manuals produced during the 1830s, especially in the Northeastern states, where the number of urban presses was rapidly increasing. Although six out of nine child-rearing manuals published in the first half of the nineteenth century advocated corporal punishment, books like John S. C. Abbott's *The Mother at Home* tried to offset the large amount of physical and psychological violence perpetrated against children of the time.[16] Abbott, although sanctioning moderate spanking, did not advocate such punishments as starving children for periods of time, locking them in closets for the entire day, or frightening them with ghost stories or horror fables. As a Congregational clergyman, he tried to counteract abuse in the spirit of evangelical Protestantism, placing his emphasis on the connection between "the christian character of the mother and the salvation of the child."[17] Since the mother was the person most likely to be raising the child, especially during its early years, she should set the tone of a loving, although disciplined and respectful, home. Therefore, he cautioned against using severe physical punishment, especially when the parent was in a state of anger. In his view, it was most important for the parents to show self-restraint while at the same time teaching the child discipline. Abbott cautioned parents against lying to children, finding fault with them too often, or of punishing them for being superstitious. Parents were advised to use quieter means of disciplining children, such as sending them out of the room until they had calmed themselves.

Whereas Helen and Lloyd might have found Abbott's advice of interest, they would not have appreciated the lengthy final chapters, which emphasized religious education, church going, and sabbath observation. Preferring to socialize within the abolitionist community, Helen also did not join one of the many popular Mother's Associations that were sprouting up. As an abolitionist, she most likely found *The Mother's Book,* by Lydia Maria Child, the most appealing of the child-rearing manuals. Child was a great admirer of Lloyd, crediting him for her own involvement in reform movements. As she wrote upon his death, Lloyd "got hold of the strings of my conscience, and pulled me into Reforms. It is of no use to imagine what might have been, if I had never met him. Old dreams vanished, old associates departed, and all things became new."[18] Child's book, published in its second edition in 1831, treated parenting as a humanistic endeavor, an approach according well with the general abolitionist belief that the home should provide a peaceful and loving environment for children. From birth, a child needed to be surrounded with bright and beautiful objects but none that intruded on the overriding calm that permeated the home. For Child, Lloyd was a perfect father, "a lion in the arena . . . a lamb at home."[19]

Child's advice that children be taught kindness toward animals as well as people matched Helen and Lloyd's own philosophy. Lloyd left orders for his children to feed his beloved cats while he was away. In one instance, his sons recalled, Lloyd left this note: "See that pussy is put down cellar . . . you will find plenty of milk for her and for yourself."[20] They also recalled how one cat mounted their father's shoulders every time he carved meat at the dinner table. Lloyd simply attributed the cat's behavior to its nature, and let it be. Even with inanimate objects, Child noted, children were to be raised to know they "should never . . . see or feel the influence of bad passions."[21] In order to achieve this goal, parents first had to rid themselves of their own extremes. Child recommended that a mother who could not control her feelings or temper should spend some time in prayer. Helen, who adopted Quaker and Unitarian beliefs, practiced gentleness, as her children often recalled, and as Child suggested, Helen also sacrificed her own needs for those of her children. "The woman, who is not willing to sacrifice a good deal in such a cause," Child wrote, "does not deserve to be a mother."[22] Helen and Lloyd, who set an example for coparenting and constantly discussed their children's upbringing, would have interpreted this to include the father as well as the mother.

Like John S. C. Abbott, Lydia Maria Child believed that parents must teach their children discipline. Both writers urged parents not to lock children in closets because this practice simply created fear and horror in them and did not lead to their understanding of good behavior. Yet both authors agreed on some types of punishment which would seem cruel by modern standards. Child, for example, sanctioned tying children in an armchair, sending them to bed in the middle of the day, putting them to sleep at night without supper, isolating them from the rest of the family at dinnertime, sending them out of the room and forbidding them to return, not allowing them to kiss their parents when they wanted to, and depriving them of some expected pleasure that they had been anxious to experience. Both authors encouraged parents to forgive any children who showed repentance for their actions. The one instance in which Child accepted the idea of severe corporal punishment was when a child did not respond to any "gentler" reprimand and kept repeating the same "crime."[23] Punishment was to be carried out in private, however, never before guests.

Whereas Helen and Lloyd certainly believed that children should behave themselves and respect their parents, they did not believe in physical retribution. In this regard, they agreed with Lucretia Mott, who stated that children misbehaved because of poor parental guidance. The compassionate Quaker leader believed that children, "like all other human beings," had "inalienable rights" that adults had to respect.[24] In this vein, Lloyd absolutely forbade anyone to touch his children in a violent manner or to chastise them in any way. Indeed, he enjoyed his offspring's self-confident assertiveness and free-spiritedness. Soon after Lloyd died in 1879, an unsigned article appeared in the *New York Times* which addressed this issue:

> He carried his theories and convictions into his own home. A believer in nonresistance and the largest liberty, he never permitted his children to be punished in any way; never repressed their natural instincts; and always encouraged them to state their own case and give their own reasons for doing or not doing anything. The consequence was that his children grew up to be independent, amiable, affectionate, and perfectly natural.[25]

Indeed, the Garrison children were treated so kindly that family friends jested about their undisciplined nature. During one of Lloyd's absences, Wendell Phillips wrote to Helen, "My time has been so hurried and filled that I have never been able to get to Pine Street, but shall yet. Those unruly boys need somebody to take them in hand. Get Francis Jackson or me to box their ears once or twice, and then they'll begin to value their nonresistant mother and father."[26] Helen responded to

Phillips in her own letter to Ann. "Tell Wendell," she wrote, "I am obliged to him for his kind offer to do my boxing. I might have occasion to call upon him if I were a professed nonresistant myself. I subscribe to the principles but am not yet prepared to carry out the measures."[27]

For all her bravado, it seems unlikely that Helen ever treated her children severely. Her few existing letters from these years give a clear impression of lively, active, unafraid children. In the same letter in which she told Wendell Phillips that she could discipline them herself, Helen described her living room: "Lizzy Pease is unmarkably well sits on the floor at my feet Wendell Charley & sis are seated at a little distance chatting and singing musicals."[28] The children, however, were not always so quietly entertained. The previous year, 1846, Helen begged Ann not to show her letters to anyone else because they were always written when the children were around her, "so noisy," she said, "I scarcely know what I am about, and I am aware they [the letters] are full of blunders which you would readily excuse in a Mother with five children."[29] In another letter, she described young Fanny as being "in such perpetual motion all the time, at this moment she is flying by me gay as a lark."[30] In yet another, Fanny and Frank were "running round the room in their night-gowns playful as kittens."[31] At one point, Helen found it almost impossible to complete a letter to Ann because young Franky kept pulling at the paper even when his mother struggled to write by holding the sheet above her head. At the same time, little Wendy "scolded" her for "blotting" her ink-wet words. Between talking with him and trying to watch Franky, Helen could scarcely keep her mind on what she was doing. "I begin to say something," she lamented, "when my attention is taken off to Frank."[32]

Helen and Lloyd tried to link any mild discipline they inflicted with learning. When the children grabbed one of their parents' pens and started scribbling on a letter or piece of paper, as so often happened, they were encouraged to continue, if not on that specific paper, then on another one within easy reach. If toddlers had temper tantrums, as Wendy often did, they were gently urged to calm down or else allowed to complete their fit. At an early age, the children were taught to care for one another. In this, they tried to emulate their parents, although their early attempts were not always successful. In 1852, when Wendy and Fanny were baby-sitting Frank at a friend's house, the then four-year-old threw a fit. As Wendy wrote his parents, "Fanny's just in a flurry with Frank who is squalling & bawling. He's been pretty good up to now; guess as how he'll get over it soon."[33] Once they passed from babyhood to childhood, all the children were expected to be reasonably approachable about their behavior. Wendell once recollected to Fanny a story told to him by one of his father's printers. One day Wendy ran into the *Liberator* office and "importuned Father for some privilege, but got a point-blank refusal." The printer recalled, "Had it been I, I should have blubbered or persisted in teasing. But you went off to play. And when it was remarked to your

Father what obedient children he had, he said: 'Yes, they generally mind well, and I never whipt one of them in my life.'"[34]

Helen, who had to handle her high-spirited offspring on a daily basis, sometimes reached a point of frustration. At such times, Lloyd felt it necessary to advise her to calm herself. In 1846, when he was in London safely away from the ruckus while Helen was alone with their five children, he imparted this advice: "As for Wendy, Charley, and Fanny, remember that they are little children, and allow them to caper as freely as they will, without chiding them too often, provided they do nothing *very* bad. Provide amusement for them in some shape or other."[35] Twelve years later, he wrote to Willie that his aim as a father was basically "to set a good example to you all, rather than to exercise a rigorous discipline or drill you doctrinally. If we do not teach by our lives, we teach in vain. An occasional admonition, words of caution, the language of reproof, all have their place; but an affectionate disposition, a benevolent spirit, a true daily life, are worth them all."[36]

In contrast to Lloyd's confidence, Helen sometimes felt that, in an effort to please her husband, she had been somewhat lax in disciplining her children. As she wrote to Fanny in 1872 upon seeing how her daughter was raising her own children, "[you] will enjoy far more in married life if the children are made to mind. You see, darling, I can preach though I was one of the class of Mothers who could never accomplish what she most desired. But I never was blinded enough not to see duties that were imposed upon me, but was deficient in will power to execute them."[37] Wendell and Frank remembered that at times, their mother, "in sheer fatigue," anxiously waited until Lloyd came home to describe "the day's naughtiness" to him in the hopes that he would either discipline the offenders or at least lend his "moral support of her censure." It was often impossible, however, for their father to bring himself to "evoke the proper warmth of reproof." "Both our parents," they wrote, "appealed to us as reasonable and affectionate beings, never using violence and seldom force with tolerably unruly subjects." Instead of inflicting punishment, Lloyd ended up playing with the children, "either romping games when small, or games of skill when older."[38]

The child-rearing manuals that emphasized the importance of providing children with a loving, affectionate home found strong proponents in the Garrisons. Lloyd, in particular, was determined that his children not suffer the abuse and abandonment that he and his siblings had. He paid close attention to Helen's and the children's needs, playing an active role in their daily, mundane activities. Wendell and Frank remembered the glee that their father demonstrated every time he returned home from a day's work. "I cannot recall," one of them wrote, "his ever coming home in other than a bright and joyous mood, bringing with him the 'eternal sunshine of the spotless mind.' Had he arrived distraught or depressed, I think the mere sight of wife and children would have gladdened him."[39] Because Helen was so overworked and the family could not afford much help, Lloyd often uncomplainingly performed certain domestic chores, even when he came home exhausted from his own work. Fanny recalled that as a rule, her father "carried the water upstairs when water was a luxury; chopped the wood, made the fires, blacked the boots, or, in case of need, made the coffee, all the while singing."[40]

During the children's youth, Boston had comparatively few restaurants or cheap boarding houses, so, as Sarah Southwick recalled, whenever an antislavery fair or convention was held, Helen and Lloyd "opened their house to any one, rich or poor." Southwick often heard guests comment that one reason why Lloyd made so many strong friends was due to Helen's "tact, efficiency, and sweet temper."[41] Because of the frequency and number of guests, however, Lloyd often had to help with the arrangements, especially at those times when he had not forewarned Helen that company was coming. Elizabeth Cady Stanton, in her own reminiscences, recalled such a scene:

> I was one of twelve at one of his impromptu tea parties. We all took it for granted that his wife knew we were coming, and that her preparations were already made. Surrounded by half a dozen children, she was performing the last act in the opera of Lullaby, wholly unconscious of the invasion downstairs. But Mr. Garrison was equal to every emergency, and, after placing his guests at their ease in the parlor, he hastened to the nursery, took off his coat, and rocked the baby until his wife had disposed of the remaining children. Then they had a consultation about the tea, and when, basket in hand, the good man sallied forth for the desired viands, Mrs. Garrison, having a hasty toilet, came down to welcome her guests. She was as genial and self-possessed as if all things had been prepared.[42]

Susan B. Anthony recalled a similar evening in 1855 when a group of participants at a woman's rights convention attended a reception in the Garrison home where they met "several of the *literati*" and were "most heartily welcomed" by Helen, "a noble, self-sacrificing woman, the loving and the loved, surrounded with healthy, happy children in that model home." At this event, Lloyd entertained guests, helped serve refreshments, and, at times, "now sooth[ed] some child to sleep."[43] "Helen's parlor," as Edmund Quincy called it, was also a popular meeting place for the Boston Garrisonians.[44] However, feeding people cost money, and Lloyd frequently commented about the cost to Helen. Sometimes a friend recognized the problem and provided assistance. One such person was Charles Hovey, who in 1855 gave Helen and Lloyd a barrel of flour to provide for the extra mouths. Another was Susan B. Anthony, who in 1858 sent the family a much appreciated bag of dried peaches. Helen did not generally complain about their numerous visitors, although in 1846, before Lloyd's western trip, she confided to Ann Phillips her wish for "a quiet retreat for a few hours to be by ourselves for thought and reflection."[45]

Music was also a most important ingredient in the children's home life. Lloyd, especially, loved to sing hymns and hum tunes, doing so while he performed his chores or thought about his professional work. Wendell and Frank recalled that their father usually sang on key, though not necessarily well. They remembered how he liked singing with such friends as Francis Jackson, Henry C. Wright, Samuel May Jr., or Oliver Johnson, whether it be in his parlor at home or at a meeting. Lloyd had a fondness for all types of music, but when he openly expressed his joy at "martial" tunes, people questioned him. How could a nonresister tolerate marches and music that glorified the military spirit? His response was simple and, as always, reflected his ability to take much in the world and adapt it to his own uses. "It is just as valuable for the moral warfare," he was heard to say.[46] Indeed, Lloyd felt that music could aid in relieving any worry. The children recalled that at those times when Helen grew despondent about their lack of money, Lloyd comforted her by putting his arm around her, walking up and down the parlor singing hymns or his favorite songs, and reassuring her with "My dear, the Lord will provide."[47]

Helen's fears, however, could not always be so easily assuaged, especially since, for several years, the family was relatively transient. When Lloyd and Helen first returned to Boston in September 1836, they stayed for a short time in the home of Joseph and Thankful Southwick. Meanwhile Thankful also took in Helen's brother Henry, tending to him during his terminal illness and refusing to accept one penny of compensation for her efforts or for the boarding of the then small Garrison family. As quickly as possible, Lloyd relocated his family to 5 Hayward Place, a boarding house run by Mary S. Parker and her sisters, Lucy, Eliza, and Abigail, all members of the Boston Female Anti-Slavery Society. Until June 1838, Helen, Lloyd, and little "Dordie Tompit" lived in one room. Helen then had no help other than Lloyd, who found the arrangement almost intolerable because he was continuously interrupted in his own writing and organizing. As he wrote to his brother-in-law George W., "as Helen has no help but myself, my time is necessarily frittered away by piece-meal, so that I bring very little to pass." Lloyd wanted to invite Helen's sister Sarah to Boston, but his wife protested, insisting that she could get along very well by herself; Lloyd did not agree. Besides his own concerns, he could not bear to see Helen's household duties keeping her "no better than a prisoner in her room from one month's end to another."[48]

When a second room at the Parkers' became available, Lloyd was able to hire a full-time domestic worker. But as time would tell, the couple was often unhappy with the servants they hired, resulting in a constant turnover over the years. Several women walked out on them, while others were fired. As Lloyd wrote to George W. in 1847, "Helen has been more troubled, in regard to her 'help,' within the last four months, than during all the previous time for more than twelve years. Girl after girl has come, and proved inexperienced or worthless—how many, I will not begin to enumerate."[49] While Lloyd and Helen each complained about their servants, neither of them ever considered the issue to be political. Domestic help was a right, low wages a given, especially when in the 1840s the Irish potato famine brought a flood of immigrant single women into the Boston labor market. Part of Helen's problem was that she sought perfection. If it was not forthcoming, she blamed herself, fearing that her friends or family would criticize her for being a poor supervisor. In April 1837, for example, a very young, petite domestic worker named Rebecca came to help Helen with the care of infant George. Rebecca was either very clumsy or incompetent, for one evening as the family went downstairs for tea, she placed George in his carriage and pushed it so hard that the poor babe was thrown headlong out of the vehicle, bruising his nose and face. The next day at dinner, she dropped him, his forehead hitting the sharp edge of a chair causing a gash an inch long which required stitches. Needless to say, Rebecca was immediately fired. Lloyd wrote to Helen's mother that his wife did not want her to know what had happened because she feared that Sally would blame her for being careless. Since a reliable replacement could not be easily found, Lloyd brought sister-in-law Sarah to Boston for a six-week visit. By the next January, Helen had finally found "an excellent girl, neat, quiet, industrious, kind, and good-natured."[50] However, there was such a demand for white domestic workers, despite the anti-Catholic sentiment of the time, that the most capable servants moved on as soon as they were offered more money. Although the Garrisons might have solved their problem by hiring an African-American servant, they rarely did so. Those few times they did, the woman usually worked as a cook. Whether politics played a role in their decision is unclear.

During the summer of 1838, the Garrison family once again left Boston to stay with Helen's family in Brooklyn. Even though the Benson women and their servants were available to take care of the two children, Lloyd still chose to be one of their primary nurturers, especially during Helen's bout with a severe grippe that lasted several weeks. Again, he complained that the care of the children prohibited him from tending to the political work at hand, such as planning for the upcoming Peace Convention and, of course, writing for the *Liberator,* but he voluntarily chose to play this role. Partly, he was trying to compensate for having as yet provided no permanent home for his dependents. In September the situation looked more promising when Lloyd arranged to rent the Boston home of the Reverend Amos Phelps, whose wife had recently died. Phelps was anxious to abandon the house, which he had rented totally furnished for $400 plus taxes a year, and offered it to Lloyd for $300 if he would take it for the full remaining year of his lease. Lloyd readily accepted. Located off Tremont Street near the Boylston Market at 2 Nassau Court, the three-story house had five bedrooms, a sitting room, parlor, and cellar, and was a virtual palace compared to the one or two rooms they had had at the Parkers' boarding house. The furnishings included carpets, beds, bedding, curtains, chairs, looking glasses, and innumerable smaller items. Situated in a quiet, working-class neighborhood, the property included an enclosed backyard for the children to play in.

The Garrisons spent a happy year in this home, but when the lease was up, they had to move once again. This time, they took a $250 per annum two-year lease on a house in Cambridgeport, directly across the Charles River from Boston. Although not as large or luxurious as the one on Nassau Court, the house afforded easy access to Boston; an omnibus arrived every half hour to carry Lloyd the two miles to his workplace. Unfortunately, however, Lloyd and Helen needed to purchase carpets, chairs, kitchen furniture, stores, grates, and other items, which added up to quite a large sum. As a result, they offered to board Oliver and Mary Ann Johnson. Neither Helen nor Lloyd enjoyed this house, blaming the location for the many illnesses that plagued the family. The house, they claimed, was musty, dank, and attracted bad air. While staying there, Helen's mother became quite ill as did her sister Anna. Helen's other sister, Mary, and Lloyd's brother, James, both died during that time. Moreover, the children always seemed to be ill with one disease or another. Although the location possibly held certain environmental dangers, it is more likely that the many illnesses and deaths plaguing the family made the place seem unhappy.

In any case, in 1843 the family had had enough of Cambridgeport and returned to Boston. This time they found a newly built red brick row house at 13 Pine Street, near Washington Street. This house was a real treat for Lloyd, as it had never been occupied. It was also much larger than any he had rented, having eleven bedrooms, two parlors, and two kitchens. In fact, the building could easily accommodate two families, so the Johnsons agreed to share it, taking three of the bedrooms, leaving the growing Garrison family with eight, one of which Lloyd turned into a study. Located in the attic, the room offered him the privacy he needed to do much of his writing and editorial work at home, an arrangement which pleased him greatly. Lloyd accepted the terms of a three-year lease for $350 per annum, cherishing the thought of living on a beautiful street which was centrally located. There, as in all his homes, he went against Helen's wishes to draw the shades in order to protect the carpets from the sun, and instead opened all the window coverings to let in the light. According to his sons, Lloyd hated "gloom, physical or mental," and identified light with energy. In addition, every item of furniture in the family's home was meant to be used, "with nothing formal, or kept for show, or too good for daily use."[51]

The family remained on Pine Street for six years, but the neighborhood grew crowded and noisy; so in 1849 they relocated to 65 Suffolk Street (later renamed Shawmut Avenue). After four years there in a narrow brick house, they moved once again in 1853 to 5 Dix Place, shortly thereafter relocating down the street to 14 Dix Place, a home they chose but which was actually purchased by Francis Jackson, who then rented it to Lloyd for $400 a year (the exact amount of his mortgage and tax payments). Jackson's devotion to the family, especially the children, gave him a strong desire to see them finally settled in their own home. Of course, Lloyd would never have been able to afford to purchase any house had it not been for the help of his friends who in 1847 had begun to raise funds for just such a purpose. Within two years, the fund had grown to $2,289, and it continued to grow to $6,837, more than enough to purchase Jackson's home. In October 1855 he sold it for its original purchase price to the Garrison fund, accepting railroad and bank stocks in place of a cash profit. "My indebtedness to you," Lloyd wrote him, "in many ways, during the period of our acquaintance, has been great. Of course, it is such as cannot be liquidated. . . . To the friends who have joined their contributions to an amount sufficient to secure the house now occupied by my family for our possession, I can only return our poor, stammering acknowledgments."[52]

The Dix Place home, three stories high with an attic, was neither bright nor luxurious. The front windows of the rather dark rooms faced directly out on a cobblestone sidewalk. The only sense of nature came from a tree and some grass in a tiny backyard. Helen, Lloyd, and their five children shared the house along with Lloyd's aunt, Charlotte Newell, who had come to the family out of destitution. Jackson, although no longer the owner, continued to maintain it. Over the years, he made several repairs to the building, in January 1859 ordering the furnace be fixed, a gift that meant a great deal to the family. "This is the first winter," Lloyd wrote his benefactor, "we have been comfortable in more than one room, a considerable portion of the time, since we came to Dix Place: now, dining room, entry and parlors are all as genial and summer-like as we can desire."[53] For Helen, a home had finally become hers. No longer did she need to think about constantly moving, carrying with her all of her material goods and her many children. Yet, she would move one more time in 1864 when the family bought its final home in the Roxbury section of Boston. By that time, all but Frank were grown and on their way to independence.

Moving from place to place was costly, for each move required an outlay of money, still a constant concern even with guaranteed incomes from Charles Hovey, Francis Jackson, and the Garrison fund committee. While Helen continued to worry, Lloyd appeared more philosophical about the situation. "Poor I am and poor I ever expect to be on earth, from principle," he wrote to a contributor, "for my spirit yearns too strongly over a world involved in misery and ruin by its alienation from God, to be tied down to the gainful pursuits of a grovelling age."[54] Yet, he, too, could not help feeling bothered about how to feed his family, fretting over the few times he lost his wallet or other possessions and lamenting his inability to ever replace what was lost. Certainly, Lloyd's profession was not lucrative, as the *Liberator*'s earnings depended on its constantly fluctuating number of subscribers. Because of the paper's importance despite its lack of profit, at Lloyd's request three of his supporters—Francis Jackson, Edmund Quincy, and William Bassett—formed a committee in 1839 to supervise the *Liberator*'s finances. Lloyd continued to receive his salary of $100 a month while the committee took the responsibility for raising money, increasing subscriptions, and paying bills—without assuming personal liability for the venture.

Managing the financial aspects of the publication was not an easy task. Early in 1841, after the schism in the movement, the newspaper showed a decline of nearly five hundred subscribers from the previous year. In addition, about three hundred delinquent payers had to be dropped. By the end of the year, the paper had fallen short of its expenses by $500. Again, in 1844, the *Liberator* suffered a similar shortfall. In 1847 a decision was made to lower the subscription price by fifty cents in the hopes that a less expensive product would attract more subscribers. Unfortunately, income went down by at least $800, with no more than one hundred new people signing up. As a result, the *Liberator* was in the red, and Lloyd was in debt as well. As he wrote to his brother-in-law, "According to my usual salary, three month's salary ($300) will be due to me on the 1st of January—every cent of which will be due to my creditors on that day."[55] The publication of Frederick Douglass's *North Star* in late 1847 brought serious competition for the available readers of abolitionist material. By the next May, Lloyd admitted to being more deeply in debt than he had ever been and could see no end to his predicament. "What to do, in order to reduce my expenses, and yet live in Boston, I know not," he admitted to George W.[56]

Lloyd's relatively meager wages could not meet the expenses of his ever-growing family, the cost of feeding and housing guests, and paying for physicians' visits for his children's illnesses. Indeed, other family members needed care as well. When Lloyd's brother, James, came to live with him, he was in very ill health. In 1842 treatment for James came to $150 over what Lloyd had in hand. When he died, the funeral expenses added fifty dollars more. At that time, Lloyd, as usual, depended on friends and supporters to help him out. In this case, however, Ellis Gray Loring, Joseph Southwick, and even Francis Jackson were strapped for funds. Jackson managed to lend Lloyd fifty dollars but could offer no more. A similar situation occurred in 1857, when Lloyd's aunt, Charlotte Newell, came to stay with him. Surprisingly, at the same time, Lloyd received a message from a bank in Baltimore that his mother had kept an account there. Although the amount she squirreled away was meager, by 1857 it had grown to $387.75. As her sole heir, it became Lloyd's. However, like all his earnings, the money did not last long. As soon as it arrived in September, it had to be turned over to pay for the cost of nursing, medical care, and burial for Charlotte. In addition, twenty dollars of the money had to be given to the Baptist Church in Baltimore for the removal and reburying of Fanny's and Elizabeth's remains when the church lost part of its land.

Of course, Lloyd's biggest expense was the upkeep of the family that he and

Helen had created. Although his love for his children was great, he also felt the weight of having to be the sole support for them. To his old friend, Samuel J. May, he confessed, "I would not have the number of our children less; but it is difficult to look after so many, and at the same time to discharge the duties of my position as a 'leading abolitionist.'"[57] Helen tried as best she could to keep household costs down, and at times Lloyd reprimanded her for being too frugal. If they needed four blankets to keep the family warm, he insisted that she not purchase only two. However, he himself marveled at the amount of money needed simply to feed them all. "How the grocery and the meat bills can amount to $45, for one month's supply, is to me inexplicable," he wrote Helen in 1848 when he was in Northampton and she in Boston. "They are so enormous, that they ought not to be paid without the most careful scrutiny."[58] Yet, children had to eat, be clothed, and housed, not to mention being educated and entertained. In an appeal to his dear friend Wendell Phillips, whom he felt he could depend on in any emergency, Lloyd listed all the bills he had to pay to keep his family going. "I am neither a spendthrift nor improvident, but careful and scrupulous, and ever anxious to keep out of debt," he told Phillips. "But, in spite of my best efforts in this respect, (seconded faithfully by dear Helen, whose dread of debt is of the strongest kind, and to whose economy in regard to personal expenditures & household affairs, I can bear grateful testimony) . . . my family is large & with increasing age the children unavoidably augment the burden of support."[59] Phillips felt happy to be able to help Lloyd. As he wrote to him in 1846, "I owe you, dear Garrison, more than you would let me express. . . . Since within the sphere of your influence, I trust I have lived a better man."[60] The children were aware of their parents' economic situation and forever grateful that they were never deprived of anything they needed.

Helen, like many women in her financial position, chose to sacrifice her own needs and desires in favor of seeing her husband and children satisfied. As the family's needs grew, she took to turning down invitations to travel along with Lloyd when there was not enough money to spare for such a luxury. At times, especially in the early years of their marriage, she had had the opportunity to visit the Motts and McKims in Philadelphia, and the Samuel J. Mays, first in Brooklyn and then on Cape Cod. She enjoyed her rare vacations in the New Hampshire lowlands or in the White Mountains, her visits to friends in nearby Lynn or Newburyport, and journeys with Lloyd to conventions—she accompanied him to New York City for the annual May meetings at least twice. During the 1840s and early 1850s, however, when her children were young and income low, Helen's mobility shrank and her social network narrowed. This may have been why she sometimes felt angry with Lloyd when he left home, especially on trips of several months, leaving her with a brood of active children, little money, and insufficient domestic help.

The financial hardships Lloyd and Helen faced did not cause any rift between them; rather, their attachment only grew stronger. A year after their first son was born, Lloyd wrote to his mother-in-law, Sally, about his feelings for her daughter: "The chains that bind us we still find to be silken—our hearts are knit together in love—and our quantum of matrimonial happiness is even more than we anticipated."[61] At about the same time, he wrote in a similar vein to Helen: "I have often thought that a man must feel queerly, who has had a leg amputated; but what is the subtraction of a leg, compared to the loss of his 'better half'? . . . Ah! The solution of the enigma is easy—our *hearts* are one, not our *bodies,* so that we can be in full communion with each other at a distance of thirty miles."[62] Helen echoed similar sentiments nine years later when she expressed her sadness to Ann Phillips that Lloyd was away from home again. "I feel lonely and forlorn without my darling," she wrote. "For who is there that can supply his place; not one. I miss his cheerful countenance, his pleasant voice which was always music to my soul. It was a severe trial to me to think of parting with him for so long a period, and for a time I could not think of it with the least composure."[63] The only reason Helen could tolerate Lloyd's absences was the knowledge that he was doing great work.

For Helen and Lloyd, their children were the reflection and extension of their deep love for each other. Lloyd enjoyed nothing more than to have his children swarm around him, bestowing hugs and kisses upon his bald head. He thrived on their tales about their activities and the lessons they had learned each day. When he traveled, any reminder of them brought on the most nostalgic of feelings. Aboard ship in 1846 on his way to England, he discovered a pair of toddler Fanny's socks in the pocket of his dressing gown. "You should have seen me when I made the discovery," he wrote to Helen, "how I smiled, how I exalted, how I kissed and pressed to my heart the tiny little things! It was next to having her in my arms, and seeing her sweet face and hearing her pleasant voice."[64] Fanny, the only daughter to survive to adulthood, was her father's "favorite daughter," as he liked to say, and received the unrestrained emotional expressions that girls were allowed. Many times he expressed to Helen and anyone else within earshot that Fanny was a special, affectionate child, whom he loved with all his might.

Lloyd felt equally loving toward his sons, although as they aged, he tended to mark each one's individuality without being overly sentimental. In 1843, for example, he described George, William, Wendell, and Charles's educational progress to Henry C. Wright. Once finished listing their accomplishments, he added, "These constitute my earthly jewels. My affection for them is strong and pure, but not idolatrous. It shall be my aim to bring them up to be a blessing to the world."[65] By 1858—when the three oldest sons were almost full-grown, Fanny was fourteen, and Frank ten—Lloyd summed up his feelings about them to his son William:

> Thus far, my happiness in my children has been without alloy. George has always been circumspect and exemplary in his conduct, to a remarkable degree; and I feel

> that he may be safely trusted. . . . Wendell has always been a model boy, mature beyond his years, unexceptionable in deportment, amiable and affectionate in spirit, and full of promise for the future. Fanny is a dear child, specially dear because she is the only daughter, of a most generous and loving nature, full of sensibility, and promising to make a noble woman. Franky is the Benjamin of the flock, around whom my heartstrings very closely twine, gentle, conscientious, most affectionate, laudably ambitious, studious and thoughtful, sensitive to blame, with a large brain and a large heart for a little boy. As for yourself, I am delighted with your ingenuousness, kindness of heart, self-forgetfulness, loving disposition, and generous regard for every member of the family.[66]

Helen and Lloyd's most profound way of proving their love was to see that their children received a good education, both intellectually and politically. Fundamental to their experience was an introduction into the world of political activism, including abolitionism, racial equality, woman's rights, and nonviolence. This part of their education took place in their home and within the social and political worlds in which their parents moved. The second part of their education proceeded through a wide variety of educational institutions, from public schools to utopian societies to wealthy private institutions of higher education. By the time the children entered the more mainstream schools, their paths as abolitionists had been set. In this, Lloyd and Helen were of one mind: when it came to their moral development, the children were to be raised as good, caring, nonsectarian Christians; but, more important, all of them would be provided with the tools to identify social injustices and the conviction to attempt to change society when necessary. As Lloyd put it to Helen just two months after George was born, "May he be trained up in the way he should go—for he has been brought into a most perilous world."[67]

With the weaknesses in their own formal education, however, neither Lloyd nor Helen saw themselves as strong aides in academic learning. Wendell and Frank reported that their father had no training in drawing or writing, and although his penmanship was "handsome," he spent a great deal of time drafting out his letters, often copying them over several times before being satisfied with the final result.[68] Lloyd was also not very good at math and, even though an expert printer, was otherwise inept at working with tools. He was unable to do household repairs or build furniture or other items for the family's use. Lloyd's children recognized, however, that their father was a gifted writer and leader, and they often listened to his advice about reading matter and political events. They were also very much aware that both their parents were on an endless journey of self-learning. Although she often found herself tied to her home, Helen was always conversant with the political issues of the day. Lloyd, who was more active in the outside world, attended concerts, debates, and lectures, often taking along one or more of his children. As a result, they grew up respecting the active pursuit of knowledge and developed the love of learning at a very early age.

Lloyd's passion for the printed word involved a certain amount of joyful playfulness, especially punning. During his and Helen's courtship, he combined his love for cats with his love for words in this reflection on a kitten that Lucretia May had given him: "I return my thanks to my lively friend Mrs. May, in *black and white,* for the feline gift which she is disposed to send me. As I am opposed to colonization, let the little sable animal remain until I visit B. I may possibly volunteer a sonnet upon it, by and by—especially if a *cat*-astrophe overtake it, so that I may say of it, 'Resquies-*cat* in pace!' in conveying its mortal remains to the *cat*-acombs."[69] Indeed, humor abounded in the Garrison home. When Charles Burleigh came to visit, his extremely long beard gave him such a fierce look that Fanny ran to her mother, crying, "Oh, mother, mother! The Devil has come!" to which her father promptly snickered, "And no wonder, hair 'em, scare 'em."[70] The children also developed a love of words, often writing articles, poems, and long letters to each other throughout their adult years.

On the more serious side, Lloyd and Helen were absolutely determined to teach their children about the evils of slavery and the need for the abolitionist movement. Top on their list of priorities was their exposure to the people involved in the movement. In addition to the abolitionists who gathered at their home, from time to time a fugitive slave would be housed for a night or two, or well-known escapees of the slave system, such as Frederick Douglass or Harriet Tubman, would visit. Sojourner Truth also frequented the Garrison home.[71] In 1896 William recalled these visits before a group of Boston high school students, emphasizing the impact that the former slaves' scars and maimed limbs had on his young mind: "How many of these I have seen and how my childish heart throbbed with pity and sympathy at these evidences of barbarism! It was a common thing in my father's house for the maid to announce, 'There's a colored man in the kitchen who has run away from slavery.' Sometimes it was a colored woman, sometimes a mother with her baby in her arms. It was so interesting to listen to the story of the escape, to hear of the long journey in the night, before the free states were reached."[72]

Besides escaped slaves, "slave saviours" also graced the Garrison home. One of these, Jonathan Walker, a ship's captain who attempted to carry a group of slaves from Florida to the free British West Indies, was captured and imprisoned in Pensacola. After his release, he occasionally visited Lloyd, sharing his tale with the children and allowing them to touch the "S.S." brand on his hand, his eternal stamp as a "slave stealer."[73] Harriet Tubman, the greatest of the "slave snatchers," made an indelible impression on William, who first saw her in 1858 when he was already twenty-years old. Never would he forget Tubman's broken teeth which, he reported, "had been partially knocked out with a stone in her own hands, because of toothache, while hiding by day on her latest escape."[74] The children also learned of their own father's greatness. This was brought home to William when his elementary school class took a trip to the Leverett Street jail just before it was torn down. There, the young son saw for himself the place his father was held in protective custody on the eventful day, October 21, 1835. The exposure to the abolitionist culture was thrilling to the children. In adulthood, Fanny recollected that there was always so much company in her home that it was not until she was fully grown that she truly realized that her father was socially ostracized by the greater society around him. In her youthful view, her family was one of the most popular in town.

The Garrison children learned a tremendous amount from their parents' guests. When deprived of this exposure, they often felt cheated. Fanny remembered that when on several occasions, young Frank was put to bed early so that Helen could tend to company, he became incensed. Frank, Fanny wrote, "told my mother between sobs, that it was not the supper that he cared for, but the conversation!" She added, "Anti-Slavery meetings were our theatre and opera, Anti-Slavery debates, meat and drink to us. What we learned was an undying devotion to the principles of justice and humanity, never-to-be abandoned, come what may. It enabled me, when pointed out at school as the daughter of an 'infidel,' to glory in the accusation."[75] When the house was empty of guests, Lloyd still exposed his children to their existence, usually through the *Liberator* or photographs he hung on the wall of the family library. Young Fanny remembered clearly her father placing her upon his shoulders, she "holding fast to his bald head, while I learned the names of the great and good women. . . . Soon, I could point them out correctly for the edification of the family and friends."[76] In Fanny's case, it was important to establish these activist women as role models. But as a young girl, she especially liked to use her father's bald head to warm her hands in the wintertime. In turn, he commented, "You come to my incendiary head to warm your cold hands, my darling."[77]

The *Liberator* was as much a part of Garrison family life as any of its human members. It was not only their financial support but also an educational tool and, for the boys, a job-training experience—for although Lloyd supported women's equality (as conceived in his time), he could not envision his daughter having a career. At a young age, all the Garrison children regularly visited their father's workplace. At first, they simply sat on a high stool and played with the spaces at the compositor's desk. Next, they were sent to the office on publication days to bring Lloyd his lunch. This job often fell to Fanny, who was always greeted warmly with "Now you have brought it to me, my darling, I must eat it."[78] Finally, the boys and Fanny helped Lloyd proofread the *Liberator* after supper on Saturday evenings. On other days, Lloyd arrived home with an armful of newspapers, tracts, and periodicals. On a regular basis, he read through them, leaving piles strewn on the floors, tables, and desks. They were always accessible to the children. Helen, who disliked disorder, noted the mess, but never disturbed it.

Through guests and the *Liberator,* the Garrison children learned how privileged their lives were in comparison to the fate of slave children. One of Fanny's earliest memories reflected the importance of this piece of her home education. "I was hardly more than an infant," she remembered, "when my father came to my crib to give me a good-night kiss. He said: 'What a nice warm bed my darling has! The poor little slave child is not so fortunate and is torn from its mother's arms. How good my darling ought to be!'" As Fanny reflected in 1924, almost eighty years later, "Thus, early, I was taught the lesson of pity for those less favored than myself and so tenderly that it remains after the lapse of more than three-quarters of a century."[79] In 1857, when Frank was nine years old, Lloyd wrote to him,

> You, my dear boy, I trust, will grow up a good abolitionist; and should your father's voice be hushed in death before the wretched slaves are set free, you must lift up, in the loudest tone, your own voice, saying—
>
> "I am an abolitionist—
> Then urge me not to pause,
> For joyfully do I enlist
> In freedom's sacred cause:
> A nobler strife the world ne'er saw,
> Th' enslaved to disenthral;
> *I am a soldier for the war*
> *Whatever may befall.*"[80]

One of the most important ways of training their children to be good abolitionists was to teach them how to read. Hence, abolitionists created an entire genre of literature geared toward exposing children to the realities of slavery and the moral issues involved. The literature was also meant to strengthen family ties by presenting little readers with settings in which mothers and fathers answered questions, reassured their offspring of the security of their parents' homes, and talked over important issues together. These portraits of close-knit, affectionate families fit in well with the nineteenth-century middle-class efforts to restructure the image of the home from the rule of the despotic father and submissive mother to one more cooperative, or "companionate" as it was then termed. Newsletters, small magazines, newspaper columns, and children's books with abolitionist themes were published on a regular basis, especially before the 1840 split in the movement caused a decline in available funds.

Henry C. Wright, the chief agent for the New England Non-Resistance Society, took on the role as the "children's agent" of the American Anti-Slavery Society.[81] Wright was well known for his interest in the political and moral education of children. As Lloyd wrote to Elizabeth Pease in 1842, "His great *forte* lies in addressing little children, over whom he exerts complete mastery. Place him in the midst of a crowded assembly of children, and he never fails to produce a deep impression upon their minds."[82] Although he was married with stepchildren of his own, Wright considered the Garrison abode his second home. In fact, he was so fond of the youngest children that in 1851 he established a $500 trust fund for Fanny and Frank from money he had inherited. Wright combined his antislavery and nonviolent beliefs in his writings for children. In his best-known book, *A Kiss for a Blow; or, A Collection of Stories for Children Showing Them How to Prevent Quarrelling,* published in 1858, Wright used examples from the behavior of children he knew, perhaps even the Garrisons, to make three points. First, children's conflicts, which erupted quickly, were caused by very small issues. Second, each conflict could actually have serious repercussions. For example, children's fights could sadden their parents or cause bodily harm. Third, every conflict could be avoided if children would simply talk with one another, be affectionate, and make every effort to compromise.

Wright may also have written articles in "The Juvenile Department" column of the *Liberator* beginning on January 22, 1831. At first a regular feature, by 1835 it had evolved into a sporadic column. The first article, "The Family Circle—No. 1," contained a fictional conversation between a mother, father, a son, and two daughters. The older daughter, Lucy, asked her parents questions about the nature of slavery, the underlying theme being the children's fear that either they or their parents could be sold into slavery. Once assured that their white skin, northern residence, and free status protected them, a discussion on race, the slave trade, and greed followed. "Was it [slavery] wicked?" small daughter Helen asked. Her sister answered: "Why Helen! . . . don't you think it would be wicked for any body to come and steal you away, and carry you off where you would never see papa, or mama, or me, or brother George, or any body who cared any thing about you again, and then sell you to be somebody's slave as long as you lived, who would make you work very hard, and whip you with a great horsewhip if he was angry with you?"[83]

A few weeks later, the column's discussion of slavery continued, describing chain gangs, auctions, and, again, the separation of child from parent, a frightening prospect for any young reader. Even worse was the idea that if youngsters were abused by a slaveholder, their parents were powerless to help them. As Lucy's mother explained, "The children may be beaten and treated very cruelly, and the mother, even if she sees it, cannot do anything to help them."[84] Over time, "The Juvenile Department" included poems, such as "From an Infant Slave to the Child of Its Mistress[,] Both Born on the Same Day" and "The White Infant's Reply." Both were outcries against slavery, the second ending on a note of optimism that "all good people of the land" would destroy the evil institution.[85] There were also stories designed to teach children racial tolerance, that African Americans, slave or free, were equal to whites; still others taught children the moral and political value of not purchasing slave-made items. Although truthful about the conditions of slavery and racism, "The Juvenile Department" had a gentle tone meant to teach children without frightening them.[86]

A very successful children's magazine emerged from the American Anti-Slavery offices at 143 Nassau Street in New York City. *The Slave's Friend,* published from 1836 to 1839, was far more strident than "The Juvenile Department." A mere two inches by three and a half inches in size, perfect for the little hands intended to hold it, each issue of *The Slave's Friend* contained several drawings and stories about slavery. Modern-day readers might find its very honest, even brutal, portrayal of slavery too strong for its intended audience, but abolitionist parents felt otherwise. In 1837, for example, an article titled "The Coffle-Yoke," gave detailed descriptions with illustrations of instruments used to torture slaves, including handcuffs, chains, and whips.[87] Unwilling to hide the reality of their times, the authors also included threats made toward their readers' abolitionist parents. These articles implied that their parents were heroic, perhaps even potential martyrs to their cause. In the second issue of 1838 there appeared a clear drawing of the "Bowie Knife" with the engraved message "Death to Abolitionism." The text stated, "People in slave states often carry such knives about them. When they get angry they draw the knife, and sometimes *stab one another!*"[88] Such was the irrational nature of supporters of slavery. The Christmas issue for the same year carried "The Tree of Slavery," a poem of dark images meant to remind children of their own safe and secure position during the season of light (see the following page).[89]

The next year, the magazine carried an article on "Mobs," warning children that mobs were the work of Satan aimed at abolitionists. These crowds were formed because of antiabolitionist lies printed in newspapers, preached by certain proslavery ministers and circulated at "grog-shops." While Jesus preached nonviolence, mobs acted out the antithesis of his teachings. The article reminded "little readers" that they had heard their parents and other older people speak of these violent masses: "They have broken into dwelling houses, into churches, into schoolhouses; they have burned furniture, anti-slavery books and pamphlets, and buildings; they have broken windows, cut off horses' tails, thrown stones and bricks and eggs at abolitionists; and they have burnt, drowned and shot men!"[90]

Besides these hard-hitting articles, *The Slave's Friend* also published stories designed to help children feel sympathy for their enslaved peers and to teach them tolerance toward people whose roots lay in Africa.[91] Several issues in 1836 contained a serial story titled "Joggy and Lorena." Joggy, aged eight, and Lorena, aged six, were African children who were brought in a brig from Angola to the United States. Separated from their parents and traveling on the ship by themselves, they met sailors who entertained themselves by teaching the girls profanities. This was

The
sin of
slavery
hardens the
heart, distempers
the mind, brutalizes
the holder, corrupts the
moral sense, inflames the
evil passions, turns men into
cruel monsters; it is "a witch
to the senses, a devil to the soul,
a thief to the pocket," a mildew to
the soil, and a curse to the nation; it
produces woe to man, woman and child,
and draws from them sighs, tears, and
groans, that reach to the ear of the great God;
it reduces man to a beast—a thing—de-
faces the image of God on the mind,
takes away the key of knowledge,
robs man of the bible and his
soul!
The
root of this evil is
SLAVERY!!!!!!

the only English they knew. Upon arriving in New York City, the captain, one Caleb Miller, took the two little orphans to "a kind lady in Broadway," where they were taught to speak proper English, to sew, and to do housework.[92] Two years later, the girls appeared in the magazine again when it was reported that President Andrew Jackson himself refused to let the woman raise them and instead placed them in the hands of "colonizationists," who sent them back to Africa. The author pointed out that since no one knew who their parents were or exactly where they were from, it would have been better for the children to remain in New York rather than becoming homeless in an African nation they were not familiar with. Another article related a story that Sarah Grimké had told a group of children in Boston. Apparently when Grimké lived on her parents' plantation in South Carolina, she was presented with a gift of an African girl right off a ship. The child, who had been stolen from her mother, was frightened by white people, afraid that they would eat her. Angelina Grimké added to her sister's tale her own recollection of seeing twenty children chained together and driven through the streets of Charleston, South Carolina, en route to the New Orleans slave market.

In an effort to help children understand the racism underlying slavery, *The Slave's Friend* addressed the color issue. In its first volume, the editors published an "Anti-Slavery Catechism." Among its tenets was the belief that the color of a person's skin was caused by climate, not biology, all human blood being the same. The unnatural hatred of whites toward blacks, therefore, was a learned prejudice. Another issue, quoting article 2 of the constitution of the Juvenile Anti-Slavery Society of Chatham Street Chapel in New York City, stated that the organization's members would press people to respect free blacks and treat them fairly as well as to obtain the freedom of the slaves. In this spirit of respect, an 1838 article analyzed the root of the word "negro." The item centered around an eleven-year-old African-American girl who wanted to know if "negroes" was the proper term for "colored people." The article traced the term to the Niger River and advised children that it was a good word to use. "But," it added, "as it has been made a term of reproach it is not best to say negro. It is better to say colored people, or people of color."[93] The final volume of the magazine carried an article titled "An African." Its purpose was to trace the evolution of slavery in the United States—to show that at first Africans had been kidnapped from their homelands and forced into slave labor. However, at this point in history, most of the slaves and free people in the country were born in the United States. In describing free African Americans, the author wrote, "This is a picture of a freeman! He is not an African, but one of those Americans *called* Africans. Either he or his forefathers were once slaves. He now breathes the sweet air of liberty, and looks like a MAN."[94] The lesson here was certainly anti–American Colonization Society, as it concluded, "A little girl about six years old, was asked this question—'Are you an abolitionist or a colonizationist?' She replied, 'I am an abolitionist. When I was between three and four years old, I was a colonizationist, but I did not know any better then.' She now loves the colored people, and does not want to have them sent to Africa."[95]

Besides learning about slavery and the proper way to behave toward fellow human beings, the Garrisons and other abolitionist children were also taught the importance of political organizing. *The Slave's Friend* encouraged children to join juvenile antislavery societies and to collect money for the cause. Children were counseled to ask their parents to help them form groups where they could make items such as pincushions or bead chains to sell to raise money for printing books, paying antislavery agents, and donating money to the adult organizations, and just as the adults convened in May in New York City for the annual American Anti-Slavery Society convention, so the children designed their own annual meeting to be held at the same time and place. Abolitionist children felt a similar loyalty to their cause as their parents did. All children in the New York City association under the age of fourteen, for instance, contributed at least one cent every month to their organization's coffers. In 1837 the Juvenile Emancipation Society of Pawtucket, Rhode Island, gave $100 to the American association, which was enough to purchase 15,000 copies of *The Slave's Friend.* The children of Whitesborough, Oneida County, New York, raised $15 to benefit schools for free black children in Cincinnati. Boston in 1837 had two Juvenile Societies, one male and one female, in which eighty boys and fifty girls claimed membership. Each group pledged to raise fifty dollars for the Massachusetts Anti-Slavery Society. Although many of these societies disbanded after 1840, when Lloyd and Helen's eldest son, George, was only four, similar informal networks survived and played an intricate role in the Garrison children's lives. The literature, even that written before their births, formed an important part of their reading matter as Lloyd, who never threw anything away, left such material scattered everywhere, freely accessible to all.

Books too were written specifically for the abolitionist child and his or her parents. Before 1831 some adult literature in the Middle Atlantic and Northeastern states had reflected antislavery stances.[96] These adult tales emphasized a moral and religious aversion to slavery and hinted at bitter feelings between the North and the South. In 1833 Lydia Maria Child published her nonfiction book *An Appeal in Favor of that Class of Americans Called Africans.* Six years later, Theodore Weld published *American Slavery As It Is: Testimony of a Thousand Witnesses,* a compilation of firsthand accounts of the slavery experience collected by himself, Angelina, and Sarah Grimké. Before the Civil War, slave narratives, such as those by Frederick Douglass and Harriet Jacobs were quite popular, especially since they offered true, dramatic accounts of slavery and escape. One novel, however, *The Slave: or, Memoirs of Archy Moore* (1836), by Richard Hildreth, the story of a slave mother and planter father, had difficulty being published, sold, or reviewed because of its interracial story line. During the 1840s and 1850s many antislavery theatrical productions were staged. *The Branded Hand,* by Sophia L. Little, which appeared in 1845, was followed by *Warren: A Tragedy* in 1850. Both plays portrayed heroes who were sent to prison for opposing slavery or for being free black citizens. Poets such as James Russell Lowell and John Greenleaf Whittier also became spokespersons for the abolitionist movement.

The passage of the Fugitive Slave Act in 1850, which entitled slaveholders to reclaim ownership of any person they could prove was an escaped slave, was incentive for several writers to create stories of runaways who faced being returned to tyrannical slave owners. The most famous of these books was Harriet Beecher Stowe's *Uncle Tom's Cabin.*[97] Published on March 20, 1852, the book became an immediate bestseller. Within three months it was selling ten thousand copies a week. By October, sales in the United States reached one hundred and fifty thousand copies. *Uncle Tom's Cabin* had various important antislavery story lines, including that of runaway slaves using the Underground Railroad to reach Canada, a slave sold from kindly owners in economic trouble to various owners including a cruel master in the deep South, and a young slave girl saved by a New England matron. The novel was so popular that it was soon adapted into folk songs and dramas. The play version was in such demand that for the first time in New York theater history, matinees were instituted to accommodate lone women and children audience members. The McLoughlin Brothers, a New York City toy and game manufacturer, even developed paper dolls of Eva St. Claire and Topsy for children to play with. Eva, the innocent white child who showed compassion for the slave Uncle Tom, had five lovely paper outfits. Poor slave Topsy was granted two identical dresses, one with an apron attached.

Children learning how to read could enjoy their own books, including *The Anti-Slavery Alphabet,* published in 1847 for the Philadelphia Anti-Slavery Fair. Each page of this small volume contained two large letters of the alphabet accompanied by a four-line poem providing a lesson on the abolitionist movement or about slavery. *A* set the tone:

A is an Abolitionist—
A man who wants to free
The wretched slave—and give to all
An equal liberty.

B stood for "Brother," a person with a darker skin but just as precious in God's eyes as the little reader. By today's standards, some verses were astonishingly direct for the small children expected to read this book or have it read to them. For example,

D is the Driver, cold and stern,
Who follows, whip in hand,
To punish those who dare to rest,
Or disobey command.

Or the four letters *I, J, K,* and *L:*

I is the Infant, from the arms
Of its fond mother torn,
And, at a public auction, sold
With horses, cows and corn.

J is the Jail upon whose floor
That wretched mother lay,
Until her cruel master came,
And carried her away.

K is the Kidnapper, who stole
  That little child and mother—
Shrieking, it clung around her, but
  He tore them from each other.

L is the Lash, that brutally
  He swung around its head,
Threatening that "if it cried again,
  He'd whip it till 'twas dead."[98]

Abolitionist children who could read on their own were provided with several books. Popular was the Peter Parley series, meant to teach children about geography and history. *Peter Parley's Tales of the Sea* included an interesting selection titled "Story of a Slave Ship." The intent was clearly antislavery but without an accusatory bent, for after introducing the reader to the cruel world of slavery, the author pointed out that some Southerners were "good people, and anxiously wish that, somehow or other, the slaves might be set free."[99]

While the Peter Parley books preached reserve, most others did not. *Juvenile Poems, for the use of Free American Children, of Every Complextion,* published in 1835 by Isaac Knapp and Lloyd, was more direct and more strident than the early columns in "The Juvenile Department." The book consisted of seventy-two pages of poems, such as "What is a Slave, Mother!" and "The Bereaved Father," each reiterating the publishers' sorrow over the cruelty of the separation of parent and child, an interesting note considering Lloyd's own personal history and the fact that the book was published when Helen was pregnant with the couple's first child. Also published by their father's printing press was *The Young Abolitionists or Conversations on Slavery,* by J. Elizabeth Jones, which carried a definite message to the Garrison children:

> The abolitionists certainly have a great work before them yet—very much remains to be done, although a great deal has been accomplished. Many have united in the work which was commenced by a very few. Where there was one in former days to labor for the slave there are now hundreds, and a great many boys and girls like you and Jennie, are helping in the work. If we all do what we can, and try to get others to do what they can, I think it will not be many years before slavery shall be no more; and the happy faces of the slave children and their gay and joyous laugh, will be a pleasant sight and sweet music to those who aided in making them and their parents free.[100]

The Hopedale community, Adin Ballou's Christian utopian society, also published books for small children. The most popular series came under the title *Lida's Tales* and included many antislavery stories. *Ralph: or I Wish He Was n't*

Black, published in 1855, told the tale of two boys, Tommy and Ralph, one white, the other black. White Ralph wanted to know why the other children did not like black Tommy. His mother went into a long explanation of slavery and Tommy's father's flight from the South, only to be returned under the provisions of the Fugitive Slave Act. Tommy, in turn, asked his mother why God loved white people better than black people. She responded, "God does not look at the *skin,* my son, but at the *heart.*"[101] In the end, the boys continued being loving friends with a new understanding of the world they lived in.

Abolitionist literature for older readers became more linguistically sophisticated, but its message remained the same. *The Two Christmas Celebrations, A.D. I. And MDCCCLV: A Christmas Story for MDCCCLVI,* by the minister Theodore Parker, told of an interracial Christmas celebration in a Massachusetts town. *The Liberty Cap,* by the Garrisons' friend Eliza Lee Follen, compared U.S. slavery to that of ancient Rome. *Aunt Judy's Story: A Tale from Real Life,* written for the Pennsylvania Anti-Slavery Fair of 1855, described the history of "Aunt Judy," a poor, elderly black woman who had been saved from slavery but separated from her husband and children. *The Envoy From Free Hearts to the Free,* published in 1840 by the Pawtucket, Rhode Island, Juvenile Emancipation Society, carried a series of sophisticated articles on the antislavery issue. The feature article, "The Envoy," described the work of William Wilberforce and Thomas Clarkson, two British abolitionists. This was followed by a poem about Benjamin Lundy and an article titled "Appeal of a Slave Mother to Mothers at the North."

While the Garrison children learned at home and within their antislavery community all about slavery and the abolitionist movement, they also needed to be prepared for life in the broader world. For this, their parents sent them to various types of schools or placed them in informal apprenticeships for vocational training. While in that outer world, however, they never forgot who their parents were or what they stood for.

SCHOOLING AND SOCIALIZING

> Your principal fault, if I may be allowed to say so, is your unsociability. . . . As father says, you are like a sponge which absorbs a great deal but requires squeezing to let anything out. . . . The best model I can think of now, is . . . father, who always makes himself agreeable and entertaining, wherever he is.
>
> William Lloyd Garrison Jr. to his brother Wendell, 1857

CHAPTER V

The Garrison children benefited greatly from the changes that the nineteenth century brought in the ways children were educated. No longer was the norm to apprentice them at an early age; the emphasis had shifted to school learning and, at least for the increasing number of middle-class boys, preparation for entry into a profession. Lloyd, who had longed for a good education, was determined that his children not have to learn on their own, as he had, but that they receive the best education he and Helen could provide. Like many women of her day, Helen, although having been raised in a middle-class environment, also had not received a formal education; she agreed with Lloyd that their own children, including Fanny, should go to school. Hence, the Garrison children attended a variety of places of learning, including traditionally oriented public and private schools, experimental alternative programs offered by utopian societies, and on-the-job training. Decisions were ultimately based on available funds, sponsorship, friendship and family ties, and each child's desires, talents, and needs.[1]

The first Garrison child to receive any formal education was the eldest son, George, who in 1840 at the age of four attended an infant school during one of Helen's extended visits to her family in Brooklyn, Connecticut. Lloyd, anxious to help his son gain an interest in reading, brought the preschooler some "nice little books" from that year's antislavery convention in New York City.[2] In the fall, however, soon after George was placed in a similar infant school in Boston, Lloyd made the rather hasty evaluation that his son was "not disposed to be very scholastic."[3] His opinion was repeated several times during George's primary school years. In early 1843, when George was seven and Willie five, the pair attended two schools: a local public district school and a small private program run by a young woman whom Helen and Lloyd felt provided a nonthreatening and permissive learning environment. Helen, in particular, needed to have the boys in this after-school program to give her respite from their wild behavior at home. As Lloyd confessed to one of his friends, both boys were very independent and stubborn, requiring "steady guidance." He also worried about their exposure to the neighborhood children, many of whom were working class or immigrant, who insulted abolitionists and used coarse language that the Garrison parents found offensive. As Lloyd put it, "Between schools, it is difficult to keep them at all times shut up in the house; and if they play out of doors, they are liable to hear improper language from vicious boys."[4] Extra hours in daycare provided the sons with a place where they were protected from this seemingly undesirable element of society while at the same time introducing them to more suitable companions.

Also, in the spring of 1843, Lloyd and Helen decided to spend the summer season from July through September in Northampton with George W. and Catherine, who in 1841 had sold the Benson farm in Brooklyn to invest in the Northampton Association of Education and Industry.[5] The focus of the community, which lasted about four and a half years and touched the lives of upward of 240 men, women, and children, was to develop a cooperative environment where all participants shared responsibilities, social life, values, and profits. Settling on land purchased from the bankrupt Northampton Silk Company, the residents hoped to reinvigorate the silk industry as a joint-stock venture based on utopian socialist principles. Northampton's major founders, including George W., Erasmus Darwin Hudson, William Adam, Joseph Conant, Earl Dwight Swift, Theodore Scarborough, and Hiram Wells, were either active or sympathetic abolitionists who embraced woman's rights, health reform, and innovative educational techniques. Together they formed one of the rare utopian societies that advocated racial equality and opened its doors to African Americans, two of whom were David Ruggles, whose water cure establishment served Lloyd and Helen, and Sojourner Truth, who spent much of her time living in George W. and Catherine's home, often helping with domestic chores.[6] Helen and Lloyd wanted to spend this particular summer with the Benson family because Helen's ailing sister, Anna, and her mother, Sally, were also in residence there. While at the community, the couple took advantage of the opportunity to enroll George and Willie in the community's school. Since George was the more difficult of the children to handle, had experienced trouble in learning, and was more physically than intellectually inclined, Helen and Lloyd hoped that an outdoor environment might motivate him to want to study. Northampton, ninety-four miles west of Boston, was in a beautiful western Massachusetts location on the Connecticut River, surrounded by mountains and filled with rivers and brooks, birds, and trees—an appealing rural environment with infinite opportunities for the boy to expend his seemingly endless energy.

William Adam, the educational director at Northampton, designed a program resembling that of Brook Farm, a utopian community in eastern Massachusetts under the leadership of Bronson Alcott. George W., who had been exposed to Brook Farm before he committed himself to Northampton, helped duplicate its educational premise that there should be a balance between school and work. In this way, children could develop the appropriate mental, physical, and moral components of good citizenship. The school, therefore, taught vocational skills as well as literature and science. Children's moral and spiritual training at Northampton included nonsectarian religious meetings and cultural events that mirrored the Garrisons' own abolitionist, nonresistant, and feminist leanings. During the summer of 1843, the school enrolled between thirty and forty children, who were divided into groups based on age. Both George and Willie fell into the coeducational infant class; once George turned eight, he would move on to the junior level, which continued up to fourteen years of age. Immediately, the boys found themselves in an environment reflective of their own home, where force of any kind was forbidden. Indeed, the teachers were so permissive that visitors described the classes as being totally uncontrolled. Nonetheless, George and Willie were exposed to many delightful experiences. Being in the infant division, they attended gym classes with girls, learned useful skills which included sewing, and listened to the works of such authors as William Shakespeare and Sir Walter Scott. Botany included field trips to the local riverbanks, where their teacher, Sophia Foord, taught her young charges how to create various geographical formations out of mud and rocks, including miniature islands, capes, promontories, peninsulas, and isthmuses. Northampton students learned from a hands-on style of pedagogy similar to that previously advocated by Emma Willard in upstate New York and later made famous during the Progressive Era by John Dewey, but rarely used during the antebellum years.

During their stay in Northampton, Helen suffered the damage to her arm in the carriage accident, so when the time came for her to return with Lloyd to Boston in September, they decided to leave George and Willie behind, largely in the care of Laura Stebbins and her husband, Armanda Wood, whom they paid for the boys' room and board. Very quickly, however, the two parents began missing their offspring, even though three-year-old Wendell, one-year-old Charley, and Helen's pregnancy offered little rest. By October, Helen had Willie sent home, but decided to leave ill-mannered George at the community's school for the entire year. Within a month, this resolve evaporated, and in early November the young boy came home, returning to the Northampton school during the summers of 1844, 1845, and 1846. In general, however, except for short summer vacations, the Garrison children never wandered far from home until they reached adulthood. George was the clear exception, his extreme activeness presenting his parents with endless consternation. When Lloyd was in London in August of 1846, he wrote to Helen that he was relieved to know that both George and Willie had gone to Northampton during his time away. If Helen was too unhappy about being separated from them, however, he urged her to bring only Willie home, as George was too much trouble for her to cope with alone. "His absence will be a great relief to you all," he wrote, "and he will be far happier in the country than in the city. As to his learning, a few weeks will make no difference worthy of a moment's consideration . . . you will have care and trouble enough with the other children."[7]

Although at first Helen complied, she missed her problem child and ordered that he be sent home, where he continued to pose more of a challenge than his siblings; his academic progress, in particular, constantly fell short of his parents' expectations.[8] In December 1843, after George had returned from Northampton the first time, Lloyd wrote anxiously to Henry Wright about the boy's failure to learn how to read and write: "George Thompson is now a very tall boy, active in work or play, but dull as a scholar. He can scarcely spell the simplest words, though he has been to school some four or five years! He abhors a book, and would much prefer that reading and writing should come by nature, than be obtained in any other method. He is far from being a dunce, but he is too restless to give any attention to his books." Lloyd felt hopeful that George would "take a sudden start" at some point, but he was at odds as to how to direct him. Willie, on the other hand, was "a much better scholar than George," but Wendy was the star, having had, at the age of three and a half, "mastered the alphabet, and is the brightest and most beautiful boy of the lot."[9] Interestingly, his characterization of the three boys foretold their future success in school.

By late October 1847, George, age eleven, Willie, nine, and Wendell, seven, were all settled in one of Boston's district public schools (also known as "common schools"), George having at last become interested in book learning and improving in skills. At the time, the family benefited from changes within the Massachusetts public school system which elevated the quality of the state's education and widened its access.[10] Improvements began in 1789, when the commonwealth passed a law formalizing district education. Almost thirty years later, in 1818, Boston legislators passed another law stating that all children between the ages of four and six had the right to a free primary school education. By the late 1820s, infant schools were created throughout Massachusetts and indeed the entire United States, setting the stage for the 1828 opening of Boston's first school designed specifically for poor children between the age of eighteen months and their entrance into primary schools. Following suit, the 1830s and 1840s witnessed a rash of reforms in the city, including the establishment of the Massachusetts Board of Education in 1837, whose first secretary, Horace Mann, believed that public education without cost was an essential element of a government representing a free people. As he stated in 1845:

> Education is to inspire the love of truth, as the supremest good, and to clarify the vision of the intellect to discern it. We want a generation of men above deciding great and eternal principles upon narrow and selfish grounds. . . . We want a generation of men taking up these complex questions, and of turning all sides of them towards the sun, and of examining them by the white light of reason. . . . We want no men who will change like the vanes of our steeples, with the course of the popular wind, but we want men, who, like mountains, will change the course of the wind. . . . We want men capable of deciding what is right in means, to accomplish what is right in principle.[11]

Mann's leadership proved highly effective. Between 1840 and 1865 the number of students enrolled in Massachusetts's winter schools increased by 53.8 percent, the number of schools statewide by 54.5 percent. Hence, the numbers of teachers also rose, leading directly to the creation of the Massachusetts's Teachers Association in 1847, an organization that rallied around issues of teaching and learning standards, working conditions, and higher wages. Within three more years, laws were attained to institute teacher certification. Massachusetts had quickly become one of the most advanced and progressive educational systems in the country and also one of the first to racially integrate, thanks to William C. Nell and other of the city's African Americans who succeeded in this effort in 1855. But while the school system was expanding, it was also becoming more bureaucratic. Teachers were required to keep attendance records and adhere to strict budgets. First in Boston and then statewide, teacher-student ratios were carefully monitored to see that money was not wasted, while structured salary scales were instituted to regularize spending.

The Garrisons were most affected by the commonwealth's 1850s adoption of an "urban pedagogy" instituted as a result of the large influx of poor immigrants, especially from Ireland, that swelled the already large number of needy African Americans and native-born whites. Those practicing urban pedagogy felt that the role of the school was one of hardening children to meet the realities of the society they lived in. Teachers were trained to see their jobs as weaning children away from their parents and teaching them self-discipline, control, and restraint while acculturating those who came from other lands. Most important of all, however, was the deep commitment to intellectual rigor.

The expanded and reformed Boston public school system played an important role in the Garrison children's lives. Although their parents may not have totally agreed with the ideas of strictness that the public schools advocated, lack of money meant that they were not totally free to choose alternative forms of education, especially as the size of the family grew. Hence, George, William, Wendell, Charley, Fanny, and Frank attended one of three district schools close to their home: the Quincy School on Tyler Street, the Dwight School, and the Winthrop School just down the block from their Dix Place home. Willie, for one, remembered his years in public school with great fondness. At an alumni reunion, he recalled his time there as a nine-year-old by reading his poem "Quincy School Memories."[12] It described his "South End" school, with both rich and poor students, as having a "mission" to "impartially . . . grind / Whatever grist was given it to find." Willie remembered the large number of Irish "impoverished . . . refugees" who attended classes with him and reflected upon the activities he and other boys participated in after school. They took "muddy baths" in Baby's Pond, skated on it in the winter and netted shrimp, speared eels, and captured minnows from the bay when there was no ice. Sometimes the schoolboys hung around the local firehouses or ran through the city to Theatre Alley playing tag. In the end, however, they all had to go home to study the great literature of "men of name."

Fanny also attended a district school, starting at the tender age of four and a half. At a time when educating girls was not a top priority for many families, Helen and Lloyd encouraged her curiosity, Helen telling Henry C. Wright that Fanny was so "desirous to go with the other children, we thought she would be happier to go. She is as determined and independent a spirit as ever, and I hope will get on the right track."[13] In Fanny's case, "the right track" was either becoming a teacher or, preferably, meeting a prosperous abolitionist man, getting married, and having babies. However, to be a good mother, she, like her brothers, needed to receive a good education. Fanny was a hard-working, bright student, eager to excel. At the Winthrop School, her studies in algebra and astronomy kept her extremely busy, but she preferred her history and language classes, especially German and French. Fanny's greatest love and talent rested in the field of music. During her youth she mastered the piano and then, in her teenage years, both music theory and technique, becoming an accomplished musician. Not only did this give her parents great joy, but it also provided additional family income for several years during which Fanny gave private lessons.

During the first half of the 1860s, Fanny also enjoyed joining her brothers at Dioclesian (Dio) Lewis's evening calisthenics classes in Boston.[14] For her exercises, Fanny wore the then scandalous bloomer costume, consisting of Turkish-style pantaloons covered by a mid-calf-length dress. Named for Amelia Bloomer, the editor of the woman's rights and temperance newspaper *The Lily*, who popularized it, the outfit was so criticized that it is unlikely that Fanny wore it outside the gymnasium; however, Dio Lewis himself encouraged such changes in clothing styles.[15] He opposed the corsets and long, heavy skirts that young women wore, believing that at least 90 percent of female physical complaints stemmed from these fashions. Rather, he preferred that women wear skirts with loose waists held up by suspenders. A temperance advocate, woman's rightist, abolitionist, and practitioner of homeopathy, Lewis was one of the first physical education teachers to insist that young and old, male and female, could benefit from a steady regimen of exercise. In fact, he became so committed to the value of exercise and dress reform for women that in 1864 he opened a school for girls. Fanny was by then too old to attend, but she continued to frequent Lewis's and other reformers' gymnasiums.

Lewis's coeducational exercise classes consisted of all sorts of calisthenics, dancing, and games. Equipment included wooden dumbbells, rings, light rods, small clubs, and beanbags for lifting and tossing. Willie, Fanny, and Frank attended classes several evenings a week while George tagged along from time to time. The boys also purchased their own equipment, including parallel bars, a horizontal bar, and exercise horses, so that they could work out each day. Wendell, William, and Frank in particular enjoyed mastering gymnastic skills on hanging rings and on the floor. At age seventeen, in a letter to Willie, Wendell drew a playful picture of himself doing a headstand while holding on to a large wooden club. Unfortunately, as his text described, he slipped and fell to the floor, "chwack! right on my nose and face!" His nose, "never too small," gushed blood for fifteen minutes, and the next day he looked like he had been in a fight. His nose was nearly doubled in size, his head ached, his lip was swollen, and he had "a great red mark" on his forehead.[16] Neither this nor any other accident kept him from attending his gym classes. In fact, the siblings consistently looked forward to their sessions, each claiming that daily exercise was responsible for their general good health.

Besides the pleasures of Dio Lewis's classes, Fanny also attended one of Massachusetts's state normal schools, the first schools opened in the United States for the formal training of teachers.[17] To qualify, she had to pass an exam, which she did in the summer of 1859 at age fourteen, answering about two-thirds of the questions correctly. Fanny attended the school in West Newton for three years but showed no great interest in becoming a teacher. As the only female Garrison child, her outlook on life differed from her brothers'. Even though the few letters and diary entries left behind from her growing-up years do not indicate an absolute determination to become a wife and mother, 90 percent of women in the United States were choosing this course; and Helen, Fanny's primary role model, was a traditional Victorian-era woman in terms of her personal life. Indeed, most of the abolitionist spokeswomen were wives and mothers, but there were single activists after whom Fanny could pattern her life. The problem was that their lifestyles did not always appeal to her. Mary Grew and Sallie Holley, for example, were good and admired friends of her mother, warm and affectionate toward the Garrison children, but both lived rather staid lives with their parents or a close woman friend.[18] Sarah Grimké was friendly enough, but her frequent visits to the

Garrison home were barely tolerated by Lloyd's favorite daughter, who portrayed Sarah in her diaries as a bore, an elderly, lonesome, somewhat demanding guest.

Susan B. Anthony, always on the go and very self-sufficient, had a more exciting lifestyle, but Fanny had no desire to emulate her, for Anthony was too much on her own, and Fanny liked to be surrounded by family. In addition, Anthony's desire that her friends' children refer to her as "Aunt Susan" seemed to highlight her aloneness to the Garrison children, who did not really spend great amounts of time with her. Unlike these unmarried abolitionist role models, Fanny thrived on parties and socializing, enjoying pretty clothes and lively cultural events, pleasures that her permissive upbringing opened to her but which her parents' friends, usually much older, did not often participate in. Her world as a young woman was less steeped in a concern to earn her own livelihood than the world of her brothers, and, indeed, Fanny left school in July 1862 with great relief, writing Frank, "Yesterday I went to school for the last time, & was truly thankful that it *was* the last time."[19]

Of the Garrison sons, only Wendy and Frank completed their high-school education in a traditional school, the highly selective Boston Latin School.[20] Founded in 1635 by the town of Boston, it is one of the oldest public schools in the United States today, antedating Harvard College by more than a year, a point of pride in the school's history. Located on Bedford Street, now the extension of Harrison Avenue, the school occupied one-half of a building erected in 1844; the English High School occupied the other half. Wendy enrolled in the fourth of six levels in 1852 at the age of twelve. Most likely, he was guided there by one of its most illustrious alumni, Wendell Phillips. The following year, Willie's education also led to the Boston Latin School, but he did not stay to graduate. Although receiving good grades and never being absent or late, Willie did not wish to remain in the program for the full four years he would have needed to finish, by which time he would have been nearly twenty years old.

Instead, in June 1855, his eighteenth year, Willie decided to enter an internship with James N. Buffum, an abolitionist and Garrison friend who owned a shoe business in Lynn. Unlike his father or his uncle, James, who faced grueling apprenticeships making shoes, Willie's plan was to learn business skills, which he did. Boarding with the Buffums in a home as active and loving as his own, he continued his self-education by joining the Old Silsbee Street Debating Club, founded by another abolitionist and nonresistant, James P. Boyce. The club required its members to do extensive reading and research in order to participate in debates concerning the most controversial political issues of the day, such as slavery, capital punishment, and political campaigns. Willie also signed up for a French class that met once every two weeks in the houses of its different members. After reading, the class, made up of five males and ten females, played games, danced, had refreshments, and engaged in conversation. Willie spent seven happy years in Lynn, leaving the shoe business in order to train as a teller at the Laighton Bank, where he remained until 1862.

Wendell, meanwhile, continued at Boston Latin. When he entered, he was one of fifty-five boys accepted into a class that included other abolitionist sons, namely Edward Blagden, William C. Gannett, Sidney Howe, Frank Howe, Edward Loring, and Waldo Merriam. According to the regulations stipulated in their 1852 catalogue, each boy had to be at least ten years old to begin his studies and "produce, from the masters of the schools they last attended, certificates of good moral character." They had to have read "common English authors," be fluent in English, skilled in arithmetic, and "able to answer the more important of Mitchell's Geographical Questions." A knowledge of both English and Latin grammar was also required.[21] The regular course of instruction lasted six years, although it could be completed in five or fewer, especially if a student did not enter on the lowest level, as was Wendy's case. That Wendy, and then Frank, were admitted into the school and graduated attests to the fine public school and home education each received.

During Wendy's first year at Boston Latin he was required to study Latin grammar, English grammar, literature, spelling, oration, penmanship, translation from Latin into English, geography, Sophocles' Greek grammar, Ovid's *Metamorphoses,* English composition, and French. Added to this in later years were advanced Greek, Latin, French, English, algebra, physical geography, Virgil, Cicero, Voltaire, and intensive history courses. Wendy did fairly well at Boston Latin; Frank, less so. Although in 1853, when most of his classmates moved up, Wendy was still in the fourth class, the next year he was promoted to the third class, and then in 1855 to the second, where at the term's end he won a prize for the best poem written in English on any subject. Wendy enjoyed the challenges offered him at Boston Latin, bragging to his brother William in October 1856 that he was at the head of the first class—although the next month he fell to third. Apparently his slip was caused by his slightly less than stellar performance in debating, where the grade was based on "delivery and ideas as well as writing."[22] Wendy's writing, like his father's, became his forte; public speaking was somewhat less of an achievement, especially in French or Greek, which intimidated him. In 1857 Wendy successfully completed his public school education, receiving the "Frankly medal" and ranking second in a class of ninety-five.

Helen and Lloyd were particularly proud of Wendy's graduation from the Boston Latin School and his admission, after intensive examinations, to Harvard College. Willie, more than any of his siblings, understood how important Wendy's success was to his parents. As he wrote to his mother after Wendy's graduation from Boston Latin, "I know that nothing in the world gives him [Lloyd] more pleasure than to witness the progress of his sons in the paths of honor and excellence, which he had invariably pointed out and counselled them to follow. May he never have cause to regret that we bear the name which he has rendered so honorable and respected by his labors in the cause of freedom and humanity."[23] Wendy's accomplishment was especially gratifying as he was named one of ten students to receive a John E. Thayer scholarship to attend Harvard, an award whose amount increased each year he was at the university. Wendell Phillips, intent on seeing that the young man carrying his name had the best education possible, also continued to help fund it. Even Theodore Parker offered assistance, giving Wendy an expensive five-volume set of the *Dictionary of Greek and Roman Biography and Mythology*, a gift that both he *and* his father greatly treasured.

Harvard offered Wendy the same type of classical education that he had begun at Boston Latin. Based on a strict system of memorization which existed well into the 1860s, he studied ancient Greek and Latin, advanced mathematics, philosophy, and English grammar, writing, and literature and began publishing articles in the school newspaper, the *Harvard Magazine*. The first, an anti-stimulant position paper titled "The Use of Tobacco in College," appeared in the March 1860 edition. Through both his Harvard experience and his lifelong "apprenticeship" at the *Liberator*, Wendy was groomed for his yet unchosen career as a newspaper writer and editor. He graduated on July 17, 1861, soon after the Civil War began, and immediately started teaching at Boston Latin as a replacement. Much to his disappointment, this opportunity lasted only a few months, after which he tutored individual students.

To a certain degree, Frank's educational path resembled Wendy's. The difference for Frank, however, was that his support and encouragement often came from his older brothers and sister rather than from his parents. Lloyd was so caught up in the impending Civil War and fatigued by his health and aging problems that he seemed content to enjoy Frank's youthfulness without worrying too much about his future. Helen, on the other hand, was too preoccupied with Fanny's entrance into the world of womanhood, her concerns over what the Civil War would mean for her draft-age sons, and her own health to chide Frank for not performing up to par. Hence, the responsibility of overseeing Franky's adolescence fell to his siblings. Willie and Wendy, in particular, pressed Frank to study and to excel. Frank, like his siblings, attended the local public school but seemed to be foundering, when, at the age of thirteen, he came under the wing of Wendy, the recent college graduate, who envisioned his own future as a teacher so he could keep his "classical knowledge . . . from rusting."[24] During the summer of 1861, Wendy actually turned down a teaching position away from Boston because he believed that Frank needed his help. With his older brother's tutoring, Frank proceeded to complete common school and move on to the Boston Latin School, where in 1863 he was in the second class along with Alfred Geist, his family physician's son, and Birney Mann, a dear friend from Sterling, Massachusetts. The next year, as a member of the first class, he received the prize "For Exemplary Conduct and Fidelity," although he did not graduate until the next term.[25]

Frank was apparently a satisfactory student, although not as excellent a scholar as Wendell, and after graduating from Boston Latin in 1865, he, too, had the opportunity to attend Harvard, thanks to a bequest left him by Francis Jackson. He decided against it because he had not enjoyed studying the classics and did not wish to become a teacher. Instead he registered in the new Technical College, founded in 1861 as a private school but adopted as the state's college for the "mechanic arts" in 1863, and later renamed the Massachusetts Institute for Technology (MIT). Lloyd and Helen were excited by their son's plans to study pharmacology, but Frank, restless and unsure what to do, postponed his decision. In January 1868 he finally entered MIT, where he studied German, English literature, and inorganic chemistry. Under the supervision of various professors and tutors, he spent innumerable hours in the school's laboratories, learning, as he put it, "chemical manipulation," but not showing great aptitude for it. On February 10, in fact, he caused an "accident" in the lab "while distilling water." Fortunately, "no body was hurt" and there was "no damage."[26] On May 15, he withdrew from the program, feeling that even though a phrenologist had told him he was a born chemist, he had learned from experience that he had no talent for or interest in the field.

While William, Wendell, Fanny, and Frank's education followed a somewhat conservative path, George's took a nontraditional twist reminiscent of his early youth in Northampton. Always considered a difficult child to interest in learning, one who had a "tremendous will of his own" and who was "very passionate," George was the only Garrison child to be sent away to school, perhaps at his own request.[27] After his experiences at Northampton and then in a local district school, at the age of fourteen, George entered school at the Hopedale community, about twenty-five miles from Boston.[28] The Garrisons had a long-lasting and friendly relationship with Adin Ballou, the founder of the community, and Henry C. Wright, who lived in Hopedale much of the year, using it as headquarters for the New England Non-Resistance Society. In 1842 Adin Ballou, himself a devout Christian who believed in nonresistance and socialism, had left his ministry in the town of Mendon in order to move his family to the 258-acre farm that he and several followers had purchased in Hopedale and turned into a utopian Christian-socialist community. At first, all twenty-eight residents at Hopedale held the property in common. Soon, however, they decided to reorganize into six separate family residences, establishing a joint-stock company with a common pool of funds and land. The community experimented with a cooperative and integrated labor system that combined agricultural, mechanical, and domestic duties. By 1853 the Hopedale community consisted of 229 members; at its peak it numbered three hundred.

The Hopedale community as a whole embraced many of the same values as Helen and Lloyd, including temperance, abolitionism, nonresistance, and social reform. Some residents were nonsmokers, others nonshavers, and all were vegetarians, stances held up as models. Although there were two or three church services each Sunday, the community was relatively nondenominational, making it acceptable to Helen and Lloyd. More important was that in 1844, Lloyd had acknowledged that Hopedale was the only community he knew of that was truly based on the beliefs of nonresistance.[29] Another attraction for Lloyd was that during the 1850s, when the United States experienced widespread fascination with spiritualism, Hopedale housed several mediums, including Abby Price, an early woman's rights activist as well as a spiritualist, and Fanny Davis. Bryan J. Butts and Harriet N. Greene, two residents who wrote several children's books, also published the newspaper *Radical Spiritualist.* Lloyd himself was a reluctant but firm believer in spiritualism, feeling that since he had no proof that contact with the spirit world was fabricated, he could not readily dismiss it. In 1852 he addressed the issue in the pages of the *Liberator:* "We have read nearly everything that has appeared, on all sides of the question," he wrote,

> and endeavored to hold the scales impartially. . . . We have heard the rappings, seen the tables moved and overturned as by an invisible power, had correct answers given to mental test questions, become acquainted with several estimable "mediums," and had many astounding statements made to us on the most reliable authority. . . . In this brief article we are unable to state in what light we regard these phenomena . . . they are so diverse and so extraordinary as both to challenge and demand a thorough investigation.[30]

In spite of his doubts, Lloyd enjoyed going to seances and playing with the planchette board with his children. He believed it when spiritualists or the board told him that Charley, Lizzy, or his own mother were visiting him, and the children, except for George, often noted that they too believed these manifestations. Helen, however, had no tolerance for the practice. Whereas Lloyd seemed to gain some comfort from contact with his deceased offspring, Helen could not bear being told that her beloved dead children were calling out to her.

In any case, feeling confident with their decision, Helen and Lloyd entrusted George's secondary education to Hopedale, especially since Adin Ballou's daughter, Abbie, had graduated from the State Normal School in West Newton and his son, Adin Augustus, from the State Normal School in Bridgewater. In addition, in 1847 the town of Milford allowed the community to become an independent school district, whereupon Abbie became coprincipal with the Reverend William Sweetser Heywood (whom she later married) of a private seminary known as the Hopedale Home School. Although the school had only one room, Abbie Ballou's skill in teaching was widely respected, alumni frequently expressing their gratitude for the privilege of having studied with her. As one woman noted, "Her methods were in advance of those in use at that day," while another remembered, "We were proud of the really remarkable maps with meridians and parallels that we used to put on the board from memory."[31] It was at Abbie's school that George settled from the fall of 1850 through the spring of 1852. There, he found himself in the company of several other abolitionist children, notably Edward May and William Reed. These children never lacked visitors, as several of their family friends and relatives came to speak and spend time at the community, including Theodore Parker, Samuel J. May, Wendell Phillips, Lucy Stone, Abby Kelley Foster, Anna Dickinson, Frederick Douglass, George's own father, and, of course, Henry C. Wright, who was often on the premises.

Even though George was away at school, his parents were determined to remain involved in his activities and anxious that he feel support from home, where he was expected for regular visits. In February 1851, for example, after a family visit to the school, Lloyd directed his son to tell his teacher, Abbie Ballou, that he had intended to speak to her about his son's progress, but time had not allowed him to do so. "I had nothing special to suggest to her," he noted, "but she may have thought it a little strange that I made no inquiries of her respecting your progress in learning." Lloyd assured his son that Hopedale was the "best place" he could think of for him away from home because he was with people who were "virtuous, upright, industrious, honest, kind, and loving." Trying to encourage George to study, he instructed him not to worry about earning money to help pay for his board; rather, he wished him to work just enough to have money for his expenses, but not for the labor to become "oppressive."[32] On his own without constant supervision and criticism, George flourished, becoming a key figure in the creation and production of a school newspaper, *The Diamond.* Edited by three abolitionist sons, William B. Reed, Edward May, and George, it was published semimonthly from March 15, 1851, until March 1, 1852, shortly before its editors completed their educational programs. The masthead of the paper, which read, "Sturdy Oaks from Little Acorns Grow," attracted students and community residents to subscribe for only twenty-five cents a year or seventeen cents for six months, all payable in advance.[33]

The Diamond was a perfect reflection of the second-generation Garrisonian abolitionists' adoption of their parents' values. In the first issue, the three young editors expressed their duty as "small men" to become involved in the important issues of the day. Determined to be "independent," to voice their opinions about all sorts of issues "fearlessly," and to seek the truth in all situations, they stated, "Our paper shall not compromise the principles of great truths, and we hope it may never become the dupe of evil geniuses. We shall endeavor to make it a healthful compound of humor, wit and good sense. . . . And as we are yet in our school-days, we hope an enlightened public will not be offended at our best bow at appearing on the stage of public life."[34] They closed this editorial with a poem that clearly reflected their common desire as young men of their time to prove their manly moral and physical strength, independence, and control over their own environments.[35]

A diamond bright! with ray of light!
  Out against wrong and error;
Our REED shall go, against the foe
  To evil works a terror.

A GARRISON! Bold, three for one,
  Against each falsehood vender,
Firmly to stand, with truth in hand,
  And never to surrender.

You seldom find, so much combined
  In one so small a paper:—
Here's MAY and might, to aid the "right"
  By the light of a diamond taper.[36]

The Diamond included short articles describing the Hopedale community and its history or extolling various values. The boys stressed how important it was to obtain an education and use it to identify and spread the truth, a constant theme in the newspaper. A regular column called "Diamond Dust" contained sayings intended to spread wisdom among the youth, such as "We gain nothing by falsehood but the disadvantage of not being believed when we speak the truth."[37] Along with truth, they encouraged good health; like his father, George valued the cold water treatment. "GOOD PRESCRIPTION.—Cold Bathing, pure water, plain diet, a clear conscience, and a clean shirt are indispensable to health and happiness."[38] The other important element to stress was having the correct political stances, especially in terms of abolitionism. Perhaps the most interesting expression of the paper's antislavery position for modern readers was the publication of "A Song" to be sung to the tune of "The Star-Spangled Banner," whose lyrics, written by D. B. Chapman, lambasted the Fugitive Slave Act. The first and final stanzas read:

Oh, say, can you see, by Freedom's clear light,
  A stain on the Banner that's over you flying;
Which enshrouds the bright stars in the blackness of night,
  And proclaims to the world that your liberty's dying?
    Hear its victims despair,
    How it bursts on the air,
  And proclaims to the world that your flag is still there;

For the Star-Spangled Banner in TRIUMPH now waves,
O'er a land where one-sixth of the people are slaves.

Oh weep! All ye lovers of liberty's name;
Oh! Weep for the utter disgrace of your nation;
And pray that her Banner be cleansed for the stain
That has worked thus her sad desolation!
With power and with might,
Strive, pray, that the night
Of oppression be pierced by the Gospel's pure light—
That the Star-Spangled Banner in triumph *may* wave,
O'er a land unpolluted by the toil of the slave.[39]

Although the song exemplified the boys' adoption of their parents' cause, a newspaper produced by a group of adolescent boys could not be all seriousness. After all, George's upbringing was filled with his father's humor, and George, of all the siblings, inherited this aspect of his father's character. Indeed, at one time or another over the years, each of his siblings commented on their eldest brother's sharp wit. One of the editors' favorite columns included "conundrums" such as, "What is the difference between a stubborn horse and a postage stamp?" (Answer: "You lick one with a stick, and stick the other with a lick") . . . or "Why may a slap on the side of the head be considered equivalent in worth to gold?" (Answer: "Because it makes the ear ring") . . . and "Why is a cook like a barber?" (Answer: "Because he dresses *hare*").[40] Humor also found a vent in politics. One "Selections, Wit, &c." column had this note: "The COMMONWEALTH has the following motto to the announcement of the Senatorial election in Massachusetts:—

Now is the WINTHROP of our discontent
Made glorious SUMNER!,

a direct reference to the antislavery favorite, Charles Sumner.[41]

A few humorous items on woman's rights also appeared. A poem in the June 1851 issue poked fun at the idea of independence for women while also reading as a social commentary of the changes in society over time:

Farmers in 1776
Men to the plough,
Wife to the cow.
Girls to the yarn.
Boy to the barn.
And all dues settled.

Farmers in 1837
Men a mere show.
Girls. Piano.
Wife, silk and satin.
Boy, Greek and Latin.
And all hands gazetted.

Farmers in 1847
Men all in debt.
Wives in a pet.
Boys, mere muscles.
Girls, snuff and bustles.
And everybody cheated.[42]

Added six months later was

Farmers in 1851
Bloomers the rage
'Mong all the sage,
Husbands delighted,
Clowns half affrighted—
Signs of 'the good time coming.'[43]

The Diamond ceased publication after its issue of March 1, 1852, the editors thanking their readers for their support and lamenting that they were to close shop, but it was time to move on. During the summer of 1851, George had worked in the law offices of Aaron F. Clark, the selectman of the town of Danvers, near Salem. When he left Hopedale the next year, he returned to Danvers to continue his work there, remaining in the position until early in 1854, his summer week off being spent at Hopedale. For the rest of his life, George had fond memories of his experiences at the community. It had proven a good option for his education, helping to boost his self-confidence and sense of independence.

When school was not in session, especially during the summers, the Garrison children had a great time socializing outside of the home and away from Boston. It was during this season that their world expanded and they practiced the socializing skills their parents had taught them. Since most of the children's friends had abolitionist parents, relationship building was easier than it would have been without common ground. The summers cemented these friendships; from early in their lives, the Garrison children spent part of their summers on vacation with their parents and as guests in the homes of their parents' friends. Having the children away from home was always emotionally trying for Helen and Lloyd, but Helen needed a break from the difficult task of raising them almost single-handedly, and both parents felt it was good for the children's health to be away from Boston during the hottest time of the year. Wendell and Ann Phillips often took one or more of the children for several weeks to Nahant, a coastal town only seven and a half miles from Boston. There they played in the ocean near the Phillipses' summer estate. It was through this connection that Wendy met Wendell Phillips's nephew Samuel, who later became his roommate at Harvard.

Another regular visiting place for the children was Providence, Rhode Island, where they stayed with Charlotte and Henry Anthony, their aunt and uncle. There the children sometimes met up with the children of their uncle George W. In the summer of 1859, for example, Fanny became better acquainted with her cousin, Mary, who, she told Helen, "makes me laugh so I can't possibly write anymore."[44] Because the cousins did not live nearby each other, these visits provided them with some sense of extended family ties. Close to Providence, in Valley Falls, the Garrison children also visited Elizabeth Buffum Chace and her family, where they became good friends with her children, Lillie, Sam, and Arnold. There they devoted their time to activities they most enjoyed: riding horses, rowing on the nearby rivers, taking walks, and indulging in huge picnic lunches. Fanny, in particular, received advice from her mother when she visited these peers. Helen reminded her to behave properly with young men and be considerate of others, something that Fanny apparently sometimes failed to do.

As an adult, Lillie wrote about her life as an abolitionist child. Her memories reflect a deep admiration for Lloyd and, indeed, the entire Garrison clan. Lillie's memory of Lloyd's portrait hanging in her parlor was but one indication of the reverence other abolitionists felt toward him, in some sense setting the family apart from the rest of the movement's participants. This adoration posed no problems for the children, who enjoyed being the offspring of a celebrity and an icon. Lillie's description of Fanny's 1861 visit to Valley Falls illustrates the young Garrison's unpretentious pleasure in being the daughter of an honored man:

> Mr. Garrison and his wife came Thursday night and in the morning Mr. Garrison went into Providence and returned bringing with him his only daughter, Miss Helen Frances Garrison—called Fanny, a pretty, bright girl of 16, overflowing with fun—in that respect resembling her respected "pater" as she termed him, only of course her fun is of a younger and more girlish sort.
>
> Saturday morning we were going huckleberrying, Mr. Garrison with us. Only think of it, going huckleberrying with a man whose name shall live fresh and green when the Napoleons are forgotten. But, alas, we were destined to be disappointed: the morning was cloudy and threatened rain. . . . Monday we went huckleberrying without Mr. Garrison, because he and his wife, and daughter thought he would get all tired and burnt. . . . We—six of us—got twenty-eight quarts, and on our return were

> greeted by all in the vestibule, Mr. Garrison, according to his habit, waving his hat to us, and Fanny, in pulling off hers to respond, pulled off her net, and down streamed her hair, nearly to her waist, so we entered the yard with screams of laughter.[45]

During the same visit, Lillie's mother, Elizabeth, gave both girls a copy of Elizabeth Barrett Browning's 1856 woman's rights poem "Aurora Leigh," hoping they would read it together. This they did, Lillie being totally "fascinated" by her idol's daughter.[46]

Young Fanny also liked visiting the Spooners in Plymouth, Massachusetts. Lydia Spooner was very fond of the entire Garrison family, and Fanny felt a particular closeness to her. She and her brothers also enjoyed rare visits to New York to see Oliver and Mary Ann Johnson, who had relocated there, or to Staten Island to stay with an abolitionist peer, Robert Gould Shaw, and his parents. On several occasions, one or another of the children, but especially Fanny and Frank, traveled to Worcester to visit Abby Kelley and Stephen Foster's daughter, Alla, who was three years younger than Fanny and a year older than Frank. At times, especially before Alla developed a spinal curvature in 1858, she reciprocated the visits. Alla was prescribed to wear a heavy surgical corset, thereby requiring intensive care; hence, the Garrison children's visits took on the guise of a diversion rather than a mutually entertaining vacation. As Helen instructed Fanny, "Dear child: do all you can to make her happy, and see that all her little wants are supplied. For you have legs, and can use them and a kind heart to feel for those who are deprived for a little while of their limbs."[47]

Throughout 1858 and into 1859 the Garrisons remained in close contact with the Fosters; on occasion Helen took care of Alla while Abby Kelley carried on business in Boston. In 1859, however, Lloyd's enthusiasm in embracing the Republican Party, and Kelley's reluctance to follow suit, led him to publicly accuse her of accepting contributions from the party under false pretenses. Although Charles Burleigh, Wendell Phillips, and others reprimanded him so that he later apologized, a rift developed that affected the children's friendship. In 1861 Willie tried to mend fences. He visited Kelley in order to express his regrets at "her alienation from our family." Although her response was "kind," and the families later experienced a reconciliation, the incident broke up their offspring's closeness.[48] The children, however, never forgot their warm feelings for Kelley. When in 1886 the four brothers attended an abolitionist reunion, Wendell wrote this of Abby Kelley Foster to his sister, "I returned to the charm she always held for me as a boy."[49]

Although Fanny and Frank enjoyed their childhood visits to Worcester, Frank much preferred staying about six miles north of Worcester in Sterling with his Boston Latin friend, Birney Mann. Several summers he spent weeks on the Manns' farm, taking long hikes and swimming several times a day (much to the consternation of his mother, who felt it to be unhealthy). When Willie moved to

Lynn, Fanny and Frank often stayed with him for a summer sojourn. Wendy, and sometimes Willie, on the other hand, had the opportunity to travel with friends like William Hovey and his parents on trips into the White Mountains of New Hampshire. Indeed, each summer the Garrison children were scattered all around New England and New York, so that at times it was difficult for family friends to keep track of them. In 1854, for example, Wendy was in Providence, Willie in Hopedale, and Fanny and Frank in Worcester. In 1858 Helen wrote to Ann Phillips, "My children are all absent from home. Mr. Hovey and Willie were going to the White Mountains and from there to Staten Island, and invited Wendell to accompany them. . . . Fannie and Frank have gone at the earnest solicitations of Mrs. Foster to pass a good part of their vacation with Alla."[50] George was on a quest in Nininger, Minnesota, for personal independence.

In 1861 George was in Connecticut, Wendell in western Massachusetts; Fanny in Providence, and Willie and Frank in the Catskills. William wrote home that Frank was "as merry as a lark" with a "little brown face and chubby body."[51] Oddly enough, it was only Frank who ever seemed to suffer from homesickness. Wendell explained his own adaptability by claiming that "novelty" and "the fact that I usually visit those who are the best of friends to our family" made his times away from home enjoyable. However, he added, "I am never weary of staying at home, nor satiated with its attractions."[52] Frank's sense of loneliness may have been a result of Helen and Lloyd's special watchfulness over this son who arrived between Lizzy's and Charley's deaths. In general, however, their parents agreed that such travels, though resulting in an all-too-quiet home for themselves, were good for the children's health and well-being.

During the heat of summer, Helen and Lloyd also received invitations to visit friends outside Boston. Most of Helen's journeys were to visit her sister Charlotte in Providence and from there to nearby Valley Falls to see the Chaces. But she also took nearby trips to Lynn to visit Willie at the Buffums, to see the Remonds in Salem, or to call upon an assortment of other abolitionists near Boston. A rare description of one of Helen's infrequent stays in Philadelphia was written by her friend Sallie Holley after she and Helen attempted to attend a Quaker meeting to support Lucretia Mott. They had heard that the church leaders were "tightening the ecclesiastical screws" on Mott for touting woman's rights as well as antislavery and being too unorthodox for conservative elements of the faith. To their great displeasure, when they arrived, the meeting had begun and the gates were closed. Holley also left behind one of the few descriptions of Helen's personality. "Mrs. Garrison," she wrote,

> is a free and easy person with the least possible pretensions, and has a very natural, artless sort of way. She told me how "awful 'fraid" she was of me when she first saw me, and when I told her that was just my embarrassment on seeing her, we both had

> a hearty laugh. We are both writing now at the same table. She asked me as we sat down if I carried a pocket dictionary with me. I nearly laughed myself into fits. "Oh, you need n't laugh so;" said she, "usually I'm not at all particular, but put down just what comes uppermost and in any way I can, but I'm going to write to Ann Phillips, and Wendell is *so* particular.". . . You would like Mrs. Garrison's talk and simple ways; no starched-up stiffness to scare a body out of their wits.[53]

Once their children were older and George and William earning wages, Lloyd thought that it would be possible for the family to afford a real vacation. In August 1860 he, Helen, Wendell, Fanny, and Frank took their first excursion together for the sole purpose of "rusticating." For nearly three weeks they stayed in Northumberland, a small town in the New Hampshire mountains. However, upon returning to Boston, Lloyd lamented to his friend Oliver Johnson about the trip's expense: "It cost me at the rate of fifty dollars a week—the railroad fare alone amounting to that sum, to say nothing of hiring horses and wagons for various excursions from our stopping-place."[54] This proved the first and last of such family excursions.

A vacation activity that Willie, Wendell, and Frank enjoyed was the "pedestrian adventure," where they and their friends walked a hundred miles or more within two to six weeks. The trip might or might not include public transportation between locations and usually involved visits with Lloyd's supporters. It was a relatively cheap but healthy vacation for young men whose parents could not afford rail or steam fares and steep hotel bills. Wendy and Frank left behind descriptions of such travels. They usually covered territory in western Massachusetts, parts of Vermont, the Lake Champlain areas of New York and Vermont and parts of New York State around Albany. A few times Lloyd met one or the other of his sons along their route, but he did not share the long-distance hiking. In 1859, for example, Wendy and his Harvard friend, John Ritchie, covered about three hundred miles, walking through portions of Connecticut, the Housatonic and Hudson River valleys to West Point, and then portions of the Catskills. In 1861 Wendy took his younger brother Frank along on an abbreviated walking vacation. The trip took them from Boston to Worcester and Sterling, where they visited Birney Mann and his parents. After some swimming and fishing they went to Baldwinville and then back to Worcester, where they caught a train to western Massachusetts to hike through Mt. Holyoke, Northampton, Warwick, and Northfield. During breaks, Wendy made sketches of local scenery and Frank read a novel, *Ruth Hall,* by the popular writer Fanny Fern. At this point Wendy returned to Boston, and Frank joined William for their trip to the Catskills. The next year, Fanny and her normal school friends Sadie Nowell, Sara Pearson, and Annie Morrill celebrated the end of their studies with a train trip to Albany (accompanied by Parker Pillsbury, for Fanny always had a male escort, which was proper). There, the young women hooked up with Susan B. Anthony, and all continued on to a convention in Ellenville.

Although the children's summer vacations away from Boston were important elements in their development, they also had active social lives within the city. Interestingly, the four oldest siblings might have actually experienced less freedom of movement than young Frank, who reached adolescence during the Civil War years. Previous to the war, abolitionist parents were watchful that their children remain within the safety of the community. Besides concentrating on their children's moral development, they worried that some bodily harm might come to them from antiabolitionist mobs—hence, all the warnings in the children's literature, family lore, and home schooling. Even though the Garrison siblings attended public schools, they mostly fraternized with other abolitionist children and their parents, for whom they felt great fondness. Within that environment, they learned that men as well as women could show affection, for unlike many nineteenth-century men, their fathers often greeted each other with a kiss on the cheek, warmly clasping each other's hands, and openly using terms of endearment. From this they learned that open emotions were not a sign of weakness.[55] Some of these caring adults, especially friends of Helen, also paid particularly close attention to the children and won their deepest affection. Ann and Wendell Phillips were major adult figures in the children's lives, Wendy being one of the few people welcome at the Phillipses' home at 26 Essex Street at any time, invited or not. As he wrote to Ann in 1858, "If there was ever a person who could lay claim to double parentage, I think it must be allowed that I am he."[56] Helen was a constant comfort to Ann, an invalid who was, by necessity, a supporter more than an activist within the movement.[57] Ann cared deeply for Helen; Wendell, for Lloyd; and both, by extension, for the children.

Carolyn Thayer, another of Helen's close friends, loved to send little Franky flowers from her garden. He in turn looked forward to receiving them. Other Boston friends whom the children were attached to through their parents' social network included Thankful and Sarah Southwick, the mother and daughter who had housed Lloyd when he returned to Boston after the 1835 mob action, the Grimké sisters, Lucretia Flagge Coffin May, and Olive Gilbert, a woman who became famous for scripting the *Narrative of Sojourner Truth,* Truth's as-told-to autobiography. Visits from Mary Grew and Sarah McKim of Philadelphia also allowed the children to bask in the attention of their mother's and father's friends, and each woman expressed deep affection for one or all of the children.

The greatest social event of the year for Helen, Lloyd, and the children—as well as for the entire abolitionist community in Boston, Philadelphia, and innumerable cities and towns around the Northeast and Midwest—was the Anti-Slavery Fair. The fair was the chief fundraising activity for the movement, but it was also a safe place for abolitionist children to congregate. The Boston Female

Anti-Slavery Society was the group responsible for organizing the fair in that city.[58] From 1834 through 1844, in fact, the Boston fair was such a successful fund-raiser that it became the national bazaar of the American Anti-Slavery Society from 1845 through 1858. Thereafter it was replaced by an appeal for monetary contributions. The first fairs were held in private homes and resembled present-day church bazaars, the emphasis being placed on the sale of used goods. Within a couple of years, the event was transferred to the mansion of Sarah and Henry Chapman Sr. on Chauncy Place. By 1845 it had grown so large that it was moved to the city's honored Faneuil Hall. While the first fairs brought in about $300 for the cause, by 1854 the proceeds were as high as $5,011. Held at the end of December, the celebrations were designed to appeal to everyone's Christmas or New Year's spirit of giving. As the years progressed and the array of items became more varied, the fair committees often advertised items that would be on sale, including clothing, knickknacks, books, household goods—many with abolitionist themes. The fairs were festive occasions at which the public shopped, ate refreshments, and socialized. Children joined their mothers in staffing the tables or ran around the room chasing one another, playing games, or, the older ones, flirting and courting.

The Boston fairs may have been the responsibility of the entire membership of the Boston Female Anti-Slavery Society, but the leading organizer was usually Maria Weston Chapman, who saw the events as vehicles for publicizing the anti-slavery cause and gaining new followers. She worked extremely hard to make each fair a not-to-be-missed event for the general public, and succeeded admirably. Besides organizing the fair in 1839, Chapman and her sisters, Anne, Deborah, and Caroline, began publication of *The Liberty Bell,* for fifteen years an annual volume of poetry, essays, biographical sketches, and short stories, produced for sale at the fair. The publication was designed to give average consumers some insight into the abolitionist cause. The fairs were so pleasurable for the abolitionists themselves that the poet James Russell Lowell wrote a poem depicting the 1846 event in Boston.[59] Titled "Letter from Boston," it was sent to James Miller McKim, the editor of the *Pennsylvania Freeman,* and contained character sketches that tickled each leader depicted. The poem gives a rare portrait of the fair and its organizers. Lowell started out with a general description of the scene:

> The great attraction now of all
> Is the "Bazaar" at Faneuil Hall,
> Where swarm the Anti-Slavery folks
> As thick, dear Miller, as your jokes.

Then he moved on to describe a variety of the abolitionists on hand, starting with Lloyd:

There's Garrison, his features very
Benign for an incendiary,
Beaming forth sunshine through his glasses
On the surrounding lads and lasses.

Lowell described the indefatigable organizer of the fair:

There was Maria Chapman, too,
With her swift eyes of clear steel-blue,
The coiled-up mainspring of the Fair
Originating everywhere
The expansive force, without a sound
That whirls a hundred wheels around.

Eliza Follen, Edmund Quincy, Wendell Phillips, Parker Pillsbury, Stephen Foster, and Abby Kelley Foster were all humorously and reverently portrayed.

The fair was the one event in which Helen became involved every year. It enabled her to participate in the movement even while taking care of the children, and she usually included them in the preparations, especially as they grew older. The fair was also an activity that she considered appropriate for a woman; in fact, Chapman saw to it that the fair remained in the hands of women even though men were encouraged to participate. By remaining in charge, Chapman was able to rescue the fair when political upheavals within the Boston Female Anti-Slavery Society caused it to disband in 1840. Members who supported a more evangelical abolitionist movement decided to leave Lloyd's cohort. Those who remained, however, continued to work with the Anti-Slavery Fair committee. Proof that Helen participated in the fair is scant, showing that her commitment was not as a leader. She signed the announcement for the fair each year and helped to organize tables. Apparently, at times, she also staffed them, but at other times she was so busy entertaining guests at her home that she barely had a chance to attend. When she did, however, she enjoyed all the attention paid to her husband and children. At the fair in 1840 she constantly walked by a bust of Lloyd that had been placed in the center of the room. At another fair, attendees poured praise upon a centrally placed huge portrait of him. Helen herself also became the focus of attention in 1836, enjoying the great fuss made over her and baby George, with friends presenting him with a pair of shoes, a pair of stockings, a pair of mittens, and a beautiful gown. Other years, the young children received antislavery handkerchiefs, books, or candy with such poems printed on the wrapping as:

Take this, my friend, you must not fear to eat.
No slave hath toiled to cultivate this sweet.[60]

The children enjoyed helping out at the tables, seeing their many friends, and playing games such as marbles, tag, blindman's buff, leapfrog, or The Mansion of Happiness, a board game developed in 1843 and popular for many years to come.[61] The game, published by D. P. Ives & Co. in Boston and S. B. Ives in Salem, was based on an English table game of 1800 but adapted for a U.S. audience. The oval drawing on the board consisted of a path that circled until it reached the center. Each block contained a number from one to sixty-seven and a label such as Justice, Piety, Honesty, Idleness, Immodesty, Chastity, and so forth. Number 67 was The Mansion of Happiness, a rectangle portraying young women dancing in a garden. Each player spun a teetotum moving the number of spaces indicated. If the block stopped on had a negative label such as Audacity, Cruelty, Immodesty, or Ingratitude, the player had to return to his former location and wait for his next turn. If the block was labeled Poverty, Whipping Post, House of Correction, Pillory, Stocks, Prison, or Ruin, the player was punished. Whoever landed on Cheat had to be sent to House of Correction and miss a turn; each such block had a different punishment. Other board games included Reward of Virtue, developed in 1850, where players moved from a dungeon to domestic bliss. Younger children could play either Master Rodbury and his Pupils or Doctor Busby, both of which taught them how to behave at school or gave them lessons in morality. By attending the fair and playing such games as these, the Garrison children combined fun with learning the values of their community.

Franky, who was ten when the fairs came to an end and twelve when the Civil War began, experienced a different adolescence from his siblings. As a young boy, he, too, enjoyed the closeness of the abolitionist community and the merriment of the Antislavery Fairs, and as he entered adolescence and young manhood, he retained his abolitionist friendships. Too young to worry about the issue of military service during the war and only sixteen at its end, he grew up in a world of fewer restrictions. Until the *Liberator* expired on December 29, 1865, Frank spent several afternoons and evenings helping his father in the office or proofreading at home. He also attended as many antislavery meetings as he could and helped package goods for African-American refugees of the war. He read newspapers and any writings on Abraham Lincoln he could find. During the war years he frequented the Boston Common to watch soldiers drill and then march off to war. In his diaries and letters he passed no judgment on the militarization until his brother George enlisted, whereupon he declared himself a nonresister.

Like William, Wendell, and Fanny, Frank carried on his normal activities during the war years, attending gymnasium sessions with Fanny and William, reading such bestsellers as Charles Dickens's *David Copperfield* and *Nicholas Nickleby,* and even hearing Dickens read in person at a local library. He also maintained a special closeness to Birney Mann, Louisa Sewall, and Hattie Pitman, and to his neighbor Lizzie Simmons. Together, they staged tableaus, a popular activity which required rehearsals and costume design for the presentation of staged illustrations of classic literature. They also performed adaptations of one-act plays and entertained themselves with such games as Accusations, Magical Music, Blowing Out a Candle, Ring Game, and Digger.[62] Frequently, friends gathered at the Garrison home for games of whist and dances, for once his older siblings had moved out and his parents relocated to a larger house, there was room for such entertainment.

In general, all the Garrison children led happy and permissive childhoods, not so unusual for abolitionist children but very different from that experienced by most of their parents. Their situation within the movement was unique, however, because their father was a revered leader. They were, they knew, the children of an extraordinary man. In later years Fanny remembered how proud she felt to be her father's daughter and the responsibility she accepted to maintain the Garrison image. As she wrote to her mother in 1874 after reading an article about Lloyd's antislavery work, "I felt my heart swell with pride, because I belong to him & he to me, although to equal him in devotion to principle is the only true way in which to prove our relationship & show myself worthy of it. So must I tell you, in strict confidence, dear Ma: my ardor is great, let the results be what they will."[63] Indeed, all the Garrison children entered adulthood feeling that there were certain expectations from their parents and the surrounding community about how they were to behave. As Willie wrote to his brother Wendy in 1858, when Wendy asked for a loan of $25:

> Never hesitate to let me know, when you think I can be of service to any of you. I should think very little of myself, indeed, if I did not contribute all in my power to aid those who have spent so much time and money in helping me. All the money I shall make for the next twenty years, should I live so long, would but poorly repay our good Father for his great example alone, that he has set us. We should be degenerate sons of a worthy sire, did we not do everything possible towards sustaining the good character of the name which he has transmitted for our safe keeping. Although unable, as we may be, to make ourselves the great benefactors of a fallen race as he has done, we can at least preserve the name that we inherit, from blight or tarnish, by living if not great lives, at least true ones. How much greater heritage does he leave to us than did John Jacob Astor to his son! How much richer shall we be with the legacy of his good name, than Wm. B. Astor of New York with his three millions in gold. I almost rejoice at the poverty of Father, since it gives me an opportunity to show him that I can appreciate his kindness to us, by extending what little aid I possess.[64]

At times, being raised largely within the abolitionist community gave rise to frustrations, the boundaries between family and community members sometimes seeming confining and unpleasant. When young, the children followed their parents' example blindly, basking in the attention paid to them and to themselves.

As they matured, however, each had to find his or her own way in the world, even if it meant questioning their much-loved and admired parents' lessons and authority. Perhaps, it even meant having to leave home, the city of Boston, the state of Massachusetts, and the United States. As usual, George led the way, this time trying to exert his independence despite his family's resistance to his actions.

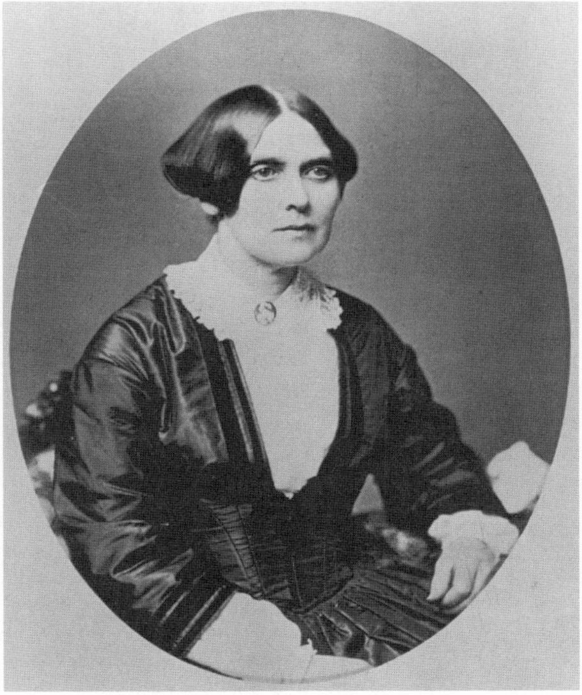

(top) Fanny Lloyd Garrison's embroidery, January 1810. By permission of the Houghton Library, Harvard University.

(bottom) Helen Eliza Benson Garrison, n.d. Photograph by Warren's Portraits. Sophia Smith Collection, Smith College.

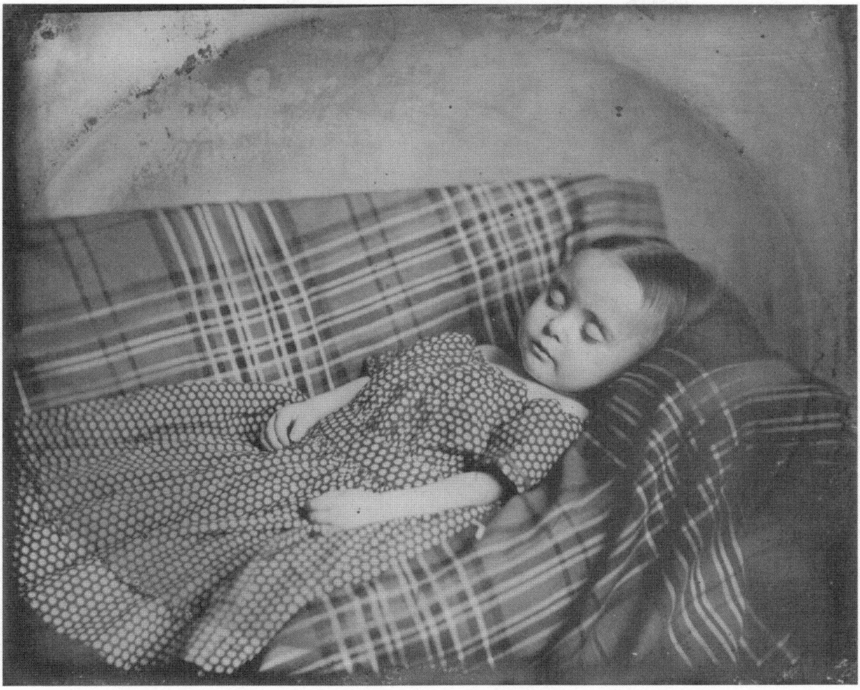

(top left) A rear view of the Garrisons' home on Dix Place, n.d. Sophia Smith Collection, Smith College.

(bottom left) Francis Jackson Garrison, March 31, 1860, age 11 years, 5 months, 2 days. Sophia Smith Collection, Smith College.

(above) Little Elizabeth Pease Garrison (Lizzy) soon after her death on April 20, 1848. Courtesy of the estate of David Lloyd Garrison.

(top left) William Lloyd Garrison Jr., April 1, 1863. Sophia Smith Collection, Smith College.

(top right) Wendell Phillips Garrison, June 1861. Photograph by C. Seaver Jr. Sophia Smith Collection, Smith College.

(bottom left) George Thompson Garrison, n.d. Photograph by C. Seaver Jr. Sophia Smith Collection, Smith College.

(above) William Lloyd Garrison with daughter Fanny, n.d. Sophia Smith Collection, Smith College.

(above) Ellen Wright with her brothers, William and Frank, 1857. Sophia Smith Collection, Smith College.

(top right) Lucy McKim, June 27, 1864. Photograph by C. H. Spielers. Sophia Smith Collection, Smith College.

(bottom right) Rockledge, August 1876. William Lloyd Garrison is at far right with Lloyd J. Garrison and the Villard family. Sophia Smith Collection, Smith College.

(top left) Henry Villard, November 1889. Photograph by Sarony. Sophia Smith Collection, Smith College.

(bottom left) Ellen, Agnes, and William Lloyd Garrison Jr., n.d. Courtesy of Daphne Harwood.

(above) Fanny Garrison Villard at Thorwood, n.d. Courtesy of the late Henry Serrano Villard.

(above) Women's Peace Society members with Fanny Garrison Villard on the far right and her car at Thorwood, n.d. By permission of the Swarthmore College Peace Collection.

(top right) The Second Generation, November 25, 1886. *From the left, standing:* George Thompson Garrison, Wendell Phillips Garrison, William Lloyd Garrison Jr.; *sitting:* Annie Anthony Garrison, Fanny Garrison Villard, Ellen Wright Garrison, Sarah Speakman McKim, and Francis Jackson Garrison. Courtesy of Daphne Harwood.

(bottom right) The Third Generation, November 25, 1886. *From the left, standing:* Charles Garrison (William's son), Harold Garrison Villard (Fanny's son), Lloyd McKim Garrison (Wendell's son), Philip McKim Garrison (Wendell's son), Oswald Garrison Villard (Fanny's son), Frank Wright Garrison (William's son); *sitting:* Rhodes Anthony Garrison (George's son), Fanny Garrison (George's daughter), Elizabeth Garrison (George's daughter), Fanny Garrison Villard holding son Henry Hilgard, Agnes Garrison (William's daughter), Eleanor Garrison (William's daughter), Helen Elise Villard (Fanny's daughter), William Lloyd Garrison III (William's son), and Katherine McKim Garrison (Wendell's daughter). Courtesy of Daphne Harwood.

THE GARRISONS AND THE CIVIL WAR

GEORGE'S SEARCH

I am young now, and now is my time to see the world, and to learn to place reliance on myself.

George Thompson Garrison, 1858

CHAPTER VI

When George Garrison reached the age of twenty-one, he felt a great need to separate himself from his parents' direct influence and find his own way in life. He saw this as a move to achieve financial success, but in the end, it became a far deeper quest to understand his own definition of abolitionism and position on nonresistance. As a child, George was seen as different from his siblings—less bright, less motivated, harder to discipline. Although in December 1837, when he was ten months old, Lloyd identified his son, "with his plump and rosy cheeks and sturdy frame, and boyish glee," as "a prodigy—of course," very soon after Willie was born, his feelings changed.[1] "I think," he wrote his mother-in-law, Sally, "George Thompson beautiful as he was as an infant, was not so fair and bright looking as is his brother."[2] George's early streak of stubbornness, his "tremendous will of his own," and his "very passionate" nature became his identifying traits.[3] His "paroxysms of disobedience" made Lloyd humorously exclaim that his son was "even more obstinate than his father." In a way, he admired George's behavior, seeing him as "a chip of [*sic*] the old block, and something more."[4] To spark his curiosity and head him in a scholarly direction, he and Helen sent George to Northampton, but even after this effort, Lloyd still thought of George as intellectually "dull" and physically "restless."[5] In spite of his family's belief that he was the least talented of the brood, George was always loved and encouraged to develop his own interests. Yet, he was treated as if he were somehow more fragile or vulnerable to life's blows than they were. George, in turn, constantly attempted to express his individuality and independence, especially as he approached his adult years.

After George left Hopedale in 1852, he had a series of apprenticeships intended to prepare him for a career as a clerk, an accountant, or a printer. None of these experiences turned out very well, however. For the two years that he worked as a clerk for Aaron F. Clark, lawyer and selectman of the town of Danvers, George was conscientious but not content, especially since his parents had pressured him to accept the appointment in spite of his desire to live at home. Although Helen and Lloyd each communicated to their sixteen-year-old son their longing to have him with them, they also tried to convince him that he would enjoy his stay in Danvers once he became better acquainted with the community. George must have found their messages somewhat contradictory, his father telling him, "Something of homesickness you will naturally feel, for the present. . . . Occasionally, you can come up to the city, and see us, and some of us will reciprocate the visit from time to time," while Helen wrote, "I think of you hourly. . . . I miss you very much."[6] Both agreed, however, that George must learn a skill for his future independence and insisted that he remain with Clark.

In the end, Lloyd must have identified with George's homesickness, for he had suffered similarly as a youth. Hence, it is not surprising that by early 1854 George was back in Boston, where he worked for eight months in G. P. Reed's music store as assistant bookkeeper. However, as Lloyd told his and Helen's friend Thomas Davis, a jewelry manufacturer in Providence, George was "not sufficiently quick at figures, or in the use of his pen," and was, therefore, dismissed. At eighteen and a half, Lloyd informed Davis, George was "'slow, but sure,' and at all times reliable."[7] Would Davis possibly have a place for him? He did not. Meanwhile, George set to work at the *Liberator* assisting the printer, James Yerrinton, a position he liked well enough except for being in extremely close proximity to his father and in a situation with low pay. Hence, in June 1855, Lloyd again tried to find George a post away from home, this time with Dr. Henry Orne Stone, a physician and farmer in Framingham, Massachusetts, but had no success. Throughout 1855, 1856, and into 1857, George worked at the *Liberator,* all the while trying to figure out what he really wanted to accomplish in life. At the same time, he was exposed to the very important changes taking place within the antislavery community, changes that would eventually affect his own choices.

George's coming-of-age years between 1850 and 1861, when he evolved from a fourteen-year-old youngster into a twenty-five-year-old man, were dramatic years in the struggle with slavery.[8] The issues that united or divided the abolitionists also came to unite or divide the Garrison family. George, in particular, began to move away from his family's nonresistant philosophy toward embracing the idea that if violence was needed to free the slaves, he could not only sanction it but also participate in it. By 1850, George was very much aware that much of the debate within the U.S. Congress centered around slavery. Where would it be allowed? Where would it not? What protections did slaveholders have in regard to ensuring that trips to the North would not result in their loss of slave property? Why did slaves remain slaves once their owners took them into free territories? Although the issue of the morality of slavery was constantly bandied about, both for government leaders and private citizens, the logistics and legal maneuverings between the slave and free states caused even greater tensions. For abolitionists, the actions taken in Congress seemed to increasingly favor the "Slave Power." As new land was added to the nation, it became apparent that slaveholders intended to exert control over the territories and force the expansion of slavery from the South into the West. When the United States entered its territorial war with Mexico in 1846, abolitionists understood this as a Southern move to gain new land. So during the war the Pennsylvania Democrat David Wilmot put forward a proviso to a military appropriations bill in Congress stating that "neither slavery nor involuntary servitude" should ever exist in any territory won from Mexico. Although the proviso did not become law, it created a new wrinkle in the slavery debate, as Southern slaveholders claimed that it was not the federal government's place to determine whether a new territory would be slave or free, as it did in 1787 in the Northwest Territory and in the Missouri Compromise of 1820, but rather, the decision should rightly be left to the settlers themselves.

From 1846 to the Emancipation Proclamation of 1863, the issue of slavery remained in the forefront of political debate. First, it affected the 1848 presidential election, when proslavery Zachary Taylor took office.[9] Next, the territory of California petitioned to enter the Union as a free state, a request that threatened to upset the delicate balance of power in the Senate. The result was the Compromise of 1850, legislation stipulating that California enter as a free state and clearly defining the boundaries of the slave state of Texas to include parts of the former Mexican lands. The territories of Utah and New Mexico, including what is now Arizona, on the other hand, were given the right to determine their own laws as long as they abided by the U.S. Constitution. Heated debate continued over whether this meant that settlers had the right to ban slavery or not. Moreover, although the Compromise of 1850 stipulated that the slave trade in the nation's capital be suppressed, it also strengthened the Fugitive Slave Law so that any slave owners who stated that one of their slaves had escaped could go into a court in their own state to file a claim. The court's transcript and a description of the runaway became legal proof of the fugitive's status. With these documents, the owners or their designated representatives had the right to travel through the North, capture the fugitive or even a free person who resembled him or her, and present their case before a federal judge or a court-appointed federal commissioner in the free state's court. Judges were forced to issue the decision that the fugitive be returned to slavery, since rarely did African Americans have the documents or opportunity to defend themselves. This was devastating news for antislavery activists and sympathizers and led to assertive, sometimes violent, action on the part of those people determined to defy the act. Indeed, it provided the motivation for Harriet Beecher Stowe's authoring *Uncle Tom's Cabin.*

At the impressionable age of fourteen, George witnessed the reaction of his father's band of abolitionists to the reinvigorated Fugitive Slave Law. Lloyd held firm in his conviction that slavery was a moral outrage. "EVERY SLAVEHOLDER IS A MANSTEALER," he reiterated to Samuel J. May, "There must be no union with slaveholders, religiously or politically. . . . The time has come to preach disunion on the highest moral and religious grounds."[10] For Lloyd, a dissolution of the Union, leaving the South to struggle economically on its own and, he believed, fail, was the answer. Still, he continued to speak against a violent solution to the slavery issue, and although he considered the Fugitive Slave Law a despicable piece of legislation and assailed it in the pages of the *Liberator,* he himself did not take part in any of the physical attempts to free African Americans brought to trial by slave owners hoping to have them returned to the South. Other Garrisonians, however, took concrete and sometimes dangerous actions in order to prevent Northern courts from re-enslaving people.[11] Members from both the white and African-American communities established vigilance committees; the one in Boston included Robert Morris Jr. and Lewis Hayden (members of the black community), and Theodore Parker, Thomas Wentworth Higginson, and Wendell Phillips (members of the white community).[12] Their involvement in blocking the exportation of free people into slavery consisted of representing cases in court as well as organizing and participating in rescues.

During his years at Hopedale and in Danvers, George read of the successful attempt in Boston to free Shadrach, a former slave, and the failure to do so for Thomas Sims, who was forcibly returned to Georgia.[13] But the fugitive case that might have had the greatest impact on him was that of Anthony Burns, who was taken into custody on May 24, 1854, when George, then eighteen, was working in G. P. Reed's music store. While George was struggling to keep a job he neither liked nor was good at, Anthony Burns, who was employed as a presser in a tailor shop, was arrested by a U.S. deputy marshal with six assistants. Burns's attorneys requested and received a five-day postponement of the trial, which gave a group of rescuers enough time to make plans. Several meetings led by Lewis Hayden and Thomas Wentworth Higginson and other members of the Boston Vigilance Committee took place in the *Liberator* office. There, George witnessed the making of secret, violent plans that Lloyd pretended to ignore.

First, the committee attempted to remove Burns by force from the prison where he was held. Fifty guards prevented the rescue but not before one of them, James

Batchelder, was killed. Next, Leonard Grimes, pastor of the Twelfth Baptist Church, arranged to purchase Burns's freedom with money he had raised after a frantic effort, but Burns's owner, John Suttle, reneged on his agreement to accept the payment. In spite of legal maneuverings and efforts to raise more money for another possible purchase, the abolitionists could not rescue Burns. On June 2, while Willie watched with shock and dismay from the second floor of a warehouse on the wharf, Burns was escorted by the U.S. marshal, militia corps, and the military to a ship that would take him back to Virginia. A month later, at the annual antislavery Fourth of July picnic in Framingham, Lloyd burned copies of the Fugitive Slave Law and the U.S. Constitution, symbols of the continued oppression of U.S. blacks. The next year, Grimes finally succeeded in purchasing Burns's freedom, the freed man then returning to Boston. The Fugitive Slave Law, however, remained in effect.

George was very impressed by the assertive action of the Boston Vigilance Committee, especially since he had known most of its members his entire life. If any of the men served as a role model, it was probably Thomas Wentworth Higginson, a man Lloyd respected but also disapproved of.[14] Born in 1823, Higginson was a Unitarian minister who had received a degree from Harvard College in 1841 and from the Harvard Divinity School in 1847. From 1847 to 1850 he served as pastor of the First Congregational Church in Newburyport, Lloyd's dear hometown. Higginson's interest in transcendentalism, literature, free thought, and especially abolitionism led to his dismissal and his subsequent appointment to the more liberal Free Church in Worcester, where he stayed from 1852 to 1858 before leaving the ministry altogether. In 1851 Higginson joined the Boston Vigilance Committee, and once in Worcester he became involved with the Underground Railroad. In 1854 he was indicted along with Theodore Parker, Wendell Phillips, and others for his participation in the attempted rescue of Anthony Burns and the murder of James Batchelder. Fortunately for them all, the case never came to trial. Higginson was neither frightened nor discouraged by his close call with the law. In 1858 he became one of the "Secret Six" who supplied the militant John Brown with weapons to attack Harpers Ferry, Virginia. Four years later, in 1862, he accepted an appointment as colonel of the first black regiment formed to fight for the North in the Civil War, the First South Carolina Volunteers, created from the ranks of freed slaves.

Higginson's militant position on abolitionism was fueled not only by the Fugitive Slave Law but also by the passage in 1854 of the Kansas-Nebraska Act, a piece of legislation that many historians feel led directly to the Civil War. When it was passed, the territories of Kansas and Nebraska encompassed land including the present states of Kansas, Nebraska, Montana, Wyoming, and parts of Colorado. The act legalized the concept of popular sovereignty for the two territories, leaving the issue of slavery up to the people who resided there. But the act aroused controversy because the new territories included lands that both the Louisiana Purchase and the Missouri Compromise of 1820 stipulated as forbidding slavery. If the people who settled them had the right to supersede these agreements and choose in favor of slavery, the balance of power between slave and nonslave territory would tip considerably in favor of the South. Furthermore, slavery would extend north to the Canadian border; and the Northern free states, with slave states both to the south and west, would be cut off from the still free California, Oregon, and Washington. The Kansas-Nebraska Act not only outraged abolitionists, but it frightened the Northern states as a whole. What would this mean for their future liberties? What would it mean in terms of industrial and commercial growth? Would the South be in control of every piece of legislation that might pass through the houses of Congress? In the North, some states took immediate action to show their disapproval of this tremendous potential growth of Slave Power, the most obvious target being the Fugitive Slave Law. Between 1855 and 1859, Connecticut, Rhode Island, Massachusetts, Michigan, Maine, Ohio, and Wisconsin all passed legislation meant to curb the laws by requiring that fugitives be given trials with juries and be mandatorily provided with legal help.

Another path Northerners took to oppose the expansion of slavery and ensure that the Kansas-Nebraska territories eventually entered the Union as free states was to settle the area themselves.[15] Hence, in April, a month after the bill was passed, the Massachusetts legislature sanctioned the creation of the Massachusetts Emigrant Aid Company, whose purpose was to "assist emigrants to settle the West." The state authorized the company to issue capital stock to sell to all those interested in investing in the new project. The New England Emigrant Aid Company (or Society), as it soon became, claimed to have no specific ideological position, but in fact most of its stockholders and clients chose to move to Kansas for both political and economic reasons. Their main goal, however, was to establish an antislavery climate in the territory so that when the time came for statehood, slavery sympathizers would either be outnumbered or have left the area entirely. Thomas Wentworth Higginson became secretary of the organization, and Massachusetts settlers, including Helen's brother George W. and his family, were among the first to head west. With financial support from industrialists and business leaders, such as John Carter Brown of Providence, Eli Thayer of Worcester, and Amos A. Lawrence of the Lawrence mill town, Kansas settlements blossomed, the most famous being Lawrence, which was founded in September 1854. By 1855 eight thousand people had settled the territory. Lawrence alone claimed a population of about four hundred, one hundred having recently arrived from New England.

In response to the Northerners' move into Kansas, numbers of proslavery settlers came in from Missouri, Kentucky, Tennessee, and in lesser numbers from Virginia and states in the Deep South. Immediately, proslavery and antislavery settlers in Kansas came into conflict, slavery sympathizers harassing and assailing their new neighbors.[16] Some tried to stake claim to land that antislavery settlers had already held but temporarily abandoned when they visited larger towns or traveled to other areas. Others formed threatening gangs who crossed the border to try to frighten abolitionists into leaving. In turn, antislavery settlers often criticized families with slaves and actively confronted Missourians who seemed to signal trouble. The hostility was exacerbated whenever an election was held. In the fall of 1854, for example, a number of armed Missourians entered Kansas to illegally vote in territorial elections while using force to keep bona fide settlers from the polls. As a result, a proslavery delegate was sent to sit in Congress in Washington. The next spring, the same tactic was used to elect an entire proslavery territorial legislature, which the settlers termed the "Bogus Legislature" and which passed a number of acts making antislavery activities punishable by long prison terms or even execution. In response, the settlers, or "free-staters," organized militias and their own separate government, which they claimed to be the only legal voice for the territory.

George was quite interested in what was taking place in "Bleeding Kansas." To the militant actions in Boston against the Fugitive Slave Law was now added a new and more aggressive form of abolitionism. The situation became even more explosive after John Brown arrived on the Kansas scene on October 7, 1855, to join his five sons who had settled in Osawatomie. Brown, originally from Torrington, Connecticut, was a dramatic figure. As a farmer, tanner, land speculator, and wool broker, he had met with only failure, his frustration with his life complicated by two marriages (his first wife having died) and seventeen children (ten who survived childhood), numerous lawsuits, and accusations of dishonesty in his business dealings. A very religious man who practiced a strict form of Calvinism, Brown was an adamant abolitionist, but never a nonresister. He believed that violence had its place in the fight against racial injustice, and several abolitionist leaders, including Lloyd and Thomas Wentworth Higginson, had a certain amount of respect and admiration for him, especially since they themselves were not prepared to take the self-sacrificing steps that Brown was. Higginson, but not Lloyd, however, saw to it that this man of little means was appropriately armed to do battle with the proslavery element.

Soon after his arrival in the territory, John Brown and his sons became part of the southeast Kansas militia company dedicated to the defense of the free-staters against the Missouri ruffians, Brown himself being named captain of his group. In this role, he grew increasingly frustrated because no assailants, even those who could be easily identified, had been indicted by proslavery grand juries, and territorial town governments began enforcing the laws of the Bogus Legislature, arresting abolitionists but not their proslavery attackers. On May 21, the day before Senator Charles Sumner of Massachusetts completed his fiery two-day antislavery speech "The Crime against Kansas" before Congress, and was subsequently caned into unconsciousness by Representative Preston Brooks of South Carolina, violence broke out in Lawrence. Free-state townspeople were arrested, the town's two newspaper offices were destroyed, the hotel was hit with cannon fire and then burned, shops were looted, and houses demolished. This "sacking" of Lawrence enraged John Brown, who took his revenge by leading a gang of men in the brutal killing of five proslavery settlers, two of them boys in their teens. Border Missourians, not taking kindly to the attack, pursued the group, capturing two of Brown's sons and turning them over to the U.S. Army troops sent to Kansas to help stave off the violence. The next morning, these same men were themselves attacked by Brown and his militia of twenty-eight men. Violence led to more violence, so that for the next four months, an all-out war between free-staters and proslavers existed in Kansas. During the war, the New England Emigrant Aid Society helped their settlers by sending clothing and relief workers; some backers also saw to it that the settlers were armed.

Newspapers and periodicals throughout the country covered the tales coming out of Bleeding Kansas, so that George, hard at work in the *Liberator* office, had plenty of material to read and think about. Having been raised a Garrison, he could sympathize with someone like John Brown, but he was not supposed to emulate him. Yet George found this type of abolitionism intriguing. At twenty-one, however, he was more in the mood for an adventure that might prove lucrative but not life threatening. He yearned to strike out on his own and discover what the West had to offer. He also wished to test his own mettle away from his family, who had come to seem overprotective. Unwilling to act too drastically, he made his initial move not to the violent territory of Kansas but to the developing territory of Minnesota, which in the 1850s had launched a campaign for settlement based upon an idealized vision of a bucolic, potentially affluent future state with good weather, fertile land, excellent river and railroad transportation, and innumerable business opportunities.[17] At the same time, he kept abreast of the situation in Kansas.

Among the most prominent of the Minnesota dreamers and developers was Ignatius Donnelly, a twenty-five-year-old Philadelphia attorney who wished to create a city to equal New York. It was he who led the effort to found the "city" of Nininger on the south bank of the Mississippi River about twenty-five miles below St. Paul. Donnelly's partner, John Nininger, also from Philadelphia but in 1856 a St. Paul businessman with an interest in land speculation, laid out the plan for the new town. After dividing the townsite into 3,800 lots, advertisements boasting the potential for great financial gain were circulated around the Northeast and mass meetings held for prospective investors. The planners promised the imminent building of a great hotel, a free ferryboat to take people across the Mississippi River, a library, and, within a short period of time, a railroad. John Nininger, who established a program for selling the lots through subscriptions, never actually lived in the city named after him, but he became rich off the profits of the land sales. Lots which initially required a mere six-dollar investment were sold for

$100 in December 1856. Soon after, some of these same lots were resold to nonsubscribers for as much as $200 or $250 each. Nininger seemed ripe to join the ranks of the "Frontier Mushroom Cities."

One of the first Massachusetts families to relocate to Nininger was that of Anthony Reed, whose son, William Bayliss Reed, had coedited *The Diamond* with George. William, two years older than George, had accompanied his parents to Nininger, where he and his father established a blind and sash business. When George decided that he wished to strike out on his own, this family connection offered him the vehicle he needed, and although Helen and Lloyd dreaded his leaving, they did not prevent it. Indeed, none of his siblings wanted him to go so far from home. As Willie wrote to Wendell, "So, Brother George has gone! You don't know how sorry I felt not to be at home and see him start. . . . and so to console myself for it, I sat down last Sunday afternoon and wrote a long letter to Wm. Reed asking him to have a brotherly care of George, and giving him, our ideas concerning G's future welfare."[18] All worried that George, the child who appeared to have the least potential for success in the world, would not be able to manage without their constant guidance.

George, however, basked in the glory of his adventure. On Tuesday morning, April 28, 1857, he left Boston with a train ticket through to Dunleith, Illinois, the twenty-nine-dollar fare paid by his father. After traveling by rail through Massachusetts and arriving in Albany the same evening, he transferred to the night train for Buffalo and Suspension Bridge. Each of the nearly thirty railway cars was full of people heading west, but after his seatmate exited at Syracuse, George was able to spread out for a two-hour nap. From Suspension Bridge, the train wound its way through part of Canada, a trip George found "long and tedious, being through a wilderness pretty much, and the train only stopping once in a while at a town containing three or four log houses."[19] Once through Canada, the train stopped in Detroit and Battle Creek, Michigan, where George stayed for five days with the family of Joseph and Phebe Hart Merritt, a Quaker abolitionist couple who had hosted his father four years earlier. A week after he had left Boston, George boarded the train at Battle Creek and within a few hours reached the great city of Chicago. There the young traveler decided to take advantage of his eight-hour layover to explore, but he found Chicago "rather too flat and muddy to suit" him and was not unhappy to reboard the train at eight o'clock on his way to Dunleith, which he reached the next morning. He immediately boarded the steamboat *City Belle,* and after a journey of two days and two nights, he reached Nininger—in all an eleven-day journey and his first long trip totally on his own. Upon landing, George saw two high bluffs on either side of the river, which presented "quite an imposing appearance."[20] He reported to his worried mother that he was "in first rate health and spirits," his only complaint being that the Mississippi River water had a bad taste. William Reed had met him at the landing and taken him in as a roommate. George found his situation most pleasant, Nininger being "a very pretty place" in a most enjoyable location.[21]

One of George's main reasons for going out west was to prove himself successful at making money. Therefore, he was very attracted to the land speculation opportunities touted in the Nininger advertisements. But he also needed to work. By May 11 he was employed at Anthony Reed's sash and blind factory, which his son William managed. George's salary amounted to seventy-five cents a day, and as he told Helen, he liked it "better than anything" he had ever tried "except printing."[22] Being a trained and competent printer, George had at first thought he could work for the *Emigrant Aid Journal,* a newspaper that had been started by Ignatius Donnelly and Philip Rohr on December 1, 1856, as part of the campaign to attract settlers to the area. After the first issue, however, the paper stopped publishing until June 20, 1857, when it started up again under the direction of A. W. MacDonald, previously of the *Scientific American,* published in New York. George's hopes for a job were soon dashed when he learned that MacDonald had already hired two other men to help him with production. As he told his brother, Willie, "I am rather glad that it happened so on the whole, as it has given me a chance to go right into the business I am in and I don't want to be a printer all my days."[23] George had not found any land he felt worth investing in, so he lent William Reed $85, charging him a rate of three per cent interest a month.

From the first moment he arrived in Nininger, George was bombarded by letters from his family, so many in fact that within two months of his leaving home, he felt compelled to write an uncharacteristically severe note telling the Garrison clan not to write to him *"oftener than once in two or three months"* and not to expect an answer, as he had always hated writing and had no intention of *"keeping up a regular correspondence."*[24] To their obvious complaints that he was not responding to their mail quickly enough, he answered that the post office was slow and that he had, indeed, answered every letter they had written. He constantly reassured them that he was happy in his new location, although he desired to leave the blind and sash factory, which bored him, to return to printing. To his father, who seemed concerned about his eldest son's ability to keep a job, George responded, "I have lost but two days work at the Sash Factory since I commenced working there; one was the fourth of July, and the other was the thirty-first of July, when I paid my road tax by working on a new road."[25]

By early August, George was able to move to the printing office of the *Emigrant Aid Journal* after the two other workers had left on the grounds that they were not being paid on time, an inauspicious sign that he chose to ignore. To his mother, who fretted that the work might prove too difficult for him, he responded that it was not. "I have nothing to do but what I am able to do," he answered her. To her inquiry as to whether he was ready to return home or not, he informed her that he had decided to remain through the winter and "had not the *slightest idea* of returning home." He closed his letter with an emphatic *"Love to all,"* lest she feel that he did not care for her.[26] George also enjoyed boarding with the MacDonalds, who had two children, a boy aged seventeen, and a six-month-old infant. His bed was in the printing office, just as his father's had been when he started the *Liberator* with Isaac Knapp, a comparison that did not escape Lloyd's notice. Shortly after George started working for the *Emigrant Aid Journal,* its founder, Ignatius Donnelly, paid him a visit. Coming forward to shake hands, Donnelly expressed his great pleasure in meeting him. "Mr. Garrison," he said, "I understand you are a son of William Lloyd Garrison, a gentleman whom I respect very much. Is that so?"[27] The incident reminded George of the pride he felt in his unique heritage. Sometimes, in fact, he even admitted to missing his family, especially at Thanksgiving and Christmas. William Reed, too, missed New England and tried, as did others, to equate Nininger with his previous home. As the *Emigrant Aid Journal* reported, Reed offered a New England toast to the territory and the town: "Minnesota—The New England of the West; Nininger—its Boston: may they ever rival their mother land in all her works of peace and good will unto men."[28]

For slightly over a year, George worked at the newspaper office. At first, the issues were produced every other week, but by mid-January 1858 the newspaper had become a weekly. Articles in the *Emigrant Aid Journal* give a good picture of frontier Nininger, with its open spaces, building explosion, and rutted paths being turned into dirt roads. It was a small community where people were concerned with each other's business, and where young and old alike hoped to invest money and reap big returns. Nininger, however, was a far cry from Boston with its big-city politics. Headlines in the *Emigrant Aid Journal* reported on the meetings of the town council rather than on the doings in eastern cities such as Washington, New York, and Boston. When George started working at the paper, many people wanted to read about the proposed constitution for the future state of Minnesota, which needed the ratification of the residents of the territory before its submission to the U.S. Congress. Equally important, however, were the weekly baseball games played by one of the first teams organized in the country, or the "hog nuisance" caused by "two or three gangs of hogs that regularly perambulate the town, calling at almost every house."[29]

Several articles described the lives of the Winnebago Indians in what appeared to be an attempt at peaceful coexistence, especially after the natives were relegated to reservations. The U.S. cavalry patrolled the border areas where the less-pacified Sioux presented some problems for the white settlers. The articles, however, were often racist, echoing much of the sentiment in nineteenth-century writings, which referred to Native Americans as childlike and animalistic, and greatly in need of the U.S. government's supervision. One article described the original residents of Minnesota as "immature," with "a childish mentality with the fully developed animal nature of man." The "whites" were the "superior race." As the author expressed it, the Native Americans "earn and practice all his [white man's] vices, but do not follow any of his good examples."[30]

African Americans, who made up less than 1 percent of the territory's population, also received some attention. Articles reprinted from eastern papers often reported on antislavery activity. Although no bylines appeared in the newspaper, making it impossible to know if George did any actual writing, these references to abolitionist work may have been obtained through his contacts back home. Unfortunately, the *Emigrant Aid Journal* was not being published when the Supreme Court made its decision in the Dred Scott case, an affair that must have interested George greatly. In 1851 Scott, a Missouri slave, had sued his owner for his freedom, claiming that since he had been taken to the free state of Illinois to live for several years and then into the Wisconsin territory where slavery was barred by the Missouri Compromise, he should be free. At first, the court decided in Scott's favor, but as the case went through various appeals, courts ruled against him. Finally, the case came before the Supreme Court, where, in March 1857, Chief Justice Roger B. Taney presented the majority decision. Scott, and all those still enslaved, were not citizens, the court declared, so residence in a free state did not make them free. The court also ruled that Congress had no authority to bar slavery from a territory. The Dred Scott decision added great fuel to the national slavery debate, remaining newsworthy for quite some time. Although never mentioned in the local paper, the issue may have arisen at the Nininger Lyceum, where George went weekly for debate and discussion. As the newspaper reported, topics at Lyceum meetings included "Should the Fugitive Slave be respected and obeyed?" and "Has the Negro suffered more injustice from the White man than the Indians?"

Whereas George found the meetings of great interest, he had no desire to participate as a debater, largely because he lacked the self-confidence to express his ideas before an audience. "Because a fellow is in a printing office," he wrote to Willie, "they seem to expect something of him here. I am not afraid to use my voice like some speakers, but the trouble with me is that I have not got the ideas, and I have no intention to make a fool of myself." Furthermore, in order to be successful in a debate, George would have had to study, and, as he wrote, "Now if there is any thing in this world that I hate it is studying. I dislike it as much now as I ever did when I went to school." Although as an adult, he understood its value, his feelings had not changed. "I will not study now any more than I would then," he added defiantly. "I know that I have got to suffer for it, but I can't help it, its in me, and always has been, and I have no desire, no wish to get it out of me."[31] Although unwilling to debate, George was desirous of expressing his opinions in less individualistic ways. In March 1858, for instance, his name appeared on a petition submitted to the town council to "restrict the sale of ardent spirits as far as practicable, and exclude it entirely from the hands of irresponsible parties."[32] Touting his family's temperance line and obviously disturbed by the alcohol abuse in this frontier town, George and others succeeded in obtaining an ordinance to license and regulate taverns, a far cry from what he might have wished for. He also lent his name to an open letter extolling the virtues of Nininger for prospective emigrants and listing Nininger's many fine qualities, including its new levee, plentiful firewood, great beauty, new hotels, mills, stores, a public hall, and its "energetic and intelligent population."[33]

Perhaps surprising is the fact that George was very sociable; although the most retiring of the Garrison children, he was far from being a recluse. In spite of Nininger's propaganda claiming Minnesota's fine weather, winters were extremely cold and snowy, and, being a frontier town, it offered far fewer options for entertainment than Boston. Yet it was in this inhospitable climate that George discovered the great pleasure of social dancing, especially after attending a New Year's Eve ball in 1857. More than eighty couples had bought the three-dollar tickets to the event, which included supper at the Handyside House followed by a carriage ride to Tremont Hall for dancing. But because of a blizzard only forty couples actually made it to the celebration. There, George danced every cotillion, although he lamented to his mother that the Nininger women were not very beautiful and did not dress in the latest fashions. The prettiest female present was a recent emigrant from Fitchburg, in his own home state. In spite of his complaints, the young man danced through the night, not arriving home until five o'clock the next morning.

After the ball, George decided to take dance lessons. "I intend to learn how to dance," he told his mother, "as it is all the rage here as well as at the East."[34] His mother, however, feared that if her son spent too much time dancing, he would not pay attention to developing his mind. In his usual fashion, he responded defensively that Nininger did not offer any place other than the Lyceum for "cultivation of the mind." The only place to read was a noisy bar downstairs in his boarding house, where the single candle sat on a table where three or four men constantly played cards. Reading in the printing office was impossible, as the small amount of precious fuel had to be reserved for the business. The sitting room in the Reeds' home was filled with "constant talking," and whenever Anthony Reed saw George he expected "to have five or six games of checkers." Hence, the only reading George was able to fit in were bits of "telegraphic news" which came into the office from the *New York Tribune*.[35] He reassured his mother that he was not idle, for on Monday nights he attended the Lyceum; on Tuesdays, Fridays, and Saturdays he read the latest news from the East or went to the Reeds' to play checkers; Wednesdays found him at the newspaper office producing the final copy of the paper, and Thursdays were reserved for dancing until midnight. He did not describe his Sundays, but it is likely that he sometimes joined friends at church and often for dinner.

That year the nation's economy took a dramatic downturn, and the ensuing Panic of 1857 had an impact on all areas of the country. Back home in Massachusetts, Willie counted his blessings that he had left James Buffum's shoe business for his position at the Laighton Bank, for had he not done so, he would have found himself in Boston without a job, a "burden" to his father instead of the help he turned out to be throughout 1857 and 1858.[36] In Minnesota, George also felt the pinch. On January 17, he had to leave the MacDonalds' home for a boarding house, as they could no longer afford to provide for him. In addition, MacDonald fell behind in George's salary, forcing him to take in a roommate, David Phillips, a twenty-seven-year-old former ship's cook. Together, they managed to live on $1.50 a week, sharing cooking and housekeeping, reading and writing together, and enjoying music, Phillips playing the violin while George sang along. The two men became such close friends that George came to jokingly refer to Phillips as "my wife."[37] As the financial times grew more difficult, however, George's situation sparked off another round of debate with his family. MacDonald came to owe George so much money that in May he gave his young employee two lots of land in lieu of $100 worth of income. Even though George was happy with the deal, for the land was in a good part of town, in reality it was worthless. Ignatius Donnelly's dream of developing a great city in Minnesota was quickly disappearing. Emigrants had stopped arriving in large numbers, and plots of land, if sold, brought in quite a bit less than when they were bought. Within a short period, MacDonald was forced to shut down the paper, an action George thought was temporary, but which turned out to be more or less permanent, the paper henceforth having a sporadic production.

Both Helen and Lloyd pressured their son to come home. They were angry that MacDonald had stopped paying George and worried that he would become hungry and homeless. Helen, however, also had another agenda. Lloyd had not been feeling very well, and James Yerrinton, only a fair proofreader, was not sufficient help. George's return could mean relief for her tired and aging husband. Lloyd, too, tried to lure his son back to the *Liberator.* "Whether you would like your old place in the Liberator office, I do not know;" he stated on New Year's Day, 1858, "but I will keep it in reserve for you, whenever you choose to return, and ultimately (when I can see the way clear) I should like to make you the printer and publisher . . . and assist you to getting all the necessary printing materials."[38] George bristled at his parents' constant pleas and responded with some anger. "You are very anxious that I should return home," he wrote, "though what great benefit it is going to be to me I can't see. I don't want to go into the *Liberator* office again if I can possibly help it and you know if I go back I shall in all probability have to go into it again. To go back and go to work in that office would settle my fate. I would have to stick to the paper as long as it lives, and would never find a chance to better my condition." If he remained in Nininger, however, he felt that he might still be able to earn some money, especially in the spring when westward migration was always at its highest. Then, he thought, business would pick up and property values double. Writing this in March, George was confident that the circulation of the *Emigrant Aid Journal* would increase and MacDonald pay him. "According to your own statement," he added, "there is a very poor chance for young men to get any employment East. . . . You want me to come back, do you? I guess I won't hurry about it yet awhile."[39]

By September, MacDonald had left Nininger to work for nearby Hasting's *Ledger*. He was in debt to George for $120, which the young Garrison was forced to take as land lots, a choice he now found deplorable. By September 30, George was jobless, lamenting to Willie that he had worked all year and had nothing "to show for it" but "lots" which he "must hold on to because the place" was "not in good financial straits." George, however, would not give in to his family's pleas to return home. "Now I suppose you want to know what I propose to do," he wrote Willie. "Have I not decided to come home? Am I not foolish in remaining West any longer? Have I not 'had Western experience enough yet?' To all of these questions I have to say no. I have not decided to come home yet. Then what do I intend to do? I will tell you. *I intend to take a boat from here to St Louis, and from there a boat to Kansas!*" Gold had been discovered in Pike's Peak. Would William be willing to send him the $50 he had offered for passage to Boston to enable him to get to Kansas? In return, he would pay his brother 2 percent a month interest and give him all his property in Nininger as security, an investment of over $400. "This Western experience is doing me a world of good, in a good many respects," he wrote, "and I have hardly got enough of it yet. . . . I have made up my mind. I am of age, and I think able to take care of myself."[40]

William was impressed by George's letter. He found it "plucky" and "good." He liked the fact that George had turned down William Reed's offer of free housing and whatever work he could give him, and he decided to share his feelings with his mother and father, who kept insisting that George return home. William convinced his parents that the only right thing to do was to commend George on his "pride" and assertiveness and send him fifty dollars and their "God speed to help him on his new undertaking." George's course was "a wise one," he told his father. "Why, the letter itself is worth fifty dollars, & the experience George is getting money won't compensate for." The adventure would add "new vigor to his character & develop that self reliance & energy that whom none more than your eldest son needs to experience. It's all for the best, Sir."[41] In the characteristic manner of the Garrison family, George's new path was eventually supported, even though his parents continued to feel that he should return home. Furthermore, Lloyd congratulated William on his generosity toward his brother while lamenting that, in general, overspeculation and greed had left the West "dead broke."[42] More to the point, Lloyd worried that George would be harassed or even harmed in Kansas once people discovered who his father was. Nothing could stop George, however, and on October 19, with $50 in his pocket, an amount that would have taken him at least another year to earn, he left for Kansas.[43]

George chose Kansas for three reasons. First, even though the Panic of 1857 was nationwide, the news of the discovery of gold near Pike's Peak had created great excitement and hope. Second, Kansas, with its reputation as an abolitionist battleground, offered a challenge to the young adventurer. For several years, he had followed the explosive events there, but not until he had tested his own survival skills did he seriously consider experiencing the place firsthand. Third, Helen's brother George W. and his family had settled there, offering George a safe and secure home away from home. To reach his destination, George traveled for seven days by steamboat to St. Louis, Missouri; five days also by steamboat to Leavenworth, Kansas; and finally several days by horse and wagon over rain-soaked roads to Lawrence—just over two weeks in all. Once there, he was immediately disappointed by the poor financial situation, which he naively supposed he had left behind. He now saw he would have to ask his brother Willie for another loan of $60 to return to Boston.

At the last minute, however, George's printing skills and his reputation as William Lloyd Garrison's son saved him. He found a job with the *Lawrence Republican,* a radical local newspaper. He quickly made plans to remain in Kansas through the winter, so that by spring he would have saved enough money to either go to Pike's Peak or return home. To his father, he wrote rather proudly, "Wherever I have been, and it has been found out that I am your son, I have always had a great deal of attention paid to me." In Lawrence people plied George with questions about Lloyd's "principles," but he found them lacking in any understanding of what nonresistance or abolitionism meant and regretted not having carried any of his father's books with him on his journey west so that he could lend them to people for their own illumination. "The Free State feeling," he continued, "seems to be very strong West, but there is very little real anti-slavery feeling connected with it. They merely look at it in a dollar and cent point of view."[44] Yet George must have seen some genuine abolitionism in Lawrence, since three months later he lauded the population's attempts to defy the Fugitive Slave Law by taking part in rescues.

Meanwhile, based upon his second plea for money from Willie, the family had believed that George was on his way home. They had prepared his room, putting in a carpet, new wardrobe, bureau, quilt, and curtains. Every time a carriage arrived, they ran to the door expecting to see George's newly bearded face, so his letter announcing his plans to stay on in Kansas greatly disappointed them. Helen, in particular, could not bear to have her son away for much longer. Although trying to support his decision, she still felt that if he had decided to remain a printer, why not come home and do the work in an atmosphere of love and friendship? She felt strongly that Pike's Peak was not a good place for him, as it was full of "cut throats." "I shall keep your room all nice for Spring," Helen wrote longingly, "and then I shall not hear of Peaks Pike. Give it all up. do."[45] Lloyd concurred, telling his son, "Of all pursuits, gold hunting is the most illusory, and generally the most demoralizing. It is usually the vicious, thriftless, unsteady and desperate, rather than the industrious, economical, sober, and well-balanced, who plunge into it. The society of such is greatly feared, and, as far as possible, to be shunned."[46]

What kept George in Lawrence was his constant fear of being trapped in the *Liberator* office with little chance of becoming his own man free from parental control and financially independent. As he wrote to Willie, by returning home he would become "tied down there all the rest of my life." If he was "ever going to see anything of the world," he had to do it then. Willie's suggestions that George consider returning home puzzled him. He could not understand why the brother who had encouraged him and lent him money had joined the voices demanding he surrender his hopes and dreams when all he wanted was to experience life's "hardships" while he was still young and unattached.[47] Willie, too, however, might have felt somewhat constrained as he continued to work to help support his parents. Should this not have been the eldest son's responsibility? William apparently envied George's ability to assert his independence and bemoaned his own incapacity to do so. As he wrote to Wendy soon after George's initial departure, "Wouldn't it have been a better thing for me if I had something to struggle against, something that would bring out and develop all my energies, and form a character worth having,—one achieved only by difficult & arduous labor?"[48] George's return home might offer Willie the opportunity to do his own searching.

In May, even though George disappointedly announced that he had postponed his Pike's Peak trip because of lack of funds, he still remained defiantly proud of his self-reliance, telling Willie, "I am able to judge for myself whether any step I may take is a good one or not, without any advice from you or any one else at home. When I ask any advice of you, you can send it along." George "hated to read" their letters, as they all harped on his desire to go prospecting.[49] Lloyd probably offended him the most by lecturing, "Only I pray you not to think too much of the money-getting, wherever you may be; for then, the passion will be to the soul what a cancer is to the body."[50] George remained defiant: "When I make up my mind fully about going anywhere, I generally go if I have the means."[51] In the end, no matter how fervently George wanted to stay on in the West, by the fall of 1859 he had to admit defeat, largely because the Panic of 1857 was followed by a devastating drought that lasted from the spring of 1859 through 1860, further crippling the economy. Records from the time show that from mid-June 1859 through November, not one rainfall produced enough moisture in Kansas to soak two inches into the ground, and during the winter there were only two light snows, neither providing enough precipitation to cover surface areas. The wheat and corn crops failed, and even vegetable gardens did not produce food for their planters.

During this period thousands of settlers left the territory. Those remaining depended on the generosity of Northern states and organizations to provide them with food. In desperation, about one hundred thousand prospectors flooded Pike's Peak. George was lucky not to have been one of them, for they found very little gold, lost all their money, and suffered innumerable hardships. Most headed back east, passing through Kansas without giving the territory a second thought. Wagons that had left with "Pike's Peak or Bust" boldly painted on their sides returned with "Busted" as their new message. Although never reaching Pike's Peak, George was one of its casualties. On September 18, he announced to Willie his plans to return home the next month and begged his brother to try to find him a job, although not at the *Liberator.* "If I get on to the 'Liberator' now," he lamented, "I shall get stuck there—don't you see."[52] When he left for home on October 17, George carried with him $137.25.

For the next two and a half years, he lived at home, once again working as a printer in the *Liberator* office. As he settled in, his eyes and mind kept absorbing the changes in the nation's political climate, but rather than being most concerned with money, his thoughts turned to those abolitionists who supported assertive, often violent, actions to end slavery. So began the second part of George's search, defining his own identity as an abolitionist and a nonresister.

Ironically, on the same day that George left Kansas to return to Massachusetts, John Brown and his followers made their unsuccessful assault on the federal armory and arsenal at Harpers Ferry, Virginia. Among Brown's band, but uninvolved in the attack and able to escape to Canada, was the Garrison sons' friend Francis Jackson Meriam, the grandson of the family's benefactor, Francis Jackson. Although history books often present Brown's assault as a lone attack by an insane man, many people did not see it that way. In fact, John Brown's final violent act through to his burial involved several abolitionists well known to the Garrison family and much admired by George, in particular. Thomas Wentworth Higginson, Theodore Parker, Samuel Gridley Howe, Gerrit Smith, George Luther Stearns, and Franklin Sanborn, the "Secret Six," saw to it that Brown's campaign had the money and weapons needed for his attack. Although Frederick Douglass declined an invitation to join the group, seeing the planned assault as suicidal, Lewis Hayden tried to raise money and recruit African-American men for the crusade, but in the end had little success. Once the raid was carried out and arrests made, Lloyd was placed in the position of having to comment upon it. In his usual style, he questioned the wisdom of such a violent turn, wondering to Oliver Johnson just what Brown had thought he would accomplish. Lloyd, however, could not help feeling sympathy for the man who had once again drawn such national attention to the necessity of overthrowing the slave system. "But, whatever may have been his errors of judgment or calculation," he wrote Johnson, "his bearing since his capture and during his trial has been truly sublime, and challenges for him all of human sympathy and respect."[53]

Perhaps most surprising to Lloyd and important in the development of George's beliefs was the fact that James Miller McKim, a most firm supporter of Garrisonianism, approved of John Brown's action. McKim's dear friend Lucretia Mott could not believe that he took such an anti-nonresistant position, but he, like other Garrisonians, now saw value in a more volatile response to slavery. Although the Harpers Ferry episode put a strain on McKim's relationship with Mott, he managed to convince her to invite Mary Ann Brown, John's wife, to stay with the Mott family throughout the trial, a gesture which greatly moved Brown and showed that even the staunchest nonresister could not turn her back on him. Two other strong Garrisonians, Lydia Maria Child and Rebecca Buffum Spring, made separate trips to visit Brown and his men in prison. After his execution on December 2, Brown's body was shipped to Philadelphia. From there, James Miller McKim and Wendell Phillips accompanied it to North Elba, New York, where Brown was buried, both McKim and Phillips speaking at the funeral. The bodies of two other members of Brown's army, Aaron D. Stephens and Albert Hazlett, were transported to New Jersey and buried on the grounds of Theodore Weld's Eagleswood School, which many abolitionist children, including Lucy McKim, attended. For George, and indeed all the Garrison children, it was becoming obvious that many of their father's friends were moving away from his strict nonviolence views. At first, they observed these changes without much discussion, but after the election of Abraham Lincoln to the presidency in 1860 and the start of the Civil War on April 12, 1861, with the firing on Fort Sumter in Charleston Harbor, South Carolina, their ideas began to take expression.

While George tried to figure out some way to once again be on his own, perhaps replicating his adventures in Minnesota and Kansas, William and Wendell took an assertive role in following their father's abolitionist stances. As early as 1858, when he was eighteen years old, for example, Wendell privately told his brother George that he supported his father's idea of disunion: "Two things only now I wish to be adjusted—the Dissolution of the Union & the establishment of a Northern Confederacy."[54] This would mean the North's separation from slavery and its establishing a new nation with a new constitution.[55] Wendell read the *Liberator* religiously and when on vacation carried along copies of his father's works, studying the articles and testing out his father's arguments in his own words. Once war broke out, he became publicly vocal about his feelings, joining the abolitionist speakers' circuit, traveling through New York, Vermont, Massachusetts, and New Hampshire raising money for the movement, then for the aid of black war refugees, and finally for reconstruction efforts in the South.

William also followed in his father's footsteps, initially writing about Abraham Lincoln's actions. Lloyd himself disdained Lincoln's position that the preservation of the Union, not the emancipation of the slaves, was the all-important issue. For Lincoln, slavery could remain in the South (but not expand into the West) as long as the country was reunited. As he wrote to Horace Greeley of the *New York Tri-*

bune, "If I could save the Union without freeing *any* slave I would do it, and if I could save it by freeing *all* the slaves I would do it; and if I could save it by freeing some and leaving others alone I would also do that."[56] Willie agreed with his father, noting to his sister, Fanny, that he was concerned that the president was "anxious for the safety of Slavery in the Southern states."[57] Shortly before the war began, William had given his first public antislavery and nonresister speech. Insecure in his own "courage and ability," he was surprised by the attention the audience paid him. As he told Lloyd, he spoke for about an hour, finding himself increasingly involved in his subject. However, it was the invocation of his parents' images that gave him self-confidence. "A new strength seemed to possess me," he wrote, "& I tried to speak as though the cause I was pleading was yours & mother's, not that of the negro far away."[58] After this event, Willie became another Garrison voice, but only on the local lecture circuit so he could continue working long days at his job. In 1864 he also volunteered at a local hospital to teach wounded veterans accounting. In some sense, William and Wendell replaced their father as a speaker, Lloyd discovering that as he aged, his vocal chords had grown weak, his ailments more frequent, and his fatigue great. Even with George working at his side, the *Liberator* still required his full attention, and he could not ease up on the time and effort needed to produce it.

Helen, too, continued to support the work of her husband, and now of her children, by upholding the last remaining vestiges of the female antislavery network in Boston. In 1861 she was one of three women, including Lydia Maria Child and Mary May, who organized the annual fund-raiser, the proceeds from which were used to circulate petitions addressed to Congress for the total abolition of slavery. Again, in December 1862, Helen joined other women in raising money, this time to keep the *Liberator* alive, the failure of the cotton crop resulting in a scarcity of paper. While the costs of publishing had risen, however, circulation had declined. In January 1863 the price of a subscription increased to three dollars a year. As Helen wrote to her friend Sallie Holley, "Our little band are desirous of persevering unto the end, for certainly it does seem as if our paper ought not to discontinue until every slave is free. And we have no other resources to obtain the means, excepting through our Festival."[59]

As the war progressed, an important question for abolitionist sons was whether to join the army or not. George, William, and Wendell, who were all of the age to either enlist or be called to serve in the military, were consumed by thoughts of war versus nonresistance. In 1861 and 1862, all three witnessed several friends' departures for the battlegrounds. Two of Wendell's classmates from Harvard, Edward Wigglesworth and Sidney Warren Thaxter, had enlisted, as had Ned and Norwood Hallowell, two Philadelphia-area abolitionist sons well known to the Garrisons. In addition, the Federal Militia Act of 1862 allowed the president to call up local militia, including all able-bodied men between the ages of eighteen and forty-five, to fight in the war.[60] It also gave him the authority to order state militias into federal service for up to nine months. This Lincoln did on August 4, 1862, ordering 300,000 men into active duty through the state militias in addition to the 300,000 three-year volunteers he had requested the previous month. By the end of 1862, the Northern army had added well over half a million new men to its ranks. Until 1863, however, there was no draft in the North, allowing the Garrison sons the luxury of contemplating their positions on war without the pressure of government repercussions for antiwar stands.

Both Willie and Wendy adopted their father's belief in nonresistance, which he publicly reiterated in two articles in the *Liberator* in 1862. Lloyd still held that nonresistance was not just the practice of not resisting authority even if unjust, as it was originally defined in seventeenth-century England, but was in fact the refusal to cooperate with such authority. The first *Liberator* article, "Drafting—The Hour of Trial," explained the difference between "Non-Resistants" and "Peace men," who were people who simply opposed war. For Lloyd, nonresisters chose to separate themselves from the government "for conscience sake" and took no part in political decision making, whereas peace proponents, who were not nonresisters, showed "no scruples" by voting, maintaining "the Constitution as it is," and holding office. Nonresisters, according to his thinking, deserved exemption from any participation in the war, for "he who believes in total abstinence from war, as a Christian duty, though a member of no religious body," should not be forced to participate in violence.[61]

In the second article, "Drafting—What is the Duty of Abolitionists?" Lloyd tackled the issue of the responsibility of those abolitionists who were not strictly nonresisters. These were people who declined to vote only because they despised the proslavery aspects of the Constitution, which included the counting of each slave as three-fifths a person (for establishing the number of representatives in the House) and the acknowledgment of the institution of slavery by ending the importation of slaves in 1808 but not ending the institution of slavery itself. For these abolitionists, participation in the war was a matter of individual conscience. What Lloyd sought to avoid was conflict within the abolitionist community. "Both parties are equally sincere," he assured his readers, "equally zealous to procure universal emancipation; and neither should deal censoriously with the other."[62] Indeed, Lloyd also needed to avoid a split at home, for whereas William, Wendell, and even fourteen-year-old Frank identified themselves as nonresisters, George did not.

On April 28, 1861, William explained his own nonresister position in a letter to his friend Edward S. Bunker, who, also raised in a nonresister home, was eager to join the army and show his support for the emancipation of the slaves. William agreed with his friend that the war was a "cheering sign of the times," for after thirty years of struggle, the warnings of the antislavery agitators had come to fruition. "It has come at last," Willie wrote, "& a bloody one it promises to be. . . .

Therefore, the abolitionists, seeing that the retributive justice can no longer be delayed, instead of feeling sad, recognize it as the 'salvation of God,' & can only say, 'Thy will be done.'" William "delighted" over the North's spirit and found the sound of the drums and the "tramp" of the soldiers' feet "welcome music" to his ears. He felt that even as a nonresister, he could revel in the idea that the North would punish and destroy the "slave-power." However, William himself could not participate in the fighting. In words that appear to contradict his own joy, Willie told Bunker that "no war is justifiable: that human life is sacred & inalienable: that it is better to be shot than to shoot, to die than to kill; that Calvary is more glorious than Bunker Hill; that Jesus acted on a higher plane than Geo. Washington or John Brown." With his "convictions" on the subject, Willie could "no more take a gun into my hand to kill a fellow creature than I could do any other horrible deed which my soul abhors." Whether for "freedom" or against "tyranny," he could not participate in a war.[63]

"Non-resistance is not cowardice," Willie assured Bunker. "To be a true non-resistant requires a loftier courage than the battle-field can furnish. It is not a state of passivity, as many suppose, but one of constant moral warfare. It is that indomitable spirit which no dangers or threats can daunt, but bearing always the unpopular but needed protest, says 'strike but hear me.'. . . Those who cannot comprehend these glorious principles must settle their differences as they can; they are surely on a lower plane than those who are willing to suffer all for righteousness' sake, without wish to retaliate." In an effort to persuade his friend not to enlist, William reminded him of their belief that the moment people forsook their "moral weapons" to take up the "carnal" was the moment they placed themselves "on equal terms with the ruffian & the blackleg. It is brute force against brute force. You smother the nobler elements of your being."[64]

Wendell's strongest statement of his opposition to war came after a desperate Congress passed the Enrollment Act of 1863, which ordered the conscription of men between the ages of twenty and forty-five to end the manpower shortage in the army. Numbers of men had been wounded or killed, while others had left service once their terms expired. Tired of war and anxious to take advantage of the booming economy in the North, they happily returned home. Responsibility for the military draft fell upon the provost marshal's bureau of the War Department, which required each congressional district to meet a quota established by the federal government. The provost marshal's job was to ensure that all eligible men enrolled. If a district met its quota through volunteers, it was not necessary for men to be drafted; this created great local pressure on men to enlist voluntarily. But many places still had to rely on one of four drafts in 1863 and 1864 to meet their goal. The first draft call came in July 1863. According to George's diary, Wendell received his draft notice on July 13. This left him with three choices: (1) He could respond to the notice and serve in the military. (2) He could hire a substitute to replace him, which would exempt him from any further draft calls. (3) He could pay a commutation fee of $300, which would release him from this call but not from future ones.

Wendell's position was stated quite clearly in a letter to the *Liberator* dated August 21, 1863. Although at first reluctant to have his response to the authorities published, he decided it was important to explain his dissent, especially since he represented one of 87,000 men who paid the fee.[65] Wendell opened his statement with an explanation of his beliefs, which closely replicated Lloyd's own. "The doctrine of the inviolability of human life," he wrote, "which I accept, will probably forever debar me from casting a ballot, as it certainly will from using a musket. I can never take office nor create an officer under any human government now existing on the face of the earth, for each rests ultimately upon the appeal to violence and the rule of might." Wendell clearly saw his duty as twofold: "to practice principles of truth and justice" and "to bear patiently the penalties for nonconformity to unjust or unenlightened enactments."[66] His position on hiring a substitute echoed Lloyd's own 1862 explanation, which stated: "It can hardly be asked of any Non-Resistant, 'How, if drafted, about hiring a substitute?' because what we do by another as our agent or representative, we do ourselves. To hire a substitute is, as a matter of principle, precisely the same as to go to the battlefield in person."[67] Wendy's explanation, while more personal, expressed the same sentiment: "I who cannot take the life of a fellow-being . . . to save my own, cannot to save others from a like destruction. . . . What I cannot do myself, I cannot do by another, and can therefore hire no substitute."[68]

Wendy did, however, find it acceptable to pay the government the $300 commutation fee. In this sense, he was acting as a true seventeenth-century nonresister by not resisting authority, no matter how unjust. Lloyd had indicated the previous year that this was a viable alternative, one to be decided by each individual. "Speaking personally," he wrote,

> we see no violation of Non-Resistant principles in paying the money. . . . In hiring a substitute yourself, you actively sustain the war, and become an armed participant in it, and so violate the principles you profess to serve. In paying a tax, you passively submit to the exaction, which in itself, commits no violence upon others, but is only a transfer of so much property to other hands. If, then, the government shall proceed to apply it to war purposes, the responsibility will rest with the government, not with you.[69]

Lloyd's sanctioning of paying the tax can be interpreted as a rationalization for supporting a just war while wishing to remain away from the violence of it. Wendell's explanation adds to the stance's puzzling nature. As a "disbeliever" in war, he felt he must "object and offer protest" to the tax. However, Wendy was just one individual, not part of a massive movement, and as such, he felt that he had no choice but to "submit to a superior force." Because his fine was against his consent, "the responsibility of this transaction, and of the uses to which my property thus taken is applied, belongs to the government, and not to me." Wendy wished to stand by his personal principles, but he also desired that the government have "complete triumph" over the slaveholding South. Therefore, he paid his fine "without a grudge." He signed his letter most emphatically, "Yours for the suppression of the slaveholders' rebellion, and the overthrow of its cause."[70]

Although verbally touting the nonresistant line, Wendell and Lloyd had actually veered from their orthodox position. While Lloyd, it is true, refused to participate in the government process and Wendy did not resist authority, both men cheered on the North to defeat the South. Wendell neither begrudged the government his money nor minded if it was used for war-related expenses (including finding another man to replace him) as long as he was not directly involved in making that decision. However, when Massachusetts organized its black regiments, Wendell contributed two dollars toward uniforms and supplies. Although his opinions and actions were widely publicized because he was "Garrison's son," Wendell did not represent all nonresisters. Alfred Love, a Philadelphia nonresister with Quaker roots though no church connection, refused to hire a substitute, pay the fine, or support the war in any way. He was called into court on several occasions, each time accompanied by Lucretia Mott. Never sentenced to prison for his beliefs, Love practiced them by not allowing his woolen commission business to sell goods for the war effort, resulting in great personal financial loss.[71] However, he maintained his strict principles, in 1866 forming the pacifist Universal Peace Union. Wendell, on the other hand, avoided government harassment and endless court appearances by cooperating with the law.

Despite their aversion to violence, all the Garrisons found great excitement in following the war's progress battle by battle. They also made several visits to Camp Meigs, the army training camp in Readville just a few miles south of Boston, to watch the troops drill. One of Wendell's first excursions there was to accompany Norwood Hallowell's mother on a visit to her son. Young Frank, a professed nonresister, made regular trips to Readville, although he more frequently observed parades and drills on Boston Common. Yet, to illustrate his principles, in early 1864 he had his father write a letter of protest in response to the Boston Latin School's intention to have its students practice military drills. Fanny often joined her brothers to cheer on the troops and reacted to many incidents of the war. In 1862, when she was a peppy, slim young woman of eighteen, Fanny heard a sermon in a Unitarian church in Concord which "showed the sin of this North in not discovering ages ago, that there were four millions of people fallen among thieves."[72] Although as a woman she was ineligible for the draft or to serve in the military, Fanny took it as her job to convince abolitionist friends, such as Shadarak Morrill, not to fight in the war. Like her mother, Fanny avidly read newspapers and frequently commented on politics. In August 1861, for example, she watched carefully as General John C. Fremont, commander of the Western Department of the military, instituted martial law in Missouri and freed the slaves of every pro-Confederate in the state. When Lincoln revoked Fremont's proclamation, abolitionists protested, and Fremont's reputation soared in their communities. Fanny felt that Fremont was a hero, writing to Willie that she wished the general would lead the entire war effort, especially since the North was not bringing the South quickly to its knees.

George himself observed all of the events from 1861 until the spring of 1863 from the *Liberator* office, taking his time to sort out his feelings and define his own beliefs. Unlike William and Wendell, he did not follow his father's strict nonresistant position; rather, he came to believe that the model set by Thomas Wentworth Higginson and James Miller McKim was more suitable. For the first two years of the war, George remained at home, working, attending military drills, going on vacations to nearby New Hampshire, and visiting his friend Thomas Bradford Drew in Plymouth. By August 1862, however, he had informed his parents that, if drafted, he would readily go. Lloyd was deeply disappointed in George's stance and maintained the same position he had expressed to his son in 1859: "Be willing to die a martyr, if need be, in the cause of liberty, and to save the oppressed, but resort to no weapons of death, even in self defense."[73] If his son insisted on being a part of the war effort, he hoped that George would at least wait until Lincoln had invoked an emancipation proclamation, for to go into the military beforehand was to "maintain 'the Union as it was, and the Constitution as it is.'"[74] Fanny echoed her father's sentiments, writing to her brother Willie, "I don't feel reconciled to having George go, till Emancipation is proclaimed. But he must do as he thinks best."[75] Fanny fretted so much over the possibility of George's being drafted or enlisting that she wrote to her brothers constantly during her 1862 summer away from home, urging them to keep her informed of his situation.

The war consumed the minds and daily activities of all members of the family. Lloyd, of course, was involved in reporting war events in the *Liberator,* his primary aim being to gain support for an Emancipation Proclamation. Throughout it all, he remained calm, "tranquil in mind."[76] Finally, on September 22, 1862, Lincoln announced that on January 1, 1863, all slaves of any state still in rebellion would be freed; those in occupied territories would be freed through other legislation which would have to be negotiated with the state legislatures. Although not the blanket law that the abolitionists desired, this proclamation was the statement needed to establish that the Civil War was indeed an antislavery crusade, a shift in policy and rhetoric that did not please many racist Northern soldiers, who then began leaving the military as their terms expired. In spite of a growing fear in the North that they would not win, Lloyd felt otherwise, vowing that until all slaves were freed he would keep the *Liberator* alive and continue to lobby for abolitionism. Young Fanny reflected her father's joy over Lincoln's September announcement. "Is not this the most glorious of all days?" she wrote her mother. "To think we have at last a proclamation of Freedom for the four million bondmen in our land. Is not Father joyous?"[77] Many years later, Fanny still vividly recalled that eventful New Year's Eve in 1862 when she, William, and their father waited together with a crowd in an African-American church in Boston for the Emancipation Proclamation to be enacted. Along with Southern-born abolitionist Moncure D. Conway, they were the only white people in attendance. After speeches and prayers, all left disappointed until, later in the day, the good news arrived, followed by a large concert in the Music Hall, where Fanny's heart filled with a "joy . . . akin to pain" as an immense crowd gave "nine cheers" for Lincoln and "three" for her father.[78]

The Emancipation Proclamation eased one of Lloyd's major reservations concerning the Civil War, but he still could not accept the fact that one of his sons would actually consider enlisting. For George, however, participation became even more attractive after Lincoln sanctioned the establishment of free "colored" regiments to fight for the North, a policy that many people had supported earlier in the war.[79] Congress had previously passed two acts regarding blacks in the military: the Confiscation Act, passed on July 17, 1862, which empowered the president to use African Americans to "suppress" the "rebellion," and a militia act, which lifted the bar on blacks serving in state militias. After these pieces of legislation were passed, the state of Indiana offered the federal government two black regiments, but Lincoln declined their aid, claiming that loyal border states such as Kentucky might leave the Union after such a move. Finally, in November 1862 two black regiments of emancipated slaves were established in South Carolina, one being Thomas Wentworth Higginson's First South Carolina Volunteers.

Following this, in early 1863, Governor John A. Andrew of Massachusetts, a diehard abolitionist, announced the formation of the Fifty-fourth Regiment of Massachusetts Volunteer Infantry. Although Andrew approved of having black officers, Edwin M. Stanton, the secretary of war, ordered there be only white leaders. The Garrison children's friend Robert Gould Shaw was invited to be the regiment's colonel, his second-in-command being another family friend, Norwood P. Hallowell. The abolitionist leaders George L. Stearns (of the Secret Six), Frederick Douglass, William Wells Brown, Charles Remond, Henry Highland Garnet, and James Miller McKim all actively recruited throughout the North to build the 54th's ten companies of one hundred men each, in total a thousand men including the officers. Contributions were raised and reported upon in the *Liberator*, George and Wendell each donating two dollars. By early May the regiment was full, and the state began filling a second, the 55th. Norwood took up the leadership of that unit, his brother Ned (Edward N. Hallowell) moving into his vacated position in the 54th.[80]

The creation of these two regiments involving his friends and peers convinced George that he, too, should sign up. This decision, which illustrated the consistency of his own beliefs and actions, served to highlight once more the contradictions in the position shared by his father and siblings, for, two days after their dismay at his announcement, Lloyd and Fanny cheered on the 54th as it left Boston for the South. Although neither Helen nor Lloyd tried to prevent their son from following his conscience, they were obviously disturbed and somewhat shocked by his choice. "Father's conviction of the wickedness of war," Willie wrote to Ellen Wright, "the utter demoralization which is inseparable from armies and the hope that his sons would all be baptized in the spirit of peace, all weigh upon his spirits. With mother I think it is the fear of bodily injury which dismays her most. She has little of the Spartan." William and Wendell regretted that George could not "comprehend & accept the higher principle of non-resistance."[81]

In June, just before accepting Norwood Hallowell's invitation to become a Second Lieutenant in the 55th, George received a final plea from his father to reconsider his actions. Lloyd reminded his son that he had not prevented him from acting in a way that met his own "highest convictions of duty," for nothing would have been gained by such behavior. But he begged George to consider certain dangers he would face, insisting, as he had when his son left Minnesota for Kansas, that he might incur extra risks because he was the offspring of William Lloyd Garrison. If the Confederates arrested George and identified his heritage, they were bound to treat him most cruelly. Like many other abolitionists, Lloyd was under the impression that the federal government intended to use the black regiments in the most "desperate" fighting. Since George would not respond to reason, Lloyd hoped that perhaps he would respond to guilt. If placed in a dangerous situation, he reminded him, his chances of falling ill or being wounded, maimed, or killed would be great. Would he not consider his mother? "It makes me tremble," Lloyd wrote, "in regard to the effect that may be produced upon the health and happiness of your mother, should any serious, especially a fatal, accident befall you. Her affection for you is intense, her anxiety beyond expression."[82] Lloyd did not go so far as to remind his son that the *Liberator* had already published the obituaries of nine abolitionist sons who had died in the war and that several others had gone unmentioned.

George could see that his father's concern had become more personal than philosophical, but still he followed his heart and sense of adventure, by mid-June having joined the 55th then in training at Camp Meigs. There George learned from such experienced officers as Colonel Norwood Hallowell, Lieutenant-Colonel Alfred S. Hartwell, and Major Charles B. Fox, who had moved to the 55th from previous regiments. As a Second Lieutenant in Company I, he came to work with the African-American men who enlisted from several states, including Massachusetts, New York, New Jersey, Pennsylvania, Rhode Island, Illinois, Indiana, the border state of Virginia, and even from Kentucky and Missouri. Over two hundred men traveled from Ohio to join up, including Joshua Dunbar, father of the future poet Paul Lawrence Dunbar. So large was the group from Ohio, in fact, that the regimental flags were stitched and donated by African-American women from that state. One unique recruit, Nicholas Saib, was a free man born in Central Africa who had spent some years enslaved in the Middle East before escaping to a free life in Turkey, Russia, Germany, and the United States. He spoke five languages, wrote in three or four, and was more educated than many officers; yet, he was not permitted to rise above the rank of sergeant because of his skin color.

At Camp Meigs, the regiment followed a strict program of military training while the men bonded into a community. Because many of them also wanted to learn how to read and write, a school was established on the camp grounds. George thrived in this atmosphere of commitment and struggle. Gone was the depression and lethargy he felt living at home and working for his father; now he was assertively sending requests to William and Wendell for various supplies and small currency bills so that he could help the men get change for the $10 and $20 bills the government had given them. Finally, on July 21, 1863, the fully prepared regiment left Camp Meigs via the Providence railroad for Boston and then the South. It was a dreary, rainy day, so that their march through Boston to Battery Wharf was not the cheerful sendoff they had hoped for. Yet the streets were thronged with people proud to cheer for their second "colored" regiment. Among them was Lloyd, who desperately wanted to say farewell to his son and give him his "parting blessing and a farewell grasp of the hand." He followed the crowd, waiting on a neighboring wharf for more than an hour to catch a glimpse of George. Eventually, the rain forced him to "beat a retreat—keenly regretting that we could not, even from a distance, shout farewell."[83]

Originally, the 55th was supposed to stop in New York, but that city was embroiled in bloody draft riots during which mainly Irish immigrants assaulted blacks, beating people, ransacking homes, and burning the Colored Orphan Asylum to the ground, leaving 233 children terrorized and homeless. As a result, the regiment headed directly to North Carolina, landing at the Morehead City wharf on July 25. As soon as they arrived, so did word of the great defeat of the 54th in its struggle to conquer Fort Wagner, the gateway to Charleston. In the battle, which made the men renowned worldwide as the "Glory" regiment, nearly half the recruits were killed, wounded, or taken captive. Robert Gould Shaw was shot down; Ned Hallowell, severely wounded. In fact, so many of the officers had either died or were wounded that nineteen-year-old Luis Emilio, the ninth captain in the chain of command, had to take over. The entire North, and especially the state of Massachusetts, was devastated by the news, as tales of the soldiers' bravery traveled quickly. Helen Garrison, already distraught over her son's enlistment, was deeply upset by the Fort Wagner tragedy. As Fanny reported to Frank,

"The horrid massacre of our brave 54th has made Mother's heart ache afresh and tremble lest it may ere long be the fate of her son & the 55th." Fanny felt wary of the federal government's disregard for the soldiers, believing there was "good reason to be suspicious of foul play in regard to the conflict," that the government had perhaps known the great risk but been unconcerned because the men were black and the leaders largely abolitionist.[84] Wendell agreed with his sister's assessment, telling William he hoped that the "sacrifice" of one regiment would be enough to "call out a proper spirit of protection from our Govt."[85]

Fanny was also saddened by Shaw's death, remembering the times she had visited him and his parents in Staten Island, and she worried about her friend Ned Hallowell's wounds.[86] Lloyd, like his wife, agonized over his son, anxiously awaiting word from him. As he wrote to George less than a month after the attack on Fort Wagner, "Not a day has passed that we have not had you in our liveliest remembrance. I miss you by my side at the table, and at the printing-office, and cannot get reconciled to the separation. Yet I have nothing but praise to give you that you have been faithful to your highest convictions, and taking your life in your hands, are willing to lay it down, even like the brave Col. Shaw and his associates, if need be, in the cause of freedom, and for the suppression of slavery and the rebellion." Still, Lloyd continued to hope that his eldest son would accept nonresistance and "ascend to what I believe a higher plane of moral heroism and a nobler method of self-sacrifice."[87]

On August 3, Helen finally received a letter from George telling her that he was in fine health and expressing his regret that he had not been able to speak with the family before leaving Massachusetts. The fact that the regiment's march through the Common was canceled for fear of similar riots as those in New York angered and embarrassed him. After all, the men were armed and trained, able to protect themselves in case of an attack, which they all doubted would occur anyway. George once again discovered that wherever he traveled, people knew that he was his father's son, for as soon as he arrived at Morehead City, he was asked by General Edward A. Wild about his father's well-being. From Morehead City, the men were taken by train to Newbern, where after just a few days, they were ordered to march to ships that carried them to Charleston to support the greatly diminished 54th. The move was so rapid that the soldiers were given a mere three days of rations and allowed to take only their knapsacks and their woolen and rubber blankets, and the officers to pack only that which they or their servants could carry—definitely not their heavy trunks. As a result, most of the men did not have even a change of clothing. Considering himself well off, George, always well-organized and composed, managed to take his knapsack with a change of clothing. A little way into the march, a "contraband boy," a former slave now residing safely behind Union lines, expressed his willingness to tag along, so George gave him his knapsack and acquired a servant who remained with him for some time, even though he paid him $7 a month while other officers offered him $13. Once in his new location, much to his parents' horror, George, in a boastful manner, wrote that the 55th might be ordered to attack Fort Wagner, in which case, their chances of being "cut up" were "as good as the 54th's."[88]

For the immediate future, however, Helen and Lloyd need not have worried too much about their rebellious son. Once settled on Morris Island and then Folly Island, part of the Sea Islands near Charleston, which had been occupied by the Union troops in November 1861, the 55th spent most of its time drilling, building fortifications, and acting as a backup for other Northern regiments. After the 55th's arrival in 1863, the 54th, which received new recruits, and the 55th usually worked in tandem, the men feeling happy with their close proximity to each other in spite of a certain amount of regimental competition. Unfortunately for the 55th, however, much of the gear they were forced to leave behind in North Carolina never caught up with them. George lost his overcoat and cap, a double blanket, a smaller blanket, a pair of boots and a musket net that had not been locked in his trunk, each item a treasured necessity not easily replaced. In spite of this, he wrote home that he was happy, assuring his family not to worry about him, as the 55th was based on the beach, a healthier location than certain inland areas. He did not mention the mosquitoes, fleas, humidity, and stifling heat, nor the fact that Folly Island was just a narrow nine-mile-long strip of sandy soil with nothing growing on it except a few bushes and shrubs. For nine months, the 55th performed fatigue duty, the tiring fortification and scouting work needed for other regiments. George detailed this work in a letter which was published in the *Liberator.* "Every night and morning," he wrote, anywhere from fifty to two hundred men were ordered to work, "mostly in unloading vessels of freight and ammunition of all kinds—in drawing heavy pieces of cannon to the front, and mounting them under the fire of the enemy—in throwing up intrenchments, covering magazines, digging parallels toward Fort Wagner."[89]

Besides acting as support for other troops, the 55th's presence was designed as protection for the abolitionists working for the Port Royal Experiment, the earliest Reconstruction effort recorded in the South.[90] Begun in 1862, the abolitionists and soldiers worked to ensure the region's peaceful transformation into a free, racially just area. At times, George had the opportunity to socialize with some of the Port Royal residents, many who were ardent Garrisonians acquainted with him or his father. On one occasion, he traveled to Hilton Head Island, where he saw the first "ladies" he had seen since leaving Boston. "Miss Lee, Miss Iveson, and Mr. and Mrs. Severance" treated him royally, but the high point of his visit was seeing Harriet Tubman, who for three months had been acting as a scout for Major General Quincy A. Gillmore, gathering important "intelligence" information from the contrabands on the island. To earn money to pay off debts and support her parents, Tubman also did laundry, ironing, and cooking for the white officers. George's hosts planned to introduce him to Tubman, but, as he wrote to Willie, "She no sooner saw me than she recognized me at once, and instantly threw her arms around me, and gave me quite an affectionate embrace, much to the amusement of those with me."[91] Once again, George's parentage and great physical resemblance to his father provided him with a special experience.

Being part of a black regiment posed unique challenges for George and the other white officers. Of major importance was the inequality of pay. Although Governor Andrew had elicited a promise from the federal government that the men in the 54th and 55th would receive the same rate of pay as white soldiers, they did not. Instead of the $13 plus a clothing allowance paid to the average soldier, the men received $7, the federal government following a previous ruling that freed slaves were to receive $10 a month with $3 deducted for uniforms. This reduced pay rate affected every black soldier from private to sergeant, including chaplains and physicians, of which there were but eight by the war's end. In contrast, the white military man's salary was graded from $13 to $21 according to rank. The men of the 54th and 55th wasted no time in protesting this outrage, but even though Governor Andrew fought constantly for equal wages, the federal government maintained that this was the proper amount given to blacks in the military. In response, the Massachusetts legislature voted on November 16, 1863, to pay the difference itself. When the paymaster of the state, Major James Sturges, accompanied by Edward W. Kinsley, a Boston merchant, arrived on Folly Island to offer the men the money, however, they declined it, saying that they would wait until the federal government paid the wages it had promised them.

The men of the 55th and the 54th considered equal pay an issue of manhood, so for over a year they refused to accept any reduced wage at all from the government. As one soldier wrote to the *Weekly Anglo-American,* "Just think of it, Mr. Editor, nearly a year has passed since the government at Washington authorized Gov. Andrew to enlist this regiment, assuring him that we should receive the same pay as other Massachusetts soldiers, and still we are *slaves;* still that precious principle—manhood—for the attainment of which we consider no hardship too great to be borne, is withheld from us. . . . MANHOOD IS OUR MOTTO. 'TIS WRITTEN IN OUR EVERY PURPOSE AND SEALED IN OUR HEART OF HEARTS."[92] As the men turned their pay away, letters began to arrive from mothers, wives, and children who desperately needed help. Some of these families ended up in poor houses and taking charity from anyone who would offer it. Anger with the injustice led a few men to rebel. Such was the case of Private Wallace Baker, who was executed on June 18, 1864, for disobeying the orders of an officer and violently assaulting him. Most men remained obedient soldiers, however, serving their country as best they could.

For George personally, money was plentiful. In December 1863, after being named acting regimental quartermaster with a promotion to first lieutenant, he was paid $435.70 for four months service. Immediately he sent $300 of it to

William to invest for him, along with another $25 that he claimed he owed his brother. He continued to save and invest money throughout the war. At the same time, he and other officers tried to convince the men under their command to accept the decreased amount of pay the government had offered, but they refused. "I cannot but admire their unanimity in refusing to take it," he wrote William, "although I think they are greatly mistaken in what they have an idea will follow if they do so."[93] George did his best to help out several soldiers, lending them money or giving them supplies when they were in need. One man who became a particularly close friend of George and the rest of his family was James Monroe Trotter, a sergeant major. Born in Mississippi in 1842 to a slave mother, Letitia, and her master, Richard S. Trotter, James, at the age of twelve, had the unusual good fortune to be taken to Cincinnati for the sole purpose of being raised free. There he attended Hiram Gilmore's school for African-American children and then a local academy. When Trotter heard that Massachusetts was initiating a black regiment, he immediately left Ohio to join up. Soon he met George, who introduced him to the rest of his family. Sixteen-year-old Franky became particularly attached to him through their correspondence, of which a few letters have survived. In those from Trotter one gets a glimpse of George's relationship with his troops, something George himself did not describe in his letters home. Trotter especially remarked on George's generosity and, in fact, that of all the Garrisons in sending letters, "coin," and supplies to the South. He also admired George's honesty as a quartermaster, a position open to much temptation, black-marketing, and dishonest behavior, especially in selling supplies that were meant to be distributed without cost. Trotter noted that George was "cheerful," "healthy," and "happy."[94]

While George attempted to help Trotter and other men on a personal level, Colonel Alfred S. Hartwell took a different approach to the pay issue. On June 13, 1864, he wrote a letter to Secretary of War Stanton demanding that the entire regiment be mustered out of service, since they were not being paid according to their contract. The letter brought no response, although Governor Andrew, other military leaders of the 54th and 55th, and private citizens continued to exert pressure upon the federal government. Finally, in late August, word arrived that the black soldiers were to receive equal pay. But before handing over any money, the government demanded that each man sign a statement pledging that he was "free" on or before April 21, 1861. For some men in the 54th and 55th, this presented a problem, for either they had been freed as a result of the war or they were officially still fugitive slaves. In response, Ned Hallowell of the 54th created the "Quaker Oath," which read, "You do solemnly swear that you owed no man unrequited labor on or before the 19th day of April, 1861. So help you God."[95] Almost every man signed, and on October 4 they began to receive their pay, the process taking three entire days to complete. Immediately, over $60,000 was sent to families back home; all debts were paid, and the regiment on the whole heaved a sigh of relief.

The other civil rights issue that involved George and the 55th was the promotion of black men to the ranks of higher officers. As ordered by the federal government, African-American soldiers could not move out of the lower ranks, some being sergeants or sergeant majors. This infuriated George, who was especially interested in seeing John F. Shorter promoted to the rank of lieutenant. Furthermore, George felt that the issue was larger than simply an order from the federal government, his greater concern being that some white officers within the regiment suffered from "colorphobia" and should never have been assigned to a black regiment. As George explained to William, Shorter had actually received a commission from Governor Andrew as a second lieutenant. To attain his higher rank, however, he had to be mustered out of service and then remustered in. At this point, Brigadier General Alexander Schimmelfenning, who had to send the papers on to his superior, noted on the back that Shorter was "of African descent." As a result, Brigadier General John Hatch, who was then in charge, refused to order Shorter's muster, saying that no man of "African descent" could become an officer in the U.S. service. Alfred Hartwell took the papers and promptly forwarded them to Secretary of War Stanton along with a letter to Governor Andrew. George sincerely wished that Hatch be reprimanded for his racist actions. "We have too many pro-slavery officers in this Department," he told William. "Although pretending and issuing orders that the colored troops should be treated the same as white troops, and that they should do exactly the same amount of fatigue work as the whites, I have noticed that, in spite of it, the colored Reg'ts have done pretty much all the fatigue duty and have not been treated the same as white troops."[96] George agreed with those officers who felt that if the black soldiers were not to be treated equally, then they should be released from service. Eventually, John Shorter, James Trotter, and William Dupree were commissioned as lieutenants in the 55th. But they were not mustered into their new roles until July 1, 1865, after the end of the war.

While George was coping with fatigue duty, small skirmishes, and the major pay and promotion issues in South Carolina, the rest of the family up North faced a major crisis at the end of 1863. On the night of December 29, at a time when she had just begun to emerge from over twenty-five years of child rearing to accompany Lloyd to public events and become more active in her own right, Helen fell victim to a severe stroke that paralyzed her left side. When the stroke occurred, she was under severe emotional strain, worried about George in the army, the possibility of William and Wendell being drafted, and Lloyd's declining health after more than thirty years of abolitionist agitation, speaking, and, especially, publishing the *Liberator* on a weekly basis. As Wendell and Frank described this totally unanticipated tragedy, "She had seldom looked more fresh and blooming than on the day that proved to be her last of active, vigorous health, and the friends on whom she called, on an errand in behalf of the freedmen, were impressed by her fine appearance."[97] Indeed, the evening of her stroke, she had attended a lecture with Lloyd and the children, but as she was getting ready for bed, she collapsed on the floor. Lloyd cried out for help, and while Wendell ran for the doctor, Frank, William, and Lloyd tried to lift her onto the bed, Lloyd's back going into a spasm during the effort, forcing Fanny to turn her attention to him. The following days and months were nightmarish for the Garrison household. At first, they did not expect Helen to survive, but she fought back and began to recover. Lloyd meanwhile assumed the role of primary caretaker, much as she had done for him over the years. Because he could not see to her every need, however, much of the responsibility became Fanny's and Frank's. George, far from home, could not offer any physical support, but for the first time in his life he could offer some monetary aid. He instructed William to use any amount of the money he had consistently sent home to pay Lloyd's debts and offset the expenses for Helen's care.

By February, Helen was beginning to regain the use of her left arm, but her recovery was long and generally unsuccessful. Although she was eventually able to walk, she dragged her left leg behind her and had great difficulty in navigating steps or the icy sidewalks of the long New England winters. Added to her misery was the fact that the month after her stroke, Wendell left Boston for a job in New York City. Unlike George, his leaving was not a struggle against his parents' authority but more a matter of economics. In late June 1863, Lloyd had written a letter to Theodore Tilton, then acting editor of the New York *Independent,* praising his son's qualifications and desire to be a writer. In fact, Wendell had written several articles over the past year for the *Liberator,* but since his father could not afford to pay a writer's salary, he was hoping that the *Independent* might have a place for him. This letter, written without Wendy's knowledge, reflected his own similar thoughts. Since he could not obtain a full-time teaching job and was not a dynamic speaker, he would pursue his other preferred route as a writer. For over two years, he had devoted much time to the lecture circuit for the cause of the war; now it was time to seek a more permanent and appropriate line of work.

The *Independent,* founded in 1848 by the Congregational church, was then the largest and most influential weekly newspaper devoted to a religious analysis of political affairs. While under the editorship of Henry Ward Beecher, the paper hired Theodore Tilton, a staunch abolitionist, as a writer.[98] When in the spring of 1863 Beecher resigned, Tilton took over as head of the *Independent,* transforming its voice from one of religion to radical abolitionism suitable for the likes of a Garrison son. Once offered the job, Wendy left home, moving first to Manhattan and then to Hicks Street in Brooklyn, where he stayed with the Anthonys, friends of the family. There he enjoyed the view of New York harbor and lower Manhattan from Brooklyn Heights and walked the half hour to the reservoir off Flatbush Avenue where, from the highest point in the city, he could see the distant Atlantic Ocean, New York harbor, and the woods and grassland of Long Island. A short ferry ride from his home in Brooklyn took him to his office at 5 Beekman Place in Manhattan.[99]

While his family faced its difficult challenges, George's regiment continued to experience the boredom of fatigue duty in South Carolina until in February 1864 the men were ordered to Jacksonville, Florida, to join an expedition under Brigadier General Truman Seymour. To their great disappointment, they saw none of the active fighting that they longed for; rather, from February 14 to 22 they performed their usual daily maintenance work. Next, they were relocated to Palatka, George's company settling in at Yellow Bluff, a point halfway between Jacksonville and the mouth of the St. John's River, where they cut down acres of pine trees, built two heavy fortifications, dug several rifle pits, built two stockades, a magazine, and a signal tower. It was in Florida that George came closest to bodily harm when on one of his trips from Palatka to Jacksonville in search of supplies, his steamer, the *Mapleleaf,* was struck by a rebel torpedo and rapidly sank. Five men were drowned, but fortunately for George, the water was so shallow that the upper deck of the boat, where the officers were, was not submerged, giving him time to escape on one of the three lifeboats that had been launched. Although the danger of capture was all too real, George felt no panic. As soon as he was safe, he retrieved his knapsack, returned to camp, and continued fatigue duty.

By April 17 the regiment was back in South Carolina where, finally, on May 21, they experienced their first skirmish, driving back a line of rebel pickets on James Island. The next day, they again exchanged shots with Confederate troops. George, meanwhile, had to face the humiliation of being relieved of duty as acting regimental quartermaster and returned to the company. For a brief time, he even found himself under arrest, a situation that James Trotter assured Frank was not unusual. "Nearly all of our excellent officers have been 'under arrest,' even Hartwell, the 'Noblest Roman of them all,'" he reassured his young friend.[100] George himself told the family that his removal was "without any just cause or reason, and is owing entirely as near as we can make out to the exertions of Lieut. Col. Fox and Major Wales to get Col. Hartwell out of the Reg't so they can be promoted." In the seven months that he was quartermaster, he had kept the accounts "perfectly straight," hearing no complaints "either directly or indirectly." Furthermore, no reason was given him for his arrest or release, nor could he find out through others why it had happened. The only reason George could see for the action was that he had disapproved of the sentiments of the other officers. Rather than being upset about his dismissal, he was actually greatly relieved to be away from such a huge "responsibility," especially since he retained his rank and, in fact, received a letter of commendation from Hartwell for his "unswerving fidelity and honesty" during his term in office.[101] Although the family wished for him to apply for a furlough so they could see for themselves that he was in good health and spirits, George, in his usual fashion, declined to do so, claiming outright that he did not want one. His brothers tried to look at the positive side of the experience. George had learned some skills as quartermaster, perhaps had gained the self-confidence they still obviously felt he lacked, and had been kept out of the line of danger. In fact, his job had been so tranquil that the young man, who was ordinarily quite thin, had gained twenty-five pounds. As his father noted, "If you have gained twenty-five pounds, Fanny has lost that amount since her mother's illness; so that the family weight suffers no diminution."[102]

George's return to active duty, however, brought him closer to the line of fire. In June he found himself on Kiawah Island, near Folly, commanding some pickets from Company I on duty to warn of an impending enemy attack. He and the men were in plain view of the Confederate pickets, but by mutual agreement, they did not fire upon each other. Life was not so peaceful once July arrived and members of the 55th were called upon to back up the 33rd U.S. Colored Regiment from South Carolina and the 103rd white regiment from New York in an attack against a Confederate battery on nearby Long Island. Successful in their duty, the men of the 55th still lost quite a number of comrades, either killed or wounded in the assault. William J. Stedman, a sergeant in George's company, was killed instantly, and Captain Fran Goodwin was shot through both thighs. In total, eleven men were killed and eighteen wounded, a light casualty list for Civil War battles.

George was not present at the initial confrontation, but on July 2 he was ordered to bring twenty of the men under his command to the conquered battery, then from Long Island to Tiger Island, and from there across a swamp to James Island, where they were to meet Brigadier General Schimmelfenning. Seeing no friendly or enemy troops during this wild-goose chase, George was leading his men back to Tiger Island when, while recrossing the swamp, they were unsuccessfully attacked by rebel soldiers. Once back on Tiger Island, he unexpectedly received orders to take his men again to Long Island, to Coles Island, and then back to Folly. By the time they returned to their base camp, they were "well used up," as George put it.[103] The fatigue and tension that the men felt was palpable in George's diary entry. So was his own frustration when three weeks later he was reprimanded for the second time that year for allowing his men to doze off while on picket duty. George, in turn, lectured them and those of other companies he discovered sleeping, all the while recognizing that overwork, lack of sleep, and boredom eventually took their toll.

George finally experienced major combat at the Battle of Honey Hill, an action taken in response to General William Tecumseh Sherman's famous "march to the sea," burning a sixty-mile path of destruction across the South from Atlanta, Georgia, to Charleston. Under the leadership of General John Porter Hatch, the accompanying attack, involving over five thousand men, took place on November 30 and was intended to destroy the Charleston and Savannah Railroad and capture the town of Grahamville, resulting in the severing of the connection between the two major cities and leaving each vulnerable to Union attack. Early in the morning of November 28, the regiment was ordered to Hilton Head Island, where they met up with Colonel Hartwell, then commanding a brigade consisting of the 54th and 55th Massachusetts regiments as well as the 102nd and 26th U.S. Colored regiments. From there, the men were carried by ship up the Broad River, heavy fog making travel slow and treacherous. The waters between the several Sea Islands were often shallow, frequently causing boats to go aground and exposing the men to enemy attack and capture. In this particular maneuver, some men were stranded in a creek about a quarter of a mile below their designated landing, Boyd's Neck. Rather than being protected by gunboats, they had to make their landing in several trips by tug boats, all arriving safely.

On the morning of November 30, the troops left Boyd's Neck for Grahamville, the 54th and 55th being ordered on this march, while the other two regiments were sent in another direction. Forward motion was difficult, however, as heavily damaged bridges hampered their movement so that by noon, they had only covered three miles. In addition, the extra amount of time needed to find lost men and repair bridges allowed the Confederates to bring in more troops. At a slightly elevated spot called Honey Hill, Confederate troops hiding in a small white roadside church opened fire. Just beyond that point, they also set fire to the grass, effectively slowing the Union troops' movement to a crawl; meanwhile Colonel Hartwell was forced to maneuver his men into position in a heavily wooded area, so it was not until one o'clock that they were ready for battle. The 54th and 55th regiments were ordered to form a double column and to move at a double-quick pace through a swamp and up a narrow roadway which was filled with artillery wagons. To do so, the files of men had to break rank, trapping many of them. Because the noise and confusion prevented Companies I, K, and E from even hearing the order to form a double column, they advanced into the woods to the right of the road rather than marching down its center. Meanwhile, the remaining troops charged and withdrew twice until they fell back in chaos and reformed under cover of the woods. The injury and death tolls were dramatic. Captain William Crane was struck in the forehead and instantly killed; Lieutenant Winthrop Boynton, his college friend and classmate, was hit several times and survived only because Lieutenant Thomas Ellsworth dragged him from under his horse to safety. Colonel Alfred Hartwell was wounded twice, his aide thrown from his horse by the effects of a shell explosion. When the color-bearer, Sergeant Robert King, a mere eighteen years old, fell victim to the explosion of a shell, Corporal Andrew Jackson Smith snatched the flag from his hand and continued to hold it high for the other men to see. George lamented in his diary that the rebels used four or five large guns which completely swept the ground in front of them. "It was a perfect massacre of our men."[104]

Major Nutt, whose horse was shot from under him, ordered George's company to remain under cover of the woods, but the fire and smoke from the battle forced them to retreat behind an old ditch a short distance away, where they kept the rebels at bay until dark. At night, after twelve hours of combat, the Union forces withdrew, the Confederates having succeeded in holding Honey Hill with only 8 dead and another 150–200 wounded. The Union, however, counted 750 casualties, the 55th itself losing 137 men within five minutes of fighting (29 dead, the others wounded). In spite of the fact that the Union did not win the Battle of Honey Hill, General Sherman captured Savannah in December. The railroad, which the troops had not destroyed, survived only two months longer, and Grahamville was burned to the ground. The men of the 55th, like their brothers of the 54th who had fought at Fort Wagner, felt that their performance at Honey Hill proved their manliness, their discipline, and their bravery under attack.

During their retreat, the soldiers carried to safety as many of their wounded as they could. There was particular reason to be concerned for their welfare, for at the beginning of the war the Confederate policy stated that captured black soldiers and their white officers were to be put to death or black soldiers were to be placed into slavery. Less than two weeks after members of the 54th had been taken at Fort Wagner, Abraham Lincoln issued a proclamation that for every Union soldier killed in violation of the laws of war, a Confederate soldier was to be executed, and for every one enslaved, a rebel soldier would be sentenced to hard labor. This policy helped alleviate some of the cruel treatment of African-American prisoners of war; however, many were tortured and murdered after being captured, and others were threatened with enslavement. After the 55th rescued its men and buried as many bodies as it could, George noted in his diary his sadness and anger at the way the battle had been handled: "In some respects, the expedition has been very badly managed, and the rebels have had plenty of time to get ready for us. . . . The fighting was all done in a very dense woods, so thick that the rebels could only be seen occasionally now and then. Our loss in killed and wounded is very heavy. The number of wounded is unusually large." George, however, counted his blessings. "I fortunately escaped without a scratch. Never felt cooler in my life than I have today."[105]

The 55th remained at Boyd's Landing until January 11, 1865, when they were ordered to Fort Thunderbold near Savannah. Although the men once again saw action in the Battle of Grimball's Causeway in February, the fighting was brief with no major casualties. Glory did come to the regiment, however, on February 18, 1865, when news arrived that the rebel army had evacuated Charleston, and Union troops grouped to march into the city. The 55th brought up the rear, collecting cattle along the way and taking charge of any contrabands they met. In each town they passed through, the men received rousing cheers from the newly freed people while the few remaining white people looked on in disdain or hid from them in fear. On February 21, to their great pride, the regiment marched into Charleston at the head of their brigade.

From the end of February into April, the men of the 55th searched for enemy forces still in the interior of South Carolina. They spent some time foraging in abandoned houses for food and supplies, helping freed people become acclimated to their new situation, and even, in one case, rescuing four members of a New York regiment from the rebel cavalry that had captured them at Moncks Corner. On James Island, which the Confederate troops had evacuated, they dismantled the guns and battery lines. Their greatest pleasure, however, came from freeing people still enslaved. In one instance, as reported in the *Liberator,* an officer approached a plantation owner, ordered him to call his slaves in from the fields, and then proclaimed them to be free. "That there was joy on that plantation, I need not tell you," the writer, obviously George, reported.[106] In April, George also had the opportunity to see his father, for Lloyd was part of a delegation of dignitaries witnessing the raising of the U.S. flag once again over Fort Sumter. George Thompson, then visiting from England, accompanied him as did Henry Ward Beecher, Senator Henry Wilson, and other honored guests. For Lloyd, this moment was most important; once an anomaly and hated, he now arrived as an abolitionist hero. A crowd of over three thousand freed people greeted him and the others on April 11, just two days after Robert E. Lee surrendered his troops to Ulysses S. Grant at Appomattox Courthouse. People pressed bouquets upon him, carried him on their shoulders, gave him gifts, and reached for his hand. George, who marched in the celebratory parade, was granted a furlough to spend some time with his father. Their joyful visit was cut short by the tragic news that Abraham Lincoln had been assassinated on April 14. Afraid that some harm might come to their visitors, they were loaded back on ship and sent home, hearts heavy and full of trepidation.

There were no serious repercussions in the South after the assassination, however, and with the ascendance of Andrew Johnson to the presidency, the 55th regiment became involved in the postwar work of Reconstruction. On May 1 the troops moved to Orangeburg, South Carolina, where they became part of the Northern District, Department of the South, their jobs including giving the oath of allegiance to Southerners, so they could prepare for the state's reentrance into the Union, and setting up a Commission on Labor to ensure that ex-masters provided freed people with equitable work contracts and fair wages. In their role as an occupying force, many soldiers heard complaints from former slaveholders of "insolence" on the part of the freed people, as the *Liberator* reported. However, they also heard freed people tell of planters who threatened to shoot them, prohibited them from leaving plantations without passes, and whipped children. For the men in the 55th, there was great urgency to break up the plantations into small farms, and, of greatest importance, "Allow the negro the ballot, get a Northern and foreign emigration to come South," so the institutions and customs of the North could "get the upperhand, and all will be well."[107] James Trotter, still in the regiment, was optimistic about his experience with the Commission of Labor. "When our Regt arrived here, nearly 2 months ago," he reported,

> we found the old system of slavery in full operation as it had always been. Matters assumed a different shape, however, in a little while. Now no one is allowed to have people working on their farms without having made a fair written contract signed by both parties, signature being witnessed, and approved by the President of this Commission. The former slaveholders wince under this new order of things. It seems to hurt them sorely—having to treat as intelligent free men and women, and draw up a written agreement to compensate for labor done by those whom they have tyrannized over with impunity, treating them as so many cattle, but they have to do it. A few do it with seeming cheerfulness. Some are too sharp to exhibit their chagrin. These contracts bind the freedmen to remain on the plantation until the present crop is harvested, this to mean its cultivation and thereby prevent starvation. Of course the colored people are all very happy, and they are working faithfully. I have several times been out on the plantations. I went 22 miles, without any guard save a good Colt revolver, which I had no occasion to call on. The Chivalry all treated me with respect and were very skillful in concealing whatever bitterness they may have felt when seeing a "nigger" with shoulder straps riding along the road to Columbia visiting their plantations in order to see that they were treating properly the colored people. We have had but a few cases of maltreatment of the freedmen by their owners.[108]

George's work in the 55th proved his commitment to abolitionism and racial justice. He had chosen the 55th as his regiment because of his belief in ending slavery and establishing equality for all African Americans, whether in the North or the South. He was indeed his parents' son, even though he chose a different path to achieve the same goals. In July, George was promoted to the rank of captain. By mid-August both the 54th and 55th regiments began preparing to return home. The Garrisons anxiously awaited for George's arrival, their dream coming true when the regiment was mustered out of service in Charleston on August 29. George left South Carolina on board the *Karnac,* arriving in Boston on September 13. With him was a fourteen-year-old African-American orphan whom he subsequently found a home for. On September 25, two days after the men of the 55th were paid and discharged, the people of Boston celebrated them with a final dress parade on Boston Common followed by the orders of dismissal. In total, 178,975 African-American soldiers had served in 166 Union regiments. Of the 32 officers (black and white) who were mustered out of the 55th, 18 had been with the regiment since its formation. Of the 822 enlisted men discharged, 653 had been at Readville in 1863.

In the September 1, 1865, issue of the *Liberator,* an anonymous author submitted the names of "prominent" male abolitionists who had "either sons, grandsons, or sons-in-law" in military service.[109] Included were Lloyd, Arthur and Lewis Tappan, James G. Birney, Gerrit Smith, Henry Ward Beecher, Francis G. Shaw, Samuel May Jr., James Forten, Robert Purvis, Frederick Douglass, S. S. Jocelyn, W. H. Burleigh, and Charles Follen.[110] Of course, there were many other less prominent abolitionists who saw loved ones go off to the war, many never to return. George was one of these second-generation abolitionist men who gave two years of their lives to the cause of freedom.

ENTER ELLIE AND LUCY

I enjoyed every minute of the time. . . . Willie Garrison . . . is a most pleasant man. . . . He is not so handsome as Wendell, but not so *kinky* & just as sincere. . . . Wendell is nice only dolorous, with a frequent and deep sigh, which speaks a world of grief & experience. George is good, but uninteresting as a prairie. Fanny is lovely & devoted to her father.

Ellen Wright to her mother, Martha, 1863

CHAPTER VII

One happenstance the Garrison family did not anticipate during the emotionally charged years of the Civil War was the appearance of two lovely young women who would capture the hearts of sons William and Wendell. In March 1863, Ellen Wright and Lucy McKim, two abolitionist daughters and lifelong friends, decided to visit Ellie's relatives near Boston. Since Lucy's father, James Miller McKim, was Lloyd and Helen's longtime friend, and Lucy had previously met the Garrison children in Philadelphia, it was natural for the young women to be invited to their Dix Place home. There they witnessed an abolitionist family that both resembled and departed from their own—for Garrisonian parents were not necessarily cut from the same cloth.

Ellen Wright, the older of the two, was raised among upstate New York abolitionists and woman's rights activists. Born on August 19, 1840, she was the daughter of David and Martha Coffin Wright of Auburn, a small town not far from Syracuse and Seneca Falls.[1] Although sympathetic to but not necessarily active in the antislavery cause, her father, David, spent his adult years struggling to build his law practice into a moderately successful endeavor. Ellie's mother, Martha, the sister of Lucretia Mott, was an energetic woman attracted to worldly pleasures, a trait that did not match her Quaker roots. The youngest of six children, she had married her first husband, army captain Peter Pelham, at the age of eighteen in

1824 and moved with him to Florida, where she soon became pregnant. Marrying outside her sect resulted in her expulsion from the Quaker community. Within a year, Pelham died from a fever, leaving Martha and her infant daughter, Marianna, without adequate support.[2] Hence, they moved north to Aurora, New York, to live with Martha's mother, herself a widow employed as head of a small girls' school. Once back in the fold, Martha resisted any return to a conservative and restrictive Quaker lifestyle. Rather, she continued to wear brightly colored clothing, read novels, go to the theater, and study art. Since her new beau, David Wright, was not closely connected with any church, there was no conflict between them on that score. Like Lloyd and Helen, they believed that religion was a matter of the heart, not institutions, and Martha herself preferred not to attend church services at all. When a friend questioned how she managed to accomplish so much work for the abolitionist and woman's rights causes and still have leisure time, she responded, "You forget that I have seven days a week while you church people have only six."[3] Martha and David wed in 1829 and had six children together: Eliza, Matthew Tallman, Ellen, William, Frank, and Charles.[4]

In 1848 Martha along with her sister, Lucretia, joined Elizabeth Cady Stanton, Mary Ann McClintock, and Jane Hunt in organizing the first Woman's Rights Convention in the United States. Ellie was only about eight years old when the Seneca Falls meeting took place, but her world thereafter revolved around abolitionism and woman's rights. "Aunt" Susan B. Anthony, Elizabeth Cady Stanton, and a slew of other early feminists including her mother became her role models; she, in turn, became their hope for the future, for from the start, Ellie was designated as one of the daughters who would carry the woman's rights struggle into the next generation, much as the Garrison children's upbringing was directed toward the continuation of the antislavery cause. Unlike the Garrisons, however, Ellie did not take to her role easily, and as she journeyed from childhood to adulthood, the pressures upon her to follow in her mother's footsteps often proved overwhelming.

Two years younger than Ellie, Lucy, born on October 30, 1842, also grew up within the abolitionist community (hers being Philadelphia and nearby Germantown), but not in the center of the emerging woman's rights movement.[5] Lucy's father, James Miller McKim, a former Presbyterian minister, was a founding member of the American Anti-Slavery Society and an agent for the Pennsylvania Anti-Slavery Society. An early friend and collaborator of Lloyd, McKim was actually schooled in the antislavery cause by Lucretia Mott. Through her, he became active in the dramatic work of the Underground Railroad, once receiving an escaped slave who had shipped himself out of the South in a crate. McKim and Mott, the Presbyterian and the Quaker, enjoyed challenging each other intellectually, filling their respective homes with constant intense debates. So close was their friendship that when it came time for Miller (as he preferred to be called) to marry, Mott encouraged him in his choice of a Quaker, Sarah Speakman, for her family also had pledged themselves to the antislavery cause, keeping a way station for fugitive slaves at their home. In 1840, after much resistance from Sarah's father, the two were wed, and subsequently, when her meeting voted for her expulsion for marrying outside the sect, Sarah boldly refused to accept their decision. Throughout her life, she remained a practicing Quaker, apparently with little interference from church leaders.

Lucretia Mott came to think of Miller and Sarah as part of her extended family. Hence, whenever young Ellie came to visit her Aunt Lucretia and Uncle James, she played with Lucy McKim, with Lucy's younger brother, Charles, and with her older adopted sister (and cousin), Annie. The first evidence of the girls' budding friendship came in the summer of 1851 when Lucy, then eight, and Ellie, ten, struck up a correspondence encouraged by Ellie's cousin, Anna Davis. In that first letter, Lucy stated her desire that Ellie come to visit her, Annie, and Charles: "we have got each of us a wax doll and a little bedstead for them to sleep in and Charley has got a Velocipede and a sweet little Pussy Cat and a pretty large yard and a play room and we have some little Toy Chairs and Tables and we have a good many flowers of different kinds."[6] In September, Ellie reported back to Anna that she had written to Lucy and she to her, and so the friendship took shape.

Although Ellie's visits to Philadelphia and the girls' correspondence fostered their acquaintance, the opportunity to form a deeper relationship came in the mid-1850s when they attended Theodore Weld's school, Eagleswood, in Perth Amboy, New Jersey, established along similar lines as the Northampton School and Hopedale. Weld, a prominent abolitionist who had married Angelina Grimké, had withdrawn from the lecture circuit so that he, his wife, and her equally activist sister, Sarah, could secure a better living for their family.[7] In 1840 they purchased a fifty-acre farm in Belleville, New Jersey, but money was scarce, so in 1848 the three decided to take in students, especially since they were already educating Angelina and Theodore's own three offspring. Ellie and her brother, Willy, attended this home school in 1853, where they studied writing, literature, history, grammar, physiology, and philosophy. Weld became known as a charismatic teacher, and Ellie early extolled his virtues, especially his permissive attitude that children experience the freedom of studying "out-of-doors," playing such games as leapfrog and whist.[8] In 1854 the Weld/Grimkés decided to relocate to the Raritan Bay Union, a 268-acre utopian community several miles south of Belleville. Situated on the beautiful Raritan River, the Union's goal was to create a manufacturing-trades-agricultural community, including private homes, workshops, artists' studios, rental apartments, a laundry, bakery, and restaurant. Weld signed on as principal and teacher of the community's school, Eagleswood, where Angelina and Sarah also taught. Ellie was so determined to continue studying with Weld that she convinced her parents to allow her to enroll even though paying the tuition and fees proved a financial hardship.

Eagleswood School, although fostering an intellectual environment, was a free-spirited, experimental institution, a larger, more ambitious endeavor than Northampton or Hopedale, one designed to prepare students for the "general duties of life, practical and professional," and for entrance into college. The curriculum was highly traditional, including English language and literature (with a great deal of Shakespeare, Milton, and translated classics), mathematics (from arithmetic, both "mental and written," to trigonometry), the physical sciences (geography, anatomy, geology, etc.), languages (Latin, Greek, French, and German), ancient and modern history, political economy, logic, ethics, and music, drawing, and painting.[9] Besides academic studies, learners at Eagleswood followed a regimented physical education, including daily drills in gymnastics and calisthenics alternating with such seasonal outdoor sports as rowing and swimming.[10] Sunday evening lectures attracted such important radical thinkers as Abby Kelley, Susan B. Anthony, Henry David Thoreau, Bronson Alcott, William Cullen Bryant, Horace Greeley, Ralph Waldo Emerson, and . . . William Lloyd Garrison.

Like Abigail Ballou at Hopedale, the Weld/Grimkés believed their duty was to raise children to identify racial and social injustices and correct them. This was a heavy responsibility, resulting in teachers who saw themselves as surrogate parents. As Sarah wrote from Belleville to her friend Elizabeth Smith Miller, "I tremble as the time approaches to receive again the charge of beings, who are to mark the age in which we live, who will shed around them influences for good or for evil to the human race, and who must feel and breathe the atmosphere of my spirit. Grant my heavenly father that I may not do them any evil."[11] To create a new generation of activists, the school committed itself to coeducational, interracial education. "To restrict each sex to schools exclusive of the other, is to ignore a law of reciprocal action vital to the highest weal of both," claimed the school's brochure. Coeducation, "under a wise supervision," gave "symmetry to mental and moral development" and fostered good habits and gentle behavior. Self-discipline helped both girls and boys develop a strong character and self-respect. Students, therefore, were to refrain from profanity, violent behavior, and "the use of tobacco, opium, or hasheesh, in any form, or all intoxicating drinks as a beverage:—in a word, habits of any kind tending to counteract the processes of nurture in others." Parents were discouraged from visiting too often or taking students away from the school, lest they distract them from learning. Likewise, giving children too much pocket money created ostentation and overindulgence. Dress was to be simple, as fashion could create "the paroxysms of a mind weak, ill-balanced, and essentially vulgar."[12] In total, fifty-six students boarded at Eagleswood at any given time. They were admitted upon application but were charged tuition from the beginning of each of the four ten-week sessions. Vacation weeks came at Christmas, at the end of the third quarter (May 6), and from the close of the school year on July 21 to the beginning of the new cycle on October 1.

Eagleswood was the preferred private school among abolitionist children. Besides the Wrights and McKims, the offspring of Robert Purvis, James Birney, Gerritt Smith, and those of the Hallowells, Potts, Chases, Motts, and Buffums all attended. The coeducational environment and Theodore Weld's popularity as a teacher, mentor, and counselor were important attractions. For the children, however, the essential feature was that the school was pure and simple fun. As one visitor noted, "It is one of the most beautiful sights in the world to see the affection the pupils have for him [Weld] and he for them. He does everything with them—joined heart and soul in a molasses candy-pull which we all had in the kitchen the other night."[13] Physical education, dramatic presentations, and social life far outweighed the difficulties in mastering the subject matter. Eagleswood offered abolitionist daughters and sons a place to grow together and to cement their friendships amidst a supportive political community. In addition, it particularly offered the young women an opportunity to become independent, equality minded, and assertive. Eagleswood was indeed the best place to train young activists. The Garrison children, however, were not among those enrolled in the school. George, the most likely candidate for Eagleswood, had already completed his education before it opened its doors. The others were the right age, but Helen and Lloyd never encouraged them to study so far from home.

The Wrights, however, were apparently willing to have Ellie, William, and Frank become part of the educational experiment. Lucy's parents, on the other hand, were hesitant even though Eagleswood was not extremely far from Philadelphia. In 1855 Miller McKim tried to convince Weld to move the school to Germantown so his children could live at home while receiving an Eagleswood education. Besides wanting Lucy nearby because of eye problems, the McKims found it difficult to afford both tuition and board. When Theodore Weld announced a necessary increase in fees in 1856, Miller was forced to notify him that Lucy and Annie could not return. Weld felt it would be such "a real affliction" to lose them that he lowered the cost for all three McKim children.[14] Like the Garrisons, the Wrights and McKims did not want to deny their children that which they desired, so Ellie, Willy, Frank, Lucy, Charley, and Annie each attended Eagleswood.

When the school opened in the fall term of 1854, Ellie was there. So were her Philadelphia friends, Hattie Purvis, who called her "her pet and kisses me twenty times a day," and Ned and Charlie Hallowell.[15] Martha, who kept in constant touch with her daughter, supervised her from afar. Unlike Helen, Martha took a rather heavy-handed approach to her daughter's political training, often criticizing and chastising her. Ellie's handwriting was sloppy, her spelling careless. Ellie in turn complained about her mother's lecturing. More than once, they disagreed over Ellie's desire to learn to play the piano. Martha had her doubts about the value of such a skill, especially since lessons required extra money, but she relented, admonishing Ellie to practice frequently and not refuse to play for anyone who asked. Martha rationalized the extra expenditure by arguing that musical skill served as a social grace and, therefore, would enhance Ellie's position in society. "I consider it as important that you should learn *to play when asked* as that you should play well," she wrote.[16]

In early spring of her first year, it became evident that Ellie was going through some kind of crisis caused by a conflict with her mother, fatigue, or the onset of puberty. At first, her symptoms pointed toward an illness brought on by running a long distance in muddy conditions. When she heard about it, Martha warned her daughter not to overtax herself: "You must remember the little girl who jumped rope so long without stopping that she killed herself. Violent exertion that heats the blood too much, some times produces consequences that last a lifetime."[17] Apparently, however, Ellie's problem was more emotional than physical. In early April she experienced such an extreme fit of hysteria that only her cousin Anna Davis and Theodore Weld could calm her. Ellie found the entire episode amusing, but Martha did not. First of all, she was concerned for her daughter's health. How had such a thing happened? Had Ellie gotten her feet wet? Had she caught a cold somehow? Had she simply overreacted to performing badly in her recitation before a stranger? Whatever the cause, Ellie had to learn not to give in to "nervous excitement," for such behavior could develop into "a most undesirable habit."[18] For the next week or so, Ellie felt so headachy, homesick, and out of sorts that Theodore Weld refused to allow her to attend classes, whereas Angelina Grimké Weld—convinced that Ellie was exaggerating and believing that activity, not whimpering like a helpless female, would cure her ills—turned her out of her room.

Ellie's erratic behavior resulted in Martha's sending her for the summer to the Clifton Sanitarium, not far from her home in Auburn. Her older sister by ten years, Eliza, accompanied her. Both young women underwent total physical examinations followed by a strict regime of rest, exercise, and healthy food. The schedule resembled that of the Northampton Water Cure: "up at 4½ . . . & down to the Cure & get a sponge bath, stay breakfast at seven, Gym's at 9¼, sitz at 10½ . . . dinner at 12½. Gymnastics at 2¼, sponge bath at 3½, dress up . . . for supper at 6½, to bed when natures wet restorer overcomes you."[19] For Eliza, this was about a half hour after dinner. Ellie soon followed, but so did her chronic headaches. Ellie grew to like the clinic and her German doctor, but she idled her time away. Martha lectured her about the adverse effects of reading popular stories rather than more intellectual material which would prepare her for independent womanhood. "Be a good girl," she wrote, "& if you ever expect to take your place with such women as Mrs. [Ernestine] Rose & Lucy Stone & *Antoinette Brown* it will only be attained by storing your mind with what is valuable. . . . so do not I beg you spend your time in reading the worse than useless trash that the idlers round you supply."[20] This "useless" trash included some of the best-selling writers of the day, for novel writing was one way a woman could become financially independent.[21] Such authors as Fanny Fern (pen name for Sara Parton), Catharine Maria Sedgwick, Caroline Howard Gilman, E.D.E.N. Southworth, Harriet Beecher Stowe, and Susan Warner all earned thousands of dollars in royalties for novels which told romantic stories of women with moral dilemmas. Some heroines became pregnant out of wedlock, faced life as poor orphans, or were conned out of their inherited wealth. Others met their Prince Charmings or death after their reputations were lost and then redeemed. In general, they were simply throwaway romance novels or episodic magazine stories not then considered to have any lasting literary value.

In order to impress upon her daughter the wonderful aspects of the woman's rights movement, Martha allowed her to briefly leave the sanitarium to attend a convention in Saratoga, which she was chairing. There, Ellie saw her heroes—Susan B. Anthony, Ernestine Rose, Antoinette Brown, and Thomas Wentworth Higginson, who invited her to accompany him to an evening get-together. Ellie's crush on Higginson escalated as they walked to and from the meetings, and she tried to assure herself a seat near him at meals. Returning to Clifton, Ellie obsessed over the "noble people" of the movement and how much she would "love to go around with them." Since Martha and David had determined she would not be returning to Eagleswood in the fall, she contemplated finding a school in Worcester, Massachusetts, to be near Higginson, a married man but with an invalid wife. Martha's plan was for Ellie to prepare herself for college and future self-reliance, an unusual path for a young woman at that time. Ellie, however, simply wanted to study music. Martha was not totally indifferent to this desire, but she dreamed that Ellie might obtain what neither she nor Ellie's two older sisters had—independence and adventure. As she told her daughter, "you can never be what I hope to see you become without steady persevering effort, & there never will be a better time than now to begin."[22] Ellie felt torn: "I cant think what is to become of me with my Woman's Rights mama, & my music mania. I cant attend to both, & would be useless to try to exist without music."[23] Besides her concerns for her fifteen-year-old daughter's mental and physical well-being, Martha was also faced with a maturing young woman. During the summer, Ellie met a young man by the name of James Wood. The two young people spent a great deal of time together, Ellie practicing her feminine wiles. Martha was quick to comment on her actions, reminding Ellie that she was no longer a little girl and that behavior that was acceptable when she was younger could now be misconstrued. Ellie was to keep a check on herself and act with "a proper and womanly decorum."[24]

Ellie's relationship with her mother was certainly problematic, although the two remained emotionally close until Martha's death in 1875. Ellie, however, seemed to know instinctively that the one way to preserve the tie was for her to remain away from home as much as possible, a much different situation from that of either Fanny Garrison or Lucy McKim, who experienced little conflict with their more traditional mothers. Therefore, she convinced Martha and David to allow her to attend the Sharon Female Seminary in Darby, Pennsylvania, quite close to Philadelphia and to her Aunt Lucretia and her friend Lucy. The school, one of a myriad of small private boarding schools for middle-class girls, was run by four Quaker women ("Aunt Rachel," whom Ellie did not care for; two preachers, Sister Jane and Sister Mary, and one lay teacher, Anne Whitson), who offered the usual subjects to the thirty-three students in attendance: grammar, philosophy, geography, arithmetic, spelling, reading, and writing. Although she was basically satisfied with her educational experience, Ellie found the living conditions at Sharon rather crude. The food tasted bad; mealtimes were too quiet (unlike the noisy scenes at Eagleswood); students could not go to their rooms during the day; there were no bureaus, and mice were getting into her storage trunk. Furthermore, Aunt Rachel was most old-fashioned when it came to woman's rights. As Ellie commented, "She dont see how any *lady* can abide the Bloomer Costume; though I believe if it was the *fashion* she'd wear her frocks among the shortest and *drawers* among the longest."[25] On the other hand, Rachel insisted upon referring to Ellie as "Lucretia Mott's Niece." Like George Garrison, whose chest swelled with pride each time a stranger asked if he was William Lloyd Garrison's son, Ellie loved the attention that came with her link to fame. "O! it's fortunate to have illustrious relatives," she noted.[26]

While at the Sharon Seminary, Ellie happily reconnected with her Philadelphia friends, especially Ned Hallowell, Richard and Beverly Chase, and Annie and Lucy McKim. As was her wont, she indulged in a bit of flirtation with two young men, the first, Ned Hallowell, whose correspondence became so intense as to be intimidating, and the second, Thomas Haskell, who wrote Ellie long, dewy-eyed letters. Ellie, with her small frame, dark hair, brown eyes, boundless energy, and warm sense of humor, had become conscious of herself as a desirable young woman. Her rapid maturation, however, continued to worry her mother, who felt Ellie was too young to become involved with men. Perhaps utilizing the themes of the many romantic novels Ellie consumed, Martha warned that such dalliances would only lead to "disappointment, sorrow, & regrets." Romantic trysts were transient, "the *devotion* of the lover, seldom survives the bridal." Martha may have also been reflecting on her second marriage when she advised Ellie that only the wife who cultivated "lasting regard & esteem" could achieve "quiet happiness, far more enduring" than romance. Determined that Ellie should devote her life to achieving the equality of the sexes, Martha urged her to plan on making her own way in the world. If, by chance, she found a suitable mate ("as Lucy Stone thinks she has done" with Henry Blackwell), so be it. If not, she would need a "disciplined" mind to lead a solo life.[27] After a year at Sharon, Martha and David allowed Ellie to return to Eagleswood, which Theodore Weld had taken on as his own after the breakup of the Raritan Bay Union. Being under the tutelage of the Grimké sisters could only do Ellie good.

Lucy, meanwhile, had her own difficulties with her education. Before entering Eagleswood, it is likely that she had attended the Chester Street Public School in Philadelphia. Her parents, who early on recognized her musical talent, saw to it that it was nurtured and developed. Unfortunately, however, Lucy suffered from an undiagnosed eye ailment that made studying difficult. In 1856 the condition resulted in a prolonged absence from school. At the height of her illness, she had to rely on her parents to read to her, Sarah McKim covering the entire Charles Dickens's novel *Nicholas Nickleby* while Miller introduced her to Plato. By early 1857 Lucy was ready to return to Eagleswood, where she and Ellie became inseparable, enjoying the beautiful sunsets over Raritan Bay, rushing to classes, sometimes playing hooky, and participating in theatrics as members of the Gamma Sigma Society. After only three months, Lucy's eye problem recurred, so that with the arrival of summer she again returned home, spending the next year, her fifteenth, giving piano lessons to local children.

After returning home that fall, Ellie spent her next year adrift. Part of the time she tried to fulfill Martha's dream for her to become a woman's rights leader; the rest was spent trying to find a mate. At first, she believed herself to be in love with a man named John, whom she prematurely decided to marry lest she end up spending her future alone. When he jilted her, Ellie experienced a surprisingly "strange feeling of freedom."[28] She then took to visiting various friends and relations in upstate New York, greatly agitating her mother with her apparent aimlessness. As Martha wrote to Ellie in November:

> as you had only to look in the glass to find a poor young woman whose education was unfinished & therefore she could not earn her bread by teaching, who couldn't bear to sew, & therefore was shut out from that avenue to wealth & distinction, who couldn't bear to sweep, and therefore could not obtain the lucrative post of chambermaid—who was "sick and tired of study" and therefore not likely ever to rise from her present poor and dependent position, and possibly destined to add one more to the thousands of helpless imbecile women, needing a protector, longing for some one to "maintain" them. . . .
>
> If you had a brother, who had no higher aim than you now seem to have, what would you think of him, Ellie?—It is of no use to say that you mean to be something, mean to do something, mean to study *next year,* mean to read to better purpose, after a while— . . . by another year a thousand unforeseen obstacles to farther study, may arise, while now there is nothing in the way of your earnestly applying yourself.[29]

Ellie's restlessness, which resembled George Garrison's, could not be channeled as his was because she was female. Venturing out west on her own was not an option she would have considered, nor was chancing a break with her parents by writing such defiant letters as George's. Rather, Ellie waffled between rebellion and compliance, in the end returning home to privately tutor three youngsters through six hours of daily study, then taking care of dusting, practicing piano, and sewing. In some way, she seemed relieved that her mother had forced her hand, telling Martha that she was glad to be there, although she missed Lucy and their walks at Eagleswood. Being home meant that Ellie could attend the local woman's rights meetings and see her "Aunt" Susan B. Anthony and her own mother in action. When unable to attend, she traced Anthony's and Elizabeth Cady Stanton's every move through the columns of the *Liberator.*

In December 1858, Ellie took a break from Auburn to visit her Philadelphia relatives. During her stay, she had a brief flirtation with Robert Purvis Jr., son of the wealthy African-American abolitionists Robert and Harriet Forten Purvis and brother of her Eagleswood friend Hattie. Due largely to initial efforts made by Lucretia Mott, it was not unusual for abolitionists in the Philadelphia area to ignore the racial divide when socializing, but dating and romance were not encouraged. In fact, one could say they were forbidden by an unspoken understanding, both groups generally fearing that intermarriage would lead only to heartache for the couple and for their offspring, who would find themselves at best isolated and at worst openly tormented by a racist society. Hence, the color line was not usually crossed on an intimate level, although those who ventured to do so continued to be part of the activist community. The details of Ellie's adventure into interracial romance appeared in a letter to her mother, who most definitely would not have approved of her actions. Ellie, however, obviously wished to display some modicum of independent thinking and daring, so she purposely included details that would test her mother's patience.

Ellie began her tale by relating her socially questionable solo journey on foot and by boat from Philadelphia to nearby Byberry, where the Purvises lived. Her cousin, Anna, was supposed to go with her; but when she was unable to, Ellie went on her own. When Roberts Sr. and Jr. met her at the wharf and whisked her off in a carriage, she suddenly felt "kinda horrid" to be so inappropriately alone with two men, especially African Americans. By that evening, however, she felt more confident as she socialized with other members of the Byberry community, including Charlotte Forten.[30] Three years her junior, this abolitionist daughter had already accomplished far more than Ellie, including having graduated from the Salem Normal School in Massachusetts two years earlier. A great admirer of Lloyd and Wendell Phillips, she had attended many abolitionist meetings and published several poems in the *Liberator,* including "The Improvement of Colored People," which showed the young woman's desire to prove to whites and blacks alike that African Americans were sincere, hard-working Christians. Ill health, however, forced Forten to return to Philadelphia rather than to accept a teaching position in Massachusetts. Back home, she signed on as a tutor for the younger Purvis children.

While at Byberry, Ellie's desire to test the boundaries of her supposed woman's rights independence led her to accept Robert Jr.'s invitation for a private horseback ride rather than a socially more acceptable group activity. After borrowing Hattie's riding outfit, a "beautiful blue velvet cap the border and ears made of handsome fur," she mounted her friend's horse and joined Robert in flirting, Ellie purposely relying on Robert to help her control her horse. Part of the time, they trotted; the rest, they walked slowly, enjoying each other's company, talking about "*everything* from books to beasts and consumption," which Robert greatly feared. When it began to snow, the two found themselves fantasizing about "some sort of romantic scene such as being snowed up," but the storm never developed, providing the pair a safe conclusion to their ten-mile ride. When they arrived home, Robert offered to help Ellie down from her horse; she, exhausted, slid off the saddle, "like so much lead," into his arms. When Martha read this description, she must have felt a deep sense of anxiety, but in actuality, she need not have worried, for Ellie, never losing sight of racial divisions, was just as skittish of racial mixing as her mother. Like so many people of her time, for example, Ellie equated shades of skin color with beauty. Charlotte Forten was "a lovely mulatto." The youngest Purvis daughter, however, was "quite dark & not at all pretty." Robert Purvis Sr., who was light-skinned, grew "more and more handsome."[31] Indeed, one suspects that Ellie's attraction to Robert Jr. would not have been as strong had he had a dark complexion. Even enlightened abolitionists used photographs of ringletted, light-skinned little slave girls to elicit sympathy from possible supporters.

Ellie's early enthusiasm for interracial relationships reversed itself just one year later when young Purvis expressed interest in her then engaged cousin, Anna. "I think," she wrote, "that there is the utmost of wretchedness in store for Bob! He is susceptible, and very sensitive. Of course no *white* person would want to fall in love with him—and of course he wouldn't marry any other than white as his father did."[32] In fact his mother, Harriet, was a daughter of the prominent African-American businessman and abolitionist leader James Forten, but she, like her husband, had very light skin. Two weeks after her first outburst, Ellie continued her attack on Purvis who, seemingly inappropriately, behaved "in such a way as to attract unpleasant observation." Yet, she could not hide her own attraction to such a dangerously unacceptable situation. As she wrote Anna, "It must be very disagreeable. It seems rather hard that you should be called upon to endure so much—unwelcome attentions from a handsome fellow of African tint!" Catching herself, she raised the most scandalous and frightening of possibilities. "Think of having an *octagoon* baby—Horrors!!" Ellie offered Anna her aid. "I have been thro' the wars and have scars and experience."[33]

Ellie was certainly an example of the conflicted race attitudes that second-generation Garrisonian abolitionists received from their parents. Love thy neighbors, no matter what the color of their skin, but do not love them too much! Indeed, when race became a point of contention between abolitionist children and those not in the movement, the antislavery children protected their reputation of being nonracist. Willie Garrison witnessed one such event when a young man asked the daughter of his father's friend Morris Davis whether she was against slavery. "'I am an abolitionist,' she replied. 'What, would you marry a nigger?' 'Yes,' was the prompt retort, 'sooner than I would a white man who could ask such a question.'"[34] The meaning of the young woman's response is ambiguous. Did she mean that the young man was naive for not understanding race relations within the abolitionist community, or did she mean that she would intermarry without question? Willie, himself, did not editorialize about it. As for Robert Purvis Jr., his fear of death was well founded. On March 19, 1862, at the age of twenty-eight, he died after a long illness. Ellie's extant letters make no mention of his passing.

In early 1859, when she was eighteen, Ellie's lack of self-esteem reached epic proportions. Her belief that people did not appreciate her musical talent and the fact that she was not as gifted a musician as Lucy snowballed into a major crisis over her ability to excel at anything. She felt she was a "*nothing* . . . absolutely a cypher."[35] If she could not succeed in such a pleasant and individualistic endeavor as playing the piano, how could she possibly live up to the expectations placed upon her by her mother and her woman's rights friends, especially Susan B. Anthony and Lucy Stone, to take on the mantle of national leadership of the cause? She convinced herself of their disappointment in her determination to study music, no matter what the cost or outcome. Would not Martha, Lucy, and Susan, "& all those dear Reformers" be saddened if she "turned out a musician and not a lecturer (which seems more impossible)"? However, she felt "that rarest gift, eloquense I am not mistress of."[36] Like George Garrison, Ellie could not envision herself as the replacement for her parent in the movement. Music did not require her to speak in public, a task that appeared increasingly horrifying as time passed.

Ellie was truly torn. "Where *does* my duty lie?" she wondered.[37] So, while Lucy's musical talent was praised by all who knew her, and while 1859 and 1860 gave her joy, adventure, and education at Eagleswood, Ellie became increasingly despondent. She felt that everyone, including her dear friend Lucy, saw her as a failure—"an impulsive, miserable creature! coquettish & charming at times. . . . That I think is Lucy's opinion but I care little for that now."[38] There is no evidence that Lucy ever expressed anything negative about her dear "Nellen." In fact, quite the opposite was evident in her April 1860 poem dedicated to her friend:

God bless thee, Nell!
It seems a many years since those rare days
When thou & I were chums at school. Rare days
Indeed!

Lucy wrote several verses of sentimental reminiscences before concluding:

Nell, I'll no more.
I need thy big, brown, sympathetic eyes
To look with me across these broken years.
But it is night; & I'm alone; & that
Was long ago. And others now sit in
Our desks, & tread our walks & worship
At our shrines. . . .[39]

Ellie's feelings of inadequacy were her own creation as she made the journey between late adolescence into adulthood.

As Ellie isolated herself from her friends, her feelings about her political activist mentors and their hopes for her fluctuated. When she suffered a break in a friendship with a peer, she commented on the reliability of "Susan & the Reformers, whose life is my life!" To them she turned in her unhappiness. Whereas her friend Petite was "graceful, & beautiful and gentle and *rich,* with winning ways," she was also fickle. Susan B. was "neither graceful nor beautiful nor rich nor winning to strangers," but she was "strong-hearted and a friend indeed."[40] During 1860, Ellie gravitated toward the activists for the emotional support she needed. In April she was in Philadelphia attending a meeting at the Antislavery Office, and in May she planned to attend a woman's rights meeting in New York City, where another second-generation abolitionist and woman's rights daughter, Elizabeth (Lizzie) Powell, would also be. Even though working within the activist community stabilized her, Ellie still suffered from mood swings whenever she heard any news or opinions that shook her self-confidence. In July, for example, an "electric shock" went through her when Martha related that Lizzie had delivered an address before the Boston Woman's Rights Convention. Her reaction was highly personal as she wrote, "I think I never will be anything."[41] Two months later, however, she felt ecstatic as she prepared to journey from Auburn to Rochester to visit with Parker Pillsbury (a leading abolitionist minister) and Susan B. "It will be delightful," she wrote. "I enjoy the anticipation to the uttermost. I want to sleep with Susan, and talk a little with her."[42] But lest she allow herself to feel *too* good, Ellie added, "She is disapptd. in me—Of course she is—isn't everybody?—I am a nonentity, *after all.*"[43]

Ellie's greatest fear was that being a failure would cause her to lose this wonderful, supportive community. She envisioned that Susan B. would "soon slip off—slide away, as tho' we had never been—for she has no time for nonentities." Ellie felt ashamed and hopeless. "I . . . try to love myself as I see so many do, who succeed in life, admirably indeed, but I cant do that, for I'm such a fool." When asked to play a piece of music, she became so anxious that her fingers shook, failing her as badly as her spirit had. She felt there was "no soul" to her playing—and no hope for a speaking career either. "I hate myself—I hate the world." The only beauty was to be found in the green trees, the blue sky, and the "nice set of . . . Reformers."[44] Susan B. Anthony was not so easily put off by her young friend, however, and continued to mentor Ellie. By mid-September she had half convinced her to serve with Lizzie Powell as secretaries at the next Woman's Rights Convention. However, as at other times, Ellie did not attend the meeting. The specter of young, successful Lizzie Powell loomed so large that she avoided making her acquaintance.

In the fall of 1860, Ellie entered Mrs. Sedgwick's Young Ladies School in Lenox, Massachusetts, in order to complete her education. Elizabeth Sedgwick, the sister-in-law of the highly popular novelist Catharine Maria Sedgwick, began the school in 1828 in a wing of her home, and it remained very popular until it closed in 1864 after her death. Mrs. Sedgwick, as she was known, referred to her establishment as a "character-factory."[45] Ellie chose it because she believed that the school's location in a peaceful Berkshire Mountains town would inspire her to master the piano. But although she loved the natural beauty of the mountains, she hated the school. The building she lived in was drafty, cold, and leaky. Music lessons, which she desired the most, cost $50 to $60 a quarter, far too much for her budget, and the basic fees ate up any money she could have used for outside lessons. In actuality, Ellie, then twenty, was getting too old for such schools, noting in her journal that it was not "half as delightful to study" as she had hoped. "There is so much committing to do, and lessons to *recite* are such a bother to learn. . . . Catch me at school again—no, no-dear!" Although other young women loved Mrs. Sedgwick's, Ellie felt it was "just nothing" compared to Eagleswood.[46] The schoolmistress did not inspire Ellie's respect, there being little rapport between them, and life was dull, even Saturday evening activities being "tabboo, no levity allowed."[47]

Furthermore, even though the Sedgwicks were known antislavery sympathizers, Ellie suspected that Mrs. Sedgwick was "no Abolitionist . . . & hardly Woman's Rights" either.[48] Being at the school awakened Ellie's ire, making her feel "more radical than ever . . . more than ever thankful to have been bred among 'Reformers.'" Indeed, she had hung a photograph of her "saint Jn. Brown" near her bed "to the holy horror of the girls."[49] Yet, nothing came of the experience. Instead, Ellie grew more depressed, stating, "I don't care much for anything now—hardly feel Enthusiastic now. It seems so much pleasanter, & is so much more to my taste, to sit down quietly & read, or hear wise people talk, or listen to music, than to *do anything*." This she rationalized as achieving maturity and being content with aging, while at the same time berating herself for disappointing "Susan & Mrs. Stanton & those" who had held such great hopes for her. "Young people keep entering the field," she wrote in her journal, "while yet I lag behind, & see no opening in my Forest of Difficulties."[50]

While Ellie was coping with her personal trials and Lucy was excelling and enjoying life in the Eagleswood environment, tensions between the North and the South accelerated until Civil War was declared. Like other Garrisonians, Lucy and Ellie had to confront the personal meaning of this war and all wars.[51] As their lively and soul-searching letters reveal, they each experienced a myriad of feelings and perceptions. Indeed, as soon as the war began, an ugly incident occurred in the most abolitionist of schools, Eagleswood. In mid-April Theodore Weld admitted four African-American children as charity cases. As a result, some of the male students, who had shared their days with middle-class African-American abolitionist children, packed their bags and left. In their minds, there was a clear demarcation between their more privileged black friends and these new, poor students. Lucy and some of the other girls cheered as the ringleader walked out the door and blessed their teacher for taking a strong stand on the rights of these refugees from the South. Ellie herself clearly welcomed the initial sounds of cannons. In April, while on a six-week visit with her family and friends in Philadelphia, she wrote home to her brother, Willy, "The Martial sound of drums inspires me, the warlike tramp of many feet." Ellie was excited by the numbers of men volunteering and women sewing soldiers' clothes for no fee. Yet, she noted, "*Every* body here is enlisting for the War & it seems very very sad."[52] Her Belleville and Eagleswood friends, Ned Hallowell and Will Potts, had already signed up, and her father, David, who was with Ellie in Philadelphia, was so caught up in the war fever that his daughter feared that as soon as they returned home, he would enlist with the New York cavalry.

Throughout 1861 and 1862, both Ellie and Lucy responded to the age-old phenomenon war creates—the reality of separation and the fear of death that results in a heightened urgency for men and women to cling to one another. In May, soon after the war began, Ellie confided to her journal that she had become attracted to her distant cousin, William Beverly Chase, an Eagleswood alumnus who lived in the Philadelphia area. Not quite eighteen, Bev, as he was called, told Ellie that he loved her "very dearly" and wanted her for a "sister."[53] When she visited Philadelphia, he brought her "pleasant things to read" and offered to escort her anywhere she wanted to go.[54] While she tried to gently warn him off, he pursued her, calling her his "meeting house" and "*guardian angel.*"[55] Ellie was flattered, indeed, and did not totally reject Bev. But she was bothered by the three-year difference in their ages, which seemed rather great to her. Ellie had some time to ruminate about the war, Bev, and singlehood while she studied at Mrs. Sedgwick's. As with most people, the very fact that war had come into her personal life consumed her thoughts, portending "destruction and waste of property, even of human blood."[56] On the other hand, if this war meant the end of the "cancer of Slavery" and "Southern arrogance," then it was a glorious endeavor indeed, and the men who offered themselves as a "sacrifice to their country" were certainly heroes.[57] Ellie and Lucy and all the young, marriage-age women soon realized that there might be a more personally devastating effect of the war, the decimation of their generation of men. This awakening resulted in Ellie's decision that she did not want to meet "the fate of 'single-blessedness.'" Women, she claimed, were not intended to live their entire lives alone, and, she, inevitably, wished "to have a large family. . . . My name 'Ellen' (Eleanor) signifies all fruitful! Hence perhaps my preference."[58]

Lucy was not as clear as Ellie about her future desires, but her awareness of the effects the war might have on her chances of finding a mate soon tempered her initial enthusiasm. When during the summer of 1861, her mother Sarah stressed to her and Annie the importance of learning domestic skills in the event they had houses of their own, Lucy burst out in a letter to Ellie, "Houses of our own! Likely prospect, when everybody is gone to the War, to come back attractive members of society on wooden pins,—moral if not physical ones!"[59] This cynicism accelerated, so that, by the end of the year, Lucy greatly lamented the contradiction of all war—its almost macabre celebration of death. Two days before New Year's, she wrote to Ellie, "In the midst of life we are in death! Never truer than in this hoary bloody '61. What has the New Year for us, I wonder? How much can we endure? Can you answer for yourself Elle? The papers say the city [Philadelphia] was never gayer than at present. There is something frightening in the wonderful recuperative power of this people. Mercy! We shall dance at funerals next year, & flirt across corpses."[60]

As 1861 passed, both Ellie and Lucy noted the people they knew who were involved in the war effort. Lucy told Ellie about Harriet Howells, who died "by overwork" in the New Jersey hospitals just before she was supposed to leave for the South.[61] Ellie responded with the numbers of African-American refugees settling in or passing through upstate New York, many of them women who had left husbands or children in the South, risking everything to follow Harriet Tubman north. She also saw her brother Willy enlist in the army, telling Lucy that he pursued "the art of War, with a might most meritorious. His sword is much more dear to him than ever his piano was & he looks upon his sash with tender affection."[62] Willy's enthusiasm was contagious, inspiring Martha to instruct him "to die before he helped to return a slave to slavery."[63] Younger brother, Frank, was jealous because he was too young to sign up. Willy's enlistment ended Ellie's attraction for young Garrisonian men who claimed to be nonresisters. To Lucy, she vented, "I wouldn't *look* at a nonresistant. What do they suppose is going to become of our firesides? Isn't Ned [Hallowell] a fine brave fellow, for all his lounging about?" The abolitionist sons' enthusiasm was so great that Ellie proposed that she and Lucy disguise themselves as men and join up with the regiment that her hero, Thomas Wentworth Higginson, was forming. "We might make Excellent warriors," she suggested.[64] Of course, the serious underlying desire for second-generation Garrisonians was to see the slaves emancipated. This was the cause upon which they had been raised to base their futures.

In January 1862, Ellie accompanied her father, her sister, and her brother-in-law, David Munson Osborne, on a trip to Washington, D.C., primarily to visit Willy, who was stationed in nearby Virginia. Ellie's reaction to the South surprised her. The favorable weather, which was delightful compared to the cold, wintry clime of Auburn, immediately lured her into thinking that her family should move there once slavery was ended and the war settled. Like other abolitionists who made the journey south, Ellie was fascinated by plantation life. Yet, she was disappointed as well. "Arlington House," the mansion that Robert E. Lee and his family had abandoned and which she toured, had "low ceilings . . . dingy walls . . . narrow plain staircases & . . . contracted entries & rooms." She had expected a more ostentatious home for ladies with beautiful gowns with trains. As she had anticipated, the slave quarters were shocking: "Horrid places—built of brick, with rickety stairs, & the slaves living in damp dirty dark cellers—with chickens and trash."[65]

On her way back home, Ellie stopped for an extended visit in Philadelphia where she spent much time with Lucy—and Bev. As usual, she enjoyed boasting about her flirtations to her mother. Bev again paid her constant attention, bringing gifts and paying her compliments. She, in turn, became increasingly delighted with his company, telling Laura Stratton she had grown "desperately enthusiastic over him."[66] Martha, hearing of this growing attachment from her sister, Lucretia, warned Ellie to distance herself from her cousin. Ellie assured her that she was not romantically involved with Bev. Had Martha not heard that Ellie's cousin Anna who had married Richard Hallowell intended to introduce her to a young man when she visited her in Massachusetts? Also, unbeknownst to Martha, Ellie once again thought she was being wooed by a man who was not Bev Chase but one William Bispham, another abolitionist child. In fact, for some reason, she believed he had proposed to her when she heard that he had become engaged to her acquaintance Laura Wyeth. Only Lucy, who, like Ellie, enjoyed the new awareness that coeducational Eagleswood and the woman's rights movement had given them of tensions between the sexes, knew about this humiliation. Greatly sympathizing with her friend, she teased Ellie about the "deceitful" and "cunning" nature of men.[67] Ellie obviously wanted to become someone's wife, a position most young women of her time achieved in their early to mid-twenties, remarking to her mother, "What can be compared to the joy of being 21–2 waiting only to say 'yes.'"[68]

While Ellie pondered her future, Lucy took an assertive step in helping the newly freed people when, a year before George Garrison arrived in South Carolina, she accompanied her father on a three-week visit to the Port Royal Experiment.[69] Throughout the history of the United States to that date, the black population of the Sea Islands far outnumbered the white, the 1860 South Carolina state census for Beaufort District indicating the presence of 939 white property owners and 33,339 African Americans, all but a few being slaves. Once the Union army took control in November 1861, the federal government was joined by volunteer groups of Northern teachers, missionaries, and managers for the abandoned plantations in assisting the freed people. James Miller McKim became a leader of one such group, the Port Royal Relief Committee, founded on March 20, 1862, and was among those abolitionists who lauded the Civil War, claiming that "A righteous war is better than a corrupt peace. . . . When war can only be averted by consenting to crime, then welcome war with all its calamities."[70] Unlike his friend Lloyd, McKim was eager to help the war effort by working with the military to ensure that former Sea Island slaves were educated for freedom and to defy any efforts their former owners might make to reclaim their abandoned lands.

Under McKim's guidance, throughout the first half of 1862, close to a hundred teachers and relief workers traveled to Port Royal. By the spring, he decided to make a visit himself in order to evaluate what supplies and assistance the Reconstruction teams needed. Lucy was ecstatic about the opportunity he offered her to serve as his secretary, immediately fitting up with what Ellie described as "a hot weather costume wh. makes her look as much like 'Sam Hill' as possible—Fancy her, arrayed in a dark calico skirt, with no width to spare, a short dressing sack as far as possible from the fashionable cut—a large hat with lace descending from the brim—a pair of spectacles upon her nose, & an extra pair in her pocket, a large bag of tracts and primers in one hand, & a blue cotton umbrella in the other."[71] Lucy's sense of drama and adventure permeated the very air she and Ellie breathed. On June 2, after several postponements, she and her father left from New York for Port Royal. For the next three weeks, the young woman experienced life in the South so intensely that one could say she underwent a conversion experience, transforming her from an antiwar observer to a pro-just-war activist.

The excitement began when Lucy first saw Hilton Head Island, an incredibly active place, even on the sabbath: "Contrabands pushing round barrels & boxes, officers riding up & down the deck; a line of baggage wagons continually on the move, & everywhere men, men, men—soldiers chiefly." As five freedmen rowed the party to Lands End, on St. Helena's Island, Lucy became acutely aware of the songs they sang and almost immediately began writing down both the tunes and lyrics of what she described to Ellie as "the wild sad songs of the negroes."[72] There, the travelers settled in at "The Oaks," a plantation once inhabited by white slaveholders but now occupied by such Reconstruction workers as Charles Ware, Arthur Sumner, Ellen Murray, Laura Towne, Nelly Winsor, and Edward and Helen Philbrick, both friends of Theodore Weld.

In all, Lucy visited four islands: Hilton Head, Port Royal, St. Helena's, and Ladies. The experience made her feel alive and self-assured, awakening in her the possibilities that an activist life could hold. As she told Ellie, traveling "is such a blessed freshening institution—gets you thoroughly out of old ruts. One can hardly realize that one lives in a cage, until accident sets you flying outside." Lucy also realized that as a gifted musician, she had a unique opportunity to record for posterity the shouts, praises, spirituals, and speech patterns she heard in the fields, homes, and makeshift churches of the freed people. By doing so, she could also help Northerners understand and appreciate African-American culture. Lucy's work as her father's secretary and a musicologist converged with her role as a student of plantation life. Once the slaves were freed, their role as paid servants fitted the Northerners' norm of class division, thereby making it possible for some to appreciate the luxuries around them while still deploring the slave labor that made them possible. In fact, the white Southern lifestyle was quite intoxicating, causing Lucy to comment, "We live in the greatest state, two cooks, three coachmen, *always* a footman, never touch our rooms!!!" She received dinners of "fricassed chickens—some splendid fish . . . hashed crabs, beets, or peas, or squashes, green corn, always rice & gov't biscuit, no meat—suppers were tea or coffee, waffles, cornbread, wafers, clauaber cakes, hot biscuit, cucumbers & figs."[73] Meals were cooked out of doors and served inside by a woman and a boy, the latter swatting the ever present flies from the diners.

Still, the freed people who "sang" and "grinned" all day also carried the visible scars of enslavement. "What horrible cruelty there has been, on this plantation! One woman's back is covered with welts. . . . There is a bent tree in the yard that Aunt Phillis says could tell a tale. It *feels smooth and human to the touch.*" Lucy, meanwhile, was deeply affected by her visits to the freed people's homes, churches, and the former slave quarters. She remarked that they introduced her to each other as "Miss Lucy, who sent the clothes, & molasses & bacon to them!" Children followed her around, gently holding her skirt and pushing others away from the privilege. The homes she saw were depressing, with people lying on the floor on bundles of rags, placing corncobs, which attracted fleas and mosquitoes, under their heads as pillows. Lucy did not know whether she wanted to "laugh" at the absurdity of life or "cry" over its horrors.[74]

Miller McKim did not react at all favorably to the Southern lifestyle. All around Port Royal, he saw the effects of slavery on people's behavior and spirit. As he told a Philadelphia audience upon his return, "Servitude is not a condition favorable to the growth of courage. Slavery, in fact as well as law, unmans its victims." However, even though *"slave education"* had created a population that relied on "deception," "petty thieving," and "scolding" to survive, McKim firmly believed that a new type of learning, which included "free-labor," would wipe away these evils.[75] McKim's commitment to Reconstruction led him to advocate for a government inquiry into the freed people's needs; his efforts contributed to the formation in March 1863 of the War Department's American Freedman's Inquiry Commission.[76] McKim was also a chief agitator for the creation of the

Bureau of Refugees, Freedmen, and Abandoned Lands (the Freedmen's Bureau), which Congress established in 1865 to help former slaves find families, jobs, become literate, and to protect their civil rights.

Once home, Lucy immediately began transcribing the slave songs she had recorded, submitting the musical arrangement for voice and piano for "Poor Rosy, Poor Gal" to *Dwight's Journal of Music,* where it appeared on November 8, 1862. As she explained in a letter to the editor, noting the music down had been most difficult because of the "odd turns made in the throat, and that curious rhythmic effect produced by single voices chiming in at different irregular intervals." To record it accurately was "almost as impossible" as scoring the "singing of birds."[77] In December, Lucy registered the arrangements for this song and "Roll, Jordan, Roll" for copyright in the District Court in Philadelphia. Apparently, she had plans to publish several other songs but never succeeded in doing so, perhaps because of poor sales and lack of interest on the part of parlor song consumers, who preferred sentimental lyrics reflective of the popular romance novels Ellie read. Lucy continued her work, however, giving private recitals of the songs and sharing her information with other collectors, including William Francis Allen, Charles Pickard Ware, Thomas Wentworth Higginson, Laura Towne, and Ellen Murray. Being home again, however, made Lucy restless for some activity as meaningful as working at Port Royal. As she told Ellie, "Oh! I'm so thankful I'm not married or engaged. There is too much to see, hear, do & feel first. Life opened so grandly in 1862 Elle, even if we 'only stand & wait' that I cannot wish to write *finis* to my history yet and of course the end of the story always is: 'So they were married, & lived happily ever after.' One dreams of every other fate but that on this historic day, the 4th of July, 1862 especially when one has been to the Sea Islands!" In the same tone that she lamented the heavy fighting going on in the Richmond, Virginia, area, she also declared, "There isn't an atom of non-resistance left in me, I believe. You propose a partnership in housekeeping. Let our menage be at Port Royal."[78]

Ellie appeared overwhelmed by Lucy's opinions and envious of her enthusiasm, and so, she responded contrarily. Since Lucy wanted adventure, Ellie suggested she think seriously about marriage and settling down. Should Lucy not show more attention to Dick Chase, who had made his feelings for her quite obvious? "Now Luce," she wrote, "dont let Dick slide. . . . If you would only be very patient you kno. you may be glad someday. . . . He is provoking of course, being a male human." To further contradict Lucy's fervor, Ellie took an uncharacteristic and momentary stand against war, a position she had not enthusiastically embraced since her brother's enlistment. "War," she wrote, "seems to me more than ever a barbarity. I am disappointed that we have not lived beyond it. Think of its after effects—of the reckless creatures thrown upon society. It doesn't seem right that we should go thro so much evil to learn a great good."[79]

Meanwhile, both Ellie and Lucy became involved in the fates of Bev and Dick Chase. Lucy acted as confidante for both Bev and Ellie, who were carrying on a somewhat secret romance. Ellie had stipulated that the two remain out of touch for three years until Bev reached the age of twenty-one; but at the same time she wanted him not to become romantically involved with anyone else. Hence, when Bev asked Lucy if she thought he and Ellie would ever be a pair, Lucy honestly answered in the negative, advising him to gather all he could from the experience and move on. Ellie was miffed by this advice to Bev, complaining, "Why do you say 'no' when I have said, 'perhaps yes'?" Echoing her mother's sentiments which she originally disdained, Ellie noted that maybe she did not believe in "Love at First Sight" anymore. Perhaps she just had faith in "good strong *friendships* which will last thro' vicissitudes, & can stand violent *concussions,* both of which married life is said to be subject to."[80] Ellie assured Lucy there had been no promises made between her and Bev. Even Bev's mother had stated such before a room full of people, and Ellie had said the same to her own mother and aunt.

In August, much to the friends' delight, both Bev and Dick Chase enlisted as privates in the Pennsylvania Volunteer Cavalry.[81] To see the two abolitionist brothers from Quaker backgrounds leave for war was very painful; yet Lucy blessed their courage and willingness to enter "this hallowed warfare. . . . 'I have enlisted,'" she wrote to Ellie, "is always an 'open sesame' to my heart."[82] Just before he signed up, Ellie wrote to Bev, "I shall be glad for all whom I love to fight in it."[83] Once the deed was done, she wrote how she "love[d] privates!"[84] The Chase brothers' enlistment reminded Lucy of her own desire to help in the war effort.[85] She felt resentful that, as a woman, there was nothing she could physically do but "pick lint & sew for the Hospitals." Because her parents would not permit her to remain on her own in Port Royal, she would sew with all the heart and spirit she had. To Ellie, she implored, "For one, I say, *never, never, never* give up! Let every cent; & every friend, & every hope go first! Rather a lifetime of loneliness & sorrow for individuals, than miss the redemption of the nation. Kneeling in that poor cabin, with those who have suffered scourgings at our hands, & listening to that . . . old preacher calling down blessings on their new friends . . . instead of cursing every Anglo-Saxon, as he had cause & right to do,—I vowed that if ever I forget them, so might Heaven forget me! & So every one that joins 'the army of the Lord,' reminds me that there is to be no interest in this life here, except as a preparation for those duties which must come."[86]

Ellie agreed and so joined the effort to collect signatures on the National Women's Loyal League petitions for an emancipation proclamation. She also had a grander scheme, however. "I am undergoing a fresh longing to start off as a nurse. & Mother desires that I shall. . . . I *know* I cd do some good," she told Lucy. If Dr. Hall, a good friend of the family, went to serve in the medical corps, she might accompany him. Although Ellie would have to miss her planned visits to

Lenox and Boston, she "could do it more willingly than I ever did anything, if one sick soldier might be benefitted by it, or one slave, liberated sooner for it."[87] Ellie's enthusiasm for nursing persisted into January of 1863, but her usual inertia settled in. As she confessed to Lucy, "I have a distinct impulse for nursing, but I shut my eyes to everything, except knitting stockings." As usual, she felt "of no other earthly service to anybody."[88]

Lucy, on the other hand, tried to soothe her own conscience. For some time, she gave up parties, gentlemen, and any "gayety" when having company. Every morning, she joined a group of other women to sew "wrappers" and shirts for the hospitals. She determined to refuse all invitations to tea parties, feeling it was "horrible to stand around grinning like a death's head."[89] She corresponded regularly with Bev Chase and knit him a pair of wristlets that he requested. In September, Bev asked Ellie to send him something she had worn, a custom between soldiers and their sweethearts, but on the advice of her mother and sister, she chose this time to finally clear up their understanding, informing Bev, "I think that until you are twentyone we should have no intercourse watever." If they met "by chance," they could be "casual and pleasant," but nothing more was to take place. If he needed a friend, he could depend on Lucy to act as a good and "safe" ear for him.[90] Two weeks later, Lucy did indeed see both the Chase men while they were on furlough. At that time, Dick gave her a friendship ring, which she readily accepted.

Lucy's enthusiasm for the war and soldiering, however, was shattered in January 1863, when she was informed of Dick's death on December 29 in the Stones River Slaughter at Murfreesboro, Tennessee. There were in all 24,988 casualties during this bloody campaign, but Dick's was the one that struck home. He was shot in the head while riding horseback alongside Bev and was laid to rest in a Nashville cemetery far from home.[91] For a short time, Bev himself was listed as missing. Lucy thought she was prepared for such an event, but she realized that as much as she believed in the cause, she could not accept the loss. "O! Elle!" she wrote. "The gapes that such stabs make let in a light to let us see the love that is hidden within us. Didn't you think when all the boys started for the War, that you were all prepared to hear of their being killed at any time? I did. I fancied myself as well drilled,—was so certain of being at least calm & philosophical!—But since that first dizzy moment when I saw 'Killed I[n]A[ction] . . . R. W. Chase,' I have been realizing the fact that I am not so ready . . . as I thought."[92] Yet, she still believed in the cause. In spite of Will Potts's worries over his fallen men, Dick's demise, Bev's disappearance, and the numerous other injuries and deaths being reported, Lucy held on to her faith that "moral force & justice" were on their side and "Tyranny" on the other.[93] The Emancipation Proclamation had been issued, and the North would succeed.

If only Lucy, as a woman, could do something active, perhaps she could deal with her heartsickness. In January she wrote to Ellie, "'They also serve who stand and wait,' is true enough, I suppose. But it is so hard! if one could *only* have something to do. Sometimes it seems as if God could not really know how willing one should be for any work, or he would give us some. Perhaps he will, if we be patient."[94] The next month, she was still frustrated by the limitations her gender placed on her. "Can anyone help being 'restless for action?' Is it not almost anguish to be a comfortable nobody in a heroic age? I have as much influence in the fate of Greece whose history I read, as I have in the fate of America, that I love with a love borne of sorrow,—The whole cry of my soul is that all the battles may not be fought without my having fired one shot, that all the pain may not have passed without my having eased one sufferer. It does not require a metaphysician to perceive a most vigorous selfishness at the bottom of such a longing. Truly I desire a place to work for my own satisfaction."[95] Ellie, too, was shocked by Dick's death, writing to her friend Laura, who had married Fitzhugh Birney, an abolitionist son who would die the next year in the war, "Dick! When I think of a dear, young, beautiful face, which as angelic, cannot be much changed, which I can never see again—and lovely violet eyes, which will never laugh into mine again, & pure brave lips, which will never call me 'Little Sister,' again, and all this grieves me. . . . I loved him dearly, and miss him sadly."[96] Her cousin Anna echoed these sentiments. "I did not know I loved the boy so well," she wrote. "Isn't it strange how many peaceful faces are found upon a battlefield."[97]

In mid-February Bev arrived home on leave rather unexpectedly, desperately needing a break from the war. His life as a private and the death of his brother before his very eyes had taken a terrible toll on him. He talked about asking for a transfer as a lieutenant of a "colored" regiment, but what he really wanted was to leave the military altogether. His mother, Mary Chase, had already lost one son, and he himself was suffering from extreme trauma. Lucy wrote Ellie that Bev looked fine but that he had developed a nervous habit of smiling and having "sudden fits of abstraction into which he falls even when one is speaking to him. He winces under allusions to his brother from almost anybody, & I have not since heard him speak his name."[98] Laura also wrote of Bev's depression, quoting Oliver Hough, another antislavery soldier who "spoke of Bev as walking up and down the streets, almost distracted."[99] Bev's psychological breakdown provided Ellie with an "insane *yearning*" to see him, but she suppressed it, begging Lucy to encourage him to talk about his feelings so that he might recover from Dick's death. In his condition, she could not believe that the army would insist on his return. "I cant bear to think of it," she wrote. "As you say, the dead make the living so precious to us."[100]

Bev did, however, return to his private's role in the army. Ellie had no more direct contact with him, arbitrarily claiming that his new habit of smoking angered her, but Lucy stayed in contact until Bev once again disappeared, this time to the

Andersonville Prison Camp in Georgia, where he died of starvation in March 1864. He was one of 13,000 men whose last days were spent among some 45,000 Union prisoners crowded into a twenty-six-acre enclosure. There many found no shelter, little food, and hardly any medical care. A great number of men were half dressed; hundreds had no clothing at all. At the war's end, the public was so incensed to learn of the inhumane conditions that Major Henry Wirz of the Confederate Army was tried and executed for war crimes. Ironically, the worst Northern prison camp was located in Elmira, New York, not far from Ellie's home.

In March 1863, Lucy and Ellie visited Anna Davis and Richard Hallowell in Medford, Massachusetts, very close to Boston. During the first week of their stay, the two young women traveled in a driving snowstorm to pay a respectful visit to the Garrison home on Dix Place, where they were warmly greeted and doted upon. William (who did not want to be called "Willie" any longer, for he considered it too childish) was immediately drawn to Ellie and she to him. Wendell was charmed by Lucy as he had been during past encounters, but she did not return his feelings. Ellie and Lucy were also most happy to discover that there were over thirty Eagleswood alumni in the area, and along with Anna and Richard they decided to throw a party, renting a hall in Boston, hiring three musicians, and ordering ice cream, cake, and coffee. On March 16 the room filled with abolitionist friends. Of the older generation, Lloyd, Dio Lewis, and Theodore Weld dominated the scene. The younger generation, numbering over forty, included Charles and Sarah Weld, Lydia Buffum, William Bassett, Frank Wright, Frank Stearns, and William, Wendell, Fanny, and Frank. Ned Hallowell, Alfred Hartwell, and John Ritchie all represented the Massachusetts 54th Colored Regiment, then in its formative stages at Camp Meigs. The music began at 7:30, couples forming to dance the night away. It soon became apparent that Ellie and William were greatly attracted to each other. To her mother, Ellie noted that she "like[d]" William "better than anyone else" she had met "in a long time." William, in turn, told her that he was "grateful . . . to meet among all these giddy girls" one who cared "anything about reform" and who sympathized with him about the issues he cared most about.[101]

For several days following the party, Lucy and Ellie stayed at Dix Place, both young women finding the Garrison children to be wonderful companions. Fanny, four years younger than Ellie and two younger than Lucy, was enthralled by the two guests. Ellie was a new face for her, but Lucy was not. She had met Lucy a few times over the years during their families' infrequent visits to either Philadelphia or Boston.[102] Each evening of their visit, Fanny undressed herself in their room, wrapped a blanket around her bedclothes, and sat on the bed with them listening to their chatter. She in turn filled them in on the antislavery social scene in Boston, letting her opinions of people flow out in the friendly atmosphere of conversation. Ellie loved Fanny's "Boston talk," but as she confided to Laura Stratton, she found William the most appealing. Wendy was very polite, perhaps "a trifle prudish & a morsel overnice possibly," so she found it entertaining to "bring him down to a lower level & to startle him out of his propriety." She also derived great pleasure from snipping off one of his "black curls" for her "hair book." However, William, although not as handsome as Wendell, was simply "capital." Ellie took "positive comfort in his society. He doesn't excite me in combativeness &c. as some of my quandam friends like to. My weary soul . . . finds a sweet rest in his presence." As for the great Lloyd, Ellie found him "genial and objective" but "rather literal too." To her young eye, Lloyd did not "seize a joke immediately, except a pun or a good conundrum which makes him quiver!" The older man, though, was a good talker and a wonderful listener, and a man totally "devoted to his wife."[103] Lucy, too, enjoyed her days at Dix Place, enchanting the family with her tales of Port Royal. There was no question that Wendell had become totally smitten with her, having been heard to "rave over the shape of her head" and seen to "inscribe sonnets to her upon the window panes."[104] Ellie, who was always trying to play matchmaker to Lucy, now thought Wendell to be her perfect mate, not Ned Hallowell as she had previously announced to her friend. Lucy's main interest at the time, however, was transcribing and performing the songs she had noted down at Port Royal, not in courting.

Once the two friends left for home, Ellie and William began an immediate correspondence. William, who was then working as a cashier in the Mattapan Bank in Dorchester, opened his heart to her. Although they did not have to test each other in the same way that Lloyd and Helen did, still, William wanted to be sure that Ellie and he were a proper match. As Ellie and the entire abolitionist community knew, William had been previously engaged to Lizzie Powell, Ellie's imagined competition as a second-generation woman's rights leader and a reminder of her own sense of failure to please her reformer friends. William and Lizzie became acquainted through her brother, Aaron, who was a lecturing agent for the American Anti-Slavery Society. His work in the movement guaranteed that whenever the Garrisons were on lecture or walking tours in New York State, they would stay with his family in Ghent. In 1858 William and Lizzie began a serious correspondence, Lloyd noting to Helen, "I find that she and Willie are in frequent correspondence, to the mutual gratification of both, I have no doubt—of one, *herself,* I am quite certain. If nothing else grows out of it, it will strengthen the bonds of friendship, and help to make them experts in literary correspondence."[105] In 1860 the two were still pursuing their relationship, William taking some time to visit Lizzie in Ghent. They became engaged, but after much soul-searching, found that while they always wanted to remain close friends, they were not suited to each other for marriage. The breakup was not easy, and for some time, neither was sure they had made the right decision. As Fanny questioned her brother, "If the engagement was mutually given up, why do you not both feel better for being released from such false positions? Why it should cause either of you heart-burns I cannot comprehend. You don't seem certain of your own minds."[106] But certain they were.

By the time William met Ellie over a year later, he was as interested in finding a mate as she was. His one concern, however, was that she be able to accept him for who he was. Since Ellie had a brother in the army, she might not be able to understand or accept his own nonresister position. Ellie was actually more willing to accept this notion than she had been a year before, explaining to Laura in April that being a nonresister took a person "of strong moral courage."[107] When William told Ellie the next month about George's enlistment, he noted that for him and Wendell, it was "more difficult to refrain from going than to go, and were we not grounded in the faith of a different duty, to-morrow would see us in the camp."[108] The brothers, after all, believed wholeheartedly that slavery had to end. Ellie responded that it seemed "unnatural for a Garrison to wield a sword," but she lauded George's bravery.[109] For Ellie, the Garrison sons somehow represented her own conundrum and that of many second-generation abolitionists raised in a spirit of nonviolence, and for this reason she provided a much needed voice of support for William's actions.

Ellie, however, was obviously traveling two roads simultaneously. This was especially difficult for her when news arrived of the May slaughter of the 54th regiment at Fort Wagner, including details of Ned Hallowell's serious injuries. Then, at the beginning of July, Ellie's own brother, Willy, was severely wounded at the Battle of Gettysburg where he served as first lieutenant of the First Independent Battery. As Ellie reported to Theodore Weld, apparently, Willy and his commanding officer, Captain Cowan, were injured in a rebel attack. The "ball" that hit Willy entered at the right breast near the top of the lung and exited near the bottom of the shoulder blade, splintering the edge of the bone. At the time, the young soldier felt no pain, "except of suffocation." Two of his men ran toward him, one probably saving his life by holding him in his arms until an ambulance took him to a farmhouse a mile outside of Gettysburg. There he remained for six weeks, always being waited upon by this one soldier. Within a week of his injury, David, Marianna, Eliza, and Frank Wright arrived to tend to him. Meanwhile, the four army surgeons present shook their heads and predicted that although his wound was "*not* necessarily mortal," his chances of surviving were "the smallest" because of the high rate of pneumonia among the patients.[110] Ellie waited and worried at home for six weeks until Willy improved enough to return to Auburn, where his family helped him make a full recovery.

Ellie and William's correspondence courtship intensified during the latter half of 1863, and on Valentine's Day of the following year, when Ellie once again paid a visit to Massachusetts, William proposed marriage. Ellie eagerly accepted. The Garrison family was overjoyed by the news, Helen, even though now very ill, enjoyed William's reading her parts of Ellie's letters. As Ellie told Lucy, once she accepted William's proposal, she had to visit Helen, "alone." Feeling extremely nervous, she trembled as she entered the room, but what she found was a frail older woman resting in "her little white bed looking very gentle, & well contented." Helen put out her hand and "two little tears rolled down her face." She and Ellie spoke for a while, and by the time she left, Helen was happy and laughing, telling Ellie how the Garrison house was now her home.[111] Fanny, Frank, and Wendell all expressed their approval; only George, who was in the South, was not yet cognizant of the news. Lloyd was equally happy, writing Ellie that he did not know her very well, but from their few visits together, he was sure that she was a "fortunate" choice for his son. As for William, he assured Ellie that he was "kind and affectionate, his principles radical and upright, his aims honorable; and his aspirations towards the perfect good." Lloyd gave the couple his "heartfelt benediction" and extended Helen's as well.[112] Ellie notified her own parents on February 17, asking them for their "full consent" to marry William, praising his good character and assuring them that this was not an impulsive act on her part. "For a long time I have been thinking of it, and I have tried to use my judgment instead of my feelings. There is now no conflict in my mind."[113]

William sent a letter to the Wrights on the same day as Ellie, apologizing for dropping his "bombshell" and not waiting for a longer courtship period to pass. However, since he was already twenty-six years old, he wished to move ahead with his and Ellie's marriage plans. William assured the Wrights that he had a good position as "confidential clerk" to Richard Hallowell, which he had assumed the previous July, and that his salary of $1,200 for the first year, although not a fortune, was a good beginning.[114] He, too, wished for Ellie's parents' blessing. Martha, however, responded directly to Ellie, stating her surprise at receiving William's letter. "It was unexpected to me," she wrote, "because I supposed he was 'as ever. Fraternally yours.'" Although she and David regretted losing their youngest daughter to marriage, they knew that she had chosen wisely, especially since William was a Garrison. "The kind and loving welcome accorded to you by his family is gratifying to us," she continued, "and must be very pleasing to you, and we can receive him with equal tenderness, not only on acct. of his own moral worth, but because he is the son of one whom we have so long regarded with reverence."[115] Aunt Lucretia Mott seconded this sentiment in her own note of congratulations to William. The first-generation Garrisonians were now seeing the success of their community rearing of children in a second generation who were forming intimate alliances. "Her co-operation with her mother in reformatory measures," Mott wrote William, "has given weight to her character—preserving her from the follies of fashionable life . . . and now we can rejoice that, in this most important step she finds a congenial spirit—for we cannot regard her cherished friend as a stranger—Your family has long seemed almost interwoven with ours, so closely allied in the slave's cause, as well as in liberal Christianity."[116] Only Ellie's sister, Marianna, disapproved of the match. Apparently, she wanted Ellie to marry someone she had in mind for her, and it took her quite some time to warm up to William.[117]

Lucy, of course, was thrilled with the match, claiming to have read Ellie's letter sixty-five times, each reading giving her more pleasure. She quickly wrote William, wondering whether she was winning or losing in this new arrangement and whether to feel jealous or not. Nevertheless, she congratulated him on his great good fortune. "You see," she explained, "we were always together while we were at school, have written shoals of letters since; . . . and indeed, never staid far apart when we could help it. In all this time, through all our experiences, many merry, some sad—she has ever been the bonniest companion, the gentlest, the most unselfish, truest, tenderest of girls. If she has a fault, it is in too much loving." Lucy worried that she would receive fewer letters from her friend now that she would be spending most of her energy writing to William. "Corresponding was the next best thing to being with her," she continued. "We have had more fun in our few years, than most people have in their whole lives. How she will make you laugh—that is when you get *real well* acquainted—until bye & bye nothing will seem worth anything unless she is with you."[118] She then jokingly told Ellie about her "shockingly (I fear) informal" letter to William, "It's all lies, too. You know I had to try & say something decent about you, & it took me a full hour of steady thinking to conjure up anything that could be twisted into a merit for you. Poor deceived young man! With such good principles too. He has my deepest sympathy."[119] Even Lizzie Powell was pleased, or so she claimed. Having finally met Ellie the previous week, Lizzie congratulated her, adding in a bittersweet tone, "It is a richer blessing than I deserve, to be held so near to you both, but I like it. I have been used to Willie's love so long that I should miss it,—And now I have not only his but yours too."[120] Lizzie obviously felt some envy toward Ellie, for she later wrote, "It would have been so terrible if I had usurped your place. The niche made for you was too large for me, and of course I could not fill it, and I am thankful beyond all word-power, that I have been spared the fearful fate of robbing you of your husband."[121] Indeed, Lizzie and Willie remained fast friends for some time, especially after she moved to the Boston area to study physical education with Dio Lewis and then to open her own gymnasium.

While both Ellie and William continued to be concerned about the war raging around them, the next six and a half months were equally filled with the joys of daily letter writing and planning for their wedding, which came sooner than most people of the time considered appropriate. During their period apart, they largely discussed personal issues, but when politics entered several of William's letters, especially in terms of George's service, his own fear of the draft, his volunteer work teaching maimed veterans accounting, or Lloyd's feelings about the controversies within the antislavery movement and in the broader political world, they both knew that they were of a similar mind. What William wanted to make perfectly clear to Ellie was that although he was the son of William Lloyd Garrison, he had certain different qualities. Most important was his commitment to financially support his own family. Both William and Ellie acknowledged that they had been raised in a very special environment, one that taught them to value "integrity and devotion to principle." The abolitionist community presented them with the opportunity "to know intimately men and women of humble means, yet of grand natures, whose lives bless every one with whom they come in contact." The world outside the antislavery movement did not value or "esteem" these people and, indeed, society had barred them from many fashionable resorts, "but in their souls," William noted, "are peace & beauty indescribable, which hallow & glorify this life." William's desire was to "keep very near such . . . in spirit & endeavor." Therefore, in deference to principle, William and Ellie might make choices that would prevent them from accumulating great sums of money. However, William promised that he would not ask Ellie to share a life "involving hardship & lack of comfort. It shall be my life's delight to place you above such possibility."[122]

William felt he owed a great debt to his family for providing him with a sound moral upbringing, but he did not wish to duplicate the financial insecurities that had always plagued his childhood home. "It has always puzzled me," he wrote Ellie, "to know how Father has been able to get along since he was married, without becoming hopelessly involved in pecuniary difficulties." William admitted that none of the Garrison children was ever deprived of anything they desired even though the family was always in financial straits. "To be sure," he continued, "it looks now, as it has every year, as if both ends could not be made to meet, Father's income receiving no increase & the necessities of life doubling in force, with the added possibility of the *Liberator* dying gracefully with the year, but we borrow no trouble, confident as ever that all will be well. I never knew Father to have fifty dollars more than he wanted & I never knew him to keep any man waiting for his pay." However, this was not the way William wanted to live, "to have this phantom of debt lying in wait for you & ready to spring out at a moment's warning."[123] Never would this happen to them.

Ellie appreciated hearing these sentiments from William, as she too had contemplated the financial and familial aspects of her future and recalled her own mother's situation. "She has suffered more than most women & is no nearer peace & happiness now than at first." In a rare piece of exposure of her family history, Ellie continued, "The children came too fast, the purse was too slender. The consequence is plain—the father nervous & overworked—no time to get acquainted with his family—the mother poor soul—half dead.—It all began by running into debt—& that isn't yet ended, & we have still to be careful of every sixpence, & if possible make it do for two sixpences—Now I have such a horror of debt, that I should rather starve, than borrow a farthing—I dont care how much I have to economise (I am well skilled in that art) if I can only be free from this responsibility."[124]

William took certain steps to ensure that his prospective family would be financially secure. First was his choice of profession. By spending seven years in Lynn learning accounting and then another two years working in banking, William had set a path for himself as a businessman. He considered his position in Richard Hallowell's wool firm an opportunity to move up the ladder in a sound venture, an opportunity that the trusted abolitionist community had created. Once on the job and engaged, he invested in life insurance. Although the annual premium from the New York Life Insurance Company was high, he felt that it was worth the investment, for after ten years all payments would cease and he would receive interest payments off the policy. Meanwhile, William's sense of responsibility maintained him through some difficult times. For starters, the wool business was unstable, especially when areas that supplied the product were involved in battles, such as Richmond, Virginia, in May 1864, or when the general economy of the country experienced panics and depressions. In addition, William learned that even though he and Richard Hallowell were politically compatible, they did not always get along with each other. At various times, Richard reprimanded William for mistakes he made in his work even when William felt the errors did not warrant the kind of strong emotional reaction they invoked in his employer. During one particular instance, William had to learn an entirely new accounting system. Although he eventually succeeded, the time it took him to master it and the errors he made along the way created an unhappy work environment. Richard often apologized to William for his outbursts, especially after William and Ellie, his wife's cousin, became engaged. In the end William learned a great deal from Richard, and despite their mutual feeling that they did not want to socialize with each other, the two men remained on friendly terms even when, after a year, William branched out on his own. William remained in the wool business for many years, in 1866 becoming part of Bailey, Jenkins, & Garrison of Boston, and in 1877 forming Garrison & Rodliff.

Together, Ellie and William determined that because of his financial situation, it was better for them to board with others than to begin their married life in their own home as their parents had done. Because William felt a strong commitment to help his ailing mother, after much discussion between them and with Lloyd and Helen, the two decided that they would move into the Garrison home itself. Although Fanny and Frank still lived there, George was in the army, and Wendell had moved to New York City. By living at home, not only would the newlyweds be saving money but William could help Lloyd and Helen with their expenses, especially since Lloyd, after all these years, had finally begun talking about retirement. William felt there were definite advantages to beginning his and Ellie's life together at Dix Place, telling his fiancée, "You will have more insight into my way of living & thinking & see the surroundings to which I have been accustomed & through these know your husband as he is."[125] Moreover, Ellie would have Fanny for company as well as the companionship of the rest of his family.

Of course, Dix Place was not the ideal home for the newlyweds, or for the Garrisons either. Over the years, the neighborhood had taken a downturn, the streets crowded with people day and night, the noise interminable. From Lloyd's perspective, the stressful environment and the still frequent visitors to the Garrison home prevented Helen's health from improving. He and the children came to believe that moving from the center of town was both desirable and necessary. With William's nuptials fast approaching, they decided that it was a good time to look for new quarters. All of the Garrisons, except George, became involved in house hunting, and within a short period they found a wonderful new home in an area then called the Roxbury Highlands. Located on a street shaded by old trees, the house was reached by a road winding uphill for several blocks from Washington Street. Ironically, it was situated less than a mile from Freedom's Cottage, where Helen and Lloyd had begun their married life.

The house itself, hidden by trees, was perched near a rocky ledge about thirty feet above the unpaved sidewalk. Lloyd at first wanted to call this new home "Bird's Nest," but the family settled on "Rockledge," a name that Fanny suggested. As William described it, the two-story wooden house, painted a straw color, had a parlor to the left of a wide entry—a square room with windows on three sides. Opposite it was a "cozy sitting room" and behind it a "good sized dining room." Then came the kitchen, a large china and silver closet, a pantry, and near the kitchen a washroom with stone tubs. On the second floor were four bedrooms and a bathroom, which had only cold water, and upstairs from that an attic with two other rooms. The house had plenty of closets and gas in every room except the attic. The entire cost was $8,000, much of which came from the sale of the Dix Place home, the rest from a mortgage. Since the family had always been "migratory," William felt that there would be no sadness over leaving their old house.[126] Within days of William and Ellie's wedding on September 14, the family moved to 125 Highland Street.

William was the first to arrive for his nuptials at the Wrights' home in Auburn, but what he found was not what he expected. Ellie was ill from her usual severe headaches as well as "a shocking cold in her lungs."[127] For three days, William comforted and encouraged her. Finally, when the wedding evening arrived, dismal and raining, Ellie summoned her will, and with the help of Fanny and Lucy, who literally had to hold her up, she got dressed. The Wrights' small parlor was festooned with autumn leaves and branches interspersed with bouquets of flowers brought by friends. The procession walked in: Wendell and Lucy first, then Fanny and Ellie's brother, Willy, and finally Ellie's niece, Emily Mott, accompanied by Frank Wright. Samuel J. May, the same Unitarian minister and friend who had joined Helen and Lloyd thirty years before, led Ellie and William in their vows. As Wendell related to George, their father's eyes "were somewhat moistened, and if he did not rub them to see if he were dreaming, he was at least puzzled to realize just what was taking place."[128] Even Wendy found it hard to believe that he had a married brother. After the shortened ceremony and reception, Ellie and William retired to her room. They had planned to honeymoon in Lenox for two or three days before journeying on to Philadelphia for another short spell, but because of Ellie's condition, they stayed in Auburn for a few days and then traveled directly to Roxbury, where Helen and Frank, who had not been at the wedding, had arranged for their room to be redecorated.

While William and Ellie were going through their courtship and engagement, Lucy and Wendell were carrying on a far less traditional romance. It was clear in March 1863 that Wendell was drawn to Lucy but that she was not enthusiastic about entering into a serious relationship with him. Unlike Ellie, Lucy was confident in herself as an independent woman, her short time in Port Royal strengthening her resolve to do more assertive work for newly freed people. In addition, still reeling from the death of Dick Chase and Bev's psychological state, she could not bring herself to believe that she was entitled to happiness just then. Having accepted Dick's ring, she may also have felt the deep loss of a not yet promised mate, but certainly a sweetheart. Complicating her feelings was the fact that Wendell was a diehard nonresister, just like William. Lucy may have found his advances unacceptable at first because she was working through her own issues of conscience. During the summer of 1863, however, the clever suitor arranged to visit the McKims in Philadelphia in order to accompany his brother, Frank, and Lucy's brother, Charley, on a walking vacation.[129] In order to pursue Lucy further, later in the summer, he paid another visit to the McKims, where he entertained the family by "playing the Raw Recruit madly on the piano & everybody else whistling & cracking bones." Even Lucy's Quaker mother, who did not participate in singing and dancing, "*did* appear." Never, Lucy wrote, had she seen "a sweeter vision!" Fred Dennis, an Eagleswood alumnus and military man soon to wed Annie McKim, liked Wendy a great deal, and even Lucy admitted to Ellie that "Wendell is admirable, unimpeachable—as perfect as this flesh allows"; but nonresisters, even Garrisons, were outsiders, and therefore suspect.[130] Lucy was more admiring of Ned Hallowell and Bev Chase than of Wendell.

Furthermore, Lucy was well aware that her father, although a great friend of Lloyd and admirer of Wendell, initially had reservations about the younger Garrison's nonresister stance. Wendell himself related to William, "Mr. McKim regrets that I have thus recorded myself on the side of the peace doctrine, thinking that . . . I may be hampered of my free will hereafter by the recollection that I am committed." Wendell, however, held strongly to his beliefs. "Of course," he added, "I cannot show him how thoroughly I have investigated the question, and am far from deeming that I have probed it to the bottom; but with my present understanding of its scope, I feel acquitted of all injury to my fellow-man when I embrace the doctrine of love to all the race, and complete obedience to the laws of God." Wendell's legacy from the antislavery struggle was the lesson that "the doctrine of peace on earth and goodwill to man is the only armor that the moral reformer can put on and find impenetrable."[131] This was indeed a difficult position for the young Garrison men to maintain when their own brother and innumerable friends were risking their lives every day to fight the war to emancipate the slaves. With this awareness and her father's doubts about Wendell's position, it is not surprising that Lucy would not immediately open her heart to him.

Lucy, however, so impressed Wendell with her tales of Port Royal that in April 1864 he decided to travel to the area to experience the work of the relief societies and also to see his brother, George. Unfortunately, by then the war had grown so intense in South Carolina that the federal government was making it very difficult for relief workers and teachers to obtain the necessary papers for the journey, so a captain of the 54th regiment agreed to take Wendell along as a "servant." William did not approve of this scheme, telling his brother that he and Lloyd were very worried about his going in such a covert manner, for, in the end, he might face repercussions from the authorities. William wrote him, "I presumed you would decide at once not to go in any assumed character, much less as a non-resistant attaché to a military officer."[132] Wendell decided against the trip, claiming he had too many lectures to give and little free time.

Meanwhile, the issue of whether Lucy and Wendell should marry became a point of discussion among William and Ellie and several other family members. Ellie saw having Lucy as a sister-in-law as the next logical step in their friendship. William also liked the idea of a match, but he warned Ellie against meddling too much in their lives. "If it is right they should come together they will, but save us from the possibility of helping in a reunion which would dwarf instead of expanding two great souls."[133] Martha Wright and Sarah McKim had suggested that Wendell not "let the grass grow," and Ellie, frustrated by the situation, told William that "If Fate doesn't mean that he shall have her, it was cruel to let him love her." However, she had to admit that Lucy was one of the "rare beings" who knew herself and "never could act upon impulse." Although she trusted Lucy's judgment, Ellie wished that she would "discover in Wendell what it is necessary for a woman to discover in the husband she chooses."[134] William also perceived that despite Wendell's nonresister position, the McKims, especially, wanted an "alliance" with the Garrison family and were putting "undue" pressure on Lucy. Although convinced that Wendell loved her more than any other woman, William feared that Lucy did not return the feeling. "I do *not* believe she loves him," he wrote Ellie, "no doubt she *likes* him. To consent to marriage with such feelings would be one of the most cruel things on her part." William trusted Lucy not to marry without love, but he distrusted her ability to resist her parents' desires. He himself simply wished that "Lucy would love Wendell."[135]

That the McKims exerted pressure on Lucy was made evident to Ellie during a visit where Miller and Sarah McKim spoke endlessly about Wendell and hinted about the possible union between him and Lucy. At one point, the two embarrassed their daughter before her friend, who reported that "she colored up to her eyes, when her father mentioned him; she declared the reason was physical, & not in the region of the heart."[136] Ellie hoped this was a sign that Lucy was warming up to Wendell, but she conceded that "If Lucy is not in love—her father & mother are. Her father thinks *she is,* and *doesn't know* it. She talks of it, reasons with herself, & wonders if the strong yet not impulsive feeling of attraction that she is conscious of, may be the divine love—I'm afraid it is not, if she can take it to pieces so calmly."[137]

Indeed, unbeknownst to the McKims, Lucy had finally accepted Wendell's proposal, but she would not tell anyone, except Ellie. For several weeks, the two refused to make the announcement even semipublic. On July 2, Wendy told William that he was amazed that Lucy had accepted him, revealing to his brother that his mind had been made up in the winter of 1862 after having visited the McKims, but before Ellie and Lucy had paid their visit to the Garrison home. He had carefully laid out his plans, making his 1863 summer trip to Pennsylvania a "courtship," even though he never called it that. When he returned to Boston in September, he had proposed to Lucy in a letter but was "put off, but not rejected." He had determined to wait a year, as Lucy had requested, but in June 1864, when he revisited the McKim home, he could not prevent himself from asking her again. He told his brother that "when the word was uttered by me, there came a revulsion, a collapse of predeterminations, and like kindred drops we mingled into one."[138] Ellie, of course, was ecstatic. "I keep a little choir in my heart," she wrote William, "& all the time the chorus sings, Lucy & Wendell. Lucy & Wendell!"[139] To Wendy, she wrote, "Young man. It is unnecessary for me to tell you what I think of Lucy. She is more dear to me than a sister, & I'm sure there will be all harmony, in the life you are to live together."[140] Lloyd and Helen were equally happy, though surprised. "As the daughter of two of my earliest and most beloved friends, to whom I have been attached by the tenderest ties," Lloyd wrote, "she will ever have special claims upon my regards."[141] To Lucy, he expressed his pleasure that the McKim and Garrison families were to be united after all these years of friendship. As for Wendell, "He is unspeakably dear to me," he told her, and though once fearful that all his sons "would live and die bachelors," he was happy to be proved wrong.[142]

For well over a month, however, the couple pretended to keep their news secret. As William told Ellie, "But it is a humbug . . . a stupendous one, this secret which every day finds a new confident. The Hoppers have been told & Lucy writes Wendell to impart the fact to Anna Hallowell at once, as it would grieve her to be kept out of the family confidence." Then, of course, Ellie had to be allowed to tell her mother, and so on. "I expect the *world* to congratulate the parties in a fortnight," Willie continued, "as it will by that time have been whispered to everybody in this country & some in Europe, & maybe will be announced in the editorial columns of the *Independent,* in italics."[143]

Wendell did not want to lose any time in making the engagement known, but Lucy remained hesitant to do so. When he suggested she go to a jewelers for a ring, she complained to Ellie that she felt it was like being fitted "for a pair of shoes." Somehow, she was embarrassed to treat the engagement as an everyday reality. But as she wrote to "Nellchen," she was surprised at how much she "likes" Wendell.[144] Whether she was pressured into marriage or simply could not admit her feelings is hard to say. When Lucy arrived at Ellie and William's wedding, in any case, she wore a bright new ring on her finger and looked "more *settled*" than she had before.[145] The two friends discussed their great good fortune in having met "two dearest brothers" who would now make them sisters, finding "new things to admire new qualities to love & not much to find fault with." They "congratulated each other, ourselves, & *them.*"[146]

Lucy and Wendell did not wed as quickly as Ellie and William. Rather, they waited well over a year to become husband and wife. Lucy was not in any hurry to marry before the customary yearlong engagement. She also needed to see that the war came to an end. Wendell, too, had to carry on his work of giving antislavery lectures and building his career in journalism. On December 6, 1865, as planned, Lucy and Wendell were wed before a "large and very select" crowd by the Unitarian minister William Henry Furness in his church at Tenth and Locust Streets in Philadelphia.[147] Annie and Fred Dennis entertained the guests in their home, and within hours the couple left by train for their rooms at 155 East 10th Street in New York City. Much to her sadness, Helen was again unable to attend her child's wedding, Frank remaining home with her a second time. Helen and Lloyd had two of their sons married within a year and a half. The festivities were not quite over, however. A month after Wendy and Lucy were wed, Fanny married Henry Villard, a German journalist who had won her heart.

THE FAMILY REDEFINED

> In the future, you should let your children go on his or her own hook, while you and mother seek some quiet resting-place, invaded only by friendly letters or by an occasional paper from the outside world.
>
> Wendell Phillips Garrison to his father, 1860

CHAPTER VIII

A turning point in the Garrison children's history came in 1864. In that year they took their first steps in becoming their parents' caretakers and also gave clearer shape to their own adult paths. By so doing, they redefined the family's structure. Among the events that pushed them in new directions were Helen's stroke, Lloyd's aging, George's service in the Civil War, William and Ellie's courtship and marriage, Wendell's move to New York and his engagement to Lucy, Fanny's growing attachment to a German national, Henry Villard, the family's move to Rockledge, and Frank's assuming the bulk of the responsibility for his parents' basic needs.

The most profound event in redefining the family was Helen's stroke on December 29, 1863. Although Lloyd wanted to accept responsibility for taking care of her, it was painfully clear to Helen's children that he could not carry this burden by himself. Almost sixty and showing great strain and fatigue from producing the *Liberator* every week for more than thirty years, he simply did not have the physical stamina for the job. His constant ailments, including back problems (perhaps a result of working over a desk all those years), incessant colds, and ever more frequent bodily aches and pains, required their own tending. Although Lloyd spent many nights sitting up with Helen, attending to her needs as best he could, it became necessary for a series of domestic workers and friends to help the family out. As tradition dictated, however, the major share of the household responsibilities initially rested on Fanny's shoulders, she being the only daughter. Fanny later recalled her daily cycle as one of endless responsibility—taking care of Helen each night and morning, ordering meals, doing housework, and giving music lessons in order to help with the family's finances. Frank, who was then fifteen, felt sorry for his sister, claiming, "Fanny has her hands full now-a-days. Mother's sickness threw the whole responsibility of the household affairs upon her, & she has had to bear a double weight. Besides this, she has nine scholars on the piano, & also takes lessons herself on it, & in German." Upon reflection, Frank felt that the shrinking of the family, with Wendell in New York and George in South Carolina, left "large gaps" that the rest of them could not fill.[1]

The family, as a whole, was very protective of Helen. Fanny, for example, prevented people from visiting her mother, fearing that any conversation might overexcite her and hamper her recovery. From Ellie's perspective, Fanny "guarded her door like a dragon," even when Helen insisted she not do so.[2] Wendell, in New York, was worried when he heard that in early February 1864, his mother had taken a fall from a chair she had been placed in. Fretting over her vulnerability, he hinted that the others should be more watchful. When Helen herself contemplated her bleak future of uselessness to her family and the abolitionist community, Wendell tried cheering her up, "No, dear Mother, I cannot think your helplessness is to be long protracted." The great care his mother had taken of him and his siblings, he promised, would now be returned; "for all the cares" she had "multiplied upon them," her children would "repay . . . in a thousandth degree."[3]

Indeed, at the end of April, when Helen finally emerged from the house for a carriage ride, William commented that the event marked "four months to the day . . . one of the saddest days of my life—when the dreadful paralytic shock came to poor mother." Even though he, Lloyd, and Fanny had to carry her downstairs, William felt hope that the "black fears" that Helen would never leave her bed again were long gone.[4] When Ellie joined the Garrisons that September, she found that Helen dined with the family but could only use her previously damaged right hand, her left hanging "like lead." It took Ellie some time to adjust to Helen's condition; she found it "dreadful to see her so disabled; I think death would be to me, far preferable."[5] Most days for the rest of her life, Helen sat in a chair in her upstairs room or downstairs by a window near the front entry, watching the outside world go by.

To the end of her life, the family sought out all available treatments for Helen. Mediums massaged her crippled limbs, offering their additional spiritualist energy to the mix while Lloyd purchased every medicine and ointment friends and homeopathic physicians recommended. Most commonly, however, Helen's attendants offered electric treatments, which had become particularly popular after the Civil War when many people believed that electricity contained a magical force that could cure a variety of ailments.[6] W. R. Wells, in his 1869 book, *A New*

Theory of Disease, espoused the idea that all illnesses had one cause, the "loss of balance of the two forces of electricity in the part or parts diseased."[7] The Garrison family placed great faith in the new electrotherapy, believing that the modern machines created for the treatment would surely cure Helen, whose paralysis seemed to them a clear sign of an imbalance in her body. Frank became the family expert on the electric battery, a device consisting of brass plates, electrodes, and various cups and sponges wired to a small wet (galvanic) cell that, when activated, sent a "modest" electrical current directly to the patient.[8] First, metal plates were attached to Helen's leg, hand, arm, and back. Then her feet were placed in a metal tub holding about an inch of hot salted water. To gradually raise the water's temperature, the electrode was dropped into the tube along with more hot water. Each treatment lasted about twenty to thirty minutes, after which Frank or another member of the family massaged Helen's paralyzed limbs. Helen suffered through these treatments for many years, sometimes feeling better afterward, often, worse. Her progress was extremely slow until it eventually stalled, then stopped.

At times, Helen's retiring personality and modest ways resulted in self-blame for her crippled body. In September 1864, when her physician remarked about her lack of progress, she interpreted that to mean that she did not work hard enough to bring about her own recovery. Her inability to be the self-sufficient woman she had always been plus her usual self-consciousness moved Lloyd to comment to Lucy McKim, "As a matter of choice, wife would much rather be at home than anywhere else, especially as an invalid, always fearing she may give some trouble, and preferring to show rather than to receive hospitality."[9] Even in her great pain and frustration, Helen tried not to be a bother to anyone. Her sons remembered watching her struggle up the flight of stairs to her room, "holding her skirt in her teeth, and dragging the useless limb from stair to stair, rather than call her daughter, who was putting her baby to sleep, to bring down the forgotten handkerchief."[10]

Helen's previous ability to serve her family and her husband's colleagues had given her a sense of contributing to the greater good. That part of her life had ended, and she missed it sorely, sorrowfully telling her husband, "I feel a longing desire to be able to do something for you, and the dear children for I am not anything to my family which depresses me exceedingly at times."[11] Ironically, what probably made her life more isolated and depressing was the move to Rockledge, which Lloyd had seen as a way of protecting Helen from the hordes of people who had constantly descended upon their home. The result, however, was to effectively cut her off from almost all people except her family and those guests who made their way out to Roxbury. Although the children and Lloyd took her for rides in specially designed carriages and even, at one point, unsuccessfully tried to get her to use a wheelchair, neither compensated for her loss.

Helen's disability and fragile health had an unanticipated effect on the family's finances as Lloyd became hesitant to travel far from home in order to give speeches.

This loss of revenue was compounded when strained relationships within the abolitionist movement resulted in diminished subscriptions and sales of the *Liberator.* Problems among Garrisonians arose over the question of what activities antislavery activists should pursue once the Civil War had begun. Some leaders, such as Lloyd and James Miller McKim, felt that the abolitionist societies should be disbanded in favor of freedmen's aid associations; others felt that the antislavery societies should remain intact.[12] The essential difference between the two positions was that abolitionist societies, basically distrustful of the government, would continue to rally against slavery and act to establish and protect the civil rights of African Americans, whether in the North or the South. The freedmen's aid associations, in cooperation with the government, would provide physical help for the newly freed people, especially in the provision of clothing, housing, and tools and in promoting literacy and traditional academic education. Of course, civil rights was also a concern of these associations, although their concentration was on the South. In early 1862, Miller McKim attempted to redefine his own position by resigning as secretary of the Pennsylvania Anti-Slavery Society in order to put his entire effort into organizing the Pennsylvania Freedmen's Relief Association. He ended up serving in both organizations, although his heart was in the freedmen's cause.

McKim and Lloyd's interest in creating a freedmen's movement as opposed to continuing the antislavery societies met with strong opposition. Lloyd's own feeling was that by creating a new movement, people who had originally opposed abolitionist work would be open to joining while, if left to their original design, membership in antislavery organizations would stagnate. Wendell Phillips did not agree with him, and although he was Lloyd's closest friend during the roughest years of the antislavery struggle, to the great distress of the Garrison children, during 1864 the friendship between the two began to unravel. Although the cause for this estrangement was obviously political disagreement, the general turmoil within the family may have clouded Lloyd's usually calm vision. In any case, the actual confrontations between Lloyd with his followers and Phillips with his arose over the issue of Abraham Lincoln's reelection. Although Lloyd, the nonresister, had never voted, over the years, he had come to believe that Abraham Lincoln was performing adequately as president. The Emancipation Proclamation in particular convinced Lloyd that Lincoln's acceptance of the antislavery mission of the war would ensure eventual political and social justice for the freed people. Phillips, however, believed that although Lincoln saw the slavery issue as a necessary element of the war, he did not define the conflict in human rights terms, and would, therefore, not pursue a civil rights path once the war ended. As a result, when the President announced his intention to once again seek the Republican Party's nomination, Lloyd supported his bid while Phillips supported that of John C. Fremont, a former Civil War general.

On May 10 and 11, at the annual meeting of the American Anti-Slavery Society in New York City, Lloyd and Phillips had a fiery debate about Lincoln. After their encounter, the membership passed Phillips's resolution expressing doubts that Lincoln would place the freedom of the slaves above all else in the war. Lloyd, momentarily defeated, continued his part of the debate in the pages of the *Liberator,* assuring his readers that this was simply a political argument without negative implications for the cohesiveness of the abolitionist community. As he wrote to Helen, "I trust nothing fell from my lips which was deemed personal or unkind by dear Phillips."[13] James Miller McKim was not as confident. Initially, he merely expressed surprise at Lloyd's infatuation with Abraham Lincoln, claiming, "I am not a Lincoln man—nor any man's man. (Nor are you)."[14] By mid-May, however, he had grown concerned that Lloyd and Wendell Phillips's disagreement would cause a split in the movement and an end to their friendship. Hence, after the New York meeting, he cautioned Lloyd, "As it is clear that he is on his guard not to say a word that would even seem to be out of keeping with the life-long friendship that has existed between you, and as I know that you mean to be equally careful, I am comparatively easy on that point. Not absolutely however I must confess; for antagonism between the best of friends when on rival points and before the public in 99 cases out of an hundred, render more or less alienation."[15]

McKim's sense of dread was proven correct when Lloyd and Phillips again created sparks, this time at the annual meeting of the New England Anti-Slavery Convention. William and Fanny, who were sitting on the speakers' platform with their father, witnessed the affair. As William admitted to Ellie, he was, of course, not an impartial observer, both because of his great devotion to his father and his own "sympathies" with those who supported Abraham Lincoln. What William witnessed was his father's decimation of Phillips's ideas before a "strongly divided" audience. Once Phillips concluded his hour-and-a-half-long speech, Lloyd took each of his comrade's points and contradicted it with quotes from Phillips's own previously favorable remarks about Lincoln made earlier in the war years. According to William, the audience "caught the joke, enjoying it hugely," but Phillips did not. He turned "pale, when at each pat quotation the whole assembly would break into shouts of laughter & the galleries echo with derisive questions."[16] A month after the incident, William claimed that all was well between the two men and that "not one unpleasant personal feeling occurs to either," but in fact their friendship had taken a negative turn, and, although remaining cordial, they lost the intimacy they had once had.[17]

Indeed, the next year, as both the war and slavery ended, Lloyd, believing that its goal had been reached, resigned from the American Anti-Slavery Society, and Phillips was elected its new president. At about the same time, Lloyd's high estimation of Lincoln was reinforced when Theodore Tilton, editor of the New York *Independent,* arranged for him to meet the president while they were attending the Republican Party convention in Baltimore. Together, on June 9 and 10, they visited the White House, first in a group, then, alone. Lincoln spent an hour with Lloyd, the latter, according to William, "telling the President frankly his short-comings,—his mistake in not making the Proclamation universal, the wicked treatment of the colored troops. . . . Not one word of congratulation did he give the President regarding his renomination."[18] However, Lloyd left the meeting with the firm conviction that Lincoln was dedicated to uprooting slavery and giving "fair play to the emancipated."[19]

Caught in the struggle between Lloyd and Wendell Phillips was son Wendell. His own feelings about Abraham Lincoln were lukewarm, largely because he detested the national leader's slowness in taking action against slavery, a common complaint within the abolitionist community. "Lincoln has been a drag," he wrote his sister. His war policies were "vacillating" and had "saved unnumbered rebels from the gallows and caused the death—the unnecessary death—of loyal thousands. He is neither a warrior nor a statesman." Wendell's motto for the upcoming election was "A better man than Lincoln if we can; Lincoln and nobody lower if we must." Furthermore, Wendell felt that Lincoln's policies would lead to "long years of vexations and unnecessary agitation to secure the black man his rights as a citizen" and a delay in "the women's movement." Unlike Phillips, however, Wendell would have supported Benjamin F. Butler for president, had he run, as Butler expressed a desire to take "both the radical and conservative sides at once."[20] Wendell's rebellious support of Butler was most likely the one way he could see to remain neutral in the battle between his father and his sponsor, the man he was named after and who had financed his Harvard College education. Indeed, Wendell was so concerned about the possible loss of Phillips's friendship that he contacted him in an attempt to smooth matters over. Phillips responded with great warmth, assuring his namesake that their relationship would always remain "very close & intimate," growing "more kindly & confidential" with each passing day. He expected no repayment for Wendell's education nor did he feel that the young Garrison owed him anything, assuring him, "The good—noble—use you have made of your opportunities far more than repays me for any share I have had in furnishing any of them."[21]

William was also disturbed about the growing schism within the abolitionist movement and the possible dissolution of a community which had nurtured him and his siblings throughout their lives. However, it took him several months to feel comfortable in verbalizing his analysis of the situation, one which clearly showed he was his father's son. To Ellie he wrote:

> Among the abolitionists there are two kinds of philosophy—one is to distrust everybody, to endeavor by every ingenious device to find evidence that the government is the enemy of the black man & every officer under it unworthy to be trusted.

> Caustic criticism, snap judgments, & wholesale asseveration mark this school, as represented by Mr. Phillips, Pillsbury, & Foster.—The other is, faith in the just intentions of a government, whose every step has been an onward, anti-slavery one, and instead of being swift to condemn, when any apparently unfavorable symptom appears, to investigate cautiously & thoroughly, not be ashamed to give full credit where credit is due.
>
> Those who accept the latter believe that the cause of the slave himself is advanced & his equal rights more speedily to be attained by swelling the grand onward current of events to their inevitable goal, assuming as undeniably as sunrise that all must & shall end in perfect & absolute justice. Those who accept the other it seems to me, have only eyes for the shadows of the night & do not see the flood of daylight which is driving the blackness away & I have no doubt that history will do justice to those who show a fair discrimination in their judgments of events & man, taking the broader view of a trustful humanity, though there be cynics to insinuate to-day, that conservatism creeps on with old age & the moral vision of the jubilant is becoming dim.[22]

The effect of all the infighting was profound on the Garrison family, for it led to a decline in income from the *Liberator.* Seeing a threat to the existence of antislavery publications in general, Lloyd's old friend Oliver Johnson, the editor of the American Anti-Slavery Society's newspaper, the *National Anti-Slavery Standard,* proposed that the two papers merge. When Wendell asked his brother George his opinion on the matter, the latter responded that since both newspapers shared many common subscribers, combining them would surely "hasten the downfall" of both. His preference was to allow the *Liberator* to "expire by a natural death." The "only possible way" George saw to save the paper was to reduce it to a half or a third of its size and fill it with Lloyd's own writings.[23] In the meantime, he offered to help his parents financially. Apparently, Lloyd agreed with George, writing Johnson in November that he desired to let the *Liberator* "remain equally distinctive to the end." Although seeing an eventual finale to publication and looking forward to his retirement from the constant work of abolitionism, Lloyd still did not wish to give up the fight until slavery had been successfully abolished through a constitutional amendment. "It [the *Liberator*] will then have accomplished its Anti-Slavery mission," he told Johnson.[24] In the meantime, in an effort to increase his income, he raised the subscription rate from $3 to $3.50, hoping that the difference would make up for the loss of readers. The paper ran at a deficit through 1865. During that time, Lloyd sought extra income by going on a five-week lecture tour to the Midwest. Finally, on December 29, 1865, just eleven days after the Thirteenth Amendment was ratified, thereby officially ending slavery, the *Liberator* concluded its run. As Lloyd had written earlier to his English friend Elizabeth Pease Nichol, "What I shall do after that time, I do not yet know; but, doubtless, the way will be opened to me in due season. The cause of the freedmen will probably demand and receive my special advocacy for some time to come."[25]

As their father's income decreased and their mother's needs increased, the Garrison children accepted increasing responsibility for their parents' support; yet, their own lives also moved along distinctive paths. When George arrived home in September 1865, he had every reason to feel optimistic; he was a victorious veteran with money in the bank and a sweetheart waiting to greet him, for during his stay in South Carolina he had begun a correspondence with Annie Keene Anthony, an abolitionist daughter three years his junior. The daughter of Anna Rhodes and the naturalist John Gould Anthony, Annie was a distant relative through marriage of George's Aunt Charlotte, Helen's sister. Although the Anthonys were of the conservative antislavery community, Lloyd and Helen were pleased with this possible match, believing that George would benefit from being married. Two months after his return, George and Annie became engaged. Within a few days, however, she changed her mind, infuriating Fanny, who complained that Annie had "accepted caresses and attentions" from her brother "as if they had been old lovers." When the young woman broke off the engagement, she told Fanny that she did not love George. "Annie is not to blame for not being able to love George," she wrote her father, "but she is to blame for making every advance. . . . I am confirmed in my original estimate of Annie's character . . . intense selfishness. Her mind is shallow and empty. The more so the farther you probe it. Her love of attention from gentlemen excessive." Annie claimed that Wendy had told her mother that George was "not good enough" for her. Fanny, intensely protective of both her older brothers, believed that Wendy had said no such thing and applauded George's response that Annie knew "that he could not be trifled with."[26]

George's difficult time with Annie did not interfere with his sense of responsibility to his parents. While spending the final months of the *Liberator*'s existence helping his father, he used his earnings from the war years to contribute to household expenses. William, too, who in 1864 worked for Richard Hallowell and lived at home, contributed greatly to his parents' income and became a member of the financial committee of the *Liberator,* an advisory group not responsible for any debt the paper incurred. Ellie's move into the family provided another helping hand in terms of home care and housework, even though at least two domestic workers, a cook and a housekeeper, resided in the Garrison home.[27] Wendell's aid to his parents came primarily through money since he was living far from home, while Frank, still attending the Boston Latin School and having no income, was a great comfort to Helen, paying close attention to her needs and taking care of the traditionally male responsibilities around the house, such as obtaining coal, feeding the furnace, and tending the yard, while also sharing in the shopping for household goods.

Fanny continued to carry the heavy burden of replacing her mother. In time, however, as a maturing young woman, she began to find the weight of these responsibilities too heavy to bear. In April 1863 she had met Henry Villard, and her thoughts were turning to having a future with him. Villard was a German national nine years Fanny's senior who had emigrated to the United States and become a journalist. Fanny, who had been an enthusiastic student of German for several years, found the twenty-eight-year-old man most attractive and intriguing. Indeed, Villard's life story up to 1863 must have seemed as exotic to the relatively untraveled Fanny as it later did to her son, Oswald Garrison Villard, who retold it in 1931 in the form of a fairy tale with kings and vassals.[28] Villard, baptized Ferdinand Heinrich Gustav Hilgard, was born on April 10, 1835, in Speyer, Germany, a small town in the Rhine area of Bavaria, and grew up in nearby Zweibrücken where he received his elementary and secondary education. Unlike Fanny, Henry's family had a long history of belonging to the bourgeoisie, and young Henry (then Heinrich) was exposed to great literature, high European culture, and a good deal of traveling on the continent. Formal schooling, however, presented a problem, for as a free-spirited young man, Henry defied any religious training, refused to pray for and honor the king, and posed such a threat to the school authorities that they expelled him.

In spite of his father's pronouncement that his formal schooling was over, Henry convinced him to send him to a semimilitary academy in the Alsatian town of Phalsbourg, where he promised to achieve the education he knew he needed to remain among the elite. Although he despised the place, he managed to excel in his studies and convince his father to allow him to return to Speyer; there he could attend school while living under the supervision of his grandmother and spinster aunt. Henry spent two happy years in Speyer, studying the classics, carousing with his fraternity friends, and honing his social-climbing skills. When it came time for him to pursue an advanced degree, however, he came in conflict with his father, a lawyer who could not tolerate his son's desire to concentrate his studies on literature and aesthetics. Gustav Hilgard ordered his son to take the course that would lead most quickly to financial independence. Contrary to his own desire to remain in Zweibrücken and study literature and writing, Henry agreed to attend a technical university in Munich. Once in that great city, he followed his heart into literature, was soon found out by his father, and given the option to study law at a more staid university or find himself in the army. After much thought and not notifying his family, the then eighteen-year-old decided to abandon Germany for the United States. Using the little money he had, he bought a second-class ticket to New York City, landing there on October 18, 1853. To reflect his new life, he changed his name to Henry Villard, an identity he borrowed from one of his former French schoolmates at Phalsbourg.[29]

Upon arriving in New York, alone with no money except for twenty dollars which some kindly fellow passengers had lent him, no acquaintances in the city, and practically no knowledge of the English language, Henry immediately contacted Theodor Adolf Engelmann, a great-uncle living in Belleville, Illinois, who, even though questioning his headstrong nephew's motives for immigrating, sent him fifty dollars. On November 19, with this money in his pocket, he headed for the Midwest, stopping in Cincinnati to visit the large Germany community which had settled there. Actually, the young traveler had chosen the ideal moment to move to the United States, as German antebellum immigration was at its peak between 1852 and 1854 with over half a million people heading for new opportunities forced upon them by continual bad harvests and the aftereffects of the 1848 revolution at home. The recent immigrants, with the help of landsmen already settled, established a German subculture in the United States complete with newspapers, local politicians, political groups, social halls, beer gardens, and self-help and charity organizations. This German community, in fact, held several links to Henry's past that helped him forge his future in his new home. In Cincinnati, for example, he stayed at an inn run by a former policeman of Zweibrücken, a man who had served under Gustav Hilgard when he was a justice of the Supreme Court of the then kingdom of Bavaria. The innkeeper and several other Rhenish Bavarians offered to find Henry a job, but his poor English and lack of vocational skills made him virtually unemployable. Unwilling to accept charity, he moved on, wandering around the German-settled areas of the Midwest, sporadically finding day labor, including canvassing German-Americans for a firm of publishers and working on a crew that carried locomotive wood fuel on the Indianapolis and Madison Railroad. It was evident from the start that Henry was a self-motivated, determined, and practically fearless young man.

Henry Villard was also a perfect example of how the German immigrant community took care of its own compatriots. In October 1854, a year after his arrival in the states, he stayed for a time in Chicago, serendipitously finding himself lodging with the elder brother of one of his childhood friends. There, his step-uncle and former schoolmate, Robert Hilgard, traced him through an ad in the German-language paper *Staats-Zeitung* and invited him to join the family in Illinois. Tired of his vagrant lifestyle, Henry accepted, traveling to Belleville via nearby St. Louis in order to become acquainted with more Hilgard relatives. Finally, he settled on his uncle Theodor's farm, becoming a part of a large family consisting of Theodor's wife and their eight children. It was Theodor who succeeded in convincing Henry to write to his parents, something he had not done since his arrival in New York. In response, his father somewhat reluctantly offered to help support him as long as he settled down to learn a skill. Within a few months of moving to Belleville, Henry, through his cousin Scheel, found a job fifty miles away copying deeds into the records for a circuit court clerk and recorder of deeds, which led to his complete immersion in the English language. Once he felt confident in his bilingual abilities, he determined to study law, convincing a Belleville lawyer, George Trumbull, to take him on as an apprentice; but again he grew restless and unhappy with the office environment. His desire to attend law school rather than continuing to train with Trumbull was thwarted by Gustav's refusal to help him out. Hence, Henry moved on.

For a time after leaving Belleville, Henry shifted from one job to another, trying traveling sales work for various companies. Along the way, he learned of the struggle over slavery in Kansas and, like many other German immigrants, sympathized with the abolitionist side. Combining his new political bent with his desire to earn money, he created a scheme to sell young Germans large tracts of land in Kansas in order to establish a German free-soil community. Interestingly, he received capital for this venture from, as he put it, "well-known and wealthy antislavery men."[30] This initial contact with abolitionists proved so unprofitable that he again changed directions, this time acting as head of the printing office of the Racine, Wisconsin, weekly German periodical, *Volksblatt.* He qualified for this job only because he was bilingual, but it ended up marking the beginning of his illustrious career as a journalist and publisher. When Henry accepted the position, the *Volksblatt* was in poor shape, the printing type on the ancient press nearly worn out, the content of the articles unexciting, and many of the farmer subscribers paying their bills with produce such as butter, eggs, and chickens rather than with cold cash. Henry was hired with the idea that a revived periodical could be used to persuade the local German community to vote Republican in any upcoming elections. This mission resulted in his intense involvement in party politics and his writing articles for other newspapers, including the *Neue Zeit,* a New York weekly. In January 1857, when the nearly bankrupt *Volksblatt* had to be abandoned, Henry expanded his newspaper contacts, working freelance for the large and prosperous *Staats-Zeitung,* the *Neue Zeit,* and the German edition of *Frank Leslie's Illustrated Weekly.*

Upon leaving Wisconsin, Henry took a position with the *Staats-Zeitung,* traveling around the midwestern states of Ohio, Indiana, Michigan, and Illinois collecting money for unpaid subscriptions, obtaining new subscribers, and writing "descriptive letters" for the paper.[31] As he spoke with local politicians, he became knowledgeable about a broad range of issues. His reporting on the Lincoln-Douglas debates, for example, brought him deeper into the intricacies of the slavery question, and his coverage of Pikes Peak gave him firsthand experience with the U.S. spirit of capitalist speculation, which he openly embraced.[32] During 1858 and 1859, Henry followed the presidential candidates for the 1860 election, filing reports in English for small papers in the Midwest until, upon meeting Horace Greeley, also on assignment, he began writing for the *New York Tribune* and the Associated Press. His work brought him interviews with Abraham Lincoln, which led to a personal relationship between the two. Henry became one of the few reporters whom Lincoln trusted and relied upon for information throughout his campaign and during the Civil War. His access to Lincoln, his ability to grab any and all opportunities, and his willingness to take risks to get his story in before other journalists helped Henry's reputation grow and netted him continuous work. By 1861 he was earning $25 a week from the *New York Herald* and also submitting articles to the *Commercial* and the *New York Tribune.* His combined income averaged about $3,000 a year, quite a decent sum of money for a single man at that time.

When the Civil War began, Henry wasted no time in joining the ranks of war correspondents. In preparation for this task, he purchased military history books so that he could master the terminology, weapons, and the strategies and tactics of war in general. By July of the war's first year, he was covering major battles, witnessing from the limb of a tree the initial July 21st battle at Bull Run. When artillery fire hit the tree trunk, he was thrown to the ground, but suffered no injury. Rather, he and two other reporters, E. C. Stedman and E. H. House, were forced to take shelter behind a farmhouse from where they observed the battle. Henry immediately wired his story to New York. The reporting was so engaging that the *Herald* immediately assigned him to Louisville to cover the action in Kentucky. There he succeeded in gaining access to the underground courier service that carried letters, documents, and news reports between Louisville and Nashville. With a few well-placed bribes, he was able to send Southern-written articles to the *Herald,* giving the newspaper a truly inside look at the South, both in terms of battles and personal-interest stories. Eighteen-sixty-two found Henry in Tennessee witnessing the capture of Nashville and the bloody campaigns at Pittsburg Landing (the battle of Shiloh) and Perryville, and then in Virginia reporting on battle at Fredericksburg. Shiloh was particularly disturbing, and it was there, after seeing over one thousand mutilated and decomposing bodies, "a spectacle . . . grim, shocking, and sickening," that he began to really contemplate the "horrors of war."[33] In order to ease the mental suffering of the soldiers, he and other journalists tried to fill them in on the events surrounding them. Since he continued having contact with Lincoln, he could offer them what seemed to be official information. Although in October of that year Henry became the Washington war correspondent for the *New York Tribune,* much of his reporting still took place on the battlefield, where he interviewed men in combat, observed battles firsthand, and lived the hard life of a soldier.

In January 1863, Henry's path again crossed that of the abolitionists when the *New York Tribune* assigned him to Port Royal and Hilton Head to report on efforts to retake Charleston and its harbor. By the time he arrived, Thomas Wentworth Higginson had organized his black regiment, the First South Carolina Volunteers, and the Port Royal Experiment was in full swing. Although primarily there to witness the war, Henry was impressed by the abolitionists' efforts, especially after Higginson explained his concept of the role of black soldiers as producing "a moral effect on the slave population" by disseminating copies of Lincoln's Emancipation Proclamation. Higginson's opinion that "nothing would end the war quicker than the employment of negro troops on the largest possible scale" seemed valid to Henry, who reported the success of black troops in battle and as spokespeople for emancipation.[34] Although he agreed with the common abolitionist view that the freed people were naive, simple, and inattentive to their personal care, he shared their faith that former slaves would ultimately evolve into responsible middle-class citizens of the United States.

After having spent two years reporting on the Civil War, the *Tribune* offered the battle-weary Henry a two-week paid vacation. Having no idea where to spend his free time, he asked Sydney Howard Gay, the paper's managing editor (and coincidentally an abolitionist and friend of Lloyd), for a recommendation. Gay urged Henry to visit Boston, the "Hub" of antislavery activity, which he did, arriving there on April 23, 1863, and leaving six days later to continue reporting on impending battles.[35] Although he was a man well used to traveling alone, Henry appreciated socializing with his ever expanding network of acquaintances. Hence, on his third day in Boston, he took a letter of introduction from the Garrisons' longtime friend Theodoric Severance, then working for the Port Royal Experiment, to Severance's wife, Caroline. The Severances' daughter, Julia, kindly invited Henry to accompany her to a class at Dio Lewis's gymnasium, where she introduced him to William and Frank Garrison. The two brothers were so enthralled with the German-accented journalist that they invited him first to accompany them to hear a Sunday sermon by the Reverend Samuel Johnson of Salem and then to dine with the Garrison family. Henry, recognizing the wonderful opportunity being offered him to meet the great antislavery leader, William Lloyd Garrison, was quick to tell the sons, somewhat didactically, of his disgust for "the incomprehensible and most contemptible prejudice in the Northern States against the inspired patriots who demanded the abolition of the horrible institution, at the risk of constant, bitter persecution and personal danger."[36] Fanny, who was also at the gym, later related that she was excluded from this conversation, a frustration since Henry's "noble presence" had "captivated" her "imagination at first sight."[37]

On the morning agreed upon, William and Frank called for Henry at his hotel, and then after the sermon, they, along with Fanny, who had attended church that morning, strolled to the Garrison home on Dix Place where Henry was, of course, warmly greeted. Like so many other guests, he had expected to meet "a fighting figure of powerful build, with thick hair, full beard, and fiery, defiant eyes" instead of the "man of middle size, completely bald and clean shaven, with kindly eyes behind spectacles, and . . . an entirely benignant expression."[38] The entire family eagerly listened to Henry's war stories and plied him with endless questions. They felt so comfortable in his company that they took to using his nickname, Harry. Frank was especially taken with him and offered to entertain him the next morning with a tour of Beacon Hill and a visit with Wendell Phillips. Consumed by the Civil War, but too young to be part of his brothers' more intimate relationship with the draft and serving in the military, Frank lived the war vicariously, grabbing at any opportunity to visit the training camp, observing drills and parades in Boston, eventually writing to James Trotter of the 55th regiment, and keeping up to date on all the battles. Speaking with a well-traveled and often published war correspondent, especially one who opposed slavery, was simply too great an opportunity for him to allow to end. When Henry left Boston to report on an impending battle in Tennessee, the youngest Garrison asked if the two might establish a correspondence. Henry, who had taken a liking to the family in general, and in particular to Fanny, "whose charms of mind and person [he] surrendered on first acquaintance," agreed.[39] Not only would the exchange be entertaining, but perhaps it could also lead to something more meaningful between himself and the Garrisons' only daughter.

Henry Villard's interest in Fanny did not go unnoticed by her parents who did not particularly welcome it. They had grave doubts about the appropriateness of a suitor who was over nine years older than their daughter, was a well-traveled foreigner, and liked to smoke cigars and drink wine, two habits of which none of the Garrisons approved. Fanny, on the other hand, found Henry almost irresistible, but because he was so different from the other young men who had begun to pay attention to her—sending her flowers, calling on her at home, and flirting at antislavery parties and gatherings—she acted cautiously. Fanny, after all, had been raised to look inside the community for socializing and marriage. Had she been attracted to a local young man brought up in the antislavery cause, her parents might have raised an eyebrow at the thought of losing her but been open to a possible match. Henry Villard, however, could pose a threat to the abolitionist cohesiveness of the family unit.

Apparently, when Henry visited the Garrisons, he joined the family for a ride to visit Camp Meigs, where the 54th Regiment was in formation. The assertive reporter used the opportunity to get to know Fanny, but being a mature man of the world, his manner was far more serious than the flirting she was accustomed to from younger abolitionist sons. Henry's maturity, his European manner, and his aggressive and unexpected attention appealed to Fanny. Indeed, she found herself feeling the thrill of love at first sight, an emotion that her parents had felt, as they had related time and again, when they first met. However, Henry had a noticeable flaw. He smoked—and both Fanny and Frank obviously remarked upon it or referred to it in some way. Hence, after their afternoon together, Henry gave Fanny a gift of his cigar case, "rather an extraordinary present for a gentleman to make to a lady," he remarked to Frank, but one with a clear message that he was willing and eager to give up the "weed" if it would make her happy. In the not too distant future, he hoped to "exchange it personally for something more suitable." As he confided to Frank, "My riddance of this expensive habit, if nothing else, will certainly cause me to remember her always. All this is, of course, 'entre nous.'"[40] Interestingly, during this rather tentative early stage of their courtship, Frank became the conduit for Fanny and Henry's news, responding the following week, "Fanny is glad to hear that you have really given up smoking, which is a little more than she expected. She hopes you will have no further temptation." As for being Henry's confidant, Frank promised, "Of course it shall be 'entre nous trois.'"[41]

For two years, Fanny's contact with Henry took place through Frank. Unlike her mother, who had written most intimately to Lloyd in 1834, Fanny's sense of propriety plus her hesitation to throw herself too deeply into this unprecedented relationship outside the abolitionist community led her to decline Henry's invitation to correspond directly to each other. In this regard, her community upbringing dictated her actions. Frank, while agreeing with Fanny's sense of Victorian right and wrong, could not contain himself from revealing his sister's true feelings: "But let me tell you, dear Villard, Fanny loves you as much as you do her, & that from the first moment she met you, she felt interested in you. Her curiosity to see your letters &c. showed me that long ago. Now all you have got to do, when you come back is to 'go in & win.'"[42] Henry was eager to hear any encouraging words, even those from an adolescent boy almost half his age. In the meantime, however, he returned to the war, covering the 1863 campaigns in the Kentucky and Tennessee areas, where, at Murfreesboro, he suffered from a severe attack of malaria which resulted in five weeks of bed rest and the end of his on-site battle coverage. Subsequently, he worked primarily from a Washington, D.C., news agency he organized with his friend Horace White of the *Chicago Tribune,* taking only short trips to battles at the Wilderness in May 1864 and Petersburg in July. With each assignment, his aversion to war and inclination toward pacifism grew stronger. Then, for the first time since his arrival in the United States in 1853, Henry returned to Germany to see his father. (His mother had died in 1859.) The visit, although not the emotional breakthrough he might have wished for, made it comfortable for Henry to contemplate a binational life.

Fanny's intimate family was acutely aware of her growing attachment to Henry Villard, William telling Ellie that Frank "imagines that his little bosom is the sole possessor of Fanny's secret." William, however, was a bit wary of this virtually invisible beau, adding in a most brotherly protective tone, "I wish I could know more of this man. I fear my sister has her affections very strongly set upon him—& yet we only saw him for three days." Fanny kept her feelings to herself, but William marked that "she betrays herself by too carefully avoiding the mention of his name & in the utter indifference & weariness which she evinces towards any man who tried to be attentive."[43] Henry, meanwhile, made some effort in getting to know the Garrisons better, paying a visit to Wendell's office in New York. Since each sibling watched out for the others, Wendell immediately notified William, who in turn told Ellie, who then wondered if Wendell, living so far from home, knew of Fanny's secret. Of course he did, but his knowledge was not as intimate as William's and Frank's. Indeed, the people most in the dark were Lloyd and Helen, who chose not to acknowledge the seriousness of the affair and simply counted each day with Fanny as a blessed one. In July 1864, when Lloyd wrote his congratulatory letter to Lucy on her engagement to Wendell, he contemplated Fanny's future: "Still unengaged, but whoever secures her will get a prize worth having—my word for it. But, you gentlemen, for the present, ask not her hand in marriage."[44]

Little did Lloyd know that at that very moment Henry was dreaming of what life would be like married to Fanny, although he doubted he could win her hand. As he confided to Frank, although "there is one being in this country, that would easily cure me of my restless, roving disposition," he felt there was "no hope" that she would.[45] Henry assumed that by now Fanny had become engaged or was, at the very least, being seriously courted by some young abolitionist. But as Frank informed him, there was only one man whom Fanny had not successfully discouraged, and that was Edward L. Pierce, collector of internal revenue for Boston. Pierce had flirted with practically every abolitionist daughter between Boston and Philadelphia, but none of the young women could tolerate him. Frank described Pierce as "conceited" with the ability to "entertain a company or an audience for a whole evening by talking about himself." In fact, Pierce had been "refused by a half dozen young ladies at least" to whom he had "offered himself," including Lucy McKim.[46] He regularly sent flowers to Fanny and several times appeared at the Garrisons' door uninvited and unwelcome. Whenever Fanny saw him approach, she escaped to her room pretending to have a headache.

On April 15, 1865, after spending six months in Germany, Henry returned to the United States intent on courting Fanny. When they first met again, however, each acted so awkwardly toward the other that Henry decided to cut the visit short and return to New York to reestablish his newspaper ties. While there, he developed his relationship with Wendell, hoping that Fanny's brother might act as his go-between. As he told Frank, he and Wendell carried on a "free exchange of views . . . concerning a certain delicate subject." Wendell even showed Henry some private letters he had received from his sister clearly indicating Fanny's deep feelings for this man she had met in person only four times. What troubled Henry and might have caused the embarrassment of his previous visit to Fanny was his relapse into smoking. Frank criticized him: he had promised to give up cigarettes, and even though Fanny had not seen him smoke, his clothing and breath probably emitted the telltale signs of tobacco use. Henry urged Frank not to discuss the issue with his sister, for, in truth, smoking was a vice he could correct; it was "not of a vital bearing upon one's morality," just a "minor defect."[47]

With Fanny's brothers obviously on his side paving the way for him, subsequent events happened quickly. The couple became engaged within a month, for as much as Henry wanted to settle down, so Fanny wanted to end the tiresome life she had been leading ever since Helen's stroke. Once the situation with Henry looked hopeful, Fanny took a major step to alleviate her burden, namely handing over all her keys to Ellie. This was not just a symbolic gesture, for the woman who held the keys in a Victorian household had the responsibility for what was in each of the closets and cupboards they opened. By handing the keys to Ellie, Fanny was relinquishing her position as female head of the household, a position she had never wanted but which she had assumed as a responsible family member who deeply loved her parents. Ellie herself was unsure how she felt about this move, telling her own mother, "It was not without a pang that I assumed the responsibility but necessity for doing brings with it a power to do, & I am not without hope to see my efforts rewarded with success."[48]

In mid-May Henry returned to Boston, where he again charmed the Garrison family, then very much aware of his and Fanny's hopes for a future together. At the time of his visit, Helen was spending an extended period in Providence under treatment of Joseph Dow, a self-trained electrotherapist who was attempting to ease her paralysis through electric treatment, diet, and physical therapy. Hence, she was not at home on the evening when Fanny and Henry summoned Lloyd into the parlor and announced that they had become engaged. Taken aback that Henry had not conferred with him before asking for Fanny's hand in marriage, Lloyd felt that he could do little but give his "fatherly sanction to the procedure." To Wendell, however, he confided his unspoken hesitation, "I had understood that, between them, there was a growing interest, which, on better acquaintance, and at some future day, might end in such an engagement; but this was so sudden as to be at least momentarily startling."[49] Helen seemed delighted and not as surprised when, in response to a letter from Henry, she also gave her "benediction," telling him, "I have enjoyed so much in my domestic life that I look upon marriage as one of the holiest relations in life, and I trust you will."[50]

William, although approving of the match, was concerned by Henry's fixation on material wealth and the fact that he had already begun to shower Fanny with "generous gifts & large ideas of living."[51] Fanny accepted these gifts but refused any money except for a few offerings from her father and brothers. Instead, she took on even more students in an effort to build her trousseau. After Henry returned to his job as Washington correspondent for the *Chicago Tribune,* both found their time apart so unbearable that they decided upon an early wedding. Fanny explained her feelings in a reassuring letter to her worried father. "Though we are in truth, strangely different," she noted, "he a mature, cultured, earnest man of the world,—and I am as you know, only a natural, affectionate, impulsive, well-meaning young lady—but spite of all this difference, love makes a bridge over the chasm, and we meet irresistibly in the centre, and cannot part. . . . I assure you that my happiness seems complete. His character is all I thought it, noble, generous, inspired with high aims—I feel confident that time will give you another son, worthy of your others."[52]

Almost a month to the day that Wendell and Lucy wed, so did Fanny and Henry, the ceremony taking place in the Garrison home at noon on January 3, 1866. Much to her great joy, Helen was at last able to witness the marriage of one of her children. George Putnam, minister of the First Religious Society of Roxbury and the Garrisons' neighbor, administered the vows before sixty-two close friends, including Wendell and Ann Phillips, Edmund Quincy, Samuel May, and all of Fanny's brothers and her two sisters-in-law. The parlor, decorated with "hanging baskets full of pure white camelias and drooping vines & evergreen, & hothouse plants in pots," hosted a small but bountiful reception of oysters, cake, and coffee catered by Joshua Bell Smith of the Boston African-American abolitionist community. When the celebration ended, Ellie wrote, "It was hard for poor Fan to get away without breaking down, but she tried hard not to stimulate mother's tears. She clung to her father & it seemed as if he couldn't let her go, but they drove off at last & Wm. fired an old slipper after them."[53] As Lloyd sorrowfully wrote to his daughter soon after the wedding, "I find it hard to give you up; for my parental affection for you has been, and through all vicissitudes will continue to be, inexpressibly great. I know, by your strong love for me and your dear mother, you will try to be as near us as you can in locality, and to sojourn with us as often as circumstances will permit."[54] Frank recalled years later "how cold the white camelias looked during the freezing days" that followed Fanny's departure and "how much sunshine went from the home with [her] dear face & presence."[55]

Fanny and Henry honeymooned on their way to their new residence in Washington, D.C., far from Fanny's only known home, the Boston area. Almost instantly, her life changed, for marrying Henry opened a world of opulence, high society, and world travel. A good journalist, an astute businessman, and a successful financier, he provided well for his wife and children. From the couple's first night together in Worcester, where the hotel owner provided them with "an immense chamber" to rest in, to their arrival in Washington, where they found their rented rooms "all lighted up and dorned with flower baskets and bouquets and a splendid dinner on the table," Henry treated Fanny with great delicacy and consideration.[56] Indeed, upon investigating her new surroundings, Fanny found that he had seen that a piano was placed in the large parlor, above whose fireplace mantel she promptly hung a portrait of her father.

Within a week of her arrival, Fanny was oriented into Washington society with an evening of receptions and parties throughout the city. Henry introduced her to Secretary of War Edwin M. Stanton, General Ulysses S. Grant, and Senator John Sherman of Ohio. At all the affairs she attended, Fanny noticed the many military officers, but, she claimed, "as I never did have a military fever they failed to impress me." In addition, at each location, wine was freely offered, which

Henry, out of consideration for his bride, politely refused. All in all, Fanny was not enthusiastic about the people she met, describing them as "a mixture of the commonest sort of odds and ends." The women, disappointingly, were artificial; "paint was plenty," and their "fancy dresses, tasteless." Both she and Henry agreed that those they were forced to socialize with were "the weakest and most brainless that we knew." On second thought, they added, "Hardly brainless, but silly and the women dressed up fools."[57] While Henry spent his days interviewing congressmen and writing articles, Fanny enjoyed the city, visiting markets, seeking out abolitionists residing and working in the area, and sitting in on sessions of Congress.[58] In February, Lloyd and Frank arrived for a ten-day visit, their descriptions of Fanny's lifestyle leaving Helen feeling somewhat envious, as she scripted to Frank, "Wish I had a fortune so that there would be no occasion for any more exertion on his [Lloyd's] part, and we could retire to quiet life for the remainder of our lives."[59] In fact, Henry had no such fortune and could therefore offer little help in supporting Lloyd and Helen.

In seeking alternate ways for their father to earn a living once the *Liberator* had ceased publication, Frank and Wendell encouraged him to write his autobiography and arranged for its production by the Boston publishers Ticknor and Fields, who were anxious to have such a book on their list. But although Lloyd promised to record his and the abolitionist movement's history, he never did. Among the reasons he gave were that he did not want to sound egotistical, nor did he trust his memory to present events the way they had actually occurred. Next, the sons offered to arrange a lecture tour, but that also did not work out, for, as in the autumn of 1865, the audiences were small, his fatigue great, and his worry about Helen intense. Besides, Lloyd had never favored lecturing, and although always a popular figure, he was not necessarily the most dynamic on the circuit. As Arthur Howard Nichols noted in 1876, Lloyd was "an indifferent speaker of unattractive appearance" who never inspired him to remember "a single sentence that he uttered in public."[60] The most feasible option for Lloyd, then, was to write articles for other papers, such as the *Independent* in New York, which he did frequently, but the fees paid were certainly not enough to live on.

A solution to these financial problems came through the "National Testimonial to Wm. Lloyd Garrison" campaign established by friends and supporters, including Massachusetts governor John A. Andrew, Samuel E. Sewall, Edmund Quincy, and Samuel May Jr., to raise $50,000 for Lloyd and Helen's retirement. The testimonial committee sent a circular signed by eighty-five well-respected abolitionists to one thousand potential contributors and to newspapers throughout the country. Samuel May Jr. also recruited several agents to solicit donations. Money flowed in, largely from New England and the Middle Atlantic states, although some arrived from Great Britain, including one from Elizabeth Pease Nichol, whose donation of one hundred British pounds, the equivalent of $688.89, was the largest. In total, $33,010.23 was placed in trust for Lloyd and Helen, enough for the couple to lead a comfortable existence. At first, the committee intended to establish a trust for Lloyd, but he would have nothing to do with such an arrangement, telling William that if the committee insisted on putting him under a "guardianship," they were "virtually saying to the world that they consider me as either incompetent to manage it, or as liable through a disposition to extravagance to squander it at no distant day."[61] Hence, for the six months until March 1868, he received only the interest on the money, at which point the entire amount was placed at his disposal to be used as he deemed best.

After Fanny's marriage in 1866 until Lloyd's death in May 1879, a period particularly marked by transformations in their personal lives, the Garrison children continued to concentrate their efforts on developing their own families and careers and taking care of their parents. William, George, and Frank continued to reside in Boston or nearby and so were most active in their parents' daily existence. Fanny's life was divided between the United States and Germany, at first spending her U.S. time in Boston but, by the autumn of 1876, making New York City and neighboring Westchester County her home. Wendell settled first in New York City, but two months after his and Lucy's wedding, James Miller McKim inquired about purchasing a home in a newly developing area in today's West Orange, New Jersey, known as Llewellyn Park. A six-hundred-acre gated community with large houses and spacious grounds, it had attracted several Philadelphia abolitionists, including Lucretia Mott's youngest daughter, Pattie, and her husband, George. The Gothic-style home McKim chose was large and roomy enough for both him and Sarah and the newly wed Wendell and Lucy plus any children the two might have. There was even some talk of including Lloyd and Helen in the plans. Lloyd, however, claimed that Orange was too isolated for Helen, even though it is highly unlikely that he himself would have chosen to leave Boston for faraway New Jersey. By May 1, 1866, McKim had received the deed to a house which Sarah found a bit "fanciful" for her taste. Designed by the architect Alexander Davis for the artist Edward W. Nichols, it had "funny pitched roofs—and clustered chimneys & Bulls eye windows, and niches for statuettes, and all sorts of artistic arrangements that dont quite suit my plain taste."[62] Sarah enjoyed the beautiful park surrounding the premises, however, and eventually grew accustomed to the house itself. She could not have guessed that within twenty years, her son, Charles Follen McKim, would become one of the most famous architects in the United States who could have designed her ideal home.

While Wendell was settling in New Jersey, William was working to attain the security he had promised Ellie during their courtship. His wool business of Bailey, Jenkins, and Garrison, situated at 164 Congress Street in Boston, experienced several ups and downs, but William worked long hours to see to its survival and success. He took the same dogged approach to his marriage. Although he and Ellie appeared to complement each other, there were times early in their marriage when William lost his temper and lashed out at her. During her summer visits to her family in Auburn, when he missed her dreadfully, he admitted to this "evil spirit."[63] The tension between them could have been caused by their cohabitation with Helen, Lloyd, George, and Frank or by Ellie's desire to have a home of her own, especially after giving birth to a daughter, Agnes, on June 14, 1866, "a little strawberry colored something" as William described her to Lucy. William, who was totally unnerved by this blue-eyed baby, added, "They told me it was a daughter & I presume it is. . . . I nearly committed infanticide by putting my knee on it."[64] Although Ellie desired some distance from her in-laws, Lloyd and Helen were ecstatic about becoming grandparents and wished for them to remain nearby. As Frank told Fanny, "I have never seen Father & Mother look so gratified as they did when they gazed upon their first grandchild, and said how it looked as all of us did at that tender age . . . and how it seemed like living their life over again."[65]

The baby's presence, however, added tension to the family dynamic, especially between Helen and Ellie. During their almost two years of living together, the two women had spoken affectionately about one another to other family members; yet there was an unspoken unease between them. Helen often related to her absent children Ellie's numerous headaches, and Ellie recorded in minute detail all of the complaints, falls, and treatments Helen experienced. Over the years, Helen confided only to Fanny her disapproval of some of Ellie's qualities, especially her mothering skills, beginning with her taking "but little care" of her newborn infant.[66] She later pitied Ellie's inability to "assume her own reins over her own children," who were apparently somewhat undisciplined. Part of Ellie's problem, according to her mother-in-law, was that she never blamed herself for her children's poor behavior, but rather the nursemaid or the children themselves. "She has a great blemish," Helen wrote, "not to see her will must be all in all, on her character to manage her children."[67] Several years later, Helen admitted to demonstrating the same quality in her own mothering. "You see darling," she told Fanny, "I can preach though I was one of the class of Mothers who could never accomplish what she most desired. But I never was blinded enough not to see duties that were imposed upon me, but was deficient in will power to execute them."[68] At the time, however, she could not acknowledge that she and her daughter-in-law were like two peas in a pod.

Indeed, Ellie spent the first summer of Agnes's life in Auburn so that her own mother could help her with child care. Now a mother herself, she seemed more tolerant of Martha's didactic manner. Once Ellie returned to Rockledge, Martha continued to be her guide, instructing her on feeding, how to prepare a warm bed, and what she should eat so as to be able to produce healthy breast milk. Ellie's continued lack of self-esteem contributed to her feelings of insecurity about mothering, sometimes resulting in impatience with her little Agnes. She complained that the baby's constantly waking up during the night was "hard on the nerves." William was more adjusted to it than she, who felt "like flying." According to Ellie, the person most successful in calming the infant was Lloyd, whom baby Agnes liked "better than anyone else!"[69] Lloyd, meanwhile, had finally achieved his wish to take care of babies. At eight months, when the infant still would not sleep through the night, Lloyd was the only one who could quiet her. As William told Frank, "When neither Ellie nor I can get her to sleep, she will go to him & nestle her little head on his breast, shut her eyes & go off in a twinkling. Indeed I think he feels himself quite necessary to her. If she cries three minutes up comes grandpa to the door to soothe her & most always does it too."[70] Whereas Ellie may have appreciated Lloyd's good intentions, she probably resented Helen's perhaps jealous comments that she had always had to get up in the night with her own babies, and so, of course, should Ellie. Hence, Ellie insisted that William find their small family its own residence, which he did in November 1867, moving them to Lambert Street, a mere five-minute walk from Rockledge but one which Helen could not manage without help. With their move, Lloyd and Helen's care fell squarely upon Frank's shoulders.

Almost a year after Agnes was born, on May 4, 1867, Lucy and Wendell also welcomed their first child, Lloyd McKim Garrison. Unlike her friend Ellie, Lucy had no difficulty adjusting to her new role, especially since Sarah McKim was by her side during the birth and shared the responsibilities of child care. Wendell was, like William, delighted about becoming a father, looking forward to the time when he could "exercise authority over my now helpless and altogether unrebellious infant." The new parents immediately discussed what they would "*not* do in the way of discipline." Wendell himself anticipated "the greatest pleasure" in "the intellectual" aspect of child rearing and renewing his own studies as he helped his son along in life.[71] Two months after the babe arrived, Wendell described him to his mother. "When asleep in bed," he reported, "covered up to the ears with a sheet, he bears a ridiculous miniature resemblance to his namesake." Lucy added, "His head, baldish on top as it is now, is ridiculously like his Grandpa Garrison's."[72] Both sets of Garrisons had more children during this period. Ellie and William greeted Charles on June 19, 1868, Frank Wright on October 18, 1871, William Lloyd III on December 5, 1874, and Eleanor on April 8, 1880; Lucy and Wendell ushered in Philip McKim on September 28, 1869, and Katherine McKim on May 10, 1873.

Fanny, meanwhile, made her first journey outside the United States, when in July 1866 she and Henry left for Germany, he to cover the brief seven-week Austro-Prussian War for the *New York Tribune*. Although she had studied the language for several years, when Fanny left New York, she could barely speak German, but by the time she returned two years later in June 1868, she was nearly bilingual. Fanny experienced new worlds on this first stay, meeting Henry's father, cousins, and favorite "tante" (aunt) Anna-Maria Pfeiffer, who lived in Heidelberg, a beautiful medieval town located in the Neckar Valley in the southwestern section of the country. While Henry reported on battles in Bohemia, Fanny remained in Heidelberg, studying German, learning about the culture, and making friends. When he rejoined her that fall, the couple moved to Munich for the winter season. By this time, Fanny was homesick and longing for her family. Coincidentally, younger brother Frank's own problems led to the reunion of the two in Germany. Frank's dilemmas had begun the previous winter shortly after he completed his studies at the Boston Latin School. For months he suffered from a cold, congested lungs, and recurring fevers, appearing so tired and worn out that his health became a major concern for his family.

Originally, Frank was to enter college in the summer of 1866; his parents and brothers advised him against it, however, suggesting instead that the young man take the summer to get as much air, sunshine, and exercise as he could. After a sociable and restful vacation, Frank would decide what to do about his education. At this point, however, Fanny suggested that he spend some time with her in Europe. Although Helen was especially loathe to see him go, the rest of the family convinced her of the potential good the experience would have for both Frank and Fanny. So, on October 10, Frank left for Germany to join his sister, Helen feeling the loss deeply. As Ellie described her mother-in-law to Fanny, "Poor Mother sits by the window in her *stiff* chair, gazing out through the darkness, as if she expected him suddenly to appear again."[73]

Fanny was most pleased to have her brother with her, especially since Henry was so busy with his own work. She took Frank sightseeing and introduced him to the social life of Munich, including many parties and balls. Because of his outgoing nature, Frank was open to all experiences offered him, but Fanny made sure that he continued his studies, particularly in German and French. Henry, meanwhile, indulged him and Fanny with riding lessons, concerts, dinners, and gifts. All was not perfect, however, for Henry suffered from severe headaches accompanied by inner roaring noises that so overpowered him that on some days he could not work and on others required a doctor's care. These headaches persisted for many years, even after German physicians tried medicines and minor surgery to cure him. The other problem Henry faced at this time was that his comparatively low income could not maintain his and Fanny's expensive tastes. Even though Lloyd took efforts to warn his daughter "not to lose [her] native simplicity in regards to manners and dress," Fanny enjoyed having nice clothes to wear to the many dinner parties and balls she both attended and hosted.[74] Henry, therefore, found himself seeking financial assistance from his brother-in-law William, who lent the money without any questions. This financial problem was solved on September 2, 1867, when Henry's father died, leaving him a sizable inheritance.

Lloyd, meanwhile, began thinking about joining Fanny and Frank in order to attend the World's Anti-Slavery Convention in Paris. His chief worry, of course, was leaving Helen largely with hired help to care for her. His hesitancy added to his wife's sense of guilt over burdening her family, so she urged him to go. After all, he had not been to Europe since 1846, and a sojourn such as this would do his health and spirits some good. On May 8, 1867, after a complicated home care arrangement was organized, Lloyd sailed for Paris, writing from the ship, "Of one thing be assured . . . that you will never be out of my thoughts for a moment."[75] Helen, in turn, urged him to "dismiss all cares about home" and "enjoy" himself.[76] Lloyd arrived in Paris on May 20, where he was greeted by Frank, Fanny, and Henry, who had been in the city since March, Henry covering the World's Fair for the *Chicago Tribune*.[77] After having their fill of the exposition, Fanny, Frank, and Lloyd left for England to visit Lloyd's longtime abolitionist friends in London, Newcastle-on-Tyne, Manchester, York, Melrose, Edinburgh (to see Elizabeth Pease Nichol), and Glasgow. Then it was back to Paris on August 10, followed in a few weeks by a trip through France to Geneva, Interlaken, Berne, and Lucerne, Switzerland.

Every so often, Henry joined the trio for a few days, but basically this was a Garrison family trip which allowed the father to relive his past and introduce two of his children to his fellow European activists.[78] In October, Frank and Lloyd traveled around Germany without Fanny, visiting Stuttgard, Heidelberg, Frankfort, Hamburg, and Cologne. By mid-October they were back in London preparing for their journey home, arriving in the United States on November 7. Frank had been away from home for over a year, Lloyd, for almost six months. During their time together, their intimacy had increased so that once home, the two continued socializing together. Frank often accompanied his father to lectures, concerts, meetings, or theatrical events, but the most enjoyment they received was from attending seances. On several occasions, the two joined other seekers in visiting local mediums but also entertained themselves with a planchette board at home. During these "remarkable" visitations, they heard from "Grandmother Garrison, Charley, Lizzie," Joshua Coffin, "Grandmother Benson," Francis Jackson, Henry C. Wright, John Brown, and Frank's friend Isaac Pitman, who had died of typhoid fever shortly after their 1866 summer hiking tour.[79] At one sitting, Abraham Lincoln attempted to communicate with them, but John Wilkes Booth blocked his spiritual path. Between socializing with his friends and entertaining his father, Frank spent his one and only term at the [Massachusetts] Institute of Technology.

On June 2, 1868, Fanny, pregnant with her first child, returned with Henry to Boston, delighting her father, who had declared that her absence had been "like a mortal bereavement" to him and Helen.[80] On June 28, just nine days after Ellie gave birth to her son, Charles, Fanny presented her family with her first child, a girl she named Helen Elise, very close in name to her mother, Helen Eliza. After

Fanny's labor pains had begun a little after three o'clock in the morning, the family's housekeeper, Mattie, woke up Frank to summon Marie Elizabeth Zakrewska, "Dr. Zak," a German-born physician who had studied midwifery before moving to the United States in 1853. Six years after receiving her M.D. from Western Reserve College in Cleveland in 1856, Dr. Zak founded the New England Hospital for Women and Children. During Ellie's first labor, Zakrewska had become the family's midwife-physician. In Fanny's case, she arrived at 4 A.M., a despondent Helen lying in the next room, unable to help her daughter at the time she felt she was needed the most. Isolated and alone, she heard the infant's cry along with the happy exclamations of her husband and son-in-law. Fanny and Henry went on to have three other children: Harold Garrison, born on December 3, 1869; Oswald Garrison, on March 13, 1872; and Henry Hilgard, on May 22, 1883.[81]

From 1868 to 1870, after Helen's birth, Henry remained in Boston, working as secretary of the newly formed American Social Science Association, where he did much to advance the cause of civil service reform and founded the *Social Science Journal.* He also published articles on foreign affairs in the *Chicago Tribune* and the *Boston Daily Advertiser.* Fanny's presence at home, of course, reminded her parents of how much they wanted the Villards to live with them at Rockledge. Lloyd tried to convince Henry to at least settle in Boston, but, in the end, the cold and damp New England climate, and the unspoken tug-of-war between him and his in-laws for Fanny's attention, led him to prefer New York and Germany for a home. Fanny, a traditional Victorian wife and very much in love with her husband, never expressed a desire to be anywhere except with him.

While William, Wendell, Fanny, and even Frank were moving ahead with their plans, George's life stagnated. His experience in the Civil War, compounded by Annie Anthony's rejection, resulted in what is today referred to as posttraumatic stress disorder, a condition neither identified nor treated at the time.[82] When George refused to visit friends or relatives outside their home, Helen simply interpreted this as symptomatic of his usual shyness, commenting to Fanny eighteen months after George had returned, "We cannot get G. to go anywhere, or see people at home if he knows they are coming. . . . It is sad to see him so averse to cultivate his social nature."[83] Helen reported that John Ritchie, also a veteran, acted in a similar manner, but she did not link the behavior to their common experience. In actuality, many Civil War veterans demonstrated difficulty in returning to their prewar existence, their recollections of constant tension, fear, and responsibility often sparking off nightmares or a sense of alienation from the people around them who had not seen the death and destruction they had. Furthermore, many experienced intense restlessness, seeing their postwar life as uneventful compared to the action and dangers of the war.

Bored with his accounting job at Bailey, Jenkins, and Garrison, despondent over Annie's rejection, and unable to find any occupation of lasting interest, George often remained alone in his room, darning socks, resting, or just gazing off into space. Depressed and unmotivated, he allowed his brothers to take care of him. Finally, in early 1868, he left William's employ to serve for two months on a superior court jury. He then worked for two months on the farm of Frank's friend Birney Mann in Sterling. This, however, was temporary seasonal employment. Wendell, recognizing George's eagerness to relocate, invited him to New York to keep the books for the *Nation,* the newspaper he was then working for.[84] In late August 1868, George settled into his own rented room in Brooklyn Heights, not far from abolitionist Henry Ward Beecher's Plymouth Congregational Church.

Every day and often into the evening, George worked with Wendell at the office. In his spare time, he slowly began to socialize, roaming the streets and neighborhoods of Manhattan and Brooklyn with new acquaintances and old abolitionist and army officer friends. Some evenings, he attended such political events as meetings of the Woman's Rights Society held in Brooklyn's Academy of Music. The one activity George did not concentrate on, however, was meeting and courting young women. Although he showed a brief interest in a different Annie Anthony (the daughter of the Brooklyn abolitionist Anthonys who rented him his room), his heart still seemed to be set on Annie Anthony of Boston. If he could not have a life with her, he apparently preferred a lonely bachelorhood. During his stay in New York, he often visited Wendell and Lucy at their home in Llewellyn Park. When on one occasion, Lucy suggested that he meet her "young & pretty neighbor," Hattie Norris, George responded that he "would have none of her."[85] In spite of George's erratic behavior, Wendell enjoyed having his companionship at the *Nation,* where they sometimes paused during their long workday for a game of chess or checkers, games which Wendell inevitably won. Although younger, Wendy watched over his brother, worrying because George overworked and did not exercise. George, in an effort to drown his unhappiness, became a workaholic, laboring all day and well into every evening. When E. L. Godkin, the editor-in-chief, acknowledged him with a $50 bonus, he felt a sense of appreciation and "esteem" he had not experienced since the war.[86]

In 1871, after nearly three years in New York, George started making plans for another move, his hope being to again test the waters in Kansas or Minnesota, especially since he still owned property in Nininger. Attempting to convince himself that he simply preferred outdoor activity to office work, he told William, "I can stand close confinement and hard work for a while, and then a time comes that I feel I must get away from it or break down." Rejecting William's offer of help in finding a new job in Boston, he ominously added, "I must 'paddle my own canoe' to get along in this world, and if I am not able to do it, the sooner I sink the better."[87] William, however, was determined to find George an opportunity so appealing that he would not leave the East Coast, thereby causing Helen undue stress and unhappiness. In March 1871, he and Henry investigated an available paper-box business on Congress Street, immediately summoning George to Boston to see it. Within three days, the eldest son had decided to buy it, returning to New York to pack while William opened the business for him. In less than two weeks, he was back home at Rockledge, reporting to his company each day in the hopes of building a successful enterprise. However, business was so slow that the next month William himself canvassed the city for paper-box orders for his brother; within a few weeks, he turned the business around. Meanwhile, William's own company thrived, clearing nearly $34,000 the first half of the year, netting William a third of the sum.

Frank, in the meantime, also discovered his career path. In January 1871, after having spent three years doing part-time accounting and secretarial work for Lloyd, Henry, and the P. T. Jackson store in Boston, he accepted the position of bookkeeper for the Riverside Press, a new and growing publishing house headed by H. G. Houghton. When at first his concern for his parents made him hesitate in taking on a full-time job, Fanny and Henry advised him from Germany to accept it. "While remembering fully what a useful, nay—almost indispensable fixture you are at home," Fanny wrote, "[Harry] thinks that filial duty hardly requires you to sacrifice what may possibly prove to be the opening of a whole life's career."[88] With his family's encouragement, Frank joined the firm where Houghton himself informed him of his intentions to teach him the publishing business. Each morning, he eagerly awoke at 5:48 to commute to Cambridgeport, arriving back home after eight o'clock every evening. Some weekends, he joined coworkers or Houghton and George Harrison Mifflin, the head of the bindery, for picnics and dinner parties. In spite of his long days, Frank retained responsibility for the care of Rockledge, his father, and his mother, giving Helen nightly leg rubs and electric treatments. He had good reason to worry. His mother took more falls and needed constant extra help, and his father, besides suffering from various ailments, showed signs of becoming forgetful. More often than not, when he went for walks, Lloyd lost his bearings, taking wrong turns and extra time to find his way home. He also made errors in his self-designed health care regimen. One September afternoon, while attempting to take a curing bath of tar and water, he put too much tar in the tub and could not extricate himself. When he arrived home at 6:00 that evening, Frank rescued his father, using lard to remove the excess tar from his back. It took Fanny, who was at Rockledge, three hours to clean the tub.

While building his career and taking care of his parents, Frank also managed to have a social life. Just as in his adolescence, Frank's friends came from the abolitionist community. Within that world, he was now an eligible young bachelor from a most respected family, who appeared to enjoy flirting with the single young women he had known for many years. Lizzie Simmons (his neighbor), Louisa Sewall, and Hattie Pitman were his favorites, although in 1868, when he was twenty, he was smitten with his mother's hired companion, Mattie Griffith. For the approximately six months Mattie lived with the family, Frank entertained her with walks, concerts, and conversations about books, and introduced her to his friends. Mattie, in turn, held several private spiritualism sessions with him in her room, bringing messages to him (and sometimes to Lloyd) from his siblings and, on one occasion, "most singular physical manifestations from Grandmother Garrison."[89] When Mattie left Rockledge, Frank was momentarily heartbroken. However, he quickly rebounded.

Although no one in his family could tell which lovely female Frank preferred, from October 1869 until May 1873 he seemed to be moving romantically closer to Louisa Sewall, the daughter of Lloyd's friend Samuel E. Sewall. To him, Louisa, two years his senior, was "as fresh and blooming as a rose, & fair & pure as a lily."[90] When they met, often with Hattie Pitman and her brother, Minot, and Lizzie Simmons, Frank enjoyed reading to her such works as John Stuart Mill's *The Subjection of Women* or articles from Lucy Stone's *Woman's Journal.* He was acutely aware that Louisa wanted to attend lectures on architecture at the [Massachusetts] Institute of Technology with the intention of having her own career, and he was livid when in 1870 the institution informed her that while she could not be a student, she could be a visitor. In an effort to be supportive, he accompanied Louisa and Hattie to "conversations" at the Woman's Club.

Meanwhile, the Garrison home became one of the socializing centers for Frank's friends. Louisa often showed up there to play croquet with other single men and women or to spend a quiet evening just with Frank. Frustrated that she could not get into a professional school, in 1871 she took a job in the office of an architect, Edward Clarke Cabot, where she worked each morning in the hopes of learning about the designing of buildings.[91] Frank, meantime, maybe because of his own hectic work and family life, continued an informal friendship with her. Watching his son with concern, Lloyd commented to Fanny that her brother was "very reticent" about "young ladies" and would give "no indication of a special regard for any one."[92] He was concerned that when Louisa's cousin, Mattie Fessenden, sent him a perfumed photograph of herself, he did not respond, and when Hattie Pitman sent him a note expressing an interest in a more serious relationship, he sat up half the night crafting a response which, while "pledging friendship," would go no further.[93] Rather, he continued to invite "angelic" Louisa to concerts and other events.[94]

Two days after attending a concert with Frank on April 9, 1873, Louisa sent him a note announcing her engagement to her employer, Edward Cabot. The news shattered the young Garrison's hopes and shocked the friends' community, for Louisa's future husband was over fifty years old and a widower with three children and two grandchildren. The message not only flabbergasted Frank but also led to his being teased by William, Ellie, and his close friends, who all knew about his infatuation with Louisa. Greatly humiliated, he rushed over to Hattie Pitman's to "compare notes," only to be met by a "blooming and happy" Louisa, who insisted on showing him photographs of her soon-to-be stepsons, aged twenty and twelve.[95] Frank could not accept this turn of events, especially since Louisa's future stepdaughter was two years older than she and married. He tried to cover up his personal hurt by attacking second marriages in general. To Fanny, he wrote, "As you perhaps know, I have always had a strong prejudice against second marriages and experience a revulsion of feeling towards people I like who enter them. . . . I am unable to reconcile it with my present faith, or to help wondering what the man will do with two wives or the woman with two husbands in the next world."[96] Frank practically accused Cabot of marrying Louisa simply to fill a void in his life. He wondered how much sincerity could exist in a man who had been married to one woman for twenty-nine years and then planned to remarry less than two years after her death.

Fanny, too, was "struck dumb with amazement." She bridled at such an "unnatural alliance" and felt that Louisa should be "more pitied than congratulated." Illustrating her own Victorian-era upbringing to be a wife and mother with no professional interests of her own, Fanny linked Louisa's marriage choice to her inability to get into the Institute of Technology and, hence, her working under Cabot's tutelage in order to learn about architecture. She fretted that Louisa's marriage would also set back the movement for woman's rights. "The query in the minds of benighted, unconverted woman's right's men," she wrote her mother, "will be fear, whether all the brave young ladies who desire to & succeed in studying architecture . . . in common with the other sex, will finally end in a common-place marriage with their teachers, even tho' they be grandfathers, staid, of course!"[97]

Louisa's marriage on October 13 did not stop Frank from seeing her, but his visits to her home became fewer, especially after Louisa became pregnant the next year.[98] Meanwhile, he seemed to be drifting into a relationship with Clara Holmes, a young woman who had previously been engaged to Ned Chace, Lillie Buffum Chace's brother, who died suddenly in 1871. For two years, the two courted, and it seemed that Frank might propose to Clara, but, again, he was taken by surprise when she abruptly announced her intention to wed the much older Frank Hall. A disturbed Lloyd commented to Fanny that Frank might need to wait until he was fifty-five or sixty before he could "find some young woman to accept a marriage proposal on his part." Lloyd continued, "See the choice of oldish men by Louisa Sewall, Lillie Chace, and Clara M. Holmes. What *is* the attraction that induces girls to marry men old enough to be their fathers—sometimes their grandfathers?"[99]

In early 1877, Frank began a new friendship with Mary Pratt of Pawtucket, Rhode Island. An acquaintance of Lillie Chace and an abolitionist daughter herself,

Mary taught kindergarten at 52 Chestnut Street in Boston. Soon after their meeting, the Garrison family again began to make comments to the then twenty-nine-year-old about his single state. Fanny insisted to her disgruntled younger brother that they all simply wanted him to be happy because his "sweet, gentle & affectionate nature" was "particularly calculated to make home-life what it ought to be."[100] Frank responded that he was not "singularly indifferent, unthinking & unappreciative about the matter,—drifting unconsciously into a bachelorhood which I should realize only too late the misery and unhappiness of."[101] With Mary, however, Frank soon became more assertive, showing up at her school on a regular basis to visit or invite her out for a walk, dinner, or cultural event. He certainly won her heart when he accepted an impromptu party invitation where he was the only man among thirteen women. He had a great time, while his father wondered why he never showed up for dinner.

For Frank and his siblings the 1870s continued to yield many new enterprises and experiences. Seven years of the decade, however, were rife with tragedies that further redefined the family, drawing it together even while deaths dispersed it. The first jarring incident took place on August 26, 1871, when the local train from Boston that carried William to nearby Lynn was rear-ended in Revere by the Boston-to-Portland express, compressing the last car of the local, where William was sitting. Twenty-seven people were killed immediately, and six others died later. In addition, thirty to forty people were badly scalded, one of them being William, who nearly died, as had the woman sitting next to him. William, however, upon hearing the express's whistle and seeing its headlight, bolted from his seat and ran to the front of the car, hoping to escape. As Fanny informed Wendell, "The engine stopped behind him & the scalding steam poured over him in a flash. Had he succeeded in reaching the outer platform, he would have been crushed with the timbers, had he been further toward the centre of the car, the engine would have done the deadly work."[102] Delirious, William somehow managed to stagger to a nearby house, where he was discovered by an acquaintance of the family who brought him to his own home and notified Ellie. All the family, except Helen, fled to William's bedside, taking turns nursing him through the day and night, alleviating Ellie, who, seven months pregnant and beside herself with worry, experienced the pangs of false labor. For over a week Frank, Wendell, and George tended their brother, changing his bandages and watching over his restless sleep. Wendell even rented a room in a nearby boarding house, where he slept during the day so he could sit up with his brother throughout the night. Lucy, in New Jersey, offered to take Agnes for a while, but Ellie preferred to keep her family together during this most difficult time. Lloyd made several trips to see his son, although at first, he could not bear to look at his badly burned head and hands.

William's condition was extremely serious, his pain so severe that he could neither remain in one position for long nor tolerate being moved. His physicians,

Christian Geist and Henry C. Ahlborn, both homeopathists, worried that potential gangrene would result in the loss of one or two of his fingers. Within a few days, however, William started to respond to their treatment, the color returning to his fingertips, and his eyes, which had been almost entirely closed, beginning to open. Although by September 10 his recovery was guaranteed, his right hand never healed, the tendons of the third and fourth fingers having been destroyed. For the rest of his life, he wore a glove on that hand. Fortunately for his family, William was insured by the Accident Insurance Company which paid him $15 a week during the entire year of his recovery. On the darker side, because he had not contributed to his firm's efforts in six months, his partners, Joseph T. Bailey and Charles E. Jenkins, decided to dissolve their partnership with him, effective March 1, 1872. To be helpful, Wendell lent his brother close to $800, which William soon returned in anticipation of the Eastern Railroad Company's settlement on his injuries. Just three weeks short of a year from the accident, he received $27,700 in damages, an amount which enabled him to comfortably support his family and establish his own wool broker business. Meanwhile, from October 8 through 10, the famous Chicago fire destroyed the office of the *Chicago Tribune,* greatly reducing Henry's investment income. In Germany since just after William's accident, Henry turned his attention to financial management, convincing a group of bankers in Frankfurt am Main and Berlin who held Oregon Railway bonds to allow him to handle their transactions in the United States. They agreed, as the near bankruptcy of the railroad frightened them into hiring a hands-on representative. From then on, he worked as a financier, particularly in the railroad and electric businesses, and as a publisher, rather than a reporter.

Unfortunately, 1872 proved as trying as the year that had passed. George's business was not doing very well, especially as William was unable to perform his usual role as advisor and legman. On January 2 the men of the family met to discuss George's $400 deficit, deciding as a group to support the enterprise only for another six months. Fanny, hearing of the meeting from her mother, sent George an encouraging, although somewhat patronizing, message saying, "'The world wasn't made in a day' & paper-box manufacturers can't expect to learn the business and make money too, the very first year. Tell him the self-reliance & sense of independence the undertaking has given him are worth more than money & will make success sure for him in the future."[103] All was not bleak for the struggling entrepreneur, however, as in February, George finally succeeded in winning Annie's hand. Even though Fanny still distrusted her, Helen felt that her son had "done better than his family could expect."[104] As she noted to her daughter, "Her health is excellent, she has a sweet disposition & everyone is delighted about it. . . . at twelve years she was left in charge of her Mothers family & fulfilled her duties faithfully."[105] Yet, months passed with no marriage taking place, largely because George did not want to start wedded life while his paper-box business stagnated.

In July, William advised him to give up on the enterprise, praising George for his untiring efforts but pointing out the disadvantages of sinking all his money into the venture. Furthermore, William could not himself continue to bail his brother out. Much to his and his family's surprise, business improved in September, and George was not only able to meet his expenses and hire sixteen young women, but he and Annie set a wedding date.

The unpredictability of life, however, continued to play havoc with George when, on November 9, a fire that began in a building on the corner of Summer and Kingston Streets in Boston destroyed George's, William's, and Richard and Ned Hallowell's businesses.[106] The conflagration consumed the greater part of downtown Boston, moving along both sides of Summer Street and then spreading to State Street and Broad Street, raging for about forty hours before the fire department got it under control. Officials estimated the damage at approximately seventy-five million dollars with the decimation of sixty-five acres of Boston's business and commercial district. George lost everything, including the machinery he had purchased and his entire paper-box stock. Even the documents in his safe turned to ashes, leaving him with just a few burnt nickels and copper pennies to show for his hard work. Because the insurance company did not have enough money to pay its claims, George collected nothing. William's new business, which had been going so well that he felt happier and more hopeful than he had since his accident, was also wiped out. Estimating his loss at close to $10,000, including a new counting-room and office which he had elegantly furnished, William, unlike George, took the optimistic approach. Within two days, he was on his feet again, having rented desk space in an office on Chauncy Street and sent out circulars.

Lloyd, Helen, and Frank had what Frank termed "a magnificent view" of the fire from their sitting-room window. They watched as "the dreadful flames" devoured the downtown area, every now and again hearing "the deep boom of an explosion" as buildings imploded and collapsed. Frank wrote Fanny, "The whole sky was aglow, & every object for miles around lighted by the flames."[107] As soon as the area was safe, Lloyd ventured out to survey the damage, also relating to Fanny, "Talk of the ruins of Pompeii and Palmyra! You should see those of our city. I wander among them awe-stricken and overwhelmed, as though they were a thousand years old, and beyond all hope of a reconstruction of those magnificant buildings which seemed to have been built to endure for many generations." Lloyd saw only one or two structures left standing on Summer street, none in Winthrop Square, and a large portion of Milk, Water, Federal, Congress, and Devonshire Streets destroyed. For several days after the blaze, he heard fire alarms, saw small fires, and witnessed people "getting very nervous at the sound of the fire-bell."[108] Helen herself took some satisfaction in seeing Jenkins & Bailey burned out, feeling they earned their punishment for the shabby way they had treated William. This uncharacteristic and harsh sentiment, of course, was written "secretly" to Fanny.[109] Perhaps owing to his childhood memory of the Newburyport fire witnessed from the safety of his mother's arms, Lloyd was so mesmerized by this one that, as a Christmas gift, William gave him a copy of James Wallace Black's four-foot-wide panoramic photograph of the devastation.

Meanwhile, much to the chagrin of the rest of the family, George and Annie's wedding was again postponed until he could find another source of income. Depressed over his loss, George once again withdrew from the outside world, spending large amounts of time sequestered in his room. Daniel Mann, the father of Frank's friend Birney, offered George an opportunity to sell his patent medicines from door to door, which George tried for a few days but gave up on. Lloyd, frustrated by his eldest son's lack of self-motivation, wrote to Wendell that any type of new work "must be found" before George gave up on himself for good.[110] The solution came in late January 1873, when William, as Frank put it, "with his usual brotherly generosity & kindness," took George on as his bookkeeper.[111] This was no easy task, as an economic depression slowed business, affecting William's own income. He and his new partner did not really need a bookkeeper, so their agreement stipulated that William pay half of George's salary from his own pocket, a detail that George was never cognizant of. With a guaranteed income in hand, finally, George, aged thirty-seven, and Annie, thirty-four, were wed on October 1, 1873. Fanny thereupon surrendered her ill feelings toward Annie, now her sister-in-law, writing to Ellie from Heidelberg, "I believe they are very well suited to each other. George's shyness must gradually disappear in the presence of so genial and sunny a person as Annie; she seems to have a talent for making friends."[112]

Helen, who was able to ride to the Anthony home in a barouche, witnessed the nuptials. The Anthonys, with the help of the Garrison sons, had constructed a special flight of steps to enable her to enter their Cambridgeport home more easily. Abolitionist friends and family, including Wendell Phillips, gathered for the two-o'clock ceremony, followed by a reception again catered by Joshua Bell Smith. Frank felt that he had never witnessed a "more simple & impressive ceremony." In fact, George looked so self-possessed that his brother was "surprised at his subsequent confession that he trembled."[113] Whether Annie finally consented to marry George out of love or social pressure will never be known, but apparently they were content with each other throughout their married years. After a honeymoon trip which took them through Cincinnati, Ohio, to visit Annie's brothers, Thomas and Edward, they returned to Boston to reside with Annie's parents. George's traveling days were over, especially after the birth of his first child, Elizabeth, on November 8, 1874. Many years later, Frank recollected the day vividly: "Entering the house solemnly and carefully hanging his hat & overcoat in the hall, he came into the sitting room & seating himself on the lounge, facing Mother, gravely said, 'Well, I'm a father!' It was one of the funniest things I ever saw but our worthy brother was incapable of perceiving the humor of it."[114]

George and Annie had two other children: Rhodes Anthony, born on October 5, 1877, and Fanny, on May 10, 1879.

As 1873 turned into 1874, Garrison family life seemed fairly peaceful. Four children were married; Frank had steady employment with the Riverside Press at an annual salary of $1,500, and Fanny and family returned to the United States in April with Henry, who in late December 1873 had suffered a mild stroke but was now in good health. No serious ailment fell upon Lloyd or Helen during this time, although both suffered from the aches and pains of aging, and Helen, in particular, had recurring falls and side effects from her paralysis. However, abolitionist friends were dying off. By early 1868, nearly half of the original signers of the "Declaration of Sentiments" had passed away, including James Mott. In late 1873, Sarah Grimké and Charles Remond died on the same day, and on June 13, 1874, James Miller McKim—Lloyd's friend, Wendell's warm and loving father-in-law, and Lucy's devoted father—passed on. When Lloyd received news that McKim could no longer get out of bed and depended on morphine to ease his pain, he immediately left for Llewellyn Park to bid him farewell. When he arrived in McKim's room, the dying man repeatedly cried out, "dear Garrison," embracing him with his weak arms. Within a day, his condition deteriorated so that he confessed to his wife, "Sarah, it is a severe ordeal," after which his breathing grew increasingly fainter until it simply stopped. "There was not a single struggle or sign of anything violent," Lucy noted. "Nothing could have been quieter."[115]

Lucy and Ellie often traveled similar paths in their lives, and so it was with the death of a parent: on January 4, 1875, Martha Wright died. She had come to visit Ellie and William in Boston, helping with the care of her grandchildren, sightseeing, and attending cultural events. One morning at breakfast, she collapsed, recovered slightly, then fell seriously ill with a "sick stomach" and a "fearful shaking chill" so strong that a frightened Ellie immediately sent for a physician. Within days, she had died of pneumonia. Martha's death left Ellie bereft, for this mother whom she had struggled with during her young adult years had become one of the most precious people in her life. "Few Mothers," she wrote to her cousin, Maria Mott Davis, "are so devoted to their grownup children as she was."[116] In her mourning, Ellie turned to her former mentor, Susan B. Anthony, who in her own grief tried to comfort her younger friend, still never losing sight of her hope that Ellie would take up the woman's rights cause. "Twelve years ago," she lamented,

> when my dear Father died, aged 69, in the full strength and vigor of body and mind, precisely as your dear Mother, it seemed to me the world and everybody in it must stop. It was months before I could recover myself, and at last it came to me, that the best way I could prove my love and respect for his memory, was to try to do more and better work for humanity than ever before, and from that day to this the feeling, in my triumphs and defeats, that my Father rejoiced and sorrowed with me, has been

> a constant stimulus to urge me ever to rally to new effort. May you even more fully come to the realization the ever present benediction of your precious mother.[117]

Ellie, although never to forget her mother's political mission, was not to assume it.

Almost a year to the day of Martha's passing, the Garrison children were faced with the death of their own dear mother. Helen's health had been in a steady, slow decline since her stroke in 1863, but in early 1876 she contracted pneumonia. Lloyd, Fanny (who had been home for just over a month), Frank, William, and Ellie kept a constant watch over her, never leaving her side, but Helen found little comfort, hardly slept, and had difficulty breathing. Frank sadly noted in his diary that his mother "threw her head & swayed her body from side to side, groaned incessantly, & wrung our hearts with her agony."[118] Day and night, he tended Helen, massaging her leg and foot, carrying her to her chair where she seemed more comfortable, and talking to her. When Frank took a break to catch some sleep or have something to eat, Fanny took over, trying her best to calm Helen by giving her baths and also constantly talking to her. Lloyd, who suffered from the same illness, sometimes lay next to her, trying to help her sleep, but his own weakness did not allow him to remain by her side incessantly.

On the morning of January 25, Helen begged to see Frank. He had always been her special child, the youngest son who reminded her of her long dead Charley. Frank carried her to the chair near her bed. That was the last anyone communicated with her, for at 8:45 A.M., she lapsed into a coma, dying at five minutes past ten. Frank, Fanny, William, and Ellie were by her side. Although their grief was great, all were also relieved that Helen's long suffering had ended. "But, oh!," Frank wrote in his diary, "how we shall miss her in this household which she has so long blessed with her dear presence, knitting us as a family closely together!"[119] Death came so quickly that neither George nor Wendell knew of its possibility until their siblings sent for them. Helen's body, meanwhile, was prepared and laid in a casket placed in the Garrison parlor, all its furniture having been removed to accommodate it. Frank carefully arranged smilax from the Tropical Grotto around Helen's photograph while Fanny positioned white camellias in the rosewood coffin and a white rose in Helen's hand. Lloyd, who had not had a chance to bid his wife farewell, was advised by his physician to remain in bed for two or three days until his health improved, but his sorrow added to his slow recovery. "From the severity of that blow I am still suffering," he told Wendell the following month, "and I wander from room to room in a state of bewilderment. . . . My grief is not for her, now delivered from all her infirmities as one emancipated from bondage, but for us who survive." About their marriage, he could only say, "No choice could have been a more fortunate one for me, and our married life was fraught with such blessings and enjoyments as have seldom been realized in a state of wedlock."[120]

On a cloudy and snowy January 27, Helen was laid to rest. The family, fearing that so many people would come to the funeral that they would not all fit in the parlor, did not publicly announce it. Yet, friends and admirers flocked in; flowers arrived from the mayor's office and also from innumerable friends.[121] Reverend Samuel May, the cousin of Samuel May Jr. led the service, but the chief eulogy was given by Wendell Phillips, who portrayed Helen as the devoted and brave abolitionist wife that she was. "And when the gallows was erected in front of the young bride's windows," he recalled, "never from that stout soul did the husband get look or word that bade him do anything but go steadily forward, and take no counsel of man." When the mob of 1835 almost lynched Lloyd, he continued, Helen was heard to say, "I know my husband will never betray his principles!" Phillips praised Helen's self-sacrificing nature, her willingness to host Lloyd's many guests, and her commitment to raise their children in a way which allowed him to act "unchecked by any distracting anxiety." Phillips closed his tribute with these sentiments: "She was not merely the mother, or the head of the home; her own life and her husband's moved hand in hand in such loving accord, seemed so exactly one, that it was hard to divide their work."[122] Others also testified to Helen's invaluable aid to the abolitionist movement. Lucy Stone attested to her "earnest interest" and "encouragement" to others, especially after her stroke left Helen unable to carry on the work herself, and the Reverend Dr. Putnam praised Helen's "kindness," noting that by sitting "at that window in the opposite parlor, day after day, year after year," she indicated to the outside world that she was still interested in its activities.[123]

Lloyd read the countless sympathy letters and eulogies, which Frank arranged to be published by the Riverside Press as *Helen Eliza Benson: A Memorial.* The book was then distributed to friends and family members. Almost every mourner emphasized Helen's kindness, her retiring personality, and her willingness to take a back seat to her husband's activism. Anne Weston remembered Helen's "meek and quiet spirit" in her work from 1835 to 1840 on the antislavery fairs, while the *Woman's Journal* marked that for forty years Helen had been "the worthy partner of his [Lloyd's] anti-slavery labors." Edmund Quincy described Lloyd and Helen's union as "perfect," while Oliver Johnson portrayed Helen as an ideal wife who put her home, husband, and children above all else. Theodore Tilton built upon that image, characterizing Helen as one of his "early ideals and typical images of matronly goodness." Only Susan B. Anthony acknowledged that Helen had some assertiveness, as being "ever ready to second every plan for work, and to start out with me to help execute it."[124] In spite of these testimonies, throughout history Helen would be portrayed simply as William Lloyd Garrison's wife, not his partner.

A little more than a month after Helen died, Wendell revealed to his father his own ability to sympathize with his loss, for just a short while before, he had felt his "hold on Lucy . . . precarious."[125] Experiencing this fear, he understood the pain his father was going through after over forty years of marriage. Wendell could not know when he wrote these sentiments that the illness that Lucy had suffered from for years was about to steal her from him forever. When Wendell and Lucy first began their life together, she was a vibrant young woman full of energy and commitment to the abolitionist cause as well as being outspoken about woman's rights. Throughout her growing-up years, she had expressed her desire for independence, taking her time before agreeing to a marriage with Wendell which naturally would result in motherhood and the assuming of many traditional female responsibilities. While Lucy eventually became chiefly a homemaker and mother, she still kept her finger on the pulse of the activist movement, usually expressing her concerns through her family network. She also tried her hand at freelance writing, reviewing children's books for various newspapers, and writing a two-part short story, "First School-Days of a Little Quaker," most likely a fictionalized memoir of her own schoolgirl experience, which appeared in *The Riverside Magazine for Young People.*[126]

As she matured, Lucy came to understand the need for woman suffrage, and even more so, for building a women's community. She often shared these thoughts with Fanny during the pair's frequent get-togethers in Llewellyn Park or New York. When, in 1869, she heard of the emergence of the New England Women's Club and New York's Sorosis, both of which provided women with space where they could gather—similar to the men's clubs with their comfortable sitting rooms and dining areas—she immediately wrote to her sister-in-law recommending that she join one, saying that she, too, might do so: "It is a good thing to belong to some organization, especially for people out of the church; & besides a thing of this sort is a relief and improvement to women confined a great deal at home by wearying household cares." Lucy added that if suffrage and "co-operative housekeeping" were in their futures, then women should become better prepared by learning from each other.[127]

Lucy practiced her brand of women's equality at home, expecting Wendell to take some initiative in performing household chores. From time to time, he was certainly up to meeting the challenge, although he did not seem to embrace the work as his father had. In one instance, when Lucy and her mother took a trip together leaving Wendell and Miller McKim on their own, his wife suggested the men board out. Wendell, however, saw this as an opportunity to prove to Lucy that men were perfectly capable of taking care of themselves. As she humorously described the incident to Lloyd,

> Wendell was set on playing housekeeper & cook, & verily I believe, more for the purpose of triumphing over us when we got back because it was "so easy," than anything else. We departed with many misgivings. Wendell was as full of self-reliance as—well, as usual! And as usual, I must admit, he proved he could do what he had a mind to.

> When we came back, everything looked real nice. My bed was made "stunningly"! The kitchen was spic & span, all the rooms orderly, clean dishes on the table, roast potatoes in the oven, etc. etc. Father declared his cooking to have been excellent. He had swept & cleaned lamps, & done almost everything but wash the dishes & keep up the fires . . . which was John's work. We consider him worth now about $3.00 a week.

Once victorious, however, Wendell settled back into his more traditional male role. "As for 'learning to like it,'" Lucy noted sarcastically, "I think that part rather fell through for we have observed he hasn't requested to be allowed to do a single thing since!"[128]

Besides woman's rights, Lucy's chief concern was fostering respect for African-American culture. Her greatest project reflected the continued influence of the Port Royal Experiment on her life. In 1867, after a year of intense work and with the assistance of Wendell's publishing ties, Lucy, along with Professor William Francis Allen of the University of Wisconsin and Charles Pickard Ware, two Port Royal alumni who had also collected slave songs, produced *Slave Songs of the United States.*[129] The three felt the book would be of great value not only in preserving the songs but in introducing African-American culture to a wider population they felt was needy of such an educational experience. A. Simpson & Co. published the collection of 136 songs with a forward by Allen, but unfortunately, when the volume appeared it did not receive many reviews, nor did it sell well. John Ross & Co. reissued it in 1871, but it again fell on deaf ears, until in 1929 the Peter Smith Co. reissued it, and its value was finally recognized. It has been available ever since, its most recent editions appearing in 1965 and again in the late 1990s.

Unlike Ellie, Lucy was interested in having some sort of career outside the home, even if it initially took the form of freelance writing. Beginning in 1868, however, she suffered health problems that grew more severe with each passing year. Initially, the illness caused a miscarriage, which sparked family concern. When the next year she again became pregnant, Wendell delayed sharing the news, explaining his hesitation to William thus: "Your rebuke about Lucy's prospects was a just one . . . & remembering our late disappointment we were not in a hurry about spreading the news."[130] At the end of October, much to his parents' delight, son Philip was born. Lucy, however, had difficulty recovering from the pregnancy. She experienced aches and pains throughout her body, which gradually worsened so that after the birth of her daughter, Katherine, in May 1873, she sought out a physician. The doctor diagnosed "simple rheumatism" and recommended she wear "rubber knee caps" to reduce the swelling and pain in her legs.[131] He could offer no help for Lucy's hands, so Wendell decided to purchase a $15 battery electrotherapy machine (a smaller version of the one used on Helen) to try to give her temporary relief. By August, Lucy could not walk without a cane. At this point, a second physician diagnosed gout, placing her on a strict diet and recommending she drink Vichy and Lithia mineral waters. Because of her weakened condition, Lucy was forced to wean Katherine when she was just six months old, news which alarmed Helen, who feared the same fate as her baby Elizabeth, but Katherine continued to thrive.

In 1874 Lucy miscarried again. By the following summer, excruciating headaches and deteriorating eyesight forced her to rely increasingly on her aging mother and Wendell to take care of the children and the household tasks. For all his bravado concerning traditional male and female roles, Wendell responded as his father had after Helen's stroke, working all day in New York and then rushing home to New Jersey to help with Lucy and their children's care. That December, Lucy had a stroke-like attack which left her paralyzed for several hours. When Wendell returned home from work, he found her crippled on her left side, her fingers curled under her palm like Helen's, her mouth drawn to the right, her right eye fixed in a stare, and her speech slurred and nonsensical. After several hours, she began to recover, and by the next day, she could walk without difficulty, her left foot scraping slightly across the floor. Lucy's physician had warned Wendell that she had, as he put it, "an ever menacing and recurring disease," and even though within two days she had almost returned to normal, Wendell felt that his life had "received one of those permanent shadows which can be ignored only by shutting one's eyes to them."[132]

Throughout 1876, Wendell attempted to protect Lucy from the knowledge that she had a progressive disease that would eventually kill her, a fact she had most likely discerned for herself. He begged his family not to discuss his wife's condition with anyone lest she hear about her prospects through the abolitionist grapevine. By the summer, she was having attacks resembling epilepsy, her speech becoming less understandable and her hearing diminishing so that she could no longer play the piano. These new complications coincided with Lloyd and Frank's discussions about a possible European trip primarily designed to help lift Lloyd's spirits. The idea came on the heels of a conversation in which George, William, Wendell, and Fanny suggested that Lloyd should leave Rockledge to live with one of the married siblings. Frank protested to Fanny, "It is too late in the day now to propose that Father shall scatter his household goods, for which, as you know, his attachment is uncommonly strong, and drift from his mooring. I believe his happiness & life depend largely on having a home, and desolate as ours now is, any substitute that we should attempt would be two-fold drearier."[133] Perhaps a trip would prove beneficial not only for Lloyd but for Lucy as well. At first, Lucy was unwilling to even consider it, saying, "What would mother and Wendell do with our three precious brats? They are nice children, but being entirely natural & not precocious, they will get dirty, quarrel, get into scrapes, burst off their buttons, and need a daily attention that mother's weakened health could not give them; and a nightly and morning and Sunday attention that would give Wendell absolutely no rest."[134] Ellie, who preferred that Lucy not travel so far, suggested she spend some time at her and William's cottage in Osterville on Cape Cod, sunbathing and enjoying the smell of the ocean and the pine trees. In this way, she could rest but be cared for by her best friend and not have to deal with the "horrid misery" of a ship.[135] Actually, once married and sisters-in-law, Ellie and Lucy saw each other less frequently than they had before. Lucy's illness added to their difficulties in keeping in touch. Once in a while, one or the other traveled for a visit, but their growing families limited their mobility. As Lucy wrote to Ellie in 1870, she wanted to see her desperately but her mothering responsibilities made a trip to Boston impossible. Would Ellie came to New Jersey? "I want to see you dreadfully. I can't write letters any more—I hate 'em, though am still capable of receiving them with the old relish."[136]

For some unknown reason, Lucy eventually consented to the Europe plan, looking "unusually bright and strong" as she did last-minute shopping for the voyage, but then, after a busy and happy day, she suffered a severe stroke, paralyzing her right side. Lucy's physician would "not even predict survival," telling Wendell that if she pulled through, her right arm would be useless, her leg "little better." Wendell sat up all night watching Lucy, wondering, "What is in store for me during the next few days or weeks I do not know."[137] Would Lucy survive, and if she did, would her life be as physically pained, her world as isolated as his mother's had been? Fanny, who had grown to love Lucy as a sister, rushed to his side from her residence in New York City, only to see Lucy's teeth and jaw so "firmly set" that she could hardly swallow or speak and "little sign of life in her hand & her foot."[138] Fanny was so upset that she almost fled the scene. Ellie also hurried to be with her lifelong friend, but there was little she could do to ease her emotional or physical pain. Lucy, meanwhile, continued to hold on to whatever small amount of independence she had. When Sarah McKim attempted to feed her, Lucy angrily fought her, shaking her head fiercely and refusing to accept any nourishment. Unable to eat, speak, or perform the simplest task for herself, she wore herself out with rage, eventually falling into a coma. She died on May 11. Once again the family convened for a funeral. As Ellie noted to her sister, Eliza, "How desolate it seems for them, & how hard for Mrs. McK—to take the motherly as well as the grandmotherly duties upon herself. . . . Wendell has always done a great deal to help Lucy, & for the last two years he has assumed almost the entire responsibility of the children so that he is well fitted for it, tho' his poor sad face, shows what a loss he has met with."[139] By focusing on Wendell and Sarah's grief, Ellie tried to ignore her own. In the coming months and years, Fanny became Wendell's main comfort and in many ways served as a surrogate mother for Katherine, Lucy's daughter.

Soon after Lucy's funeral, Frank and Lloyd left for England, not returning until September 4. They spent their time visiting Lloyd's former abolitionist contacts throughout Great Britain and Ireland. In order to accompany his father, Frank had taken a leave from his job at the Riverside Press and bid a hopefully temporary farewell to Mary Pratt. As soon as he returned to the United States, he began courting Mary in earnest. As his life took a different turn, so did those of George and Fanny. In October 1877, George's father-in-law died, leaving him and Annie responsible for Anna Anthony's care and support until her death in 1898. At the end of the year during a trip west, Henry caught a cold which quickly turned to pneumonia. San Francisco physicians gave him little chance of surviving, but, as in the past, Henry called upon his seemingly endless reserve of inner strength and pulled through. The following year Fanny, in New York, caught a strange virus which caused the loss of all her hair. Until it grew back, she had to wear a wig which she detested. Lloyd tried to put a humorous spin on his daughter's unfortunate circumstance. "In the matter of shaving your head," he wrote, "I trust it will prove advantageous, as it certainly did not in my case; for the more the razor was applied to my cranium, the more my baldness was promoted."[140] He added in all seriousness that in her case, illness was the culprit; in his, it was hereditary.

The traumatic decade ended with Lloyd's death. In May 1879, concerned about his weakened condition, Fanny requested that her father come to New York to see her physician, Leonard Weber, who diagnosed bladder and kidney trouble and prescribed four or five months of rest and quiet. Lloyd remained with Fanny for about a month, throughout that time finding it so uncomfortable to lie down that he spent most days propped up with pillows, with his feet resting upon a footstool. On May 22, Fanny cabled Henry in Oregon that "Poor father is slowly dying."[141] Lloyd's children and Ellie rushed to be with him for the end. Annie, who had just given birth to her daughter, Fanny, on May 10, could not travel, and Mary Pratt, who, much to Lloyd's delight, had become engaged to Frank in April, did not feel it appropriate to be at such an intimate family gathering. On the morning of May 23, when Dr. Weber asked Lloyd if there was anything he wanted, he purportedly replied, "To finish it up!"[142] To make the act of dying easier, his children sang his favorite hymns while massaging his hands and feet. He, in turn, acknowledged their presence, bidding each a silent, loving farewell. At one point, as Frank lay beside him on the bed, he suddenly turned, threw his left arm over him, and embraced him with great strength. All through May 23 and 24, Lloyd's children carried out their death watch until, at eleven o'clock on the evening of the twenty-fourth, he left them.

The Garrison children saw to it that their father was buried next to Helen in the Forest Hills Cemetery in Roxbury. The funeral services, led by Samuel May, were held at the First Religious Society; as per Lloyd's request, the church blinds were fully open to allow in as much cheerful light as possible.[143] Flowers rested atop the pulpit, and the chosen hymns, sung by a quartet of Lloyd's African-American friends, were one of "cheer and inspiration," songs that Lloyd had enjoyed and which his children had sung to him at his deathbed. The pallbearers were old friends, including Wendell Phillips, Samuel May, Samuel E. Sewall, Robert F. Wallent, Theodore Weld, Oliver Johnson, Lewis Hayden, and Charles Mitchell. Most of the comments at the funeral reiterated Lloyd's own words from the *Liberator,* repeating his many victories and struggles in the abolitionist movement. Some, however, referred to his private life. Wendell Phillips reflected, "His was the happiest life I ever saw. No need for pity. No man gathered into his bosom a fuller sheaf of blessing, delight, and joy. . . . Every one of his near friends will agree with me that this was the happiest life God has granted in our day to any American standing in the foremost rank of influence and effort."[144] Lucy Stone thanked Lloyd for his work for woman's rights. "He saw that it was a question of human rights," she wrote. "In my heart of hearts I am grateful to him for the great work he did. The veneration of all who appreciate the meaning of the words, 'Equal rights for woman,' will be paid to his memory forever."[145]

After the funeral, the children saw to it that their father's accomplishments were praised in innumerable obituaries. No less than seventy-five newspapers throughout the United States and Europe printed tributes which summarized and praised Lloyd's life and work. Many talked about his simple beginnings; others mentioned his close and happy family life. Largely they sought to cement his historical image as the great abolitionist that he was. Some newspapers, however, were happy that their nemesis had finally died. The Okolona, Mississippi, paper, for example, wrote, "Wm. Lloyd Garrison, one of the wickedest men of his day, is dead."[146] In Augusta, Georgia, mourners were criticized for demonstrating outside the courthouse in Lloyd's memory. The numerous articles, letters, and commentaries were preserved in two scrapbooks which became part of the family's archives.

In spite of all the sadness, the decade ended on a happy note when on August 25, 1879, Frank and Mary Pratt became husband and wife. The couple composed their own wedding vows, advised the minister to offer no prayer, and exchanged rings before their families and close friends. Fanny, again in Germany until the end of the year, was the only family member not in attendance. Frank remained in Rockledge after Lloyd's death, making slight alterations to the rooms and furnishings to accommodate his new life there with Mary. Together, they decided to preserve the sitting room as it was and to place in it books from the antislavery movement, a full run of the *Liberator* in a specially made case, and many of Lloyd's writings in a designated drawer. They also kept family and abolitionist photographs on the walls. Still, for some time, Frank found the house desolate.

The decade that had begun with the entire Garrison family in tact had ended with the loss of Helen, Lloyd, and Lucy; the tragic crippling of William's hand, and the loss of his and George's businesses. Over the ten years, while the children oversaw their parents' care, the dynamics among them shifted. In spite of his accident, William took on the responsibility of ensuring George's security, Henry acting as both brothers' financial advisor. Frank, the chief on-site caretaker for his parents, finally gained independence at the age of thirty-one, but only after Lloyd's death. Wendell, although independent, became the sibling most in need of emotional support, which he received tenfold. Fanny replaced her mother as the beloved female figure of the family. As the children and their own children, thirteen in all, began the new decade, the family continued to expand, and the Garrison siblings pushed forward on the political work begun by their parents.

A LEGACY OF SOCIAL CONSCIOUSNESS AND POLITICAL ACTIVISM

THEIR PARENTS' SONS

> Our reward was great and lasting, for the men and women who came in such numbers, through a long series of years, to receive our hospitality, were the salt of the earth. I wish it were in my power adequately to portray them, and to tell of the enlivening talk, the animated discussions on moral questions, and, in hours of relaxation, the wit and merriment, which made all outside attractions pale beside those of our own home. In them and in the daily lives of our parents we had everything to instruct, ennoble and inspire.
>
> Francis Jackson Garrison, 1904

CHAPTER IX

After May 1879, the Garrison children no longer had their parental role models to determine what urgent causes they should concentrate on. But they had learned their lessons well. Immediately following Lloyd's death, all five picked up his uncompleted work of sending goods, blankets, clothing, and money to the African-American "exodusters" fleeing the violent postwar South for Kansas. Throughout the rest of their lives, each offspring attended meetings where racism, woman's rights, and peace were motivating forces for action, but their efforts took shape around each one's political bent, interests, experiences, and personal lifestyles. From the time of the Civil War, when they still had their parents' examples to follow, into the early twentieth century, the sons found their individual professional and political voices while Fanny, as a wife and mother, remained on the sidelines. Their lives as brothers and sister, however, remained intricately intertwined, their concern for each other's happiness and welfare apparent in their letters, diaries, and everyday behavior.

Although he despised racism and supported woman's rights, George's shyness and lack of business success led to his becoming the least politically involved of the siblings. Where his sentiment particularly diverged from theirs was on the antiwar issue. Serving in the 55th regiment had convinced the now eldest Garrison that not all conflicts could be settled peacefully. Hence, when his brothers and sister spoke out against militarism, George remained silent. Indeed, two of his favorite activities were attending the annual reunion of his fellow Civil War veterans and creating scrapbooks on the regiment's history. In many ways, George was the son who most resembled Helen. Except for his youthful effort to build a life in Minnesota and his participation in the Civil War, he enjoyed the role of supporter. Had he been born a woman, his parents would have been content with his nature, for he was responsible and goodhearted, carrying his share of household responsibilities and making financial contributions with nary a complaint. George, however, was born a son—the *first* son, and as such, he was always somewhat of a disappointment to his father, who felt frustrated by his restlessness and inability to secure a job without the help of his brothers. Helen, meanwhile, tried to protect George by pressuring him to remain home rather than venturing out on his own, a behavior which made him feel even more discontent. That several family meetings were held to discuss his paper-box business and other plans for his future, whereas none were called about other members of the clan, must have deeply humiliated him, but, in the end, his resentment gave way to compliance.

William, in many ways, took on the role of surrogate father to George, seeing that his brother always had an income by hiring him as an employee and advising him about business investments. In fact, it was rare for William to make a business decision without keeping George's needs in mind. Although appreciative of all the financial help that William gave him over the years, George often balked at the advice that came along with it. In 1880, for example, George felt proud when his four hundred shares of Pullman Company stock jumped from twenty-three to forty-two dollars a unit within one week. William dampened his brother's pleasure, however, when, "like a father," he warned him to be cautious with his money, perhaps selling some shares but not purchasing others. When George would not listen to him, William, somewhat nastily predicted to Fanny, "When the panic comes along some fine day he will see how it is himself."[1]

For the next year, George continued to do so well in the stock market that he purchased an estate in the Boston suburb of West Newton for the enormous sum of $17,000. The property, consisting of a large house and barn situated on 75,000 square feet of land with a three-hundred-foot frontage on the street, was a mere two-minute walk from the Boston-bound train. Feeling "as happy as a twelve-pound Oregon—no, Puget Sound clam, at high tide," George planned on spending an additional two to three thousand dollars to modernize the place, having hired an architect to complete the work.[2] William seemed to resent his brother's using his profits in such an extravagant way instead of saving them or establishing his own business. Although often cautioning and criticizing George, however, William himself liked to play the stock market and seek out new ways of expanding his own financial base. In his case, Henry assumed the role of advisor and guardian. When in 1881, after several years of spending their summers in Osterville on Cape Cod, William and Ellie decided to invest in property there, Henry went into partnership with them on a twenty-two room "cottage," which they named "Wayside." Each summer, William and Ellie rented out most of the rooms to abolitionist friends, keeping a private area of four rooms for the Villards and another few for their own family.

By July 1882 an economic downswing, created in the aftermath of President James Garfield's assassination, soured both George's and William's investments. Henry, still successful, helped the two out of their difficulties, warning them to "beware of getting in again." The next year, however, he found himself saving William from another dangerous financial loss by purchasing some of his brother-in-law's stock in the Oregon & Transcontinental Railroad, which he headed, and skillfully extricating him from declining wool investments.[3] William's inn at Osterville and a loan on more stable bank securities helped fill the financial gap, but he also decided to give up on the volatile wool business. His retirement left George once again without employment. Although both brothers' investment income kept food on the table, each accepted a personal loan from Henry who established a $10,000 bank account for the two brothers to draw upon as needed. While George, looking worn out and depressed, traveled to Boston every day to look for work, William despondently told Fanny, "I wish I could see a place for him to fill. It is time that he & I subsisted upon our own exertions. The thought of our indebtedness & embarrassment is bitter, especially our burdening Harry at this harassing time."[4]

Henry, however, had an excellent track record in investing, having manipulated the creation of the Oregon Railway & Navigation Company out of two railroads and a steamship line. As a man with great business acumen, he turned his eyes toward a new energy source—electricity, helping to establish the Edison Electric Illuminating Company in 1880. Thomas Alva Edison himself recognized Henry's outstanding instincts, proclaiming, "In pioneering, you have to have a man with nerves to adopt your ideas. I have found the man. He is Henry Villard."[5] Henry saw a way to help William through the newly renamed Edison Electric Company, which signed him on to sell towns such as Brockton, a manufacturing center not far from Boston, on the idea of substituting electric lighting for gas lighting. If successful, William was promised a position with Edison's Boston management team. After several months of seemingly fruitless efforts, in December 1883 the electric business in Brockton took off, a hotel owner ordering thirty lamps and the opera house director some one hundred lights for the theater. By mid-January, William had single-handedly seen to the placement of 830 electric lamps in the town. While he proved a capable agent for the Edison Company, the management could not afford to offer William a full-time, paid position. Instead, in December 1884, they suggested an agent post if he would accept shares of stock in lieu of salary, an arrangement he chose not to accept. Hence, he resigned, although for some time to come, he continued to represent those people he had involved in the endeavor.

Soon after leaving Edison, William established his own investment brokerage firm, enlisting the still unemployed George as his aide. Within eight months, he had sold "two & a half millions of dollars & manage[d] to sift in a few mortgages."[6] His hope was to earn enough to afford George a living wage, thereby releasing the rest of the family from supporting him. Although the business kept both men afloat for four years, in 1888, William had to give it up. As a result, George had to put his house on the market, an effort he soon forsook when enterprising William opened yet another new business, "Garrison & Howe—Commercial Paper & Investment Securities." This more lucrative endeavor provided a basic income for both brothers through their retirements. Over the years, however, the family continued to help support George. Frank, still at the Riverside Press (reorganized first as Houghton, Osgood & Company and then as Houghton, Mifflin and Company), provided George with regular financial assistance as did Wendell, when he could. Fanny also continually sent George money, including $500 in January 1890; $5,000 in 1893, and another unstated sum in November 1901, at that point promising to send him whatever he needed to meet his future needs. In addition, Henry saw to it that the money George had invested in the Chicago & Northern Pacific Railroads in his children's names was protected until George used it to send his son, Rhodes, to Harvard and his daughter Fanny to Smith College. George, in hindsight, noted that it would have been prudent to have sent them to less expensive schools.

While George and William struggled with their numerous financial schemes and businesses, Wendell and Frank continued in their more secure salaried positions at the *Nation* and Houghton, Mifflin and Company respectively. At first, it appeared that Wendell's career would most continue his parents' political work. Throughout much of 1863 and 1864, when his father was still alive, Wendell had traveled around the Northeast giving abolitionist speeches, and in late 1864 he had joined Miller McKim's effort to support the newly formed Baltimore Association for the Moral and Intellectual Improvement of the Freed People and the Pennsylvania Freedmen's Relief Association, traveling to Washington with McKim and Lucy to visit freed people's schools and makeshift refugee camps for those who had flocked to the nation's capital.[7] He then believed that he would be relocating to Baltimore to oversee McKim's reconstruction efforts, but in the interim, his career took a turn toward journalism. On February 19, 1864, Wendell made his debut as a regular columnist for the *Liberator* under the pseudonym "Maladie du Pays" (translated from French as "the country's illness"). Echoing his father's opinions in his guise as du Pays, Wendell supported aid to the freed people and wrote of the need for reconstruction efforts to guarantee them civil rights, full suffrage, education, vocational training, and land. He considered it most important that the newly freed people have a say in any postwar plans for the South, for without that stipulation guaranteed by Congress, all efforts were doomed to fall into the hands of racist white bureaucrats who would quickly reclaim power. After the war ended, du Pays expressed his desire for harsh treatment for the Confederacy: no amnesty for its president, Jefferson Davis, and no pardons for former Confederate landowners. Except for his opposition to Lincoln's reelection, Wendell, as M. du Pays, played the dutiful son.

In July 1865, after writing for the *Independent* and the *Anti-Slavery Standard,* Wendell was hired as the associate editor in charge of literary contributions to the *Nation,* the independent newspaper founded by James Miller McKim, George L. Stearns, Frederick Law Olmsted, Wendell Phillips, and several other abolitionists.[8] In seeking out seed money for the endeavor, McKim fostered the message that the new periodical would represent the voice of the freedmen's associations. With this understanding, he set out to raise $25,000 from Philadelphia and Baltimore sympathizers. Stearns and Charles E. Norton promised to obtain $50,000 from Boston supporters, and Edwin Lawrence Godkin, the proposed editor, aimed for $25,000 in New York City. With this sum, it would be possible to establish a periodical with an editor earning $5,000 a year plus 12½ percent of whatever annual profits were left after paying a 6 percent dividend to the stockholders. Godkin was an interesting choice as editor of the *Nation.* Born in 1831 in Ireland, but with English parents, he had worked as a reporter for the London *Daily News,* serving for a time as a war correspondent in the Crimea. In 1856 he emigrated to the United States, where he studied law at the office of David Dudley Field. Two years later, Godkin was admitted to the New York bar, but before long, returned to journalism, writing articles for a series of publications. During his stay in the United States, Godkin had become friendly with Charles E. Norton, who had personally contributed a large sum to the creation of the *Nation.* Wishing to secure his friend the position of editor, the liberal-minded Norton pushed the other planners to hire him without informing them that Godkin was not a radical abolitionist. In fact, the Englishman knew little about the issues of greatest importance to the *Nation*'s antislavery backers. When he discovered that Wendell Phillips and George L. Stearns, the men interviewing him for the job, held sacred such ideals as African-American suffrage, Godkin immediately adopted their rhetoric, convincing them that he agreed with all of their uncompromising stands on Reconstruction. He revealed his true feelings only after he was securely ensconced behind the editor's desk.

Although Wendell could count his parentage, his experience on the *Liberator,* and his assistant editorship of the *Independent* as qualifications for his own editorial position, in reality, it was his father-in-law who arranged the job offer. Extremely happy to receive it, the young Garrison immediately designed a letterhead for the business's stationery, mailed out advertising circulars, wrote several book reviews, and began recruiting potential literary contributors. He then took on the writing of book reviews, a column on freed people's issues, and a weekly news summary. He and Godkin got along well from the start, partly because Wendell valued the intellectual nature of his work and was willing to compromise on the values behind his Garrisonian political upbringing.

Touted on its masthead as "A Weekly Journal of Politics, Literature, Science & Art," initially the *Nation* endorsed several abolitionist goals designed to completely alter the previously slave-based society of the South through the Freedmen's Bureau, the Civil Rights Bill of 1866, and the Reconstruction Acts of 1867.[9] Adopting a stance similar to his support of the Civil War, despite his nonresistance beliefs, Wendell agreed with the *Nation*'s sanctioning of the use of force to ensure that blacks were protected from revengeful whites. He had no objection to the North's military occupation of the South and felt no need for Congress to rush to readmit the Southern states into the Union. The paper's first editorial acknowledged that there was no easy remedy to the racist practices in the South: "Anybody who expects Southern whites and blacks to settle down into their true and just relations to each other without breaking one another's heads a good deal, knows little either of history or human nature." Where the editorial diverged from the abolitionists' viewpoint, however, was in its position that any suffrage should be based on "quality, not quantity, in the electorate."[10] Under Godkin's leadership, from the start, the *Nation* voiced the opinion that universal suffrage was not necessarily a good policy. Rather, voting should be based on age, residence, sanity, literacy level, lack of a criminal record, and state of employment. Those existing on charity should not be allowed to vote at all.

In terms of woman suffrage, the editors were circumspect. Once all educated, propertied men had the vote, then one could consider women's right to the elective franchise. This conservative position resulted as much from the original makeup and approach of its creators as it did from Godkin's influence. When Miller McKim had initially approached his friend Lucretia Mott for a donation for the paper's establishment, Mott turned him down flat because there were no women being considered for staff positions and no stated concern for the struggle for woman's rights. "I told him," Mott wrote her sister, Martha, "it was objected that woman was ignored in their new organization, and if it really were a reconstruction for the nation, she ought not so to be, and that it would be rather humiliating for our anti-slavery women and Quaker women to consent to be thus overlooked, after suffering the Anti-Slavery Society to be divided in 1840 rather than yield, and after claiming our right so earnestly in London to a seat in the World's Convention." McKim, taken aback by Mott's protest, responded that if there seemed a "necessity" for women, they would be admitted. "*Seemed a necessity!!* For *one half* the nation to act with you!" Mott retorted, apparently leaving McKim speechless.[11] It was no surprise to Mott that the new periodical appeared with no women on board and only one female contributor, Gail Hamilton (the pen name for Mary Abigail Dodge), an essay writer who supported woman's rights. In general, ignoring the need for women to vote continued to be the paper's policy, causing Fanny to complain in 1870 that she wished the *Nation* "were not so bitter (it seems to grow more so) toward the cause of women."[12] Indeed, the next year, an article which came out in support of a taxpayer qualification for African-American voters in New York City also stated its "fear" of giving women the vote, lest their "female charms" proved dangerous when plied on "susceptible legislators."[13]

Although Wendell and Miller McKim privately favored a more radical Garrisonian approach to journalism, neither put up a fuss over Godkin's more conservative positions. Indeed, McKim stated soon after publication began, "The *Nation* is not the organ of the Freedmen's Movement. It is established and is to be conducted in the interest of all virtue. Therefore we Freedmens men—who are also more than Freedmens men—favor and support it."[14] Wendell Phillips, George L. Stearns, and other Boston stockholders, however, were so outraged by the shift in the paper's political stance that within a year they withdrew their financial backing, in effect giving Godkin carte blanche over the *Nation*'s direction. He turned the paper into a newsy compilation of articles whose main emphasis was on literature, science, and the arts with lesser attention paid to political controversy. Within a month of the first issue, dated July 6, 1865, in fact, Godkin had assumed control. Wendell quickly took his side, defending him even to his own family. When William complained that the paper's writing had quickly changed from political reporting to intellectual posturing, Wendell shot back: "You are moving in the atmosphere which is most hostile to the *Nation* . . . a periodical which is the product of ripe thought must necessarily seem dull and stupid. . . . You say the *Nation* is bloodless and without warmth. I interpret that to mean that we argue rather than declaim, and prefer to understate rather than to overstate." To Lloyd's critical observation that Godkin did not know what he was doing, Wendell retorted, "Father doesn't know Mr. Godkin. No better man could be appointed to the place he now fills. He is a cautious, careful man, and in his judgment, an independent and ready thinker, an excellent critic . . . temperate in all respects, clean in his personal habits, a most agreeable, unassuming companion."[15]

E. L. Godkin may have played an important role in Wendell's life at the time because, it appears, the third son was going through a search to determine his self-identity. While his intellectual Harvard education swayed him to support Godkin, his political upbringing haunted him. How could he follow his literary bent while still holding on to the family values he cherished? Until the end of 1865, Wendell resolved the dilemma by adhering to and defending Godkin's philosophy at the *Nation* while at the same time continuing to submit articles to the *Liberator*. Once the family paper ceased publication, however, his avenues for political self-expression became limited. Wendell then moderated his politics, a shift his father criticized him for, accusing him of surrendering his individuality to Godkin. Wendell, however, did not see the issue in the light of defection from his past. "It is unpleasant for me to differ from you, dear Father," he told Lloyd. "I know so intimately the nature of Mr. Godkin's mind and the sincerity of his aims, and the absolute independence with which he expresses his views on all occasions that I am ever glad of an opportunity to praise him for all these noble qualities." Not wishing to cause a break with the father he so loved and admired, Wendell tried to win Lloyd over to Godkin's side. "He differs as much from me as from you in his way of looking at a subject, and yet I am sure you would share my admiration if you knew him. He is a very democratic, a very social, genial and tolerant man."[16] Lloyd continued to pressure Wendell to admit that Godkin was an insincere conservative, but his son would not listen to his argument, not even when Lloyd pointed to Wendell's exploitative salary. Wendell was happy and content where he was, noting, "I decidedly prefer low wages for serving the *Nation* to a fat salary in any other place."[17]

During the time the siblings still had their parents around, political differences were sometimes expressed, although always with deference to the older pair. After Lincoln's assassination, for instance, Lloyd, Helen, and their children carried on a serious discussion about the presidency of Andrew Johnson, a Southerner. At first, it appeared to most abolitionists that Johnson would proceed with Lincoln's plans for reconstructing the South, plans that, although lenient to white landholders, also sought racial justice. However, it soon became clear that Johnson's intention was to reestablish the Union as quickly as possible without demanding sweeping civil rights legislation. Whereas former Confederate states had to take loyalty oaths and rewrite their constitutions to eliminate all vestiges of slavery, Johnson turned away from any suggestions of land redistribution or universal suffrage. Abolitionists tried to impress upon the new president that he had been elected a Republican, thereby promising to secure equality and safety for the newly freed people, but their pleas fell upon deaf ears. Early in Johnson's administration, feelings about him among members of the Garrison family fluctuated. Like his father, William was willing to give the president a fighting chance, noting to his mother-in-law, Martha, "I feel anxious at Pres. Johnson's course & think he mistakes it lamentably by his method of reconstruction, but . . . I prefer to believe in his good intentions & integrity till otherwise convinced."[18] Within a few months, William, recognizing Johnson's growing rigidity, was no longer confident that he would protect black rights.

When in March 1866 the president vetoed a civil rights bill—which became law only when Congress overrode his veto—the family's feeling toward him deteriorated further, although their faith in Congress, usually skeptical, grew. Frank reflected this sentiment soon after returning from a visit with Fanny in D.C., "Things begin to look a little brighter, and if we can only keep the two-thirds majority obtained for the bill, we can snap our fingers at the wretched occupant of the White House."[19] His sister, however, was cynical, observing that in Washington the general attitude toward Johnson was "distrustful," the Republican Party, which her parents supported, either "disunited," "luke-warm in sentiment," and often "deferential and yielding." Fanny, then a budding woman's rightist though not an activist, was especially annoyed by the politicians' open distrust of and aversion to women's opinions, noting to her mother, "One is almost tempted to believe here that all men are liars & hypocrites & the truth is not in them."[20] At least the passage and ratification of the Fourteenth Amendment in 1868 granting the freed people citizenship gave the abolitionists some sense of accomplishment.

As abolitionist anger mounted, talk of asking for Andrew Johnson's impeachment circulated freely. Wendell Phillips, for one, felt that the Fourteenth Amendment, although a step in the right direction, did not mean that Reconstruction had succeeded. Rather, Johnson's subsequent actions had proved just the opposite. When the president dismissed Secretary of War Edwin M. Stanton without his successor being approved by Congress as stipulated in the Tenure of Office Act of 1867, the Republicans called for impeachment. Although a Senate trial was held, Johnson was not convicted of the charges and continued his term in office. Meanwhile the debates and arguments over the issue reverberated through the abolitionist community, this time including the second generation. Wendell felt angriest about the call issued by his mentor, Wendell Phillips, for Johnson's impeachment. Believing that some of the old guard needed to move aside to make room for the new, he complained to his father, "I am firmly persuaded that on this side of the grave neither the original rebels nor the latter-day abolition saints and martyrs will ever change their minds, recognize the tendency of things about them, their own anachronism, uselessness and folly, or abate one jot of their prejudices and presumption." No longer did Phillips seem heroic to Wendell, even though Miller McKim and Lloyd, who believed that the most important issue at stake was the "movement for the freedmen," continued to seem so.[21]

As the Reconstruction efforts of the 1870s wound down, and racist landowners and politicians reassumed control over state and local governments, the first- and second-generation abolitionists continued to speak out, the voices of the younger activists growing louder as their parents' voices were silenced by old age and, finally, death. The Garrison children's opinions proceeded to take clearer shape, one or another of them now seemingly embarrassed by their father's usual outspokenness. Lloyd's support of the Republican president Ulysses S. Grant's 1872 proposal that the United States annex the Dominican Republic was a case in point. Senator Charles Sumner of Massachusetts attacked the idea on the grounds that it would lead to certain imperialism, a concept Sumner considered against the intent of the nation's founders. As in the past, at first, Lloyd opposed such expansionism, but his admiration for Grant convinced him to take his side against his former abolitionist supporter. When Sumner made the decision to support Horace Greeley in the presidential race against Grant, the senator delivered a speech titled "Republicanism vs. Grantism" and then published an open letter to the African-American community urging them to support Greeley over Grant. Lloyd communicated to Sumner that his action was "ill judged, ill-timed, and so extravagant in its charges and bitter in its personalities as to neutralize whatever of just criticism can be found in it."[22]

Fanny, who believed that Ulysses S. Grant was a poor excuse for a Republican, was upset by what she perceived as her father's support of the conservative side in the election. Petulantly, she pointed out, "I should have thought that our radical father would, as usual, have steered clear of conservatism, and taken the radical side!"[23] When she suggested that perhaps he should not express these views publicly, he railed against her in one of his rare displays of temper toward his daughter. Just as he had always in the past praised Sumner, why should he not also criticize him if he saw the need? For over forty years, he had taken part in the public debate on political issues. Why should he not do so now? Lloyd was so upset with Fanny that he attacked her personally, pointing out, "This is the first time, since her marriage that I have known my daughter to take any interest in radicalism, or any exception to conservatism. Your father is still as radical and as anti-conservative as ever; . . . So long as I confront them and they me, my daughter need give herself no concern about her father's 'conservatism,' nor cherish the hope that he will be dumb and a passive looker-on when the most tremendous issues are pending."[24]

Lloyd's tone struck a deep chord within Fanny, especially his claim that her concern about his becoming conservative "amused" him. In fact, she was so aghast that she was not even sure that she should issue a response, especially since she was raised to believe that even though it was one's duty to express oneself morally and politically, it was not acceptable to cause ill will at home. In this case, however, Fanny was so outraged at her father that she could not contain herself. The argument continued its personal bent. Fanny expressed long-denied frustration with being expected to be the traditionally obedient daughter while Lloyd expressed the hurt of the disregarded father. "The matter seems to me to stand thus:" she responded, "if I express an opinion which does not coincide with your own, it serves only to 'amuse' you, it being extraordinarily funny that your daughter should pretend to have an interest in the questions of radicalism or conservatism, the first time 'since her marriage,' that she has done so. On the other hand, if I remain silent, you take it for granted that I am incapable of taking an interest in affairs that especially concern the welfare of my own country. Which horn of the dilemma shall I choose?" Fanny explained that her father had misunderstood her previous letter; she had no intention of "dictat[ing]" to him what course of action he should take on any issue. However, his attacks on Sumner and defense of Grant indicated that he was acting like a "political partisan," a position he had avoided his entire life. Although "astonished" that her father could see no fault with Grant's administration, she agreed with his estimation of Horace Greeley, finding the idea that "such a scatter-brains" could become president almost too much to bear.[25]

Fanny could not help ending her letter with further discussion of her father's apparent inability to take her seriously and accept any dissent from her. "Well, it is useless to try to carry on an argument on paper," she concluded,

> and as I am far from wishing to incur further chances of displeasing you, I shall henceforth choose the other horn & remain silent. Not, however, without feeling a trifle humiliated, that in spite of my added years, you regard me as unable to form an independent opinion, or in fact 'to take interest' enough to have any opinions about public matters at all. . . . if that is the case, you have a right to be ashamed of your only daughter, who has certainly had the rare advantage of being brought up in the midst of people who have felt proud to give their whole life up to the furtherance of the public good. But, I am, nevertheless your admiring & most tenderly loving Fanny.[26]

It is clear from Fanny's letter that even though her father was a strong advocate for woman's rights, his daughter felt that he did not completely believe that women, at least the women in his family, could be as politically astute as he was.

Wendell, who had his own share of run-ins with his father, also took umbrage with Fanny's sentiments. Although he agreed in part with his sister's feeling that Lloyd had perhaps exaggerated his case, he could not understand how Fanny could criticize her father's right to express his opinions. "But how can you question Father's right to take an interest in political movements of such overwhelming importance to the country," he countered Fanny, "to form a judgment upon them, and to express his mind about them? He always has done so, and always must. That is neither to be partisan nor to be a politician. It is against his nature to be indifferent."[27] Frank, too, defended his father, as did Helen her husband. Frank felt Lloyd's letter to Sumner was "a crusher" and would ensure that the black vote went in favor of Grant. He assured Fanny that he had heard nothing but "expressions of delight" from all sides in support of Lloyd.[28] Helen later added that the African-American community was "as clear sighted as can be & well know that Grant is the one for them to vote for." She implied that this was thanks to Lloyd's work.[29] When election day came, the nonresistant, nonvoting Lloyd, who could not see that his electioneering indicated participation in the electoral process, expressed some hope that Frank would go to the polls and cast a ballot for Grant. His son did not do so, but Grant easily won the election anyhow.

While Lloyd might have been disappointed in his children's discussions of his own behavior, he should not have been surprised by their outspokenness. After all, he and Helen had raised them to have confidence in themselves and to stand up for their beliefs. The first in the family to openly defy his parents' values had been George, but the family had stood behind him in his commitment to join the military during the Civil War. During the 1870s, however, as Wendell continued to move further away from his father's positions on Reconstruction, Lloyd became increasingly perturbed. Wendell had always been the intellectual apple of his father's eye. Lloyd had watched this intelligent son move through the Boston Latin School and Harvard, tramp the abolitionist lecture circuit, and then become a writer for what Lloyd at first perceived to be the replacement paper for the *Liberator*. However, as E. L. Godkin's rhetoric took the *Nation* to a more conservative position and Wendell followed suit, Lloyd's disappointment grew. What most annoyed him was the *Nation*'s stand on civil rights. The paper consistently spoke of the need for "an intelligent, educated citizenry" which would see to it that the U.S. government moved away from its present nineteenth-century mode of corruption to a "rule in accordance with the principles of laissez-faire."[30] In order to achieve "good government," Southern leaders themselves needed to offer limited voting rights for African Americans. Lloyd and the other abolitionists maintained their sentiment that any former Confederate or believer in slavery could not possibly create new state governments committed to racial equality. Even if these leaders eventually accepted the reality of African Americans as free people, they would see to it that economically, legally, politically, and socially, blacks lived second-class lives.

In this father-son struggle over Reconstruction politics, Wendell tried to reason with his father but often found the elder Garrison unmovable. "I see, of course," he wrote Lloyd in early 1875, "why it is useless for you and me to exchange arguments on this matter. You see in every Southern issue a race issue, and your sympathies are naturally with the (nominally) weaker side. I try to judge each one according to the facts and the principles involved, holding fast to this maxim: that good government is first to be thought of and striven for, and that the incidental loss which it may seem to occasion to either race is far less mischievous than the incidental protection accorded to either by bad government." Wendell defended the *Nation* against his father's accusation that it was "a Southern organ," claiming that the paper was neutral, not favoring the North or the South, but presenting the issues of the entire country in a nonpartisan way.[31] Recognizing that Lloyd's constant attacks on the *Nation* specifically targeted Godkin himself, Wendell may have perceived that not only was his father angry with Godkin's politics, but he was also jealous of Godkin's influence over his son, fearing that the editor had taken his place as political mentor, turning Wendell away from his parents' more radical positions. Might not a growing difference in political opinion result in a loss of filial affection?

During the nation's centennial celebration in 1876, father and son again conflicted, this time over what appeared to be a trivial issue—the move on the part of several wealthy Bostonians to save the Old South Church from demolition and then to refurbish it. Wendell was all in favor of preserving the 1729 institution, which had been used as a meeting place during the War of Independence. He felt that at a time when the country was in such strong conflict over Reconstruction, any effort to highlight the spirit of liberty was positive. Lloyd, however, disagreed, believing that the nation should be reminded of the shame of slavery and the poor way that Reconstruction was being handled. Preserving the Old South Church, whose reverend, George Washington Blagden, had been "conspicuously pro-slavery," merely fed people's patriotic fervor with no consideration of the country's true past and present failures concerning civil rights. When Lloyd's views appeared in the July 6 issue of the *Independent,* Wendell expressed his great displeasure. Lloyd, while commending his son for speaking his mind, also criticized him for becoming part of the "gush" and "glorification" which simply helped the nation overlook the "criminality" of racism practiced toward its black citizens ever since independence.[32]

Lloyd's displeasure with his son did not prevent Wendell from continuing to opine that ridding the government of corruption through an educated electorate would end racism.[33] With each apparent mimicking of Godkin's sentiments, however, members of the family became more irate. In 1874, when the *Nation* excused Ku Klux Klan activity, Frank lambasted his brother for allowing his name to be connected with it, but Wendell felt that Southern whites were simply reacting to "bad government." Until corruption ceased, in fact, African-American leaders should refrain from taking a leading role in politics and spend more effort in aiding their constituency in learning "the gospel of education, thrift, industry, and chastity."[34] Echoing the ideas of Charles Darwin, whom he considered "*the* man of our epoch, the greatest scientist & the greatest theologian of recent times," Wendell wondered why, if it had taken whites centuries to achieve their present state of civilization, people would expect former slaves to be able to accomplish this in just a few years.[35] Much to his family's dismay, in his enthusiasm to support Godkin's program, Wendell did not consider the historical role of free African Americans in the United States, including his father's fellow activists, nor did he seek out information about the great civilizations in African history. William opposed Wendell's stance, even when, during his own visit to the South in 1875, he discovered that popular opinion held that newly freed people were not yet ready for full citizenship. William was appalled by the racist attitudes he witnessed, pledging that he would continue the family's equal rights and social justice struggles.

In November 1876, when the Republican candidate Rutherford B. Hayes gained the presidency in one of the nation's most controversial elections, Wendell and Lloyd's differences almost caused a break in their relationship. Hayes's Democratic opponent, Samuel J. Tilden, it appeared, had gained a majority of the popular vote and enough electoral votes to win. But when the Republicans disputed twenty of these votes, Congress created the mandatory special electoral commission, consisting of five senators, five representatives, and five Supreme Court justices, to decide the case. The majority of these officials were loyal Republicans, who determined that Hayes should receive all the disputed votes. Congress accepted the commission's decision even though Democrats controlled the House, leading to much public speculation about secret deals hatched between Hayes and Southern Democrats. Hayes's victory spelled defeat for the proponents of Reconstruction, as one of the new president's first actions was to remove the occupying Northern military troops from the South, leaving African Americans without the support they needed to further their efforts for civil rights. Of all the Garrisons, Wendell alone supported the Hayes administration. Much to his father's chagrin, he continued to espouse his position that the vote for blacks was not the most important issue. If Hayes managed to calm some of the tensions in the South by removing the last vestiges of Northern occupation, a safer and more prosperous life was bound to come to its African-American residents.

Throughout 1877, father and son bickered over Hayes. Then, in early 1878, the Boston *Globe* and the New York *Herald* published an open letter from Lloyd to William E. Chandler, a New England politician who had accused Hayes of having made an agreement with Southern Democrats to end Reconstruction in exchange for gaining the presidency.[36] Wendell, apparently, wrote his father a scathing letter of reproach, for Lloyd, in turn, complained to Fanny, "I have just received a letter from Wendell. And such a letter from a son to a father!" What upset Lloyd was Wendell's seemingly "accordance with the Rebel side of the question" and his including with his correspondence articles from Northern and Southern Democratic newspapers "in fiercest denunciation" of Lloyd himself. Lloyd could not believe that Wendell had moved so far from his sphere of influence as to become an adversary. "Not the slightest feeling does he exhibit in view of such dirty and murder-exciting attacks upon me," he lamented. "He is only apprehensive that I may feel my position strengthened and justified by them! . . . The grief I feel over his letter is extremely poignant."[37] To Wendell, he responded with a chilly nod for the offending articles and stiff-lipped assurances that he would continue to follow his own path and express his own opinions, no matter what his opponents or his errant son had to say about him, concluding, "When you speak of 'the restoration of the South to self-government—i.e. government as it is in Massachusetts'—you confound all distinctions, and utterly reverse the truth of history. And when you profess to find 'a certain resemblance' between my state of mind and that of the editor of the Petersburg *Index-Appeal,* who thinks the gallows ought to be my doom, I can only ask, with parental solicitude, whether my son is in his right senses."[38]

Fanny, in an effort to placate the situation, suggested that father and son no longer discuss politics with each other. Lloyd responded that he had not intended to communicate with Wendell about the Chandler letter, "knowing his state of mind," but he could not fail to respond to his "tone," which had "both surprised and grieved" him. In truth, he desired to avoid any more confrontations with his son, especially during this final, lonely stage of his life. To Fanny, he noted, "Of course, I do not for a moment suppose that Wendell intended to wound my feelings, and here I wish the matter to end." If blame were to be placed, it belonged to Wendell's boss, for "alas the day that he ever became connected with Godkin and The Nation!" [39] What Lloyd did not comprehend was the extent that his son's own loneliness cemented his relationship with Godkin. Over the course of ten years, he had lost two babies through miscarriage, Lucy, his father-in-law, and his mother. Living in New Jersey isolated him from his siblings and friends, and even though Sarah McKim remained with him to help raise his children, she did not serve as his intellectual and personal soul mate as had Lucy and Miller McKim. E. L. Godkin and the *Nation* filled a gap for Wendell, providing the intellectual stimulation he craved and enough of an income for him to take care of himself and his family. Godkin felt similarly, claiming in 1883, "If anything goes wrong with you, I will retire into a monastery. You are the one steady and constant man I ever had to do with."[40]

In general, Wendell kept his unending sense of loss over Lucy's death private. Sometimes his need for companionship led him to Fanny, but most of his time he spent at work or taking care of his children. It was through them that he still felt in touch with his lost love, and it was they who led him to an interest in how children could be taught to be literate, educated, and moral.[41] In 1887 Wendell published *Bedside Poetry: A Parent's Assistant in Moral Discipline,* a compilation of poems by such famous writers as Ralph Waldo Emerson, William Shakespeare, William Wordsworth, Leigh Hunt, John Greenleaf Whittier, Samuel Coleridge, and Robert Burns. Dedicated to Lucy, it provided classic poetry for parents to read to children during the precious pre-bedtime hour, when "Sweeter or more impressive relations than those thus established cannot be hoped for in this life."[42]

Wendell authored two other children's books.[43] The first, *What Mr. Darwin Saw,* adapted abstracts from Charles Darwin's journals, with the famed scientist's approval.[44] The second, *Parables for School and Home* (1898), was a delightful collection of short essays on topics as varied as treating animals kindly, taking care of possessions, listening to adults, being patriotic, learning about national flags, accepting death as a natural part of life, and honoring the equality of the sexes. Wendell's writing style was straightforward but interesting, with a spark of Garrison humor to it. For example, in his section on why boys and girls should be treated the same, he played on the concept of women as the housekeepers of society, a popular notion during the Progressive Era: "She may now, for all he cares, do almost everything a man does except vote and be voted for, though there is nothing difficult about that. Government is only a kind of housekeeping, and it is surely woman's business to keep house."[45] On a more serious note, in his section on property, Wendell reminded his turn-of-the-century audience of the anguish of slavery, relating his eyewitness account of the capture and re-enslavement of Anthony Burns.

Wendell also composed poetry, much of it reflecting his longing for Lucy. In his anger and despair immediately following her death, he had destroyed most of Lucy's letters, especially those written during their courtship, and kept only a few photographs and a portrait that he hung in the parlor, largely so that the children might remember her. In 1898, more than twenty years later, Wendell published a small book titled *Sonnets and Lyrics of the Ever-Womanly,* dedicating it "To You My Sister and to the Memory of Our Dear Mother." A small oval photograph of Lucy's face graced the frontispiece. One sonnet, "Reality," told of the poet's imagining that a portrait of his deceased lover had come to life:

Whether my fancy or truth it be,
   I know not: in its frame her portrait turned
   Profile to full face on me, who had earned
This boon by deepest longing. You be free
To reject the miracle, and nothing see
   Save one poor brain that mused by fire that burned,
   And lids that feebly sleep's caresses spurned;
And write Illusion o'er my Verity.
I will not argue. Not more real I found
   Her condescension that she would be mine,
Those dear confiding arms which clasped me
   Or that immortal voice, as with wind bound,
Quickened my pulse in words that still resound—
   "The kindest eyes in all the world are thine!"[46]

Although nothing ever successfully filled the gap left by Lucy's death, Wendell's father and siblings held such a special place in his life that no political disagreement, no matter how intense, could ever cause him to break that bond. Hence, it is not surprising that throughout his tussles with Lloyd, he also worked to honor his parents' memories. When Wendell and Frank realized that their father was never going to write the much-desired autobiography and history of the abolitionist movement, the two decided to take on the project themselves. While Lloyd was still alive, the brothers began sifting through his letters and writings, searching out their family's history. Individually, each had already preserved various segments of the abolitionists' stories. Wendell in 1872 had privately published *The Benson Family of Newport, R.I.,* a genealogical account of his maternal background. Frank, meanwhile, had used the auspices of the Riverside Press and Houghton's *Atlantic Monthly* to publish various memoirs and books about his family and other abolitionists, including those by or about Wendell, Helen and Lloyd, his brother-in-law Henry, James and Lucretia Mott, and Sarah Southwick.[47]

By 1876, Frank and Wendell were thoroughly engrossed in writing Lloyd's biography. They placed ads in several periodicals asking for letters and papers connected with their father's life. Whenever any of the brothers had a chance to visit those abolitionists still alive, they took it. In April 1880, for example, they attended Samuel May's seventieth birthday celebration, where they reminisced with Wendell Phillips, Maria Weston Chapman, Deborah Weston, Theodore Weld, Sarah Southwick, the Buffum family, and Parker Pillsbury. Also in the 1880s, they met at Lucy Stone's home, adding to their list of sources Elizabeth B. Chase, Harriet and Samuel Sewall, Zilpha Spooner, and Henry Blackwell. William helped by copying over letters from Edmund Quincy, each resulting in thirty to forty pages in his own handwriting. George also collected data and copied over letters. The brothers enjoyed reliving their parents' and their own past, William relating to Fanny, "Every item of anti-slavery interest is detailed, with no end of personal gossip, bandinage, etc. I get fascinated in the work. At first I intended to copy only the most important things, but so far, I have included everything disliking to omit even the trivialities."[48] While researching and writing the biography, they also served on a committee in Boston which commissioned the sculptor Olin L. Warner to design a statue of Lloyd, which in 1886 took its place on Commonwealth Avenue. Although pleased with the idea, Frank, unlike Wendell, did not approve of the statue's likeness of his father and was disappointed that few people came to witness its unveiling. From its inception, William had hated the "shabby caricature" which would "make another bad statue for Boston."[49] In 1893 another statue of Lloyd was dedicated, this one in Newburyport. William was not very enamored of this likeness of his father either, claiming it was "without inspiration" and had "no claim to rank as a work of art."[50] Much to their joy, however, the dedication ceremony attracted over five hundred of Lloyd's African-American admirers.

Working on their father's biography helped the brothers through some difficult personal times. For Wendell, it was the loss of Miller McKim and Lucy. For Frank, it was a similar tragedy. During their first happy years together, he and Mary succeeded in making Rockledge their own, and in 1881, much to their delight, Mary became pregnant. Being physical fitness advocates, the couple saw to it that she ate healthily, took long walks, and got plenty of rest. Yet, when the baby was ready to appear on July 27, Mary went through a torturous eighteen-hour labor at the end of which ten-pound Ruth Phillips Garrison was stillborn. According to Fanny, who had hurried to be with her brother and sister-in-law, the baby's head was too large to exit the womb, and when the doctor attempted to deliver her, she was "mutilated" and Mary "torn."[51] Mary herself suffered greatly and died within a couple of days. Friends and family flocked to Frank's side, Samuel May and Wendell Phillips leading the final services for mother and child. Sarah McKim, who went to Boston on Wendell's behalf, could not contain her grief, noting to her son-in-law, "Poor Frank—poor Mary. One short week ended all their lovely bright prospects. O *horrible, horrible.* It seems *too* dreadful to be true."[52] Wendell

Phillips concurred, "It was, as you say, very sad—so overwhelmingly sad that one could only sit with him & press his hand."[53]

Soon after the funeral, Fanny convinced her brother to stay with her for awhile in New York. Unable to fathom how such a healthy pregnancy could turn so tragic, Frank mulled over the physicians' shock and Mary's own disbelief in the turn of events. In the end, he became so disoriented in his mourning that his old friend Lizzie Simmons was summoned to accompany him back home to Boston.[54] Although Fanny did not think it wise for Frank to live alone at Rockledge, he returned there, summing up his feelings to a "dear friend": "It is a great change for me, to be left alone in the old home with its three vacant chairs, but few men have been so richly blessed as I in the past. . . . Heaven gave me one of the purest, loveliest & most perfect women that ever lived, for my wife, and our three years of married life were years of perfect, unalloyed bliss."[55] Frank remained alone until 1891, when he wed Theresa Holmes, a former friend of his and Mary's. They had two children together: Wendell Holmes, born in 1894, and David Holmes, born in 1897 but succumbing to diphtheria only sixteen months later.

While working on his father's biography, Wendell's personal life also took a new turn. In 1883 Annie, Lucy's sister, and her husband, Fred Dennis, moved to Orange to be near the McKim-Garrison clan. The couple had had two children of their own whose deaths in their teen years had resulted in Fred's mental and physical breakdown. In 1886 he collapsed on a New York street, dying within days. Soon after, Annie moved in with her mother, Wendell, and the two children still living at home. January 1891 brought the death of Sarah McKim, who had become a substitute mother to Wendell, helping to raise his children and taking care of his home for fifteen years. That March, Annie and Wendell married, an appropriate move considering their personal attachment and their residing under the same roof. Frank was delighted when he received the "bombshell," assuring his brother that he felt only "gladness . . . that a new burst of joy and sunshine has come into your life after so many years of sad loneliness, so sweetly & heroically borne."[56] For a year and a half, Annie and Wendell lived together contentedly, but Annie, too, suffered from a lingering illness. Short of funds, her brother, Charles McKim, covered the costs of her medical treatment, refusing repayment from Wendell. After her death on September 22, 1893, Charles insisted that investments that Annie had bequeathed to him be turned over to Wendell's daughter, Katharine. Annie was buried, as she requested, near Fred Dennis in Auburn, New York. Wendell was once again alone.

During all of their personal travails, Wendell and Frank continued working on the biography, writing to each other almost daily. As Frank later described the experience to Fanny, "How many points there were for investigation, discussion, & settlement! And how much I owe my dear brother for his long & patient years of teaching & training which, all unconsciously to us both, was qualifying me for a partnership with him in our filial task. Certainly we worked in the completest harmony, with deference to each other's views on doubtful points, & with, as he wrote, 'never a crack in the bond.'"[57] In 1885, after more than ten years of collaboration, the Century Company in New York published the first two volumes as *William Lloyd Garrison, 1805–1879: The Story of His Life Told by His Children.* As Wendell and Frank noted in the introduction, the work was intended to represent "the largest and the most important collection of anti-slavery autographs in existence," its documentation including letters (many with personal anecdotes) and articles from the *Liberator* and other periodicals. Hence, for them, the book was both biography and the history of the abolitionist movement. The brothers admitted that they could not avoid being biased, but they had penned the narrative "in a spirit emulous of the absolute fairness which distinguished our father" and "the hope" that Lloyd's "unfinished work" would be "promoted by this review of his fortunate career" and the furthering of "the doctrine of Peace."[58]

The second two volumes appeared four years later in 1889, bearing at the end of the "Valediction" the notice "THE TENTH ANNIVERSARY OF OUR FATHER'S DEATH." Acknowledging their pleasure at the praise their first two volumes received, the brothers accepted the label "autobiography," which several readers had attached to the work. They warned the public, however, to be aware of the "defects of reminiscence" and of their own input.[59] In 1894, five years after the original publication of the final two volumes, Houghton, Mifflin and Company reissued all four books. The brothers followed up their work by placing complete runs of the *Liberator* in various libraries, notably the Boston Public Library, the New York Public Library, the Library of Congress, and the British Museum in London.[60] The correspondence used to enhance the story was placed in the Boston Public Library, although Garrison family papers were also entrusted to the Massachusetts Historical Society and later, by Lloyd's and the children's descendants, to Harvard University and Smith College.

William Lloyd Garrison, the most complete history of the abolitionist movement of its time, pleased its authors and their brothers, who praised the work profusely. Only Fanny, angered by her brothers' presentation of their mother, criticized the final chapter of the fourth volume in which Wendell and Frank drew a picture of their version of their parents' relationship. Although she would not have wanted one word about her father removed, Fanny complained that Wendell and Frank "did not do Mother justice" by portraying Helen as "inferior" to her husband "in conversation." With a growing sensibility of the contradiction between her father's pro–woman's rights politics and his behavior at home, Fanny countered that Lloyd "did not know the meaning of conversation, for he alone spoke, & that was one reason why Mother, (& I too) were afraid to have any opinions, that differed from his, or at least to express them." Fanny wished that her brothers had used more "tact & judgment" in depicting their parents' lives."[61]

Wendell balked at Fanny's criticism, retorting, "I did not say that Mother had 'inferior powers of conversation' in the absolute sense, but in comparison to Father's—an incontestable fact."[62] In the end, the siblings agreed to disagree. Critics, in general, wrote favorably about the biography, the *New York Tribune* claiming that the first two volumes "told their story in such a way that no reader who cares for the subject at all will wish to leave it unfinished."[63] The *Philadelphia Ledger and Transcript* praised the volumes' "completeness of a labor of love . . . free from the defects of the too familiar hand."[64] The *Brooklyn Union* applauded the objective treatment, while the *Boston Daily Advertiser* considered volumes three and four "a masterpiece of modern historical biography."[65]

Eleven years after the publication of the homage to his father, Frank finally decided to move from Rockledge to a new house in Lexington, a town William and Ellie had relocated to in 1903. After much discussion and negotiating, in 1904, the children sold their family home to the Episcopalian order of the Sisters of St. Margaret, who turned it into St. Monica's Home for Sick and Infirm Colored Women and Children, naming one of its wards after Lloyd. Today, the structure is a modern state-of-the-art nursing home, while the original rooms of the Garrison home have been preserved as a historical landmark. In 1905 Boston observed the Garrison Centennial, two days of celebration dedicated to the memory of Lloyd and the abolitionist movement. Activities were organized by the Boston Suffrage League, St. Monica's Home, and various other organizations, especially those of the African-American community who kept Lloyd's story and reputation alive. By the time of the 1905 festivities, when several black leaders joined Frank in speaking about Lloyd, he and his abolitionist cohorts had effectively been diminished in traditional white historical memory, not to resurface in any major way until the 1950s and 1960s when the Civil Rights movement reached its peak.[66] Wendell and Frank followed up on the 1905 festivities by collecting some of Lloyd's writings and publishing them as *The Words of Garrison: A Centenary Selection (1805–1905)*.[67]

As well as striving to preserve their father's memory, the Garrison children continued to work for causes that they had been raised to believe in, namely racial justice, woman's rights, and peace. It was particularly important to them to see that civil rights gains and improvements in education for African Americans in the South succeeded.[68] Only Wendell, who continued to question whether the first generation of freed people could really match in intellectual capacity their white counterparts, reflected a conservative bent. In 1881 Henry Villard purchased the New York *Evening Post,* hiring E. L. Godkin as its associate editor and the next year promoting him to editor-in-chief. At the same time, the *Evening Post* absorbed the *Nation,* diminishing its status to that of a weekly edition of the larger paper. Wendell remained with the *Nation,* its tone, unfortunately, becoming even more conservative as his influence grew, sparking his nephew, Oswald Garrison Villard, to admit in 1925 that under his uncle's influence the *Nation* "lost much of its spontaneity," becoming "less and less polemical and more and more the organ of intense scholarship."[69] Wendell, it appeared, cared little about how the news was presented.

In 1884, however, in an expression of disgust for the way the Republican Party had failed to complete Reconstruction efforts and protect black civil rights, Wendell, William, and Frank joined in voting for a Democrat, Grover Cleveland, in the presidential election. Unlike their father, the brothers continued to vote, again supporting Cleveland in his 1888 reelection bid. When Thomas Wentworth Higginson, still active in the struggle for political equality, ran for Congress on the Democratic ticket, William supported his efforts, claiming that the party had not proven to be any worse than the Republicans. The brothers saw voting as a way to pressure Congress to build upon the freedmen's associations and to further the American Missionary Society's work in creating a school system, albeit racially segregated, to educate blacks. Fanny and her son Oswald were also involved in this effort, concentrating their work in raising funds for the Manassas Industrial School, founded in Virginia in 1894 by the African-American educator Jennie Dean, and joining the brothers in fundraising drives in support of Booker T. Washington's Tuskegee Institute.[70]

Indeed, Booker T. Washington himself became an issue for the Garrison children. Born a slave, Washington committed his life to providing vocational education for blacks after the Civil War so that they could find work as quickly as possible. His efforts to build Tuskegee Institute were greeted favorably both in the North and the South, for while the school provided good workers, it also fostered a respectful attitude toward whites. Although many racial justice proponents considered Washington an apologist, he continued to seek his own way of ameliorating racism in the South by convincing white businessmen that African Americans would prove to be more dedicated and subservient workers than the large influx of immigrants then entering the country. In 1895 Washington accepted an invitation to deliver a speech at the Cotton States and International Exposition in Atlanta, Georgia, an event held to commemorate thirty years of industrial and agricultural progress in the post–Civil War south. His comments were intended to deflate racist attitudes that blocked the hiring of black workers, but they also could easily be interpreted as "Uncle Tomish." "Cast down your buckets among these people who have . . . tilled your fields, cleared your forests, builded your railroads and cities," he said,

> While doing this, you can be sure in the future, as in the past, that you and your families will be surrounded by the most patient, faithful, law-abiding, and unresentful people that the world has seen. As we have proved our loyalty to you in the past, in nursing your children, watching by the sick-bed of your mothers and fathers, and

> often following them with tear-dimmed eyes to their graves, so in the future, in our humble way, we shall stand by you with a devotion that no foreigner can approach, ready to lay down our lives if need be, in defense of yours, interlacing our industrial, commercial, civil, and religious life with yours in a way that shall make the interests of both races one.[71]

As the years passed, however, rather than improving, race relations in the South grew more tense. Jim Crow laws mandated extensive restrictions on the black community; the number of lynchings increased, and the 1896 Supreme Court decision *Plessy v. Ferguson* legalized segregation with its sanctioning of a "separate but equal" doctrine. Abolitionist children were angered by the reversals of the laws and initiatives made after the Civil War, especially efforts to give African Americans the vote. William, for one, felt that voting was "the first and most important essential in a republic. It antedates the school of letters for it is itself the greatest school. Better that the door of every school-house in the South were closed, than that the ballot should be wrested from black hands. With the ballot sacredly guarded, school-houses will, in time, take care of themselves."[72] Without the elective franchise guaranteed and protected, blacks in the South had little control over what happened to themselves or their communities. The 1890s, in particular, was a decade of lynchings, its peak reaching 255 in 1892, 155 of them African Americans. By the end of the decade, 68 percent of all lynching victims were black; in the early 1900s the number increased to 89 percent.

Lynchings were not all secret midnight murders but had turned into public spectacles with people coming from all directions to watch hangings, burnings, and torture. For the second-generation abolitionist Garrisons, these outrages upon humanity provided a new impetus to their campaign, echoing their parents' outrage at the inhumane treatment of slaves. After all, learning about torture and killing had been a part of their upbringing; as children they had read about it and they had listened to the stories of runaway slaves hiding in their home. William channeled his anger into giving speeches sponsored by the Massachusetts Anti-Lynching League, explaining that he would seek all avenues to stop the violence except retaliation, which contradicted his nonresistant philosophy. William's journalist nephew, Oswald, however, felt perfectly comfortable in advocating the death sentence for lynchers, stating in an article in the New York *Evening Post,* "What have we left of civilization? The old saying, 'Scratch a Russian and find a Tartar' should be amended so as to read: 'Scratch an American and find a savage.'"[73]

The children's anger at Northern racism was equally strong since news of intolerance in the North provided the South with an excuse to escalate its own practices. In this vein Wendell—who, despite his conservative leanings, could not abide intolerance—finally used the pages of the *Nation* to give examples of racial discrimination throughout the country's legal system, and Frank convinced Houghton,

Mifflin and Company to allow the *Atlantic Monthly* to print "The Heart of the Race Problem" by Quincy Ewing, a white Episcopalian clergyman from Louisiana. But George, William, Wendell, and Frank had begun to believe that the South had reverted so far back into its pre–Civil War mind-set that there was no hope of achieving equality. As William wrote to the *Boston Globe* in 1901, his father and his friends would be most disheartened to see "a race contempt unabated by emancipation, and lynching cruelties that exceed in savagery the deeds of Simon Legree," the evil slave owner in Harriet Beecher Stowe's *Uncle Tom's Cabin.*[74] Wendell added that even large protest meetings reminiscent of abolitionist days seemed to have no effect on Northern public opinion about crimes based on racial hatred.

The children's greatest disappointment, however, was the behavior of their former hero, Booker T. Washington. As supporters of nonviolence, the Garrisons embraced Washington's approach favoring black reconciliation with Southern whites. Frank, especially, became Washington's good friend, helping to raise money for the educator's much needed vacation during the spring of 1899. In 1900 William, as a favor to Washington, appeared as a featured speaker at the first convention of the National Negro Business League in Washington, D.C. At the same time, W. E. B. Du Bois, the Massachusetts-raised African-American leader, also allied with Washington. In the early 1900s, however, the Garrisons and Du Bois grew disenchanted with Washington because he would not take a strong stand against lynching and disfranchisement. Frank feared that if Washington did not speak out, Southern whites might believe he was "silently assenting to inequity."[75] Washington, however, felt that a race war could result in the South if he began making inflammatory comments. Did Frank want to see all the work accomplished since 1865 evaporate into thin air? Had he not noticed that Washington had successfully stopped Georgia from taking the vote away from its black citizens? Even though he felt uncomfortable with the man's apparent meekness, Frank continued to raise funds for him. At the same time, Washington covertly supported action against states, but he forbade his name to be used in any public way. Oswald also supported Washington's efforts when, in 1901, he and other supporters founded the Southern Education Board; but two years later, he and Frank grew wary of the all-white board's emphasis on vocational training. During the first decade of the twentieth-century, as a result, Garrison support of Washington dwindled, the brothers and their nephew feeling that his accommodationism gave more help to the cause of white supremacy than it did to black equality.

Out of desperation, second- and third-generation abolitionists and black leaders, such as W. E. B. Du Bois, began to look for a new way to achieve racial justice. No longer willing to sit by while newspapers reported race riots, lynchings, and racial discrimination in jobs and schools, and while politicians such as President Theodore Roosevelt expressed nostalgic and conciliatory thoughts about the old South, they began to move toward a more militant strategy. Among the

Garrisons, the impetus for action fell upon their third generation, particularly Oswald, whose Uncle William claimed it was time for "colored people to organize for lawful self-defense and for white lovers of liberty to stand up for equal rights."[76] Oswald used the tools that he had inherited from his family to launch his battle, including pen, a press, money, an ability to deliver effective speeches, and the support and encouragement of his mother and uncles, not to mention the spirit of his grandfather.

Even though he maintained a friendly but cool relationship with Booker T. Washington, often using information the latter supplied to him in his speeches and articles, Oswald and the family as a whole had decided to place their hopes in W. E. B. Du Bois's assertive Niagara Movement, whose 1905 "Declaration of Principles" indicated that the period of accommodationism was at an end. It stated, "The Negro race in America stolen, ravished and degraded, struggling up through difficulties and oppression, needs sympathy and receives criticism; needs help and is given hindrance, needs protection and is given mob-violence, needs justice and is given charity, needs leadership and is given cowardice and apology, needs bread and is given a stone. This nation will never stand justified before God until these things are changed."[77] As Du Bois himself later added, African Americans claimed for themselves "every single right that belongs to a freeborn American, political, civil and social; and until we get these rights we will never cease to protest and to assail the ears of America."[78] These were certainly sentiments which the Garrison children could support, for as William put it, "Why is it that the white South is laying such stress on the industrial, as distinguished from the intellectual education of the Negro? Because an educated Negro intellect is dangerous to a community where race rule is decreed and caste ideas are as firmly rooted as in India. . . . the master race desires an efficient subject labor system, educated hands, unthinking heads. A dream, of course, but when were tyrants other than dreamers?"[79]

In 1906 Oswald and other organizers for civil rights, settlement houses, suffrage, and urban welfare—both whites and blacks—began to think about creating an interracial organization to work assertively for racial equality, tentatively naming it the Committee for the Advancement of the Negro Race.[80] For three years this informal coalition discussed various options, until in 1909, under the leadership of Oswald, Du Bois, Mary White Ovington, Florence Kelley, William English Walling, Lillian Wald, Charles E. Russell, the AME Zion bishop Alexander Walters, and the black Baptist clergyman William Henry Brooks, it organized a National Negro Conference. Oswald was chosen to draft a call for the event, which led the next May to the creation of a permanent organization, the National Association for the Advancement of Colored People (NAACP). Frank and Fanny were both active members of the group, Frank in the Boston branch, Fanny in New York City. The NAACP was, perhaps, the greatest legacy that the Garrison children left behind in terms of racial equality. They were just participants in the organizing force, but their spirit, money, and access to the print media helped to forge the NAACP into the respected organization it remains to this day.

Although racial equality was the most dominant cause handed down from parents to children, woman's rights was also an issue of great importance to them. Whereas Fanny would not become actively involved with woman suffrage until 1906, William was intricately involved with the movement from the early 1880s. Even though raised by a woman-rightist father, it is likely that William's involvement was a direct effect of his being married to Ellie, who continued her lifelong friendship with Susan B. Anthony. Since Ellie always claimed she did not want to be a public speaker or leading personality in the movement, it appears that William took on that role for her. Indeed, Ellie was such a reluctant activist that she did not even want her name listed as an officer of a suffrage organization, claiming that the Garrison name was not really hers, and so she had qualms about "loaning" it out. Desiring to take "no public part" in the movement, she told her mentor that she preferred instead to "keep in my corner, & raise up children, who perhaps will do better service for the world."[81] As an adult, Ellie and William's daughter Eleanor became an ardent suffragist and woman's rights activist, but until that time, her father was her family's sole public voice for women's equality.

By the time William became a spokesperson for woman's rights, however, the movement had suffered a major split over the issue of black manhood suffrage versus woman suffrage, as Congress and various states were not willing to grant both. When the Fifteenth Amendment to the Constitution ensuring black men the vote was proposed to Congress, the woman suffrage movement divided into two. Susan B. Anthony, Elizabeth Cady Stanton, and their supporters, representing the radical wing, denounced the amendment as it, in tandem with the Fourteenth Amendment, excluded women from the elective franchise. The more moderate wing, led by Lucy Stone, Henry Blackwell, Wendell Phillips, and Thomas Wentworth Higginson, supported the Fifteenth Amendment in the hope that a future piece of legislation would enfranchise women. In 1868 this group formed the New England Suffrage Association, which in 1869 became the American Woman Suffrage Association (AWSA), an organization that stood by the Republican Party and supported Reconstruction efforts while working for state constitutional amendments to give women the vote. A short while later, Stanton and Anthony created the National Woman Suffrage Association (NWSA), which denounced the Republican Party and Reconstruction and proposed to dedicate itself to working for a federal constitutional amendment for woman suffrage.[82] In 1890 the two groups unified as the National American Woman Suffrage Association (NAWSA), largely because as the old guard gave way to the new, younger women could not differentiate between the two and often ended up with dual memberships.

Still alive at its founding, Lloyd himself favored the AWSA's belief that suffrage for African-American men was of primary importance, woman suffrage to come next. When the first was constitutionally achieved, he worked wholeheartedly for the second, noting to Lucy Stone in 1869 that women and men "were created equal, in the same divine image; they were designed for each other—to stand side by side in all the relations and liabilities of life—to take counsel together as equally concerned in whatever pertains to the general welfare; and neither can be elevated or depressed at the expense of the other, without injury to both. The only reason given why a man should be allowed to vote is, that he is a man. It is as conclusive that a woman should have the same right because she is a woman."[83] Lloyd's basic complaint against Stanton and Anthony was that they had become involved with George Francis Train, an opportunistic speculator who helped the two women found their suffrage newspaper, *The Revolution.* Lloyd felt that Train was a "semi-lunatic" who was "one of the greatest despisers of the negro race living." Their collaboration and "glorification" of Train had "greatly lessened" his "respect for and confidence in them."[84]

William, who believed in immediate suffrage for everyone without any restrictions, was somehow able to maintain a relationship with both organizations, thereby not having to choose between lifelong friends of his family's and Ellie's. Susan B. Anthony, for example, felt perfectly comfortable in asking Ellie, William, and Frank to research past *Liberator* articles to be used as references for the multi-volumed *History of Woman Suffrage* that she was producing along with Elizabeth Cady Stanton, Matilda Joslyn Gage, and Ida Husted Harper. She also resided with William and Ellie whenever in Boston. As a group, the siblings attended conventions and meetings of both the NWSA and the AWSA, sometimes comparing their character more than their content. In May 1881, after one such meeting, William wrote Fanny that with regard to spirit, "Mrs. Stanton & Susan's beats Lucy's all hollow."[85] The next year, William made his debut as a second-generation abolitionist suffrage speaker at a "Woman Suffrage Banquet" held in Boston. Over five hundred people, including Frank, heard him honor the dedication of the "Women of the Anti-Slavery Movement," the audience "cheer[ing], applaud[ing] and wav[ing] handkerchiefs for 2–3 minutes" even before he had uttered one word. During his initial short speech, Lucy Stone's eyes filled with tears, her handkerchief frequently blotting them away, while Henry Blackwell said he could hear Lloyd's own "tones" coming from William's mouth, and a spiritualist in the crowd swore that he saw Lloyd standing behind William, encouraging him on.[86]

Throughout the 1880s William was a frequent speaker at suffrage meetings and legislative hearings on woman's rights, usually in Boston. In January 1883, for example, he spoke before the Massachusetts legislature and the next year, in the hopes of supporting women's participation, he attempted to get elected to the local school committee, but lost by an overwhelming majority. He made up for it by addressing a large woman suffrage meeting in Providence where, along with such first-generation celebrities as Frederick Douglass, Lucy Stone, and Susan B. Anthony, William faced a crowd so large that it overflowed its assigned room at the Rhode Island State House. Ellie often accompanied her spouse to meetings and also went to larger suffrage conventions with her sister, Eliza, but William did the public speaking.

In February 1890, William, feeling as frustrated as the suffrage leaders that their cause had not yet been won, told the Massachusetts Woman Suffrage Association membership that men who opposed suffrage because they feared competition from women who might enter the professions were shortsighted. In particular, William faulted political party leaders who used the woman suffrage issue to manipulate voters. He claimed that it was time to take the issue to the general public and escalate efforts to reach the average male voter: "The people make the legislature, and when the people are earnest about woman suffrage, the legislature will reflect the sentiment very quickly." William felt it was necessary to stop speaking to the "rulers" and to speak to the ruled instead.[87] Anna Howard Shaw, president of the NAWSA from 1904 to 1915, thought of William as having a "rare quality in men"—the ability to understand women's point of view. She praised him for knowing that woman's rights included not only the vote but also the "right of every citizen, man and woman, to the opportunity to earn an honest livelihood, without being degraded into a mere human machine using all its powers simply to supply fuel to keep the machine at work." People deserved to aspire to greater heights, and according to Shaw, William fought for this right by seeking for people the ability to have "free action and free desire."[88]

The one time William expressed disdain for the suffrage movement itself was in 1895 when the NAWSA, meeting for its first time in the South, spoke in favor of an educated electorate. Following this, the organization tried to win favor with Southern suffragists by avoiding discussion of racial issues and discouraging black women from marching in suffrage parades. In 1903, after remaining with the group in spite of its continued failings on the issues of Jim Crow laws and black women's right to organize and join suffrage efforts, William resigned. Ellie, however, who had taken out a life membership in 1900, remained loyal and attended national conventions. William continued his work through his other suffrage organization, the Massachusetts Men's League for Woman Suffrage. In spite of his misgivings, in 1906 he delivered a eulogy at Susan B. Anthony's funeral and never gave up on the cause of woman's rights.

As it turned out, William became the son most like his father. Until 1888 he worked for racial equality and woman's rights, echoing the ideals and principles upon which he had been raised, including the importance of avoiding the use of violence as a solution for any conflict. In 1888, however, as the Progressive Era produced innumerable reform movements, such as labor, public welfare, politics, education, and the environment in addition to civil rights and women's equality, William was exposed to the thinking of Henry George, the founder and advocate of the "single tax" movement. After much thought, reading, and discussion, he became a committed single-taxer, using the concept as the umbrella for all the other issues he fought for—civil rights, woman's rights, free trade, anti-imperialism, and nonviolence. Born in 1839, Henry George, a printer, journalist, and then managing editor of the *San Francisco Times,* used his belief in individualism and personal freedom to develop a creed.[89] After observing the great disparity between the rich and the poor in the United States, he wrote a pamphlet titled *Our Land and Land Policy, National and State,* which laid out the basic tenets he fostered until his death in 1897. In general, George felt that land should not be allowed to become private property, as by rights it belonged to all. Landlords who charged others rent in order to gain wealth for themselves robbed society of its just rewards and caused people to fall into poverty. To compensate for this, George felt that the government should charge taxes on the full value of property whose owners did not generate wealth from its natural use. The money was to be used for the greater society. This single tax to replace all others would reward those who worked hard and penalize those who lived off the sweat of others. Although George's premise sounded socialistic, it was not, as single-taxers disdained tight central government control and embraced laissez-faire.

The single-tax idea made perfect sense to William, who portrayed George's followers as "the new Abolitionists, because our object is to be attained purely by the abolition of vicious taxes, taking off one by one, until land values alone supply government with revenue. While working for the ideal society where justice shall make charity obsolete, we strike directly at the obstacles which lie nearest our hand." The basic proposition of the single tax, that people had a "right to the use of the earth so long as all wealth is drawn from that source by the application of labor," pointed society in the direction of equality. William saw manufacturers and wealthy people who placed taxes upon propertyless people to benefit themselves as "a feudal relic, and an anachronism." Laws that exempted property owners from paying taxes were unfair. With the single tax, farmers would not be taxed on their homes or improvements to the land. Land values, not the land itself, would be taxed, so that farmers who used their land and improved it would actually benefit. "Two farms, side by side," William explained, "having the same site value, are taxed to-day in proportion to their working, and the thrifty farmer is made to pay heavily because of his industry, and his shiftless neighbor is let off with a small contribution. Thrift is punished and neglect rewarded."[90] William liked the fact that with the single-tax system, labor would keep all its earnings, while wealthy urbanites who owned large homes, stores, and factories which they did not work in themselves would be most heavily taxed.

From 1890 until his death in 1909, almost twenty years later, William's public speeches and writing reflected George's philosophy. He became the most visible of the Garrison sons, his reputation growing so that he became respected for his own, not his father's, accomplishments. While his single-tax ideology reverberated in his work for civil rights and woman suffrage, William's involvement with Henry George led him into other issues, such as free trade, tariff reform, and anti-imperialism, all of which lined up with what William understood to be George's commitment to "concentrate and express the long hidden agony of a disinherited world." William agreed that the single tax was "the only rod that can draw off the lightening from this cloud," transcending "all geographical bounds," suiting "every nation of God's earth," and acting as "the handmaid of peace and brotherly love" with "no use for forts, ironclads, and armies."[91]

Hand-in-hand with this philosophy came William's belief that tariffs were simply governmental interference in free trade. Indeed, his own unfortunate experience as a wool merchant gave him personal knowledge of the damage which tariffs did to a business. Congress's tariff of 1867, for example, had sparked off a downward spiral in the wool market. At first, merchants had believed that new domestic markets would open in Ohio, Michigan, and California, but the wool produced in these states was inferior, often "greasy and burry," and its variety was negligible. Within a short period of time, wool merchants were swamped with an overabundance of a poor product, which brought the values of the wool down. After twenty years of being limited in what he and other merchants could afford to import because of the high tariffs, William lambasted the government for its intrusion into his profits. "It follows of necessity, that our manufacturers must either import the wools not grown in this country, or limit the range and quality of their product. In other words, we must be content with inferior cloth, or subject ourselves to an onerous tax in order to make the higher fabrics." The tariff, in other words, did not protect the pricing of domestic goods but, rather, brought down prices and quality in the United States. For William, a tariff simply controlled whom manufacturers could buy from, depriving them of freedom of trade:

> Under the high tariff the wool-grower has not prospered, the sheep of the country have not increased as expected, nor have factories had a normal growth, and in neither occupation is the condition of affairs satisfactory. Further than this, the tariff fails to keep out the goods of foreign competitors and to secure the home market for Americans. It encourages fraudulent importations and smuggling. For all purposes for which it was enacted, it has been an utter failure. It has not even added a cent to the wages of operatives in woolen mills, but has taken from their pay a part of its natural purchasing power. It "with one hand drops a penny in the cap of poverty, and with the other takes a shilling out."[92]

Free trade was "an inalienable right, whether a majority want it or not."[93] Tariffs curtailed people's freedom, and furthermore, resulted in lower wages than in unprotected products.

As his belief in the single-tax movement grew stronger, William's view of politics expanded. By the late 1890s, when the United States became involved in Western imperialism, William had defined himself as a citizen of the world, all of his causes merging into one. Echoing the abolitionist children's lesson that all blood was the same, William embraced the globe, claiming, "I belong to the human race. I know no distinction of birth or color. I believe that we are only one race. There never were created different species. I believe that environment and climate have differentiated us, and for one to appear lordly over the other is contrary to all ideas of Christianity or democracy."[94] For William, tariffs created racist competition between workers and discrimination of industrialists toward laborers. Indeed, "protection" was "the international law of the Devil." In order to enforce tariffs and "protect" domestic labor and products, "armies, navies, forts, arsenals, revenue cutters, expensive custom houses, spies, perjurers, useless law suits, special privileges, [and] political corruption" were needed. By 1895, he noted that the proposed annexation of Hawaii was simply caused by "the old land disease, mixed with the tariff cause." Greed and racism on the part of U.S. sugar growers, "not the character of the native Queen" Liliukalani, were the true motivating forces.[95]

Already a member of the American Free Trade League (where he later served as secretary and then president and which Lloyd had also briefly belonged to) and the Massachusetts Single Tax League (where he served as president for ten years), William became one of the central figures in the creation of the Anti-Imperialist League, founded on November 19, 1898, in protest of U.S. political interference in the internal affairs of Cuba, Puerto Rico, Guam, and the Philippines as a result of the Spanish-American War of 1898.[96] Although the actual fighting with Spain lasted a little over three months, the ensuing war pitting the U.S. military against the indigenous Filipino forces led by Emilio Aguinaldo lasted until 1902, when Aguinaldo was captured and the islands finally conquered. Basically, the many national and local organizations of the Anti-Imperialist League considered the taking of foreign lands contradictory to the intent of the Declaration of Independence and the U.S. Constitution, which had no provisions for such action. Some League members found U.S. imperialism to be immoral; others, with racist sentiments, protested that the new colonies would invite the influx of people of color into the United States, thereby threatening the white majority, flooding the labor market, and bringing wages down. In addition, social reformers worried that U.S. energy and money would be spent on expansionism rather than on addressing poverty, underpaid workers, and other issues at home.

William's opposition to U.S. imperialism was based on his abhorrence of violence of any kind in conjunction with his single-tax ideas about tariffs, free trade, and democracy. Also wrapped up in his continued nonresistant position was his hatred of racism and sexism. As he explained to a meeting of African-American anti-imperialists, "The same race prejudice that justified your enslavement is rampant in the islands of the East and among the United States soldiers, who from the refuge of Manila, make their bloody raids upon an unoffending people."[97] Indeed, the same U.S. government that had criticized Spain for starving and torturing Cubans was now doing the same thing in the Philippines, causing anywhere from 250,000 to 650,000 Filipino deaths, many of them civilian. The documented evidence of U.S. military atrocities inflamed people's anger, as did the seemingly unnecessary death of 7,000 U.S. soldiers. The use of dumdum bullets (which upon impact leave gaping holes in the body), the development of the .45-caliber bullet for the Colt gun, the Gatling machine gun, and bombs using dynamite all pointed to the escalating inhumanity of war.[98] William believed that in order to attain world peace or at least stem the tide of U.S. imperialism, it would help to have an enfranchised female population, since "Women's votes would tend to peace"; and although some women disproved his theory by supporting imperialist war efforts, others joined local branches of the Anti-Imperialist League or women's organizations, such as the Woman's Christian Temperance Union's Department of Peace and Arbitration, the National Council of Women, and local groups like the Utah Congress of Mothers.[99]

William's anger at the U.S. war with the Philippines led him to romanticize Emilio Aguinaldo in a poem he wrote in March 1899. The Filipino leader became for William a symbol of freedom versus oppression. Indeed, William's vision of democracy and freedom resembled that of his father. Part of the poem "Aguinaldo" encapsulated William's anguish over U.S. culpability for the war:

> Thine, AGUINALDO, is the common fate
> Of all who seek, in Freedom's holy cause,
> Deliverance from foreign yokes and laws,
> Against a foe of overwhelming weight.
>
> . . . .
>
> Take heart and comfort if thy soul be sad.
> Not lost nor wasted thy heroic stand:
> Thou hast unmasked a nation falsely clad
> In altruistic garb, revealed a land
> Blind to distinctions between good and bad,
> And smiting Liberty with ruthless hand.[100]

Even more compelling, however, were the words to William's subsequent poem, "Onward, Christian Soldier," which reflected the sentiment of many of those in the Anti-Imperialist League:

The Anglo-Saxon Christians, with Gatling gun and sword,
In serried ranks are pushing on the gospel of the Lord;
On Afric's soil they press the foe in war's terrific scenes,
And merrily the hunt goes on throughout the Philippines.

What though the Boers are Christians; the Filipinos, too!
It is a Christian act to shoot a fellow-creature through,
The bombs with dynamite surcharged their deadly missiles fling,
And gayly on their fatal work the dum-dum bullets sing.
The dead and mangled bodies, the wounded and the sick,
Are multiplied on every hand, on every field, are thick;
"O gracious Lord," the prayer goes up, "to us give victory swift!"
The chaplains on opposing sides the same petitions lift.

. . . .

The outworn, threadbare precept, to lift the poor and weak,
The fallacy that this great earth is for the saintly meek,
Have both gone out of fashion, the world is for the strong;
That might shall be the Lord of right is now the Christian song.

. . . .

How natural that a change should come in nineteen hundred years,
And Bibles take a place behind the bullets and the beers!
We need a new Messiah to lead the latest way,
And gospel version well revised to show us how to prey.

Then, onward, Christian soldier! through fields of crimson gore,
Behold the trade advantages beyond the open door!
The profits of our ledgers outweigh the heathen loss;
Set thou the glorious stars and stripes above the ancient cross![101]

In the summer of 1899, William revived the pledge his father had written for the 1838 Peace Convention, which had resulted in the formation of the New England Non-Resistance Society. By doing so, he pledged himself anew to the spirit of nonresistance and to the memory of his parents. The somewhat revamped pledge read, in part:

> Our country is the world, our countrymen are all mankind. We love the land of our nativity only as we love all other lands. . . . We register our testimony, not only against all wars, whether offensive or defensive, but all preparations for war; against every naval ship, every arsenal, every fortification; against the militia system and a standing army; against all military chieftains and soldiers; against all monuments, commemorative of victory over a foreign foe, all trophies won in battle, all celebra-

> tions in honor of military or naval exploits; against all appropriations for the defense of a nation by force of arms on the part of any legislative body; against every edict of government requiring of its subjects military service. Hence we deem it unlawful to bear arms, or to hold a military office.[102]

For his children, Lloyd's words were still relevant, as was his sentiment that children should not be taught to use violence. When the Boston school system appropriated money to purchase muskets for young boys to use in practice drills, William lodged a sound complaint. Not only was it morally wrong to teach children how to carry on violent acts, but encouraging a connection with the military fostered the use of alcohol, tobacco, and profanities, and using his tax dollars to do so was a blatant misuse of people's money, proving the "state of barbarism in which this country, which boasts of its civilization and Christianity, is at present groveling" before.[103]

Several years later, in an address before the Progressive Friends of Longwood, Pennsylvania, a group which Lloyd had visited numerous times, William continued his discourse on nonresistance and his opposition to military training. "The only strong position," he noted, "is one of constant and uncompromising opposition to the taking of human life either by capital punishment or war. Instead of admiring the uniformed soldiers, we should lament that reasonable men can adopt such a wicked trade, for all the governments in the world can no more make human slaughter good than they can make black white."[104] However, his anti-imperialist stance also came in conflict with his nonresistance belief, much as his father's antislavery position had during the Civil War. Intellectually, William believed that just as the United States had had the right to fight for its independence from an oppressive England, so did the Filipinos have the same right to fight the United States, which was "crushing out" its attempt to govern itself.[105] While William himself deplored violence, he accepted the necessity of it for the oppressed. One of the problems in the United States, as he viewed it, was that people had become too "patriotic," so much so, in fact, that they were unable to see when the nation was acting immorally. As he expressed it in 1899, the "fetish of patriotism" was "an unreasoning sentiment" producing "only lies, violence, and murder," a reasoning previously voiced by the Russian nonresistant, Leo Tolstoy.[106]

In linking the war with the issue of free trade, William felt that there was quite a "debit" side for the nation. First, going to war meant the loss of production "by distracting men from labor to murder innocent people against whom they had no enmity or grievance." Second, the cost of the war would have to be paid through taxes, thereby lessening the ability of the average wage earner and consumer to buy things. Third, war created political corruption, which led to the fourth debit, the loss of the people's trust in government institutions. "More than all else," he felt, "we have weakened faith in ideals; accustomed ourselves to brutality; retrograded to slaveholding views as regards the treatment of so-called inferior races; discarded the saving and immortal essence of Lincoln's Gettysburg address and Lowell's supreme gospel of democracy." William's role as the abolitionist son was clear; so was his ability to use strong images and language, just as his father had, when, for example, he stated, "Brotherly love, self-respect, honesty, character, decency, all these we are asked to barter for the Philippines with their inevitable train of new wars, hatreds, self-contempt, murder, disease, indecencies and all the baleful brood. Take up the white man's burden and let go the humble and the contrite heart."[107] William's anger stemmed from his interpretation that the emergency tariff to cover war expenses was a mechanism for "enriching manufacturers," the added tax creating more poor people while the republican form of government previously honored in the country turned into "a despotism, the basest and most brutal." Power was in the hands of a relatively few wealthy men, including those who ran the Standard Oil Company and the sugar, tobacco, and steel monopolies, who favored war and strong government in order to add more wealth to their personal coffers. What William feared was that only "an uprising of the people, like that of 1861" would end the government's march to despotism.[108]

Even Wendell, more conservative, was irked by the imperialist posturing of the United States. Soon after the fighting ended with Spain in 1898, he voiced his concern that U.S. imperialism was intertwined with racism. Those Filipinos who would flee war and poverty by coming to the United States would be treated no better than Native Americans while the people of a conquered Cuba would be governed by the same principles of jim crowism as African Americans in the South. It was a better idea for the nation to concentrate on solving its "own scandalous abuses rather than to extend the system under which they have arisen to other peoples."[109] Making the connection between racism and imperialism brought Wendell back to his roots as an abolitionist child, reawakened his radicalism, and pushed him to take up controversial political issues with new fervor. "The great debate of the last century will be renewed in our latter years as it seemed settled in Father's," he told Frank. "If we are silent now about the great reaction, where shall we be 100 years hence?"[110] From 1898 until his retirement from the *Nation* in 1905, he took an assertive approach to the issues of imperialism and racism, whether it be domestic or international, seeing to it that book reviews and articles did not reflect racist sentiments even if it meant personally censoring authors' biased remarks.

Wendell received encouragement and support from his nephew, Oswald, who had joined the *Evening Post*'s editorial board in 1897, becoming editor-in-chief of the *Post* and the *Nation* in 1900 and sharing ownership of the periodical with his mother.[111] Fanny had raised Oswald to stand tall in respect to his heritage, and as a result, he determined to refashion the newspapers after the spirit of the *Liberator*. "All the Garrison blood in me has been moving me to bear testimony," he told his mother. "We are in this fight to stay."[112] Under Oswald's leadership the *Nation* became consistent in its outspokenness, opposing all buildups of arms and claiming, in 1904, that "War is a game which kings would not play if their subjects were wise. It is the duty of those who make and unmake statesmen—namely, the people who have to pay the taxes and furnish their bodies as food for cannon—to insist by voice and pen and note that war, and the huge armaments that lead to war shall be kept out of their thoughts and plans."[113] Wendell himself blamed politicians for causing war and its subsequent problems, lamenting in 1905 the country's "present state of shattered republican ideals, our tyrannous subjection of 'inferior peoples,' our all-prevalent militarism."[114]

Although newly committed to his politics, Wendell continued to value intellectual endeavors above all else. In 1895 Harvard University had awarded him an honorary master's degree for his literary work, proof that his meticulous editing of articles for grammar, usage, and vocabulary, his book reviewing, and his own articles and poems had not gone unnoticed. His love of language led him in 1898 to write a short piece titled "The New Gulliver," a "musing" about speech and linguistics. "Without speech," he wrote, "abstract thought can be carried but a little way, and ratiocination not far. Yet the glory of our development and differentiation from the beasts of the field has been used to terrify us with vain misgivings of a world to come, whereas we have invented ethics and religion along with our vocabulary. It is all of human manufacture, and man may criticize his own product."[115] "The New Gulliver" told the story of Theophilus Brocklebank, a graduate of Yale College, who found himself stranded on the same island as Gulliver had. There, Theophilus met a descendant of the Houyhnhnms, the talking, civilized horses whom Gulliver had befriended. He and his equine host held a lengthy discussion about language, Theophilus insisting that it could be acquired and carried no moral sense with it, the Houyhnhnm insisting that language was a gift from a Great Creator who implanted thought and morality together. In the end, this most gracious and pacifistic host gave his life to save Theophilus from a collapsing building caused by an earthquake. "The New Gulliver" reflected Wendell's thoughts about Darwin's theory of survival of the fittest and the evolution of species, the Houyhnhnms being a higher form of animal themselves.

Wendell's greatest joy may have been intellectual, but his greatest comfort in life was his three children, Lloyd, Philip, and Katherine, his remaining tie with Lucy. Lloyd, especially, had shown himself to be a true Garrison descendant when, in 1885, he asked to be excused from mandatory prayers at Harvard on the basis of, as Wendell put it, "his disbelief in the 'doctrines of Christianity.'"[116] While at the university, the young Garrison also gave several speeches in favor of woman suffrage and against racism, all resulting in 1888 in his suspension for his outspokenness although he was allowed to receive his diploma on time. Three years later, Lloyd earned a law degree, also from Harvard, and began working for the law firm of Gould and Wilkie in New York City, where he became a partner. His reputation secured, in December 1898, several months after the Spanish-American War ended, he and his partner were appointed by the U.S. government to go to Cuba to translate the Spanish Criminal Code and make recommendations for its transformation into a system more reflective of that of the United States. After a short while there, Lloyd became ill with a fever, returned home, and continued to weaken until on October 4, 1900, he died. He left behind his wife, Alice Kirkham, and their two children, Lloyd Kirkham and Clarinda. Wendell continued to drown his personal sorrows in work until on July 6, 1905, he retired from the *Nation* after forty years of service.[117]

Indeed, all four Garrison sons had devoted part of their later years to some political cause. For George, it was the yearly reunions and collecting of articles on the work of the 55th Massachusetts Colored Regiment and his attendance at political meetings. For William, it was the single-tax movement, which served as an umbrella for his work for racial justice, woman suffrage, and peace. For Wendell, it was the *Nation* and his books on the Garrison family's history. For Frank, it was his work for racial equality, his memberships in the Men's League for Woman Suffrage, the Massachusetts Woman Suffrage Association, and the New England Woman Suffrage Association, and his efforts to preserve the historical record of the abolitionist movement. From 1880 through much of the first decade of the twentieth century, the sons made their voices heard in one way or another. For Fanny, the only daughter, the timetable was different, at least in terms of her radical work in the suffrage and peace movements, for, like many women, her calendar was determined by her roles as wife and mother.

ANOTHER FANNY'S STORY

> When in 1900 my father died . . . there began the third epoch of my mother's life. She had naturally been overshadowed by the personality with whom she had shared those [thirty-five] years. She reached out now to build a life of her own. . . . For her it was a summoning to devote her remaining years to the reforms in which she was profoundly interested, notably woman suffrage and peace.
>
> Oswald Garrison Villard, 1939

CHAPTER X

From 1866 until early in the 1900s, a period when her brothers built their careers and defined their positions on political issues, Fanny devoted her life to the needs of her husband, Henry, and their four children, Helen, Harold, Oswald, and Hilgard.[1] Having been raised to emulate Helen, there was no conflict in her mind over the choice of a domestic role over activism, nor did she envision combining the two. Furthermore, her constantly moving back and forth between the United States and Europe prevented Fanny from becoming too involved in any organized activity until the family made New York City its permanent home. Even then, six months of every year from 1880 on were spent at the family's estate, Thorwood, located in Dobbs Ferry, Westchester County, New York, which meant that twice a year trunks of clothing and household items, plus some furniture, had to be packed, shipped, and unpacked. But Fanny never forgot her roots, and in her later years she finally became a political activist.

Fanny's upper-class lifestyle was a direct result of Henry's great business acumen, for in spite of setbacks or failures, he always rebounded. During the 1860s and 1870s, he had carefully built business bases in both the United States and Germany, but most of his success came from representing German banking interests in the United States. Henry and his investors (and Fanny as well) had come to believe that a fortune could be made by fostering the development of the Pacific

Northwest, especially through the development of transportation systems. Northwestern Oregon had particularly fertile river valleys, while the area east of the Cascade Mountains had great potential for raising cattle. The territory also had abundant redwood and other trees to entice lumber companies. All that Oregon needed, it seemed to these businessmen, was more settlers, a good transportation system, and business investments.

For the eleven years between 1873 and 1884, Henry concentrated his efforts on building up the Pacific Northwest. Besides his plan to dominate the railroad and steamship lines, he also led the way in attracting immigrants to the area, particularly those from Northern Europe. To this end, he saw to the publication of brochures in German, English, Norwegian, and Swedish. It was Henry's steamers that carried these folk from San Francisco to Portland, and his railroad lines that helped to bring them from the East. Fanny enjoyed this empire building as much as Henry did; indeed, in private, they liked to jokingly refer to themselves as the "Duke and Duchess of Oregon."[2] They imagined their domain in Boston as the entry point for people heading west. Henry's efforts were tremendously successful. As a result of his work, the population of Oregon boomed. Between 1870 and 1880, it almost doubled, reaching 317,000.

When in 1879 the owners of the Oregon Steamship Company decided to sell, Henry organized a syndicate to purchase it, shortly after taking over the Oregon Steam Navigation Company as well. After merging the two businesses into the Oregon Railway & Navigation Company, he created the Oregon Improvement Company, becoming the head of both ventures. Seeing that western investment could be very lucrative, in 1881 he convinced a group of friends to entrust twenty million dollars to him through a "blind trust" (or "blind pool") which he then used to gain control of the Northern Pacific Railroad, creating the Oregon & Transcontinental Company. He was so successful that at this point he virtually controlled the transportation network in the Northwest. He added to his growing influence by also purchasing the *Evening Post* and the *Nation.*

Owing to Henry's hard work in obtaining European investors, the laying of the transcontinental tracks of the Northern Pacific Railroad reached completion in 1883. The work, involving 40,000 men, included building bridges and tunnels, leveling hills and filling valleys, constructing trestles, and blasting through mountains. To commemorate the project's conclusion, U.S. government officials, including those from the seven new states that the railroad crossed, joined leading journalists, business leaders, and foreign guests from Great Britain and Germany in a luxurious Villard-sponsored railroad journey. Four special trains came from the East, including a private car for the family, and one special train from the West. Fanny and her children, including three-month-old Hilgard, accompanied Henry and watched proudly as throngs of people in Chicago, St. Paul, Minneapolis, and Bismarck honored his work. On September 3, when east and west met in Gold Creek, a small settlement in western Montana, for a grand ceremony celebrating the driving in of the final spike, Henry held baby Hilgard up to the cheering crowd, kissed him, and placed his tiny hands upon it. From then on, Hilgard was known to his family as "the little spike-driver."[3] Unfortunately for the Villards, the venture had surpassed its budget by fourteen million dollars, an amount which proved impossible to raise because of another economic downturn. As a result, several stockholders sold their holdings; Henry himself used most of his and Fanny's own money in an attempt to purchase enough shares to save his and his backers' investment. In December, exhausted and close to a nervous breakdown, he accepted an offer made by a committee of friends and supporters that he take their financial help to avoid personal bankruptcy and to save the Oregon and Transcontinental Company. In exchange, he was forced to use everything he owned as collateral and tender his resignation as president of both the Oregon and Transcontinental and the Oregon Railway and Navigation Companies. At the request of his English backers, he retained only the Oregon and California Railroad Company.[4]

Henry's financial situation was complicated by his and Fanny's expensive taste. During the final years of the railroad's completion, the two had spent huge sums of money on their homes in Dobbs Ferry and New York City.[5] In 1880, soon after purchasing their country house on its 225 acres, they commissioned Charles McKim's architectural firm, McKim, Mead, & White, later noted for such designs as the 1883 World's Columbus Exposition in Chicago, the Boston Public Library, and much of Columbia University's present campus, to make renovations.[6] It was the trio's first commission for redesigning a large country house. Interior changes to Thorwood added up to well over $28,000 over the course of two years, after which Fanny and Henry made several additions onto the house and purchased and redecorated a second mansion on their property for guests. At about the same time, Henry also invested $260,000 in a two-hundred-foot-long square parcel of land on Manhattan's Madison Avenue between East 50th and 51st Streets directly behind the newly completed St. Patrick's Cathedral. The land was not in a fashionable district then (it is now part of the New York Palace Hotel); it fell between the horsecar route on Madison Avenue and the smoky steam locomotives of the New York & Harlem Railroad that raced by on nearby Fourth Avenue, now known as Park Avenue. Within a few months of the purchase, Henry announced his plan to have McKim's firm erect several connected houses with private entrances opening onto a garden. Actual construction of the building started on May 4, 1882, Henry and Fanny's house at 451 Madison Avenue being the first. The initial costs for planning and construction totaled $213,679.28, an amount which quickly escalated: an additional $99,000 for woodworking, over $50,000 for furniture, and thousands more for fixtures and decorative arts.

Fanny, Henry, and the children moved into their Madison Avenue home on

December 17, 1883, in order to save on hotel bills. The work had just about been completed, but not all the furnishings were in place. Very quickly, any joy they felt was overshadowed by Henry's fragile mental state and the family's great financial loss, causing Fanny to lament that they all had "heavy hearts, for Harry's affairs look gloomy & the house, beautiful as it is, is only trying to us."[7] To run it was so expensive, in fact, that it took the pleasure out of living there. The electric bill for the month of February 1884 reached $5,000. When newspaper reporters hounded Henry about his bankruptcy, he responded that he was truly destitute, but did not mention that some of the family's assets, including their homes, the *Evening Post,* and the *Nation,* were in Fanny's name. So intense were the media's attacks on him, however, that by early spring Henry and the family moved to Dobbs Ferry, never returning to the Madison Avenue houses which still bear their name and are registered as historical landmarks.

Leaving Fanny and the children in Dobbs Ferry, a depressed Henry and lonely Wendell left for Germany, where Henry was surprised to find himself greeted as a celebrity. For years he had donated money to the charities and schools in Speyer and Zweibrücken, and his good-heartedness far outweighed his U.S. business humiliation. In the fall, Fanny and the children joined him while Wendell returned home. For the next two years, the Villards basked in the glow of German optimism and faith in Henry's financial skills. It was easy for them to subsist on the $10,000 yearly salary voted for Henry by the Northern Pacific Railroad and other income from existing investments, including the newspapers. The house in Manhattan was put into the hands of trustees, who saw to it that it was sold, the final buyers, Elisabeth and Whitelaw Reid, paying the full indenture of $350,000 and taking possession in 1886. The Villards returned to New York in October of that year, once again to Thorwood at Dobbs Ferry and their lavish previously rented apartment on East 72nd Street in Manhattan. By this time Henry had put together a full array of business ventures, handling the Deutsche Bank's U.S. investments, rejoining the board of the Oregon & Transcontinental Company and then assuming its presidency, recommitting as chair of the finance committee of the Northern Pacific Railroad, and heading General Electric. He continued to work until his retirement in 1893.

While it is clear that Fanny was aware of most of Henry's business dealings and a partner in some of them, she was never included in the actual financial affairs. Rather, her chief responsibilities included seeing to the household and the couple's four children and living Henry's dream of wealth and prominence. The three eldest children—Helen, eighteen years old in 1886; Harold, seventeen; and Oswald, fourteen—had been raised in a bicultural, bilingual world, living part of their lives in the United States and part in Germany. Oswald's name, in fact, was chosen to represent his German roots. The first time Helen and Lloyd met Oswald, he could speak no English at all, which greatly disturbed his grandfather.

Hilgard, born eleven years after Oswald, was only two-and-a-half when his parents returned to the United States for good, so was not raised in a binational setting. The three older Villard children attended schools on both sides of the Atlantic and were well versed in both German and U.S. literature, music, and politics. Fanny, who continued her own studies in piano, saw to it that her children learned to play musical instruments: Oswald and Helen, the violin, and Harold, the cello. Often over the years, the siblings and their mother formed duets, trios, or quartets to entertain guests or play at charitable events.

As a woman with money, Fanny existed in a whirlwind of activity. Living in the middle of Manhattan, first near Union Square and 17th Street, then at 334 Fifth Avenue, and later on Madison Avenue and 72nd Street, she had easy access to museums, concerts, theatrical events, meetings, lectures, dinner parties, and balls. Almost every day of the year, she entertained anywhere from one to over thirty guests at her home, many calling on her for tea and conversation. She entertained members of the city's elite—the Barnards, Rockefellers, Carnegies, Tiffanies, Astors, and Vanderbilts. She also welcomed into her home German guests passing through New York or friends and business associates of Henry's. At least three or four evenings a week, she, Henry, and their children attended concerts, lectures, and plays. When Helen reached the courting age, Fanny and Henry took her to cultural events, balls, and dinner parties so that she could meet young men of her own class. In 1887, when she was nineteen, they gave her a "coming-out party" attended by two hundred guests. Helen, however, often suffered from headaches, back and neck pains, and anxiety, which may have derived from a childhood fall down an elevator shaft at the Westmoreland House, the first apartment building in the city to have an elevator. On several occasions, her mother called in physicians and surgeons or accompanied Helen to spas in Europe; in 1888, Helen spent time on her own in Eisenach, a German clinic where she learned a "cure" for her anxiety.[8]

For the Villard children, growing up in New York City was exciting. At first, the family resided in the Westminster Hotel, a residence located near Union Square. Then, in 1877, they moved to the nearby, newly built, and more luxurious Westmoreland House, where they had first one apartment and then two. It was here that Lloyd spent his final days. Living near such famous stores as Tiffany's, Brentano's, and Huyler's (which introduced ice cream sodas into the world), the children absorbed the energetic city life.[9] But 17th Street, though a hubbub during the day, was quiet at night. Often the only noise came from a tiny one-horse streetcar making its way down the block at irregular intervals. Although the children enjoyed riding on the public buses whose floors were covered with straw and whose roof had a small hole through which to watch the driver, Henry preferred that they have their own coachman and horses to escort them on trips around the city. He also insisted that Harold and Oswald attend a private school run by Harvard-trained James Herbert Morse and that Helen go to a private school for girls. Eventually finding the rooms in the Westmoreland too small, the Villards moved uptown, first to their house at 451 Madison Avenue and then, after their extended stay in Europe, to the Tiffany House on the corner of East 72nd Street and Madison Avenue, a large, sunny apartment a block away from Central Park.

Unlike the rest of the Garrisons, Fanny (and Henry) thrived on material possessions that reflected and enhanced their status. Almost daily, Fanny went shopping, buying new clothes for herself, items for the family's homes, clothes and gifts for the children, and at least twice a year, a wardrobe for Wendell's daughter, Katherine. She also enjoyed receiving gifts, especially from Henry, who showered her with expensive items, especially during the two weeks surrounding her birthday and Christmas. In 1881, for example, Fanny received a pearl pendant set in diamonds from her husband. The next year, it was "a large flower piece, consisting of a bed of violets from which sprang 38 roses." In addition, he presented her with a "silk umbrella with a silver handle, pearl opera glasses, and a gold thimble."[10] In 1888 he brought her "a wonderful necklace of most exquisite pearls, of large size, beautiful color and fifty-four in number."[11] Still modest in her attitudes, Fanny never took Henry's generosity for granted. On several occasions, she expressed her gratitude, musing to Wendell in 1889, "But how did it happen, that I came to be married to a man of such singularly unselfish and high aims . . . as Harry? It is surely more than I deserve."[12]

Once Henry and Fanny obtained Thorwood, the children spent long summers in Dobbs Ferry. The estate, which had a breathtaking view of the Hudson River, was Fanny's favorite home, one she never tired of. Although in the country, however, neither she nor Henry lost access to urban society and culture, for they invited innumerable guests into the estate's six living rooms, its paneled library complete with comfortable leather chairs, and its white and gold music room designed by Charles McKim himself. Fanny ordered a white and gold grand piano to match the decor and spent many happy hours practicing and taking lessons, even when she reached her sixties and seventies. The dining room, with a table that sat well over twenty people, had full-length stained-glass windows, one bearing the words "Peace be unto this house," that afforded views of the lawn and river. Needless to say, as soon as electricity was available in 1888, the house was entirely wired, adding to its comfort.

Outdoor activity was a joy at Thorwood, with carriage (and later automobile) rides to nearby Tarrytown and Sleepy Hollow, excursions to the river for boating or viewing the sunsets, horseback riding and playing with the many pedigree dogs which Henry kept in the stable. Fanny despised having animals inside the house, although she made two exceptions.[13] The first was a mastiff that attached itself to Henry, running away from its owner so many times that the man eventually gave him to the dog's chosen master. The other was a small dog named Tommy Dot who was a gift for little Hilgard. At every opportunity the family took endless walks, played lawn games, and hosted picnics, outdoor concerts, and meetings; and each spring the young girls attending Miss Master's school climbed the steep hill to Thorwood for a special picnic and entertainment designed just for them.[14] People seemed drawn to Thorwood by some magical means; in actuality, they came because of Fanny's well-known hospitality, her energy, and her uncanny ability to sense what activities guests would enjoy. Her children and grandchildren thrived on her love for life. Harold's daughter, Mariquita, recalled her "short, plump" grandmother's "puckish . . . mischievous sense of humor."[15] Yet she also experienced Fanny's Victorian sense of decorum; even when the children were enjoying their annual Easter-egg hunt, they were expected to dress and act properly. In that vein, Mariquita's brother, Henry, remembered his "Gros Mama" as a dominant personality, "a matriarch in essence," a woman who ran her affairs in a circumscribed manner most likely attained in her adulthood, her childhood home having been somewhat haphazard. Henry recalled the many Christmas eve parties he spent with his grandmother, where everybody had an assigned chair in the living room with a "carefully tailored gift" on it.[16] The large, exquisitely decorated tree, which was visited by groups of children from neighboring schools and charity institutions, dominated the room. Oswald's son, Oswald Jr., remembered Fanny as a warmhearted woman who "had more charm and less tact than anyone else in the world."[17] It seemed impossible for her not to speak her mind even if it meant criticizing any and all who did not agree with her.

Even though Fanny raised her children to consider themselves part of the elite, she also adhered to the moral and political values she herself was brought up with—sometimes more in theory than in practice. For example, like her parents, Fanny did not allow alcohol to grace her table or servants to smoke. Family members recalled with laughter how surprised guests were to find that the wine carafe held nothing but water while Henry kept a bottle of wine or beer under the table. Apparently, her turning a blind eye or playing dumb merely egged people on. When one of the cooks at Thorwood served sherry-covered ice cream, Fanny thought it very tasty, until she found out the magic ingredient. The cook was soundly reprimanded, but no serious repercussions ensued. Although Fanny was a teetotaler, she appeared to make exceptions to her practice, a fact that annoyed her brother Frank, who complained about her serving a "claret punch" at Helen's coming-out party. "I must confess that it gave me unspeakable pain," he noted. "Time was when I should have deemed it incredible that your father's and mother's daughter, who has taught the boys that total abstinence is the wisest and best habit for them to adopt through life, would deliberately provide alcoholic drink of any sort for her guests." Frank felt that Fanny was accepting a certain amount of "indulgence" as acceptable. "I wonder," he added, "that with your training, and with the daily opportunities which we all have of seeing and knowing the deadly work which intemperance is doing in the land, you dare take the responsibility of offering wine to any guest, and of setting an example inconsistent with what have been your teachings to your own children."[18] Fanny did not respond but instead continued acting with a certain purposeful naiveté to break with tradition. When, for example, she found a servant's tobacco pouch on the floor of her car, she announced its contents to be "flea powder."[19]

Fanny was not always inconsistent, however, especially when it came to the issue of nonviolence. It was important to her that the children be taught never to solve any conflict, whether with their siblings or friends, with violence. Her belief in nonresistance and the search for world peace extended to such practices as not allowing her children to play with war toys. When, early in her marriage, she sent a photo of Harold to Lloyd in which the child was holding a toy gun, her father expressed his disappointment. Fanny, embarrassed, blamed the image on the photographer, an explanation that Lloyd accepted but not without a warning: "But if *you* should at any time buy him sword or gun, and make him a soldier's paper cap, by way of amusement, I should be sorry for the bias it might give to his mind."[20] Fanny never did, although the Villards, like the rest of the Garrison family, gathered to watch military drills and parades. Fanny took advantage of raising the children in two countries and exposing them to guests from all over the world to foster attitudes of tolerance. Even though, like her parents, she did not take her children to any specific church, they were taught Christian ethics, identified themselves as Christians, and referred to Christianity and Jesus in their letters, articles, and speeches. Henry, a self-proclaimed agnostic, accepted the Garrison position.

Like her brothers, Fanny also taught her children to believe in and work for racial equality. Stories about Lloyd and the abolitionists were a common part of their everyday lives, as were visits from elderly abolitionists, including members of the Hallowell family, the Motts, and even Harriet Tubman. On March 13, 1879, Fanny used seven-year-old Oswald's birthday party to instruct him about racism. When the entertainer whom she had hired announced his plan to impersonate an African American trying to scrub off his color, Fanny demanded he change his program or leave. Seven years later, the fruits of her labor began to blossom when one of her sons, while visiting his cousin Philip, inspired Wendell to comment, "Your tall boy—only a hair's-breadth shorter than Phil—is sitting behind me reading the Life of Harriet Tubman. Proof that he has safely arrived."[21] While brothers and sister usually made nothing but positive remarks about each other's parenting skills, occasionally one or the other could not help but express their disapproval of some small diversion from the accepted family path. Frank, of course, reprimanded Fanny for her failure in not following the temperance line. Fanny, unwilling to hurt George's feelings, privately noted in her diary that his son, Rhodes, although a "splendid" child, was undisciplined.[22] Wendell did not approve of Fanny's willingness to allow her daughter to dress in the latest styles, especially that of wearing low-cut dresses to balls. In 1891 he expressed relief that his own daughter, Katherine, would not be wearing such attire to a charity ball which Fanny was taking her to. "My feeling of aversion to it arises from general considerations as to balls and ball costumes," he wrote. He wished to ensure that his daughter grew up to be like her mother, "simple, unconscious, unaffected, best on serious & spiritual" matters. He also expressed disapproval of William's allowing his son Frank to join a fraternity at college, feeling they were "the worst society in college & . . . calculated for the profligate sons of the rich."[23]

Fanny's life, although more comfortable and worldly than her brothers', was not all joy and endless activity. Henry's business problems added stress, as did his constant bouts of severe headaches and the continuing problem of hearing noises in his head, conditions diagnosed by physicians both in Germany and the United States as anything from blocked ear passages to nervous tension, but never cured. Still, he persevered, his illness never diminishing his inexhaustible energy for carrying on business. In March 1890, however, Fanny and Henry faced one of their most difficult challenges when their youngest and most fragile son, Hilgard, at age seven, became ill with pneumonia. Fanny watched over him intensely, taking him to Thorwood in the hopes that the country air would help him gain strength. Three months after he took ill, the child was suddenly stricken with peritonitis, dying on June 11. Both Fanny and Henry were overwhelmed with grief, Fanny "too dazed to know what it means."[24] Hilgard was buried in Sleepy Hollow Cemetery, where Fanny visited his grave at least once a year.

Six years later, Fanny and Henry faced another crisis when Helen traveled to Germany to visit family and be treated for her physical and emotional problems. Soon after his daughter left, Henry suffered two attacks during which he had difficulty breathing and experienced severe pain in his arm. His physician, Leonard Weber, the same man who had treated Lloyd during his final days, prescribed medication and gave him an injection to ease his anxiety. It is likely that Henry had suffered a mild heart attack from which he soon recovered. Meanwhile Helen checked herself into a hospital in Dresden where she stayed for ten days. Once out on her own again, she became romantically involved with James W. Bell, a British schoolteacher who lived in Germany.

Although their family's letters concerning Bell and Helen only hint at their situation, it seems likely that the two decided to live together, a behavior most scandalous at the time and certainly to the Garrison and Villard families. Indeed, Fanny experienced such great "misery" about Helen that it hampered her celebration of Harold's engagement to Mariquita Serrano.[25] In her attempt to help her daughter regain her sense of morality and proper decorum, Fanny wrote several letters which were returned unopened. To her great dismay, Helen then went further astray, arranging to access her parents' German savings without their permission, causing Henry to rush to Europe to stop his errant daughter from creating any further havoc. His trip was wasted, as he made "no progress toward peace" with Helen and found Jim Bell a "bothersome" stumbling block.[26] Oswald, who accompanied his father to Germany, also tried to intervene in the family crisis, but the two men just kept uncovering more of Helen's deceptions with the banks. Fanny, anxiously awaiting any word from Europe, found her letters from Oswald "heart-sickening," but her anger gave way to maternal concern over Helen's psychological state. "My poor, poor daughter!" she wrote in her diary. "She needs all the pity that a Mother can give a child. I fear that her health is in a very delicate condition."[27] At the end of October, when Henry and Oswald returned home with no success, the family became estranged from Helen, cutting off most of her funds and turning a deaf ear to any requests she made for financial assistance. The next June, when Harold visited her and Jim in Dresden, he found his sister amenable to conversation but, to him, for some "incomprehensible" reason, extremely angry with her parents.[28] On July 10, 1897, Helen and Jim married, their now socially acceptable status easing the tensions between daughter and parents, so that the next summer, when Fanny traveled to Germany, she found a friendly, although reserved, Helen.

Helen kept in touch with the family until the end of 1900. Then disaster struck. Throughout the year Henry had suffered from various bouts of pain and indigestion, indications of a worsening heart condition and, as his autopsy later showed, cancer of the rectum. By October he appeared to a very worried Fanny as "broken in spirit as well as body."[29] Because he could no longer take care of himself, Fanny hired a male nurse to tend to his needs and to carry him downstairs at Thorwood, where he was then forced to use a wheelchair. As the weeks passed, he grew more unable to perform the simplest tasks and lost all desire for food. In his final weeks he subsisted basically on milk, castor oil, and a bit of whiskey from time to time until he lapsed into a coma. During the evening of November 8, as he neared "the end," and Fanny tried to keep up her spirits by entertaining a visiting Ellie with fancy dinners and chatty conversation, a bolt of lightning struck Thorwood's greenhouse. The ensuing fire consumed "the beautiful blooming roses, chrysanthemums, [and] carnations" while a helpless Ellie and Fanny watched on. Ellie noted to William that even the chaos of firefighters and the frightening threat of a possible explosion of the Villard's "electricity plant" and boiler did not rouse Henry from his coma.[30] On November 10 and 11, with only the sound of high winds roaring about her, a sorrowful Fanny sat by Henry's side as he faded away, dying just after midnight on November 12. Three days later he was buried in Sleepy Hollow Cemetery next to Hilgard.

Although family and friends gathered around her, for months, even years, after his death, Fanny could find no comfort. When William came to share her first New Year's Eve as a widow, the two went to bed early, neither feeling any joy in seeing "the old century out & the new one in."[31] Three days later, on her and Henry's thirty-fifth wedding anniversary, Fanny noted, "It seems so strange, so impossible. . . . I feel the uselessness of trying to become accustomed to his loss."[32] To honor Henry and to keep his memory alive, Fanny helped edit the memoirs he had been working on during his final years. The two volumes were published in 1904 by Houghton, Mifflin and Company as *Memoirs of Henry Villard, Journalist and Financier, 1835–1900*. As Fanny stated in her preface, Henry's language was purposely left to reflect his German origin. "The man speaks for himself," she wrote, stressing his strong character, love for his two nations, and his generous heart, "but his philanthropy is only faintly portrayed by his own hand; of its full extent he alone was aware."[33] Both Henry and Hilgard were later remembered in Germany. Fanny and Henry had seen that an orphanage in Zweibrücken was funded in Hilgard's memory. For Henry, the people of Speyer placed a tablet on his birthplace in commemoration of his many charitable gifts to the town's hospitals and schools.

At first, Henry's death seemed to bring Helen back into the family fold, for immediately after learning the news, she wrote an agonized letter to Oswald, expressing her guilty conscience over the break with her parents but also reminding him of her "bitter conviction" that her parents had "never made an effort at reconciliation." In any case, Helen longed to help her mother. Assuming that Fanny would not wish to travel to Europe "since she would miss her conveniences," Helen suggested that a friend or relative move in with her so that she would not suffer in her "isolation."[34] Little did she know of her mother's great resiliency, for although in deep and continuous mourning, Fanny kept up her many social, organizational, and family activities. That spring, she decided to travel to Europe, first in the company of William, Ellie, and Oswald and then to Germany with Oswald alone. There on May 22, she reunited with Helen, who was "much overcome" on seeing her.[35] The stress on Fanny, however, created its own health hazard, for a few days later, she fainted. Her physician pronounced that she had weak heart muscles and would need to avoid great activity and stress for the remainder of her life, a piece of advice that Fanny neglected to heed until her final two years when poor health forced her to. Meanwhile, mother and daughter continued seeing each other throughout Fanny's visit until her departure in late August. The next summer, Helen and Jim spent three months with the Villard family in Dobbs Ferry, leaving Fanny to believe that her daughter was back in her life for good.

Fanny's hope of having a close-knit family was short-lived, however. During her spring 1903 visit to Germany, Helen, then thirty-five, belatedly complained about the terms of her father's will, claiming that Fanny and Henry had neglected her because she had refused to live her life according to their precepts. Upset and hurt, Fanny avoided contact for two weeks, when Jim showed up and convinced her that Helen was justified in her anger and coerced Fanny into signing a statement acknowledging the unfairness of Henry's will. When the next day she begged Jim to destroy the document, he refused. Acting upon the advice of Emil Hilgard, a relative of hers, Fanny fled Germany, feeling exhausted and "sick at heart."[36] Once at home, she received a "real shock" when Helen filed a lawsuit claiming that Harold, Oswald, and Fanny "brought undue influence to bear upon" Henry when he wrote his will.[37] When the *New York Sun* carried the story, Fanny felt particularly saddened and humiliated, especially since many of the bequests and the inheritance taxes had already been paid and, if the Westchester County Supreme Court ruled in Helen's favor, she would have had to ask the money be returned.[38]

Henry's last will and testament, although not equal in its allocations, had not left Helen penniless.[39] Considering the family's great wealth, however, Helen's anger is understandable. In addition, the document, of course, did not mention those assets already in Fanny's name, including Thorwood, the two newspapers, and certain investments, making her very rich in her own right. To Fanny, Henry left all his jewelry, clothing, and other personal effects, all horses, carriages, harnesses, books, and the sum of $250,000, an amount equal to nearly $4,780,000 in 1998. To Oswald went $50,000; Harold received no definite sum as his father had given him the equivalent amount of Oswald's inheritance when Harold got married. However, if Oswald died, his inheritance would revert to Harold and Helen. Helen received $25,000 outright plus $25,000 held in trust by the Farmers Loan and Trust Company of New York, the trustees to invest the money, giving Helen regular payments from the interest. Helen had the right to control the funds "free of debts, control or interference of any husband she may have" and to bequeath it to anyone she chose. If she died intestate, the money was to revert back to her siblings. Henry, apparently choosing to limit Helen's access to half her inheritance because of her previous poor management and swindling of her family's money, also stipulated she receive a yearly sum of $6,000 to be paid quarterly.

Although Helen interpreted her father's final action as manipulative and unfair, he may have been operating on a traditional male bias in both German and U.S. culture that women were not capable of managing their own fortunes. Indeed, although he placed wealth in Fanny's name, he did so to protect his own interests, for Fanny herself made no individual decisions on its use. Henry, in not trusting Jim or Helen, sought to protect his daughter's future by limiting her immediate access to her money and spreading her payments over her lifetime. After hearing of Henry's other bequests, Helen must surely have felt that she was entitled to a larger sum, especially since her father left considerable amounts to charities in Zweibrücken and Speyer as well as to various institutions in the United States.[40] Harvard University and Columbia University each received $50,000; another $25,000 went to the New York Society for Prevention of Cruelty to Children; $10,000 to the New York Infirmary for Women and Children, and smaller amounts of $5,000 to the New York Medical College and Hospital for Women, the Dobbs

Ferry Hospital Association, the American Museum of Natural History, and the Metropolitan Museum of Art. William, Wendell, and Frank, but not George, each received $5,000, and Henry's private secretary of many years, Charles A. Spofford, $20,000. Helen's contesting of the will and her lawsuit concerning ownership of the *Evening Post,* which was in Fanny's and Oswald's hands, dragged on for over two years, in the end the courts ruling in Fanny's favor. During the turmoil, however, Fanny grew so despondent that at times she wished she "had never been born."[41]

Adding to her embarrassment over the public airing of the family's personal concerns was Fanny's worry about her brother George's health. The first indication of a quick decline came in December 1903, when Frank, in one of his weekly letters to his sister, noted that George had "much color in his face," but it was "not the flush of health."[42] For the past several months, he had grown weak and was generally housebound. Fanny, always conscious that George had little extra money, made sure that he had regular visits from a physician and any medicine he needed, but toward the end of the next month, paralysis of his throat, which prevented eating or speaking, marked a near end. As he sat by the fire, looking bent and feeble, with "no light or smile in his countenance," George indicated to Annie that he was "failing." Frank could hardly bear to watch, sharing his despair with Fanny: "I am very sad at heart at such a spectacle of decay of a man only sixty-eight years old. I cannot wish him to linger thus, for a more joyless existence it would be hard to conceive."[43] George died on January 26, 1904, the first of the Garrison children to pass on. As he requested, Frank and William made arrangements for his cremation, the two complaining that the cost of even the cheapest coffin was an outrage, considering it was to be immediately incinerated. However, they paid the $40 and had their brother's body transported to Mt. Auburn Cemetery, where a Unitarian minister led a brief service before a small group including all four siblings. George, the least political, the least financially successful, but a most warm-hearted and beloved brother, was gone. The immediate family circle had begun to shrink.

From 1876 until 1905, Fanny's life had generally evolved around activities in New York City and Dobbs Ferry. Although during these years, her main role was as wife of a business entrepreneur and a mother, she also joined in many charitable causes. Indeed, for her and many women like her who followed a traditional Victorian way of life, the Progressive Era offered innumerable opportunities to help others in a socially acceptable, moderate environment. Many middle- and upper-class women, especially in towns and cities, were attracted to reform efforts, including health care, prison reform, city beautification projects, self-improvement clubs, education, labor issues, and settlement houses. Women of Fanny's type chose those activities which did not challenge their roles as wives and mothers, although they were willing, even eager, to place their causes before public opinion and push them into the political arena. Sometimes work in causes that initially appeared related only to women's domestic sphere led to commitment to the more controversial issues of woman's rights or peace. With Fanny's familial history, it is not surprising that her activism followed this path.

Throughout the Progressive Era, Fanny attended the meetings of many organizations or sat on their boards. These organizations benefited from her insights and financial support. A sampling includes the Women's Exchange, the Union League, the Association for the Higher Education of Women, the Woman's Infirmary for Women and Children, the University Settlement House, the Tarrytown and Dobbs Ferry Hospital boards, the Hampton [College] Association, the Women's String Orchestra, the Household Economic Association, the Woman's Committee of the Municipal League, and the Women's Political League. She was also attracted to various kindergarten efforts for African-American and Jewish children living in the poor sections of New York City, including the Columbus Hill Day Nursery for African-American infants and the East Side Jewish Kindergarten, both for mothers who were part of the paid labor force.

Other organizations that Fanny served throughout her later years include the Barnard Club and the Wednesday Afternoon Club, whose meetings Fanny attended weekly for over thirty years. The Wednesday Afternoon Club was a self-improvement organization where women gathered to discuss readings and share ideas. At the meetings, members with little experience giving public addresses learned how to coherently present their ideas in written and oral forms. Members of the Barnard Club, created specifically to gain support for Barnard College, which opened in 1889 as the female annex for Columbia University, also learned how to develop public relations activities and raise money. In the same vein, she devoted several years to the board of trustees of the Constantinople Women's College and added her voice to those who succeeded in creating Radcliffe College in Cambridge, Massachusetts, the female annex for Harvard.

Fanny was intensely dedicated to advancing educational opportunities for women, perhaps because she felt she had been deprived of that right herself. Angrily, she wrote to Wendell in 1877 that a letter she had written at the age of nineteen showed poor "style & penmanship" and that her schooling had been "superficial." More damningly, her education illustrated "how completely parental discipline and interest in my mental progress was lacking." Had it not been for Wendell, Fanny believed, "the few sparks of ambition that smouldered" in her breast would have died, as they did after he left home for New York.[44] In the talks she presented before her sister club members, Fanny reflected on her own sense of loss, although she chose to generalize it. "If we look back only a generation," she liked to point out, "we find woman still deprived of the one essential element of all intellectual development—adequate opportunities for obtaining a thorough education." Schools were dedicated to proving that young women had "weak minds" and that they would never be capable of leaving their designated "sphere," the home. Mathematics were never taught with great seriousness, but "the Bible was made to oppress her with the weight of its authority." In this new progressive era, however, women were proving that they had "quick intelligence and large sympathy" which would help to move the cause of education forward. Indeed, women had achieved great recognition for their work in charitable and reform organizations, so much so that they had become entitled to the training needed to "enable her to play her part in the field of human labor as well as man." Education would, then, lead to equality between men and women. In a nod to her nineteenth-century upbringing, however, Fanny added that women's "superior education" would make them "better wives and mothers. . . . Knowledge is indeed power for women as well as men." With educated women still the creators of a happy home life, "the real foundation of perfect government" would be achieved.[45]

As she grew older, Fanny finally came to see that the two realms of womanhood—the private and the public—were intertwined. Hence, as she spoke more about how her foremothers recognized that both the woman's rights and abolitionist causes dealt with the freedom of humanity, her speeches and writings began to reflect her upbringing. To guarantee the highest level of performance, women had to be educated not only as well as men but also alongside them. Therefore, Fanny spoke of the need for coeducation, stressing that separate women's colleges were desirable only if they had the same high standards as men's schools, which the nineteenth-century academies did not. In 1893, addressing the Women's Unitarian League, Fanny outlined the reasons why she believed coeducation was of primary importance to the advancement of women. By being educated together, she claimed, the "moral and intellectual standard" of both young men and young women would be raised. Each sex would learn to respect the other and to work cooperatively in a competitive environment. It made no sense to Fanny for men and women to socialize publicly in theaters, at balls, on the street, and even at home but not be educated together. Women's colleges could be acceptable if they were not consistently underfunded and if they employed male professors with years of study and experience until a cadre of women professors were so trained. "Ought we not all to be painfully conscious of the fact that 'woman's cause is man's,'" she noted, "'they rise or sink together, dwarfed or godlike, bond or free?'"[46]

Besides her concern about women's education, Fanny was extremely interested in health care, hence her presence on the many boards of hospitals, infirmaries, kindergartens, and nurseries. There were two organizations, however, in which she was particularly involved—the Riverside Rest Association and the Diet Kitchen Association. The Rest was a halfway house where recently released prisoners from city houses of detention and other homeless people could find temporary housing. Fanny's work there, which began in 1887, included finding furniture for the home, raising money through concerts and charity dinners, and, for a time during her ten active years as a member, working as a hostess to those who resided in the house. Her greatest dedication, however, was to the Diet Kitchen Association, an organization she first mentioned in her 1878 diary and continued to work with practically up to the day she died, having served as its president for twenty-five years.[47] Incorporated under the laws of New York in 1873, the Diet Kitchen Association, as Fanny described it in a speech and article, was at first intended to give some relief to the "destitute sick" by providing them with "suitable nourishment, properly prepared." Middle- and upper-class women established "kitchens" near medical dispensaries so that physicians and nurses could screen patients and refer those needing aid to them. Neither soup kitchens nor cooking schools, the Diet Kitchens were "depots from which pure milk, more than anything else" was distributed at no charge to the "sick poor." A member of the patient's family or "some kind neighbor," after showing physician-signed requisition forms, picked up the milk and took it to the proper recipient. The physicians noted how much milk each patient was entitled to, renewing the request at the end of each week. At first, the Diet Kitchens provided a variety of products, including barley, gruel, rice, beef tea, arrowroot, and milk. By 1892, when the organization's name was changed to the New York Diet Kitchen Association, only "pure milk,—the very best,—up to the standard of the Board of Health" was distributed.[48]

The first Diet Kitchen opened on April 24, 1873, before Fanny made New York City her home. Located next to the Demilt Dispensary, it covered a large area which extended from 14th Street to 42nd Street and from the East River to Fifth Avenue in Manhattan. Operating on a budget of about $2,000 per year, the kitchen fulfilled every request for two years. Then, to serve more clients, a second facility was opened on the west side of Manhattan, at the corner of Ninth Avenue and 36th Street. A former abolitionist and Garrison family friend, Abby Hopper Gibbons, became the association's president, a position she held for twenty-one years. In 1876 another kitchen opened. By 1884 the number of people serviced by the three Diet Kitchens added up to 7,228, with over 50,000 filled requisitions, one center reporting a daily high of 112 applicants. With each passing day, physicians gained more respect for the association and aided in raising money for new kitchens linked with health care dispensaries. By 1902 the number of people served had increased to 34,215 and the budget had grown to $11,433, all but about $3,000 being used for the purchase of milk. In 1903 the women of the New York Diet Kitchen Association developed an endowment fund of $38,883, which allowed the number of kitchens to increase, almost all of them provided rent free owing to the generosity of those women who sponsored them. At least eight kitchens were named after benefactors, including the Gibbons Kitchen at 140 East 97th Street and eventually the Villard Kitchen on 100th Street.[49] By 1911 the organization dispensed a total of 1,000,900 quarts of milk through these establishments.

Fanny truly loved her work with the Diet Kitchen, whose presidency she assumed after Gibbons's death. Many times she held meetings, luncheons, and musical entertainment for members at her home in New York City, and at least once a week, often more, she visited various kitchens to see that they were being run efficiently and properly. Helen, Harold, and Oswald gave periodic concerts for the clients, and each year they joined other children in partying at the annual Diet Kitchen Fair, a fund-raiser reminiscent of the antislavery fairs Fanny attended as a child. No matter what ups and downs she faced in her personal life, Fanny met her responsibilities to the Diet Kitchen. Her summers in Dobbs Ferry may have curtailed her activity somewhat, but she still oversaw the organization's work, often hosting members at Thorwood for luncheons, drives in the countryside, and overnight stays. Only her visits to Europe and extended stays in Germany prevented her efforts, but, immediately upon returning home, she picked up where she left off, not only with the Diet Kitchen Association but also with her social clubs as well.

During Henry's lifetime, Fanny did not involve herself in political activism, although she never forsook her roots, supporting all efforts toward African-American civil rights and women's equality and remaining aware and committed to the ideas of nonresistance and peace. However, she went no further than expressing them in writing or in talks before small, carefully chosen, groups of women. For example, whereas in her 1893 talk before the Women's Unitarian League, Fanny voiced the need for women to support peace, she herself did not organize around the issue. She simply claimed that women suffered greatly from war, perhaps even more than men did, and, therefore, if women protested against war, "it could no longer be the curse of the world."[50] When the Spanish-American War broke out in 1898, she expressed her disdain for the "Jingo spirit" she recognized among the members of the Wednesday Afternoon Club and lamented over the "disgraceful session" held by the members of the House of Representatives who voted for U.S. intervention in Cuba, noting, "Rainy, gloomy day, like our thoughts, for Congress has done its wicked work & we are to have war, unless a miracle saves us."[51] When Wendell's son Lloyd tried to enlist to fight in the war, Fanny thought him to be taking the "cowardly" path.[52] With all her talk, however, she took no individual action.

After Henry's death, Fanny's life was initially swept up in her problems with Helen and her support of Oswald's work opposing educational discrimination facing the black population of the South. But her personal path soon started moving in a more assertive direction, first with the issue of peace and then, as a component of that spirit, active participation in the woman suffrage campaign. The impetus for her becoming active in the peace movement may have been a letter written to the siblings in 1904 by the great Russian author and nonresistant, Leo Tolstoy, in which he attested that his beliefs were based on those of Fanny's father.

Later in life, Fanny recollected that her "joy" at reading the letter was "at that time mingled with bewilderment" at Tolstoy's wonder that Lloyd's beliefs "could have been so hushed up" as to appear new to most people fifty years after his death.[53] The next year, while never giving up her charity work, Fanny began attending peace meetings and hosting woman suffrage gatherings in her homes. The suffrage meetings proved far more interesting than the meetings of the New York Peace Society, where women attendees were in the minority and usually given no voice. Hence, Fanny sought out the suffragists, especially those like Elizabeth Cady Stanton's daughter, Harriot Stanton Blatch, who were connected in some way to her childhood.[54]

When Fanny entered the suffrage struggle in 1906, only four western states had granted women a vote equal to men's.[55] In the new century, with efforts in several more states gaining in strength, Fanny became excited to join. With Harriot Stanton Blatch, who represented the spirit of suffrage militancy she had adopted from the British, Fanny made her first public appearance as a campaigner when in March 1906 a group traveled to Albany, New York, to speak before a joint committee on woman suffrage.[56] At the same time, she became entranced with a more traditional organizer, Carrie Chapman Catt, who led the NAWSA and the New York State Woman Suffrage Association, and with Anna Howard Shaw, the previous head of the NAWSA and a great admirer of William. Like her brothers, Fanny was able to work with opposing factions of the movement, fostering relations with Catt, Shaw, and Blatch with no apparent conflicts. Two months after testifying with Blatch, Fanny traveled to London to attend a woman suffrage meeting. There she grew deeply excited by the "enthusiasm & more forceful & earnest" approach of the English suffragists she had heard positive stories about from Blatch.[57] When she later learned that these women used violent means of demonstrating, such as throwing rocks, breaking up parliamentary meetings, and forcing their way in to see male legislators, she changed her mind.

Fanny's excitement over her new activity was dampened by the news upon her return to the United States of Wendell's broken health. When she saw him in September 1906, she commented that he looked "so yellow & so like a skeleton" that her heart ached.[58] Two months later, she recognized that her brother was "doomed," so that when surgery took place in December, revealing an inoperable cancer, she held out little hope.[59] On February 27, 1907, at age sixty-seven, Wendell died "as peacefully & gently as if a babe were sleeping."[60] He was buried beside Lucy and their son Lloyd, the family receiving over twelve hundred letters of condolence from people who knew him through his work on the *Nation.* Oswald later honored his uncle in his book, *The Disappearing Daily: Chapters in American Newspaper Evolution.*[61] About a week after Wendell died, Fanny received the last letter he had written to her. Dated December 21, 1906, her brother thanked her for all the consideration she and Henry had displayed toward him and his children, including paying for Lloyd's and Philip's education, seeing that Katherine was well dressed and educated, and emotionally and financially supporting his own work at the *Nation*. With so much in life still undone, Wendell did not feel ready to die, but, still, he went "without apprehension or hesitation." "I embrace you for the last time as the family good angel," he concluded, "with the assurance that the thought of me will be a joy rather than a grief—affection calling to affection as deep into deep."[62]

While Wendell lay dying, Fanny divided her time between visiting him and becoming more involved with peace and suffrage issues. In October 1906 she took a break from her family worries to attend a suffrage meeting in Syracuse, where she delivered an address on the same platform as Anna Howard Shaw. Ellie also attended this meeting, and together the sisters-in-law visited their Auburn relatives. Upon her return home, Fanny presented the same speech before sixteen members of the William Lloyd Garrison Equal Rights Club, a small interracial organization she founded and fostered throughout her involvement in the suffrage campaign. Meanwhile, the New York Peace Society meetings continued to frustrate her, causing her to remark that the male leaders "certainly do not know what peace is."[63] Nevertheless, she agreed to play an active role in organizing a Peace Congress held in Carnegie Hall from April 14 to 17, 1907, taking the opportunity to create a special women's session with May Wright Sewall chairing and a children's meeting as well. From Fanny's point of view, the addresses given by Andrew Carnegie, William Jennings Bryan, and Edward Everett Hale were as unsatisfactory as were those by male leaders at the Peace Conference at The Hague that June. "The object of it in the main," she noted, "is how to preserve the noble art of war."[64]

Fanny was particularly upset when a delegation of women she was a part of was refused admission to the Peace Congress at The Hague. Instead they were forced to meet privately with a few male leaders and then hold their own meetings, one addressed by the 1905 Nobel Peace Prize laureate, Bertha von Suttner. Fanny, who addressed the women's meeting, linked the causes of peace and woman suffrage, a perspective she continued to expand upon for the next thirteen years. In an undated speech titled "Peace and Woman Suffrage," Fanny asked why the peace movement always seemed to move so slowly. Her own answer was simple—the movement's "primary advocates," largely men, were "for the most part, lukewarm . . . [with] timidity . . . [and] a cowardly and temporizing spirit." As she saw it, the greatest setback to the peace movement was that it did not embrace nonresistance, "the overcoming of evil with good . . . a willingness to lose one's life in a good cause, while refusing to take the life of another." After having seen the lack of assertive action after The Hague Peace Conference of 1907, Fanny claimed to have felt "sick at heart, discouraged and depressed." In that state, she found "consolation" in the woman suffrage movement, where the enfranchisement of women signaled the possibility "to create a dominating public opinion against war" because women, as the "Mothers of the race," felt an innate repulsion toward violence. Fanny's hope was that the suffrage movement would also operate as a peace movement, with massive numbers of women speaking out against the government's squandering of money for weapons development rather than using it "for the civilizing influences of education and the arts of peace." For Fanny, the key to success was the "power of the ballot," an idea that her brothers, but not her father, embraced.[65]

With this as her guiding ideal, Fanny continued to assert herself in both the peace and suffrage movements, using whatever platform she mounted to address both issues. In 1908 she advocated the vote to a group at a Harlem church, where her topic was "Some Dangerous Social Tendencies," that is, alcohol abuse and gambling. She also campaigned for her two favorite reforms at the Ethical Culture School, the Portia Law Club, the Beaver City History Club (a high-school organization), the Colony Club, and the League of Women for Political Education. When not given in her own home, these speeches took her around New York City and local communities in Westchester County, including Yonkers, Tarrytown, Dobbs Ferry, Mt. Vernon, New Rochelle, and further north to Poughkeepsie. In February, Fanny joined other New York suffragists in addressing a committee in the Senate chamber and then before a larger evening meeting in Assembly Hall. Her stately presence as a beautiful older woman of sixty-three, with her white curly hair, elegant clothing, and Victorian poise, along with her reputation as the daughter of William Lloyd Garrison and the widow of Henry Villard, made her admired not only by suffrage supporters but by state legislators as well, who gave her their undivided attention. Fanny had become a symbol of a bygone age, a small elite group whose numbers decreased daily. Whenever the leaders of the movement found an opportunity, they asked her to say a few words, to sit on the platform, to walk at the head of a demonstration, to be part of a delegation to a government leader. For her part, Fanny still felt young and vibrant, reflecting on her sixty-fourth birthday that her age was "a fact I can't fathom."[66]

In May 1908, when Fanny traveled to the famous Quaker-founded Mohonk Mountain House in New Paltz, New York, to participate in yet another peace meeting, the men in attendance were shocked when she spoke against their "namby-pamby" ideas and reluctance to pass a resolution in favor of world disarmament, a rather obvious stance to Fanny for a peace organization to assume.[67] She promptly followed up this meeting by traveling several hours further northwest to Seneca Falls, New York, where she read a paper about Lucretia Mott before a celebration organized by Harriot Stanton Blatch to bring attention to the 1848 Woman's Rights meeting. After a summer in Europe, she returned once again to work for suffrage and peace, attending a large women's conference in Buffalo in October, where Anna Howard Shaw persuaded her to give a short impromptu speech.

Fanny continued this work with several gatherings at her home in New York City, becoming acquainted for the first time with Caroline Lexow, a Barnard College alumna who spoke for the Collegiate Equal Suffrage League and who would become an important part of Fanny's post–World War I work.

During the summer of 1908, however, Fanny again faced the prospect of losing another brother, as William's health began to fail. In hopes of building his strength, she suggested that he follow an eating regimen prescribed by the Diet Kitchen, one where he would consume small amounts of food several times during the day and always "on the stroke of the clock," not at other times.[68] Meals of eggs, white meat, cheese, fish, vegetables, and salad with French dressing were to alternate with servings of fruit. William's problems, however, could not be easily solved through diet, for like Wendell, he was suffering from cancer. During the next year, while William's health deteriorated, Fanny continued her political work around the New York area, except for a short trip to a meeting of the International Council of Women in Ottawa, followed by a brief visit to Seattle with a group of women including Anna Howard Shaw and Carrie Chapman Catt.

On September 12, 1909, Fanny rushed to Lexington to see William one last time before he died. He passed away at the age of seventy-one a few hours after she and Oswald arrived and was cremated on September 14. Three days later, at the age of sixty-two, Charles McKim was put to rest. All of the McKims, three of Fanny's brothers, and Henry were now gone. Even though she and Frank had children and grandchildren, and Frank still had Theresa, the two siblings felt oddly alone. It was not surprising then that Fanny found herself longing for her daughter, but she could not bring herself to reopen the wounds which Helen's lawsuits had created. Even though Oswald, Harold, and their families were a constant source of comfort and Ellie wrote frequently and occasionally visited with one of her daughters, Fanny anxiously awaited Frank's weekly letters and periodic visits, the only direct remaining link to her Garrison past.[69] Meanwhile, she relied upon her suffrage and peace activism, the Diet Kitchen, and her other innumerable club and social activities to keep herself going.

From 1910 through the first half of 1914, when several more states granted women equal suffrage, Fanny participated in suffrage and peace actions almost weekly.[70] On February 23, 1910, she gave a speech at a hearing before the Massachusetts legislature in Boston in support of woman suffrage. In her home state, she easily drew upon her famed background to remind government officials of her long claim to equal rights, stating, "My father, Wm. Lloyd Garrison, and my brother of the same name have successively pleaded this cause before Committees of the Massachusetts legislature. I feel it all the more a privilege and a duty, now that their voices are stilled, to renew the appeal." Fanny insisted that the fact that Massachusetts women still did not have equal rights should bring "a blush of shame to the cheeks of liberty-loving Bostonians." Since women made up the largest group of philanthropists, Fanny remarked, their charity work acted like a tax, for women were always called upon "to save the victims of bad laws, or the non-enforcement of good laws."[71] In her usual manner, she easily slid to the issue of war, claiming that antisuffragists argued that women should not have the right to vote because they were ineligible for military service. For this very reason, Fanny noted, they would make excellent voters, for as noncombatants, women more easily understood and believed in peace.

Fanny also got caught up in the fervor created by New York State suffragists pushing the state legislature for a referendum on suffrage. Sometimes working with Harriot Stanton Blatch's Women's Political Union and sometimes with Anna Howard Shaw and Carrie Chapman Catt's rather small New York State Woman Suffrage Association, Fanny, at the age of sixty-six, took to the streets, organizing large demonstrations. On May 6, for instance, 3,000 marchers, the majority of them women attired in white dresses with purple sashes to signify their suffrage stance, walked down Fifth Avenue from 54th Street to 17th Street in Manhattan. The next year, Oswald and eighty-three other men marched with the women. Although harassed and harangued all along the route, he felt "elated" by the experience.[72] In 1912 the "Great Parade of Women," which wended its way from 11th Street to 57th Street, numbered 15,000.[73] Although she walked the entire length of each and every march even when, after the age of seventy, the fatigue that followed resulted in three days of bed rest, Fanny liked following up each demonstration with a speech from her car.

For three years, until 1913 when the state referendum was achieved, Fanny worked tirelessly. She attended endless "useless" and "unendurable" suffrage committee meetings, yearning for action rather than strategizing.[74] Never having been trained to lead a political campaign, she had little understanding or tolerance for planning sessions. Rather, Fanny preferred to perform the legwork and the fundraising, even though these jobs demanded more physical energy than she had. She rightly saw that she could be most effective as a symbol of a continuum with the past and as a celebrity of sorts whose stature, age, and personality increased the movement's attractiveness with the older and wealthier set. Fanny, who still had her youthful spirit, enjoyed being a participant in the drama of this final and rapidly unfolding chapter of suffrage history.

In January 1913, Fanny attended the celebratory suffrage ball designed to mark the beginning of the campaign to get the New York State referendum passed. Sponsored by the Women's Political Union, it drew over eight thousand guests and raised five thousand dollars from the fifty-cent entrance fee. This was followed by a spurt of suffrage dinners, teas, lunches, and a birthday celebration on February 15 in honor of the memory of Susan B. Anthony. Fanny's closest allies in the state suffrage association were Carrie Chapman Catt, Harriet Burton Laidlaw, and Harriet May Mills, but because of disagreements among the leaders, Fanny preferred to exercise her authority over her own small local group in Westchester and the William Lloyd Garrison Equal Suffrage Club. Besides local events, in March on the day before Woodrow Wilson's inauguration, Fanny participated in the now infamous suffrage parade in Washington, D.C., where the women were "scandalously treated . . . by a crowd of low men making ribald jests all the way along," the police making no effort to protect them from either verbal or physical abuse.[75] Troops had to be called in to quell the mobs who resented the intrusion of women activists into what had traditionally been a celebration of male electoral politics. Here, as in other parades, she was accompanied by William and Ellie's daughter Eleanor, who had moved to New York City in 1912 in order to work with Catt. Two days after the parade, Oswald, in Washington in his role as a journalist, took his mother to the White House to meet the new president.

Like her father and three of her brothers, Fanny opposed using violence to confront violence. Being a nonresister herself, she sought ways to foster a nonviolent approach to organizing. Upon returning home from the D.C. demonstration, she utilized the auspices of the William Lloyd Garrison Equal Rights Club, over which she held virtual authority, to voice her opposition to the move toward using violent tactics in the U.S. suffrage movement, similar to those being used in Great Britain. On May 6 the group adopted a resolution which stated that its membership was "wholly opposed to the lawless methods employed by the long-suffering, misguided militant suffragettes & unhesitatingly declare that 'doing evil that good may come' is fraught with worse consequences for mankind than any existing wrong, however intolerable it may seem."[76]

Although her work for suffrage and peace dominated her days, Fanny had many social and family concerns to fill her life. One of the most painful tasks she had to perform was convincing her son Harold that he was incompetent as a business man. Harold had tried to follow in his father's footsteps, playing the stock market and investing in high-risk enterprises. In early 1911, Fanny spoke to him about his losing great sums of money which Henry and she had given him plus a considerable sum of her own. Six months later, Harold finally agreed to give up his risky investments and take some time to reevaluate his options. Soon after, he and his wife, Mariquita, and their three children left for Europe. Fanny assumed financial support for the family during their entire stay abroad. In return, Mariquita signed over ownership of their 57th Street house, which Fanny sold in 1920, putting the proceeds into a trust fund for Mariquita, the income to be hers for life and the principle to revert to her children after Mariquita's death. In total, Fanny guaranteed Harold and Mariquita a fixed annual income of $17,380, a comfortable sum which Fanny hoped would cover their needs, free them from continuous debt, and, as she put it, "add to your happiness."[77] Meanwhile, Harold's leaving for Europe meant that only Oswald and his wife, Julia, along with their children, Dorothea and Henry Hilgard, would be Fanny's immediate family contact. Julia, although often considerate of Fanny, thought of her mother-in-law as overbearing when it came to Oswald.[78] A Southerner who avoided contact with African Americans, she also did not always see eye to eye with Fanny. However, each remained cordial to the other so as not to alienate Oswald. Fortunately for Fanny, Oswald ignored any tensions between his wife and mother and maintained an extremely close relationship with Fanny. In fact, soon after Harold's business failure, he urged her to rent an apartment at 525 Park Avenue to be nearer to him. She, in turn, doted upon him, noting in her diary that Oswald was her most successful and responsible child, "A dearer son never lived."[79]

As Fanny became more aware of society's use of women as objects of derision, criticism, exploitation, and abuse, she grew more sensitive to her participation in events that upheld these norms. In February 1913, for example, her attendance at one of her many costume parties, which she had so often thrived upon, brought the point home. At this particular Cleopatra-themed fete hosted by an acquaintance, Louis C. Tiffany, Fanny noted that the Egyptian theme was "all too vividly portrayed to suit my taste," and she regretted exposing her now aging, but newly feminist, flesh to the public in her revealing costume.[80] It would be easy to claim that Fanny's reaction was created by her Victorian modesty rather than by her consciousness-raising about women's roles, but Fanny had eagerly chosen her costume, as she had so often in the past, with an eye toward having a good time at the party. It was only when she observed the interaction between the men and women at the scene that she realized that her political work had added a new layer of depth of understanding to her personal life.

In 1914 world tensions came to dominate Fanny's every waking moment. Intermittent war in the Balkans, which began the year before between Bulgaria and Turkey, had expanded to include Greece, Russia, Albania, and Serbia, and dangerous tensions on the Alsace-Lorraine border threatened peace between Germany and France. Europe's age-old border disputes, nationalistic struggles among various ethnic groups, competition in trade and imperialism, and increasing weapons development added fuel to these fires. Although the suffrage movement still commanded a great deal of her time and energy, working for peace became more urgent. As the year progressed, the two issues finally came together organizationally in Fanny's life, largely because as a result of the anti-imperialist impetus which began during the Spanish-American War, many women who supported suffrage now made the connection between the violence of militarism and war and violence against women. Only the complete end of institutionalized violence, they believed, could lead to a just world and guarantee women physical safety as well as economic, political, and social equality. Of course, for women who had no right to vote, it appeared that the answer to all their inequities was enfranchisement. Fanny had voiced this opinion many times, one of the most succinct expressions of it being in 1911, when she told a Tarrytown meeting, "Men can protest at the ballot-box against the fearful waste of the war-power, but only in a few states can women do so."[81]

By April 1914 the worsening situation in Europe drew Fanny into a more intense involvement with peace organizations, as she joined other women in creating a "Protest Meeting against War" at Cooper Union which attracted over two thousand concerned citizens.[82] From that meeting came a committee that called itself "The Woman's Anti-War Committee," whose job it was to make presentations before existing organizations in order to create more antiwar meetings and demonstrations, such as the one on May 2 which took Fanny and her "well-decorated Peerless" car to Washington Square and then to Morningside Park.[83] Of course, Fanny's concern was seated not simply in her pacifist feelings but also, and in this case even more so, in her connection with Germany, her second homeland. Her Hilgard relatives still resided there, as did her daughter, so Fanny grew frightened when Archduke Francis Ferdinand and his wife were assassinated in Sarajevo on June 28. Within a month, there was war between Austria-Hungary and Serbia, followed by Germany's declaration of war on Russia and France, then Britain's declaration on Germany, Austria on Russia, Serbia and Montenegro on Germany, France and Britain on Austria, Austria on Belgium, and Russia, France, and Britain on Turkey. Chaos reigned in Europe and then its colonies in what became known as "the Great War," "the war to end all wars," and, eventually, "World War I."

On July 28, Fanny was filled with "consternation"; two days later, she was consumed by "horror."[84] On August 1, she could only say, "The world seems to be going under in blood, hatred & revenge."[85] She, however, was not one to sit around moaning, so on August 12 she joined other women in forming the Peace Parade Committee, a group which reflected a clear coalition of suffrage, social work, labor, and peace activists. It included Harriot Stanton Blatch, Carrie Chapman Catt, Lillian Wald, Lavinia Dock, Leonora O'Reilly, Rose Schneiderman, and Charlotte Perkins Gilman. When Carrie Chapman Catt, May Shaw, and Lillian Wald all refused the nomination as chair, Fanny was elected to the position, her response reiterating her commitment to nonresistance: "I . . . suggest this is a time for a new peace movement; . . . the preservation of human life under all circumstances."[86]

The committee's initial call for action claimed that women had a unique concern about war and peace: "We know that deep in the hearts of all women lies an instinctive abhorrence of war . . . that though this woman instinct may be overwhelmed for the hour by the drum beat and the bugle call, it can be expected to reassert itself above every other consideration."[87] The parade itself was meant, as Lillian Wald, the founder of the Henry Street Settlement House, put it, to "strip war of its glamour and see only the realities of brute force." Women alone, she felt, could make this point clearly by reaffirming "their unalterable faith in peace, in the practicability of arbitration, and in their belief that the centuries have been set back by what has occurred."[88] To expand its outreach, the parade committee attempted to recruit working women as well as middle-class and wealthy activists. Letters were sent to department store managers requesting that a flier be posted in the women's lunch rooms or toilets—B. Altman's and Macy's approving, Abraham & Strauss, not.

Although President Woodrow Wilson's August 20th endorsement helped publicize the event, newspapers criticized the woman-only nature of the parade. To this, the women responded with a strongly worded, but humorous, press release:

> It is the consensus of opinion among the women . . . that it should be carried through as a feminine achievement. The idea was originated by women, and it appears if the men wish to make a protest they will have to organize a parade of their own.
>
> One pretty dodger distributor [of handbills] . . . said she never knew before how many men like to start an argument on the slightest provocation . . . she devised a clever means of disarming the argumentative ones. . . .
>
> "Why do you want a parade? What good will it do?"
>
> "That is quite simple. . . . You see, we think so much of you men that we can't afford to let you go to war and be shot to pieces."
>
> The young lady says that this has proven the best way she knows to stop all arguments.[89]

The parade from 58th Street to Union Square took place on August 29, the committee requesting that each of the fifteen hundred participants don black or light dresses with a black band on their left arms. Although ill with fever and tonsillitis the few days before the procession, Fanny showed up to lead it. Together with her niece, Eleanor, she passed at least twenty thousand spectators, who watched, "touchingly sympathetic, the men often uncovering as we passed."[90] Sick and tired of the slow-acting, conservative, male-run American and New York Peace Societies, she hoped the parade would result in the creation of an all-women's peace organization. To this effect, she addressed the remnants of the Peace Parade Committee at its final meeting on September 21, impressing upon the group that other organizations were "weak and ineffectual" because they were concerned only with compromise. "They assert in one breath that war is wrong and wicked," she complained, "and then with perfect equanimity and amazing in consistency they say that a recourse to war is sometimes justifiable, notably in self-defense."[91]

Fanny, of course, desired an organization that would be strongly rooted in nonresistance, but she also wanted to place her faith in one that was all female. Remembering all too well the abolitionist sons who had died in the Civil War, she cried out, "Too long have women been controlled by the teachings of men who demand of them that they permit their fathers, husbands and sons, at the word of command, to perish on the field of battle." Women were expected to stand by and patch up the men before sending them back to get injured or cause injury to others once again. "We denounce it as an infamous means of blotting out the spirituality of all motherhood," she concluded, "to which men have acknowledged their indebtedness."[92] Fanny's dream of a women's peace organization was not reached at this moment, for the Peace Parade Committee disbanded with no permanent group formed out of it.

At the same time that Fanny's hopes in the Peace Parade Committee were being deflated, another group of women in New York, some of whom Fanny knew, were thinking in a similar vein.[93] They were the younger, more militant suffragists who lived in Greenwich Village and moved in bohemian circles. Madeline Zabrisky Doty and Crystal Eastman, two graduates of New York University's law school and friends of John Reed and Eugene O'Neill, had become involved with Alice Paul's breakaway suffrage group, the Congressional Union, which believed that U.S. women should take a more violent and aggressive approach to suffrage campaigning, much as their British counterparts were doing. Although Fanny certainly did not sanction their approach, she joined in their successful efforts in creating the Woman's Peace Party of New York, a result of visits from British suffragist Emmeline Pethick-Lawrence and Austrian-Hungarian suffragist Rosika Schwimmer, each seeking help in convincing Woodrow Wilson to instigate peace talks among European leaders. Soon after the Woman's Peace Party of New York was formed on October 31, Fanny started attending its meetings, spending time with both Pethick-Lawrence and Schwimmer and viewing *Lay Down Your Arms!*, the film version of Bertha von Suttner's best-selling antiwar novel, *Die Waffen Nieder!* Therefore, when Jane Addams, one of the most honored women in the country for her settlement house work at Hull House in Chicago, and Carrie Chapman Catt sent out a call for a meeting to organize a national women's peace organization, Fanny was eager to comply.

On January 8, 1915, Fanny traveled to Washington, D.C., for the two-day meeting that resulted in the formation of the national Woman's Peace Party, headquartered in Chicago where Jane Addams could easily serve as chair. Three thousand women, including seventy-seven delegates representing such diverse organizations as the Daughters of the American Revolution, the Congressional Union, the Woman's Christian Temperance Union, the American Peace Society, the General Federation of Women's Clubs, the Women's Trade Union League, and the Women's National Committee of the Socialist Party, eagerly discussed how war impacted on women and what they, as activists, could do about it. Although Fanny lamented that the new organization did not embrace the nonresistance principle, she was pleased that the preamble of its program spoke of the unique role "the mother half of humanity" played in the world. Women, it claimed, had "a peculiar moral passion of revolt against both the cruelty and waste of war." As their nineteenth-century foremothers, these twentieth-century women were disgusted with the "reckless destruction" wrought by unenlightened men in power in governments the world over. If women were put in charge of "the future of childhood and with the care of the helpless and the unfortunate," they would no longer "endure without protest that added burden of maimed and invalid men and poverty stricken widows and orphans" which war created. Most important of all, women wanted "a share in deciding between war and peace," a share that could only be achieved through equality in all aspects of their lives.[94] The Woman's Peace Party was, in effect, an antiwar suffragist organization, the perfect combination of ideals for Fanny to dedicate herself to. It was indeed, as she herself expressed it, "all that I wished."[95]

Fanny kept up her suffrage work, attending hearings in Albany and Washington, D.C., and participating in innumerable suffrage parades, lectures, dinners, and balls. But the escalating war spirit in the country led her to pay closest attention to the work of the Woman's Peace Party, where she joined Jane Addams, Grace Hoffman White, and Alice Post on the national board's executive council. On the local level, Fanny volunteered to work on the New York branch's publicity committee, giving countless speeches around New York City—at the Women's Republican Club, a Sorosis luncheon, a club for girls, the Brooklyn Woman Suffrage Club, Thorwood, and in her New York City apartment. When forty-seven women, including Jane Addams, left the country that April to meet with other suffragists for peace at The Hague, Fanny attended two farewell dinners held in their honor. As 1915 passed, however, she found it more difficult to deliver her soapbox speeches. For example, on May 7, 1915, after the *Lusitania* was hit by a German U-boat and sunk, Fanny tried to convince a crowd on the busy corner of Broadway and 110th Street that war should be avoided at any cost. Their response was less than generous, and after browbeating her they rushed to the nearby Hudson River where a display of fireworks celebrated the presence of a fleet of battleships. Whereas in the past, Fanny would have eagerly joined the revelers, she now looked upon them with disdain. Disappointed, she returned home. Her only relief came from the news that Helen and Jim Bell had left Germany for England.

Throughout much of 1916 the Democratic Party president, Woodrow Wilson, while supporting a military preparedness campaign in case of German aggression, sustained his position that the United States remain neutral in the war that was raging around the world. Since he continued to oppose woman suffrage, when he came up for reelection in the fall, suffragist pacifists faced a dilemma. Should they back the Republican candidate, Charles Evans Hughes, who supported suffrage but would not promise to keep the nation out of the war, or Wilson, who took the exact opposite position? They decided to stick with Wilson, having faith that the ever-growing numbers of those supporting the vote would win the day, even over the president's opposition. Although Fanny agreed with that point of view, at age seventy-one she no longer had the stamina to work on as many issues as she had in the past. Of equal importance with her work with the Diet Kitchen Association came her efforts for peace—suffrage, which seemed near at hand, increasingly falling under that rubric. Feeling that it was imperious for the nation to stay out of the war, she fought hard, but not always successfully, against those favoring militarism. At the national Woman's Peace Party convention in January, she proposed more radically nonresistant "Peace Resolutions," which were defeated largely because with war growing more threatening, less radical pacifists questioned whether the Woman's Peace Party program was really suitable for them at all. The loudest voice of conservatism came from the Massachusetts Branch of the Woman's Peace Party, led by Lucia Ames Mead, a longtime peace activist.

Fanny's frustration over the slow progress of the suffrage campaign and the public's growing interest in war created in her an uncharacteristic sense of anger at those people who could not understand that it was men's values and men's power that had created such extreme havoc in the world. Whereas attending a talk on motherhood would once have pleased her, on March 31, 1916, her reaction was just the opposite: "I listened to a stupid talk about the care of babies & the great profession of Motherhood. I asked about fatherhood & why the lives we are asked to preserve are slaughtered by men—quite a bomb."[96] While the participation of twenty thousand women in an anti-preparedness parade on May 13 delighted her, she was disgusted that children in public schools were expected to participate in military drills. Like her father and brothers, Frank and William, before her, Fanny found this aspect of education both harmful and unnatural.

In August, in the midst of her campaigning against preparedness, Fanny visited Frank in Boston, only to learn that he, like his brothers, was suffering from cancer. Actually, Frank had been intermittently ill since 1891, but the family had decided that his problems stemmed from lack of exercise, and they urged him to return to the physically active life he had led as a younger man, which he could not. By 1911, he had "lost all desire" even to go to meetings or into nearby Boston to see a play or have dinner.[97] Although he continued to attend local NAACP meetings and added his voice to protest the war, he did not lend his efforts to the types of activities that Fanny did, largely because, despite his illness, he continued to work for Houghton Mifflin, not retiring until August 1915, after forty-four and a half years of continuous service to the company. All he wanted to do once his work life had ended was act "like a hibernating bear," living off the "generous pension" given him by the company.[98]

Frank planned to use his time to travel, read, write, and to do simply whatever pleased him. However, when on September 6, a month after he retired, Theresa died, he seemed to lose his will to live. The next year, when the cancer was detected, Frank prepared himself for the inevitable, telling Fanny that he was going through his papers and books, being sure that his affairs were in order. Once again expressing gratitude for being raised a Garrison, he noted, "It is a joy to me and great, to think of all the dear children of the fourth generation who are to bear down our name & strain, & who promise to do it so worthily."[99] Frank died at the age of sixty-eight on December 11, a few hours before Fanny arrived in Boston to be with him. Two days later, she noted, "I am dazed & unable to realize that the end has come."[100] Like George and William before him, Frank's body was cremated at Mt. Auburn Cemetery near Boston.

Fanny, the last surviving Garrison child, depended on her long-held belief in nonresistance, and her personal abhorrence at the thought of the children of her two homelands maiming and killing each other, to spur her on to action. None of the results of aging—fatigue, some hearing loss, deteriorating teeth, aches and pains, or heart palpitations—prevented her from using her status, wealth, and organizational abilities to help the peace movement. In August 1916, as a member of the American Neutral Conference Committee, Fanny served on a delegation which met with Woodrow Wilson. Although received most graciously, the group was told in no uncertain terms that the present administration was not interested in leading an effort to bring the warring parties together. As an Anglophile, Wilson had consistently favored England in its war with Germany, allowing merchant marine ships to intercept and relay German messages and supporting huge bank loans to the British government, neither the actions of a truly neutral country. When after his reelection, Wilson issued his famous "Peace without Victory" speech, urging all nations to take care of their own concerns and not to interfere in those of other countries, peace activists hoped that the United States, at least, would stay out of the war. Their hopes were short-lived, for on January 31, 1917, Germany announced plans to resume the use of unrestricted submarine warfare on all ships, armed or not, neutral or belligerent, that sailed through designated areas. Three days later, on February 3, the United States severed diplomatic relations with them.

With the U.S. government seemingly determined to enter the war, Fanny joined other peace activists in a last-ditch effort to prevent it. For the first three months of 1917, she often attended two or three meetings in one day, her efforts centering around the Woman's Peace Party and the Emergency Peace Federation, the second incarnation of the American Neutral Conference Committee. For the latter group, she traveled to Washington, D.C., in February to lobby senators who appeared shy of war, and as a result found herself, much like Jane Addams and Oswald, the recipient of letters and editorials in newspapers labeling her a coward and a puppet of the German government. Such public name-calling placed her work in other organizations in jeopardy. After one article, for example, a leading member of the Diet Kitchen Association offered her resignation if Fanny was reelected president, but the executive board stood by its long-term and most dedicated officer. Once Wilson asked for a declaration of war on April 2 and Congress granted his wish, in despair, Fanny resigned from the Emergency Peace Federation, feeling that nothing more could be done.

Feeling "tired" and hopeless, she was emotionally unprepared for the news that her daughter had died in England after a bout with the grippe followed by anemia.[101] Sending Jim Bell $1,000 to help with funeral expenses could not assuage the deep grief and regret which she felt, for Helen's death, of course, marked the end of any hope for a future reconciliation between mother and daughter. In addition, she was faced with the decision of Harold's son, Henry, to sign up with the Red Cross to serve in Italy. At first, Henry had taken part in the mandatory ROTC classes at Harvard, but he soon realized that he would never be able to bayonet another man. Because he agreed with the U.S. position on the war, however, he chose to go on "a mission of mercy to save lives." Reluctant to discuss the issue with his grandmother, whom he thought would only be "angry and hurt" by his decision, he was, in the end, surprised by her reaction. Although concerned for his safety, she did not deride him, but, rather, gave him a trench coat to keep him warm and dry. As an older man in his nineties, he remembered her act as one illustrative of "her generosity and good spiritedness."[102]

Once war was declared, Fanny's voice, like many others, was almost totally silenced by government suppression of dissent assured through two 1917 acts of Congress. The Threats against the President Act made it treasonous to criticize Wilson in any way, while the Espionage Bill called for up to $10,000 in fines and twenty years in prison for disloyalty, refusal to serve in the armed forces, interfering with the recruitment or enlisting of soldiers, and "aiding the enemy" in any way. It also allowed for the banning from the mails of any antiwar or antigovernment materials. These two laws frightened many women away from the Woman's Peace Party and made it virtually impossible to carry out antiwar work. Fanny's own close ties to German culture, language, and family put her in a particularly vulnerable position. As co-owners of the *Nation,* she and Oswald faced continual opposition from their pro-war staff, which in early 1917 printed the opinion that "if war should come, it is certain that the Government could count upon all the volunteers whom it could train and equip."[103] The editors blamed all parties for the war—polititians, the Kaiser and German militarism, and the Anglo-Saxon doctrine of superiority. Since appearing to be pro-German could endanger the paper's existence, the two owners decided not to discourage what they perceived as their writers' middle-of-the-road stances. Instead, they settled for mild editorials—such as the one that described the Selective Service Act, passed in May 1917, as being un-American, unnecessary, and a menace to the nation's democratic institutions—rather than attacking U.S. participation in and capitalist motivation for the war. In January 1918, however, Oswald finally lost patience with the *Nation*'s bias and took over the chief editorial position, using the paper's pages for true dissent. In defending the rights of conscientious objectors and socialists to speak out and skewering the government for stamping on citizens' civil liberties, he opened the way for government attacks.

Fanny, in the meantime, turned her attention once again to the suffrage movement, for although radical, it was less hated than pacifism. When women in New York State were granted the vote in November 1917, she happily joined others at a grand "Jubilee" meeting at Cooper Union, reminiscent of the similarly named events held after the Emancipation Proclamation was signed in 1863 and at the end of the Civil War two years later. Even she, who had seen slavery end, could hardly believe that it was "really true" that she could now vote.[104] This great victory, however, could not make up for the awful events of the war. Fanny, for one, was relieved to bid 1917 farewell, as, for her, it was "the worst of all years for human-misery-man-made."[105] With the state vote won, Fanny bade farewell to her suffrage groups—the NAWSA, the New York State Woman Suffrage Association, the Hudson River Equal Franchise Society, and the William Lloyd Garrison Equal Rights Club. It was only a matter of time before the peace movement called to her once more. The Great War ended on November 11, 1918, a day on which Fanny could rejoice, feeling it was "wonderful" with lots of "sunshine & hope."[106] Little did she know that the repression of freedom of speech which had begun during the war would escalate into a full-blown Red Scare, a time when the government and media joined forces to silence and punish the dissenting voices in the country, including pacifists, suffragists, labor activists, socialists—indeed many who had expressed liberal or leftist opinions during the Progressive Era and World War I.

The purpose of the Red Scare was to frighten people away from the idea of communism, which had gained in popularity once the Russian Revolution of 1917 had created the first socialist nation in world history. As a result, Woman's Peace Party leaders such as Jane Addams and Emily Greene Balch were taken to task for their actions. Balch was fired from her position on the faculty of Wellesley College because of her peace work. At the age of fifty-two, she found herself unemployed after twenty-one years of service. Addams still had Hull House, but she was unwelcome to speak at many public functions, and her membership in the Daughters of the American Revolution was discontinued. In January 1919, the Overman subcommittee in the Senate produced a list of sixty-two people whom they considered dangerous to the ideals of the country. The next year, the Lusk Commission of New York State published its report on "Revolutionary Radicalism." Considering her links to Germany, including hosting innumerable German guests during her peace and suffrage activities, it is surprising that Fanny was not attacked in these documents. In fact, the Lusk Report portrayed her as an "influential local" woman who was more or less duped by the socialist influences in the Emergency Peace Federation and the New York Woman's Peace Party.[107] In contrast, Louis Lochner, also in the peace movement and with ties to Germany, was portrayed as a German and Russian agent.

On an individual level, Fanny felt the brunt of the Red Scare far less than others. Although she witnessed the government's censorship of the *Nation* and read newspaper articles that described Oswald's pacifist views as unpatriotic, she herself was hardly mentioned.[108] In Oswald's and others' defense, she wrote a letter which was published in the *Boston Globe,* again using to advantage her position as William Lloyd Garrison's daughter. "If my father were alive today," she stated, "I am confident that he would regard the aspersions cast upon pacifists as 'deluded, unpatriotic members of society,' as indicating that the peace cause is advancing." Attacks meant that apathy no longer dominated society's thoughts on peace, "a very hopeful sign" of a rising national consciousness about the real horrors of war.[109] In the wake of World War I, Fanny turned her eyes back to the issue of nonresistance, leaving the final push of the national suffrage campaign for a constitutional amendment up to others, not even noting in her diary the passage of the resolution through the House in 1918, the Senate in 1919, or its ratification on August 26, 1920. Rather, when the Versailles Treaty was negotiated in 1919, which blamed Germany for the war, punished it economically, and caused starvation and internal violence, Fanny felt that her final years must be devoted to peace.

While the Versailles Treaty was being negotiated, members of the Woman's Peace Party joined with their international counterparts in Zurich to create the Women's International League for Peace and Freedom (WILPF), which is still thriving today. In New York City, when the local branch joined WILPF, Fanny remained a member, hoping that it would become the voice for nonresistance which she yearned for. However, when in March 1919 the leaders held a Woman's Freedom Conference, in which the more than six hundred participants addressed woman's rights issues rather than peace, some women began to feel that the group had moved away from peace toward a "violent revolutionary attitude" favorable to socialist Russia.[110] A splinter group formed by much younger women, some of whom Fanny had met in the suffrage campaign—including the lawyer Elinor Byrns, the New York suffrage leader Caroline Lexow Babcock, the birth control advocate Mary Ware Dennett, and the educator Katherine Devereux Blake—formed a new organization dedicated to peace alone, claiming that their commitment to war resistance kept them divided from WILPF. Not wishing to alienate themselves from friends and an organization they might wish to continue working with in a less intense manner, the women noted that, for them, the New York City branch of WILPF simply reflected "in its small way the chaos in which the whole world was struggling."[111] After several conversations with Fanny at her apartment, twenty-five women created the Women's Peace Society and "begged" Fanny to act as chair.[112]

Convinced that her father's beliefs were as relevant in 1919 as they had been in 1831, for the next month Fanny worked unceasingly to draft a nonresistance platform for the new peace organization, which, after much debate, was accepted. As a 1921 pamphlet written to describe the Women's Peace Society demonstrated,

Elinor Byrns, the author, brought Fanny's dream to life, declaring that the organization was built on "moral principle and not just anti-war activity." Women interested in joining the society had to agree not to aid in or sanction any war, whether offensive or defensive, international or civil, nor make or handle munitions, subscribe to war loans, use their labor to set others free for war work, or raise money or work for relief organizations. They had to oppose bloodshed even under circumstances that seemed just, such as "preserving law and order, or defending liberty and property, or on the plea of securing the safety of women and children."[113]

The key to understanding the Women's Peace Society was the knowledge that nonresistance was not "a state of passivity."[114] Rather, it meant being active in ridding the world of war and other forms of violence through complete disarmament with no compromises. Free trade, although not of munitions, would lead to peace and prosperity. For twenty-five cents as dues and the signing of a pledge claiming it wrong to destroy human life under any circumstances, a woman could become a member. In many ways, the statement of purpose reflected the *Declaration of Sentiments* which Lloyd had written upon the creation of the New England Non-Resistance Society in 1838, but it differed in one crucial aspect. It had an obvious feminist slant, which came as a result of its founders' suffrage voice, including Fanny's own:

> Whereas we women have secured our enfranchisement without the destruction of a single life, thus bringing about by peaceful methods one of the greatest revolutions in history . . . we call upon all other women to help us, knowing that women can never have true freedom or equality with men in a society dominated by force, and believing that women should not want rights, privileges or protection secured for them at the cost of men's lives.[115]

Fanny retained her membership in WILPF as well as leading the Women's Peace Society, enjoying the social contact of women with whom she felt an affinity and pushing her nonresistance platform as often as possible. WILPF leaders, however, had no intention of supporting a resolution claiming the organization to be nonresistant, for such a position would have ended any chance of attracting large numbers of women who supported peace but did not define it in such a strict way. Nonetheless, Fanny persisted in trying to get this largest of the women's peace organizations to go her way. In November 1919 she attended the national meeting of WILPF in Philadelphia, where she expressed her views on nonresistance but declined an invitation to serve on the national board.[116] She wrote letters to women in Europe proposing that a second international women's peace organization was necessary, one that was based on nonresistance—an idea that annoyed Emily Greene Balch and other WILPF leaders who wanted to build one strong international organization rather than two weaker ones.[117]

In 1921 Fanny traveled to Vienna to present her ideas before the WILPF international convention. Once there, however, she felt that she had wasted her time, claiming that more women were interested in talking about communism "& things irrelevant" than the real issue of peace. She was further frustrated when the chair, Jane Addams, allowed her to speak only "at the eleventh hour," giving her a mere three minutes in which to present her ideas. Although a majority of those present favored her resolution for nonresistance, the chair of the British section pointed out that it would change the basis of membership. Hence, Addams insisted a vote be an expression of individual opinion only, "committing no one to it."[118] As Fanny lamented, "It passed as an expression of sympathy only. Strange Jane Addams."[119] At the annual U.S. WILPF meeting in 1922, Fanny again attempted to propose a resolution. Out of respect, Addams gave her time to speak and then recommended that the suggestion be taken up by the Resolutions Committee where it was politely, but effectively, killed.

Encouraged by 1920s popular opinion which favored an end to all war, Fanny was not deterred. Back home in New York, except for her continued work with the Diet Kitchen Association, she put all her efforts into the Women's Peace Society. As peace organizations nationwide multiplied in number, her optimism grew. She noticed that many people believed that business interests had led Woodrow Wilson into a war of greed, not one of humanitarian concerns, and that consequently the government was investigating ways to legislate world peace. In this generally optimistic climate, the Women's Peace Society sought to link the theme of nonresistance with the peaceful revolution of suffrage, a great change in society brought about without resorting to any violent means. The women in the organization had great faith not only in the strategies, tactics, and results of the suffrage campaign but also in the ability of women to use the newly gained vote as an entrance into the international political sphere in order to peacefully eliminate war. In that vein, lobbying, as in the suffrage days, was perhaps the most widespread action used by the Women's Peace Society and other organizations.

Hence when Representative Edwin D. Brooks of Illinois, feeling great concern over a possible naval arms race among the United States, Great Britain, and Japan, proposed a resolution asking Wilson to invite representatives from all nations to a disarmament conference, Jessie Hardy MacKaye of the Women's Peace Society board lobbied for it, then arranged for members of the organization to speak in favor of the idea at the resolution's hearings. When the Washington Naval Conference was eventually held from November 11, 1921, through February 6, 1922, Women's Peace Society members felt great satisfaction. For Fanny, one of the most important issues that the organization addressed during her final years was opposing military training in public schools. For this purpose, the women turned their eyes to Albany, where, in the state capitol, they held a hearing in March 1920 on the abolition of the Military Training Commission of New York State.

By the end of 1920, the society had supporters in Milwaukee, Cincinnati, Boston, and Washington, D.C., as well as individual members throughout the United States, Mexico, and in various European countries. It eventually claimed a membership of about two thousand, although no more than twenty or so were actually active. During its first two years the organization was quite busy, but all was not well among its leadership, for while the pledge and leaflets clearly indicated that the Women's Peace Society was a nonresistant organization, some members, led by Elinor Byrns, felt their position needed to be more explicit. Hence, Byrns wrote Fanny that she intended to propose changing the pledge in order "to keep out those who would help in a war" through buying war bonds or knitting socks or doing some such activity.[120] Byrns and Caroline Lexow Babcock wanted to alter the wording, "Believing that under no circumstances is it right to take human life, I hereby apply for membership in the Women's Peace Society and pledge myself to further its high aims by every means in my power," to include the following: "And I declare it is my intention never to aid in or sanction war, offensive or defensive, international or civil, in any way, whether by making or handling munitions, subscribing to war loans, using my labor for the purpose of setting others free for war service, helping by money or work any relief organization which supports or condones war."[121] In addition, Byrns wanted Fanny and herself to agree on the way in which nonresistance could be practiced rather than simply held as a principle. She further claimed that while Fanny thought it wise to recruit a large number of members, she herself felt that a small membership of about fifty women would be preferable if they all agreed on the theory and practice of nonresistance. By April the issue of the pledge had become so controversial that Fanny feared several women would leave the organization, including Elinor Byrns, whom she had come to rely upon for the physical leadership she could no longer provide.

In fact, the pledge was just a sign of a deeper problem, that of a generation gap. The younger women in the activist core of the group began to feel that Fanny was inflexible, favoring rhetoric over action. They did not take into account that Fanny's style of organizing reflected an earlier generation's practices and that, at her age, she found it impossible to change. Almost all of the Women's Peace Society members had come out of the suffrage and peace movements prior to and during World War I. In their thirties, they represented the "new woman" of the 1920s, who often had a career or job, an active social life, and political interests. Fanny represented the older, more privileged woman who kept control over the money and, therefore, unfairly dominated the group. These younger New York City women tended to be somewhat socialistic in their thinking, and so when Fanny expressed her belief that peace could be achieved under the present capitalist system, several of them questioned her political astuteness, especially Byrns, who had run on the Socialist Party ticket in 1920 for state representative from

Staten Island. In addition to all these differences, Fanny had developed the habit of referring to the Women's Peace Society as "my organization," which irked her younger coworkers.[122]

In a strange but interesting turn of events, Elinor Byrns accused Fanny of not being a true nonresister. She claimed that Fanny not only admitted to having bought Liberty Bonds during World War I but also denied having pledged not to support any wars. Of course, Fanny herself could not discard her abolitionist support of the Civil War, but this history most likely never crossed Byrns's mind, 1861 seeming light years away. In addition, Byrns told other members that Fanny said she would not sign "such a drastic pledge" as the one she and Caroline Babcock had created, and this was true, as Fanny would never have turned her back on her grandson, Henry, or her brother, George, both of whom had supported a war effort in some way.[123] Eventually, the argument led to the one result Fanny did not want, the resignation of a core group of members who went on to form the Women's Peace Union, an organization which led a campaign for a constitutional amendment to make war illegal. Upon hearing of the organizing conference that spawned the new society, Fanny was circumspect, claiming to rejoice over the news, perhaps not totally comprehending that the founding of the new meant the death of the old. Rather, in her usual optimistic spirit of compromise, she chose to treat both organizations as one. Hence, on November 12, 1921, when joining a march of seventeen hundred people from 58th Street to Washington Square, Fanny delighted in seeing "Our Peace Society & Peace Union banners" being carried side by side.[124] However, within a few months, when most of the younger women had decided to work with the Women's Peace Union or WILPF rather than with Fanny, the Women's Peace Society became basically one that published pamphlets, encouraged letter-writing campaigns, and attended demonstrations, meetings, and hearings organized by other, larger groups.

From 1922 on, Fanny spent increasing amounts of time at home and with her family rather than at peace meetings, held most Diet Kitchen meetings at her home, and raised money to help the war survivors in Germany. In March 1922 the death of Annie Anthony, her sister-in-law, left only her and Ellie from their generation; by the next year, she herself was experiencing more bouts of illness. In 1901 a German physician had warned Fanny that she had a heart ailment, but for the next twenty-three years, she had continued her busy life with few physical complaints. In 1924, however, this condition worsened, with Fanny often feeling her heart missing a beat or being, as she called it, "a tired heart."[125] She suffered from frequent pains and indigestion which prevented her from sleeping and also resulted in fainting spells. Realizing that she was nearing her end, the remaining members of the Women's Peace Society sponsored a luncheon in her honor on the occasion of Fanny's eightieth birthday. Nearly three hundred people joined her at the Hotel Astor, where representatives of the various organizations she belonged to sang her praises. Meta Lilienthal, the spokesperson for the Women's Peace Society, must have pleased Fanny immensely when she said, "We of the Women's Peace Society are proud to call Fanny Garrison Villard our leader. We know her as an uncompromising pacifist. So young is she in spirit that despite her eighty years she is still a radical and like her honored father she still says, 'I will not compromise.'"[126] Another member, Margaret Loring Thomas, wrote a sonnet for the event titled "Fanny Garrison Villard":

> December's Daughter, we now honor thee,
> A prophet come to swell among us here,
> When days are overbrief and nights are drear
> And life is dormant in each seed and tree,
> Thy spirit's call is heard from sea to sea.
> "Work on for brighter days. The Spring is near.
> Awake mankind! Bring in a better year!
> Come, open door for trade, it shall be free."
> It was her father by whose sainted hands
> The slaves were set free from tyrant bands.
> Humanity she would emancipate
> From war and murder, bloodshed and blind hate.
> In dreams she sees the end of rule by might
> And force; the victory of love and right.[127]

Perhaps the greatest compliment, however, came from W. E. B. Du Bois, who claimed, "Mrs. Villard represents peculiarly a unity of ideas of the emancipation of the black race, the emancipation of women, the freeing of the world from that organized murder which we call war. I know of no one who represents these three ideas in a more beautiful unity than the person whom we are here to honor today."[128]

Fanny was "almost overcome with emotion" by the outpouring of love and admiration shown her at the luncheon, noting that it was "hard to find words in which to thank them for such a brilliant occasion & one of such tenderness & affection for one who is 80 years old."[129] The event inspired her to carry on in spite of her declining health. When not ill, she attended peace and Diet Kitchen meetings and worked on a small volume she titled *William Lloyd Garrison on Non-Resistance Together with a Personal Sketch by His Daughter, Fanny Garrison Villard.* Published in 1924 by the Nation Press Printing Company, it consisted of small segments of Lloyd's writings on nonresistance and some of Fanny's recollections of her childhood, largely adapted from her brothers' biography of their father. Time, however, was not on her side. Twice in 1926 she tripped and fell in her home, and many nights she had trouble breathing. Her condition worsened so that in June of that year she had to use a wheelchair to get around. However,

Fanny was not one to allow herself to remain immobile, and as soon as she could manage, she stood on her own two feet, greeting her Diet Kitchen and Women's Peace Society associates for yet another meeting at her home. Oswald and Harold visited every day, worrying that each might be her last. On December 16, 1927, she marveled that she was now eighty-three, sighing, "It seems like a dream."[130]

Fanny began 1928 by writing an open letter for the Women's Peace Society's newsletter, reminding each member "to do all in her power to spread the Christian doctrine of Peace undaunted by any and all opposition." In her usual humble manner, she thanked all those who had sent birthday greetings, which Annie E. Gray, the executive secretary, had collected into a scrapbook. "I want you to know," she wrote, "that I have read every kind tribute to me with real humility of spirit, for I did not know before my 80th birthday that I had ever accomplished anything worth remembering."[131] On April 7 she visited the Villard Diet Kitchen, and on May 14 she held a Women's Peace Society meeting. Then she ran out of steam. For several weeks, Fanny remained at home, usually in bed, until on July 5, at 8:30 A.M., she died at her home in Dobbs Ferry, Harold and Oswald by her side. She was buried beside Henry and Hilgard in the Sleepy Hollow Cemetery, only Ellie surviving her until her own death on February 12, 1931.

Fanny had lived to see many reforms made in her favorite causes. Although nowhere near her version of perfection, equal rights for African Americans had advanced considerably by 1928. Fanny saw around her the blossoming of the Harlem Renaissance and the political presence of W. E. B. Du Bois and Mary Church Terrell, two people whom she especially admired. Women had the vote, and although she felt that they did not use it properly to achieve peace, she treasured her trips to the polls. In addition, she had witnessed the explosion of women into the political arena, the work force, and the leadership of cultural institutions. In terms of peace, the Kellogg-Briand Pact of 1928 pledged sixty-two nations to discuss their problems before starting a war, while the League of Nations and the World Court, although flawed, provided countries with possible avenues to prevent war. Fanny exited this world at a time of relative peace. She did not live to see the rise of Hitlerism and the extermination of twelve million people by her beloved Germany, followed by that nation's division into East and West during the Cold War. She also did not live to see her own country develop and use the atomic bomb. These disasters would have deeply grieved her, but, in the end, they would most likely not have altered her lifelong view that nonresistance was the answer to violence and injustice. As a true Garrison child, Fanny lived with the belief that people could achieve an equal and humane world if they would simply try.

A NOTE ON SOURCES

Writing a book about the children of a famous historical figure presented some interesting challenges, the most striking being the lack of information about their lives—and indeed about the lives of any abolitionist children—in secondary sources. While books and articles on William Lloyd Garrison are numerous, they are, as one would expect, concerned with Garrison as an abolitionist leader; little is said of Garrison the family man. Yet, after studying this family for over ten years, I find myself hard-pressed to say which was more important in his life—his family or his cause. My own conclusion is that even though his rhetoric indicated he would die for his cause, I doubt that William Lloyd would have voluntarily left his family. There was simply too much evidence of dedication to his wife's welfare and his children's upbringing, and pure joy in family life, to believe that he would act on his "martyr complex," as other biographers have labeled it.

Few biographers have looked deeply enough into this man's personal life to uncover his dedication to his role as a husband and father. The first to do so was one of Garrison's closest friends and cohorts, Oliver Johnson, who just after "the liberator's" death wrote *William Lloyd Garrison and His Times.*[1] In a few sections, Johnson emphasized that Garrison was first and foremost a loving husband and father, a man who forbade violence in his home, who shared in the responsibility of caring for his children, and who helped his wife with household chores. Johnson tried to deflate the public's view of Garrison as a firebrand with a narrow vision by revealing some of his firsthand knowledge of his friend's private life. Like most political biographies, however, Johnson's tale emphasizes the man's all-important work to improve society.

In the period from 1879 to the 1950s, Garrison virtually disappeared from the telling of U.S. history. At first, his life was honored by the placement of statues in Boston (1886) and Newburyport (1893) and by the centennial of his birth, commemorated in 1905 by the two groups most dedicated to keeping his memory alive: African Americans who remembered Garrison's devotion to the antislavery cause, and Garrison's own children, who pledged to each other that they would see that the United States remembered him and the other abolitionists who had worked so hard for freedom. But after this generation passed on, few people cared to remember the blot of slavery, the national pain of the Civil War, or those who fought the government to abolish the "peculiar institution." One who remembered was Godwin Smith, who used the sons' biography of their father to weave together a short political biography titled *The Moral Crusader: William Lloyd Garrison.*[2] Another was John Jay Chapman, himself an abolitionist descendant, who wrote *William Lloyd Garrison.*[3] Published in 1913, this so-called biography of Garrison is more of an extolment of the abolitionist movement and its leader—almost a demigod for Chapman—than an objective study. In fact, Chapman's narrative reads like a passionate but angry polemic meant to shame the reading public into remembering and honoring William Lloyd Garrison and his fellow radicals. Certainly, this climate allowed little room for the softer edges of the firebrand. Yet those soft spots are precisely what made him such a passionate leader.

Happily for those interested in seeing the abolitionist movement obtain its deserved place in the study of U.S. history, beginning in the 1950s the growth of Civil Rights activism in the South encouraged interest in the antislavery movement and in Garrison in particular. However, as in the past, there was little interest in preserving anything but the man's political persona. Russel B. Nye, who wrote the first of several new studies of Garrison, *William Lloyd Garrison and the Humanitarian Reformers,* revived the spirit of the abolitionists but did little to inform the reader about Garrison's personal life.[4] A brief overview of his boyhood and two references to "Mrs. Garrison," his wife, were all he offered.

In 1963 appeared Walter M. Merrill's groundbreaking biography, *Against Wind and Tide: A Biography of Wm. Lloyd Garrison.*[5] Merrill was the first modern historian to give some insight into Garrison's personality, including glimpses, however spotty, into the man's homelife. Most prominent is Merrill's portrait of Garrison's boyhood years with his mother, Fanny, and an entertaining chapter on the courtship of Garrison and Helen. Merrill, however, was greatly influenced by Freudian psychology, and his portraits of both women relies heavily on the image of the controlling mother, the rebellious son, and the meek, adoring wife. Mention of Garrison's seven children is scant, except in the case of young Charles. *Against Wind and Tide,* a serious and valuable political biography, spawned several other studies, including John L. Thomas's *The Liberator: William Lloyd Garrison: A Biography,* George M. Fredrickson's *William Lloyd Garrison,* and James Brewer Stewart's *William Lloyd Garrison and the Challenge of Emancipation.*[6] Of great importance, also, was the publication in six volumes of Garrison's letters, edited by Merrill and Louis Ruchames.[7] The annotated footnotes and introductions to each volume provided more information about the family's homelife than any other source to date, but, to be quite candid, who but diehard Garrison addicts like myself would read these massive books?

Garrison's story, then, became pat. New interpretations of the workings of the abolitionist movement came out, but no in-depth consideration of the man as a whole. This was partly remedied in 1998 with the publication of Henry Mayer's *All on Fire: William Lloyd Garrison and the Abolition of Slavery.*[8] Mayer's mammoth book traces in detail Garrison's political beliefs and actions. It also gives a better sense of Garrison family life than any other book to date. Mayer traces Garrison's heritage, offers a balanced portrait of his parents' relationship and his boyhood years, and intersperses political history with glimpses into life inside the Garrison home. For the first time in biographies of Garrison, Helen and the children come to life. However, Mayer's object was to paint a political actor; including a full portrait of the family would have doubled the length of his otherwise definitive work.

Interestingly, the one work that offers a personal portrait of Garrison is the previously mentioned biography written by his sons Wendell and Frank. *William Lloyd Garrison, 1805–1879, The Story of His Life Told by His Children* is a compendium of Garrison's personal and political relationships, revealing, particularly in its final chapter, many fascinating family stories, some of which I have included in this book.[9]

There is no question that recording the history of the abolitionist movement and its major players is essential for an honest rendering of U.S. history. Feeling the need to ensure its representation in the nation's canon, a few abolitionist children have recorded their parents' or even grandparents' stories or edited memoirs or collections of letters, in the process preserving small parts of their own childhood memories. The Garrison sons' work was the greatest of these efforts, but others are noteworthy for their glimpses into abolitionist life. In each book, the second-generation author primarily mentions the profound effect exposure to their parents' activist friends had on their youth, the exciting debates that took place in their homes, the joyful dinners, picnics, and sing-alongs, and the profoundly serious antislavery and human rights messages conveyed to youngsters in the most loving tones. Such was the picture painted in memoirs by Sarah Southwick and Lillie Buffum Chace, and in the journals and letters of Lucretia and James Mott, Charlotte Forten Grimké, Elizabeth Cady Stanton, Lucy Stone, and Alice Stone Blackwell.[10]

The fuzzy line between abolitionist and woman's rights activism in women's history complicates the tracking of second-generation Garrisonians, for many of their stories were framed around the history of the suffrage movement. In the case of Elizabeth Cady Stanton, for example, biographers have spent much effort discussing the effects that Henry Stanton's abolitionist lecturing tours had on Elizabeth, especially since, unlike in Abby Kelley and Stephen Foster's marriage, Henry took little direct care of his offspring. In presenting Cady Stanton's political career, therefore, emphasis was placed on her strong sense of entrapment, inequality, and boredom as motivating forces behind her becoming a leader in the woman's rights struggle.[11] *Harriot Stanton Blatch and the Winning of Woman Suffrage,* Ellen Carol DuBois's study of Cady Stanton's daughter, also emphasizes the woman's rights movement aspect of Blatch's heritage. DuBois does acknowledge Blatch's abolitionist roots, however: Blatch, upon the death of her brother Theodore in 1925, wrote Fanny Garrison Villard's son Oswald, "The former abolitionist stock is falling away. What is there to take its place? Only milk & water I fear."[12]

Particularly insightful to me was a comment in Alice Stone Blackwell's biography of her mother, the abolitionist Lucy Stone. Born in 1857, too late to feel the full impact of the abolitionist movement, Alice Stone Blackwell was the right age for the woman's rights movement, in which she played an active role. Her casual comment in *Lucy Stone: Pioneer of*

Woman's Rights about her childhood reaction to the movement, taken in conjunction with Ellen Wright's and Lizzie Powell's (discussed in this book), raises fascinating questions about second-generation woman's rightists: "Brought up by such parents, I naturally came to share their views. In my childhood, I heard so much about woman suffrage that I was bored by it and thought I hated it, until one day I came across a magazine article on the other side and found myself bristling up like a hen in defense of her chickens. This happened when I was about twelve years old. After that I never had any doubt as to whether I believed in it."[13]

The historical study of second-generation Garrisonians is now gaining momentum, perhaps as a response to the fascinating peeks into family life offered in studies of the abolitionist community and biographies of specific individuals, especially women. One of the earliest of these to address the issue of marriage and, by extension, child rearing is Blanche Glassman Hersh's *The Slavery of Sex: Feminist-Abolitionists in America.*[14] This wonderfully spirited book offers an analysis of fifty-one women in abolitionist circles, examining their backgrounds, political formation, and entrance into woman's rights. Although not an investigation of childhood experiences, it raises questions in readers' minds about what sort of homelife these children had. Following Hersh's study came Lawrence J. Friedman's classic *Gregarious Saints: Self and Community in American Abolitionism, 1830–1870,* a detailed investigation of the Garrisonian "Boston Clique."[15] Again, although insightful into the personal relationships between women and men, the book gives only a hint of what an abolitionist child might have experienced. More recently, Chris Dixon's book *Perfecting the Family: Antislavery Marriages in Nineteenth-Century America* illustrates the importance of the traditional nuclear family structure to the abolitionist community through an analysis of eight prominent couples, the Garrisons among them.[16] Dixon, however, does not disclose much information on their child-rearing practices.

To date, biographies of women in the abolitionist movement have provided the most detail about child rearing, primarily because that role fell to women. But these books, in an effort to prove the importance of their subjects' political work in a focused way, necessarily truncate the discussion of raising children. Also, once the subject of the biography dies, of course, the book ends. In my case, narrating the lives of Garrison's grandchildren would have virtually constituted a new project, so I purposely chose not to involve myself with them too deeply. Gerda Lerner's *The Grimké Sisters from South Carolina* clearly illustrates how even biographies of women cannot include every aspect of their lives.[17] Angelina Grimké, who gave birth to her first child at the then late age of thirty-four, was greatly aided in child care by her sister, Sarah. But Lerner, who aimed her study at the sisters' political ideas (even after they dropped out of public lecturing), had to avoid focusing too narrowly on their children's experiences. Still, in those places where she cites Angelina's feelings about motherhood and marriage, she tells the reader a great deal. So too does Andrea Moore Kerr in *Lucy Stone: Speaking Out for Equality,* which analyzes Lucy Stone's work in the abolitionist and woman's rights movements.[18] Margret Hope Bacon follows suit in her *Valiant Friend: The Life of Lucretia Mott,* where the vibrancy of the children's lives illuminates that of their parents.[19] In her more recent study, *Abby Hopper Gibbons: Prison Reformer and Social Activist,* Bacon draws the abolitionist link in more detail in order to illustrate how Gibbons, an abolitionist daughter herself, became involved in her later reform activities.[20] Still, despite their understandably political focus, all three books do give the reader a sense of the women's feelings about mothering as well as a taste of their children's experiences.

Of those authors who have written about abolitionist women, Dorothy Sterling is the most successful in interweaving the children's lives into those of their parents. Her early work, *Lucretia Mott,* which was aimed at a young adult readership, included many examples of what children experienced in the Mott home—their reactions to meeting such famous celebrities as Charles Dickens, their attendance at antislavery fairs, their impressions of other abolitionists, and their distress when Lucretia, their nonviolent role model, drowned a litter of kittens—to name just a few.[21] A more sophisticated characterization of a child's life, however, is found in Sterling's *Ahead of Her Time: Abby Kelley and the Politics of Antislavery,* in which the author grapples with the effects of Abby Kelley's and Stephen Foster's activism on their daughter, Alla.[22] Because both parents dedicated their lives to the cause, in a manner unique for their times, they shared child care, as well as occasionally relying on Foster's sister to stand in for them. But although Alla's story surfaces in Sterling's book, it has no independence of its own and does not continue after her parents' deaths.

In my search for stories of the children raised in this fascinating community, I uncovered only two works distinctly dedicated to the lives of second-generation Garrisonians—and both are currently in dissertation form. Sibyl Ventress Brownlee's study of Sarah Parker Remond of Salem, Massachusetts, traces the effects of being raised in an African-American abolitionist family.[23] In "'Out of Abundance of the Heart': Sarah Ann Parker Remond's Quest for Freedom," Brownlee illustrates how Sarah Remond's parents, John and Nancy Remond, fought for the integration of Salem's public schools and for the rights of their children to quality education. Both Sarah and her brother, Charles, grew up to be abolitionist speakers. Brownlee follows Sarah's evolution from an abolitionist to an expatriate medical doctor in nineteenth-century Italy. A work of even greater detail is Elizabeth Cooke Stevens's "'From Generation to Generation': The Mother and Daughter Activism of Elizabeth Buffum Chace and Lillie Chace Wyman."[24] Stevens has uncovered numerous documents which give insight into the mothering and fathering practices, school experiences, friendship patterns, and political education of the abolitionist child, pushing to the forefront the ins and outs, tensions and diversions, and thoughts and feelings of abolitionist parents and children. In addition, the reader appreciates the effects of the childhood home on the adult woman when Lillie Chace Wyman became involved in the woman suffrage campaign. These two works indicate how exciting an intergenerational study of political activists can be.

Although throughout this work I cite from many wonderful secondary sources, which enhance both the narrative and our knowledge of the 150 years separating the colonial era and the period between the two world wars, the majority of my citations refer to the many letters, diaries, speeches, articles, books, and artifacts carefully archived by the five Garrison children and their descendants. The three major archives are the Houghton Library of Harvard University, the Sophia Smith Collection of Smith College, and the Manuscript Division of the Wichita State University Library. One could spend years in each; in fact, I did. Other personal papers are located in the various collections named in the list of abbreviations preceding the notes.

The huge number of documents allowed me to incorporate a great deal of the children's own words. In fact, rather than paraphrasing letters or using a few quotes here and there, I have inserted as much of their thoughts as possible, allowing their words to dominate that part of the narrative which directly describes their lives and thoughts. I have corrected only those misspellings that interfere with understanding (and have refrained from inserting *sic*'s). With the Garrison children's documents to guide me, I have attempted to create a narrative history that brings their lives forward while pushing the exemplary life of their father into the background. At times the task proved nearly impossible, for even at the end of their lives, they identified themselves as children of the great abolitionist that was William Lloyd Garrison.

ABBREVIATIONS

AAS	American Antiquarian Society, Worcester, Massachusetts
ASC:BPL	Antislavery Collection: Boston Public Library, Department of Rare Books and Manuscripts, Boston, Massachusetts
AG	Abijah Garrison
b.	box
BA	Boston Athenaeum, Boston, Massachusetts
BML:Hopedale	Bancroft Memorial Library, Hopedale, Massachusetts
BPL	General Collection in Boston Public Library
BW:CU	Burt Green Wilder Papers, Collection no. 14-26-95: Rare and Manuscript Collections, Carl A. Kroch Library, Cornell University, Ithaca, New York
EW	Ellen Wright (EWG after marriage)
EWG	Ellen Wright Garrison
f.	file folder
FG	Helen Frances Garrison, better known as Fanny (FGV after marriage)
FGV	Fanny Garrison Villard
FGV:HHU	bMSAm1321, Fanny Garrison Villard Papers: Houghton Library of Harvard University, Cambridge, Massachusetts
FJG	Francis Jackson Garrison
FLG	Fanny Lloyd Garrison

GF:BPL	Garrison Family Collection: Boston Public Library, Department of Rare Books and Manuscripts, Boston, Massachusetts
GF:HHU	bMSAm1906, Garrison Family Papers: Houghton Library of Harvard University, Cambridge, Massachusetts
GF:PC	Garrison Family: Personal Collection
GF:SC	Garrison Family Papers: Sophia Smith Collection, Smith College, Northampton, Massachusetts
GF:WSU	Eunice McIntosh Merrill Collection of William Lloyd Garrison Family Papers: Wichita State University Library Special Collections, Wichita, Kansas
GTG	George Thompson Garrison
GWB	George W. Benson
HBG	Helen Benson Garrison
HEB	Helen Eliza Benson (HBG after marriage)
HV	Henry Villard
HV:HHU	bMSAm1322, Henry Villard Papers: Houghton Library of Harvard University, Cambridge, Massachusetts
KF:WHM	Abby Kelley/Stephen Foster Papers: Worcester Historical Museum, Worcester, Massachusetts
Letters 1–6	Walter M. Merrill and Louis Ruchames, eds., *The Letters of William Lloyd Garrison,* 6 vols. (Cambridge: Belknap Press of Harvard University Press, 1971–81)
LMcK	Lucy McKim (LMcKG after marriage)
LMcKG	Lucy McKim Garrison
Life 1–4	Wendell Phillips Garrison and Francis Jackson Garrison, *William Lloyd Garrison, 1805–1879, The Story of His Life Told by His Children,* 4 vols. (New York: Century Company, 1885–89)
McK:BPL	James Miller McKim Papers: Boston Public Library, Department of Rare Books and Manuscripts, Boston, Massachusetts
MF	Martha Farnham
MMcG:NYPL	William J. Maloney and Margaret McKim Maloney Collections of Historical Papers: Maloney Collection of McKim-Garrison Family Papers: The New York Public Library, Rare Books and Manuscripts Division, Astor, Lenox and Tilden Foundations, New York, New York
MW	Martha Wright
n.d.	no date
NYC-WPP:SCPC	New York City branch of the Woman's Peace Party: Swarthmore College Peace Collection, Swarthmore, Pennsylvania
NYPL	General Research Library: The New York Public Library, Astor, Lenox and Tilden Foundations, New York, New York
OGV	Oswald Garrison Villard
OGV:HHU	bMSAm1323, Oswald Garrison Villard Papers: Houghton Library of Harvard University, Cambridge, Massachusetts

S/L:NYPL	Rosika Schwimmer/Lola Maverick Lloyd Collection: The New York Public Library, Rare Books and Manuscripts Division, Astor, Lenox and Tilden Foundations, New York, New York
WLG	William Lloyd Garrison
WLG:MHS	William Lloyd Garrison Papers: Massachusetts Historical Society, Boston, Massachusetts
WLGJR	William Lloyd Garrison Jr.
WP:BPL	Wendell Phillips Papers: Boston Public Library, Department of Rare Books and Manuscripts, Boston, Massachusetts
WPG	Wendell Phillips Garrison
WPG:HHU	bMSAm1169, Wendell Phillips Garrison Papers: Houghton Library of Harvard University, Cambridge, Massachusetts
WP:HHU	bMSAm1153, Crawford-Blagden Collection of Wendell Phillips Papers: Houghton Library of Harvard University, Cambridge, Massachusetts
WPS:SCPC	Women's Peace Society Papers: Swarthmore College Peace Collection, Swarthmore, Pennsylvania
WPU:SCPC	Women's Peace Union Papers: Swarthmore College Peace Collection, Swarthmore, Pennsylvania

NOTES

PROLOGUE

–Epigraph: FJG to FGV, January 25, 1880, bMSAm1321, f. 784, FGV:HHU.

1. WPG to HV, May 24, 1879, bMSAm1321, f. 814, FGV:HHU.

2. FGV to Elizabeth Pease Nichol, May 27, 1879, bMSAm1906, f. 630, GF:HHU.

3. See Wendell Phillips Garrison and Francis Jackson Garrison, *William Lloyd Garrison, 1805–1879, The Story of His Life Told by His Children,* 4 vol. (New York: Century Company, 1885–89).

1. FANNY'S STORY

–Epigraph: WLG to WPG, December 12, 1878, *Letters* 6:538–539.

1. Fanny's father, Andrew, came from Kinsale County Munster, Ireland; her mother, Mary, of Irish and English parentage, came from Limerick. The couple wed on March 30, 1771, and had eleven children: Catherine, Ellenore, William, Nancy, Frances, Edward, Charles, John, Plato, David, and Charlotte. The available records show no dates for the births, so Fanny's placement in the family line is unclear. It is likely, however, that she was born in 1776.

2. Information on the appeal of Baptism to women in the eighteenth century is culled from Susan Juster, *Disorderly Women: Sexual Politics & Evangelicalism in Revolutionary New England* (Ithaca, N.Y.: Cornell University Press, 1994) and Janet Moore Lindman, "'A Dear Sister in Christ': The Devotional Culture of Baptist Women in the 18th Century"

(paper presented at the annual meeting of the Organization of American Historians, Washington, D.C., April 1995).

3. Abijah's father, Joseph Garrison, and his mother, Mary Palmer, were settlers of the Jemseg River area of New Brunswick, Canada, near St. John. They wed on August 14, 1764, and had nine children: Hannah, Elizabeth, Joseph, Daniel, Abijah, Sarah, Nathan, Silas, and William. Abijah was born on June 18, 1773.

4. WLG as quoted in *People's Journal,* September 12, 1846, p. 141, as cited in *Life* 1:14–15.

5. Ibid., pp. 12–13.

6. AG to his parents, April 4, 1805, b. 1, f. 5, GF:SC.

7. All subsequent information on Newburyport in this chapter was gleaned from Benjamin W. Labaree, *Patriots and Partisans: The Merchants of Newburyport, 1764–1815* (Cambridge: Harvard University Press, 1962); Stephan Thernstrom, *Poverty and Progress: Social Mobility in a Nineteenth Century City* (Cambridge: Harvard University Press, 1964), and Daniel Vickers, *Farmers and Fishermen: Two Centuries of Work in Essex County, Massachusetts, 1630–1850* (Chapel Hill: University of North Carolina Press, 1994). An interesting book on women and the world of the sea is Margaret S. Creighton and Lisa Norling, ed., *Iron Men, Wooden Women: Gender and Seafaring in the Atlantic World, 1700–1920* (Baltimore: Johns Hopkins University Press, 1996).

8. At its high point in 1805, about fifty-five or sixty cod ships sailed from Newburyport. By 1807 the prosperous town also touted a population numbering 7,500.

9. The town records say December 12, but the family claims the 10th. Also, until 1835, William Lloyd Garrison believed he had been born in 1804.

10. Earlier in 1807, the town's businesses boomed. In that year alone, smaller sized vessels made ninety-three voyages to the West Indies. Thirteen large ships took products to Europe. On the average, the town's merchants were exporting goods from the West Indies worth as much as $1,500,000 annually through Newburyport to Europe.

11. Newburyport *Herald,* May 13 and July 15, 1808, as cited in Labaree, *Patriots and Partisans,* p. 154. In 1809, Congress replaced the Embargo Act with the Non-Intercourse Act, which allowed trade with everyone but England and France. Since these nations were the biggest customers, nothing improved. In 1810, trade with England and France was allowed as long as neither attacked U.S. shipping. This also failed. Impressment of U.S. sailors onto British ships also escalated. Tensions soon led to the June 1, 1812, U.S. declaration of war against England.

12. For more information on alcohol and temperance, see Robert L. Hampel, *Temperance and Prohibition in Massachusetts, 1813–1852* (Ann Arbor: UMI Research Press, 1982); information on alcoholism and wife abuse can be found in Elizabeth Pleck, *Domestic Tyranny: The Making of Social Policy against Family Violence from Colonial Times to the Present* (New York: Oxford University Press, 1987).

13. *Life* 1:25.

14. Lloyd later remembered her as Maria Elizabeth until he saw the Newburyport town records in 1878, which showed him her real name.

15. Susan Grigg, *The Dependent Poor of Newburyport: Studies in Social History, 1800–1830* (Ann Arbor: UMI Research Press, 1984), p. 1.

16. See ibid., p. 53, for another interpretation; also Overseers' Minutes, no. 66, New-

buryport Library, as cited in John L. Thomas, *The Liberator: William Lloyd Garrison: A Biography* (Boston: Little, Brown, 1963), pp. 20–22, as cited in Grigg, *Dependent Poor of Newburyport*, p. 53.

17. Information on Lynn and the shoe business adapted from Mary H. Blewett, *Men, Women, and Work: Class, Gender, and Protest in the New England Shoe Industry, 1780–1910* (Urbana: University of Illinois Press, 1988), p. 22.

18. James Holley Garrison, *Behold Me Once More: The Confessions of James Holley Garrison, Brother of William Lloyd Garrison*, ed. Walter McIntosh Merrill (Boston: Houghton Mifflin, 1954), p. 7. The original manuscript of this work is housed in MMcG:NYPL. While I have looked through the original, I have chosen to cite Walter Merrill's edited version for ease and clarity. In all fairness to James, it must be noted that drinking was very popular among men, especially those of the working class. Employees frequently considered it part of their responsibility to supply their workers with a daily portion of rum or gin. In addition, workers often drank beer, hard cider, and homemade whiskey during breaks, on weekends, and to celebrate just about anything. Learning to drink was actually part of James's apprenticeship.

19. Ibid.

20. FLG to MF, May 26, 1814, b. 26, f. 752, GF:SC.

21. Ibid.

22. FLG to "Sister," April 5, 1814, Ac. 74–6, b. 1, f. 10, GF:WSU.

23. FLG to MF, "Dear Sister," July 20, 1814, b. 26, f. 752, GF:SC.

24. FLG to "Brother," August 21, 1814, b. 26, f. 751, GF:SC.

25. FLG to "Sister," April 5, 1814, Ac. 74–6, b. 1, f. 10, GF:WSU.

26. WLG to FGV, August 14, 1857, bMSAm1321, f. 823, FGV:HHU.

27. *Life* 1:30.

28. Ibid., pp. 31–32.

29. Information on Baltimore is culled from Gary Lawson Browne, *Baltimore in the Nation, 1789–1861* (Chapel Hill: University of North Carolina Press, 1980). Fanny's journal of the voyage reflected her role as a seaman's wife. Her knowledge of nautical terminology and the ways of the sea indicate that she and Abijah had indeed communicated often about his work. The journal also related a frightening incident when a British ship's crew boarded the ship in mid sea. Fanny feared that James would be impressed, but the British sailors did not take any action at all.

30. FLG to MF, October 22, 1815, Ac. 74–6, b. 1, f. 12, GF:WSU.

31. FLG to WLG, May 5, 1819, bMSAm1906, f. 655, GF:HHU.

32. FLG to WLG, October 5, 1819, Ac. 74–6, b. 1, f. 3, GF:WSU.

33. FLG to WLG, November 30, 1819, Ac. 74–6, b. 1, f. 4, GF:WSU.

34. FLG to MF, January 17, 1820, Ac. 74–6, b. 1, f. 13, GF:WSU.

35. FLG to "M.E.," added to FLG to WLG, June 13, 1820, Ac.74–6, b. 1, f. 7, GF:WSU.

36. FLG to WLG, September 20, 1820 (probably), bMSAm1906, f. 655, GF:HHU.

37. FLG to WLG, July 1, 1822 (probably), bMSAm1906, f. 655, GF:HHU.

38. Ibid.

39. FLG to WLG, June 3, 1823, Ac. 74–6, b. 1, f. 9, GF:WSU.

40. Fanny's letter relating Elizabeth's death reflected her emotional and mental distress.

Full of missing words (which her grandson Wendell later penciled in with some guesswork) and grammatical errors, she, nonetheless, told Lloyd of his sister's own premonition of her end. Two nights before her death, Elizabeth had had a nightmare in which a voice asked, "Are you prepared to die?" Upset that she would never see her brother again, she asked her mother to take her into her bed. Two days later, she was dead. FLG to WLG, December 4, 1822, bMSAm1906, f. 655, GF:HHU.

41. WLG to Ephraim Allen, July 7, 1823, as cited in *Life* 1:52–53.

42. *Life* 1:53.

43. AG to Joanna Palmer, July 27, 1814, bMSAm1906, f. 559, GF:HHU, also AG to Cousin, July 27, 1814, b. 1, f. 7a, GF:SC.

44. WPG to FGV, August 1, 1873, bMSAm1321, f. 814, FGV:HHU.

45. William A. Garrison to WPG, July 13, 1874, bMSAm1906, f. 196, GF:HHU.

46. WLG to the secretary of the navy, James K. Paulding, December 14, 1839, as cited in Garrison, *Behold Me Once More,* p. 101.

47. A message from WLG to James Garrison in HBG to James Holley Garrison, May 1840 (probably), bMSAm1906, f. 566, GF:HHU.

48. At first, Lloyd bought into the political agenda of the American Colonization Society, which pushed for the removal of free blacks to Africa (Liberia). Once he identified this as a slaveholder-backed, racist effort to keep only enslaved African Americans in the country, Lloyd turned his back on the Society. In 1832 he wrote a book-length diatribe, *Thoughts on African Colonization,* against the colonization scheme.

49. WLG to Harriet Minot, April 9, 1833, *Letters* 1:218–220.

11. LLOYD AND HELEN

–Epigraph: *Life* 1:421–422.

1. Wendell Phillips Garrison, *The Benson Family of Newport, Rhode Island* (New York: Nation Press, 1872); "Privately Published."

2. Information on Brown, Benson & Ives was culled from James B. Hedges, *The Browns of Providence Plantations: The Nineteenth Century* (Providence: Brown University Press, 1968).

3. The *Rising Sun,* whose maiden voyage began on January 15, 1792, carried Spanish coins, cordage, bar iron, steel, whale oil, rum, beef, and flour. Subsequent trips took place on the *George Washington, Ann, Hope, John Jay,* and *Friendship.* Their cargoes included fish, tobacco, rice, indigo, and New England rum.

4. In 1795, for example, five ships had been sent to Europe full of rice and flour. Only one made a profit. Two were seized by the British, one was wrecked and repaired at great cost, and one was lost at sea. In 1796 the fall in the price of rice cost the company $35,000 while a storm off the Irish coast resulted in the loss of the *Elizabeth,* then carrying $5,000 worth of flour.

5. The children included Frances (b. 1794), Mary (b. 1797), Sarah (b. 1799), Anne Elizabeth, called Anna (b. 1801), Charlotte (b. 1803), George (1806–7), George William (b. 1808), Helen Eliza (b. 1811), and Henry Egbert (b. 1814).

6. Information on the Benson home courtesy of the Rhode Island Historical Society Library.

7. Hedges, *Browns of Providence Plantations,* p. 38.

8. Information on the history of Friendship Valley and parts of Brooklyn, Connecticut, courtesy of Beverly and Charles Yates, proprietors of Friendship Valley Bed and Breakfast Inn, Brooklyn, Connecticut.

9. William Lloyd Garrison, *Helen Eliza Benson: A Memorial* (Cambridge, Mass.: Riverside Press, 1876), p. 9; "Printed for Private Presentation."

10. For more on the Underground Railroad, see Horatio T. Strother, *The Underground Railroad in Connecticut* (Middletown, Conn.: Wesleyan University Press, 1962); and Wilbur H. Siebert, *The Underground Railroad in Massachusetts* (Worcester, Mass.: American Antiquarian Society, 1936). In order to maintain security, only a few people were knowledgeable of the entire railroad network. Included in this group were Samuel J. May, Harriet Tubman, and Frederick Douglass.

11. For detailed studies on pacifism during the nineteenth century, see Peter Brock, *Pacifism in the United States: From the Colonial Era to the First World War* (Princeton, N.J.: Princeton University Press, 1968); and Charles Chatfield, *The American Peace Movement: Ideals and Activism* (New York: Twayne Publishers, 1992).

12. Throughout this book, general information on William Lloyd Garrison's background and politics that does not derive from primary sources is adapted from William E. Cain, ed., *William Lloyd Garrison and the Fight against Slavery* (Boston: Bedford Books of St. Martin's Press, 1995); John Jay Chapman, *William Lloyd Garrison* (New York: Moffat, Yard, 1913); George M. Fredrickson, *William Lloyd Garrison* (Englewood Cliffs, N.J.: Prentice-Hall, 1968); Oliver Johnson, *William Lloyd Garrison and His Times* (Boston: B. B. Russell, 1879); Henry Mayer, *All on Fire: William Lloyd Garrison and the Abolition of Slavery* (New York: St. Martin's Press, 1998); Walter M. Merrill, *Against Wind and Tide: A Biography of Wm. Lloyd Garrison* (Cambridge: Harvard University Press, 1963); James Brewer Stewart, *William Lloyd Garrison and the Challenge of Emancipation* (Arlington Heights, Ill.: Harlan Davidson, 1992); and John L. Thomas, *The Liberator: William Lloyd Garrison: A Biography* (Boston: Little, Brown, 1955). Information about abolitionism in general is based upon many sources, including Richard O. Curry and Lawrence B. Goodheart, "'Knives in their Heads': Passionate Self-Analysis and the Search for Identity in American Abolitionism," *Canadian Review of American Studies* 14, no. 4 (winter 1983): 401–414; Martin Duberman, ed., *The Antislavery Vanguard: New Essays on the Abolitionists* (Princeton, N.J.: Princeton University Press, 1965); Aileen S, Kraditor, *Means and Ends in American Abolitionism: Garrison and His Critics on Strategy and Tactics,* 1834–1850 (New York: Pantheon Books, 1967); and Lewis Perry, *Radical Abolitionism* (Ithaca, N.Y.: Cornell University Press; reprint, Knoxville: University of Tennessee Press, 1995). Many other secondary sources on abolitionism are listed in notes throughout the text.

13. Lloyd had just left Benjamin Lundy's *Genius of Universal Emancipation* and was new on the lecture trail. Samuel J. May's acquaintance with Lundy led him to Lloyd's lecture.

14. *Liberator* 1, no. 1 (January 1, 1831): 1. For an interesting take on events surrounding the nation at this time, see Louis P. Masur, *1831: Year of Eclipse* (New York: Hill and Wang, 2001).

15. For other versions of the courtship, see Mayer, *All on Fire;* and Walter McIntosh Merrill, "'A Passionate Attachment': William Lloyd Garrison's Courtship of Helen Eliza

Benson," *New England Quarterly* 29, no. 2 (June 1956): 182–203, which was adapted into a chapter in his book, *Against Wind and Tide.*

16. *Life* 1:422.

17. For more on Prudence Crandall, see Susan Strane, *A Whole-Souled Woman: Prudence Crandall and the Education of Black Women* (New York: W. W. Norton, 1990); and "The Prudence Crandall Museum," Routes 14 and 169, Canterbury, Connecticut (brochure).

18. "The Prudence Crandall Museum."

19. WLG to GWB, November 25, 1833, *Letters* 1:119.

20. Garrison, *Helen Eliza Benson,* p. 18.

21. For a detailed discussion of the "cult of true womanhood," see Barbara Welter, "The Cult of True Womanhood: 1820–1860," *American Quarterly* 18 (1966): 151–174.

22. An Old Bachelor to the editor of the Boston *Courier,* December 16, 1828, *Letters* 1:71.

23. Garrison, *Helen Eliza Benson,* p. 12.

24. *Life* 1:422–423.

25. WLG to HEB, January 18, 1834, bMSAm1906, f. 44, GF:HHU.

26. WLG to HEB, February 18, 1834, bMSAm1906, f. 44, GF:HHU.

27. WLG to HEB, March 8, 1834, bMSAm1906, f. 44, GF:HHU.

28. WLG to HEB, March 19, 1834, bMSAm1906, f. 44, GF:HHU.

29. HEB to WLG, March 21, 1834, bMSAm1906, f. 13, GF:HHU.

30. WLG to HEB, March 26, 1834, bMSAm1906, f. 44, GF:HHU.

31. WLG to GWB, March 29, 1834, bMSAm1906, f. 44, GF:HHU.

32. HEB to WLG, April 3, 1834, bMSAm1906, f. 13, GF:HHU.

33. WLG to HEB, April 5, 1834, bMSAm1906, f. 44, GF:HHU.

34. HEB to WLG, May 22, 1834, bMSAm1906, f. 13, GF:HHU.

35. WLG to HEB, May 30, 1834, bMSAm1906, f. 44, GF:HHU.

36. WLG to HEB, May 23, 1834, bMSAm1906, f. 44, GF:HHU.

37. WLG to HEB, May 16, 1834, bMSAm1906, f. 44, GF:HHU.

38. HEB to WLG, May 22, 1834, bMSAm1906, f. 13, GF:HHU.

39. WLG to HEB, May 30, 1834, bMSAm1906, f. 44, GF:HHU.

40. WLG to HEB, June 2, 1834, bMSAm1906, f. 44, GF:HHU.

41. HEB to WLG, June 2, 1834, bMSAm1906, f. 13, GF:HHU.

42. HEB to WLG, June 9, 1834, bMSAm1906, f. 13, GF:HHU.

43. In one of the poems that remained private, the first letters of each line spell Helen's full name, "Helen Eliza Benson."

> **H**ow beautiful is morn upon the hills!
> **E**'en so art thou whose sight my bosom thrills:
> **L**ove kindles in my heart its vestal flame,
> **E**lectrifies and runs through all my frame;
> **N**or would I from this soft captivity
>
> **E**nfranchisement desire, away from thee.
> **L**et Heaven bear witness to the pledge I give—

In weal or wo to love thee while I live;
Zealous to strow thy path with fadeless flowers,
And gild with rapture's rays the flying hours.

Beautiful girl! my chosen one! my pride!
Elect as mistress—soon to be my bride—
Not all the strong attractions of the earth
Shall draw my heart like thy magnetic worth:
Obedient—constant—kind, I'll ever be,
Nor doubt to meet a sweet return from thee.
WLG to HEB, June 25, 1834, bMSAm1906, f. 44, GF:HHU.

44. "A Letter, My Love!" *Liberator* 4, no. 16 (April 19, 1834): 64.

45. As quoted in WLG to HEB, May 1, 1834, bMSAm1906, f. 44, GF:HHU.

46. WLG to HEB, May 23, 1834, bMSAm1906, f. 44, GF:HHU.

47. HEB to WLG, June 2, 1834, bMSAm1906, f. 13, GF:HHU.

48. HEB to WLG, June 16, 1834, bMSAm1906, f. 13, GF:HHU.

49. WLG to HEB, June 21, 1834, bMSAm1906, f. 44, GF:HHU.

50. WLG to GWB, September 12, 1834, *Letters* 1:411–414.

51. Garrison, *Helen Eliza Benson,* p. 21.

52. Interestingly, during their first year of marriage, Lloyd had the opportunity to accompany his aunt Charlotte to New Brunswick. The two went in search of a supposed inheritance from Fanny's family. For the first time since 1810, when he was a small child, Lloyd saw Fanny's sister Nancy, who "sobbed and wept like a child, for gladness of heart" when she saw the two relatives. Nancy and her husband, John Delap, had a comfortable life, owning two farms and many cattle. As Lloyd questioned his aunt and uncle, he learned that the inheritance due him and Charlotte consisted of a small amount of property, part of sixty acres of land on Deer Island about three miles from Eastport. Fanny's brother, Plato Lloyd, had long since taken possession of the property, and although he promised the two he would help seek an equitable settlement, they knew this could not be done without a lawyer. Lloyd figured that his share, about ten acres, was worth about five hundred dollars, the rocky and sterile soil lowering its value. He also figured, correctly, that he would never see a penny of the money. WLG to HBG, July 25, 1835, *Letters* 1:479–481.

53. WLG to Henry E. Benson, September 12, 1835, *Letters* 1:525–526.

54. WLG to GWB, September 12, 1835, *Letters* 1:527.

55. WLG to GWB, September 17, 1835, *Letters* 1:529–530.

III. ESTABLISHING THE FAMILY

–Epigraph: Fanny Garrison Villard, *William Lloyd Garrison on Non-Resistance Together with a Personal Sketch by His Daughter, Fanny Garrison Villard* (New York: Nation Press Printing, 1924), pp. 20–21.

1. *Life* 1:xiv.

2. Information on the Boston Female Anti-Slavery Society is culled from primary

sources, including Maria Weston Chapman, *Right and Wrong in Boston* (ASC:BPL), and Sarah H. Southwick, *Reminiscences of Early Anti-Slavery Days* (Cambridge, Mass.: Riverside Press, 1893); and Debra Gold Hansen, *Strained Sisterhood: Gender and Class in the Boston Female Anti-Slavery Society* (Amherst: University of Massachusetts Press, 1993).

3. Theodore Lyman, *Papers Relating to the Garrison Mob* (Cambridge, Mass.: Welch, Bigelow, 1870).

4. WLG as cited in *Life* 2:12.

5. Maria Weston Chapman as cited in *Life* 2:15.

6. WLG to GWB, October 26, 1835, *Letters* 1:544.

7. HBG to Caroline Weston, October 31, 1835, ASC:BPL.

8. Information on family planning is culled from James Reed, *The Birth Control Movement and American Society: From Private Vice to Public Virtue* (Princeton, N.J.: Princeton University Press, 1978).

9. Neither Helen nor Lloyd actually wrote about their feelings on family planning. Helen, in particular, was far too self-conscious to discuss the issue, and Lloyd respected her sense of privacy. The pattern was set in the aftermath of the mob when Lloyd wrote in the *Liberator* that "the delicate state of Mrs. Garrison's health" was one of the main reasons he took refuge in Brooklyn. Apparently Helen reprimanded him for referring so publicly to her pregnancy. He responded that the reference was necessary in order to help dispel the image of him as a coward. However, he admitted to his readers that he "expected" Helen's "gentle scolding. . . . My dear wife is much more sensitive than the Queen of England, in a matter like this." *Liberator* 5, no. 45 (November 7, 1835): 179; WLG to HBG, November 14, 1835, *Letters* 1:555.

10. *Life* 4:232.

11. "Private Life and Last Hours," letter from Oliver Johnson in the *New York Tribune,* May 25, 1879, in Garrison Family Scrapbook, bMSAm1906, f. 688–689, GF:HHU.

12. All sonnet quotes taken from WLG, "To My First-Born," in *Sonnets and Other Poems* (Boston: Oliver Johnson, 1843), pp. 44–47; and "Sonnets," *Liberator* 6, no. 8 (February 20, 1836): 31.

13. WLG to Sarah T. Benson, January 20, 1838, *Letters* 2:336–338. There seems to be a confusion about the exact date of William's birth. Although this letter was dated January 20, all future references to William's birthdate, including obituaries and family letters, give it as January 21. Lloyd must have misdated this letter.

14. WLG to HBG, July 3, 1840, *Letters* 2:659–660.

15. WLG to HBG, May 15, 1840, *Letters* 2:611–612.

16. WLG to HBG, May 16, 1840, *Letters* 2:614.

17. WLG to HBG, May 19, 1840, *Letters* 2:615–617.

18. WLG to HBG, June 14, 1840, *Letters* 2:642–643.

19. WLG to Elizabeth Pease, November 15, 1846, *Letters* 3:452.

20. WLG to GWB, September 10, 1842, *Letters* 3:100.

21. The family's spelling of "Fanny," "Charley," "Franky," and "Lizzy" was inconsistent. From time to time, each ended in an *-ie.* For consistency, I have chosen to use the more common spelling, "Charley," "Fanny," "Franky," and "Lizzy" unless spelled otherwise in a direct quote.

22. WLG to Louisa Gilman Loring, January 11, 1845, *Letters* 3:275–276.

23. WLG to GWB, December 11, 1846, *Letters* 3:460.

24. WLG to Elizabeth Pease, April 1, 1847, *Letters* 3:474–475.

25. WLG to Elizabeth Pease, May 3, 1848, *Letters* 3:555–557.

26. Ibid.

27. HBG to Ann Greene Phillips, August 9, 1848, bMSAm1953, f. 1427, WP:HHU.

28. Information on medical treatments is culled from Paul Starr, *The Social Transformation of American Medicine* (New York: Basic Books, 1982).

29. WLG to GWB, March 10, 1838, *Letters* 2:341–342.

30. Information on water cures is adapted from Susan E. Cayleff, *Wash and Be Healed: The Water-Cure Movement and Women's Health* (Philadelphia: Temple University Press, 1987).

31. WLG to Maria W. Chapman, July 19, 1848, *Letters* 3:566.

32. HBG to Ann Phillips, August 13, 1848, bMSAm1953, f. 1427, WP:HHU.

33. WLG to Elizabeth Pease, June 20, 1849, *Letters* 3:618–622.

34. Ibid.

35. Ibid.

36. HBG to Ann Phillips, n.d., bMSAm1953, f. 1427, WP:HHU.

37. HBG to Henry C. Wright, July 15, 1849, Ac. 74–6, b. 3, f.1, GF:WSU.

38. Mary Grew to HBG, October 14, 1849, Ms.A.1.2, v. 18, p. 78, GF:BPL.

39. The following description of WLG is derived from Harriet Martineau, *Retrospect of Western Travel* (London: Saunders and Otley, 1838), pp. 216–220.

40. WLGJR to WPG, February 25, 1857, b. 3, f. 51, GF:SC.

41. WLGJR to WLG, January 3, 1859, b. 3, f. 55, GF:SC.

42. Inscription in WLGJR's Bible "on the completion of his 37th birthday, January 21, 1875." b. 3, f. 60, GF:SC.

43. WLG to GWB, November 27, 1835, *Letters* 1:560–561.

44. Lloyd also felt that a nonresister could pay the government's fine for refusing to participate in militia training. If that money was then used to pay a replacement "to do the work of butchery," he claimed, "mine is not the responsibility. The government is doubly guilty; first, in exacting the money—and secondly, in perverting it to such horrid use." These thoughts and even these exact words would be used by sons William and Wendell in chapter 6 with reference to the Civil War. WLG to Charles Stearns, February 10, 1840, *Letters* 2:561.

45. For more on this aspect of peace movement history, see Lawrence R. Jannuzzi, "William Lloyd Garrison and the Crisis of Nonresistance," *Historical Journal of Massachusetts,* winter 1994, pp. 21–43; and Valarie H. Ziegler, *The Advocates of Peace in Antebellum America* (Bloomington: Indiana University Press, 1992).

46. The militia episode is adapted from Walter M. Merrill, *Against Wind and Tide: A Biography of Wm. Lloyd Garrison* (Cambridge: Harvard University Press, 1963), pp. 31–32.

47. WLG to John Farmer, June 6, 1837, *Letters* 2:265.

48. WLG to Elizabeth Pease, April 1, 1847, *Letters* 3:476.

49. WLG to John W. LeBarnes, April 29, 1858, *Letters* 4:521.

50. WLG to Joseph H. Kimball, August 16, 1837, *Letters* 2:285.

51. WLG to Levi Woodbury, March 14, 1845, *Letters* 3:292.

52. Information on the Grimké sisters is adapted from Gerda Lerner, *The Grimké Sisters from South Carolina* (New York: Schocken Books, 1967); Edward T. James et. al, *Notable American Women*, vol. 2 (Cambridge: Belknap Press of Harvard University Press, 1971), pp. 97–99; and Pamela Robinson-Durso, "'The Power of Woman': Sarah Moore Grimké, Abolitionist and Feminist of the 1830s" (Ph.D. diss., Baylor University, 1992). Information on Garrisonians and woman's rights can be found in Lori D. Ginzberg, *Women in Antebellum Reform* (Wheeling, Ill.: Harlan Davidson, 2000); Blanche Glassman Hersh, *The Slavery of Sex: Feminist-Abolitionists in America* (Urbana: University of Illinois Press, 1978); Kristin Hoganson, "Garrison Abolitionists and the Rhetoric of Gender, 1850–1860," *American Quarterly* 45, no. 4 (December 1993): 558–595; Nancy Gale Isenberg, "'Coequality of the Sexes': The Feminist Discourse of the Antebellum Women's Rights Movement in America" (Ph.D. diss., University of Wisconsin, 1990); Julie Roy Jeffrey, *The Great Silent Army of Abolitionism: Ordinary Women in the Antislavery Movement* (Chapel Hill: University of North Carolina Press, 1998); Kathryn Kish Sklar, *Women's Rights Emerges within the Antislavery Movement, 1830–1870* (New York: Bedford Books of St. Martin's Press, 2000); and "'Women Who Speak for an Entire Nation': American and British Women Compared at the World Anti-Slavery Convention, London, 1840," *Pacific Historical Review*, November 1990, pp. 453–499; Anna M. Speicher, "'Faith Which Worketh by Love': The Religious World of Female Antislavery Lecturers" (Ph.D. diss., Georgetown University, 1996); Dorothy Sterling, *Ahead of Her Time: Abby Kelley and the Politics of Antislavery* (New York: W. W. Norton, 1991); Clare Taylor, *Women of the Anti-Slavery Movement: The Weston Sisters* (New York: St. Martin's Press, 1995); and Jean Fagan Yellin and John C. Van Horne, eds., *The Abolitionist Sisterhood: Women's Political Culture in Antebellum America* (Ithaca, N.Y.: Cornell University Press, 1994).

53. Angelina E. Grimké, "Appeal to the Christian Women of the South," reprinted in Larry Ceplair, ed., *The Public Years of Sarah and Angelina Grimké* (New York: Columbia University Press, 1989), pp. 36–79; quotes from pp. 55–57.

54. WLG to Harriott Plummer, March 4, 1833, *Letters* 1:208.

55. Information on the Philadelphia abolitionists is adapted from Margret Hope Bacon, *Valiant Friend: The Life of Lucretia Mott* (New York: Walker, 1980).

56. WLG to HBG, September 21, 1838, *Letters* 2:390.

57. *Declaration of Sentiments* as reprinted in *Life* 2:231.

58. WLG to Oliver Johnson, May 22, 1840, *Letters* 2:627.

59. Information on African-American support for WLG is culled from primary sources and Patrick T. J. Browne, "'To Defend Mr. Garrison': William Cooper Nell and the Personal Politics of Antislavery," *New England Quarterly* 70 (September 1997): 415–442; Lawrence J. Friedman, *Gregarious Saints: Self and Community in American Abolitionism, 1830–1870* (New York: Cambridge University Press, 1982); James Oliver Horton and Lois E. Horton, *Black Bostonians: Family Life and Community Struggle in the Antebellum North* (New York: Holmes and Meier Publishers, 1979); Donald M. Jacobs, ed., *Courage and Conscience: Black and White Abolitionists in Boston* (Bloomington: Indiana University Press, 1993); Benjamin Quarles, *Black Abolitionists* (New York: Oxford University Press,

1969); and Shirley J. Yee, *Black Women Abolitionists: A Study in Activism, 1828–1860* (Knoxville: University of Tennessee Press, 1992).

60. *Liberator* 11, no. 46 (November 17, 1832): 183.

61. Charlotte Forten Grimké, *The Journals of Charlotte Forten Grimké,* ed. Brenda Stevenson (New York: Oxford University Press, 1988), p. 64.

62. WLG as cited in Janice Sumler-Lewis, "The Forten-Purvis Women of Philadelphia and the American Anti-Slavery Crusade," *Journal of Negro History* 65–66 (1980–81): 281–288.

63. Conversation with David Lloyd Garrison, May 8, 1995, in Lincoln, Massachusetts.

64. Information on Frederick Douglass is culled from primary sources and Frederick Douglass, *Narrative of the Life of Frederick Douglass, An American Slave: Written by Himself,* ed. David W. Blight (Boston: Bedford Books of St. Martin's Press, 1993); and William S. McFeely, *Frederick Douglass* (New York: W. W. Norton, 1991).

65. WLG as cited in McFeely, *Frederick Douglass,* p. 95.

66. WLG to HBG, October 20, 1847, *Letters* 3:532–533.

IV. RAISING LITTLE GARRISONS

–Epigraph: WPG to WLG, March 2, 1876, bMSAm1321, f. 814, FGV:HHU.

1. Fanny Garrison Villard, *William Lloyd Garrison on Non-Resistance Together with a Personal Sketch by His Daughter, Fanny Garrison Villard* (New York: Nation Press Printing Co., 1924), pp. 20–21.

2. Background information on abolitionist families is culled from primary sources and Margret Hope Bacon, "Abby Hopper Gibbons: Pioneer in Prison Reform" (typescript, 1993); Ira V. Brown, *Mary Grew: Abolitionist and Feminist (1813–1896)* (Selinsgrove, Pa.: Susquehanna University Press, 1991); Sibyl Ventress Brownlee, "'Out of Abundance of the Heart': Sarah Ann Parker Remond's Quest for Freedom" (Ph.D. diss.: University of Massachusetts Amherst, 1997); Elizabeth Buffum Chace and Lucy Buffum Lovell, *Two Quaker Sisters* (New York: Liveright Publishing Corporation, 1937); Chris Dixon, *Perfecting the Family: Antislavery Marriages in Nineteenth-Century America* (Amherst: University of Massachusetts Press, 1997); Eve Lewis Perera and Lucille Salitan, ed., *Virtuous Lives: Four Quaker Sisters Remember Family Life, Abolitionism, and Women's Suffrage* (New York: Continuum Publishing Company, 1994); Dorothy Burnett Porter, *The Remonds of Salem, Massachusetts: A Nineteenth-Century Family Revisited* (Worcester: American Antiquarian Society, 1986); Elizabeth Cooke Stevens, "'From Generation to Generation': The Mother and Daughter Activism of Elizabeth Buffum Chace and Lillie Chace Wyman" (Ph.D. diss.: Brown University, 1993).

3. WLG to HBG, April 18, 1853, *Letters* 4:232.

4. The average number of children born to women in the United States was 6.4 in 1800 and 4.9 in 1850.

5. Edmund Quincy as quoted in *Life* 3:71–72.

6. Laura P. Boyle to Abby Kelley, April 15, 1845, f. 2.B, KF:WHM.

7. Wendell Phillips as quoted in *Life* 3:154.

8. WLG to Phoebe Jackson, May 1–June 10, 1843, *Letters* 3:155.

9. Edmund Quincy as cited in *Life* 4:323.

10. WLG to Drs. Clark and Potter, January 23, 1851, *Letters* 4:47.

11. WLG to HBG, February 19, 1857, *Letters* 4:435.

12. HEB to Rebecca Buffum, 1833, WLG:MHS.

13. WLG to HBG, June 1, 1836, *Letters* 2:118; William Andrus Alcott, *The Young Mother, or Management of Children in Regard to Health,* 2nd ed. (Boston: Light and Stearns, 1836).

14. Villard, *William Lloyd Garrison on Non-Resistance,* pp. 1–2.

15. FGV as cited in *Life* 4:332

16. John S. C. Abbott, *The Mother at Home* (Boston: Crocker and Brewster, 1833). Information on violence against children is culled from Elizabeth Pleck, *Domestic Tyranny: The Making of Social Policy against Family Violence from Colonial Times to the Present* (New York: Oxford University Press, 1987).

17. Abbott, *Mother at Home,* p. 12.

18. Lydia Maria Child as quoted in Deborah Pickman Clifford, *Crusader for Freedom: A Life of Lydia Maria Child* (Boston: Beacon Press, 1992), p. 97.

19. Ibid.

20. WLG as cited in *Life* 4:312.

21. Lydia Maria Child, *The Mother's Book,* 2nd ed. (Boston: Carter and Hendee, 1831), p. 9.

22. Ibid., pp. 15–16.

23. Ibid., p. 37.

24. Lucretia Mott as cited in Margret Hope Bacon, *Valiant Friend: The Life of Lucretia Mott* (New York: Walker, 1980), p. 83.

25. Unsigned, *New York Times,* June 4, 1879, Garrison Family Scrapbook, bMSAm1906, GF:HHU. (The author was most likely Oliver Johnson, whose biography of Garrison carried the same sentiment.)

26. Wendell Phillips to HBG, August 20, 1847, Ms.A.1.2 v. 17, p. 64, GF:BPL.

27. HBG to Ann Phillips, August 24, 1847, bMSAm1953, f. 1427, WP:HHU.

28. Ibid.

29. HBG to Ann Phillips, August 8, 1846, bMSAm1953, f. 1427, WP:HHU.

30. HBG to Ann Phillips, n.d., bMSAm1953, f. 1427, WP:HHU.

31. HBG to Ann Phillips, September 21, 1851, bMSAm1953, f. 1427, WP:HHU.

32. HBG to Ann Phillips, July 22, 1850, bMSAm1953, f. 1427, WP:HHU.

33. WPG to parents, October 19, 1852, bMSAm1906, f. 372, GF:HHU.

34. WPG to FG, April 20, 1865, bMSAm1321, f. 814, FGV:HHU.

35. WLG to HBG, August 13, 1846, *Letters* 3:368.

36. WLG to WLGJR, January 7, 1858, *Letters* 4:503.

37. HBG to FGV, July 11, 1872, bMSAm1321, f. 813, FGV:HHU.

38. *Life* 4:331–332.

39. Ibid., p. 331.

40. Villard, *William Lloyd Garrison on Non-Resistance,* pp. 1–2.

41. Sarah H. Southwick, *Reminiscences of Early Anti-Slavery Days* (Cambridge, Mass.: Riverside Press, 1893), pp. 9–10. Privately printed.

42. Elizabeth Cady Stanton, *Eighty Years and More: Reminiscences 1815–1897* (T. Fisher Unwin, 1898; reprint, New York: Schocken Books, 1971), pp. 128–129.

43. Susan B. Anthony quoted in *Life* 3:429. The date the Garrison sons gave for this citation is a bit problematic, since in 1855 Franky was already seven and Fanny eleven.

44. Edmund Quincy as quoted in Henry C. Wright, "Diary to Maria," December 2, 1847, ASC:BPL, as cited in *Letters* 3:540.

45. HBG to Ann Phillips, July 18, 1846, WP:HHU.

46. *Life* 4:313.

47. Ibid., p. 340; Villard, *William Lloyd Garrison on Non-Resistance,* p. 8.

48. WLG to GWB, January 4, 1837, *Letters* 2:201.

49. WLG to GWB, December 17, 1847, *Letters* 3:538.

50. WLG to Sarah T. Benson, January 20, 1838, *Letters* 2:338.

51. *Life* 4:329.

52. WLG to Francis Jackson, October 11, 1855, *Letters* 4:347. At approximately the same time that he received this gift, Charles Hovey granted the family a yearly sum equal to the interest on a legacy he was contemplating for Lloyd.

53. WLG to Francis Jackson, January 2, 1859, *Letters* 4:605.

54. WLG to Harriet Foster, January 14, 1839, *Letters* 2:424.

55. WLG to GWB, December 17, 1847, *Letters* 3:539.

56. WLG to GWB, May 17, 1848, *Letters* 3:558.

57. WLG to Samuel J. May, December 19, 1846, *Letters* 3:462.

58. WLG to HBG, October 10, 1848, *Letters* 3:596.

59. WLG to Wendell Phillips, January 1851, *Letters* 4:46–47.

60. Wendell Phillips as quoted in James Brewer Stewart, *Wendell Phillips: Liberty's Hero* (Baton Rouge: Louisiana State University Press, 1986).

61. WLG to Sarah T. Benson, April 8, 1837, *Letters* 2:255.

62. WLG to HBG, July 1, 1837, *Letters* 2:269.

63. HBG to Ann Phillips, July 18, 1846, bMSAm1953, f. 1427, WP:HHU.

64. WLG to HBG, 1846, bMSAm1906, f. 44, GF:HHU.

65. WLG to Henry C. Wright, December 16, 1843, *Letters* 3:240.

66. WLG to WLGJR, December 31, 1858, *Letters* 4:602.

67. WLG to HBG, April 18, 1836, *Letters* 2:82.

68. *Life* 4:309.

69. WLG to HEB, June 6, 1834, bMSAm1906, f. 44, GF:HHU.

70. FGV biography, typescript, n.d., bMSAm1321, f. 896, FGV:HHU.

71. Truth continued to visit the family through the years. In 1870, when youngest son, Frank, was twenty-two, he noted a visit from the then eighty-year-old woman. As he noted in his diary, "Sojourner Truth . . . is a wonderfully wise person. Wm. asked her why she didn't learn to read, & said people as old as she had learned. 'Pshaw, child, they don't know anything. I know too much & think too much to learn.'" FJG diary, August 8, 1870, Ac. 74–1, GF:WSU. At one point, Wendell complained that because Truth could not read, she needed constant entertaining when she visited him and Lucy.

72. WLGJR, "Abolitionists, Part I," *Chronicle,* February 8, 1896, b. 73, f. 2066, GF:SC.

73. WLGJR, "Abolitionists, Part II," *Chronicle,* February 15, 1896, b. 73, f. 2066, GF:SC.

74. WLGJR, "The Story of Harriet Tubman," *The Republican,* n.d., b. 73, f. 2066, GF:SC.

75. Villard, *William Lloyd Garrison on Non-Resistance,* p. 10.

76. Ibid., pp. 5–6.

77. FGV biography, typescript, n.d., bMSAm1321, f. 896, FGV:HHU.

78. Villard, *William Lloyd Garrison on Non-Resistance,* p. 7.

79. Ibid., p. 5.

80. WLG to FJG, August 17, 1857, *Letters* 4:474. WLG composed the "Song of the Abolitionist" in 1843. This is the second stanza.

81. Information on Henry C. Wright is adapted from primary sources and Lewis Perry, *Childhood, Marriage, and Reform: Henry Clarke Wright, 1797–1870* (Chicago: University of Chicago Press, 1980).

82. WLG to Elizabeth Pease, July 2, 1842, *Letters* 3:90–91.

83. "Juvenile Department," *Liberator* 1, no. 4 (January 22, 1831): 13. Information on similar literature for English children can be found in J. R. Oldfield, "Anti-slavery Sentiment in Children's Literature, 1750–1850," *Slavery and Abolition* 10, no. 1 (May 1989): 44–59.

84. "Juvenile Department," *Liberator* 1, no. 8 (February 19, 1831): 31.

85. *Liberator* 1, no. 13 (March 26, 1831): 51.

86. Besides "The Juvenile Department" in the *Liberator,* there is evidence that Lloyd also created a children's publication called *Youth's Cabinet.* An announcement and prospectus for the planned publication appeared in the May 12, 1837, issue of the paper. It was to be published every Friday in order to promote "the physical, intellectual, moral, and religious education of children." The magazine was to be edited by the Reverend Nathaniel Southard, a member of the New England Anti-Slavery Society. By May 19, three issues had been published although few subscriptions had been attained. By October 27, twenty-six issues had been published and there was a subscription base of 580. After this point, however, little mention of the magazine appeared in the *Liberator.* Although no copies of the short-lived newspaper appear to have survived, a *Liberator* advertisement for it gives a good idea of the contents. The sixth issue, for example, carried articles titled "The Boy who Would not Swear," "Runaway's Song," and "The Goodness of the Lord." Announcement of *Youth's Cabinet, Liberator* 7, no. 20 (May 12, 1837): 79; *Youth's Cabinet* advertisement, *Liberator* 7, no. 24 (June 9, 1837): 95.

87. All references taken from volumes 1–4 of *The Slave's Friend,* AAS.

88. *The Slave's Friend* 3, no. 2 (1838): 1.

89. *The Slave's Friend* 3, no. 9 (1838): 2.

90. *The Slave's Friend* 4, no. 11 (1839): 1.

91. An interesting story about George Washington noted his supposed courtesy to all people, regardless of race, but neglected to add that the first President was a slaveholder. *The Slave's Friend* 1, no. 2 (1836): 4–5.

92. *The Slave's Friend* 1, no. 3 (1836): 1.

93. *The Slave's Friend* 1, no. 6 (1836): 13.

94. *The Slave's Friend* 4, no. 1 (1839): 6.

95. Ibid.

96. Information on adult antislavery literature is adapted from Lorenzo Down Turner, *Anti-Slavery Sentiment in American Literature Prior to 1865* (1929; reprint, Port Washington, N.Y.: Kennikat Press, 1966); and Elizabeth B. Clark, "'The Sacred Rights of the

Weak': Pain, Sympathy, and the Culture of Individual Rights in Antebellum America," *Journal of American History* (September 1995): 463–493.

97. Ann Douglas, "Introduction: The Art of Controversy," in *Uncle Tom's Cabin or Life among the Lowly,* by Harriet Beecher Stowe (New York: Penguin Books, 1981).

98. *The Anti-Slavery Alphabet,* Philadelphia Anti-Slavery Fair, 1847, BA.

99. *Peter Parley's Tales of the Sea* (Philadelphia: DeSilver, Thomas, 1836), p. 123.

100. J. Elizabeth Jones, *The Young Abolitionists or Conversations on Slavery* (Boston: Anti-Slavery Office, 1848), p. 129, AAS.

101. *Ralph: or I Wish He Was n't Black* (Hopedale, Mass.: E. Gay, Publishers, 1855), AAS.

v. SCHOOLING AND SOCIALIZING

–Epigraph: WLGJR to WPG, September 2, 1857, b. 3, f. 51, GF:SC.

1. Sons Wendell and Frank, in particular, benefited from being named after well-to-do abolitionists, for both Wendell Phillips and Francis Jackson invested considerable sums of money in their namesakes' education.

2. WLG to HBG, May 19, 1840, *Letters* 2:617.

3. WLG to James Garrison, September 17, 1840, *Letters* 2:704.

4. WLG to Hannah Webb, March 1, 1843, *Letters* 3:130.

5. Information on the Northampton Association of Education and Industry is culled from primary sources and Christopher Clark, *The Communitarian Moment: The Radical Challenge of the Northampton Association* (Ithaca, N.Y.: Cornell University Press, 1995); and Charles A. Sheffeld, ed., *The History of Florence, Massachusetts, Including a Complete Account of the Northampton Association of Education and Industry* (Florence, Massachusetts: Published by the Editor, 1895).

6. For more on Sojourner Truth, see Nell Irvin Painter, *Sojourner Truth: A Life, A Symbol* (New York: W. W. Norton, 1996).

7. WLG to HBG, August 13, 1846, *Letters* 3:367.

8. George's lack of interest in learning may have been caused by hyperactivity, constantly changing schools, or simple childhood immaturity. His later letters and journals seem to rule out dyslexia, although he may have suffered from another type of learning disorder.

9. WLG to Henry C. Wright, December 16, 1843, *Letters* 3:240.

10. Background information on education in Massachusetts is culled from Carl F. Kaestle and Maris A. Vinovskis, *Education and Social Change in Nineteenth-Century Massachusetts* (New York: Cambridge University Press, 1980); Michael B. Katz, *The Irony of Early School Reform: Educational Innovation in Mid-Nineteenth Century Massachusetts* (Cambridge: Harvard University Press, 1968); and Marvine Lazerson, *Origins of the Urban School: Public Education in Massachusetts, 1870–1915* (Cambridge: Harvard University Press, 1971).

11. Horace Mann, *Lectures on Education* (Boston: W. B. Fowle and N. Capen, 1845).

12. WLGJR, "Quincy School Memories," n.d., bMSAm1906, f. 686–687, GF:HHU.

13. HBG to Henry C. Wright, July 15, 1849, Ac. 74–6, b. 3, f. 1, GF:WSU.

14. Background information on Dio Lewis is adapted from Mary F. Eastman, *The Biography of Dio Lewis, A.M., M.D.* (New York: Fowler and Wells, 1891); Harvey Green, *Fit*

for America: Health, Fitness, Sport and American Society (New York: Pantheon Books, 1986); and Dio Lewis, *Five-minute chats with Young Women and Certain Other Parties* (New York, 1874).

15. Lewis was educated at Auburn Academy in upstate New York. At the age of eighteen, he had become a well-respected temperance speaker and advocate. In 1856, Lewis journeyed to Europe to study German and Swedish gymnastics, which he then adapted for his use in the United States.

16. WPG to WLGJR, April 12, 1857, b. 30, f. 846, GF:SC.

17. Information on normal schools is culled from Richard J. Altenbaugh and Kathleen Underwood, "The Evolution of Normal Schools," in *Places Where Teachers Taught,* ed. John I. Goodlad, Roger Soder, and Kenneth A. Sirotnik, pp. 136–186 (San Francisco: Jossey-Bass Publishers, 1990); Merle L. Borrowman, ed., *Teacher Education in America: A Documentary History* (New York: Columbia University, Teachers College Press, 1965).

18. The historian Carroll Smith-Rosenberg indicates that Mary Grew and her sister abolitionist Margaret Burleigh were lifelong companions. See Carroll Smith-Rosenberg, "The Female World of Love and Ritual: Relations Between Women in Nineteenth-Century America," *Signs: Journal of Women in Culture and Society* 1 (1975): 1–30.

19. FG to FJG, July 13, 1862, bMSAm1321, f. 848, FGV:HHU.

20. I am indebted to David L. Reed, an alumnus of the Boston Latin School, for tracking down and sending me an overview of the school's history as it appeared in his copy of the December 1969 school catalogue.

21. "A Catalogue of the Scholars in the Latin Grammar School in Boston, October, 1852," AAS.

22. WPG to WLGJR, October 7, 1856, b. 30, f. 845, GF:SC.

23. WLGJR to HBG, July 24, 1857, b. 3, f. 48, GF:SC.

24. WPG to FG, August 25, 1861, bMSAm1169, f. 362–371, WPG:HHU.

25. "A Catalogue of the Scholars in the Latin Grammar School in Boston, 1864," p. 21, AAS.

26. FJG diary, February 10, 1868, Ac. 74–6, GF:WSU.

27. WLG to GWB, September 30, 1839, *Letters* 2:533.

28. Information on Hopedale is culled from primary sources and Adin Ballou, *Autobiography of Adin Ballou, 1803–1890,* ed. William S. Heywood (Lowell: Vox Populi Press, 1896); Ann Braude, *Radical Spirits: Spiritualism and Women's Rights in Nineteenth-Century America* (Boston: Beacon Press, 1989); Lewis Perry, *Radical Abolitionism* (Ithaca, N.Y.: Cornell University Press, 1973; reprint, Knoxville: University of Tennessee Press, 1995); and Edward K. Spann, *Hopedale: From Commune to Company Town, 1840–1920* (Columbus: Ohio State University Press, 1992).

29. *Liberator* 14, no. 44 (November 8, 1844): 174.

30. *Liberator* 22, no. 19 (May 7, 1852): 74.

31. Sarah E. Bradbury and Willie Fish as quoted in *Hopedale Reminiscences: Papers Read Before the Hopedale Ladies' Sewing Society and Branch Alliance, April Twenty-Seventh, Nineteen Hundred and Ten* (Hopedale School Press), BML:Hopedale.

32. WLG to GTG, February 18, 1851, Ac. 74–6, b. 1, f. 77, GF:WSU.

33. All quotes from *The Diamond,* vols. 1 and 2, BML:Hopedale.

34. *The Diamond* 1, no. 1 (May 1, 1851): 2.

35. For more on nineteenth-century boyhood and manhood, see E. Anthony Rotundo, *American Manhood: Transformations in Masculinity from the Revolution to the Modern Era* (New York: Basic Books, 1993). On childhood in general, see Paula S. Fass and Mary Ann Mason, eds., *Childhood in America* (New York: New York University Press, 2000).

36. *The Diamond* 1, no. 1 (March 15, 1851): 3.

37. *The Diamond* 1, no. 4 (May 15, 1851): 20.

38. *The Diamond* 1, no. 10 (August 1, 1851): 39.

39. D. B. Chapman, "A Song," *The Diamond* 2, no. 7 (December 15, 1851): 76. D. B. Chapman may have been Deborah Chapman, Maria's sister. The other stanzas read:

'Mong the hills of the North, where we boast to the world
That no slave dwells with us by permission,
The folds of that Flag by our homesteads unfurl'd,
Is but a slave-catcher's commission:
To stalk through our home,
And our neighbors to doom,
To a life of despair more dread than the tomb;
For wherever the spot that that Banner doth wave
There's nought but despair in store for the slave.

Oh! Ye who have boasted your earlier fame,
Behold now with shame your country's prostration;
Deep in infamy's pit be buried the name
That makes war to enslave a free nation;
And make her domains
But a market for chains,
While thus to the world she her vileness proclaims;
That the Star-Spangled Banner floats not o'er the brave,
But o'er *cowards* whose glory's the weak to enslave.

Behold, how the sons of your virtuous brave,
Who were martyr'd in freedom's endeavor,
Are compelled to betray the poor fugitive slave,
Who has striven his bonds to dissever.
And your statesmen combined,
O'er his limbs and his mind,
The fetters of ign'rance and iron to bind;
For the Star-Spangled Banner in triumph doth wave
O'er the land of the tyrant and the thrall of the slave.

40. *The Diamond* 1, no. 4 (May 1, 1851): 16.

41. *The Diamond* 1, no. 6 (June 1, 1851): 23.

42. *The Diamond* 1, no. 7 (June 15, 1851): 27.

43. *The Diamond* 2, no. 7 (December 15, 1851): 75.

44. FG to HBG, August 7, 1859, bMSAm1321, f. 869, FGV:HHU.

45. Lillie Buffum Chace to Lucy F. Lovell, August 13, 1861, as quoted in Lillie Buffum Chace Wyman and Arthur Crawford Wyman, *Elizabeth Buffum Chace, 1806–1899, Her Life and Its Environment,* vol. 1 (Boston: W. B. Clarke, 1914), pp. 222–223.

46. Ibid.

47. HBG to FG, August 9, 1858, Ac. 74–6, b. 1, f. 86, GF:WSU.

48. WLGJR to WLG, August 22, 1861, b. 3, f. 58, GF:SC.

49. WPG to FGV, July 5, 1886, bMSAm1321, f. 816, FGV:HHU.

50. HBG to Ann Phillips, August 9, 1858, bMSAm1953, f. 1427, WP:HHU.

51. WLGJR to FG, August 17, 1861, f. 824, FGV:HHU.

52. WPG to HBG, August 16, 1857, b. 30, f. 847, GF:SC.

53. Sallie Holley quoted in John White Chadwick, *A Life for Liberty: Anti-Slavery and Other Letters of Sallie Holley* (G. P. Putnam's Sons, 1899; reprint, New York: Negro Universities Press, 1969).

54. WLG to Oliver Johnson, August 9, 1860, *Letters* 4:686.

55. For more on the behavior of abolitionist men toward each other, see Donald Yacovone, "Abolitionists and the Language of Fraternal Love," in *Meanings for Manhood: Constructions of Masculinity in Victorian America,* ed. Mark C. Carnes and Clyde Griffen, pp. 85–95 (Chicago: University of Chicago Press, 1990).

56. WPG to Ann Phillips, July 21, 1858, bMSAm1953, f. 1427, WP:HHU.

57. Before her confinement to her bed, Ann Greene Phillips had been extremely outspoken. In 1840 she was one of the female U.S. representatives to the World Anti-Slavery Convention in London who were refused seats on the convention floor. When her husband stepped forward to propose that the women be allowed their place at the meeting, Ann sent him a message written on the back of the official program. "Please to maintain the floor—no matter what they do," she wrote. "Wendell, don't shilly-shally." Ann Phillips to Wendell Phillips, June 12, 1840, as quoted in James Brewer Stewart, *Wendell Phillips: Liberty's Hero* (Baton Rouge: Louisiana State University Press, 1986), p. 81.

58. Background information on the antislavery fairs is culled from primary sources and Lee Chambers-Schiller, "'A Good Work among the People': The Political Culture of the Boston Antislavery Fair," in *The Abolitionist Sisterhood: Women's Political Culture in Antebellum America,* ed. Jean Fagan Yellin and John C. Van Horne, pp. 249–274 (Ithaca, N.Y.: Cornell University Press, 1994); and Debra Gold Hansen, *Strained Sisterhood* (Amherst: University of Massachusetts Press, 1993), pp. 124–139.

59. James Russell Lowell, "Letter from Boston," as quoted in *Life* 3:178–184.

60. Cited in Margret Hope Bacon, *Valiant Friend: The Life of Lucretia Mott* (New York: Walker, 1980), p. 41.

61. "The Mansion of Happiness Game," AAS.

62. FJG diary, December 22, 1868, Ac. 74–1, GF:WSU.

63. FGV to HBG, February 14, 1874, bMSAm1321, f. 871, FGV:HHU.

64. WLGJR to WPG, January 3, 1858, b. 3, f. 53, GF:SC.

VI. GEORGE'S SEARCH

–Epigraph: GTG to WLGJR, September 5, 1858, b. 28, f. 787, GF:SC.

1. WLG to GWB, December 9, 1837, *Letters* 2:330.

2. WLG to Sarah T. Benson, March 5, 1838, *Letters* 2:340.

3. WLG to GWB, September 30, 1839, *Letters* 2:533–534.

4. WLG to GWB, January 4, 1840, *Letters* 2:555.

5. WLG to Henry C. Wright, December 16, 1843, *Letters* 3:240.

6. WLG to GTG, June 10, 1852, Ac. 73–1, b. 1, GF:WSU, HBG to GTG, June 10, 1852, Ac. 73–1, b. 1, GF:WSU.

7. WLG to Thomas Davis, October 6, 1854, *Letters* 4:319–320.

8. Information on the politics of the antislavery movement between 1850 and 1865 is culled from primary sources and James M. McPherson, *The Struggle for Equality: Abolitionists and the Negro in the Civil War and Reconstruction* (Princeton, N.J.: Princeton University Press, 1964). For an interesting look at one year, see Kenneth M. Stampp, *America in 1857: A Nation on the Brink* (New York: Oxford University Press, 1990).

9. The 1848 election pitted a Democratic Northerner, Lewis Cass, and the Free Soil nominee Martin Van Buren against Zachary Taylor, a Southern Whig. Both Cass and Taylor supported "popular sovereignty" of those in the territories to decide whether to have slavery or not. In response, the newly organized Free Soil Party, consisting of former Liberty Party members and other antislavery voices, adopted the slogan "Free soil, free speech, free labor, and free men." They stood in favor of the Wilmot Proviso.

10. WLG to Samuel J. May, January 13, 1850, *Letters* 4:4.

11. Information on fugitive slave cases and the Boston Vigilance Committee is based on primary sources and Benjamin Quarles, *Black Abolitionists* (New York: Oxford University Press, 1969); Jane H. Pease and William Pease, *They Who Would be Free: Blacks' Search for Freedom, 1830–1861* (Urbana: University of Illinois Press, 1974); James Brewer Stewart, *Holy Warriors: The Abolitionists and American Slavery* (New York: Hill and Wang, 1976); Joel Strangis, *Lewis Hayden and the War Against Slavery* (North Haven, Conn.: Shoestring Press, 1999); and Albert J. Von Frank, *The Trials of Anthony Burns: Freedom and Slavery in Emerson's Boston* (Cambridge: Harvard University Press, 1998).

12. Lewis Hayden, one of the most prominent leaders of Boston's African-American community, was a fugitive himself, having escaped from Kentucky in 1844. Hence, rescue work was particularly dangerous in his case. See Strangis, *Lewis Hayden,* for more on his life and work.

13. Shadrach was defended in court by an interracial team of abolitionists, including Richard Henry Dana, Jr., Robert H. Morris, Charles G. Davis, Charles List, Ellis Gray Loring, and Samuel Sewall. During the preliminary hearings, a crowd from the African-American community rushed into the courtroom, surrounded Shadrach, and whisked him away within a matter of minutes. Sometime later he arrived in Canada. Lewis Hayden, Robert H. Morris, Elizur Wright, James Scott, and Charles G. Davis were all arrested and tried for planning the action, but none of the juries could reach a verdict, so the cases were dismissed. In Sims's case, Thomas Wentworth Higginson planned an escape and

Wendell Phillips offered a bribe to the ship's captain scheduled to take Sims south, but neither effort succeeded. In another case, that of the successful October 1851 rescue of Jerry McHenry in Syracuse, twelve black and fourteen white abolitionists were indicted, the only one convicted being Enoch Reed, the single African American to come to trial. (Several others fled to Canada.) Samuel J. May and Gerrit Smith were not indicted because government officials feared their eagerness to test the constitutionality of the Fugitive Slave Law. Henceforth, rescuers became known as "Jerries" and the anniversary of McHenry's rescue was celebrated each year by abolitionist communities all over the free states.

14. Information on Thomas Wentworth Higginson is culled from R. D. Madison, introduction to *Army Life in a Black Regiment and Other Writings,* by Thomas Wentworth Higginson (1870; reprint, New York: Penguin Books, 1997); and Edward J. Renehan Jr., *The Secret Six: The True Tale of the Men Who Conspired with John Brown* (Columbia: University of South Carolina Press, 1997).

15. Information on Kansas Territory is culled from Kenneth S. Davis, *Kansas: A Bicentennial History* (New York: W. W. Norton; Nashville: American Association for State and Local History, 1976); and Samuel A. Johnson, *The Battle Cry of Freedom: The New England Emigrant Aid Company in the Kansas Crusade* (Lawrence: University of Kansas Press, 1954).

16. Henry Ward Beecher, the Brooklyn, New York, abolitionist minister, did not help matters when in 1855 he donated to each adult male of his congregation who left for Kansas a Bible, a hymnal, and a Sharps rifle, the last of which became nicknamed "Beecher's Bible." The Sharps rifle was one of the earliest breechloaders and could fire ten shots a minute. This was a much greater range than most rifles of the time and made a clear statement to proslavery settlers that these abolitionists were not of the nonresistant variety. The Brooklyn residents joined up with a group of Congregationalists from New Haven, Connecticut, led by the Reverend C. B. Lines. Together, they founded the town of Wabaunsee, thirteen miles downstream from Manhattan, Kansas. Their church became known as the "Beecher Bible and Rifle Church."

17. Background information on Nininger, Minnesota, is culled from Dudley S. Brainard, "Nininger, A Boom Town of the Fifties," *Minnesota History* 13 (June 1932): 127–151; and Theodore C. Blegen, *Minnesota: A History of the State* (Minneapolis: University of Minnesota Press, 1963).

18. WLGJR to WPG, May 3, 1857, b. 3, f. 51, GF:SC.

19. GTG to Henry C. Wright, May 2, 1857, b. 28, f. 786, GF:SC.

20. GTG to Henry C. Wright, August 9, 1857, b. 28, f. 786, GF:SC.

21. GTG to HBG, May 10, 1857, b. 28, f. 783, GF:SC.

22. GTG to HBG, June 9, 1857, b. 28, f. 783, GF:SC.

23. GTG to WLGJR, June 1, 1857, b. 28, f. 787, GF:SC.

24. GTG to WLG, July 8, 1857, b. 28, f. 783, GF:SC.

25. GTG to WLG, August 9, 1857, b. 28, f. 783, GF:SC.

26. GTG to HBG, September 20, 1857, b. 28, f. 783, GF:SC.

27. GTG to WPG, August 16, 1857, b. 28, f. 785, GF:SC.

28. "A Toast," *Emigrant Aid Journal* 1, no. 4 (July 18, 1857): 2.

29. "The Hog Nuisance," *Emigrant Aid Journal* 1, no. 2 (June 20, 1857): 3.

30. "The Indians of Minnesota," *Emigrant Aid Journal* 1, no. 11 (October 24, 1857): 2.

31. GTG to WLGJR, January 10, 1858, b. 28, f. 787, GF:SC.
32. "Proceedings of the Town Council," *Emigrant Aid Journal* 1, no. 25 (March 10, 1858): 2.
33. "Dear Sir," *Emigrant Aid Journal* 1, no. 32 (May 5, 1858): 2.
34. GTG to HBG, January 10, 1858, b. 28, f. 784, GF:SC.
35. GTG to HBG, February 7, 1858, b. 28, f. 784, GF:SC.
36. WLGJR to WPG, October 20, 1857, b. 3, f. 51, GF:SC.
37. GTG to HBG, May 13, 1858, b. 28, f. 784, GF:SC.
38. WLG to GTG, January 1, 1858, GF:PC.
39. GTG to HBG, March 14, 1858, b. 28, f. 784, GF:SC.
40. GTG to WLGJR, September 5, 1858, b. 28, f. 787, GF:SC.
41. WLGJR to WLG, October 11, 1858, b. 3, f. 52, GF:SC.
42. WLG to WLGJR, October 15, 1858, *Letters* 4:565–566.
43. George never made any money from the Nininger lots. In fact, by 1869 Nininger had even ceased to exist.
44. GTG to WLG, November 28, 1858, b. 28, f. 784, GF:SC.
45. HBG to GTG, December 12, 1858, Ac. 74–6, b. 1, f. 88, GF:WSU.
46. WLG to GTG, February 11, 1859, GF:PC.
47. GTG to WLGJR, December 26, 1858, b. 28, f. 787, GF:SC.
48. WLGJR to WPG, May 3, 1857, b. 3, f. 51, GF:SC.
49. GTG to WLGJR, May 8, 1859, b. 28, f. 787, GF:SC.
50. WLG to GTG, February 11, 1859, GF:PC.
51. GTG to WLGJR, May 8, 1859, b. 28, f. 787, GF:SC.
52. GTG to WLGJR, September 18, 1859, b. 28, f. 787, GF:SC.
53. WLG to Oliver Johnson, November 1, 1859, *Letters* 4:661.
54. WPG to GTG, April 25, 1858, Ac. 74–6, b. 1, f. 82, GF:WSU.
55. Interestingly, two months earlier, Helen had expressed the same sentiment to George when she wrote, "I think this country is doomed without a speedy dissolution of the Union takes place." HBG to GTG, February 23, 1858, Ac. 74–6, b. 1, f. 88, GF:WSU.
56. Horace Greeley as quoted in McPherson, *The Struggle for Equality*, p. 116.
57. WLGJR to FG, August 22, 1861, bMSAm1321, f. 824, FGV:HHU.
58. WLGJR to WLG, March 25, 1861, b. 3, f. 58, GF:SC.
59. HBG to Sallie Holley, December 14, 1862, bMSAm1906, f. 563, GF:HHU.
60. Background information on the draft is culled from primary sources and James M. McPherson, *Battle Cry of Freedom: The Civil War Era* (New York: Oxford University Press, 1988), pp. 490–494, 600–601.
61. WLG, "Drafting—The Hour of Trial," *Liberator* 32, no. 38 (September 19, 1862): 2.
62. WLG, "Drafting—What is the Duty of Abolitionists?" *Liberator* 32, no. 39 (September 26, 1862): 2.
63. WLGJR to Edward S. Bunker, April 28, 1861, b. 3, f. 58, GF:SC.
64. Ibid.
65. Seventy-four thousand others hired substitutes.
66. WPG, "The Trial Hour," *Liberator* 33, no. 34 (August 21, 1863): 2.
67. WLG, "Drafting—The Hour of Trial."
68. WPG, "The Trial Hour."

69. WLG, "Drafting—The Hour of Trial."

70. WPG, "The Trial Hour."

71. The court decided that because Love was partially deaf, he would not be useful in the military anyway.

72. FG to HBG, July 27, 1862, bMSAm1321, f. 869, FGV:HHU.

73. WLG to GTG, February 11, 1859, GF:PC.

74. WLG to Elizabeth Buffum Chace, August 7, 1862, *Letters* 5:106–107.

75. FG to WLGJR, August 12, 1862, bMSAm1321, f. 869, FGV:HHU.

76. HBG to FG, September 5, 1862, Ac. 74–6, b. 1, f. 97, GF:WSU.

77. FG to HBG, September 23, 1862, bMSAm1321, f. 869, FGV:HHU.

78. FGV, "How Boston Received the Emancipation Proclamation" in *The American Review of Reviews,* c. 1913, pp. 177–178, bMSAm1906, f. 100, GF:HHU.

79. Background information on black regiments in the Civil War is culled from primary sources and Peter Burchard, *"We'll Stand by the Union": Robert Gould Shaw and the Black 54th Massachusetts Regiment* (New York: Facts on File, 1993); Clinton Cox, *Undying Glory: The Story of the Massachusetts 54th Regiment* (New York: Scholastic, 1991); Joseph Russell Duncan, *Where Death and Glory Met: Colonel Robert Gould Shaw and the 54th Massachusetts Infantry* (Athens: University of Georgia Press, 1999); T. Glatthaar, *Forged in Battle: The Civil War Alliance of Black Soldiers and White Officers* (New York: Penguin Books, 1990); Thomas Wentworth Higginson, *Army Life in a Black Regiment and Other Writings;* Thomas H. O'Connor, *Civil War Boston: Home Front and Battlefield* (Boston: Northeastern University Press, 1997); Edwin S. Redkey, ed., *A Grand Army of Black Men: Letters from African-American Soldiers in the Union Army, 1861–1865* (New York: Cambridge University Press, 1992); and Susie King Taylor, *A Black Woman's Civil War Memoir,* ed. Patricia W. Romero and Willie Lee Rose (New York: Markus Wiener Publishing, 1988).

80. The history of the 55th Massachusetts Regiment is culled from primary sources and *Record of the Service of the Fifty-fifth Regiment of Massachusetts Volunteer Infantry* (1868; reprint, Salem, N.H.: Ayer Company, Publishers, 1991); Jack Abramowitz, "Documents: A Civil War Letter: James M. Trotter to Francis J. Garrison," *The Midwest Journal* 4 (summer 1952): 117–122; Noah Andre Trudeau, ed., *Voices of the 55th: Letters from the 55th Massachusetts Volunteers, 1861–1865* (Dayton, Ohio: Morningside House, 1996); Trudeau, *Like Men of War: Black Troops in the Civil War, 1862–1865* (Boston: Little, Brown, 1998); and Burt G. Wilder, *The Fifty-fifth Regiment of the Massachusetts Volunteer Infantry Colord* [sic] *June 1863–September 1865* (Brookline, Mass.: Riverdale Press, 1919).

81. WLGJR to EW, May 26, 1863, b. 3, f. 60, GF:SC.

82. WLG to GTG, June 11, 1863, *Letters* 5:160.

83. WLG to GTG, August 6, 1863, *Letters* 5:167.

84. FG to FJG, July 29, 1863, bMSAm1321, f. 880, FGV:HHU.

85. WPG to WLGJR, August 2, 1863, bMSAm1169.2, f. 296, WPG:HHU.

86. Ned's brother, Richard, who lived near Boston and would become William's employer, went to the battle area to accompany his brother home to Philadelphia. John Ritchie, another family friend and officer in the 54th, had not been in the battle—a great relief to all.

87. WLG to GTG, August 6, 1863, *Letters* 5:167.

88. GTG to HBG, August 3, 1863, b. 28, f. 788, GF:SC.

89. "Fifty Fifth Regiment Massachusetts Colored Volunteers—Extracts from Private Letters to the Editor," *Liberator* 33, no. 38 (September 18, 1863): 3.

90. James Miller McKim was one of the chief organizers of the Port Royal Experiment. More on this episode appears in chapter 7.

91. GTG to WLGJR, February 10, 1864, b. 28, f. 790, GF:SC.

92. Mon to editor, May 21, 1864, as cited in Trudeau, *Voices of the 55th*, pp. 98–99.

93. GTG to WLGJR, December 10, 1863, b. 28, f. 789, GF:SC.

94. James M. Trotter to FJG, August 2, 1864, as cited in Trudeau, *Voices of the 55th*, p. 140; and Jack Abramowitz, "Documents: A Civil War Letter."

95. Cox, *Undying Glory*, p. 127.

96. GTG to WLGJR, June 14, 1864, b. 28, f. 790, GF:SC.

97. *Life* 4:93–94.

98. For the twisted relationship between Beecher and Tilton, see Barbara Goldsmith, *Other Powers: The Age of Suffrage, Spiritualism and the Scandalous Victoria Woodhull* (New York: Alfred A. Knopf, 1998).

99. While with the *Independent*, Wendell also wrote articles for the *Liberator* under the pseudonym Maladie du Pays, and for the New York *Anti-Slavery Standard*. These are discussed in more detail in chapter 9.

100. James M. Trotter to FJG, August 2, 1864, as cited in Trudeau, *Voices of the 55th*, p. 140.

101. GTG to HBG, June 7, 1864, b. 28, f. 790, GF:SC.

102. WLG to GTG, June 10, 1864, bMSAm1321, f. 782, FGV:HHU.

103. GTG's diary excerpts, July 3, 1864, as cited in BW:CU.

104. GTG's diary excerpts, November 30, 1864, as cited in BW:CU.

105. Ibid.

106. "Mass. Fifty-Fifth Reg. Col. Vols," *Liberator* 35, no. 13 (March 31, 1865): 3.

107. "From South Carolina," *Liberator* 35, no. 30 (July 28, 1865): 4.

108. James M. Trotter to Edward W. Kinsley as cited in Trudeau, *Voices of the 55th*, pp. 182–183.

109. "Abolitionists in the War," *Liberator* 35, no. 35 (September 1, 1865): 3.

110. Others included William Jay, Joshua Leavitt, Salmon P. Chase, Abraham L. Cox, Joseph W. Alden, Charles Jewett, John Rankin, Samuel Fessenden, Leonard Brown, Jacob Heaton, H. I. Bowditch, Joseph Thompson, the Reverend Dr. Ide, Charles G. Finney, Henry Wilson, Joshua R. Giddings, and William Slade.

VII. ENTER ELLIE AND LUCY

–Epigraph: EW to MW, March 9, 1863, b. 14, f. 395, GF:SC.

1. Background information on Martha Wright is culled from Margret Hope Bacon, *Valiant Friend: The Life of Lucretia Mott* (New York: Walker, 1980).

2. There appears to be some discrepancy in the spelling of Marianna's first name. James D. Livingston, who is working on Martha's biography, discovered that Ellie's sister's name was originally Mary Anna, but Martha spelled it *Marianna*. Ellie spelled it with one *n:*

Mariana. I have chosen to use Martha's spelling, but it may be that Marianna later changed the spelling herself. James D. Livingston to author, December 21, 2000.

3. MW as quoted in Anna Davis Hallowell, *James and Lucretia Mott: Life and Letters* (Boston: Houghton Mifflin, 1884), p. 380.

4. Matthew Tallman died at age twenty-two in a drowning accident; Charles died at age one.

5. Some background information on the McKim family is culled from Wendell Phillips Garrison, *In Memoriam Sarah A. McKim 1813–1891* (New York: DeVinne Press, 1891).

6. LMcK to EW, July 6, 1851, b. 29, f. 796, GF:SC.

7. Information on Theodore Weld and Eagleswood School is culled from primary sources and Benjamin P. Thomas, *Theodore Weld: Crusader for Freedom* (New Brunswick, N.J.: Rutgers University Press, 1950).

8. EW to Hettie Wood, April 25, 1854, b. 14, f. 362, GF:SC.

9. Eagleswood School brochure, n.d., b. 65, f. 1963, GF:SC. The goals of the school included preparing students "for the general duties of life, practical and professional. Those preparing for College will be fitted for the Freshman Class, or for an advanced standing."

10. Eagleswood faculty included Theodore Weld, Angelina Grimké Weld, Sarah Grimké, Elizabeth Palmer Peabody, Catharine Iness Ireland, and Mary Mann.

11. Sarah Grimké to Elizabeth Smith Miller, September 18, 1852, as cited in Anna M. Speicher, "'Faith Which Worketh by Love': The Religious World of Female Antislavery Lecturers" (Ph.D. diss., Georgetown University, 1996), p. 182.

12. Eagleswood School brochure, n.d., b. 65, f. 1963, GF:SC.

13. Barbara Leigh Smith Bodichon, *An American Diary, 1857–8,* ed. Joseph W. Reed Jr. (London: Routledge and Kegan Paul, 1972), p. 142.

14. Theodore Weld to James Miller McKim, June 23, 1856, b. 2, MGF13, MMcG:NYPL.

15. EW to Sister, October 20, 1854, b.14, f. 360, GF:SC.

16. MW to EW, October 20, 1854, b. 35, f. 918, GF:SC.

17. MW to EW, April 3, 1855, b. 35, f. 923, GF:SC.

18. MW to EW, April 13, 1855, b. 35, f. 923, GF:SC.

19. EW to MW, August 3, 1855, b.14, f. 364, GF:SC.

20. MW to EW, August 27, 1855, b. 35, f. 923, GF:SC.

21. Information on women writers is culled from Mary Kelley, *Private Woman, Public Stage: Literary Domesticity in Nineteenth-Century America* (New York: Oxford University Press, 1984).

22. MW to EW, August 27, 1855, b. 35, f. 923, GF:SC.

23. EW's Journal, December 7, 1855, b. 90, GF:SC.

24. MW to EW, September 1, 1855, b. 35, f. 923, GF:SC.

25. EW to MW, November 12, 1855, b. 14, f. 364, GF:SC.

26. EW's Journal, December 7, 1855, b. 90, GF:SC.

27. MW to EW, January 13, 1856, b. 36, f. 929, GF:SC.

28. EW to Anna Davis, October 7, 1857, b. 14, f. 359, GF:SC.

29. MW to EW, November 20, 1857, b.36, f. 935, GF:SC.

30. EW to MW, December 13, 1858, b. 14, f. 369, GF:SC; Charlotte Forten's background

information is culled from Charlotte Forten Grimké, *The Journals of Charlotte Forten Grimké,* ed. Brenda Stevenson (New York: Oxford University Press, 1988).

31. EW to MW, December 13, 1858, b. 14, f. 369, GF:SC.

32. EW to Anna Davis, December 21, 1859, b. 14, f. 372, GF:SC.

33. EW to Anna Davis, January 6, 1860, b. 14, f. 372, GF:SC.

34. WLGJR to EW, March 11, 1864, b. 3, f. 63, GF:SC.

35. EW to LMcK, February 25, 1859, b. 14, f. 374, GF:SC.

36. EW's Journal, August 28, 1859, b. 90, GF:SC.

37. Ibid.

38. EW's Journal, September 29, 1859, b. 90, GF:SC.

39. Poem written April 18, 1860, in letter from LMcK to EW, March 12, 1861, b. 29, f. 796, GF:SC.

40. EW's Journal, March 5, 1860, b. 90, GF:SC.

41. EW's Journal, July 8, 1860, b. 90, GF:SC.

42. Whereas Ellie's words and obvious emotional feeling for both her peers and the older women reformers reflect the intimate world of women portrayed by Carroll Smith-Rosenberg ("The Female World of Love and Ritual: Relations Between Women in Nineteenth-Century America," *Signs: Journal of Women in Culture and Society* 1 [1975]), there did seem to be ample contact with men for these abolitionist daughters, especially at schools such as Eagleswood, Northampton, and Hopedale.

43. EW's Journal, September 4, 1860, b. 90, GF:SC.

44. Ibid.

45. Elizabeth Sedgwick quoted in R. DeWitt Mallary, *Lenox and the Berkshire Highlands* (New York: G. P. Putnam's Sons, 1902), p. 82.

46. EW's Journal, November 1860, b. 90, GF:SC.

47. EW to LMcK, January 1, 1861, b. 14, f. 378, GF:SC.

48. EW to MW, November 1860, b. 14, f. 376, GF:SC.

49. EW to LMcK, January 1, 1860, b. 14, f. 378, GF:SC.

50. EW's Journal, March 23, 1861, b. 90, GF:SC.

51. For more on abolitionist women and the war, see Wendy Hamand Venet, *Neither Ballots nor Bullets: Women Abolitionists and the Civil War* (Charlottesville: University Press of Virginia, 1991).

52. EW to Willy Wright, April 23, 1861, b. 14, f. 385, GF:SC.

53. EW's Journal, May 11, 1861, b. 90, GF:SC.

54. EW to Laura Stratton, April 1861, b. 14, f. 373, GF:SC.

55. EW's Journal, May 11, 1861, b. 90, GF:SC.

56. EW's Composition Book, May 1861 essay, b. 90, GF:SC.

57. Ibid., as well as second essay, May 1861, b. 90, GF:SC.

58. EW to LMcK, June 16, 1861, b. 14, f. 378, GF:SC.

59. LMcK to EW, August 26, 1861, b. 29, f. 799, GF:SC.

60. LMcK to EW, December 29, 1861, b. 29, f. 799. GF:SC.

61. LMcK to EW, August 26, 1861, b. 29, f. 799, GF:SC.

62. EW to LMcK, November 16, 1861, b. 14, f. 378, GF:SC.

63. MW cited in EW to Wm. Beverly Chase, December 3, 1861, b. 14, f. 382, GF:SC.

64. EW to LMcK, November 16, 1861, b. 14, f. 378, GF:SC.

65. EW to MW, January 12, 1862, b. 14, f. 387, GF:SC.

66. EW to Laura Stratton, May 26, 1862, b. 14, f. 388, GF:SC.

67. LMcK to EW, June 1, 1862, b. 69, f. 800, GF:SC.

68. EW to MW, May 17, 1862, b. 14, f. 387, GF:SC.

69. Information on the Port Royal Experiment and Lucy McKim's involvement in it is culled from primary sources and Dena J. Epstein, "Lucy McKim Garrison, American Musician," *NYPL Bulletin* (New York Public Library) 65 (October 1963): 529–546; Dena J. Epstein, *Sinful Tunes and Spirituals: Black Folk Music to the Civil War* (Urbana: University of Illinois Press, 1977); and Willie Lee Rose, *Rehearsal for Reconstruction: The Port Royal Experiment* (New York: Bobbs-Merrill, 1964).

70. James Miller McKim as cited in *The Underground Railroad* (no documentation), p. 665, MMcG:NYPL.

71. EW to MW, May 17, 1862, b. 14, f. 387, GF:SC.

72. "Extracts from Lucy's letter, St. Helena's Island, June 12, 1862" by EW to Wm. Beverly Chase, b. 29, f. 800, GF:SC.

73. Ibid.

74. Ibid.

75. James Miller McKim as cited in James M. McPherson, *The Struggle for Equality: Abolitionists and the Negro in the Civil War and Reconstruction* (Princeton, N.J.: Princeton University Press, 1964), p. 166.

76. McKim was not named as one of the Commission's three members. These were Robert Dale Owen, Samuel Gridley Howe, and James McKaye.

77. LMcK, from *Dwight's Journal of Music,* November 1, 1862, as reprinted in *Liberator* 32, no. 48 (November 28, 1862): 3.

78. LMcK to EW, July 3, 1862, b. 29, f. 800, GF:SC.

79. EW to LMcK, July 7, 1862, b.14, f. 378, GF:SC.

80. EW to LMcK, July 21, 1862, b. 14, f. 378, GF:SC.

81. Information on the experiences of the Chase brothers and others in the Civil War is culled from primary sources and Bruce Catton, *The Civil War* (Boston: Houghton Mifflin Company, 1960); Winston Groom, *Shrouds of Glory: From Atlanta to Nashville: The Last Great Campaign of the Civil War* (New York: Atlantic Monthly Press, 1995); James M. McPherson, *What They Fought For, 1861–1865* (New York: Doubleday, 1995); and Page Smith, *Trial by Fire* (New York: McGraw-Hill Book Company, 1982).

82. LMcK to EW, August 12, 1862, b. 29, f. 800, GF:SC.

83. EW to Wm. Beverly Chase, August 5, 1862, b. 14, f. 389, GF:SC.

84. EW to Wm. Beverly Chase, August 12, 1862, b. 14, f. 389, GF:SC.

85. For an interesting look at women's sense of patriotism, see Alice Fahs, "The Feminized Civil War: Gender, Northern Popular Literature, and the Memory of the War, 1861–1900," *Journal of American History* (March 1999): 1461–1494. Also on abolitionist daughters and the war, see Lori D. Ginzberg, *Women and the Work of Benevolence: Morality, Politics, and Class in the 19th-Century United States* (New Haven: Yale University Press, 1990).

86. LMcK to EW, August 12, 1862, b. 29, f. 800, GF:SC.

87. EW to LMcK, August 15, 1862, b. 14, f. 378, GF:SC.

88. EW to LMcK, January 24, 1863, b. 14, f. 378, GF:SC.

89. LMcK to EW, September 5, 1862, b. 29, f. 800, GF:SC.

90. EW to Wm. Beverly Chase, September 16, 1862, b. 14, f. 389, GF:SC.

91. An undated newspaper clipping of the time claimed that Dick had been reciting lines from Tennyson's "Morte D'Arthur" at the time he was shot. Biography file, GF:SC.

92. LMcK to EW, January 21, 1863, b. 29, f. 801, GF:SC.

93. LMcK to EW, February 1, 1863, b. 29, f. 801, GF:SC.

94. LMcK to EW, January 21, 1863, b. 29, f. 801, GF:SC.

95. LMcK to EW, February 1, 1863, b. 29, f. 801, GF:SC.

96. EW to Laura Stratton Birney, January 17, 1863, b. 14, f. 388, GF:SC.

97. Anna Davis Hallowell to EW, January 20, 1863, b. 51, f. 1399, GF:SC.

98. LMcK to EW, February 10, 1863, b. 29, f. 801, GF:SC.

99. Laura Stratton Birney to EW, January 24, 1863, b. 45, f. 1139, GF:SC.

100. EW to LMcK, February 12, 1863, b. 14, f. 392, GF:SC.

101. EW to MW, March 16, 1863, b. 14, f. 395, GF:SC.

102. Since Lucy and Fanny lived so far apart, their friendship did not strengthen until they became sisters-in-law. At that time, Lucy and Wendell lived in New Jersey; Fanny and her husband, Henry Villard, in New York City.

103. EW to Laura Stratton Birney, March 23, 1863, b. 14, f. 388, GF:SC. Interestingly, Ellie's impressions were similar to those made by the newest abolitionist speaking sensation, Anna E. Dickinson, who the year before had described William as "splendid . . . a specimen of simple, natural, dignified,—attractive manhood." Wendell, she thought, was the most handsome and intelligent of the sons, but "not especially lovable"; George, reserved, "the 'most stillest'" young man she knew. Fanny was "handsome, talented, & cultivated . . . full of life," while Franky, the youngest, was "the beauty and genius of the family." Anna E. Dickinson, April 28, 1862, as cited in Walter M. Merrill, *Against Wind and Tide: A Biography of Wm. Lloyd Garrison* (Cambridge: Harvard University Press, 1963), p. 282.

104. EW to Laura Stratton Birney, March 23, 1863, b. 14, f. 388, GF:SC.

105. WLG to HBG, October 28, 1858, *Letters* 4:593.

106. FG to WLGJR, January 19, 1862, b. 60, f. 1869, GF:SC.

107. EW to Laura Stratton Birney, April 20, 1863, b. 14, f. 388, GF:SC.

108. WLGJR to EW, May 26, 1863, b. 3, f. 60, GF:SC.

109. EW to WLGJR, June 13, 1863, b. 14, f. 396, GF:SC.

110. EW to Theodore Weld, September 4, 1863, b. 14, f. 398, GF:SC.

111. EW to LMcK, February 18, 1864, b. 15, f. 401, GF:SC.

112. WLG to EW, February 19, 1864, *Letters* 5:188–189.

113. EW to MW and David Wright, February 17, 1864, b. 15, f. 403, GF:SC.

114. WLGJR to MW and David Wright, February 17, 1864, b. 3, f. 62, GF:SC.

115. MW to EW, February 21, 1864, b. 38, f. 969, GF:SC.

116. Lucretia Mott to WLGJR, 3 mo. 4th. 1864, b. 74, f. 2079, GF:SC.

117. Marianna married her first cousin, Thomas Mott, a choice that her own family members had expressed concern over.

118. LMcK to WLGJR, March 1, 1864, b. 74, f. 2079, GF:SC.

119. LMcK to EW, March 1, 1864, b. 74, f. 2079, GF:SC.
120. Lizzie Powell to EW, February 16, 1864, b. 74, f. 2079, GF:SC.
121. Lizzie Powell to EW, March 1864, b. 74, f. 2079, GF:SC.
122. WLGJR to EW, February 26, 1864, b. 3, f. 63, GF:SC.
123. WLGJR to EW, July 30, 1864, b. 3, f. 69, GF:SC.
124. EW to WLGJR, July 26, 1864, b. 15, f. 405, GF:SC. As Martha's biographer, James D. Livingston, points out, David's law practice was reasonably successful, but he and Martha pinched their pennies. This may have given Ellie the impression that money was scarcer than it really was. James D. Livingston to author, December 21, 2000.
125. WLGJR to EW, May 9, 1864, b. 3, f. 67, GF:SC.
126. WLGJR to EW, August 19, 1864, b. 3, f. 71, GF:SC.
127. FG to HBG, September 13, 1864, bMSAm1321, f. 869, FGV:HHU.
128. WPG to GTG, September 17, 1864, b. 30, f. 853, GF:SC.
129. Frank and Charley were acquainted with each other as children, just as Fanny and Lucy were. However, since boys had more freedom to travel and have adventures, they grew closer in their teens than their sisters did. During the war years, Charley worked with the Philadelphia Office of Supervisory Committee for Recruiting Colored Regiments, an activity that the nonresistant Frank would not have chosen to participate in.
130. LMcK to EW, August 31, 1863, b. 29, f. 801, GF:SC.
131. WPG to WLGJR, August 23, 1863, b. 30, f. 851, GF:SC.
132. WLGJR to WPG, April 11, 1864, b. 3, f. 61, GF:SC.
133. WLGJR to EW, February 29, 1864, b. 3, f. 63, GF:SC.
134. EW to WLGJR, March 3, 1864, b. 15, f. 403, GF:SC.
135. WLGJR to EW, April 14, 1864, b. 3, f. 64, GF:SC.
136. EW to WLGJR, May 18, 1864, b. 15, f. 403, GF:SC.
137. EW to WLGJR, May 31, 1864, b. 15, f. 403, GF:SC.
138. WPG to WLGJR, July 2, 1864, b. 30, f. 852, GF:SC.
139. EW to WLGJR, June 28, 1864, b. 15, f. 405, GF:SC.
140. EW to WPG, July 14, 1864, b. 15, f. 401, GF:SC.
141. WLG to WPG, June 30, 1864, *Letters* 5:217.
142. WLG to LMcK, July 11, 1864, b. 1, f. 24, GF:SC.
143. WLGJR to EW, July 22, 1864, b. 3, f. 69, GF:SC.
144. LMcK to EW, August 11, 1864, b. 29, f. 802, GF:SC.
145. EW to WLGJR, August 29, 1864, b.15, f. 405, GF:SC.
146. EW to WLGJR, September 2, 1864, b. 15, f. 405, GF:SC.
147. WLG to Samuel J. May, December 10, 1865, *Letters* 5:356.

VIII. THE FAMILY REDEFINED

–Epigraph: WPG to WLG, August 12, 1860, bMSAm1169.2, f. 3, WPG:HHU.
1. FJG to HV, March 25, 1864, bMSAm1322, f. 136, HV:HHU.
2. EW to MW, February 6, 1864, b. 14, f. 399, GF:SC.
3. WPG to HBG, February 11, 1864, bMSAm1169.2, f. 182, WPG:HHU.
4. WLGJR to EW, April 29, 1864, b. 3, f. 64, GF:SC.

5. EWG to MW, September 25, 1864, b. 14, f. 399, GF:SC.

6. For an excellent discussion of the use of electricity, see Harvey Green, *Fit for America: Fitness, Sport and American Society* (New York: Pantheon Books, 1986), pp. 167–180.

7. W. R. Wells cited in ibid., p. 168.

8. Green paraphrased and quoted in ibid., p. 171.

9. WLG to LMcK, July 11, 1864, *Letters* 5:218.

10. *Life* 4:342.

11. HBG to WLG, September 8, 1864, Ac. 74-b, b. 1, f. 31, GF:WSU.

12. Background information on political differences within the abolitionist movement is culled from primary sources and James M. McPherson, *The Struggle for Equality: Abolitionists and the Negro in the Civil War and Reconstruction* (Princeton, N.J.: Princeton University Press, 1964).

13. WLG to HBG, May 13, 1864, *Letters* 5:203.

14. James Miller McKim to WLG, March 18, 1864, Ms.A.1.2.v. 33, p. 29b, McK:BPL.

15. James Miller McKim to WLG, May 14, 1864, Ms.A.1.2.v. 33, p. 54A, McK:BPL.

16. WLGJR to EW, May 29, 1864, b. 3, f. 67, GF:SC.

17. WLGJR to EW, June 27, 1864, b. 3, f. 67, GF:SC.

18. Ibid.

19. WLG to HBG, June 11, 1864, *Letters* 5:212.

20. WPG to FG, May 16, 1864, bMSAm1169.2, f. 362–371, WPG:HHU. Butler later served in Congress as a Republican and then as governor of Massachusetts as a Democrat.

21. Wendell Phillips to WPG, July 12, 1864, Ms.Am.123.50, WP:BPL.

22. WLGJR to EWG, February 14, 1865, b. 3, f. 76, GF:SC.

23. GTG to WPG, August 12, 1864, b. 28, f. 790, GF:SC.

24. WLG to Oliver Johnson, November 26, 1864, *Letters* 5:239–242.

25. WLG to Elizabeth Pease Nichol, October 9, 1865, *Letters* 5:302.

26. FG to WLG, November 12, 1865, Ac. 74–6, b. 1, f. 42, GF:WSU.

27. As in years past, there were frequent changes in household help, both due to the ability for Irish servants to move frequently to more lucrative or appealing positions or to the demands of taking care of an invalid and the many children and guests who frequented the house. In general, all the Garrisons, although continuously hiring Irish servants, complained about them incessantly and did not consider them appropriate providers of child care, mainly because of their Catholic views.

28. Background information on Henry Villard is culled from primary sources and Thomas Fuchs, "Henry Villard: A Citizen of Two Worlds" (Ph.D. diss., University of Oregon, 1991); Alexandra Villard de Borchgrave and John Cullen, *Villard: The Life and Times of an American Titan* (New York: Doubleday, 2001); and Henry Villard, *Memoirs of Henry Villard, Journalist and Financier,* vol. 1, *1825–1862;* vol. 2, *1863–1900* (Boston: Houghton Mifflin, 1904); Oswald Garrison Villard, "Henry Villard: A True Fairy Tale," in *What I Owe My Father,* ed. Sidney Strong (New York: Henry Holt, 1931), pp. 147–158.

29. Henry was affectionately known as "Harry." For consistency, I have chosen to use "Henry" throughout the text.

30. Villard, *Memoirs,* 1:53.

31. Ibid., p. 90.

32. Henry claimed to dislike Lincoln's fondness for telling "risky" [risqué] stories and off-color jokes. Ibid., p. 90.

33. Ibid., p. 251. Approximately 25,000 soldiers were injured at Shiloh, at least 3,500 of them dying during the fighting.

34. Ibid., 2:19.

35. Ibid., p. 52.

36. Ibid., p. 53.

37. FGV, biography (typed manuscript), n.d., bMSAm1321, f. 896, FGV:HHU.

38. Villard, *Memoirs,* 2:53.

39. Ibid., p. 55.

40. HV to FJG, May 3, 1863, bMSAm1322, f. 541, HV:HHU.

41. FJG to HV, May 10, 1863, bMSAm1322, f. 135, HV:HHU.

42. FJG to HV, September 25, 1864, bMSAm1322, f. 136, HV:HHU.

43. WLGJR to EW, March 29, 1864, b. 3, f. 63, GF:SC.

44. WLG to LMcK, July 11, 1864, *Letters* 5:219.

45. HV to FJG, August 10, 1864, bMSAm1322, f. 541, HV:HHU.

46. FJG to HV, September 25, 1864, bMSAm1322, f. 136, HV:HHU.

47. HV to FJG, April 27, 1865, bMSAm1322, f. 542, HV:HHU.

48. EWG to MW, May 1, 1865, b. 15, f. 407, GF:SC.

49. WLG to WPG, May 25, 1865, b.1, f. 24, GF:SC.

50. HBG to HV, May 25, 1865, bMSAm1322, f. 144, HV:HHU.

51. WLGJR to HBG, May 30, 1865, b. 3, f. 79, GF:SC.

52. FG to WLG, June 1865, bMSAm1321, f. 881, FGV:HHU.

53. EWG to MW, January 8, 1866, b. 15, f. 415, GF:SC.

54. WLG to FGV, January 7, 1866, bMSAm1321, f. 823, FGV:HHU.

55. FJG to FGV, January 2, 1916, bMSAm1321, f. 812, FGV:HHU.

56. FGV to HBG, January 4, 1866, HV to HBG, January 13, 1866, bMSAm1321, f. 869, FGV:HHU.

57. FGV to EWG, January 19, 1866, bMSAm1321, f. 846, FGV:HHU.

58. At one point, Fanny visited Campbell Hospital, a facility used to help newly freed people get on their feet. There she met up with Sojourner Truth.

59. HBG to FJG, February 20, 1866, Ac. 74–6, b. 2, f. 8, GF:WSU.

60. "Extract from the Journal of Dr. Arthur Howard Nichols, 1876," Ac. 73–1, b. 8, GF:WSU.

61. WLG to WLGJR, September 11, 1867, Ac. 73–1, b. 1, GF:WSU.

62. Sarah McKim to Charles McKim, June 7, 1866, b. 1MGF, MMcG:NYPL.

63. WLGJR to EWG, August 15, 1865, b. 3, f. 77, GF:SC.

64. WLGJR to LMcKG, June 24, 1866, b. 3, f. 84, GF:SC.

65. FJG to FGV, June 17, 1866, bMSAm1321, f. 782, FGV:HHU.

66. HBG to FGV, August 23, 1866, Ac. 73–1, b. 1, GF:WSU.

67. HBG to FGV, n.d., bMSAm1321, f. 813, FGV:HHU.

68. HBG to FGV, July 11, 1872, bMSAm1321, f. 813, FGV:HHU.

69. EWG to MW, December 3, 1866, b. 15, f. 415, GF:SC.

70. WLGJR to FJG, February 24, 1867, b. 15, f. 417, GF:SC.

71. WPG to WLG, May 5, 1867, bMSAm1169.2, f. 42, WPG:HHU.

72. WPG and LMcKG to HBG, July 7, 1867, bMSAm1169.2, f. 218, WPG:HHU.

73. EWG to FGV, October 10, 1866, b. 15, f. 413, GF:SC.

74. WLG to FGV, February 19, 1867, bMSAm1321, f. 823, FGV:HHU.

75. WLG to HBG, May 15, 1867, *Letters* 5:483.

76. HBG to WLG, May 19, 1867, bMSAm1906, f. 13, GF:HHU.

77. While in Paris, the Garrisons and Henry visited the African-American abolitionist Sarah Remond and her sister, Caroline Putnam, who had emigrated from Salem, Massachusetts, to Europe in order to live in a racially more tolerant society. Remond attended medical school in Italy and, for a time, practiced medicine there.

78. During the summer, Henry was summoned to Munich, where his father lay dying. He died on September 1.

79. Just a few of the references to spiritualism include FJG diaries, January 21, February 11, 12, 13, March 7, 8, April 29, May 2, 1868, Ac. 74–1, GF:WSU.

80. WLG to FGV, December 12, 1867, *Letters* 5:559.

81. In December 1869, Helen again felt isolated and useless when Fanny's labor came on so unexpectedly and quickly that baby Harold arrived ten minutes before the doctor and thirty minutes before Ellie arrived. Fanny and the Garrison's cook, Ellen Cronan, delivered the child. As Frank noted in his diary, "Poor Mother was alone in bed & couldn't get to Fanny & Ellen, the cook was the only one with Fanny." FJG diary, December 3, 1869, Ac. 74–1, GF:WSU.

82. For discussions on posttraumatic stress disorder during and after the Civil War, see Eric T. Dean, *Shook Over Hell: Post-Traumatic Stress, Vietnam, and the Civil War* (Cambridge: Harvard University Press, 1997); and Gordon Jones, "*Gone for a Soldier:* Transformed by War, 1861–1865," *Atlanta History* 37 (fall 1993): 36–49.

83. HBG to FGV, April 28, 1867, Ac. 74–6, b. 2, f. 42, GF:WSU.

84. Wendell's career at the *Nation* is covered in some detail in chapter 9.

85. LMcKG to EWG, July 9, 1869, b. 29, f. 803, GF:SC.

86. GTG to HBG, January 29, 1871, bMSAm1169.2, f. 240, WPG:HHU.

87. At this time, Wendell helped George apply for a patent for a "snuff and pen holder," but apparently nothing came of it. GTG to WLGJR, February 13, 1871, b. 28, f. 791a, GF:SC.

88. FGV to FJG, July 31, 1870, bMSAm1321, f. 848, FGV:HHU.

89. FJG diary, March 15, 1868, Ac. 74–1, GF:WSU.

90. FJG diary, April 23, 1870, Ac. 74–1, GF:WSU.

91. In September 1872, Louisa tried again to enter MIT as a student. Again, she was turned down because of her gender. To placate her and other women, the college offered a Saturday afternoon course on English literature and some classes describing women's traditional arts and crafts. These classes were for women only. FJG to FGV, September 25, 1872, bMSAm1321, f. 782, FGV:HHU. Cabot designed the Boston Athenaeum and the Boston Theatre. Information on the Cabot family is culled from L. Vernon Briggs, *History and Genealogy of the Cabot Family, 1475–1927,* vol. 2 (Boston: Charles E. Goodspeed, 1927), pp. 686–693.

92. WLG to FGV, April 19, 1872, bMSAm1321, f. 823, FGV:HHU.

93. FJG diary, December 17, 1872, Ac. 74–1, GF:WSU.

94. FJG diary, March 8, 1873, Ac. 74–1, GF:WSU.

95. FJG diary, April 18, 1873, Ac. 74–1, GF:WSU.

96. FJG to FGV, April 23, 1873, bMSAm1321, f. 782, FGV:HHU. Frank would live to wonder about these words when he, himself, took a second wife after the death of his first.

97. FGV to HBG, May 3, 1873, bMSAm1321, f. 871, FGV:HHU.

98. Louisa and Edward Cabot had three children together: Sewall in 1875, Norman in 1876, and Lucy in 1890.

99. WLG to FGV, September 3, 1878, bMSAm1321, f. 823, FGV:HHU. Although this may not have been the case with Frank's friends, many women faced a world of fewer marriageable men as a result of the high Civil War death toll.

100. FGV to FJG, February 22, 1877, bMSAm1321, f. 848, FGV:HHU.

101. FJG to FGV, February 25, 1877, bMSAm1321, f. 783, FGV:HHU.

102. FGV to WPG, August 29, 1871, bMSAm1321, f. 880, FGV:HHU.

103. FGV to HBG, January 21, 1872, bMSAm1321, f. 870, FGV:HHU.

104. HBG to FGV, March 19, 1872, Ac. 74–6, b. 2, f. 83, GF:WSU.

105. HBG to FGV, March 29, 1872, Ac. 74–6, b. 2, f. 78, GF:WSU.

106. Facts on the fire are taken from primary sources and Thomas H. O'Connor, *Bibles, Brahmins, and Bosses: A Short History of Boston* (Boston: Boston Public Library, 1991), pp. 165–166.

107. FJG to FGV, November 13, 1872, bMSAm1321, f. 782, FGV:HHU.

108. WLG to FGV, November 22, 1872, bMSAm1321, f. 823, FGV:HHU.

109. HBG to FGV, December 9, 1872, bMSAm1321, f. 813, FGV:HHU.

110. WLG to WPG, January 3, 1873, *Letters* 6:264.

111. FJG to FGV, January 29, 1873, bMSAm1321, f. 782, FGV:HHU.

112. FGV to EWG, September 23, 1873, bMSAm1321, f. 846, FGV:HHU.

113. FJG to FGV, October 7, 1873, bMSAm1321, f. 782, FGV:HHU.

114. FJG to FGV, February 19, 1911, bMSAm1321, f. 807, FGV:HHU.

115. LMcKG to unknown, n.d., MGF14, MMcG:NYPL.

116. EWG to Maria Mott Davis, January 28, 1875, b. 16, f. 445, GF:SC.

117. Susan B. Anthony to EWG, January 22, 1875, b. 45, f. 1107, GF:SC.

118. FJG diary, January 24, 1876, Ac. 74–6, GF:WSU.

119. Ibid., January 25, 1876.

120. WLG to WPG, February 27, 1876, *Letters* 6:400.

121. Suzie Munro, Lizzie Stodder, Mary Wells, Ellen Fisher, Julia Burrage, and Mary Wiley were among those who sent flowers.

122. William Lloyd Garrison, *Helen Eliza Benson: A Memorial* (Cambridge, Mass.: Riverside Press, 1876), pp. 40–41.

123. Ibid., pp. 44, 46.

124. Ibid., pp. 55–67.

125. WPG to WLG, March 2, 1876, bMSAm1321, f. 814, FGV:HHU.

126. LMcKG, "First School-Days of a Little Quaker," *The Riverside Magazine for Young People* 3, no. 30 (June 1869): 241–246; no. 31 (July 1869): 301–307, no. 32 (August 1869): 363–367.

127. LMcKG to FGV, March 2, 1869, bMSAm1169, f. 50, WPG:HHU.

128. LMcKG to WLG, January 29, 1867, bMSAm1169, f. 44–46, WPG:HHU.

129. William Francis Allen, Charles Pickard Ware, and Lucy McKim Garrison, *Slave Songs of the United States* (1867; reprint, New York: Oak Publications, 1965; Bedford, Mass.: Applewood Books, n.d.).

130. WPG to WLGJR, March 25, 1869, bMSAm1169.2, f. 351, WPG:HHU.

131. WPG to HBG, August 30, 1873, bMSAm1169.2, f. 270, WPG:HHU.

132. WPG to WLGJR, December 11, 1875, b. 30, f. 859, GF:SC.

133. FJG to FGV, February 18, 1877, bMSAm1321, f. 783, FGV:HHU.

134. LMcKG to FJG, February 18, 1877, bMSAm1169, f. 39–41, WPG:HHU.

135. EWG to LMcKG, April 17, 1877, b. 16, f. 44, GF:SC.

136. LMcKG to EWG, October 9, 1870, b. 29, f. 804, GF:SC.

137. WPG to FGV, April 28, 1877 (probably), bMSAm1321, f. 814, FGV:HHU.

138. FGV to WLG, April 22, 1877, bMSAm1321, f. 881, FGV:HHU.

139. EWG to Eliza Osborne, May 25, 1877, b. 16, f. 452, GF:SC.

140. WLG to FGV, November 22, 1878, bMSAm1321, f. 823, FGV:HHU.

141. Telegram from FGV to HV, May 22, 1879, bMSAm1906, f. 632, GF:HHU.

142. *Life* 4:305.

143. Funeral descriptions are culled from *Tributes to William Lloyd Garrison, At the Funeral Services, May 28, 1879* (Boston: Houghton, Osgood; Cambridge, Mass.: Riverside Press, 1879).

144. Ibid., p. 47.

145. Ibid., p. 18.

146. Undated clipping in scrapbook, bMSAm1906, f. 688–689, GF:HHU.

IX. THEIR PARENTS' SONS

–Epigraph: FJG, "A Memory of William Lloyd Garrison," *The Woman's Journal,* June 25, 1904, bMSAm1906, f. 686–687, GF:HHU.

1. WLGJR to FGV, December 31, 1880, bMSAm1321, f. 824, FGV:HHU.

2. FJG to FGV, October 30, 1881, bMSAm1321, f. 783, FGV:HHU.

3. FGV to EWG, July 16, 1882, bMSAm1321, f. 846, FGV:HHU.

4. WLGJR to FGV, November 4, 1883, bMSAm1321, f. 824, FGV:HHU.

5. Thomas A. Edison as quoted in D. Joy Humes, *Oswald Garrison Villard, Liberal of the 1920's* (Syracuse: Syracuse University Press, 1960), p. 3.

6. WLGJR to FGV, February 1886, bMSAm1321, f. 824, FGV:HHU.

7. While in Alexandria, Virginia, Lucy and Wendell visited the former fugitive slave and author Harriet Jacobs and her daughter. In 1861 Jacobs had published her autobiography under the pseudonym Linda Brent.

8. Background information on the *Nation* is culled from primary sources and William M. Armstrong, "The Freedmen's Movement and the Founding of the *Nation,*" *Journal of American History* 53 (1967): 708–726; Wendell Phillips Garrison, *Letters and Memorials of Wendell Phillips Garrison: Literary Editor of "The Nation," 1865–1906* (Cambridge, Mass.: Riverside Press, 1908); Alan Pendelton Grimes, *The Political Liberalism of the New York*

"Nation," 1865–1932 (Chapel Hill: University of North Carolina Press, 1953); and James M. McPherson, *The Abolitionist Legacy: From Reconstruction to the NAACP* (Princeton, N.J.: Princeton University Press, 1975); and McPherson, *The Struggle for Equality: Abolitionists and the Negro in the Civil War and Reconstruction* (Princeton, N.J.: Princeton University Press, 1964).

9. Masthead, *Nation* 1, no. 2 (July 13, 1865): 34.

10. Editorial, *Nation* 1, no. 1 (July 6, 1865): 1.

11. Mott as cited in Anna Davis Hallowell, *James and Lucretia Mott: Life and Letters* (Boston: Houghton Mifflin, 1884), pp. 415–416.

12. FGV to WPG, November 7, 1870, bMSAm1321, f. 880, FGV:HHU.

13. *Nation* 12 (1871): 271, as cited in Grimes, *Political Liberalism,* p. 52.

14. James Miller McKim, July 10, 1865, as cited in Armstrong, "Freedmen's Movement," p. 726.

15. WPG to WLGJR, August 3, 1865, bMSAm1169.2, f. 306, WPG:HHU.

16. WPG to WLG, January 17, 1867, bMSAm1169.2, f. 38, WPG:HHU.

17. WPG to WLG, May 7, 1868, bMSAm1169.2, f. 56, WPG:HHU.

18. WLGJR to MW, July 9, 1865, as cited in McPherson, *Struggle for Equality,* p. 330.

19. FJG to FGV, April 8, 1866, as cited in ibid., p. 350.

20. FGV to HBG, March 23, 1866, bMSAm1321, f. 869, FGV:HHU.

21. WPG to WLG, April 4, 1868, bMSAm1169.2, f. 53, WPG:HHU.

22. WLG to Charles Sumner, June 1, 1872, *Letters* 6:231.

23. FGV as quoted in WLG to FGV, July 11, 1872, bMSAm1321, f. 823, FGV:HHU.

24. WLG to FGV, July 11, 1872, bMSAm1321, f. 823, FGV:HHU.

25. FGV to WLG, August 1, 1872, bMSAm1321, f. 870, FGV:HHU.

26. Ibid.

27. WPG addendum to HBG to FGV, September 15, 1872, bMSAm1321, f. 813, FGV:HHU.

28. FJG addendum to HBG to FGV, August 7, 1872, bMSAm1321, f. 813, FGV:HHU.

29. HBG to FGV, September 19, 1872, bMSAm1321, f. 813, FGV:HHU.

30. Cited in Grimes, *Political Liberalism,* p. 12.

31. WPG to WLG, February 7, 1875, bMSAm1169.2, f. 118, WPG:HHU.

32. WLG to WPG, July 21, 1876, *Letters* 6:410–411.

33. Discussion on Reconstruction arguments within the Garrison family and efforts toward education of African Americans is based on primary sources and McPherson, *Abolitionist Legacy.*

34. WPG as cited in McPherson, *Abolitionist Legacy,* p. 39.

35. WPG as cited in ibid., pp. 54–55.

36. Lloyd hated Hayes so much that he criticized Fanny for allowing Henry's cousin, Julius Erasmus Hilgard, a civil engineer working with the United States Coast Survey, to introduce her to the president. The meeting was, as he put it, "well meant, but malapropos." WLG to FGV, January 25, 1878, *Letters* 6:510.

37. WLG to FGV, February 2, 1878, b. 1, f. 46, GF:SC.

38. WLG to WPG, February 5, 1878, *Letters* 6:511–512.

39. WLG to FGV, February 7, 1878, b. 1, f. 46, GF:SC.

40. E. L. Godkin to WPG, 1883, as cited in Garrison, *Letters and Memorials,* p. 9. Although I found no documentation, there may be another reason for Wendell's closeness to Godkin. In May 1875, Godkin's daughter died soon after birth; his wife died a few days later. Just a year later, Wendell lost Lucy.

41. Until she was the age of twelve, Lucy and Wendell's daughter, Katherine, slept in a "crib" in Wendell's room. At that point, she received a room of her own. WPG to FGV, March 15, 1885, bMSAm1321, f. 815, FGV:HHU.

42. Wendell Phillips Garrison, *Bedside Poetry: A Parent's Assistant in Moral Discipline* (Boston: D. Lothrop, 1887), p. viii; republished as *Good-Night Poetry: A Parent's Assistant in Moral Discipline* (Boston: Ginn, 1891).

43. The books seem to be appropriate for what would be today's fourth- through eighth-grade readers.

44. Wendell Phillips Garrison, *What Mr. Darwin Saw* (New York: Harper and Brothers, n.d.).

45. Wendell Phillips Garrison, *Parables for School and Home* (New York: Longmans, Green, 1898), p. 97.

46. Wendell Phillips Garrison, *Sonnets and Lyrics of the Ever-Womanly* (Jamaica, N.Y.: Marion Press, 1898), p. 25.

47. In 1872 Frank tried to convince Houghton to publish Sarah Grimké's memoirs, but the publisher claimed the book "would not interest the public and sell well." Grimké felt that the problem was not the antislavery content but the book's portrayal of that part of her family history in which "a quadroon . . . *married* a planter." Sarah Grimké to FJG, May 30, 1872, Ms. A. 1.2.v.37, p. 33a, GF:BPL.

48. WLGJR to FGV, April 21, 1882, bMSAm1321, f. 824, FGV:HHU.

49. WLGJR to FGV, February 9, 1883, bMSAm1321, f. 824, FGV:HHU.

50. WLGJR to WPG, July 6, 1893, bMSAm1906, f. 94, GF:HHU.

51. FGV diary, July 27, 1882, bMSAm1321, f. 900.

52. Sarah McKim to WPG, August 3, 1882, b. 53, f. 1523, GF:SC.

53. Wendell Phillips to WPG, August 13, 1882, Ms.Am.123.49, WP:BPL.

54. Lizzie and Frank remained friends throughout their lives. Their relationship was unusually close for an unrelated man and woman. Letters indicate that Lizzie may have wished for more than a platonic relationship, but Frank never reciprocated the feeling.

55. FJG to "My dear friend," October 11, 1882, MS.Am.1067 (30), GF:BPL.

56. FJG to WPG, February 24, 1891, bMSAm1906, f. 184, GF:HHU.

57. FJG to FGV, January 17, 1915, bMSAm1321, f. 811, GF:HHU.

58. *Life* 1:ix–xiv.

59. *Life* 3:iii–v.

60. The other depositories included the Portland (Maine) Public Library, the Boston Athenaeum, Harvard College Library, Malden (Massachusetts) Public Library, the American Antiquarian Society (Worcester, Massachusetts), the Rhode Island Historical Society (Providence), Yale College Library, the Long Island Historical Society (Brooklyn, New York), Cornell University Library, the Library Company (Philadelphia), the Cincinnati (Ohio) Public Library, the Newberry Library (Chicago), and the Kansas Historical Society (Topeka). *Life* 3:vi.

61. FGV to WPG, February 9, 1889, bMSAm1321, f. 880, FGV:HHU.

62. WPG to FGV, February 9, 1889, bMSAm1321, f. 817, FGV:HHU.

63. *New York Tribune* clipping, bMSAm1906, f. 686–687, GF:HHU.

64. *Philadelphia Ledger and Transcript* clipping, bMSAm1906, f. 686–687, GF:HHU.

65. "Books and Authors," *Boston Daily Advertiser,* December 10, 1889, bMSAm1906, f. 686–687, GF:HHU.

66. Among the speakers was Mary Church Terrell, founder in 1896 of the National Association of Colored Women. She also later worked in the woman suffrage campaign and with the Women's International League for Peace and Freedom, causes which Fanny also joined.

67. William Lloyd Garrison, *The Words of Garrison: A Centenary Selection (1805–1905)* (Boston: Houghton, Mifflin, 1905).

68. Much of the interpretation of the Garrison children's post-Reconstruction work is informed by McPherson, *Abolitionist Legacy.*

69. OGV as quoted in Grimes, *Political Liberalism,* p. viii.

70. Richard and Norwood Hallowell, the Garrisons' friends, became Tuskegee's chief fund-raisers in Massachusetts.

71. Booker T. Washington, "Atlanta Exposition Address," in *Up From Slavery: A Biography* (New York: Doubleday, Page, 1901), pp. 218–225.

72. WLGJR as quoted in McPherson, *Abolitionist Legacy,* p. 302.

73. OGV as quoted in ibid., p. 309.

74. WLGJR as quoted in ibid., p. 356.

75. FJG as quoted in ibid., p. 362.

76. WLGJR as quoted in ibid., p. 372.

77. Cited in David Levering Lewis, *W. E. B. Du Bois: Biography of a Race, 1868–1919* (New York: Henry Holt, 1993), p. 322.

78. Ibid., p. 330.

79. WLGJR, "Industrial Education—Will It Solve the Negro Problem?" in *The Colored American Magazine,* n.d., p. 248, b. 80, f. 2190, GF:SC.

80. The founding of the NAACP is culled from primary sources and Lewis, *W. E. B. Du Bois;* McPherson, *Abolitionist Legacy;* and Mary White Ovington, *Black and White Sat Down Together: The Reminiscences of an NAACP Founder* (New York: Feminist Press at the City University of New York, 1995). For a more local view relevant to the Garrisons, see Mark Schneider, "Confronting Jim Crow: Boston's Anti-Slavery Tradition, 1890–1920," *Historical Journal of Massachusetts,* winter 1996, pp. 68–89.

81. EWG to Susan B. Anthony, October 7, 1882, b. 15, f. 404, GF:SC.

82. In 1870 Frank heard from Lucy Stone that there was "a movement afoot" to merge the AWSA and NWSA. His response was, "Cool!" Both were disappointed that the merger did not happen. FJG diary, March 21, 1870, Ac. 74–1, GF:WSU.

83. WLG to Lucy Stone, May 8, 1869, *Letters* 6:109.

84. WLG to Elizabeth Pease Nichol, September 26, 1869, *Letters* 6:129.

85. WLGJR to FGV, May 27, 1881, bMSAm1321, b. 824, FGV:HHU.

86. FJG to FGV, June 4, 1882, bMSAm1321, f. 784, FGV:HHU.

87. "Mr. Garrison's Address," *Woman's Journal,* February 8, 1890, b. 73, f. 2066, GF:SC.

88. "Address by Reverend Anna H. Shaw," in *William Lloyd Garrison: Memorial Meeting,* October 16, 1909, pp. 26–30, b. 80, f. 2198, GF:SC.

89. Background information on Henry George is culled from primary sources and Charles Albro Barker, *Henry George* (New York: Oxford University Press, 1955); Anna George de Mille, *Henry George: Citizen of the World* (Chapel Hill: University of North Carolina Press, 1950); and David Montgomery, "Henry George," in John A. Garraty and Mark C. Carnes, *American National Biography,* vol. 8 (New York: Oxford University Press, 1999), pp. 849–852.

90. WLGJR, "The New Abolition," in *The Standard,* extra no. 14 (September 12, 1891), b. 80, f. 2193, GF:SC.

91. WLGJR, "The Philosophy of the Single Tax Movement" (New York: Sterling Publishing, 1895), b. 80, f. 2193, GF:SC.

92. WLGJR, "The Wool Question," in *Tariff Reform* 2, no. 19 (December 15, 1889), b. 80, f. 2192, GF:SC.

93. WLGJR, "The Ethics of Free Trade," March 15, 1892, speech before the New England Tariff Reform League, b. 80, f. 2193, GF:SC.

94. WLGJR as cited in "Address of Professor W. E. B. Du Bois," in *William Lloyd Garrison: Memorial Meeting,* October 16, 1909, p. 6, b. 80, f. 2198, GF:SC.

95. WLGJR, "The Things that Make for Peace," *The Sterling Library* 2, no. 23, (October 21, 1895), b. 80, f. 2193, GF:SC.

96. Background information on the Anti-Imperialist League and other antiwar groups is culled from Jim Zwick's website, http://www.boondocksnet.com/ and Harriet Hyman Alonso, *Peace as a Women's Issue: A History of the U.S. Movement for World Peace and Women's Rights* (Syracuse: Syracuse University Press, 1993); Charles Chatfield, *The American Peace Movement: Ideals and Activism* (New York: Twayne Publishers, 1992); and Charles DeBenedetti, *The Peace Reform in American History* (Bloomington: Indiana University Press, 1980). Each of these books includes an extensive bibliography of peace movement history.

97. "Wm. L. Garrison on Imperialism," n. d., b. 73, f. 2066, GF:SC.

98. Information on the weaponry of war is culled from John Whiteclay Chambers II, "The American Debate over Modern War, 1871–1914," in *Anticipating Total War: The German and American Experience, 1871–1914,* ed. Manfred F. Boemeke, Roger Chickering, and Stig Forster (New York: Cambridge University Press, 1999), pp. 241–279.

99. "The War with Spain," *The Woman's Journal,* April 30, 1898, b. 80, f. 2190, GF:SC.

100. WLGJR, "Aguinaldo," March 19, 1899, in *The Nation's Shame: Sonnets,* 1899, Pamphlet Collection: NYPL.

101. WLGJR, "Onward, Christian Soldier," December 4, 1899, in *American Poetry* collection of pamphlets, NYPL.

102. WLGJR, "No Compromise with War," address before Summer Peace Institute, Mystic, Connecticut, August 25, 1899, b. 80, f. 2193, GF:SC.

103. WLGJR, "Muskets for Boston Schools," *Christian Neighbor,* n.d., b. 80, f. 2190, GF:SC.

104. WLGJR, "Non-Resistance a Better Defence Than Armies and Navies," address before Yearly Meeting of Progressive Friends, Longwood, Pennsylvania, June 6, 1908, b. 80, f. 2195, GF:SC.

105. WLGJR to HV, July 4, 1899, bMSAm1906, f. 100, GF:HHU.

106. WLGJR as cited in *New York Daily Tribune* obituary, September 1909, bMSAm1906, f. 686–687, GF:HHU.

107. WLGJR, speech before New England Free Trade League, February 20, 1899, as cited in *Boston Transcript* obituary, September 1909, bMSAm1906, f. 686–687, GF:HHU.

108. WLGJR, "The Root of Imperialism," speech before the Henry George Club, April 7, 1900, b. 80, f. 2190, GF:SC.

109. WPG as cited in McPherson, *Abolitionist Legacy,* p. 327.

110. WPG as cited in ibid., p. 330.

111. E. L. Godkin retired from the newspaper business in 1899, leaving Wendell free to fall under Oswald's influence and return to his roots. Godkin and Wendell had worked together for thirty-seven years.

112. OGV as cited in McPherson, *Abolitionist Legacy,* p. 331.

113. *Nation* 79 (1904): 288–289, as cited in Grimes, *Political Liberalism,* p. 80.

114. WPG, "Forty Years of the *Nation,*" *Nation* 81 (July 13, 1905): 30, as cited in Garrison, *Letters and Memorials,* p. 145.

115. WPG, "The New Gulliver," reprinted in Garrison, *Letters and Memorials,* p. 275.

116. WPG to FGV, March 15, 1885, bMSAm1321, f. 815, FGV:HHU.

117. In honor of his forty years of service, Wendell was presented with a silver vase with the inscription "Presented to Wendell Phillips Garrison as a token of gratitude for the service rendered to his country by his forty years of able, upright, and truly patriotic work in the editorship of The Nation, 6th July 1905." Vase inscription cited in Garrison, *Letters and Memorials,* p. 141.

x. ANOTHER FANNY'S STORY

–Epigraph: OGV, *Fighting Years: Memoirs of a Liberal Editor* (New York: Harcourt, Brace, 1939), pp. 21–22.

1. As early as 1871, Henry saw to it that Fanny and the children would be well protected financially should he die. In that year, he purchased $5,000 worth of life insurance from the State Mutual Incorporated Company in Worcester and $7,500 worth from the Northwestern Mutual Company in Milwaukee. FJG diary, 1871, paper slipped into back of book, Ac. 74–1, GF:WSU.

2. Katherine N. Villard as cited in Thomas Fuchs, "Henry Villard: A Citizen of Two Worlds" (Ph.D. diss., University of Oregon, 1991), p. 205.

3. FGV, "Biographical Sketch," typewritten manuscript, pp. 19–20, n.d., bMSAm1321, f. 896, FGV:HHU.

4. In spite of his financial downfall, Henry Villard has received much of the credit for ending the isolation of the Pacific Northwest and opening it to tourism, increased settlement, and development. See Fuchs, "Henry Villard."

5. Background information on the Villards' houses and the McKim, Mead, & White architectural firm is culled from primary sources and Barry Bergdoll, *Mastering McKim's Plan: Columbia's First Century on Morningside Heights* (New York: Meriam and Ira D. Wallach Art Gallery, Columbia University in the City of New York, 1997); and William C.

Shopsin and Mosette Glaser Broderick, *The Villard Houses: Life Story of a Landmark* (New York: Viking Press, 1980).

6. McKim's partners were William Rutherford Mead and Stanford White. By 1883 the three owned the world's largest architectural firm.

7. FGV diary, December 24, 1883, bMSAm1321, b. 900, FGV:HHU.

8. FGV diary, June 12, 1888, bMSAm1321, b. 900, FGV:HHU.

9. The Villard children's early experiences are culled from Villard, *Fighting Years,* pp. 24–44.

10. FGV diary, December 16, 1882, bMSAm1321, b. 900, FGV:HHU.

11. FGV to EWG, December 25, 1888, bMSAm1321, f. 846, FGV:HHU.

12. FGV to WPG, December 17, 1889, bMSAm1321, f. 880, FGV:HHU.

13. Conversations with David Lloyd Garrison, May 8, 1995, in Lincoln, Mass.; Mariquita Serrano Platov, July 26, 1993, in Tannersville, N.Y.; Henry Serrano Villard, April 7, 1994, in Los Angeles; and Oswald Garrison Villard Jr., September 9, 1998, by phone to Palo Alto, Calif. See also David Lloyd Garrison, *Early and Late: Early Years and Later Comments* (Lincoln Center, Mass.: Heritage House Publishers, 1994).

14. In May 1896, the tireless Fanny learned how to ride a tricycle so she could cover more of Thorwood's grounds on her exercise outings.

15. Conversation with Mariquita Serrano Platov.

16. Conversation with Henry Serrano Villard.

17. Conversation with Oswald Garrison Villard Jr.

18. FJG to FGV, February 20, 1887, bMSAm1169, f. 15–16, WPG:HHU. In 1871 Frank had taken a firm stand on temperance when he voted "no" on the local Boston referendum "Shall any person be allowed to manufacture, sell, or keep for sale, Ale, Porter, Strong Beer, or Lager Beer, in this City?" FJG diary, July 1, 1871, Ac. 74–1, GF:WSU.

19. Conversation with Mariquita Serrano Platov.

20. WLG to FGV, October 16, 1873, *Letters* 6:282.

21. WPG to FGV, September 19, 1886, bMSAm1321, f. 816, FGV:HHU.

22. FGV diary, August 30, 1882, bMSAm1321, f. 900, FGV:HHU. Even Ellie got in the act, claiming in 1877 that if Annie would "spank" her small daughter, the child would no longer have temper tantrums. EWG to FGV, November 30, 1877, bMSAm1321, f. 781, FGV:HHU.

23. WPG to FGV, December 9, 1891, bMSAm1169.2, f. 382–392, WPG:HHU.

24. FGV diary, June 11, 1890, bMSAm1321, f. 900, FGV:HHU.

25. FGV diary, September 11, 1896, bMSAm1321, f. 900, FGV:HHU.

26. HV cable quoted in FGV diary, October 10, 1896, bMSAm1321, f. 900, FGV:HHU.

27. FGV diary, October 17, 1896, bMSAm1321, f. 900, FGV:HHU.

28. Harold Villard as quoted in FGV diary, June 8, 1897, bMSAm1321, f. 900, FGV:HHU.

29. FGV diary, October 12, 1900, bMSAm1321, f. 900, FGV:HHU.

30. EWG to WLGJR, November 8, 1900, bMSAm1906, f. 82, GF:HHU.

31. FGV diary, December 31, 1900, bMSAm1321, f. 900, FGV:HHU.

32. FGV diary, January 3, 1901, bMSAm1321, f. 900, FGV:HHU.

33. FGV in HV, *Memoirs,* vol. 1, "Preface," p. vi.

34. Helen Villard Bell to OGV, November 12, 1900, bMSAm1323, f. 194, OGV:HHU. The original letter was written in German. I would like to thank Robert Pois for translating the letter into English.

35. FGV diary, May 23, 1901, bMSAm1321, f. 900, FGV:HHU.

36. FGV diary, August 5, 1903, bMSAm1321, f. 900, FGV:HHU.

37. FGV diary, November 23, 1903, bMSAm1321, f. 900, FGV:HHU.

38. "The Villard Will Fight," *New York Sun,* December 4, 1903, p. 1.

39. The stipulations in Henry Villard's will are based upon "Last Will and Testament of Henry Villard. Dated 23rd day of June, 1900," bMSAm1322, f. 640, HV:HHU.

40. Henry's German donations over the years included those for the construction of two model worker's homes in Zweibrücken (1880); to his old school, the Zweibrücken Gymnasium; to the Diakonissen, a Protestant nursing order in Speyer; the Speyer Gymnasium; Speyer Urkundenbuch (a collection of medieval documents); the trade museum, Kaiserslautern Gewerbemuseum; the Palatine Club-Pfalzischer Verschonerungsverein; and the Zweibrücken orphanage.

41. FGV to FJG, December 14, 1903, bMSAm1321, f. 867.3, FGV:HHU.

42. FJG to FGV, December 13, 1903, bMSAm1321, f. 799, FGV:HHU.

43. FJG to FGV, January 24, 1904, bMSAm1321, f. 800, FGV:HHU.

44. FGV to WPG, June 24, 1877, bMSAm1321, f. 880, FGV:HHU.

45. FGV, "The Social Status of Woman To-day," n.d., bMSAm1321, f. 896, FGV:HHU.

46. FGV, "Reform and Reformers," read before the Women's Unitarian League, February 3, 1893, bMSAm1321, f. 897, FGV:HHU.

47. Information on the Diet Kitchen Association is culled from FGV, untitled speech, n.d., bMSAm1321, f. 897, FGV:HHU; and FGV, "The New York Diet Kitchen Association," in *Social Service,* November 1903, pp. 85–89, bMSAm1321, f. 896, FGV:HHU.

48. FGV, "New York Diet Kitchen Association."

49. Others included the Raymond Kitchen at 423 West 41st Street, the Wickham Kitchen at 137 Centre Street, the Rusch Kitchen at 146 East 7th Street, the Freeman Kitchen at 205 East 66th Street, the Hackley Kitchen at 26 Barrow Street, and the Anne Barbara Kitchen at 205 West 62nd Street. The records do not give a definite address for the Villard Kitchen.

50. FGV, "Reform and Reformers," read before the Women's Unitarian League, February 3, 1893, bMSAm1321, f. 897, FGV:HHU.

51. FGV diary, April 19, 1898, bMSAm1321, f. 900, FGV:HHU.

52. FGV diary, April 21, 1898, bMSAm1321, f. 900, FGV:HHU.

53. Fanny Garrison Villard, *William Lloyd Garrison on Non-Resistance Together with a Personal Sketch by His Daughter, Fanny Garrison Villard* (New York: Nation Press Printing Co., 1924), pp. 46–47.

54. In 1907 Blatch founded the Equality League of Self-Supporting Women, a suffrage organization aimed at expressing the needs and support of working-class women for the vote. In 1910 the league evolved into the Women's Political Union, a suffrage organization which allied with wealthy women while also holding on to the idea of suffrage for workers.

55. These included Wyoming (1890), Colorado (1893), Utah (1896), and Idaho (1896).

56. Supplemental information on the New York suffrage campaign is culled from Carrie Chapman Catt and Nettie Rogers Shuler, *Woman Suffrage and Politics: The Inner Story of the Suffrage Movement* (New York: Scribner's, 1923); Ellen Carol DuBois, *Harriot Stanton Blatch and the Winning of Woman Suffrage* (New Haven: Yale University Press, 1997); Robert Booth Fowler, *Carrie Catt: Feminist Politician* (Boston: Northeastern University Press, 1986); and Anna Howard Shaw, *The Story of a Pioneer* (New York: Harper and Brothers, 1915).

57. FGV diary, May 19, 1906, bMSAm1321, f. 900, FGV:HHU.

58. FGV diary, September 11, 1906, bMSAm1321, f. 900, FGV:HHU.

59. FGV diary, November 21, 1906, bMSAm1321, f. 900, FGV:HHU.

60. FGV diary, February 27, 1907, bMSAm1321, f. 900, FGV:HHU.

61. Oswald Garrison Villard, *The Disappearing Daily: Chapters in American Newspaper Evolution* (New York: Alfred A. Knopf, 1944).

62. WPG to FGV, December 21, 1906 (copy in FGV's hand, dated March 4, 1907), bMSAm1169.2, f. 382–392, WPG:HHU.

63. FGV diary, January 7, 1907, bMSAm1321, f. 900, FGV:HHU.

64. FGV diary, June 18, 1907, bMSAm1321, f. 900, FGV:HHU.

65. FGV, "Peace and Woman Suffrage," n.d., bMSAm1321, f. 896, FGV:HHU.

66. FGV diary, December 16, 1908, bMSAm1321, f. 901, FGV:HHU.

67. FGV diary, May 19, 1908, bMSAm1321, f. 901, FGV:HHU.

68. FGV to WLGJR, August 1, 1908, bMSAm1321, f. 883, FGV:HHU.

69. Neither of William and Ellie's daughters (Agnes and Eleanor) married.

70. These states included Washington (1910), California (1911), Oregon (1912), Arizona (1912), Kansas (1912), and Nevada and Montana (1914).

71. FGV, "The Boston Hearing, 1910," bMSAm1321, f. 896, FGV:HHU.

72. Villard, *Fighting Years,* p. 199.

73. FGV diary, May 4, 1912, bMSAm1321, f. 901, FGV:HHU.

74. FGV diary, April 1, 1910, bMSAm1321, f. 901, FGV:HHU.

75. FGV diary, March 3, 1913, bMSAm1321, f. 901, FGV:HHU.

76. FGV diary, May 6, 1913, bMSAm1321, f. 901, FGV:HHU.

77. FGV to Mariquita Villard, May 27, 1920, bMSAm1321, f. 896, FGV:HHU.

78. Conversation with Mariquita Serrano Platov.

79. FGV diary, March 13, 1912, bMSAm1321, f. 901, FGV:HHU.

80. FGV diary, February 4, 1913, bMSAm1321, f. 901, FGV:HHU.

81. FGV, "Tarrytown Meeting: Address by Mrs. Henry Villard," March 16, 1911, bMSAm1321, f. 896, FGV:HHU.

82. FGV diary, April 21 and 23, 1914, bMSAm1321, f. 901, FGV:HHU.

83. FGV diary, May 2, 1914, bMSAm1321, f. 901, FGV:HHU.

84. FGV diary, July 28 and 30, 1914, bMSAm1321, f. 901, FGV:HHU.

85. FGV diary, August 1, 1914, bMSAm1321, f. 901, FGV:HHU.

86. Peace Parade Committee meeting transcript, August 12, 1914, bMSAm1323, f. 3993, OGV:HHU.

87. "Initial Call," Peace Parade Committee, n.d., bMSAm1323, f. 3993, OGV:HHU.

88. Lillian Wald, Peace Parade Committee meeting transcript, August 12, 1914, bMSAm1323, f. 3993, OGV:HHU.

89. Press release, n.d., bMSAm1323, f. 3993, OGV:HHU.

90. FGV diary, August 29, 1914, bMSAm1321, f. 901, FGV:HHU.

91. FGV, "Mrs. Villard's Address One. . . . Peace Address by Mrs. Henry Villard at the Hotel McAlpine, September 21, 1914," reprinted as "A Real Peace Society," *The World Aflame Magazine,* November 1915, bMSAm1321, f. 897, FGV:HHU.

92. Ibid.

93. Much of the information on the women's peace movement from 1915 through Fanny's death in 1928 first appeared in Harriet Hyman Alonso, *Peace as a Women's Issue: A History of the U.S. Movement for World Peace and Women's Rights* (Syracuse: Syracuse University Press, 1993); and Alonso, *The Women's Peace Union and the Outlawry of War, 1921–1942* (Knoxville: University of Tennessee Press, 1989; reprint, Syracuse: Syracuse University Press, 1997). See also Jane Addams, *The Second Twenty Years at Hull-House: September 1909 to September 1929* (New York: Macmillan, 1930).

94. "Woman's Peace Party Preamble and Platform Adopted at Washington, January 10, 1915," Subject Files 463, S/L:NYPL.

95. FGV diary, January 10, 1915, bMSAm1321, f. 901, FGV:HHU.

96. FGV diary, March 31, 1916, bMSAm1321, f. 901, FGV:HHU.

97. FJG to FGV, May 8, 1911, bMSAm1321, f. 807, FGV:HHU.

98. FJG to FGV, July 18, 1915, bMSAm1321, f. 811, FGV:HHU.

99. FJG to FGV, August 20, 1916, bMSAm1321, f. 812, FGV:HHU.

100. FGV diary, December 13, 1916, bMSAm1321, f. 901, FGV:HHU.

101. FGV diary, April 6, 1917, bMSAm1321, f. 901, FGV:HHU.

102. Conversation with Henry Serrano Villard. During World War I, Henry was stationed at a hospital in Italy where the young Ernest Hemingway recovered from a war-related injury. There, Hemingway had a brief love affair with Agnes Von Kurowsky, a nurse. Henry, a friend of both, came into possession of Von Kurowsky's papers, which he later edited and published as *Hemingway in Love and War: The Lost Diary of Agnes Von Kurowsky: Her Letters and Correspondence of Hemingway* (Boston: Northeastern University Press, 1989). Henry's son, Dmitri Villard, a movie producer, later made the story into the film *In Love and War,* starring Sandra Bullock and Chris O'Donnell.

103. *Nation* 104 (1917): 150, as cited in Alan Pendelton Grimes, *The Political Liberalism of the New York "Nation," 1865–1932* (Chapel Hill: University of North Carolina Press, 1953), p. 83.

104. FGV diary, November 6, 1917, bMSAm1321, f. 901, FGV:HHU.

105. FGV diary, December 31, 1917, bMSAm1321, f. 901, FGV:HHU.

106. FGV diary, November 11, 1918, bMSAm1321, f. 901, FGV:HHU.

107. *Report of the Joint Legislative Committee Investigating Seditious Activities, Filed 24 January in the Senate of New York: Revolutionary Radicalism,* pt. 1, vol. 1, Clayton R. Lusk, chairman (Albany: J. B. Lyon, 1920), pp. 1000, 1005, 1031.

108. An article in the New York *Herald* in 1918 claimed that the *Nation* was popular reading among "the interned [German] enemy aliens at Fort Oglethorpe, Georgia." The

article stated that, "The articles in the *Nation* appeal so much to the interned aliens that they gather in groups evenings and read it aloud so that those who do not subscribe may have the benefit of it." "Says *Nation* Was Popular Reading in Internment Camp," New York *Herald,* September 16, 1918, bMSAm1906, f. 686–687, GF:HHU.

109. FGV to the editor, *Boston Globe,* August 26, 1924, bMSAm1906, f. 686–687, GF:HHU. For a look at Oswald's activities, see Michael Wreszin, *Oswald Garrison Villard: Pacifist at War* (Bloomington: Indiana University Press, 1965).

110. Elinor Byrns to WIL Board Members, May 16, 1919, NYC-WPP:SCPC.

111. FGV, Elinor Byrns, Katherine Devereux Blake, Mary Ware Dennett, Caroline Lexow Babcock et al to Members: WIL-NYS, September 12, 1919, WPS:SCPC.

112. FGV diary, September 30, 1919, bMSAm1321, f. 901, FGV:HHU.

113. Elinor Byrns, "The Women's Peace Society: A Non-Resistant Organization—Founded October, 1919—Its Aim, Program and Arguments," June 1921, WPU:SCPC.

114. Ibid.

115. Resolution, n.d., WPS:SCPC.

116. At that meeting, Fanny took pleasure in telling Jane Addams about the creation of the Women's Peace Society. Much to Fanny's delight, Addams responded that she "had done enough" for peace just by bringing Oswald into the world. FGV diary, November 3, 1919, bMSAm1321, f. 901, FGV:HHU.

117. Information on Fanny's efforts to expand the Women's Peace Society through WILPF channels is based on Anne Marie Pois, "'Practical' and Absolute Pacifism in the Early Years of the U.S. Women's International League for Peace and Freedom," in *Challenge to Mars: Essays on Pacifism from 1918 to 1945,* ed. Peter Brock and Thomas P. Socknat (Toronto: University of Toronto Press, 1999), pp. 199–217.

118. FGV diary, July 15, 1921, bMSAm1321, f. 901, FGV:HHU. See also Florence Kelley, "The Women's Congress at Vienna," in *Social Justice Feminists in the United States and Germany: A Dialogue in Documents, 1885–1933,* ed. Kathryn Kish Sklar, Anja Schüler, and Susan Strasser (Ithaca, N.Y.: Cornell University Press, 1998), pp. 269–270.

119. FGV diary, July 17, 1921, bMSAm1321, f. 901, FGV:HHU.

120. Elinor Byrns to FGV, n.d., WPS:SCPC.

121. Cited in Mary Abbott to Elinor Byrns, April 10, 1921, WPS:SCPC.

122. Elinor Byrns to Mary Abbott, April 11, 1921, WPS:SCPC.

123. Ibid.

124. FGV diary, November 12, 1921, f. 901, FGV:HHU.

125. FGV diary, March 11, 1924, f. 901, FGV:HHU.

126. Meta Lilienthal, speech in "Luncheon Given by the Women's Peace Society in Celebration of Mrs. Henry Villard's 80th Birthday" program, Hotel Astor, New York City, December 20, 1924, b.83, f. 2275, GF:SC.

127. Margaret Loring Thomas, "Fanny Garrison Villard," in "Luncheon Given by the Women's Peace Society . . ." program.

128. W. E. B. Du Bois, speech in "Luncheon Given by the Women's Peace Society . . ." program.

129. FGV diary, December 20, 1924, f. 901, FGV:HHU.

130. FGV diary, December 16, 1927, f. 901, FGV:HHU.

131. FGV, "Greetings from Our Chairman" and following letter, *Newsletter* (WPS) 2, no. 3 (February 1928), b. 83, f. 2275, GF:SC.

NOTE ON SOURCES

1. Oliver Johnson, *William Lloyd Garrison and His Times* (Boston: B. B. Russell & Company, 1879).

2. Godwin Smith, D.C. L., *The Moral Crusader: William Lloyd Garrison* (New York: Funk & Wagnalls, 1892).

3. John Jay Chapman, *William Lloyd Garrison* (New York: Moffat, Yard, 1913).

4. Russel B. Nye, *William Lloyd Garrison and the Humanitarian Reformers* (Boston: Little, Brown, 1955).

5. Walter M. Merrill, *Against Wind and Tide: A Biography of Wm. Lloyd Garrison* (Cambridge: Harvard University Press, 1963).

6. John L. Thomas, *The Liberator: William Lloyd Garrison: A Biography* (Boston: Little, Brown, 1963); George M. Fredrickson, *William Lloyd Garrison* (Englewood Cliffs, N.J.: Prentice-Hall, 1968); and James Brewer Stewart, *William Lloyd Garrison and the Challenge of Emancipation* (Arlington Heights, Ill.: Harlan Davidson, 1992).

7. Walter M. Merrill and Louis Ruchames, eds., *The Letters of William Lloyd Garrison,* 6 vols. (Cambridge: Belknap Press of Harvard University Press, 1971–81).

8. Henry Mayer, *All on Fire: William Lloyd Garrison and the Abolition of Slavery* (New York: St. Martin's Press, 1998).

9. Wendell Phillips Garrison and Francis Jackson Garrison, *William Lloyd Garrison, 1805–1879, The Story of His Life Told by His Children,* 4 vols. (New York: Century Company, 1885–89).

10. Alice Stone Blackwell, *Growing Up in Boston's Guilded Age: The Journal of Alice Stone Blackwell, 1872–1874,* ed. Marlene Deahl Merrill (New Haven: Yale University Press, 1990); Charlotte Forten Grimké, *The Journals of Charlotte Forten Grimké,* ed. Brenda Stevenson (New York: Oxford University Press, 1988); Anna Davis Hallowell, *James and Lucretia Mott: Life and Letters* (Boston: Houghton Mifflin, 1884); Sarah H. Southwick, *Reminiscences of Early Anti-Slavery Days* (Cambridge, Mass.: Riverside Press, 1893), ACS:BPL; Elizabeth Cady Stanton, *Eighty Years and More: Reminiscences, 1815–1897* (1898; reprint, Boston: Northeastern University Press, 1993); Leslie Wheeler, ed., *Loving Warriors: Selected Letters of Lucy Stone and Henry B. Blackwell, 1853–1893* (New York: Dial Press, 1981); and Lillie Buffum Chace Wyman and Arthur Crawford Wyman, *Elizabeth Buffum Chace, 1806–1899, Her Life and Its Environment,* 2 vols. (Boston: W. B. Clarke, 1914).

11. Lois Banner, *Elizabeth Cady Stanton: A Radical for Woman's Rights* (Boston: Little, Brown, 1980); and Elisabeth Griffith, *In Her Own Right: The Life of Elizabeth Cady Stanton* (New York: Oxford University Press, 1984).

12. Cited in Ellen Carol DuBois, *Harriot Stanton Blatch and the Winning of Woman Suffrage* (New Haven: Yale University Press, 1997), p. 245.

13. Cited in Alice Stone Blackwell, *Lucy Stone: Pioneer of Woman's Rights* (Norwood, Mass.: Plimpton Press, 1930), p. 271.

14. Blanche Glassman Hersh, *The Slavery of Sex: Feminist-Abolitionists in America* (Urbana: University of Illinois Press, 1978).

15. Lawrence J. Friedman, *Gregarious Saints: Self and Community in American Abolitionism, 1830–1870* (New York: Cambridge University Press, 1982).

16. Chris Dixon, *Perfecting the Family: Antislavery Marriages in Nineteenth-Century America* (Amherst: University of Massachusetts Press, 1997).

17. Gerda Lerner, *The Grimké Sisters from South Carolina* (New York: Schocken Books, 1967).

18. Andrea Moore Kerr, *Lucy Stone: Speaking Out for Equality* (New Brunswick, N.J.: Rutgers University Press, 1992).

19. Margret Hope Bacon, *Valiant Friend: The Life of Lucretia Mott* (New York: Walker, 1980).

20. Margret Hope Bacon, *Abby Hopper Gibbons: Prison Reformer and Social Activist* (Albany: State University of New York Press, 2000).

21. Dorothy Sterling, *Lucretia Mott* (New York: Feminist Press of the City University of New York, 1964).

22. Dorothy Sterling, *Ahead of Her Time: Abby Kelley and the Politics of Antislavery* (New York: W. W. Norton, 1991).

23. Sibyl Ventress Brownlee, "'Out of the Abundance of the Heart': Sarah Ann Parker Remond's Quest for Freedom" (Ph.D. diss.: University of Massachusetts, Amherst, 1997).

24. Elizabeth Cooke Stevens, "'From Generation to Generation': The Mother and Daughter Activism of Elizabeth Buffum Chace and Lillie Chace Wyman" (Ph.D. diss.: Brown University, 1993).

ACKNOWLEDGMENTS

Growing Up Abolitionist took over ten years to complete. During that time I accumulated many personal and professional debts to people who helped me locate information and find my way. Most of all, I owe thanks to several members of the Garrison family who shared stories, materials, and photographs and encouraged me to tell a tale I so wanted to tell. Two generations of Garrison children opened their homes and hearts to me. Of William Lloyd and Helen Benson Garrison's great-grandchildren and their spouses, I thank Oswald Garrison Villard Jr., Arnold Garrison, and George and Nancy Garrison; and I acknowledge the late Henry Serrano Villard, the late David Lloyd Garrison, and the late Mariquita Serrano Villard Platov. Of the great-great-grandchildren and their relatives, I wish to thank Edith Garrison Griffin, Nancy Garrison, Elinor Bliss, Alexandra Villard de Borchgrave, Daphne Harwood, Ruth Emerson Wortis, Frank Garrison, Chris Backrecker, Sherry Penney, and James D. Livingston. I am particularly indebted to James Gould for allowing me to use elements of his family tree.

To the many librarians whose assistance has been invaluable, I offer great thanks and appreciation. These include George Heerman of the Illinois State Historical Library; Wendy E. Chmielewski of the Swarthmore College Peace Collection; Mark Levine of the Brooklyn Public Library; Brigid Shields of the Minnesota Historical Society; Jennifer Tolpa of the Massachusetts Historical Society; Julia Barrow of the Worcester Historical Museum; the librarians of the New York Public Library, especially the Rare Books and Manuscripts Division; Michael Kelly of the Wichita State University Libraries; Laura Wasowicz of the American Antiquarian Society; Bruce McSheehy, Jerry Greene, and Robert Foley of the Fitchburg State College Library; Jean Therrien of the Rhode Island Historical Society; Leslie A. Morris and the staff of the Houghton Library of Harvard University; Peter Meyer Filard of the Tamiment Library at New York University; Lorna Knight of the Cornell University Library; Eugene Zepp of the Boston Public Library's Department of Rare Books and Manuscripts; the staff of the Boston Athenaeum; Elaine Malloy of the Bancroft Memorial Library in Hopedale; Sherrill Redmon, Amy Hague, and Susan Boone of the Sophia Smith Collection at Smith College, and Sister Esther of St. Monica's Home.

In 1994 I attended the Writing Narrative History conference at the California Institute of Technology. There I met people who have become role models for me in demonstrating how history can be written to appeal to a broader audience. Most of all, I would like to thank Robert Rosenstone, the organizer of the conference, for his support over the past eight years of this project. I would also like to acknowledge advice from John Demos and Min Soo Kang, who read and commented on an early version of "Fanny's Story."

My long-standing membership in the Women Writing Women's Lives group in New York City has paid off greatly. Monthly meetings kept me centered on controversial issues of writing biography, of working in a narrative style, and on keeping women's stories at the center of this book. I would particularly like to thank Nell Painter, Adrienne Bloch, Louise Bernikow, Norah Chase, Dorothy Helly, Jean Fagin Yellin, and Brooke Kreuger for their insights and support and the entire group for its exciting and challenging discussions.

The Peace History Society has been my intellectual and scholarly base for well over sixteen years. With the wonderful inspiration from conversations, panel discussions, emails, and phone calls provided by the warm peace history community, I wrote two books, *The Women's Peace Union and the Outlawry of War, 1921–1942* and *Peace as a Women's Issue: A History of the U.S. Movement for World Peace and Women's Rights,* which led me directly to this project. For feedback and support on this effort, I particularly want to thank Anne Marie Pois, Jim Zwick, Cynthia Maude, Anne Kjelling, Charles Chatfield, Frances Early, John Chambers, and Dee Garrison. I would also like to acknowledge the friendship, support, and great humor of the late Scott Bills.

For over seven years of this project, I was a member of the faculty of Fitchburg State College in Massachusetts. Although without many resources, the school granted me two terms as a Graduate Research Fellow, two Professional Development grants, which allowed me to hire Rachelle Lappinen and Ann Marie Flynn as work-study students, and a Harrod lectureship. Besides thanking Rachelle and Ann Marie for stellar work, I would like to thank several other friends and colleagues for reading and commenting on parts of the manuscript, providing articles and leads to sources, and for being there with advice and moral support even after I left the college. These include Roberta Adams, Margot Kempers, Nan Wiegersma, Shirley Wagner, Michele Zide, Sibyl Brownlee, Tom Murray, Nancy Kelly, LeAnn Erickson, Pat Micciche, Ed Thomas, Susan Williams, David Reed, and Betsy True. At the City College of New York, where I landed in 1999, I would like to thank Provost Zeev Dagan for his support during the final stages of this work.

A thank-you to other friends and colleagues who have read chapters and given friendly advice, namely Kathleen Dalton, Bonnie Anderson, Robert Pois, Walter Merrill, Nancy Tomes, Kathryn Kish Sklar, Rob Forbes, Elizabeth Stevens, Melanie Gustafson, Gela Kline, Kate Clifford Larson, and the late Henry Mayer. I also acknowledge the warm support and friendship of the late Ed Rivera. A special thanks to Tony Rotundo for helping me over a particularly rough spot . . . and to Charles and Beverly Yates of the Friendship Valley Bed and Breakfast in Brooklyn, Connecticut—a really great place to stay. I would also like to thank Zayra Minaya for clerical assistance with the layout and typing of the Garrison family tree and four excellent City College students for help with the final proofreading—Amoi Bonny, Sharae Belton, Adrienne Hill, and Arline Edwards-Bones.

I consider myself very fortunate to have this book published by the University of Massachusetts Press, headed by Bruce Wilcox. Paul Wright, who acquired the manuscript, has been a constant support. I especially appreciate his insistence that I forge on when I had reached the point of giving up on the seemingly endless revisions. His contribution greatly improved this book. After the manuscript left his office, it came under the caring eye of Carol Betsch. Since that time, I have felt a surge of support for the work. With the greatest professionalism and a large dose of humor, the Garrisons' story has moved from hand to hand until its completion. I would especially like to thank all those at the press who helped with the production work, especially Carol Betsch, and copy editor John LeRoy.

A heartfelt hug to my family members who read parts of the manuscript and encouraged me with loving words and thoughts—Clara Hyman, Carolyn Beck, Terri Randall, Avner Tavori, and Miguel, Pablo, Lucinda, and Victor Alonso. Also, a special thanks to my grandson, Joseph, . . . just for being.

INDEX

Note: Illustrations in the picture gallery following page 134 are referenced as *illus.*